A GUIDE TO ECONOMETRICS

A GUIDE TO ECONOMETRICS

FOURTH EDITION

PETER KENNEDY

Simon Fraser University

The MIT Press
Cambridge, Massachusetts

Printed and bound in The United Kingdom by TJ International.

ISBN 0–262 11235–3 (hardcover), 0–262–61140–6 (paperback)
Library of Congress Catalog Card Number: 98–65110

CONTENTS

PREFACE

In the preface to the third edition of this book I noted that upper-level undergraduate and beginning graduate econometrics students are as likely to learn about this book from their instructor as by word-of-mouth, the phenomenon that made the first edition of this book so successful. Sales of the third edition indicate that this trend has continued – more and more instructors are realizing that students find this book to be of immense value to their understanding of econometrics.

What is it about this book that students have found to be of such value? This book supplements econometrics texts, at all levels, by providing an overview of the subject and an intuitive feel for its concepts and techniques, without the usual clutter of notation and technical detail that necessarily characterize an econometrics textbook. It is often said of econometrics textbooks that their readers miss the forest for the trees. This is inevitable – the terminology and techniques that must be taught do not allow the text to convey a proper intuitive sense of "What's it all about?" and "How does it all fit together?" All econometrics textbooks fail to provide this overview. This is not from lack of trying – most textbooks have excellent passages containing the relevant insights and interpretations. They make good sense to instructors, but they do not make the expected impact on the students. Why? Because these insights and interpretations are broken up, appearing throughout the book, mixed with the technical details. In their struggle to keep up with notation and to learn these technical details, students miss the overview so essential to a real understanding of those details. This book provides students with a perspective from which it is possible to assimilate more easily the details of these textbooks.

Although the changes from the third edition are numerous, the basic structure and flavor of the book remain unchanged. Following an introductory chapter, the second chapter discusses at some length the criteria for choosing estimators, and in doing so develops many of the basic concepts used throughout the book. The third chapter provides an overview of the subject matter, presenting the five assumptions of the classical linear regression model and explaining how most problems encountered in econometrics can be interpreted as a violation of one of these assumptions. The fourth chapter exposits some concepts of inference to provide a foundation for later chapters. Chapter 5 discusses general approaches to the specification of an econometric model, setting the stage for the next six chapters, each of which deals with violations of an assumption of the classical linear regression model, describes their implications, discusses relevant tests, and suggests means of resolving resulting estimation problems. The remaining eight chapters and Appendices A, B and C address selected topics. Appendix D provides some student exercises and Appendix E offers suggested answers to the even-numbered exercises. A set of suggested answers to odd-numbered questions is available from the publisher upon request to instructors adopting this book for classroom use.

There are several major changes in this edition. The chapter on qualitative and limited dependent variables was split into a chapter on qualitative dependent variables (adding a section on count data) and a chapter on limited dependent variables (adding a section on duration models). The time series chapter has been extensively revised to incorporate the huge amount of work done in this area since the third edition. A new appendix on the sampling distribution concept has been added, to deal with what I believe is students' biggest stumbling block to understanding econometrics. In the exercises, a new type of question has been added, in which a Monte Carlo study is described and students are asked to explain the expected results. New material has been added to a wide variety of topics such as bootstrapping, generalized method of moments, neural nets, linear structural relations, VARs, and instrumental variable estimation. Minor changes have been made throughout to update results and references, and to improve exposition.

To minimize readers' distractions, there are no footnotes. All references, peripheral points and details worthy of comment are relegated to a section at the end of each chapter entitled "General Notes". The technical material that appears in the book is placed in end-of-chapter sections entitled "Technical Notes". This technical material continues to be presented in a way that supplements rather than duplicates the contents of traditional textbooks. Students should find that this material provides a useful introductory bridge to the more sophisticated presentations found in the main text. Students are advised to wait until a second or third reading of the body of a chapter before addressing the material in the General or Technical Notes. A glossary explains common econometric terms not found in the body of this book.

Errors in or shortcomings of this book are my responsibility, but for improvements I owe many debts, mainly to scores of students, both graduate and undergraduate, whose comments and reactions have played a prominent role in shaping this fourth edition. Jan Kmenta and Terry Seaks have made major contributions in their role as "anonymous" referees, even though I have not always followed their advice. I continue to be grateful to students throughout the world who have expressed thanks to me for writing this book; I hope this fourth edition continues to be of value to students both during and after their formal coursework.

DEDICATION

To ANNA and RED who, until they discovered what an econometrician was, were very impressed that their son might become one. With apologies to K. A. C. Manderville, I draw their attention to the following, adapted from *The Undoing of Lamia Gurdleneck*.

"You haven't told me yet," said Lady Nuttal, "what it is your fiancé does for a living."

"He's an econometrician." replied Lamia, with an annoying sense of being on the defensive.

Lady Nuttal was obviously taken aback. It had not occurred to her that econometricians entered into normal social relationships. The species, she would have surmised, was perpetuated in some collateral manner, like mules.

"But Aunt Sara, it's a very interesting profession," said Lamia warmly.

"I don't doubt it," said her aunt, who obviously doubted it very much. "To express anything important in mere figures is so plainly impossible that there must be endless scope for well-paid advice on how to do it. But don't you think that life with an econometrician would be rather, shall we say, humdrum?"

Lamia was silent. She felt reluctant to discuss the surprising depth of emotional possibility which she had discovered below Edward's numerical veneer.

"It's not the figures themselves," she said finally, "it's what you do with them that matters."

INTRODUCTION

1.1 WHAT IS ECONOMETRICS?

Strange as it may seem, there does not exist a generally accepted answer to
this question. Responses vary from the silly "Econometrics is what econometricians do" to the staid "Econometrics is the study of the application of
statistical methods to the analysis of economic phenomena," with sufficient
disagreements to warrant an entire journal article devoted to this question
(Tintner, 1953).

This confusion stems from the fact that econometricians wear many different
hats. First, and foremost, they are *economists*, capable of utilizing economic theory to improve their empirical analyses of the problems they address. At times
they are *mathematicians*, formulating economic theory in ways that make it
appropriate for statistical testing. At times they are *accountants*, concerned with
the problem of finding and collecting economic data and relating theoretical economic variables to observable ones. At times they are *applied statisticians*,
spending hours with the computer trying to estimate economic relationships or
predict economic events. And at times they are *theoretical statisticians*, applying
their skills to the development of statistical techniques appropriate to the empirical problems characterizing the science of economics. It is to the last of these
roles that the term "econometric theory" applies, and it is on this aspect of
econometrics that most textbooks on the subject focus. This guide is accordingly
devoted to this "econometric theory" dimension of econometrics, discussing the
empirical problems typical of economics and the statistical techniques used to
overcome these problems.

What distinguishes an econometrician from a statistician is the former's pre-
occupation with problems caused by violations of statisticians' standard assumptions; owing to the nature of economic relationships and the lack of controlled
experimentation, these assumptions are seldom met. Patching up statistical
methods to deal with situations frequently encountered in empirical work in economics has created a large battery of extremely sophisticated statistical techniques. In fact, econometricians are often accused of using sledgehammers to
crack open peanuts while turning a blind eye to data deficiencies and the many

questionable assumptions required for the successful application of these techniques. Valavanis has expressed this feeling forcefully:

> Econometric theory is like an exquisitely balanced French recipe, spelling out precisely with how many turns to mix the sauce, how many carats of spice to add, and for how many milliseconds to bake the mixture at exactly 474 degrees of temperature. But when the statistical cook turns to raw materials, he finds that hearts of cactus fruit are unavailable, so he substitutes chunks of cantaloupe; where the recipe calls for vermicelli he used shredded wheat; and he substitutes green garment die for curry, ping-pong balls for turtle's eggs, and, for Chalifougnac vintage 1883, a can of turpentine. (Valavanis, 1959, p. 83)

How has this state of affairs come about? One reason is that prestige in the econometrics profession hinges on technical expertise rather than on hard work required to collect good data:

> It is the preparation skill of the econometric chef that catches the professional eye, not the quality of the raw materials in the meal, or the effort that went into procuring them. (Griliches, 1994, p. 14)

Criticisms of econometrics along these lines are not uncommon. Rebuttals cite improvements in data collection, extol the fruits of the computer revolution and provide examples of improvements in estimation due to advanced techniques. It remains a fact, though, that in practice good results depend as much on the input of sound and imaginative economic theory as on the application of correct statistical methods. The skill of the econometrician lies in judiciously mixing these two essential ingredients; in the words of Malinvaud:

> The art of the econometrician consists in finding the set of assumptions which are both sufficiently specific and sufficiently realistic to allow him to take the best possible advantage of the data available to him. (Malinvaud, 1966, p. 514)

Modern econometrics texts try to infuse this art into students by providing a large number of detailed examples of empirical application. This important dimension of econometrics texts lies beyond the scope of this book. Readers should keep this in mind as they use this guide to improve their understanding of the purely statistical methods of econometrics.

1.2 THE DISTURBANCE TERM

A major distinction between economists and econometricians is the latter's concern with disturbance terms. An economist will specify, for example, that consumption is a function of income, and write $C = f(Y)$ where C is consumption and Y is income. An econometrician will claim that this relationship must also include a *disturbance* (or *error*) term, and may alter the equation to read

$C = f(Y) + \varepsilon$ where ε (epsilon) is a disturbance term. Without the disturbance term the relationship is said to be *exact* or *deterministic*; with the disturbance term it is said to be *stochastic*.

The word "stochastic" comes from the Greek "stokhos," meaning a target or bull's eye. A stochastic relationship is not always right on target in the sense that it predicts the precise value of the variable being explained, just as a dart thrown at a target seldom hits the bull's eye. The disturbance term is used to capture explicitly the size of these "misses" or "errors." The existence of the disturbance term is justified in three main ways. (Note: these are not mutually exclusive.)

(1) *Omission of the influence of innumerable chance events* Although income might be the major determinant of the level of consumption, it is not the only determinant. Other variables, such as the interest rate or liquid asset holdings, may have a systematic influence on consumption. Their omission constitutes one type of *specification error*: the nature of the economic relationship is not correctly specified. In addition to these systematic influences, however, are innumerable less systematic influences, such as weather variations, taste changes, earthquakes, epidemics and postal strikes. Although some of these variables may have a significant impact on consumption, and thus should definitely be included in the specified relationship, many have only a very slight, irregular influence; the disturbance is often viewed as representing the net influence of a large number of such small and independent causes.

(2) *Measurement error* It may be the case that the variable being explained cannot be measured accurately, either because of data collection difficulties or because it is inherently unmeasurable and a proxy variable must be used in its stead. The disturbance term can in these circumstances be thought of as representing this measurement error. Errors in measuring the explaining variable(s) (as opposed to the variable being explained) create a serious econometric problem, discussed in chapter 9. The terminology *errors in variables* is also used to refer to measurement errors.

(3) *Human indeterminacy* Some people believe that human behavior is such that actions taken under identical circumstances will differ in a random way. The disturbance term can be thought of as representing this inherent randomness in human behavior.

Associated with any explanatory relationship are unknown constants, called *parameters*, which tie the relevant variables into an equation. For example, the relationship between consumption and income could be specified as

$$C = \beta_1 + \beta_2 Y + \varepsilon$$

where β_1 and β_2 are the parameters characterizing this consumption function. Economists are often keenly interested in learning the values of these unknown parameters.

The existence of the disturbance term, coupled with the fact that its magnitude is unknown, makes calculation of these parameter values impossible. Instead, they must be *estimated*. It is on this task, the estimation of parameter values, that the bulk of econometric theory focuses. The success of econometricians' methods of estimating parameter values depends in large part on the nature of the disturbance term; statistical assumptions concerning the characteristics of the disturbance term, and means of testing these assumptions, therefore play a prominent role in econometric theory.

1.3   ESTIMATES AND ESTIMATORS

In their mathematical notation, econometricians usually employ Greek letters to represent the true, unknown values of parameters. The Greek letter most often used in this context is beta (β). Thus, throughout this book, β is used as the parameter value that the econometrician is seeking to learn. Of course, no one ever actually learns the value of β, but it can be estimated: via statistical techniques, empirical data can be used to take an educated guess at β. In any particular application, an estimate of β is simply a number. For example, β might be estimated as 16.2. But, in general, econometricians are seldom interested in estimating a single parameter; economic relationships are usually sufficiently complex to require more than one parameter, and because these parameters occur in the same relationship, better estimates of these parameters can be obtained if they are estimated together (i.e., the influence of one explaining variable is more accurately captured if the influence of the other explaining variables is simultaneously accounted for). As a result, β seldom refers to a single parameter value; it almost always refers to a set of parameter values, individually called $\beta_1, \beta_2, \ldots, \beta_k$ where k is the number of different parameters in the set. β is then referred to as a vector and is written as

$$\beta = \begin{bmatrix} \beta_1 \\ \beta_2 \\ \vdots \\ \beta_k \end{bmatrix}.$$

In any particular application, an estimate of β will be a set of numbers. For example, if three parameters are being estimated (i.e., if the dimension of β is three), β might be estimated as

$$\begin{bmatrix} 0.8 \\ 1.2 \\ -4.6 \end{bmatrix}.$$

In general, econometric theory focuses not on the estimate itself, but on the *estimator* – the formula or "recipe" by which the data are transformed into an actual estimate. The reason for this is that the justification of an estimate computed from a particular sample rests on a justification of the estimation method (the estimator). The econometrician has no way of knowing the actual values of the disturbances inherent in a sample of data; depending on these disturbances, an estimate calculated from that sample could be quite inaccurate. It is therefore impossible to justify the estimate itself. However, it may be the case that the econometrician can justify the estimator by showing, for example, that the estimator "usually" produces an estimate that is "quite close" to the true parameter value regardless of the particular sample chosen. (The meaning of this sentence, in particular the meaning of "usually" and of "quite close," is discussed at length in the next chapter.) Thus an estimate of β from a particular sample is defended by justifying the estimator.

Because attention is focused on estimators of β, a convenient way of denoting those estimators is required. An easy way of doing this is to place a mark over the β or a superscript on it. Thus $\hat{\beta}$ (beta-hat) and β^* (beta-star) are often used to denote estimators of beta. One estimator, the ordinary least squares (OLS) estimator, is very popular in econometrics; the notation β^{OLS} is used throughout this book to represent it. Alternative estimators are denoted by $\hat{\beta}$, β^*, or something similar. Many textbooks use the letter b to denote the OLS estimator.

1.4   GOOD AND PREFERRED ESTIMATORS

Any fool can produce an estimator of β, since literally an infinite number of them exists; i.e., there exists an infinite number of different ways in which a sample of data can be used to produce an estimate of β, all but a few of these ways producing "bad" estimates. What distinguishes an econometrician is the ability to produce "good" estimators, which in turn produce "good" estimates. One of these "good" estimators could be chosen as the "best" or "preferred" estimator and be used to generate the "preferred" estimate of β. What further distinguishes an econometrician is the ability to provide "good" estimators in a variety of different estimating contexts. The set of "good" estimators (and the choice of "preferred" estimator) is not the same in all estimating problems. In fact, a "good" estimator in one estimating situation could be a "bad" estimator in another situation.

The study of econometrics revolves around how to generate a "good" or the "preferred" estimator in a given estimating situation. But before the "how to" can be explained, the meaning of "good" and "preferred" must be made clear. This takes the discussion into the subjective realm: the meaning of "good" or "preferred" estimator depends upon the subjective values of the person doing the estimating. The best the econometrician can do under these circumstances is to recognize the more popular criteria used in this regard and generate estimators that meet one or more of these criteria. Estimators meeting certain of these criteria could be called "good" estimators. The ultimate choice of the "preferred" estimator, however, lies in the hands of the person doing the estimating, for it is his or her value judgements that determine which of these criteria is the most important. This value judgement may well be influenced by the purpose for which the estimate is sought, in addition to the subjective prejudices of the individual.

Clearly, our investigation of the subject of econometrics can go no further until the possible criteria for a "good" estimator are discussed. This is the purpose of the next chapter.

GENERAL NOTES

1.1   What is Econometrics?

- The term "econometrics" first came into prominence with the formation in the early 1930s of the Econometric Society and the founding of the journal *Econometrica*. The introduction of Dowling and Glahe (1970) surveys briefly the landmark publications in econometrics. Pesaran (1987) is a concise history and overview of econometrics. Hendry and Morgan (1995) is a collection of papers of historical importance in the development of econometrics. Epstein (1987), Morgan (1990a) and Qin (1993) are extended histories; see also Morgan (1990b). Hendry (1980) notes that the word econometrics should not be confused with "economystics," "economic-tricks," or "icon-ometrics."

- The discipline of econometrics has grown so rapidly, and in so many different directions, that disagreement regarding the definition of econometrics has grown rather than diminished over the past decade. Reflecting this, at least one prominent econometrician, Goldberger (1989, p. 151), has concluded that "nowadays my definition would be that econometrics is what econometricians do." One thing that econometricians do that is not discussed in this book is serve as expert witnesses in court cases. Fisher (1986) has an interesting account of this dimension of econometric work. Judge et al. (1988, p. 81) remind readers that "econometrics is *fun*!"

- A distinguishing feature of econometrics is that it focuses on ways of dealing with data that are awkward/dirty because they were not produced by controlled experiments. In recent years, however, controlled experimentation in economics has become more common. Burtless (1995) summarizes the nature of such experimentation and argues for its continued use. Heckman and Smith (1995) is a strong defense of using traditional data sources. Much of this argument is associated with the selection bias phenomenon (discussed in chapter 16) – people in an experimental program inevitably are not a random selection of all people, particularly with respect to their unmeasured attributes, and so results from the experiment are compromised. Friedman and Sunder (1994) is a primer on conducting economic experiments. Meyer (1995) discusses the attributes of "natural" experiments in economics.

- Mayer (1933, chapter 10), Summers (1991), Brunner (1973), Rubner (1970) and Streissler (1970) are good sources of cynical views of econometrics, summed up dramatically by McCloskey (1994, p. 359) "... most allegedly empirical research in economics is unbelievable, uninteresting or both." More comments appear in this book in section 9.2 on errors in variables and chapter 18 on prediction. Fair (1973) and Fromm and Schink (1973) are examples of studies defending the use of sophisticated econometric techniques. The use of econometrics in the policy context has been hampered by the (inexplicable?) operation of "Goodhart's Law" (1978), namely that all econometric models break down when used for policy. The finding of Dewald et al. (1986), that there is a remarkably high incidence of inability to replicate empirical studies in economics, does not promote a favorable view of econometricians.

- What has been the contribution of econometrics to the development of economic science? Some would argue that empirical work frequently uncovers empirical regularities which inspire theoretical advances. For example, the difference between time-series and cross-sectional estimates of the MPC prompted development of the relative, permanent and life-cycle consumption theories. But many others view econometrics with scorn, as evidenced by the following quotes:

> We don't genuinely take empirical work seriously in economics. It's not the source by which economists accumulate their opinions, by and large. (Leamer in Hendry et al., 1990, p. 182);

> Very little of what economists will tell you they know, and almost none of the content of the elementary text, has been discovered by running regressions. Regressions on government-collected data have been used mainly to bolster one theoretical argument over another. But the bolstering they provide is weak, inconclusive, and easily countered by someone else's regressions. (Bergmann, 1987, p. 192);

> No economic theory was ever abandoned because it was rejected by some empirical econometric test, nor was a clear cut decision between competing theories made in light of the evidence of such a test. (Spanos, 1986, p. 660); and

> I invite the reader to try . . . to identify a meaningful hypothesis about economic behavior that has fallen into disrepute because of a formal statistical test. (Summers, 1991, p. 130)

This reflects the belief that economic data are not powerful enough to test and choose among theories, and that as a result econometrics has shifted from being a tool for testing theories to being a tool for exhibiting/displaying theories. Because economics is a non-experimental science, often the data are weak, and because of this empirical evidence provided by econometrics is frequently inconclusive; in such cases it should be qualified as such. Griliches (1986) comments at length on the role of data in econometrics, and notes that they are improving; Aigner (1988) stresses the potential role of improved data.

- Critics might choose to paraphrase the Malinvaud quote as "The art of drawing a crooked line from an unproved assumption to a foregone conclusion." The importance of a proper understanding of econometric techniques in the face of a potential inferiority of econometrics to inspired economic theorizing is captured nicely by Samuelson (1965, p. 9): "Even if a scientific regularity were less accurate than the intuitive hunches of a virtuoso, the fact that it can be put into operation by thousands of people who are not virtuosos gives it a transcendental importance." This guide is designed for those of us who are not virtuosos!
- Feminist economists have complained that traditional econometrics contains a male bias. They urge econometricians to broaden their teaching and research methodology to encompass the collection of primary data of different types, such as survey or interview data, and the use of qualitative studies which are not based on the exclusive use of "objective" data. See MacDonald (1995) and Nelson (1995). King, Keohane and

Verba (1994) discuss how research using qualitative studies can meet traditional scientific standards.

- Several books focus on the empirical applications dimension of econometrics. Some recent examples are Thomas (1993), Berndt (1991) and Lott and Ray (1992). Manski (1991, p. 49) notes that "in the past, advances in econometrics were usually motivated by a desire to answer specific empirical questions. This symbiosis of theory and practice is less common today." He laments that "the distancing of methodological research from its applied roots is unhealthy."

1.2   The Disturbance Term

- The error term associated with a relationship need not necessarily be additive, as it is in the example cited. For some nonlinear functions it is often convenient to specify the error term in a multiplicative form. In other instances it may be appropriate to build the stochastic element into the relationship by specifying the parameters to be random variables rather than constants. (This is called the random-coefficients model.)
- Some econometricians prefer to define the relationship between C and Y discussed earlier as "the mean of C conditional on Y is $f(Y)$," written as $E(C|Y) = f(Y)$. This spells out more explicitly what econometricians have in mind when using this specification.
- In terms of the throwing-darts-at-a-target analogy, characterizing disturbance terms refers to describing the nature of the misses: are the darts distributed uniformly around the bull's eye? Is the average miss large or small? Does the average miss depend on who is throwing the darts? Is a miss to the right likely to be followed by another miss to the right? In later chapters the statistical specification of these characteristics and the related terminology (such as "homoskedasticity" and "autocorrelated errors") are explained in considerable detail.

1.3   Estimates and Estimators

- An estimator is simply an algebraic function of a potential sample of data; once the sample is drawn, this function creates an actual numerical estimate.
- Chapter 2 discusses in detail the means whereby an estimator is "justified" and compared with alternative estimators.

1.4   Good and Preferred Estimators

- The terminology "preferred" estimator is used instead of the term "best" estimator because the latter has a specific meaning in econometrics. This is explained in chapter 2.
- Estimation of parameter values is not the only purpose of econometrics. Two other major themes can be identified: testing of hypotheses and economic forecasting. Because both these problems are intimately related to the estimation of parameter values, it is not misleading to characterize econometrics as being primarily concerned with parameter estimation.

TECHNICAL NOTES

1.1 What is Econometrics?

- In the macroeconomic context, in particular in research on real business cycles, a computational simulation procedure called *calibration* is often employed as an alternative to traditional econometric analysis. In this procedure economic theory plays a much more prominent role than usual, supplying ingredients to a general equilibrium model designed to address a specific economic question. This model is then "calibrated" by setting parameter values equal to average values of economic ratios known not to have changed much over time or equal to empirical estimates from microeconomic studies. A computer simulation produces output from the model, with adjustments to model and parameters made until the output from these simulations has qualitative characteristics (such as correlations between variables of interest) matching those of the real world. Once this qualitative matching is achieved the model is simulated to address the primary question of interest. Kydland and Prescott (1996) is a good exposition of this approach.

  Econometricians have not viewed this technique with favor, primarily because there is so little emphasis on evaluating the quality of the output using traditional testing/assessment procedures. Hansen and Heckman (1996), a cogent critique, note (p. 90) that "Such models are often elegant, and the discussions produced from using them are frequently stimulating and provocative, but their empirical foundations are not secure. What credibility should we attach to numbers produced from their 'computational experiments,' and why should we use their 'calibrated models' as a basis for serious quantitative policy evaluation?" King (1995) is a good comparison of econometrics and calibration.

2 CRITERIA FOR ESTIMATORS

2.1 INTRODUCTION

Chapter 1 posed the question, What is a "good" estimator? The aim of this chapter is to answer that question by describing a number of criteria that econometricians feel are measures of "goodness." These criteria are discussed under the following headings:

(1) Computational cost
(2) Least squares
(3) Highest R^2
(4) Unbiasedness
(5) Efficiency
(6) Mean square error
(7) Asymptotic properties
(8) Maximum likelihood

Since econometrics can be characterized as a search for estimators satisfying one or more of these criteria, care is taken in the discussion of the criteria to ensure that the reader understands fully the meaning of the different criteria and the terminology associated with them. Many fundamental ideas of econometrics, critical to the question, What's econometrics all about?, are presented in this chapter.

2.2 COMPUTATIONAL COST

To anyone, but particularly to economists, the extra benefit associated with choosing one estimator over another must be compared with its extra cost, where cost refers to expenditure of both money and effort. Thus, the computational ease and cost of using one estimator rather than another must be taken into account whenever selecting an estimator. Fortunately, the existence and ready availability of high-speed computers, along with standard packaged routines for most of the popular estimators, has made computational cost very low. As a result, this criterion does not play as strong a role as it once did. Its influence is now felt only when dealing with two kinds of estimators. One is the case of an atypical estimation procedure for which there does not exist a readily available packaged computer program and for which the cost of programming is high. The second is an estimation method for which the cost of running a packaged program is high because it needs large quantities of computer time; this could occur, for example, when using an iterative routine to find parameter estimates for a problem involving several nonlinearities.

2.3   LEAST SQUARES

For any set of values of the parameters characterizing a relationship, estimated values of the dependent variable (the variable being explained) can be calculated using the values of the independent variables (the explaining variables) in the data set. These estimated values (called $\hat{y}$) of the dependent variable can be subtracted from the actual values (y) of the dependent variable in the data set to produce what are called the *residuals* ($y - \hat{y}$). These residuals could be thought of as estimates of the unknown disturbances inherent in the data set. This is illustrated in figure 2.1. The line labeled $\hat{y}$ is the estimated relationship corresponding to a specific set of values of the unknown parameters. The dots represent actual observations on the dependent variable y and the independent variable x. Each observation is a certain vertical distance away from the estimated line, as pictured by the double-ended arrows. The lengths of these double-ended arrows measure the residuals. A different set of specific values of the

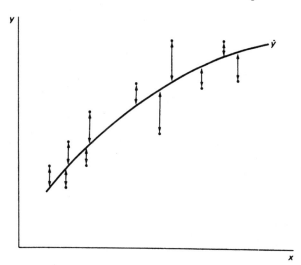

Figure 2.1   Minimizing the sum of squared residuals

parameters would create a different estimating line and thus a different set of residuals.

It seems natural to ask that a "good" estimator be one that generates a set of estimates of the parameters that makes these residuals "small." Controversy arises, however, over the appropriate definition of "small." Although it is agreed that the estimator should be chosen to minimize a weighted sum of all these residuals, full agreement as to what the weights should be does not exist. For example, those feeling that all residuals should be weighted equally advocate choosing the estimator that minimizes the sum of the absolute values of these residuals. Those feeling that large residuals should be avoided advocate weighting larger residuals more heavily by choosing the estimator that minimizes the sum of the squared values of these residuals. Those worried about misplaced decimals and other data errors advocate placing a constant (sometimes zero) weight on the squared values of particularly large residuals. Those concerned only with whether or not a residual is bigger than some specified value suggest placing a zero weight on residuals smaller than this critical value and a weight equal to the inverse of the residual on residuals larger than this value. Clearly a large number of alternative definitions could be proposed, each with appealing features.

By far the most popular of these definitions of "small" is the minimization of the sum of squared residuals. The estimator generating the set of values of the parameters that minimizes the sum of squared residuals is called the *ordinary least squares* estimator. It is referred to as the OLS estimator and is denoted by β^{OLS} in this book. This estimator is probably the most popular estimator among researchers doing empirical work. The reason for this popularity, however, does *not* stem from the fact that it makes the residuals "small" by minimizing the sum of squared residuals. Many econometricians are leery of this criterion because minimizing the sum of squared residuals does not say anything specific about the relationship of the estimator to the true parameter value β that it is estimating. In fact, it is possible to be too successful in minimizing the sum of squared residuals, accounting for so many unique features of that *particular sample* that the estimator loses its general validity, in the sense that, were that estimator applied to a new sample, poor estimates would result. The great popularity of the OLS estimator comes from the fact that in some estimating problems (but not all!) it scores well on some of the other criteria, described below, that are thought to be of greater importance. A secondary reason for its popularity is its computational ease; all computer packages include the OLS estimator for linear relationships, and many have routines for nonlinear cases.

Because the OLS estimator is used so much in econometrics, the characteristics of this estimator in different estimating problems are explored very thoroughly by all econometrics texts. The OLS estimator *always* minimizes the sum of squared residuals; but it does *not* always meet other criteria that econometricians feel are more important. As will become clear in the next chapter, the subject of econometrics can be characterized as an attempt to find alternative estimators to the OLS estimator for situations in which the OLS estimator does not meet the estimating criterion considered to be of greatest importance in the problem at hand.

2.4 HIGHEST R^2

A statistic that appears frequently in econometrics is the coefficient of determination, R^2. It is supposed to represent the proportion of the variation in the dependent variable "explained" by variation in the independent variables. It does this in a meaningful sense in the case of a linear relationship estimated by OLS. In this case it happens that the sum of the squared deviations of the dependent variable about its mean (the "total" variation in the dependent variable) can be broken into two parts, called the "explained" variation (the sum of squared deviations of the estimated values of the dependent variable around their mean) and the "unexplained" variation (the sum of squared residuals). R^2 is measured either as the ratio of the "explained" variation to the "total" variation or, equivalently, as 1 minus the ratio of the "unexplained" variation to the "total" variation, and thus represents the percentage of variation in the dependent variable "explained" by variation in the independent variables.

Because the OLS estimator minimizes the sum of squared residuals (the "unexplained" variation), it automatically maximizes R^2. Thus maximization of R^2, as a criterion for an estimator, is formally identical to the least squares criterion, and as such it really does not deserve a separate section in this chapter. It is given a separate section for two reasons. The first is that the formal identity between the highest R^2 criterion and the least squares criterion is worthy of emphasis. And the second is to distinguish clearly the difference between applying R^2 as a criterion in the context of searching for a "good" estimator when the functional form and included independent variables are known, as is the case in the present discussion, and using R^2 to help determine the proper functional form and the appropriate independent variables to be included. This latter use of R^2, and its misuse, are discussed later in the book (in sections 5.5 and 6.2).

2.5 UNBIASEDNESS

Suppose we perform the conceptual experiment of taking what is called a *repeated* sample: keeping the values of the independent variables unchanged, we obtain new observations for the dependent variable by drawing a new set of disturbances. This could be repeated, say, 2,000 times, obtaining 2,000 of these repeated samples. For each of these repeated samples we could use an estimator β^* to calculate an estimate of β. Because the samples differ, these 2,000 estimates will not be the same. The manner in which these estimates are distributed is called the *sampling distribution* of β^*. This is illustrated for the one-dimensional case in figure 2.2, where the sampling distribution of the estimator is labeled $f(\beta^*)$. It is simply the probability density function of β^*, approximated

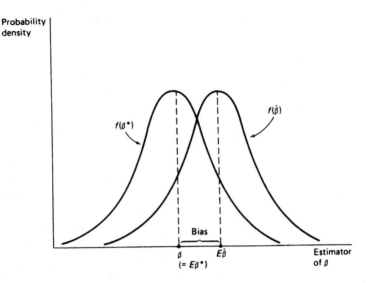

Figure 2.2   Using the sampling distribution to illustrate bias

by using the 2,000 estimates of β to construct a histogram, which in turn is used to approximate the relative frequencies of different estimates of β from the estimator β*. The sampling distribution of an alternative estimator, β̃, is also shown in figure 2.2.

This concept of a sampling distribution, the distribution of estimates produced by an estimator in repeated sampling, is crucial to an understanding of econometrics. Appendix A at the end of this book discusses sampling distributions at greater length. Most estimators are adopted because their sampling distributions have "good" properties; the criteria discussed in this and the following three sections are directly concerned with the nature of an estimator's sampling distribution.

The first of these properties is unbiasedness. An estimator β* is said to be an *unbiased* estimator of β if the mean of its sampling distribution is equal to β, i.e., if the average value of β* in repeated sampling is β. The mean of the sampling distribution of β* is called the expected value of β* and is written Eβ*; the bias of β* is the difference between Eβ* and β. In figure 2.2, β* is seen to be unbiased, whereas β̃ has a bias of size (Eβ̃ − β). The property of unbiasedness does not mean that β* = β; it says only that, if we could undertake repeated sampling an infinite number of times, we would get the correct estimate "on the average."

The OLS criterion can be applied with no information concerning how the data were generated. This is not the case for the unbiasedness criterion (and all other criteria related to the sampling distribution), since this knowledge is required to construct the sampling distribution. Econometricians have therefore developed a standard set of assumptions (discussed in chapter 3) concerning the way in which observations are generated. The general, but not the specific, way in which the disturbances are distributed is an important component of this. These assumptions are sufficient to allow the basic nature of the sampling distribution of many estimators to be calculated, either by mathematical means (part of the technical skill of an econometrician) or, failing that, by an empirical means called a Monte Carlo study, discussed in section 2.10.

Although the mean of a distribution is not necessarily the ideal measure of its location (the median or mode in some circumstances might be considered superior), most econometricians consider unbiasedness a desirable property for an estimator to have. This preference for an unbiased estimator stems from the *hope* that a particular estimate (i.e., from the sample at hand) will be close to the mean of the estimator's sampling distribution. Having to justify a particular estimate on a "hope" is not especially satisfactory, however. As a result, econometricians have recognized that being centered over the parameter to be estimated is only *one* good property that the sampling distribution of an estimator can have. The variance of the sampling distribution, discussed next, is also of great importance.

2.6 EFFICIENCY

In some econometric problems it is impossible to find an unbiased estimator. But whenever one unbiased estimator can be found, it is usually the case that a large number of other unbiased estimators can also be found. In this circumstance the unbiased estimator whose sampling distribution has the smallest variance is considered the most desirable of these unbiased estimators; it is called the *best unbiased* estimator, or the *efficient* estimator among all unbiased estimators. Why it is considered the most desirable of all unbiased estimators is easy to visualize. In figure 2.3 the sampling distributions of two unbiased estimators are drawn. The sampling distribution of the estimator $\hat{\beta}$, denoted $f(\hat{\beta})$, is drawn "flatter" or "wider" than the sampling distribution of β^*, reflecting the larger variance of $\hat{\beta}$. Although both estimators would produce estimates in repeated samples whose average would be β, the estimates from $\hat{\beta}$ would range more widely and thus would be less desirable. A researcher using $\hat{\beta}$ would be less certain that his or her estimate was close to β than would a researcher using β^*.

Sometimes reference is made to a criterion called "minimum variance." This criterion, by itself, is meaningless. Consider the estimator $\beta^* = 5.2$ (i.e., whenever a sample is taken, estimate β by 5.2 ignoring the sample). This estimator has a variance of zero, the smallest possible variance, but no one would use this estimator because it performs so poorly on other criteria such as unbiasedness. (It is interesting to note, however, that it performs exceptionally well on the computational cost criterion!) Thus, whenever the minimum variance, or "efficiency," criterion is mentioned, there must exist, at least implicitly, some additional constraint, such as unbiasedness, accompanying that criterion. When the

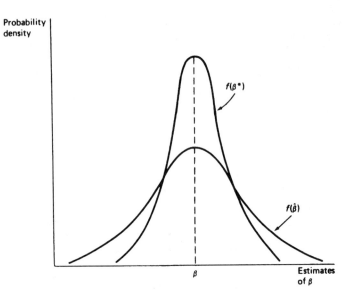

Figure 2.3 Using the sampling distribution to illustrate efficiency

additional constraint accompanying the minimum variance criterion is that the estimators under consideration be unbiased, the estimator is referred to as the *best unbiased* estimator.

Unfortunately, in many cases it is impossible to determine mathematically which estimator, of all unbiased estimators, has the smallest variance. Because of this problem, econometricians frequently add the further restriction that the estimator be a *linear* function of the observations on the dependent variable. This reduces the task of finding the efficient estimator to mathematically manageable proportions. An estimator that is linear and unbiased and that has minimum variance among all linear unbiased estimators is called the *best linear unbiased estimator* (BLUE). The BLUE is very popular among econometricians.

This discussion of minimum variance or efficiency has been implicitly undertaken in the context of a unidimensional estimator, i.e., the case in which β is a single number rather than a vector containing several numbers. In the multidimensional case the variance of $\hat{\beta}$ becomes a matrix called the variance–covariance matrix of $\hat{\beta}$. This creates special problems in determining which estimator has the smallest variance. The technical notes to this section discuss this further.

2.7 MEAN SQUARE ERROR (MSE)

Using the best unbiased criterion allows unbiasedness to play an extremely strong role in determining the choice of an estimator, since only unbiased esti-

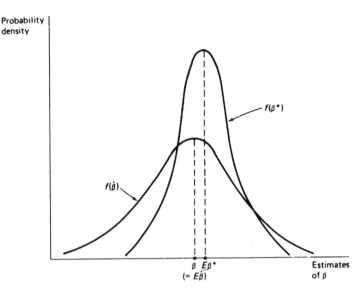

Figure 2.4   MSE trades off bias and variance

mators are considered. It may well be the case that, by restricting attention to only unbiased estimators, we are ignoring estimators that are only slightly biased but have considerably lower variances. This phenomenon is illustrated in figure 2.4. The sampling distribution of $\hat{\beta}$, the best unbiased estimator, is labeled $f(\hat{\beta})$. β^* is a biased estimator with sampling distribution $f(\beta^*)$. It is apparent from figure 2.4 that, although $f(\beta^*)$ is not centered over β, reflecting the bias of β^*, it is "narrower" than $f(\hat{\beta})$, indicating a smaller variance. It should be clear from the diagram that most researchers would probably choose the biased estimator β^* in preference to the best unbiased estimator $\hat{\beta}$.

This trade-off between low bias and low variance is formalized by using as a criterion the minimization of a weighted average of the bias and the variance (i.e., choosing the estimator that minimizes this weighted average). This is not a viable formalization, however, because the bias could be negative. One way to correct for this is to use the absolute value of the bias; a more popular way is to use its square. When the estimator is chosen so as to minimize a weighted average of the variance and the square of the bias, the estimator is said to be chosen on the *weighted square error* criterion. When the weights are equal, the criterion is the popular mean square error (MSE) criterion. The popularity of the mean square error criterion comes from an alternative derivation of this criterion: it happens that the expected value of a loss function consisting of the square of the difference between β and its estimate (i.e., the square of the estimation error) is the same as the sum of the variance and the squared bias. Minimization of the expected value of this loss function makes good intuitive sense as a criterion for choosing an estimator.

In practice, the MSE criterion is not usually adopted unless the best unbiased criterion is unable to produce estimates with small variances. The problem of multicollinearity, discussed in chapter 11, is an example of such a situation.

2.8 ASYMPTOTIC PROPERTIES

The estimator properties discussed in sections 2.5, 2.6 and 2.7 above relate to the nature of an estimator's sampling distribution. An unbiased estimator, for example, is one whose sampling distribution is centered over the true value of the parameter being estimated. These properties do not depend on the size of the sample of data at hand: an unbiased estimator, for example, is unbiased in both small and large samples. In many econometric problems, however, it is impossible to find estimators possessing these desirable sampling distribution properties in small samples. When this happens, as it frequently does, econometricians may justify an estimator on the basis of its *asymptotic* properties – the nature of the estimator's sampling distribution in extremely large samples.

The sampling distribution of most estimators changes as the sample size changes. The sample mean statistic, for example, has a sampling distribution that is centered over the population mean but whose variance becomes smaller as the sample size becomes larger. In many cases it happens that a biased estimator becomes less and less biased as the sample size becomes larger and larger – as the sample size becomes larger its sampling distribution changes, such that the mean of its sampling distribution shifts closer to the true value of the parameter being estimated. Econometricians have formalized their study of these phenomena by structuring the concept of an *asymptotic distribution* and defining desirable asymptotic or "large-sample properties" of an estimator in terms of the character of its asymptotic distribution. The discussion below of this concept and how it is used is heuristic (and not technically correct); a more formal exposition appears in appendix C at the end of this book.

Consider the sequence of sampling distributions of an estimator $\hat{\beta}$, formed by calculating the sampling distribution of $\hat{\beta}$ for successively larger sample sizes. If the distributions in this sequence become more and more similar in form to some specific distribution (such as a normal distribution) as the sample size becomes extremely large, this specific distribution is called the asymptotic distribution of $\hat{\beta}$. Two basic estimator properties are defined in terms of the asymptotic distribution.

(1) If the asymptotic distribution of $\hat{\beta}$ becomes concentrated on a particular value k as the sample size approaches infinity, k is said to be the *probability limit* of $\hat{\beta}$ and is written plim $\hat{\beta} = k$; if plim $\hat{\beta} = \beta$, then $\hat{\beta}$ is said to be *consistent*.

(2) The variance of the asymptotic distribution of $\hat{\beta}$ is called the *asymptotic variance* of $\hat{\beta}$; if $\hat{\beta}$ is consistent and its asymptotic variance is smaller than

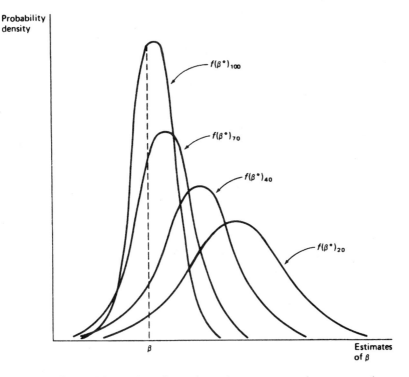

Figure 2.5   How sampling distribution can change as the
sample size grows

the asymptotic variance of all other consistent estimators, $\hat{\beta}$ is said to be
asymptotically efficient.

At considerable risk of oversimplification, the plim can be thought of as the
large-sample equivalent of the expected value, and so plim $\hat{\beta} = \beta$ is the large-
sample equivalent of unbiasedness. Consistency can be crudely conceptualized
as the large-sample equivalent of the minimum mean square error property,
since a consistent estimator can be (loosely speaking) thought of as having, in
the limit, zero bias and a zero variance. Asymptotic efficiency is the large-sample equivalent of best unbiasedness: the variance of an asymptotically efficient
estimator goes to zero faster than the variance of any other consistent estimator.

Figure 2.5 illustrates the basic appeal of asymptotic properties. For sample
size 20, the sampling distribution of β^* is shown as $f(\beta^*)_{20}$. Since this sampling
distribution is not centered over β, the estimator β^* is biased. As shown in figure 2.5, however, as the sample size increases to 40, then 70 and then 100, the
sampling distribution of β^* shifts so as to be more closely centered over β (i.e.,
it becomes less biased), and it becomes less spread out (i.e., its variance
becomes smaller). If β^* were consistent, as the sample size increased to infinity

the sampling distribution would shrink in width to a single vertical line, of infinite height, placed exactly at the point β.

It must be emphasized that these asymptotic criteria are only employed in situations in which estimators with the traditional desirable small-sample properties, such as unbiasedness, best unbiasedness and minimum mean square error, cannot be found. Since econometricians quite often must work with small samples, defending estimators on the basis of their asymptotic properties is legitimate only if it is the case that estimators with desirable asymptotic properties have more desirable small-sample properties than do estimators without desirable asymptotic properties. Monte Carlo studies (see section 2.10) have shown that in general this supposition is warranted.

The message of the discussion above is that when estimators with attractive small-sample properties cannot be found one may wish to choose an estimator on the basis of its large-sample properties. There is an additional reason for interest in asymptotic properties, however, of equal importance. Often the derivation of small-sample properties of an estimator is algebraically intractable, whereas derivation of large-sample properties is not. This is because, as explained in the technical notes, the expected value of a nonlinear function of a statistic is not the nonlinear function of the expected value of that statistic, whereas the plim of a nonlinear function of a statistic is equal to the nonlinear function of the plim of that statistic.

These two features of asymptotics give rise to the following four reasons for why asymptotic theory has come to play such a prominent role in econometrics.

(1) When no estimator with desirable small-sample properties can be found, as is often the case, econometricians are forced to choose estimators on the basis of their asymptotic properties. As example is the choice of the OLS estimator when a lagged value of the dependent variable serves as a regressor. See chapter 9.

(2) Small-sample properties of some estimators are extraordinarily difficult to calculate, in which case using asymptotic algebra can provide an indication of what the small-sample properties of this estimator are likely to be. An example is the plim of the OLS estimator in the simultaneous equations context. See chapter 10.

(3) Formulas based on asymptotic derivations are useful approximations to formulas that otherwise would be very difficult to derive and estimate. An example is the formula in the technical notes used to estimate the variance of a nonlinear function of an estimator.

(4) Many useful estimators and test statistics may never have been found had it not been for algebraic simplifications made possible by asymptotic algebra. An example is the development of LR, W and LM test statistics for testing nonlinear restrictions. See chapter 4.

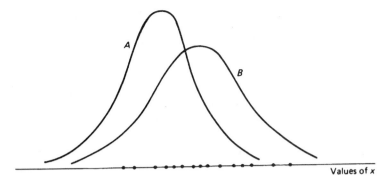

Figure 2.6 Maximum likelihood estimation

2.9 MAXIMUM LIKELIHOOD

The maximum likelihood principle of estimation is based on the idea that the sample of data at hand is more likely to have come from a "real world" characterized by one particular set of parameter values than from a "real world" characterized by any other set of parameter values. The maximum likelihood estimate (MLE) of a vector of parameter values β is simply the particular vector β^{MLE} that gives the greatest probability of obtaining the observed data.

This idea is illustrated in figure 2.6. Each of the dots represents an observation on x drawn at random from a population with mean μ and variance σ^2. Pair A of parameter values, μ^A and $(\sigma^2)^A$, gives rise in figure 2.6 to the probability density function A for x, while the pair B, μ^B and $(\sigma^2)^B$, gives rise to probability density function B. Inspection of the diagram should reveal that the probability of having obtained the sample in question if the parameter values were μ^A and $(\sigma^2)^A$ is very low compared with the probability of having obtained the sample if the parameter values were μ^B and $(\sigma^2)^B$. On the maximum likelihood principle, pair B is preferred to pair A as an estimate of μ and σ^2. The maximum likelihood estimate is the particular pair of values μ^{MLE} and $(\sigma^2)^{\text{MLE}}$ that creates the greatest probability of having obtained the sample in question; i.e., no other pair of values would be preferred to this maximum likelihood pair, in the sense that pair B is preferred to pair A. The means by which the econometrician finds this maximum likelihood estimate is discussed briefly in the technical notes to this section.

In addition to its intuitive appeal, the maximum likelihood estimator has several desirable asymptotic properties. It is asymptotically unbiased, it is consistent, it is asymptotically efficient, it is distributed asymptotically normally, and its asymptotic variance can be found via a standard formula (the Cramer-Rao lower bound – see the technical notes to this section). Its only major theoretical drawback is that in order to calculate the MLE the econometrician must assume a *specific* (e.g., normal) distribution for the error term. Most econometricians seem willing to do this.

These properties make maximum likelihood estimation very appealing for situations in which it is impossible to find estimators with desirable small-sample properties, a situation that arises all too often in practice. In spite of this, however, until recently maximum likelihood estimation has not been popular, mainly because of high computational cost. Considerable algebraic manipulation is required before estimation, and most types of MLE problems require substantial input preparation for available computer packages. But econometricians' attitudes to MLEs have changed recently, for several reasons. Advances in computers and related software have dramatically reduced the computational burden. Many interesting estimation problems have been solved through the use of MLE techniques, rendering this approach more useful (and in the process advertising its properties more widely). And instructors have been teaching students the theoretical aspects of MLE techniques, enabling them to be more comfortable with the algebraic manipulations it requires.

2.10 MONTE CARLO STUDIES

A Monte Carlo study is a simulation exercise designed to shed light on the small-sample properties of competing estimators for a given estimating problem. They are called upon whenever, for that particular problem, there exist potentially attractive estimators whose small-sample properties cannot be derived theoretically. Estimators with unknown small-sample properties are continually being proposed in the econometric literature, so Monte Carlo studies have become quite common, especially now that computer technology has made their undertaking quite cheap. This is one good reason for having a good understanding of this technique. A more important reason is that a thorough understanding of Monte Carlo studies guarantees an understanding of the repeated sample and sampling distribution concepts, which are crucial to an understanding of econometrics. Appendix A at the end of this book has more on sampling distributions and their relation to Monte Carlo studies.

The general idea behind a Monte Carlo study is to (1) model the data-generating process, (2) generate several sets of artificial data, (3) employ these data and an estimator to create several estimates, and (4) use these estimates to gauge the sampling distribution properties of that estimator. This is illustrated in figure 2.7. These four steps are described below.

(1) *Model the data-generating process* Simulation of the process thought to be generating the real-world data for the problem at hand requires building a model for the computer to mimic the data-generating process, including its stochastic component(s). For example, it could be specified that N (the sample size) values of X, Z and an error term generate N values of Y according to $Y = \beta_1 + \beta_2 X + \beta_3 Z + \varepsilon$, where the β_i are specific, known numbers, the N val-

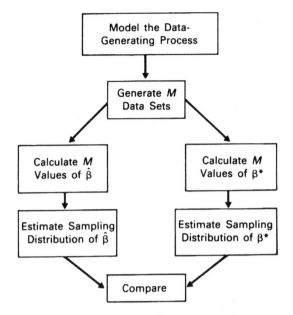

Figure 2.7   Structure of a Monte Carlo study

ues of X and Z are given, exogenous, observations on explanatory variables, and the N values of ε are drawn randomly from a normal distribution with mean zero and known variance σ^2. (Computers are capable of generating such random error terms.) Any special features thought to characterize the problem at hand must be built into this model. For example, if $\beta_2 = \beta_3^{-1}$ then the values of β_2 and β_3 must be chosen such that this is the case. Or if the variance σ^2 varies from observation to observation, depending on the value of Z, then the error terms must be adjusted accordingly. An important feature of the study is that all of the (usually unknown) parameter values are *known* to the person conducting the study (because this person chooses these values).

(2) *Create sets of data*   With a model of the data-generating process built into the computer, artificial data can be created. The key to doing this is the stochastic element of the data-generating process. A sample of size N is created by obtaining N values of the stochastic variable ε and then using these values, in conjunction with the rest of the model, to generate N values of Y. This yields one complete sample of size N, namely N observations on each of Y, X and Z, corresponding to the particular set of N error terms drawn. Note that this artificially generated set of sample data could be viewed as an *example* of real-world data that a researcher would be faced with when dealing with the kind of estimation problem this model represents. Note especially that the set of data obtained depends crucially on the particular set of error terms drawn. A different set of

error terms would create a different data set *for the same problem.* Several of these examples of data sets could be created by drawing different sets of N error terms. Suppose this is done, say, 2,000 times, generating 2,000 set of sample data, each of sample size N. These are called repeated samples.

(3) *Calculate estimates*   Each of the 2,000 repeated samples can be used as data for an estimator $\hat{\beta}_3$, say, creating 2,000 estimated $\hat{\beta}_{3i}$ ($i = 1, 2, \ldots, 2,000$) of the parameter β_3. These 2,000 estimates can be viewed as random "drawings" from the sampling distribution of $\hat{\beta}_3$.

(4) *Estimate sampling distribution properties*   These 2,000 drawings from the sampling distribution of $\hat{\beta}_3$ can be used as data to estimate the properties of this sampling distribution. The properties of most interest are its expected value and variance, estimates of which can be used to estimate bias and mean square error.

(a)   The *expected value* of the sampling distribution of $\hat{\beta}_3$ is estimated by the average of the 2,000 estimates:

$$\text{estimated expected value} = \bar{\hat{\beta}} = \left(\sum_{i=1}^{2,000} \hat{\beta}_{3i} \right) / 2,000.$$

(b)   The *bias* of $\hat{\beta}_3$ is estimated by subtracting the known true value of β_3 from the average:

$$\text{estimated bias} = \bar{\hat{\beta}}_3 - \beta_3.$$

(c)   The *variance* of the sampling distribution of $\hat{\beta}_3$ is estimated by using the traditional formula for estimating variance:

$$\text{estimated variance} = \sum_{i=1}^{2,000} (\hat{\beta}_{3i} - \bar{\hat{\beta}}_3)^2 / 1,999.$$

(d)   The *mean square error* of $\hat{\beta}_3$ is estimated by the average of the squared differences between $\hat{\beta}_3$ and the true value of β_3:

$$\text{estimated MSE} = \sum_{i=1}^{2,000} (\hat{\beta}_{3i} - \beta_3)^2 / 2,000.$$

At stage 3 above an alternative estimator β_3^* could also have been used to calculate 2,000 estimates. If so, the properties of the sampling distribution of β_3^* could also be estimated and then compared with those of the sampling distribution of $\hat{\beta}_3$. (Here $\hat{\beta}_3$ could be, for example, the ordinary least squares estimator and β_3^* any competing estimator such as an instrumental variable estimator, the least absolute error estimator or a generalized least squares estimator. These estimators are discussed in later chapters.) On the basis of this comparison, the person conducting the Monte Carlo study may be in a position to recommend one estimator in preference to another for the sample size N. By repeating such a study for progressively greater values of N, it is possible to investigate how quickly an estimator attains its asymptotic properties.

2.11 ADDING UP

Because in most estimating situations there does not exist a "super-estimator" that is better than all other estimators on all or even most of these (or other) criteria, the ultimate choice of estimator is made by forming an "overall judgement" of the desirableness of each available estimator by combining the degree to which an estimator meets each of these criteria with a subjective (on the part of the econometrician) evaluation of the importance of each of these criteria. Sometimes an econometrician will hold a particular criterion in very high esteem and this will determine the estimator chosen (if an estimator meeting this criterion can be found). More typically, other criteria also play a role on the econometrician's choice of estimator, so that, for example, only estimators with reasonable computational cost are considered. Among these major criteria, most attention seems to be paid to the best unbiased criterion, with occasional deference to the mean square error criterion in estimating situations in which all unbiased estimators have variances that are considered too large. If estimators meeting these criteria cannot be found, as is often the case, asymptotic criteria are adopted.

A major skill of econometricians is the ability to determine estimator properties with regard to the criteria discussed in this chapter. This is done either through theoretical derivations using mathematics, part of the technical expertise of the econometrician, or through Monte Carlo studies. To derive estimator properties by either of these means, the mechanism generating the observations must be known; changing the way in which the observations are generated creates a new estimating problem, in which old estimators may have new properties and for which new estimators may have to be developed.

The OLS estimator has a special place in all this. When faced with any estimating problem, the econometric theorist usually checks the OLS estimator first, determining whether or not it has desirable properties. As seen in the next chapter, in some circumstances it does have desirable properties and is chosen as the "preferred" estimator, but in many other circumstances it does not have desirable properties and a replacement must be found. The econometrician must investigate whether the circumstances under which the OLS estimator is desirable are met, and, if not, suggest appropriate alternative estimators. (Unfortunately, in practice this is too often not done, with the OLS estimator being adopted without justification.) The next chapter explains how the econometrician orders this investigation.

GENERAL NOTES

2.2 Computational Cost

- Computational cost has been reduced significantly by the development of extensive computer software for econometricians. The more prominent of these are ET,

GAUSS, LIMDEP, Micro-FIT, PC-GIVE, RATS, SAS, SHAZAM, SORITEC, SPSS, and TSP. The *Journal of Applied Econometrics* and the *Journal of Economic Surveys* both publish software reviews regularly. All these packages are very comprehensive, encompassing most of the econometric techniques discussed in textbooks. For applications they do not cover, in most cases specialized programs exist. These packages should only be used by those well versed in econometric theory, however. Misleading or even erroneous results can easily be produced if these packages are used without a full understanding of the circumstances in which they are applicable, their inherent assumptions and the nature of their output; sound research cannot be produced merely by feeding data to a computer and saying SHAZAM.

- Problems with the accuracy of computer calculations are ignored in practice, but can be considerable. See Aigner (1971, pp. 99–101) and Rhodes (1975). Quandt (1983) is a survey of computational problems and methods in econometrics.

2.3   Least Squares

- Experiments have shown that OLS estimates tend to correspond to the average of laymen's "freehand" attempts to fit a line to a scatter of data. See Mosteller et al. (1981).
- In figure 2.1 the residuals were measured as the vertical distances from the observations to the estimated line. A natural alternative to this vertical measure is the orthogonal measure – the distance from the observation to the estimating line along a line perpendicular to the estimating line. This infrequently seen alternative is discussed in Malinvaud (1966, pp. 7–11); it is sometimes used when measurement errors plague the data, as discussed in section 9.2

2.4   Highest R^2

- R^2 is called the coefficient of determination. It is the square of the correlation coefficient between y and its OLS estimate $\hat{y}$.
- The total variation of the dependent variable y about its mean, $\Sigma(y - \bar{y})^2$, is called SST (the total sum of squares); the "explained" variation, the sum of squared deviations of the estimated values of the dependent variable about their mean, $\Sigma(\hat{y} - \bar{\hat{y}})^2$ is called *SSR* (the regression sum of squares); and the "unexplained" variation, the sum of squared residuals, is called *SSE* (the error sum of squares). R^2 is then given by *SSR/SST* or by $1 - (SSE/SST)$.
- What is a high R^2? There is no generally accepted answer to this question. In dealing with time series data, very high R^2s are not unusual, because of common trends. Ames and Reiter (1961) found, for example, that on average the R^2 of a relationship between a randomly chosen variable and its own value lagged one period is about 0.7, and that an R^2 in excess of 0.5 could be obtained by selecting an economic time series and regressing it against two to six other randomly selected economic time series. For cross-sectional data, typical R^2s are not nearly so high.
- The OLS estimator maximizes R^2. Since the R^2 measure is used as an index of how well an estimator "fits" the sample data, the OLS estimator is often called the "best-fitting" estimator. A high R^2 is often called a "good fit."
- Because the R^2 and OLS criteria are formally identical, objections to the latter apply

to the former. The most frequently voiced of these is that searching for a good fit is likely to generate parameter estimates tailored to the particular sample at hand rather than to the underlying "real world." Further, a high R^2 is not necessary for "good" estimates; R^2 could be low because of a high variance of the disturbance terms, and our estimate of β could be "good" on other criteria, such as those discussed later in this chapter.

- The neat breakdown of the total variation into the "explained " and "unexplained" variations that allows meaningful interpretation of the R^2 statistic is valid only under three conditions. First, the estimator in question must be the OLS estimator. Second, the relationship being estimated must be linear. Thus the R^2 statistic only gives the percentage of the variation in the dependent variable explained *linearly* by variation in the independent variables. And third, the linear relationship being estimated must include a constant, or intercept, term. The formulas for R^2 can still be used to calculate an R^2 for estimators other than the OLS estimator, for nonlinear cases and for cases in which the intercept term is omitted; it can no longer have the same meaning, however, and could possibly lie outside the 0–1 interval. The zero intercept case is discussed at length in Aigner (1971, pp. 85–90). An alternative R^2 measure, in which the variations in y and $\hat{y}$ are measured as deviations from zero rather than their means, is suggested.

- Running a regression without an intercept is the most common way of obtaining an R^2 outside the 0–1 range. To see how this could happen, draw a scatter of points in (x,y) space with an estimated OLS line such that there is a substantial intercept. Now draw in the OLS line that would be estimated if it were forced to go through the origin. In both cases *SST* is identical (because the same observations are used). But in the second case the *SSE* and the *SSR* could be gigantic, because the $\hat{\varepsilon}$s and the $(\hat{y} - \bar{y})$s could be huge. Thus if R^2 is calculated as $1 - SSE/SST$, a negative number could result; if it is calculated as SSR/SST, a number greater than one could result.

- R^2 is sensitive to the range of variation of the dependent variable, so that comparisons of R^2s must be undertaken with care. The favorite example used to illustrate this is the case of the consumption function versus the savings function. If savings is defined as income less consumption, income will do exactly as well in explaining variations in consumption as in explaining variations in savings, in the sense that the sum of squared residuals, the unexplained variation, will be exactly the same for each case. But in *percentage* terms, the unexplained variation will be a higher percentage of the variation in savings than of the variation in consumption because the latter are larger numbers. Thus the R^2 in the savings function case will be lower than in the consumption function case. This reflects the result that the expected value of R^2 is approximately equal to $\beta^2 V/(\beta^2 V + \sigma^2)$ where V is $\Sigma(x - \bar{x})^2$.

- In general, econometricians are interested in obtaining "good" parameter estimates where "good" is not defined in terms of R^2. Consequently the measure R^2 is not of much importance in econometrics. Unfortunately, however, many practitioners act as though it is important, for reasons that are not entirely clear, as noted by Cramer (1987, p. 253):

> These measures of goodness of fit have a fatal attraction. Although it is generally conceded among insiders that they do not mean a thing, high values are still a source of pride and satisfaction to their authors, however hard they may try to conceal these feelings.

Because of this, the meaning and role of R^2 are discussed at some length throughout this book. Section 5.5 and its general notes extend the discussion of this section. Comments are offered in the general notes of other sections when appropriate. For example, one should be aware that R^2 from two equations with different dependent variables should not be compared, and that adding dummy variables (to capture seasonal influences, for example) can inflate R^2, and that regressing on group means overstates R^2 because the error terms have been averaged.

2.5   Unbiasedness

- In contrast to the OLS and R^2 criteria, the unbiasedness criterion (and the other criteria related to the sampling distribution) says something specific about the relationship of the estimator to β, the parameter being estimated.
- Many econometricians are not impressed with the unbiasedness criterion, as our later discussion of the mean square error criterion will attest. Savage (1954, p. 244) goes so far as to say: "A serious reason to prefer unbiased estimates seems never to have been proposed." This feeling probably stems from the fact that it is possible to have an "unlucky" sample and thus a bad estimate, with only cold comfort from the knowledge that, had all possible samples of that size been taken, the correct estimate would have been hit on average. This is especially the case whenever a crucial outcome, such as in the case of a matter of life or death, or a decision to undertake a huge capital expenditure, hinges on a single correct estimate. None the less, unbiasedness has enjoyed remarkable popularity among practitioners. Part of the reason for this may be due to the emotive content of the terminology: who can stand up in public and state that they prefer *biased* estimators?
- The main objection to the unbiasedness criterion is summarized nicely by the story of the three econometricians who go duck hunting. The first shoots about a foot in front of the duck, the second about a foot behind; the third yells, "We got him!"

2.6   Efficiency

- Often econometricians forget that although the BLUE property is attractive, its requirement that the estimator be linear can sometimes be restrictive. If the errors have been generated from a "fat-tailed" distribution, for example, so that relatively high errors occur frequently, linear unbiased estimators are inferior to several popular nonlinear unbiased estimators, called robust estimators. See chapter 19.
- Linear estimators are not suitable for all estimating problems. For example, in estimating the variance σ^2 of the disturbance term, quadratic estimators are more appropriate. The traditional formula $SSE/(T - K)$, where T is the number of observations and K is the number of explanatory variables (including a constant), is under general conditions the best quadratic unbiased estimator of σ^2. When K does not include the constant (intercept) term, this formula is written as $SSE(T - K - 1)$.
- Although in many instances it is mathematically impossible to determine the best unbiased estimator (as opposed to the best *linear* unbiased estimator), this is not the case if the *specific* distribution of the error is known. In this instance a lower bound, called the *Cramer–Rao lower bound*, for the variance (or variance–covariance matrix)

of unbiased estimators can be calculated. Furthermore, if this lower bound is attained (which is not always the case), it is attained by a transformation of the maximum likelihood estimator (see section 2.9) creating an unbiased estimator. As an example, consider the sample mean statistic $\bar{X}$. Its variance, σ^2/T, is equal to the Cramer–Rao lower bound if the parent population is normal. Thus $\bar{X}$ is the best unbiased estimator (whether linear or not) of the mean of a normal population.

2.7 Mean Square Error (MSE)

- Preference for the mean square error criterion over the unbiasedness criterion often hinges on the use to which the estimate is put. As an example of this, consider a man betting on horse races. If he is buying "win" tickets, he will want an unbiased estimate of the winning horse, but if he is buying "show" tickets it is not important that his horse wins the race (only that his horse finishes among the first three), so he will be willing to use a slightly biased estimator of the winning horse if it has a smaller variance.
- The difference between the variance of an estimator and its MSE is that the variance measures the dispersion of the estimator around its mean whereas the MSE measures its dispersion around the true value of the parameter being estimated. For unbiased estimators they are identical.
- Biased estimators with smaller variances than unbiased estimators are easy to find. For example, if $\hat{\beta}$ is an unbiased estimator with variance $V(\hat{\beta})$, then $0.9\hat{\beta}$ is a biased estimator with variance $0.81V(\hat{\beta})$. As a more relevant example, consider the fact that, although $(SSE/(T-K))$ is the best quadratic unbiased estimator of σ^2, as noted in section 2.6, it can be shown that among quadratic estimators the MSE estimator of σ^2 is $SSE/(T-K+2)$.
- The MSE estimator has not been as popular as the best unbiased estimator because of the mathematical difficulties in its derivation. Furthermore, when it can be derived its formula often involves unknown coefficients (the value of β), making its application impossible. Monte Carlo studies have shown that approximating the estimator by using OLS estimates of the unknown parameters can sometimes circumvent this problem.

2.8 Asymptotic Properties

- How large does the sample size have to be for estimators to display their asymptotic properties? The answer to this crucial question depends on the characteristics of the problem at hand. Goldfeld and Quandt (1972, p. 277) report an example in which a sample size of 30 is sufficiently large and an example in which a sample of 200 is required. They also note that large sample sizes are needed if interest focuses on estimation of estimator variances rather than on estimation of coefficients.
- An observant reader of the discussion in the body of this chapter might wonder why the large-sample equivalent of the expected value is defined as the plim rather than being called the "asymptotic expectation." In practice most people use the two terms synonymously, but technically the latter refers to the limit of the expected value, which is usually, but not always, the same as the plim. For discussion see the technical notes to appendix C.

2.9   Maximum Likelihood

- Note that β^{MLE} is *not*, as is sometimes carelessly stated, the most probable value of β; the most probable value of β is β itself. (Only in a Bayesian interpretation, discussed later in this book, would the former statement be meaningful.) β^{MLE} is simply the value of β that maximizes the probability of drawing the sample actually obtained.
- The asymptotic variance of the MLE is usually equal to the Cramer–Rao lower bound, the lowest asymptotic variance that a consistent estimator can have. This is why the MLE is asymptotically efficient. Consequently, the variance (not just the asymptotic variance) of the MLE is estimated by an estimate of the Cramer–Rao lower bound. The formula for the Cramer–Rao lower bound is given in the technical notes to this section.
- Despite the fact that β^{MLE} is sometimes a biased estimator of β (although asymptotically unbiased), often a simple adjustment can be found that creates an unbiased estimator, and this unbiased estimator can be shown to be best unbiased (with no linearity requirement) through the relationship between the maximum likelihood estimator and the Cramer–Rao lower bound. For example, the maximum likelihood estimator of the variance of a random variable x is given by the formula

$$\sum_{i=1}^{T}(x_i - \bar{x})^2/T$$

which is a biased (but asymptotically unbiased) estimator of the true variance. By multiplying this expression by $T/(T-1)$, this estimator can be transformed into a best unbiased estimator.
- Maximum likelihood estimators have an invariance property similar to that of consistent estimators. The maximum likelihood estimator of a nonlinear function of a parameter is the nonlinear function of the maximum likelihood estimator of that parameter: $[g(\beta)]^{\text{MLE}} = g(\beta^{\text{MLE}})$ where g is a nonlinear function. This greatly simplifies the algebraic derivations of maximum likelihood estimators, making adoption of this criterion more attractive.
- Goldfeld and Quandt (1972) conclude that the maximum likelihood technique performs well in a wide variety of applications and for relatively small sample sizes. It is particularly evident, from reading their book, that the maximum likelihood technique is well-suited to estimation involving nonlinearities and unusual estimation problems. Even in 1972 they did not feel that the computational costs of MLE were prohibitive.
- Application of the maximum likelihood estimation technique requires that a specific distribution for the error term be chosen. In the context of regression, the normal distribution is invariably chosen for this purpose, usually on the grounds that the error term consists of the sum of a large number of random shocks and thus, by the Central Limit Theorem, can be considered to be approximately normally distributed. (See Bartels, 1977, for a warning on the use of this argument.) A more compelling reason is that the normal distribution is relatively easy to work with. See the general notes to chapter 4 for further discussion. In later chapters we encounter situations (such as count data and logit models) in which a distribution other than the normal is employed.
- Maximum likelihood estimates that are formed on the incorrect assumption that the errors are distributed normally are called quasi-maximum likelihood estimators. In

many circumstances they have the same asymptotic distribution as that predicted by assuming normality, and often related test statistics retain their validity (asymptotically, of course). See Godfrey (1988, p. 40–2) for discussion.

- Kmenta (1986, pp. 175–83) has a clear discussion of maximum likelihood estimation. A good brief exposition is in Kane (1968, pp. 177–80). Valavanis (1959, pp. 23–6), an econometrics text subtitled "An Introduction to Maximum Likelihood Methods," has an interesting account of the meaning of the maximum likelihood technique.

2.10   Monte Carlo Studies

- In this author's opinion, understanding Monte Carlo studies is one of the most important elements of studying econometrics, not because a student may need actually to do a Monte Carlo study, but because an understanding of Monte Carlo studies guarantees an understanding of the concept of a sampling distribution and the uses to which it is put. For examples and advice on Monte Carlo methods see Smith (1973) and Kmenta (1986, chapter 2). Hendry (1984) is a more advanced reference. Appendix A at the end of this book provides further discussion of sampling distributions and Monte Carlo studies. Several exercises in appendix D illustrate Monte Carlo studies.
- If a researcher is worried that the specific parameter values used in the Monte Carlo study may influence the results, it is wise to choose the parameter values equal to the estimated parameter values using the data at hand, so that these parameter values are reasonably close to the true parameter values. Furthermore, the Monte Carlo study should be repeated using nearby parameter values to check for sensitivity of the results. Bootstrapping is a special Monte Carlo method designed to reduce the influence of assumptions made about the parameter values and the error distribution. Section 4.6 of chapter 4 has an extended discussion.
- The Monte Carlo technique can be used to examine test statistics as well as parameter estimators. For example, a test statistic could be examined to see how closely its sampling distribution matches, say, a chi-square. In this context interest would undoubtedly focus on determining its size (type I error for a given critical value) and power, particularly as compared with alternative test statistics.
- By repeating a Monte Carlo study for several different values of the factors that affect the outcome of the study, such as sample size or nuisance parameters, one obtains several estimates of, say, the bias of an estimator. These estimated biases can be used as observations with which to estimate a functional relationship between the bias and the factors affecting the bias. This relationship is called a *response surface*. Davidson and MacKinnon (1993, pp. 755–63) has a good exposition.
- It is common to hold the values of the explanatory variables fixed during repeated sampling when conducting a Monte Carlo study. Whenever the values of the explanatory variables are affected by the error term, such as in the cases of simultaneous equations, measurement error, or the lagged value of a dependent variable serving as a regressor, this is illegitimate and must not be done – the process generating the data must be properly mimicked. But in other cases it is not obvious if the explanatory variables should be fixed. If the sample exhausts the population, such as would be the case for observations on all cities in Washington state with population greater than 30,000, it would not make sense to allow the explanatory variable values to change during repeated sampling. On the other hand, if a sample of wage-earners is drawn

from a very large potential sample of wage-earners, one could visualize the repeated sample as encompassing the selection of wage-earners as well as the error term, and so one could allow the values of the explanatory variables to vary in some representative way during repeated samples. Doing this allows the Monte Carlo study to produce an estimated sampling distribution which is not sensitive to the characteristics of the particular wage-earners in the sample; fixing the wage-earners in repeated samples produces an estimated sampling distribution conditional on the observed sample of wage-earners, which may be what one wants if decisions are to be based on that sample.

2.11   Adding Up

- Other, less prominent, criteria exist for selecting point estimates, some examples of which follow.

  (a) *Admissibility*   An estimator is said to be admissible (with respect to some criterion) if, for at least one value of the unknown β, it cannot be beaten on that criterion by any other estimator.

  (b) *Minimax*   A minimax estimator is one that minimizes the maximum expected loss, usually measured as MSE, generated by competing estimators as the unknown β varies through its possible values.

  (c) *Robustness*   An estimator is said to be robust if its desirable properties are not sensitive to violations of the conditions under which it is optimal. In general, a robust estimator is applicable to a wide variety of situations, and is relatively unaffected by a small number of bad data values. See chapter 19.

  (d) *MELO*   In the Bayesian approach to statistics (see chapter 13), a decision-theoretic approach is taken to estimation; an estimate is chosen such that it minimizes an expected loss function and is called the MELO (minimum expected loss) estimator. Under general conditions, if a quadratic loss function is adopted the mean of the posterior distribution of β is chosen as the point estimate of β and this has been interpreted in the non-Bayesian approach as corresponding to minimization of average risk. (Risk is the sum of the MSEs of the individual elements of the estimator of the vector β.) See Zellner (1978).

  (e) *Analogy principle*   Parameters are estimated by sample statistics that have the same property in the sample as the parameters do in the population. See chapter 2 of Goldberger (1968b) for an interpretation of the OLS estimator in these terms. Manski (1988) gives a more complete treatment. This approach is sometimes called the *method of moments* because it implies that a moment of the population distribution should be estimated by the corresponding moment of the sample. See the technical notes.

  (f) *Nearness/concentration*   Some estimators have infinite variances and for that reason are often dismissed. With this in mind, Fiebig (1985) suggests using as a criterion the *probability of nearness* (prefer $\hat{\beta}$ to β^* if prob $(|\hat{\beta} - \beta| < |\beta^* - \beta|) \geq 0.5$) or the *probability of concentration* (prefer $\hat{\beta}$ to β^* if prob $(|\hat{\beta} - \beta| < \delta) > $ prob $(|\beta^* - \beta| < \delta)$.

- Two good introductory references for the material of this chapter are Kmenta (1986, pp. 9–16, 97–108, 156–72) and Kane (1968, chapter 8).

TECHNICAL NOTES

2.5   Unbiasedness

- The expected value of a variable x is defined formally as $Ex = \int x f(x) dx$ where f is the probability density function (sampling distribution) of x. Thus $E(x)$ could be viewed as a weighted average of all possible values of x where the weights are proportional to the heights of the density function (sampling distribution) of x.

2.6   Efficiency

- In this author's experience, student assessment of sampling distributions is hindered, more than anything else, by confusion about how to calculate an estimator's variance. This confusion arises for several reasons.

(1)   There is a crucial difference between a variance and an estimate of that variance, something that often is not well understood.

(2)   Many instructors assume that some variance formulas are "common knowledge," retained from previous courses.

(3)   It is frequently not apparent that the derivations of variance formulas all follow a generic form.

(4)   Students are expected to recognize that some formulas are special cases of more general formulas.

(5)   Discussions of variance, and appropriate formulas, are seldom gathered together in one place for easy reference.

Appendix B has been included at the end of this book to alleviate this confusion, supplementing the material in these technical notes.

- In our discussion of unbiasedness, no confusion could arise from β being multidimensional: an estimator's expected value is either equal to β (in every dimension) or it is not. But in the case of the variance of an estimator, confusion could arise. An estimator β^* that is k-dimensional really consists of k different estimators, one for each dimension of β. These k different estimators all have their own variances. If all k of the variances associated with the estimator β^* are smaller than their respective counterparts of the estimator $\hat{\beta}$, then it is clear that the variance of β^* can be considered smaller than the variance of $\hat{\beta}$. For example, if β is two-dimensional, consisting of two separate parameters β_1 and β_2

$$\left(\text{i.e., } \beta = \begin{bmatrix} \beta_1 \\ \beta_2 \end{bmatrix} \right),$$

an estimator β^* would consist of two estimators β_1^* and β_2^*. If β^* were an unbiased estimator of β, β_1^* would be an unbiased estimator of β_1^*, and β_2^* would be an unbiased estimator of β_2. The estimators β_1^* and β_2^* would each have variances. Suppose their variances were 3.1 and 7.4, respectively. Now suppose $\hat{\beta}$, consisting of $\hat{\beta}_1$ and $\hat{\beta}_2$, is another unbiased estimator, where $\hat{\beta}_1$ and $\hat{\beta}_2$ have variances 5.6 and 8.3, respectively. In this example, since the variance of β_1^* is less than the variance of $\hat{\beta}_1$ and the variance of β_2^* is less than the variance of $\hat{\beta}_2$, it is clear that the "variance" of β^* is less than the variance of $\hat{\beta}$. But what if the variance of $\hat{\beta}_2$ were 6.3 instead of 8.3? Then it is *not* clear which "variance" is smallest.

- An additional complication exists in comparing the variances of estimators of a multidimensional β. There may exist a nonzero covariance between the estimators of the separate components of β. For example, a positive covariance between $\hat{\beta}_1$ and $\hat{\beta}_2$ implies that, whenever $\hat{\beta}_1$ overestimates β_1, there is a tendency for $\hat{\beta}_2$ to overestimate β_2, making the complete estimate of β worse than would be the case were this covariance zero. Comparison of the "variances" of multidimensional estimators should therefore somehow account for this covariance phenomenon.

- The "variance" of a multidimensional estimator is called a variance–covariance matrix. If β^* is an estimator of k-dimensional β, then the variance–covariance matrix of β^*, denoted by $V(\beta^*)$, is defined as a $k \times k$ matrix (a table with k entries in each direction) containing the variances of the k elements of β^* along the diagonal and the covariances in the off-diagonal positions. Thus,

$$V(\beta^*) = \begin{bmatrix} V(\beta_1^*), & C(\beta_1^*, \beta_2^*), & \ldots, & C(\beta_1^*, \beta_k^*) \\ & V(\beta_2^*) & & \ddots \\ & & & V(\beta_k^*) \end{bmatrix}$$

where $V(\beta_k^*)$ is the variance of the kth element of β^* and $C(\beta_1^*, \beta_2^*)$ is the covariance between β_1^* and β_2^*. All this variance–covariance matrix does is array the relevant variances and covariances in a table. Once this is done, the econometrician can draw on mathematicians' knowledge of matrix algebra to suggest ways in which the variance–covariance matrix of one unbiased estimator could be considered "smaller" than the variance–covariance matrix of another unbiased estimator.

- Consider four alternative ways of measuring smallness among variance–covariance matrices, all accomplished by transforming the matrices into single numbers and then comparing those numbers:

   (1) choose the unbiased estimator whose variance–covariance matrix has the smallest *trace* (sum of diagonal elements);
   (2) choose the unbiased estimator whose variance–covariance matrix has the smallest *determinant;*
   (3) choose the unbiased estimator for which any given linear combination of its elements has the smallest variance;
   (4) choose the unbiased estimator whose variance–covariance matrix minimizes a *risk* function consisting of a weighted sum of the individual variances and covariances. (A risk function is the expected value of a traditional loss function, such as the square of the difference between an estimate and what it is estimating.)

This last criterion seems sensible: a researcher can weight the variances and covariances according to the importance he or she subjectively feels their minimization should be given in choosing an estimator. It happens that in the context of an unbiased estimator this risk function can be expressed in an alternative form, as the expected value of a quadratic function of the difference between the estimate and the true parameter value; i.e., $E(\hat{\beta} - \beta)'Q(\hat{\beta} - \beta)$. This alternative interpretation also makes good intuitive sense as a choice criterion for use in the estimating context.

If the weights in the risk function described above, the elements of Q, are chosen so as to make it impossible for this risk function to be negative (a reasonable request, since if it were negative it would be a gain, not a loss), then a very fortunate thing occurs. Under these circumstances all four of these criteria lead to the same choice of estimator. What is more, this result does *not* depend on the particular weights used in the risk function.

Although these four ways of defining a smallest matrix are reasonably straightforward, econometricians have chosen, for mathematical reasons, to use as their definition an equivalent but conceptually more difficult idea. This fifth rule says, choose the unbiased estimator whose variance–covariance matrix, when subtracted from the variance–covariance matrix of any other unbiased estimator, leaves a non-negative definite matrix. (A matrix A is non-negative definite if the quadratic function formed by using the elements of A as parameters $(x'Ax)$ takes on only non-negative values. Thus to ensure a non-negative risk function as described above, the weighting matrix Q must be non-negative definite.)

Proofs of the equivalence of these five selection rules can be constructed by consulting Rothenberg (1973, p. 8), Theil (1971, p. 121), and Goldberger (1964, p. 38).

- A special case of the risk function is revealing. Suppose we choose the weighting such that the variance of any one element of the estimator has a very heavy weight, with all other weights negligible. This implies that each of the elements of the estimator with the "smallest" variance–covariance matrix has individual minimum variance. (Thus, the example given earlier of one estimator with individual variances 3.1 and 7.4 and another with variances 5.6 and 6.3 is unfair; these two estimators could be combined into a new estimator with variances 3.1 and 6.3.) This special case also indicates that in general covariances play no role in determining the best estimator.

2.7   Mean Square Error (MSE)

- In the multivariate context the MSE criterion can be interpreted in terms of the "smallest" (as defined in the technical notes to section 2.6) MSE matrix. This matrix, given by the formula $E(\hat{\beta} - \beta)(\hat{\beta} - \beta)'$, is a natural matrix generalization of the MSE criterion. In practice, however, this generalization is shunned in favor of the sum of the MSEs of all the individual components of $\hat{\beta}$, a definition of *risk* that has come to be the usual meaning of the term.

2.8   Asymptotic Properties

- The econometric literature has become full of asymptotics, so much so that at least one prominent econometrician, Leamer (1988), has complained that there is too much of it. Appendix C of this book provides an introduction to the technical dimension of this important area of econometrics, supplementing the items that follow.
- The reason for the important result that $Eg(x) \neq g(Ex)$ for g nonlinear is illustrated in figure 2.8. On the horizontal axis are measured values of $\hat{\beta}$, the sampling distribution of which is portrayed by $pdf(\hat{\beta})$, with values of $g(\hat{\beta})$ measured on the vertical axis. Values A and B of $\hat{\beta}$, equidistant from $E\hat{\beta}$, are traced to give $g(A)$ and $g(B)$. Note that $g(B)$ is much farther from $g(E\hat{\beta})$ than is $g(A)$: high values of $\hat{\beta}$ lead to values of $g(\hat{\beta})$ considerably above $g(E\hat{\beta})$, but low values of $\hat{\beta}$ lead to values of $g(\hat{\beta})$ only slightly below $g(E\hat{\beta})$. Consequently the sampling distribution of $g(\hat{\beta})$ is asymmetric, as shown by $pdf[g(\hat{\beta})]$, and in this example the expected value of $g(\hat{\beta})$ lies above $g(E\hat{\beta})$.

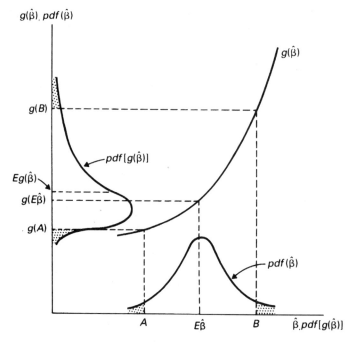

Figure 2.8 Why the expected value of a nonlinear function is not the nonlinear function of the expected value

If g were a linear function, the asymmetry portrayed in figure 2.8 would not arise and thus we would have $Eg(\hat{\beta}) = g(E\hat{\beta})$. For g nonlinear, however, this result does not hold.

Suppose now that we allow the sample size to become very large, and suppose that plim $\hat{\beta}$ exists and is equal to $E\hat{\beta}$ in figure 2.8. As the sample size becomes very large, the sampling distribution $pdf(\hat{\beta})$ begins to collapse on plim $\hat{\beta}$; i.e., its variance becomes very, very small. The points A and B are no longer relevant since values near them now occur with negligible probability. Only values of $\hat{\beta}$ very, very close to plim $\hat{\beta}$ are relevant; such values when traced through $g(\hat{\beta})$ are very, very close to g(plim $\hat{\beta}$). Clearly, the distribution of $g(\hat{\beta})$ collapses on g(plim $\hat{\beta}$) as the distribution of $\hat{\beta}$ collapses on plim $\hat{\beta}$. Thus plim $g(\hat{\beta}) = g$(plim $\hat{\beta}$), for g a continuous function.

For a simple example of this phenomenon, let g be the square function, so that $g(\hat{\beta}) = \hat{\beta}^2$. From the well-known result that $V(x) = E(x^2) - (Ex)^2$, we can deduce that $E(\hat{\beta}^2) = (E\hat{\beta})^2 + V(\hat{\beta})$. Clearly, $E(\hat{\beta}^2) \neq (E\hat{\beta})^2$, but if the variance of $\hat{\beta}$ goes to zero as the sample size goes to infinity then plim$(\hat{\beta}^2) = (\text{plim}\beta)^2$. The case of $\hat{\beta}$ equal to the sample mean statistic provides an easy example of this.

Note that in figure 2.8 the modes, as well as the expected values, of the two densities do not correspond. An explanation of this can be constructed with the help of the "change of variable" theorem discussed in the technical notes to section 2.9.

- An approximate correction factor can be estimated to reduce the small-sample bias discussed here. For example, suppose an estimate $\hat{\beta}$ of β is distributed normally with mean β and variance $V(\hat{\beta})$. Then exp $(\hat{\beta})$ is distributed log-normally with mean exp $[\beta + \frac{1}{2}V(\hat{\beta})]$, suggesting that exp (β) could be estimated by exp $[\hat{\beta} - \frac{1}{2}\hat{V}(\hat{\beta})]$ which, although biased, should have less bias than exp (β). If in this same example the original error were not distributed normally, so that $\hat{\beta}$ was not distributed normally, a Taylor series expansion could be used to deduce an appropriate correction factor. Expand exp $(\hat{\beta})$ around $E\hat{\beta} = \beta$ to get

$$\exp(\hat{\beta}) = \exp(\beta) + (\hat{\beta} - \beta)\exp(\beta) + \frac{1}{2}(\hat{\beta} - \beta)^2\exp(\beta)$$

plus higher-order terms which are neglected. Taking the expected value of both sides produces

$$E\exp(\hat{\beta}) = \exp\beta[1 + \frac{1}{2}V(\hat{\beta})]$$

suggesting that exp β could be estimated by

$$\exp(\hat{\beta})[1 + \frac{1}{2}\hat{V}(\hat{\beta})]^{-1}.$$

For discussion and examples of these kinds of adjustments, see Miller (1984), Kennedy (1981a, 1983) and Goldberger (1968a). An alternative way of producing an estimate of a nonlinear function $g(\beta)$ is to calculate many values of $g(\beta^* + \varepsilon)$, where ε is an error with mean zero and variance equal to the estimated variance of β^*, and average them. For more on this "smearing" estimate see Duan (1983).

- When g is a linear function, the variance of $g(\hat{\beta})$ is given by the square of the slope of g times the variance of $\hat{\beta}$; i.e., $V(ax) = a^2 V(x)$. When g is a continuous nonlinear function its variance is more difficult to calculate. As noted above in the context of figure 2.8, when the sample size becomes very large only values of $\hat{\beta}$ very, very close to plim $\hat{\beta}$ are relevant, and in this range a linear approximation to $(\hat{\beta})$ is adequate. The slope of such a linear approximation is given by the first derivative of g with respect to $\hat{\beta}$. Thus the asymptotic variance of $g(\hat{\beta})$ is often calculated as the square of this first derivative times the asymptotic variance of $\hat{\beta}$, with this derivative evaluated at $\hat{\beta} = $ plim $\hat{\beta}$ for the theoretical variance, and evaluated at $\hat{\beta}$ for the estimated variance.

2.9 Maximum Likelihood

- The likelihood of a sample is often identified with the "probability" of obtaining that sample, something which is, strictly speaking, not correct. The use of this terminology is accepted, however, because of an implicit understanding, articulated by Press et al. (1986, p. 500): "If the y_i's take on continuous values, the probability will always be zero unless we add the phrase, '. . . plus or minus some fixed Δy on each data point.' So let's always take this phrase as understood."
- The likelihood function is identical to the joint probability density function of the given sample. It is given a different name (i.e., the name "likelihood") to denote the fact that in this context it is to be *interpreted* as a function of the parameter values (since it is to be maximized with respect to those parameter values) rather than, as is usually the case, being interpreted as a function of the sample data.
- The mechanics of finding a maximum likelihood estimator are explained in most econometrics texts. Because of the importance of maximum likelihood estimation in

the econometric literature, an example is presented here. Consider a typical econometric problem of trying to find the maximum likelihood estimator of the vector

$$\beta = \begin{bmatrix} \beta_1 \\ \beta_2 \\ \beta_3 \end{bmatrix}$$

in the relationship $y = \beta_1 + \beta_2 x + \beta_3 z + \varepsilon$ where T observations on y, x and z are available.

(1) The first step is to specify the nature of the distribution of the disturbance term ε. Suppose the disturbances are identically and independently distributed with probability density function $f(\varepsilon)$. For example, it could be postulated that ε is distributed normally with mean zero and variance σ^2 so that

$$f(\varepsilon) = (2\pi\sigma^2)^{-\frac{1}{2}} \exp\{- \varepsilon^2/2\sigma^2\}.$$

(2) The second step is to rewrite the given relationship as $\varepsilon = y - \beta_1 - \beta_2 x - \beta_3 z$ so that for the ith value of ε we have

$$f(\varepsilon_i) = (2\pi\sigma^2)^{-\frac{1}{2}}\exp\left\{- \frac{1}{2\sigma^2}(y_i - \beta_1 - \beta_2 x_i - \beta_3 z_i)^2\right\}.$$

(3) The third step is to form the *likelihood function*, the formula for the joint probability distribution of the sample, i.e., a formula proportional to the probability of drawing the particular error terms inherent in this sample. If the error terms are independent of each other, this is given by the product of all the $f(\varepsilon)$s, one for each of the T sample observations. For the example at hand, this creates the likelihood function

$$L = (2\pi\sigma^2)^{-T/2}\exp\left\{- \frac{1}{2\sigma^2}\sum_{i=1}^{T}(y_i - \beta_1 - \beta_2 x_i - \beta_3 z_i)^2\right\}$$

a complicated function of the sample data and the unknown parameters β_1, β_2 and β_3, plus any unknown parameters inherent in the probability density function f– in this case σ^2.

(4) The fourth step is to find the set of values of the unknown parameters (β_1, β_2, β_3 and σ^2), as functions of the sample data, that maximize this likelihood function. Since the parameter values that maximize L also maximize lnL, and the latter task is easier, attention usually focuses on the log-likelihood function. In this example,

$$\ln L = - \frac{T}{2} \ln (2\pi\sigma^2) - \frac{1}{2\sigma^2}\sum_{i=1}^{T}(y_i - \beta_1 - \beta_2 x_i - \beta_3 z_i)^2.$$

In some simple cases, such as this one, the maximizing values of this function (i.e., the MLEs) can be found using standard algebraic maximizing techniques. In most cases, however, a numerical search technique (described in section 6.3) must be employed to find the MLE.

- There are two circumstances in which the technique presented above must be modified.

(1) *Density of y not equal to density of ε* We have observations on y, not $ε$. Thus, the likelihood function should be structured from the density of y, not the density of $ε$. The technique described above implicitly assumes that the density of y, $f(y)$, is identical to $f(ε)$, the density of $ε$ with $ε$ replaced in this formula by $y - Xβ$, but this is not necessarily the case. The probability of obtaining a value of $ε$ in the small range $dε$ is given by $f(ε)$ $dε$; this implies an equivalent probability for y of $f(y)|dy|$ where $f(y)$ is the density function of y and $|dy|$ is the absolute value of the range of y values corresponding to $dε$. Thus, because of $f(ε)$ $dε = f(y)|dy|$, we can calculate $f(y)$ as $f(ε) |dε/dy|$.

In the example given above $f(y)$ and $f(ε)$ are identical since $|dε/dy|$ is one. But suppose our example were such that we had

$$y^λ = β_0 + β_1x + β_2z + ε$$

where $λ$ is some (known or unknown) parameter. In this case,

$$f(y_i) = λy_i^{λ-1} f(ε_i)$$

and the likelihood function would become

$$L = λ^T \prod_{i=1}^{T} y_i^{λ-1} Q$$

where Q is the likelihood function of the original example, with each y_i raised to the power $λ$.

This method of finding the density of y when y is a function of another variable $ε$ whose density is known, is referred to as the *change-of-variable technique*. The multivariate analogue of $|dε/dy|$ is the absolute value of the *Jacobian* of the transformation – the determinant of the matrix of first derivatives of the vector $ε$ with respect to the vector y. Judge et al. (1988, pp. 30–6) have a good exposition.

(2) *Observations not independent* In the examples above, the observations were independent of one another so that the density values for each observation could simply be multiplied together to obtain the likelihood function. When the observations are not independent, for example if a lagged value of the regressand appears as a regressor, or if the errors are autocorrelated, an alternative means of finding the likelihood function must be employed. There are two ways of handling this problem.

(a) *Using a multivariate density* A multivariate density function gives the density of an entire vector of $ε$ rather than of just one element of that vector (i.e., it gives the "probability" of obtaining the entire set of $ε_i$). For example, the multivariate normal density function for the vector $ε$ is given (in matrix terminology) by the formula

$$f(ε) = (2πσ^2)^{-T/2}|\det Ω|^{-1/2}\exp\left\{\frac{1}{-2σ^2} ε'Ω^{-1}ε\right\}$$

where $\sigma^2\Omega$ is the variance–covariance matrix of the vector ε. This formula itself can serve as the likelihood function (i.e., there is no need to multiply a set of densities together since this formula has implicity already done that, as well as taking account of interdependencies among the data). Note that this formula gives the density of the vector ε, not the vector y. Since what is required is the density of y, a multivariate adjustment factor equivalent to the univariate $|d\varepsilon/dy|$ used earlier is necessary. This adjustment factor is $|\det d\varepsilon/dy|$ where $d\varepsilon/dy$ is a matrix containing in its ijth position the derivative of the ith observation of ε with respect to the jth observation of y. It is called the *Jacobian* of the transformation from ε to y. Watts (1973) has a good explanation of the Jacobian.

(b) *Using a transformation*   It may be possible to transform the variables of the problem so as to be able to work with errors that are independent. For example, suppose we have

$$y = \beta_1 + \beta_2 x + \beta_3 z + \varepsilon$$

but ε is such that $\varepsilon_t = \rho\varepsilon_{t-1} + u_t$ where u_t is a normally distributed error with mean zero and variance σ^2_u. The εs are not independent of one another, so the density for the vector ε cannot be formed by multiplying together all the individual densities; the multivariate density formula given earlier must be used, where Ω is a function of ρ and σ^2 is a function of ρ and σ^2_u. But the u errors are distributed independently, so the density of the u vector can be formed by multiplying together all the individual u_t densities. Some algebraic manipulation allows u_t to be expressed as

$$u_t = (y_t - \rho y_{t-1}) - \beta_1(1 - \rho) - \beta_2(x_t - \rho x_{t-1}) - \beta_3(z_t - \rho z_{t-1}).$$

(There is a special transformation for u_1; see the technical notes to section 8.3 where autocorrelated errors are discussed.) The density of the y vector, and thus the required likelihood function, is then calculated as the density of the u vector times the Jacobian of the transformation from u to y. In the example at hand, this second method turns out to be easier, since the first method (using a multivariate density function) requires that the determinant of Ω be calculated, a difficult task.

● Working through examples in the literature of the application of these techniques is the best way to become comfortable with them and to become aware of the uses to which MLEs can be put. To this end see Beach and MacKinnon (1978a), Savin and White (1978), Lahiri and Egy (1981), Spitzer (1982), Seaks and Layson (1983), and Layson and Seaks (1984).

● The Cramer–Rao lower bound is a matrix given by the formula

$$-\left[E\frac{\partial^2 \ln L}{\partial\theta^2} \right]^{-1}$$

where θ is the vector of unknown parameters (including σ^2) for the MLE estimates of which the Cramer–Rao lower bound is the asymptotic variance–covariance matrix. Its estimation is accomplished by inserting the MLE estimates of the unknown parameters. The inverse of the Cramer–Rao lower bound is called the *information matrix*.

• If the disturbances were distributed normally, the MLE estimator of σ^2 is *SSE/T*. Drawing on similar examples reported in preceding sections, we see that estimation of the variance of a normally distributed population can be computed as $SSE/(T - 1)$, *SSE/T* or $SSE/(T + 1)$, which are, respectively, the best unbiased estimator, the MLE, and the minimum MSE estimator. Here *SSE* is $\Sigma(x - \bar{x})^2$.

2.11   Adding Up

• The analogy principle of estimation is often called the *method of moments* because typically moment conditions (such as that $EX'\varepsilon = 0$, the covariance between the explanatory variables and the error is zero) are utilized to derive estimators using this technique. For example, consider a variable x with unknown mean μ. The mean μ of x is the first moment, so we estimate μ by the first moment (the average) of the data, $\bar{x}$. This procedure is not always so easy. Suppose, for example, that the density of x is given by $f(x) = \lambda x^{\lambda - 1}$ for $0 \le x \le 1$ and zero elsewhere. The expected value of x is $\lambda/(\lambda + 1)$ so the method of moments estimator λ^* of λ is found by setting $\bar{x} = \lambda^*/(\lambda^* + 1)$ and solving to obtain $\lambda^* = \bar{x}/(1 - \bar{x})$. In general we are usually interested in estimating several parameters and so will require as many of these moment conditions as there are parameters to be estimated, in which case finding estimates involves solving these equations simultaneously.

  Consider, for example, estimating α and β in $y = \alpha + \beta x + \varepsilon$. Because ε is specified to be an independent error, the expected value of the product of x and ε is zero, an "orthogonality" or "moment" condition. This suggests that estimation could be based on setting the product of x and the residual $\varepsilon^* = y - \alpha^* - \beta^* x$ equal to zero, where α^* and β^* are the desired estimates of α and β. Similarly, the expected value of ε (its first moment) is specified to be zero, suggesting that estimation could be based on setting the average of the ε^* equal to zero. This gives rise to two equations in two unknowns:

$$\Sigma(y - \alpha^* - \beta^* x)x = 0$$
$$\Sigma(y - \alpha^* - \beta^* x) = 0$$

which a reader might recognize as the normal equations of the ordinary least squares estimator. It is not unusual for a method of moments estimator to turn out to be a familiar estimator, a result which gives it some appeal. Greene (1997, pp. 145–53) has a good textbook exposition.

  This approach to estimation is straightforward so long as the number of moment conditions is equal to the number of parameters to be estimated. But what if there are more moment conditions than parameters? In this case there will be more equations than unknowns and it is not obvious how to proceed. The *generalized method of moments* (GMM) procedure, described in the technical notes of section 8.1, deals with this case.

3

THE CLASSICAL LINEAR
REGRESSION MODEL

3.1 TEXTBOOKS AS CATALOGS

In chapter 2 we learned that many of the estimating criteria held in high regard by econometricians (such as best unbiasedness and minimum mean square error) are characteristics of an estimator's sampling distribution. These characteristics cannot be determined unless a set of repeated samples can be taken or hypothesized; to take or hypothesize these repeated samples, knowledge of the way in which the observations are generated is necessary. Unfortunately, an estimator does not have the same characteristics for all ways in which the observations can be generated. This means that in some estimating situations a particular estimator has desirable properties but in other estimating situations it does *not* have desirable properties. Because there is no "superestimator" having desirable properties in all situations, for each estimating problem (i.e., for each different way in which the observations can be generated) the econometrician must determine anew which estimator is preferred. An econometrics textbook can be characterized as a catalog of which estimators are most desirable in what estimating situations. Thus, a researcher facing a particular estimating problem simply turns to the catalog to determine which estimator is most appropriate for him or her to employ in that situation. The purpose of this chapter is to explain how this catalog is structured.

The cataloging process described above is centered around a standard estimating situation referred to as the *classical linear regression model* (CLR model). It happens that in this standard situation the OLS estimator is considered the optimal estimator. This model consists of five assumptions concerning the way in which the data are generated. By changing these assumptions in one way or another, different estimating situations are created, in many of which the OLS estimator is no longer considered to be the optimal estimator. Most econometric problems can be characterized as situations in which one (or more) of these five assumptions is violated in a particular way. The catalog works in a straightforward way: the estimating situation is modeled in the general mold of the CLR model and then the researcher pinpoints the way in which this situation differs from the standard situation as described by the CLR model (i.e., finds out which assumption of the CLR model is violated in this problem); he or she then turns to the textbook (catalog) to see whether the OLS estimator retains its desirable properties, and if not what alternative estimator should be used. Because econometricians often are not certain of whether the estimating situation they face is one in which an assumption of the CLR model is violated, the catalog also includes a listing of techniques useful in testing whether or not the CLR model assumptions are violated.

3.2 THE FIVE ASSUMPTIONS

The CLR model consists of five basic assumptions about the way in which the observations are generated.

(1) The *first assumption* of the CLR model is that the dependent variable can be calculated as a linear function of a specific set of independent variables, plus a disturbance term. The unknown coefficients of this linear function form the vector β and are assumed to be constants. Several violations of this assumption, called specification errors, are discussed in chapter 6:

(a) *wrong regressors* – the omission of relevant independent variables or the inclusion of irrelevant independent variables;
(b) *nonlinearity* – when the relationship between the dependent and independent variables is not linear;
(c) *changing parameters* – when the parameters (β) do not remain constant during the period in which data were collected.

(2) The *second assumption* of the CLR model is that the expected value of the disturbance term is zero; i.e., the mean of the distribution from which the disturbance term is drawn is zero. Violation of this assumption leads to the *biased intercept* problem, discussed in chapter 7.

(3) The *third assumption* of the CLR model is that the disturbance terms all have the same variance and are not correlated with one another. Two major econometric problems, as discussed in chapter 8, are associated with violations of this assumption:

(a) *heteroskedasticity* – when the disturbances do not all have the same variance;
(b) *autocorrelated errors* – when the disturbances are correlated with one another.

(4) The *fourth assumption* of the CLR model is that the observations on the independent variable can be considered fixed in repeated samples; i.e., it is possible to repeat the sample with the same independent variable values. Three important econometric problems, discussed in chapters 9 and 10, correspond to violations of this assumption:

(a) *errors in variables* – errors in measuring the independent variables;
(b) *autoregression* – using a lagged value of the dependent variable as an independent variable;
(c) *simultaneous equation estimation* – situations in which the dependent variables are determined by the simultaneous interaction of several relationships.

(5) The *fifth assumption* of the CLR model is that the number of observations is greater than the number of independent variables and that there are no exact linear relationships between the independent variables. Although this is viewed as an assumption for the general case, for a specific case it can easily be checked, so that it need not be assumed. The problem of *multicollinearity* (two or more independent variables being approximately linearly related in the sample data) is associated with this assumption. This is discussed in chapter 11.

All this is summarized in table 3.1, which presents these five assumptions of the CLR model, shows the appearance they take when dressed in mathematical notation, and lists the econometric problems most closely associated with violations of these assumptions. Later chapters in this book comment on the meaning and significance of these assumptions, note implications of their violation for the OLS estimator, discuss ways of determining whether or not they are violated, and suggest new estimators appropriate to situations in which one of these assumptions must be replaced by an alternative assumption. Before we move on to this, however, more must be said about the character of the OLS estimator in the context of the CLR model, because of the central role it plays in the econometrician's "catalog."

3.3 THE OLS ESTIMATOR IN THE CLR MODEL

The central role of the OLS estimator in the econometrician's catalog is that of a standard against which all other estimators are compared. The reason for this is that the OLS estimator is extraordinarily popular. This popularity stems from the fact that, in the context of the CLR model, the OLS estimator has a large number of desirable properties, making it the overwhelming choice for the "optimal" estimator when the estimating problem is accurately characterized by the CLR model. This is best illustrated by looking at the eight criteria listed in chapter 2 and determining how the OLS estimator rates on these criteria in the context of the CLR model.

(1) *Computational cost* Because of the popularity of the OLS estimator, many packaged computer routines exist, and for simple cases hand-held calculators can be used to perform the required calculations quickly. (Some hand-held calculators have OLS estimation built in.) Whenever the functional form being estimated is linear, as it is in the CLR model, the OLS estimator involves very little computational cost.

Table 3.1 The assumptions of the CLR model

Assumption	Mathematical expression		Violations	Chapter in which discussed
	Bivariate	*Multivariate*		
(1) Dependent variable a linear function of a specific set of independent variables, plus a disturbance	$y_t = \beta_0 + \beta_1 x_t + \varepsilon_t$, $t = 1, \ldots, T$	$Y = X\beta + \varepsilon$	Wrong regressors Nonlinearity Changing parameters	6
(2) Expected value of disturbance term is zero	$E\varepsilon_t = 0$, for all t	$E\varepsilon = 0$	Biased intercept	7
(3) Disturbances have uniform variance and are uncorrelated	$E\varepsilon_t \varepsilon_r = 0, t \neq r$ $= \sigma^2, t = r$	$E\varepsilon\varepsilon' = \sigma^2 I$	Heteroskedasticity Autocorrelated errors	8
(4) Observations on independent variables can be considered fixed in repeated samples	x_t fixed in repeated samples	X fixed in repeated samples	Errors in variables Autoregression Simultaneous equations	9 10
(5) No exact linear relationships between independent variables and more observations than independent variables	$\sum_{t=1}^{T}(x_t - \bar{x})^2 \neq 0$	Rank of $X = K \leq T$	Perfect multicollinearity	11

The mathematical terminology is explained in the technical notes to this section. The notation is as follows: Y is a vector of observations on the dependent variable; X is a matrix of observations on the independent variables; ε is a vector of disturbances; σ^2 is the variance of the disturbances; I is the identity matrix; K is the number of independent variables; T is the number of observations.

(2) *Least squares* Because the OLS estimator is designed to minimize the sum of squared residuals, it is automatically "optimal" on this criterion.

(3) *Highest R^2* Because the OLS estimator is optimal on the least squares criterion, it will automatically be optimal on the highest R^2 criterion.

(4) *Unbiasedness* The assumptions of the CLR model can be used to show that the OLS estimator β^{OLS} is an unbiased estimator of β.

(5) *Best unbiasedness* In the CLR model β^{OLS} is a linear estimator; i.e., it can be written as a linear function of the errors. As noted earlier, it is unbiased. Among all linear unbiased estimators of β, it can be shown (in the context of the CLR model) to have the "smallest" variance–covariance matrix. Thus the OLS estimator is the BLUE in the CLR model. If we add the additional assumption that the disturbances are distributed normally (creating the CNLR model – the *classical normal linear regression model*), it can be shown that the OLS estimator is the best unbiased estimator (i.e., best among *all* unbiased estimators, not just linear unbiased estimators).

(6) *Mean square error* It is not the case that the OLS estimator is the minimum mean square error estimator in the CLR model. Even among linear estimators, it is possible that a substantial reduction in variance can be obtained by adopting a slightly biased estimator. This is the OLS estimator's weakest point; chapters 11 and 12 discuss several estimators whose appeal lies in the possibility that they may beat OLS on the MSE criterion.

(7) *Asymptotic criteria* Because the OLS estimator in the CLR model is unbiased, it is also unbiased in samples of infinite size and thus is asymptotically unbiased. It can also be shown that the variance–covariance matrix of β^{OLS} goes to zero as the sample size goes to infinity, so that β^{OLS} is also a consistent estimator of β. Further, in the CNLR model it is asymptotically efficient.

(8) *Maximum likelihood* It is impossible to calculate the maximum likelihood estimator given the assumptions of the CLR model, because these assumptions do not specify the functional form of the distribution of the disturbance terms. However, if the disturbances are assumed to be distributed normally (the CNLR model), it turns out that β^{MLE} is identical to β^{OLS}.

Thus, whenever the estimating situation can be characterized by the CLR model, the OLS estimator meets practically all of the criteria econometricians consider relevant. It is no wonder, then, that this estimator has become so popular. It is in fact *too* popular: it is often used, without justification, in estimating situations that are not accurately represented by the CLR model. If some of the CLR model assumptions do not hold, many of the desirable properties of the OLS estimator no longer hold. If the OLS estimator does not have the properties that are thought to be of most importance, an alternative estimator must be found. Before moving to this aspect of our examination of econometrics, however, we will spend a chapter discussing some concepts of and problems in inference, to provide a foundation for later chapters.

GENERAL NOTES

3.1 Textbooks as Catalogs

- The econometricians' catalog is not viewed favorably by all. Consider the opinion of Worswick (1972, p. 79): "[Econometricians] are not, it seems to me, engaged in forging tools to arrange and measure actual facts so much as making a marvellous array of pretend-tools which would perform wonders if ever a set of facts should turn up in the right form."

- Bibby and Toutenberg (1977, pp. 72–3) note that the CLR model, what they call the GLM (general linear model), can be a trap, a snare and a delusion. They quote Whitehead as saying: "Seek simplicity . . . and distrust it," and go on to explain how use of the linear model can change in undesirable ways the nature of the debate on the phenomenon being examined in the study in question. For example, casting the problem in the mold of the CLR model narrows the question by restricting its terms of reference to a particular model based on a particular set of data; it trivializes the question by focusing attention on apparently meaningful yet potentially trivial questions concerning the values of unknown regression coefficients; and it technicalizes the debate, obscuring the real questions at hand, by turning attention to technical statistical matters capable of being understood only by experts.

  They warn users of the GLM by noting that "it certainly eliminates the complexities of hardheaded thought, especially since so many computer programs exist. For the soft-headed analyst who doesn't want to think too much, an off-the-peg computer package is simplicity itself, especially if it cuts through a mass of complicated data and provides a few easily reportable coefficients. Occam's razor has been used to justify worse barbarities: but razors are dangerous things and should be used carefully."

- If more than one of the CLR model assumptions is violated at the same time, econometricians often find themselves in trouble because their catalogs usually tell them what to do if only *one* of the CLR model assumptions is violated. Much recent econometric research examines situations in which two assumptions of the CLR model are violated simultaneously. These situations will be discussed when appropriate.

3.3 The OLS Estimator in the CLR Model

- The process whereby the OLS estimator is applied to the data at hand is usually referred to by the terminology "running a regression." The dependent variable (the "regressand") is said to be "regressed" on the independent variables ("the regressors") to produce the OLS estimates. This terminology comes from a pioneering empirical study in which it was found that the mean height of children born of parents of a given height tends to "regress" or move towards the population average height. See Maddala (1977, pp. 97–101) for further comment on this and for discussion of the meaning and interpretation of regression analysis. Critics note that the *New Standard Dictionary* defines regression as "The diversion of psychic energy . . . into channels of fantasy."

- The result that the OLS estimator in the CLR model is the BLUE is often referred to as the Gauss–Markov theorem.

- The formula for the OLS estimator of a specific element of the β vector usually

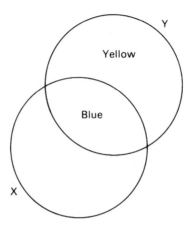

Figure 3.1   Defining the Ballentine Venn diagram

involves observations on *all* the independent variables (as well as observations on the dependent variable), not just observations on the independent variable corresponding to that particular element of β. This is because, to obtain an accurate estimate of the influence of one independent variable on the dependent variable, the simultaneous influence of other independent variables on the dependent variable must be taken into account. Doing this ensures that the jth element of β^{OLS} reflects the influence of the jth independent variable on the dependent variable, holding all the other independent variables constant. Similarly, the formula for the variance of an element of β^{OLS} also usually involves observations on all the independent variables.

- Because the OLS estimator is so popular, and because it so often plays a role in the formulation of alternative estimators, it is important that its mechanical properties be well understood. The most effective way of exposing these characteristics is through the use of a Venn diagram called the Ballentine. Suppose the CLR model applies, with Y determined by X and an error term. In figure 3.1 the circle Y represents variation in the dependent variable Y and the circle X represents variation in the independent variable X. The overlap of X with Y, the blue area, represents variation that Y and X have in common in the sense that this variation in Y can be explained by X via an OLS regression. The blue area reflects information employed by the estimating procedure in estimating the slope coefficient β_x; the larger this area, the more information is used to form the estimate and thus the smaller is its variance.

Now consider figure 3.2, in which a Ballentine for a case of two explanatory variables, X and Z, is portrayed (i.e., now Y is determined by both X and Z). In general, the X and Z circles will overlap, reflecting some collinearity between the two; this is shown in figure 3.2 by the red-plus-orange area. If Y were regressed on X alone, information in the blue-plus-red area would be used to estimate β_x, and if Y were regressed on Z alone, information in the green-plus-red area would be used to estimate β_z. What happens, though, if Y is regressed on X and Z together?

In the multiple regression of Y on X and Z together, the OLS estimator uses the

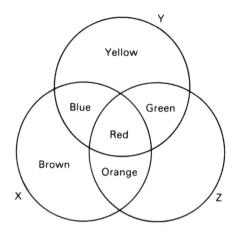

Figure 3.2   Interpreting multiple regression with the Ballentine

information in the blue area to estimate β_x and the information in the green area to estimate β_z, *discarding the information in the red area.* The information in the blue area corresponds to variation in Y that matches up uniquely with variation in X; using this information should therefore produce an unbiased estimate of β_x. Similarly, information in the green area corresponds to variation in Y that matches up uniquely with variation in Z; using this information should produce an unbiased estimate of β_z. The information in the red area is not used because it reflects variation in Y that is determined by variation in *both X and Z,* the relative contributions of which are not *a priori* known. In the blue area, for example, variation in Y is all due to variation in X, so matching up this variation in Y with variation in X should allow accurate estimation of β_x. But in the red area, matching up these variations will be misleading because not all variation in Y is due to variation in X.

- Notice that regression Y on X and Z together creates unbiased estimates of β_x and β_z whereas regressing Y on X and Z separately creates biased estimates of β_x and β_z because this latter method uses the red area. But notice also that, because the former method discards the red area, it uses less information to produce its slope coefficient estimates and thus these estimates will have larger variances. As is invariably the case in econometrics, the price of obtaining unbiased estimates is higher variances.
- Whenever X and Z are orthogonal to one another (have zero collinearity) they do not overlap as in figure 3.2 and the red area disappears. Because there is no red area in this case, regressing Y on X alone or on Z alone produces the same estimates of β_x and β_z as if Y were regressed on X and Z together. Thus, although in general the OLS estimate of a specific element of the β vector involves observations on *all* the regressors, in the case of orthogonal regressors it involves observations on only one regressor (the one for which it is the slope coefficient estimate).
- Whenever X and Z are highly collinear and therefore overlap a lot, the blue and green areas become very small, implying that when Y is regressed on X and Z together very

little information is used to estimate β_x and β_z. This causes the variances of these estimates to be very large. Thus, the impact of multicollinearity is to raise the variances of the OLS estimates. Perfect collinearity causes the X and Z circles to overlap completely; the blue and green areas disappear and estimation is impossible. Multicollinearity is discussed at length in chapter 11.

- In figure 3.1 the blue area represents the variation in Y explained by X. Thus, R^2 is given as the ratio of the blue area to the entire Y circle. In figure 3.2 the blue-plus-red-plus-green area represents the variation in Y explained by X and Z together. (Note that the red area is discarded only for the purpose of estimating the coefficients, not for predicting Y; once the coefficients are estimated, all variation in X and Z is used to predict Y.) Thus, the R^2 resulting from the multiple regression is given by the ratio of the blue-plus-red-plus-green area to the entire Y circle. Notice that there is no way of allocating portions of the total R^2 to X and Z because the red area variation is explained by *both*, in a way that cannot be disentangled. Only if X and Z are orthogonal, and the red area disappears, can the total R^2 be allocated unequivocally to X and Z separately.

- The yellow area represents variation in Y attributable to the error term, and thus the magnitude of the yellow area represents the magnitude of σ^2, the variance of the error term. This implies, for example, that if, in the context of figure 3.2, Y had been regressed on only X, omitting Z, σ^2 would be estimated by the yellow-plus-green area, an overestimate.

- The Ballentine was named, by its originators Cohen and Cohen (1975), after a brand of US beer whose logo resembles figure 3.2. Their use of the Ballentine was confined to the exposition of various concepts related to R^2. Kennedy (1981b) extended its use to the exposition of other aspects of regression. A limitation of the Ballentine is that it is necessary in certain cases for the red area to represent a negative quantity. (Suppose the two explanatory variables X and Z each have positive coefficients, but in the data X and Z are negatively correlated: X alone could do a poor job of explaining variation in Y because, for example, the impact of a high value of X is offset by a low value of Z.) This suggests that the explanations offered above are lacking and should be revised; for example, the result that regressing on X alone reduces the variance of its coefficient estimate should be explained in terms of this regression incorporating a greater range of variation of X (i.e., the entire X circle as opposed to just the blue-plus-brown area). This problem notwithstanding, the interpretation advanced earlier is retained in this book, on the grounds that the benefits of its illustrative power outweigh the danger that it will lead to error. The Ballentine is used here as a metaphoric device illustrating some regression results; it should not be given meaning beyond that.

- An alternative geometric analysis of OLS, using vector geometry, is sometimes used. Davidson and MacKinnon (1993, chap. 1) have a good exposition.

TECHNICAL NOTES

3.2 The Five Assumptions

- The regression model $y = g(x_1, \ldots, x_k) + \varepsilon$ is really a specification of how the conditional means $E(y|x_1, \ldots, x_k)$ are related to each other through x. The population regression function is written as $E(y|x_1, \ldots, x_k) = g(x)$; it describes how the average or expected value of y varies with x. Suppose g is a linear function so that the regression function is $y = \beta_1 + \beta_2 x_2 + \beta_3 x_3 + \ldots + \beta_k x_k + \varepsilon$. Each element of β^{OLS} (β_4^{OLS}, for example) is an estimate of the effect on the conditional expectation of y of a unit change in x_4, with all other x held constant.

- In the CLR model, the regression model is specified as $y = \beta_1 + \beta_2 x_2 + \ldots + \beta_k x_k +$ disturbance, a formula that can be written down T times, once for each set of observations on the dependent and independent variables. This gives a large stack of equations, which can be consolidated via matrix notation as $Y = X\beta + \varepsilon$. Here Y is a vector containing the T observations on the dependent variable y; X is a matrix consisting of K columns, each column being a vector of T observations on one of the independent variables; and ε is a vector containing the T unknown disturbances.

3.3   The OLS Estimator in the CLR Model

- The formula for β^{OLS} is $(X'X)^{-1}X'Y$. A proper derivation of this is accomplished by minimizing the sum of squared errors. An easy way of remembering this formula is to premultiply $Y = X\beta + \varepsilon$ by X' to get $X'Y = X'X\beta + X'\varepsilon$, drop the $X'\varepsilon$, and then solve for β.
- The formula for the variance–covariance matrix β^{OLS} is $\sigma^2 (X'X)^{-1}$ where σ^2 is the variance of the disturbance term. For the simple case in which the regression function is $y = \beta_1 + \beta_2 x_2$ this gives the formula $\sigma^2/\Sigma(x_2 - \bar{x}_2)^2$ for the variance of β_2^{OLS}. Note that, if the variation in the regressor values is substantial, the denominator of this expression will be large, tending to make the variance of β^{OLS} small.
- The variance–covariance matrix of β^{OLS} is usually unknown because σ^2 is usually unknown. It is estimated by $s^2(X'X)^{-1}$ where s^2 is an estimator of σ^2. The estimator s^2 is usually given by the formula $\hat{\varepsilon}'\hat{\varepsilon}/(T - K) = \Sigma\hat{\varepsilon}_i^2/(T - K)$ where $\hat{\varepsilon}$ is the estimate of the disturbance vector, calculated as $(Y - \hat{Y})$ where $\hat{Y}$ is $X\beta^{OLS}$. In the CLR model s^2 is the best quadratic unbiased estimator of σ^2; in the CNLR model it is best unbiased.
- By discarding the red area in figure 3.2, the OLS formula ensures that its estimates of the influence of one independent variable are calculated while controlling for the simultaneous influence of the other independent variables, i.e., the interpretation of, say, the jth element of β^{OLS} is as an estimate of the influence of the jth explanatory variable, holding all other explanatory variables constant. That the red area is discarded can be emphasized by noting that the OLS estimate of, say, β_x can be calculated from either the regression of Y on X and Z together or the regression of Y on X "residualized" with respect to Z (i.e., with the influence of Z removed). In figure 3.2, if we were to regress X on Z we would be able to explain the red-plus-orange area; the residuals from this regression, the blue-plus-brown area, is called X residualized for Z. Now suppose that Y is regressed on X residualized for Z. The overlap of the Y circle with the blue-plus-brown area is the blue area, so exactly the same information is used to estimate β_x in this method as is used when Y is regressed on X and Z together, resulting in an identical estimate of β_x.

  Notice further that, if Y were also residualized for Z, producing the yellow-plus-blue area, regressing the residualized Y on the residualized X would also produce the same estimate of β_x since their overlap is the blue area. An important implication of this result is that, for example, running a regression on data from which a linear time trend has been removed will produce exactly the same coefficient estimates as when a linear time trend is included among the regressors in a regression run on raw data. As another example, consider the removal of a linear seasonal influence; running a regression on linearly deseasonalized data will produce exactly the same coefficient estimates as if the linear seasonal influence were included as an extra regressor in a regression run on raw data.

- A variant of OLS called *stepwise regression* is to be avoided. It consists of regressing Y on each explanatory variable separately and keeping the regression with the highest R^2. This determines the estimate of the slope coefficient of that regression's explanatory variable. Then the residuals from this regression are used as the dependent variable in a new search using the remaining explanatory variables and the procedure is repeated. Suppose that, for the example of figure 3.2, the regression of Y on X produced a higher R^2 than the regression of Y on Z. Then the estimate of β_x would be formed using the information in the blue-plus-red area. Note that this estimate is biased.

- The Ballentine can be used to illustrate several variants of R^2. Consider, for example, the simple R^2 between Y and Z in figure 3.2. If the area of the Y circle is normalized to be unity, this simple R^2, denoted R^2_{yz}, is given by the red-plus-green area. The *partial* R^2 between Y and Z is defined as reflecting the influence of Z on Y *after* accounting for the influence of X. It is measured by obtaining the R^2 from the regression of Y corrected for X on Z corrected for X, and is denoted $R^2_{yz\cdot x}$. Our earlier use of the Ballentine makes it easy to deduce that in figure 3.2 it is given as the green area divided by the yellow-plus-green area. The reader might like to verify that it is given by the formula

$$R^2_{yz\cdot x} = (R^2 - R^2_{yx})/(1 - R^2_{yx}).$$

- The OLS estimator has several well-known mechanical properties with which students should become intimately familiar – instructors tend to assume this knowledge after the first lecture or two on OLS. Listed below are the more important of these properties; proofs can be found in most textbooks. The context is $y = \alpha + \beta x + \varepsilon$.

  (1) If $\beta = 0$ so that the only regressor is the intercept, y is regressed on a column of ones, producing $\alpha^{OLS} = \bar{y}$, the average of the y observations.
  (2) If $\alpha = 0$ so there is no intercept and one explanatory variable, y is regressed on a column of x values, producing $\beta^{OLS} = \Sigma xy/\Sigma x^2$.
  (3) If there is an intercept and one explanatory variable

$$\beta^{OLS} = \Sigma(x - \bar{x})(y - \bar{y})/\Sigma(x - \bar{x})^2 = \Sigma(x - \bar{x})y/\Sigma(x - \bar{x})^2.$$

  (4) If observations are expressed as deviations from their means, $y^* = y - \bar{y}$ and $x^* = x - \bar{x}$, then $\beta^{OLS} = \Sigma x^* y^*/\Sigma x^{*2}$. This follows from (3) above. Lower case letters are sometimes reserved to denote deviations from sample means.
  (5) The intercept can be estimated as $\bar{y} - \beta^{OLS}\bar{x}$ or, if there are more explanatory variables, as $\bar{y} - \Sigma\beta_i^{OLS}\bar{x}_i$. This comes from the first normal equation, the equation that results from setting the partial derivative of *SSE* with respect to α equal to zero (to minimize the *SSE*).
  (6) An implication of (5) is that the sum of the OLS residuals equals zero; in effect

the intercept is estimated by the value that causes the sum of the OLS residuals to equal zero.

(7) The predicted, or estimated, y values are calculated as $\hat{y} = \alpha^{OLS} + \beta^{OLS}x$. An implication of (6) is that the mean of the $\hat{y}$ values equals the mean of the actual y values: $\bar{\hat{y}} = \bar{y}$.

(8) An implication of (5), (6) and (7) above is that the OLS regression line passes through the overall mean of the data points.

(9) Adding a constant to a variable, or scaling a variable, has a predictable impact on the OLS estimates. For example, multiplying the x observations by 10 will multiply β^{OLS} by one-tenth, and adding 6 to the y observations will increase α^{OLS} by 6.

(10) A linear restriction on the parameters can be incorporated into a regression by eliminating one coefficient from that equation and running the resulting regression using transformed variables. For an example see the general notes to section 4.3.

(11) The "variation" in the dependent variable is the "total sum of squares" $SST = \Sigma(y - \bar{y})^2 = y'y - N\bar{y}^2$ where $y'y$ is matrix notation for Σy^2, and N is the sample size.

(12) The "variation" explained linearly by the independent variables is the "regression sum of squares," $SSR = \Sigma(\hat{y} - \bar{y})^2 = \hat{y}'\hat{y} - N\bar{y}^2$.

(13) The sum of squared errors from a regression is $SSE = (y - \hat{y})'(y - \hat{y}) = y'y - \hat{y}'\hat{y} = SST - SSR$. (Note that textbook notation varies. Some authors use SSE for "explained sum of squares" and SSR for "sum of squared residuals," creating results that look to be the opposite of those given here.)

(14) SSE is often calculated by $\Sigma y^2 - \alpha^{OLS}\Sigma y - \beta^{OLS}\Sigma xy$, or in the more general matrix notation $\Sigma y^2 - \beta^{OLS'}X'y$.

(15) The coefficient of determination, $R^2 = SSR/SST = 1 - SSE/SST$ is maximized by OLS because OLS minimizes SSE. R^2 is the squared correlation coefficient between y and $\hat{y}$; it is the fraction of the "variation" in y that is explained linearly by the explanatory variables.

(16) When no intercept is included, it is possible for R^2 to lie outside the zero to one range. See the general notes to section 2.4.

(17) Minimizing with some extra help cannot make the minimization less successful. Thus SSE decreases (or in unusual cases remains unchanged) when an additional explanatory variable is added; R^2 must therefore rise (or remain unchanged).

(18) Because the explanatory variable(s) is (are) given as much credit as possible for explaining changes in y, and the error as little credit as possible, ε^{OLS} is uncorrelated with the explanatory variable(s) and thus with $\hat{y}$ (because $\hat{y}$ is a linear function of the explanatory variable(s)).

(19) The estimated coefficient of the ith regressor can be obtained by regressing y on this regressor "residualized" for the other regressors (the residuals from a regression of the ith regressor on all the other regressors). The same result is obtained if the "residualized" y is used as the regressand, instead of y. These results were explained earlier in these technical notes with the help of the Ballentine.

4
INTERVAL ESTIMATION AND
HYPOTHESIS TESTING

4.1   INTRODUCTION

In addition to estimating parameters, econometricians often wish to construct confidence intervals for their estimates and test hypotheses concerning parameters. To strengthen the perspective from which violations of the CLR model are viewed in the following chapters, this chapter provides a brief discussion of these principles of inference in the context of traditional applications found in econometrics.

Under the null hypothesis most test statistics have a distribution that is tabulated in appendices at the back of statistics books, the most common of which are the standard normal, the t, the chi-square, and the F distributions. In small samples the applicability of all these distributions depends on the errors in the CLR model being normally distributed, something that is not one of the CLR model assumptions. For situations in which the errors are not distributed normally, it turns out that in most cases a traditional test statistic has an asymptotic distribution equivalent to one of these tabulated distributions; with this as justification, testing/interval estimation proceeds in the usual way, ignoring the small sample bias. For expository purposes, this chapter's discussion of inference is couched in terms of the classical normal linear regression (CNLR) model, in which the assumptions of the CLR model are augmented by assuming that the errors are distributed normally.

4.2   TESTING A SINGLE HYPOTHESIS: THE t TEST

Hypothesis tests on and interval estimates of single parameters are straightforward applications of techniques familiar to all students of elementary statistics. In the CNLR model the OLS estimator β^{OLS} generates estimates that are distributed joint-normally in repeated samples. This means that β_1^{OLS}, β_2^{OLS}, ..., β_k^{OLS} are all connected to one another (through their covariances). In particular, this means that β_3^{OLS}, say, is distributed normally with mean β_3 (since the OLS estimator is unbiased) and variance $V(\beta_3^{OLS})$ equal to the third diagonal element of the variance–covariance matrix of β^{OLS}. The square root of $V(\beta_3^{OLS})$ is the standard deviation of β_3^{OLS}. Using the normal table and this standard deviation, interval estimates can be constructed and hypotheses can be tested.

A major drawback to this procedure is that the variance–covariance matrix of β^{OLS} is not usually known (because σ^2, the variance of the disturbances, which appears in the formula for this variance–covariance matrix, is not usually known). Estimating σ^2 by s^2, as discussed in the technical notes to section 3.3, allows an estimate of this matrix to be created. The square root of the third diagonal element of this matrix is the standard error of β_3^{OLS}, an estimate of the standard deviation of β_3^{OLS}. With this estimate the t-table can be used in place of the normal table to test hypotheses or construct interval estimates.

The use of such t tests, as they are called, is so common that most packaged computer programs designed to compute the OLS estimators (designed to run OLS regressions) have included in their output a number called the t statistic for each parameter estimate. This gives the value of the parameter estimate divided by its estimated standard deviation (the standard error). This value can be compared directly to critical values in the t-table to test the hypothesis that that parameter is equal to zero. In some research reports, this t statistic is printed in parentheses underneath the parameter estimates, creating some confusion because sometimes the standard errors appear in this position. (A negative number in parentheses would have to be a t value, so that this would indicate that these numbers were t values rather than standard errors.)

4.3   TESTING A JOINT HYPOTHESIS: THE F TEST

Suppose that a researcher wants to test the joint hypothesis that, say, the fourth and fifth elements of β are equal to 1.0 and 2.0, respectively. That is, he wishes to test the hypothesis that the sub-vector

$$\begin{bmatrix} \beta_4 \\ \beta_5 \end{bmatrix}$$

is equal to the vector

$$\begin{bmatrix} 1.0 \\ 2.0 \end{bmatrix}$$

This is a different question from the two separate questions of whether β_4 is equal to 1.0 and whether β_5 is equal to 2.0. It is possible, for example, to accept the hypothesis that β_4 is equal to 1.0 and also to accept the hypothesis that β_5 is equal to 2.0, but to *reject* the joint hypothesis that

$$\begin{bmatrix} \beta_4 \\ \beta_5 \end{bmatrix}$$

is equal to

$$\begin{bmatrix} 1.0 \\ 2.0 \end{bmatrix}$$

The purpose of this section is to explain how the F test is used to test such joint hypotheses. The following section explains how a difference between results based on separate tests and joint tests could arise.

The F statistic for testing a set of J linear constraints in a regression with K parameters (including the intercept) and T observations takes the generic form

$$\frac{[SSE \text{ (constrained)} - SSE \text{ (unconstrained)}]/J}{SSE \text{ (unconstrained)}/(T - K)}$$

where the degrees of freedom for this F statistic are J and $T - K$. This generic form is worth memorizing – it is extremely useful for structuring F tests for a wide variety of special cases, such as Chow tests (chapter 6) and tests involving dummy variables (chapter 14).

When the constraints are true, because of the error term they will not be satisfied exactly by the data, so the SSE will increase when the constraints are imposed – minimization subject to constraints will not be as successful as minimization without constraints. But if the constraints are true the per-constraint increase in SSE should not be large, relative to the influence of the error term. The numerator has the "per-constraint" change in SSE due to imposing the constraints and the denominator has the "per-error" contribution to SSE. (The minus K in this expression corrects for degrees of freedom, explained in the general notes.) If their ratio is "too big" we would be reluctant to believe that it happened by chance, concluding that it must have happened because the constraints are false. High values of this F statistic thus lead us to reject the null hypothesis that the constraints are true.

How does one find the constrained SSE? A constrained regression is run to obtain the constrained SSE. The easiest example is the case of constraining a coefficient to be equal to zero – just run the regression omitting that coefficient's variable. To run a regression constraining β_4^{OLS} to be 1.0 and β_5^{OLS} to be 2.0, subtract 1.0 times the fourth regressor and 2.0 times the fifth regressor from the dependent variable and regress this new, constructed dependent variable on the remaining regressors. In general, to incorporate a linear restriction into a regression, use the restriction to solve out one of the parameters, and rearrange the resulting equation to form a new regression involving constructed variables. An explicit example is given in the general notes.

4.4 INTERVAL ESTIMATION FOR A PARAMETER VECTOR

Interval estimation in the multidimensional case is best illustrated by a two-dimensional example. Suppose that the sub-vector

$$\begin{bmatrix} \beta_4 \\ \beta_5 \end{bmatrix}$$

is of interest. The OLS estimate of this sub-vector is shown as the point in the center of the rectangle in figure 4.1. Using the t-table and the square root of the fourth diagonal term in the estimated variance–covariance matrix of β^{OLS}, a 95% confidence interval can be constructed for β_4. This is shown in figure 4.1 as the interval from A to B; β_4^{OLS} lies halfway between A and B. Similarly, a 95% confidence interval can be constructed for β_5; it is shown in figure 4.1 as the interval from C to D and is drawn larger than the interval AB to reflect an assumed larger standard error for β_5^{OLS}.

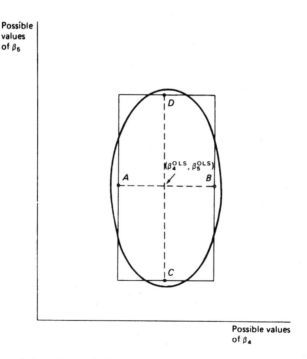

Figure 4.1   A confidence region with zero covariance

An interval estimate for the sub-vector

$$\begin{bmatrix} \beta_4 \\ \beta_5 \end{bmatrix}$$

is a *region* or area that, when constructed in repeated samples, covers the true value (β_4, β_5) in, say, 95% of the samples. Furthermore, this region should for an efficient estimate be the smallest such region possible. A natural region to choose for this purpose is the rectangle formed by the individual interval estimates, as shown in figure 4.1. If β_4^{OLS} and β_5^{OLS} have zero covariance, then in repeated sampling rectangles calculated in this fashion will cover the unknown point (β_4, β_5) in $0.95 \times 0.95 = 90.25\%$ of the samples. (In repeated samples the probability is 0.95 that the β_4 confidence interval covers β_4, as is the probability that the β_5 confidence interval covers β_5; thus the probability for both β_4 and β_5 to be covered simultaneously is 0.95×0.95.)

Evidently, this rectangle is not "big" enough to serve as a 95% joint confidence interval. Where should it be enlarged? Because the region must be kept as small as possible, the enlargement must come in those parts that have the greatest chance of covering (β_4, β_5) in repeated samples. The corners of the rectangle will cover (β_4, β_5) in a repeated sample whenever β_4^{OLS} and β_5^{OLS} are simultaneously a long way from their mean values of β_4 and β_5. The probability in repeated samples of having these two unlikely events occur simultaneously is very small. Thus the areas just outside the rectangle near the points A, B, C, and D are more likely to cover (β_4, β_5) in repeated samples than are the areas just outside the corners of the rectangle: the rectangle should be made bigger near the points A, B, C, and D. Further thought suggests that the areas just outside the points A, B, C, and D are more likely, in repeated samples, to cover (β_4, β_5) than the areas just *inside* the corners of the rectangle. Thus the total region could be made smaller by chopping a lot of area off the corners and extending slightly the areas near the points A, B, C, and D. In fact, the F statistic described earlier allows the econometrician to derive the confidence region as an ellipse, as shown in figure 4.1.

The ellipse in figure 4.1 represents the case of zero covariance between β_4^{OLS} and β_5^{OLS}. If β_4^{OLS} and β_5^{OLS} have a positive covariance (an estimate of this covariance is found in either the fourth column and fifth row or the fifth column and fourth row of the estimate of the variance–covariance matrix of β^{OLS}), whenever β_4^{OLS} is an overestimate of β^4, β_5^{OLS} is likely to be an overestimate of β_5, and whenever β_4^{OLS} is an underestimate of β_4, β_5^{OLS} is likely to be an underestimate of β_5. This means that the area near the top right-hand corner of the rectangle and the area near the bottom left-hand corner are no longer as unlikely to cover (β_4, β_5) in repeated samples; it also means that the areas near the top left-hand corner and bottom right-hand corner are even less likely to cover (β_4, β_5). In this case the ellipse representing the confidence region is tilted to the right, as shown in figure 4.2. In the case of negative covariance between β_4^{OLS} and β_5^{OLS}, the

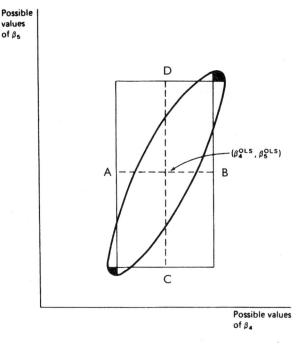

Figure 4.2 A confidence region with positive covariance

ellipse is tilted to the left. In all cases, the ellipse remains centered on the point $(\beta_4^{OLS}, \beta_5^{OLS})$.

This two-dimensional example illustrates the possibility, mentioned earlier, of accepting two individual hypotheses but rejecting the corresponding joint hypothesis. Suppose the hypothesis is that $\beta_4 = 0$ and $\beta_5 = 0$, and suppose the point $(0,0)$ lies inside a corner of the rectangle in figure 4.1, but outside the ellipse. Testing the hypothesis $\beta_4 = 0$ using a t test concludes that β_4 is insignificantly different from zero (because the interval AB contains zero), and testing the hypothesis $\beta_5 = 0$ concludes that β_5 is insignificantly different from zero (because the interval CD contains zero). But testing the joint hypothesis

$$\begin{bmatrix} \beta_4 \\ \beta_5 \end{bmatrix} = \begin{bmatrix} 0 \\ 0 \end{bmatrix},$$

using an F test, concludes that

$$\begin{bmatrix} \beta_4 \\ \beta_5 \end{bmatrix}$$

is significantly different from the zero vector because (0,0) lies outside the ellipse. In this example one can confidently say that *at least one* of the two variables has a significant influence on the dependent variable, but one cannot with confidence assign that influence to either of the variables individually. The typical circumstance in which this comes about is in the case of multicollinearity (see chapter 11), in which independent variables are related so that it is difficult to tell which of the variables deserves credit for explaining variation in the dependent variable. Figure 4.2 is representative of the multicollinearity case.

In three dimensions the confidence region becomes a confidence volume and is represented diagrammatically by an ellipsoid. In higher dimensions diagrammatic representation is impossible, but the hyper-surface corresponding to a critical value of the F statistic can be called a multidimensional ellipsoid.

4.5 LR, W, AND LM STATISTICS

The F test discussed above is applicable whenever we are testing linear restrictions in the context of the CNLR model. Whenever the problem cannot be cast into this mold – for example, if the restrictions are nonlinear, the model is nonlinear in the parameters or the errors are distributed non-normally – this procedure is inappropriate and is usually replaced by one of three asymptotically equivalent tests. These are the *likelihood ratio* (LR) test, the *Wald* (W) test), and the *Lagrange multiplier* (LM) test. The test statistics associated with these tests have unknown small-sample distributions, but are each distributed asymptotically as a chi-square (χ^2) with degrees of freedom equal to the number of restrictions being tested.

These three test statistics are based on three different rationales. Consider figure 4.3, in which the log-likelihood (lnL) function is graphed as a function of β, the parameter being estimated. β^{MLE} is, by definition, the value of β at which lnL attains its maximum. Suppose the restriction being tested is written as $g(\beta) = 0$, satisfied at the value β_R^{MLE} where the function $g(\beta)$ cuts the horizontal axis:

(1) *The LR test* If the restriction is true, then lnL_R, the maximized value of lnL imposing the restriction, should not be *significantly* less than lnL_{max}, the unrestricted maximum value of lnL. The LR test tests whether $(lnL_R - lnL_{max})$ is significantly different from zero.

(2) *The W test* If the restriction $g(\beta) = 0$ is true, then $g(\beta^{MLE})$ should not be *significantly* different from zero. The W test tests whether β^{MLE} (the unrestricted estimate of β) violates the restriction by a significant amount.

(3) *The LM test* The log-likelihood function lnL is maximized at point A where the slope of lnL with respect to β is zero. If the restriction is true, then the slope of lnL at point B should not be *significantly* different from zero. The LM test tests whether the slope of lnL, evaluated at the restricted estimate, is significantly different from zero.

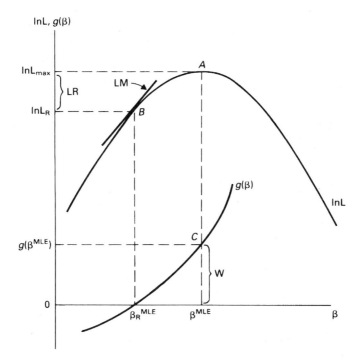

Figure 4.3 Explaining the LR, W, and LM statistics

When faced with three statistics with identical asymptotic properties, econometricians would usually choose among them on the basis of their small-sample properties, as determined by Monte Carlo studies. In this case, however, it happens that computational cost plays a dominant role in this respect. To calculate the LR statistic, both the restricted and the unrestricted estimates of β must be calculated. If neither is difficult to compute, then the LR test is computationally the most attractive of the three tests. To calculate the W statistic only the unrestricted estimate is required; if the restricted but not the unrestricted estimate is difficult to compute, owing to a nonlinear restriction, for example, the W test is computationally the most attractive. To calculate the LM statistic, only the restricted estimate is required; if the unrestricted but not the restricted estimate is difficult to compute – for example, when imposing the restriction transforms a nonlinear functional form into a linear functional form – the LM test is the most attractive.

4.6 BOOTSTRAPPING

Testing hypotheses exploits knowledge of the sampling distributions of test statistics when the null is true, and constructing confidence intervals requires knowledge of estimators' sampling distributions. Unfortunately, this "knowledge" is often questionable, or unavailable, for a variety of reasons:

(1) Assumptions made concerning the distribution of the error term may be false. For example, the error may not be distributed normally, or even approximately normally, as is often assumed.
(2) Algebraic difficulties in calculating the characteristics of a sampling distribution often cause econometricians to undertake such derivations assuming that the sample size is very large. The resulting "asymptotic" results may not be close approximations for the sample size of the problem at hand.
(3) For some estimating techniques, such as minimizing the median squared error, even asymptotic algebra cannot produce formulas for estimator variances.
(4) A researcher may obtain an estimate by undertaking a series of tests, the results of which lead eventually to adoption of a final estimation formula. This search process makes it impossible to derive algebraically the character of the sampling distribution.

One way of dealing with these problems is to perform a Monte Carlo study: data are simulated to mimic the process thought to be generating the data, the estimate or test statistic is calculated and this process is repeated several thousand times to allow computation of the character of the sampling distribution of the estimator or test statistic. To tailor the Monte Carlo study to the problem at hand, initial parameter estimates are used as the "true" parameter values, and the actual values of the explanatory variables are employed as the "fixed in repeated samples" values of the explanatory variables. But this tailoring is incomplete because in the Monte Carlo study the errors must be drawn from a known distribution such as the normal. This is a major drawback of the traditional Monte Carlo methodology in this context.

The bootstrap is a special Monte Carlo procedure which circumvents this problem. It does so by assuming that the unknown distribution of the error term can be adequately approximated by a discrete distribution that gives equal weight to each of the residuals from the original estimation. Assuming a reasonable sample size, in typical cases most of the residuals should be small in absolute value, so that although each residual is given equal weight (and thus is equally likely to be chosen in random draws from this distribution), small residuals predominate, causing random draws from this distribution to produce small values much more frequently than large values. This procedure, which estimates sampling distributions by using only the original data (and so "pulls itself up by its own bootstraps") has proved to be remarkably successful. In effect it substitutes computing power, the price of which has dramatically decreased, for theorem-proving, whose price has held constant or even increased as we have adopted more complicated estimation procedures.

The bootstrap begins by estimating the model in question and saving the residuals. It performs a Monte Carlo study, using the estimated parameter values as the "true" parameter values and the actual values of the explanatory variables as the fixed explanatory variable values. During this Monte Carlo study errors are drawn, with replacement, from the set of original residuals. In this way account is taken of the unknown distribution of the true errors. This "residual-based" technique is only appropriate whenever each error is equally likely to be drawn for each observation. If this is not the case, an alternative bootstrapping method is employed. See the general notes to this section for further discussion.

GENERAL NOTES

4.1 Introduction

- It is extremely convenient to assume that errors are distributed normally, but there exists little justification for this assumption. Tiao and Box (1973, p. 13) speculate that "Belief in universal near-Normality of disturbances may be traced, perhaps, to early feeding on a diet of asymptotic Normality of maximum likelihood and other estimators." Poincaré is said to have claimed that "everyone believes in the [Gaussian] law of errors, the experimenters because they think it is a mathematical theorem, the mathematicians because they think it is an empirical fact." Several tests for normality exist; for a textbook exposition see Maddala (1977, pp. 305–8). See also Judge et al. (1985, pp. 882–7). The consequences of non-normality of the fat-tailed kind, implying infinite variance, are quite serious, since hypothesis testing and interval estimation cannot be undertaken meaningfully. Faced with such non-normality, two options exist. First, one can employ robust estimators, as described in chapter 18. And second, one can transform the data to create transformed errors that are closer to being normally distributed. For discussion see Maddala (1977, pp. 314–17).

- Testing hypotheses is viewed by some with scorn. Consider for example the remark of Johnson (1971, p. 2): "The 'testing of hypotheses' is frequently merely a euphemism for obtaining plausible numbers to provide ceremonial adequacy for a theory chosen and defended on *a priori* grounds." For a completely opposite cynical view, Blaug (1980, p. 257) feels that econometricians "express a hypothesis in terms of an equation, estimate a variety of forms for that equation, select the best fit, discard the rest, and then adjust the theoretical argument to rationalize the hypothesis that is being tested."

- It should be borne in mind that despite the power, or lack thereof, of hypothesis tests, often conclusions are convincing to a researcher only if supported by personal experience. Nelson (1995, p. 141) captures this subjective element of empirical research by noting that "what often really seems to matter in convincing a male colleague of the existence of sex discrimination is not studies with 10,000 'objective' observations, but rather a particular single direct observation: the experience of his own daughter."

- Hypothesis tests are usually conducted using a type I error rate (probability of rejecting a true null) of 5%, but there is no good reason why 5% should be preferred to some other percentage. It is chosen so often that it has become a tradition, prompting Kempthorne and Doerfler (1969, p. 231) to opine that "statisticians are people whose aim in life is to be wrong 5% of the time!"

- For a number of reasons, tests of significance can sometimes be misleading. A good discussion can be found in Bakan (1966). One of the more interesting problems in this respect is the fact that almost any parameter can be found to be significantly different from zero if the sample size is sufficiently large. (Almost every relevant independent variable will have *some* influence, however small, on a dependent variable; increasing the sample size will reduce the variance and eventually make this influence statistically significant.) Thus, although a researcher wants a large sample size to generate more accurate estimates, too large a sample size might cause difficulties in interpreting the usual tests of significance. McCloskey and Ziliak (1996) look carefully at a large number of empirical studies in economics and conclude that researchers seem not to appreciate that statistical significance does not imply economic significance. One must ask if the magnitude of the coefficient in question is large enough for its explanatory variable to have a meaningful (as opposed to "significant") influence on the dependent variable. This is called the *too-large sample size problem*. It is suggested that the significance level be adjusted downward as the sample size grows; for a formalization see Leamer (1978, pp. 88–9, 104–5). See also Attfield (1982). Leamer would also argue (1988, p. 331) that this problem would be resolved if researchers recognized that genuinely interesting hypotheses are neighborhoods, not points.

  Another interesting dimension of this problem is the question of what significance level should be employed when replicating a study with new data; conclusions must be drawn by considering both sets of data as a unit, not just the new set of data. For discussion see Busche and Kennedy (1984). A third interesting example in this context is the propensity for published studies to contain a disproportionately large number of type I errors; studies with statistically significant results tend to get published, whereas those with insignificant results do not. For comment see Feige (1975). Yet another example that should be mentioned here is pre-test bias, discussed in chapter 12.

- Inferences from a model may be sensitive to the model specification, the validity of which may be in doubt. A *fragility analysis* is recommended to deal with this; it examines the range of inferences resulting from the range of believable model specifications. See Leamer and Leonard (1983) and Leamer (1983a).

- Armstrong (1978, pp. 406–7) advocates the use of the method of multiple hypotheses, in which research is designed to compare two or more reasonable hypotheses, in contrast to the usual advocacy strategy in which a researcher tries to find confirming evidence for a favorite hypothesis. (Econometricians, like artists, tend to fall in love with their models!) It is claimed that the latter procedure biases the way scientists perceive the world, and that scientists employing the former strategy progress more rapidly.

4.2   Testing a Single Hypothesis: the t Test

- A t test can be used to test any single linear constraint. Suppose $y = \alpha + \beta x + \delta w + \varepsilon$ and we wish to test $\beta + \delta = 1$. A t test is formulated by rewriting the constraint so that it is equal to zero, in this case as $\beta + \delta - 1 = 0$, estimating the left-hand side as $\beta^{BOLS} + \delta^{BOLS} - 1$ and dividing this by the square root of its estimated variance to form a t statistic with degrees of freedom equal to the sample size minus the number of parameters estimated in the regression. Estimation of the variance of $(\beta^{OLS} + \delta^{OLS} - 1)$ is a bit messy, but can be done using the elements in the estimated variance–covariance matrix from the OLS regression. This messiness can be avoided by using an F test, as explained in the general notes to the following section.

- Nonlinear constraints are usually tested by using a W, LR or LM test, but sometimes an "asymptotic" t test is encountered: the nonlinear constraint is written with its right-hand side equal to zero, the left-hand side is estimated and then divided by the square root of an estimate of its asymptotic variance to produce the asymptotic t statistic. It is the square root of the corresponding W test statistic. The asymptotic variance of a nonlinear function was discussed in chapter 2.

4.3   Testing a Joint Hypothesis: the F Test

- If there are only two observations, a linear function with one independent variable (i.e., two parameters) will fit the data perfectly, *regardless* of what independent variable is used. Adding a third observation will destroy the perfect fit, but the fit will remain quite good, simply because there is effectively only one observation to explain. It is to correct this phenomenon that statistics are adjusted for *degrees of freedom* – the number of "free" or linearly independent observations used in the calculation of the statistic. For all of the F tests cited in this section, the degrees of freedom appropriate for the numerator is the number of restrictions being tested. The degrees of freedom for the denominator is $T - K$, the number of observations less the number of parameters being estimated. $T - K$ is also the degrees of freedom for the t statistic mentioned in section 4.2.

- The degrees of freedom of a statistic is the number of quantities that enter into the calculation of the statistic minus the number of constraints connecting these quantities. For example, the formula used to compute the sample variance involves the sample mean statistic. This places a constraint on the data – given the sample mean, any one data point can be determined by the other $(N - 1)$ data points. Consequently there are in effect only $(N - 1)$ unconstrained observations available to estimate the sample variance; the degrees of freedom of the sample variance statistic is $(N - 1)$.

- A special case of the F statistic is automatically reported by most regression packages – the F statistic for the "overall significance of the regression." This F statistic tests the hypothesis that all the slope coefficients are zero. The constrained regression in this case would have only an intercept.

- To clarify further how one runs a constrained regression, suppose for example that $y = \alpha + \beta x + \delta w + \varepsilon$ and we wish to impose the constraint that $\beta + \delta = 1$. Substitute $\beta = 1 - \delta$ and rearrange to get $y - x = \alpha + \delta(w - x) + \varepsilon$. The restricted

SSE is obtained from regressing the constructed variable $(y - x)$ on a constant and the constructed variable $(w - x)$. Note that because the dependent variable has changed it will not be meaningful to compare the R^2 of this regression with that of the original regression.

- In the preceding example it should be clear that it is easy to construct an F test of the hypothesis that $\beta + \delta = 1$. The resulting F statistic will be the square of the t statistic that could be used to test this same hypothesis (described in the preceding section). This reflects the general result that the square of a t statistic is an F statistic (with degrees of freedom one and the degrees of freedom for the t test). With the exception of testing a single coefficient equal to a specific value, it is usually easier to perform an F test than a t test.

- By dividing the numerator and denominator of the F statistic by *SST*, the total variation in the dependent variable, F can be written in terms of R^2 and ΔR^2. This method is not recommended, however, because often the restricted *SSE* is obtained by running a regression with a different dependent variable than that used by the regression run to obtain the unrestricted *SSE* (as in the example above), implying different *SST*s and incomparable R^2s.

- An F statistic with p and n degrees of freedom is the ratio of two independent chi-square statistics, each divided by its degrees of freedom, p for the numerator and n for the denominator. For the standard F statistic we have been discussing, the chi-square on the denominator is *SSE*, the sum of squared OLS residuals, with degrees of freedom $T - K$, divided by σ^2. Asymptotically, $SSE/(T - K)$ equals σ^2, so the denominator becomes unity, leaving F equal to the numerator chi-square divided by its degrees of freedom p. Thus, asymptotically pF is distributed as a chi-square with degrees of freedom p. This explains why test statistics derived on asymptotic arguments are invariably expressed as chi-square statistics rather than as F statistics. In small samples it cannot be said that this approach, calculating the chi-square statistic and using critical values from the chi-square distribution, is definitely preferred to calculating the F statistic and using critical values from the F distribution.

- One application of the F test is in testing for causality. It is usually assumed that movements in the dependent variable are caused by movements in the independent variable(s), but the existence of a relationship between these variables proves neither the existence of causality nor its direction. Using the dictionary meaning of causality, it is impossible to test for causality. Granger developed a special definition of causality which econometricians use in place of the dictionary definition; strictly speaking, econometricians should say "Granger-cause" in place of "cause," but usually they do not. A variable x is said to Granger-cause y if prediction of the current value of y is enhanced by using past values of x. This definition is implemented for empirical testing by regressing y on past, current and future values of x; if causality runs one way, from x to y, the set of coefficients of the future values of x should test insignificantly different from the zero vector (via an F test), and the set of coefficients of the past values of x should test significantly different from zero. Before running this regression both data sets are transformed (using the same transformation), so as to eliminate any autocorrelation in the error attached to this regression. (This is required to permit use of the F test; chapter 8 examines the problem of autocorrelated errors.) Great controversy exists over the appropriate way of conducting this transformation and the extent to which the results are sensitive to the transformation chosen. Other criticisms focus on the possibility of expected future values of x affecting the current value of y, and, in general, the lack of full correspondence between Granger-causality and causality. (Consider, for example, the fact that Christmas card sales Granger-cause Christmas!) Bishop (1979) has a concise review and references to the major studies on this topic. Darnell (1994, pp. 41–3) has a concise textbook exposition.

4.4 Interval Estimation for a Parameter Vector

- Figure 4.2 can be used to illustrate another curiosity – the possibility of accepting the hypothesis that

$$\begin{bmatrix} \beta_4 \\ \beta_5 \end{bmatrix} = \begin{bmatrix} 0 \\ 0 \end{bmatrix}$$

on the basis of an F test while rejecting the hypothesis that $\beta_4 = 0$ and the hypothesis that $\beta_5 = 0$ on the basis of individual t tests. This would be the case if, for the sample at hand, the point $(0, 0)$ fell in either of the small shaded areas (in the upper right or lower left) of the ellipse in figure 4.2. For a summary discussion of the possible cases that could arise here, along with an example of this seldom encountered curiosity, see Geary and Leser (1968).

4.5 LR, W, and LM Statistics

- Figure 4.3 is taken from Buse (1982) who uses it to conduct a more extensive discussion of the W, LR and LM statistics, noting, for example, that the geometric distances being tested depend on the second derivatives of the log-likelihood function, which enter into the test statistics through variances (recall that these second derivatives appeared in the Cramer–Rao lower bound). Engle (1984) has an extensive discussion of the W, LR and LM test statistics. Greene (1990, pp. 126–33) is a good textbook exposition.
- The name of the LM statistic comes from an alternative derivation of this statistic. To maximize subject to restrictions, the Lagrange multiplier technique is usually employed; if the restrictions are not binding, the vector of Lagrange multipliers is zero. Thus, when maximizing the log-likelihood subject to restrictions, if the restrictions are true they should be close to being satisfied by the data and the value of the Lagrange multiplier vector should be close to zero. The validity of the restrictions could therefore be tested by testing the vector of Lagrange multipliers against the zero vector. This produces the LM test.
- Critical values from the χ^2 distribution are used for the LR, W and LM tests, in spite of the fact that in small samples they are not distributed as χ^2. This is a weakness of all three of these tests. Furthermore, it has been shown by Berndt and Savin (1977) that in linear models in small samples the values of these test statistics are such that $W \geqslant LR \geqslant LM$ for the same data, testing for the same restrictions. Consequently, it is possible for conflict among these tests to arise in the sense that in small samples a restriction could be accepted on the basis of one test but rejected on the basis of another. Zaman (1996, pp. 411–12) argues that the third-order terms in the asymptotic

expansions of the W, LR and LM tests are different and upon examination the LR test is to be favored in small samples. Dagenais and Dufour (1991, 1992) conclude that W tests and some forms of LM tests are not invariant to changes in the measurement units, the representation of the null hypothesis and reparameterizations, and so recommend the LR test.

- Because it requires estimation under only the null hypothesis, the LM test is less specific than other tests concerning the precise nature of the alternative hypothesis. This could be viewed as an advantage, since it allows testing to be conducted in the context of a more general alternative hypothesis, or as a disadvantage, since it does not permit the precise nature of an alternative hypothesis to play a role and thereby increase the power of the test. Monte Carlo studies, however, have shown that this potential drawback is not of great concern.

- For the special case of testing linear restrictions in the CNLR model with σ^2 known, the LR, W and LM tests are equivalent to the F test (which in this circumstance, because σ^2 is known, becomes a χ^2 test). When σ^2 is unknown, see Vandaele (1981) for the relationships among these tests.

- In many cases it turns out that the parameters characterizing several misspecifications are functionally independent of each other, so that the information matrix is block-diagonal. In this case the LM statistic for testing all the misspecifications jointly is the sum of the LM statistics for testing each of the misspecifications separately. The same is true for the W and LR statistics.

- A nonlinear restriction can be written in different ways. For example, the restriction $\alpha\beta - 1 = 0$ could be written as $\alpha - 1/\beta = 0$. Gregory and Veall (1985) find that the Wald test statistic is sensitive to which way the restriction is written. For this example, they recommend the former version.

4.6 Bootstrapping

- Jeong and Maddala (1993) is a good survey of bootstrapping in an econometric context. Li and Maddala (1996) extend this survey, concentrating on time series data. Veall (1987, 1992) are good examples of econometric applications, and Veall (1989, 1998) are concise surveys of such applications. Efron and Tibshirani (1993) is a detailed exposition.

- An implicit assumption of bootstrapping is that the errors are exchangeable, meaning that each error, which in this case is one of the N residuals (sample size N), is equally likely to occur with each observation. This may not be true. For example, larger error variances might be associated with larger values of one of the explanatory variables, in which case large errors are more likely to occur whenever there are large values of this explanatory variable. A variant of the bootstrap called the complete bootstrap is employed to deal with this problem. Each of the N observations in the original sample is written as a vector of values containing an observation on the dependent variable and an associated observation for each of the explanatory variables. Observations for a Monte Carlo repeated sample are drawn with replacement from the set of these vectors.

  This technique introduces three innovations. First, it implicitly employs the true, unknown errors because they are part of the dependent variable values, and keeps these unknown errors paired with the original explanatory variable values with which they were associated. Second, it does not employ estimates of the unknown parameters, implicitly using the true parameter values. And third, it no longer views the explanatory variable values as fixed in repeated samples, assuming instead that these values were drawn from a distribution adequately approximated by a discrete distribution giving equal weight to each observed vector of values on the explanatory variables. This makes sense in a context in which the observations are a small subset of a large population of similar observations. Unfortunately, it does not make sense if the original observations exhaust the population, as would be the case, for example, if they were observations on all large Canadian cities. Nor would it make sense in a context in which a researcher selected the values of the explanatory variables to suit the study rather than via some random process. It also would not be suitable for a problem in which the errors are autocorrelated in that the error for one observation is related to the error for another; in this case a bootstrapping residuals technique would have to be used with an appropriate modification to create the desired error correlation in each bootstrapped sample. The message here is that the bootstrapping procedure must be carefully thought out for each application.

- An alternative computer-based means of estimating a sampling distribution of a test statistic is that associated with a randomization/permutation test. The rationale behind this testing methodology is that if an explanatory variable has no influence on a dependent variable then it should make little difference to the outcome of the test statistic if the values of this explanatory variable are shuffled and matched up with different dependent variable values. By performing this shuffling thousands of times, each time calculating the test statistic, the hypothesis can be tested by seeing if the original test statistic value is unusual relative to the thousands of test statistic values created by the shufflings. Notice how different is the meaning of the sampling distribution – it no longer corresponds to "what would happen if we drew different bundles of errors"; now it corresponds to "what would happen if the independent variable values were paired with different dependent variable values." Hypothesis testing is based on viewing the test statistic as having resulted from playing a game of chance; the randomization view of testing claims that there is more than one way to play a game of chance with one's data! For further discussion of this testing methodology in the econometrics context see Kennedy (1995) and Kennedy and Cade (1996). Noreen (1989) is a good elementary reference.

TECHNICAL NOTES

4.1   Introduction

- A *type I error* is concluding the null hypothesis is false when it is true; a *type II error* is concluding the null hypothesis is true when it is false. Traditional testing methodologies set the probability of a type I error (called the *size*, usually denoted α, called the *significance level*) equal to an arbitrarily determined value (typically 5%) and then maximize the *power* (one minus the probability of a type II error) of the test. A test is called *uniformly most powerful* (UMP) if it has greater power than any other test of the same size for all degrees of falseness of the hypothesis. Econometric theorists work hard to develop fancy tests with high power, but, as noted by McAleer (1994,

p. 334), a test that is never used has zero power, suggesting that tests must be simple to perform if they are to have power.

- A test is *consistent* if its power goes to one as the sample size grows to infinity, something that usually happens if the test is based on a consistent estimate. Many tests are developed and defended on the basis of asymptotics, with most such tests being consistent; this creates a dilemma – how can the power of such tests be compared when asymptotically they all have power one? This problem is solved through the concepts of a *local alternative* and *local power*. For the null hypothesis $\beta = \beta_0$, the alternative hypothesis is indexed to approach the null as the sample size T approaches infinity, so that, for example, the alternative $\beta \neq \beta_0$ becomes the local alternative $\beta_T = \beta_0 + \Delta\beta/\sqrt{T}$. Now an increase in T increases power, but this is balanced by a move of the alternative towards the null; the local alternative is in general constructed so as to make the power approach a well-defined limit as T approaches infinity. This limit is called the local power, and is what is used to compare consistent tests.

4.3   Testing a Joint Hypothesis: The F Test

- The ΔSSE that appears in the numerator of the F statistic sometimes appears in other guises in textbooks. If, for example, the test is for β equal to a specific vector β_0, then $\Delta SSE = (\beta^{OLS} - \beta_0)'X'X(\beta^{OLS} - \beta_0)$. This can be shown algebraically, but it is instructive to see why it makes sense. Assuming the CNLR model applies, under the null hypothesis β^{OLS} is distributed normally with mean β_0 and variance–covariance matrix $\sigma^2(X'X)^{-1}$. Thus $(\beta^{OLS} - \beta_0)$ is distributed normally with mean zero and variance $\sigma^2(X'X)^{-1}$, implying that $(\beta^{OLS} - \beta_0)'X'X(\beta^{OLS} - \beta_0)/\sigma^2$ is distributed as a chi-square. (This is explained in the technical notes to section 4.5.) This chi-square is the numerator chi-square of the F statistic (an F statistic is the ratio of two independent chi-squares, each divided by its degrees of freedom); the σ^2 gets canceled out by a σ^2 that appears in the denominator chi-square.

4.5   LR, W, and LM Statistics

- The LR test statistic is computed as $-2 \ln \lambda$ where λ is the *likelihood ratio*, the ratio of the constrained maximum of the likelihood (i.e., under the null hypothesis) to the unconstrained maximum of the likelihood.
- The W statistic is computed using a generalized version of the χ^2 which is useful to know. A sum of J independent, squared standard normal variables is distributed as χ^2 with J degrees of freedom. (This in effect defines a χ^2 distribution in most elementary statistics texts.) Thus, if the J elements θ_j of θ are distributed normally with mean zero, variance σ_j^2 and zero covariance, then $Q = \Sigma\theta_j^2/\sigma_j^2$ is distributed as a χ^2 with J degrees of freedom. This can be written in matrix terminology as $Q = \theta'V^{-1}\theta$ where V is a diagonal matrix with σ_j^2 as its diagonal elements. Generalizing in the obvious way, we obtain $\theta'V^{-1}\theta$ distributed as a χ^2 with J degrees of freedom, where the $J \times 1$ vector θ is distributed multivariate normally with mean zero and variance–covariance matrix V.

For the W statistic, θ is a vector of $\hat{g}$ of the J restrictions evaluated at β^{MLE}, and V, the variance–covariance matrix of $\hat{g}$, is given by $G'CG$ where G is the $(K \times J)$ matrix of derivatives of $\hat{g}$ with respect to β and C is the Cramer–Rao lower bound, representing the asymptotic variance of β^{MLE}. (Recall the technical notes of section 2.8 for an explanation of why the asymptotic variance of $\hat{g}$ is given by $G'CG$.) Placing hats over G and C to indicate that they are evaluated at β^{MLE}, we obtain $W = \hat{g}'[\hat{G}'\hat{C}\hat{G}]^{-1}\hat{g}$.

- Calculation of the LM statistic can be undertaken by the formula $\hat{d}'\hat{C}\hat{d}$, sometimes referred to as the *score* statistic. $\hat{d}$ is a $K \times 1$ vector of the slopes (first derivatives) of lnL with respect to β, evaluated at β_R^{MLE}, the restricted estimate of β. $\hat{C}$ is an estimate of the Cramer–Rao lower bound. Different ways of estimating the Cramer–Rao lower bound give rise to a variety of LM statistics with identical asymptotic properties but slightly different small-sample properties. For discussion of the various different ways of computing the LM statistic, and an evaluation of their relative merits, see Davidson and MacKinnon (1983).

- If the model in question can be written as $Y = h(x; \beta) + \varepsilon$ where h is either a linear or nonlinear functional form and the ε are distributed independent normally with zero mean and common variance, an auxiliary regression can be employed to facilitate calculation of the LM statistic for a test of some portion of β equal to a specific vector. Consider H, the vector of the K derivatives of h with respect to β. Each element of this vector could be evaluated for each of the N observations, using β_R^{MLE}, the restricted estimate of β. This would give a set of N "observations" on each of the K derivatives. Consider also $\hat{\varepsilon}$, the vector of N residuals resulting from the calculation of β_R^{MLE}. Suppose $\hat{\varepsilon}$ is regressed on the K derivatives in H. Then the product of the resulting R^2 and the sample size N yields the LM statistic: $LM = NR^2$. For a derivation of this, and an instructive example illustrating its application, see Breusch and Pagan (1980, pp. 242–3). Additional examples of the derivation and use of the LM statistic can be found in Godfrey (1978), Breusch and Pagan (1979), Harvey (1981, pp. 167–74), and Tse (1984).

- It is noted in appendix A that there are three different ways of estimating the information matrix. This implies that there are three different ways of estimating the variance–covariance matrix needed for calculating the W and LM tests. In general, the OPG variant is inferior to the alternatives and should be avoided; see, for example, Bera and McKenzie (1986). Unfortunately, however, some of the computationally attractive ways of calculating the LM statistic implicitly have built into them the OPG calculation for the variance–covariance matrix of the MLE, causing the size of the resulting LM statistic to be too large. In particular, versions of the LM test that are calculated as the explained sum of squares from regressing a column of ones on first derivatives are suspect. Davidson and MacKinnon (1983) suggest an alternative way of calculating the LM statistic for a wide variety of applications, through running what they call a *double-length regression* (DLR), which retains the computational attractiveness of the OPG variant of the LM test, but avoids its shortcomings. Godfrey (1988, pp. 82–4) has a good discussion. See also Davidson and MacKinnon (1988). Davidson and MacKinnon (1993, pp. 492–502) is a good textbook exposition.

4.6 Bootstrapping

- When drawing OLS residuals for bootstrapping they should be adjusted upwards by multiplying by the square root of n/(n − k) to account for the fact that although the

OLS residuals are unbiased estimates of the errors, they underestimate their absolute value.

- To find the sampling distribution of a test statistic on the null hypothesis, the null-hypothesis parameter values should be used when creating Monte Carlo repeated samples. In general, as with all Monte Carlo studies, every effort should be made to create the bootstrap samples in a way that incorporates all known facets of the data-generating process.

- The bootstrap should investigate the sampling distribution of an "asymptotically pivotal" statistic, a statistic whose sampling distribution does not depend on the true values of the parameters. For example, rather than estimating the sampling distribution of a parameter estimate, the sampling distribution of the associated t statistic should be estimated. The sampling distribution of the t statistic can be used indirectly to produce confidence intervals, rather than calculating confidence intervals directly using the sampling distribution of the parameter estimate.

5

SPECIFICATION

5.1 INTRODUCTION

At one time econometricians tended to assume that the model provided by economic theory represented accurately the real-world mechanism generating the data, and viewed their role as one of providing "good" estimates for the key parameters of that model. If any uncertainty was expressed about the model specification, there was a tendency to think in terms of using econometrics to "find" the real-world data-generating mechanism. Both these views of econometrics are obsolete. It is now generally acknowledged that econometric models are "false" and that there is no hope, or pretense, that through them "truth" will be found. Feldstein's (1982, p. 829) remarks are typical of this view: "in practice all econometric specifications are necessarily 'false' models.... The applied econometrician, like the theorist, soon discovers from experience that a useful model is not one that is 'true' or 'realistic' but one that is parsimonious, plausible and informative." This is echoed by an oft-quoted remark attributed to George Box – "All models are wrong, but some are useful" – and another from Theil (1971, p. vi): "Models are to be used, but not to be believed."

In light of this recognition, econometricians have been forced to articulate more clearly what econometric models are. There is some consensus that models are metaphors, or windows, through which researchers view the observable world, and that their acceptance and use depends not upon whether they can be deemed "true" but rather upon whether they can be said to correspond to the facts. Econometric specification analysis is a means of formalizing what is meant by "corresponding to the facts," thereby defining what is meant by a "correctly specified model." From this perspective econometric analysis becomes much more than estimation and inference in the context of a given model; in conjunction with economic theory, it plays a crucial, preliminary role of searching for and evaluating a model, leading ultimately to its acceptance or rejection.

Econometrics textbooks are mainly devoted to the exposition of econometrics for estimation and inference in the context of a given model for the data-generating process. The more important problem of specification of this model is not given much attention, for three main reasons. First, specification is not easy. In the words of Hendry and Richard (1983, p. 112), "the data generation process is complicated, data are scarce and of uncertain relevance, experimentation is uncontrolled and available theories are highly abstract and rarely uncontroversial." Second, most econometricians would agree that specification is an innovative/imaginative process that cannot be taught: "Even with a vast arsenal of diagnostics, it is very hard to write down rules that can be used to guide a data analysis. So much is really subjective and subtle.... A great deal of what we teach in applied statistics is *not* written down, let alone in a form suitable for formal encoding. It is just simply 'lore' " (Welsch, 1986, p. 405). And third, there is no accepted "best" way of going about finding a correct specification.

There is little that can be done about items one and two above; they must be lived with. Item three, however, is worthy of further discussion: regardless of how difficult a specification problem, or how limited a researcher's powers of innovation/imagination, an appropriate methodology should be employed when undertaking empirical work. The purpose of this chapter is to discuss this issue; it should be viewed as a prelude to the examination in chapter 6 of specific violations of the first assumption of the CLR model.

5.2 THREE METHODOLOGIES

Until about the mid-1970s, econometricians were too busy doing econometrics to worry about the principles that were or should be guiding empirical research. Sparked by the predictive failure of large-scale econometric models, and fueled by dissatisfaction with the gap between how econometrics was taught and how it was applied by practitioners, the profession began to examine with a critical eye the way in which econometric models were specified. This chapter is in part a summary of the state of this ongoing methodological debate. At considerable risk of oversimplification, three main approaches to the specification problem are described below in stylized form.

(1) AVERAGE ECONOMIC REGRESSION (AER)

This approach describes what is thought to be the usual way in which empirical work in economics is undertaken. The researcher begins with a specification that is viewed as being known to be correct, with data being used primarily to determine the orders of magnitude of a small number of unknown parameters. Significant values of diagnostic test statistics, such as the Durbin–Watson statistic, are initially interpreted as suggesting estimation problems that should be dealt with by adopting more sophisticated estimation methods, rather than as pointing to a misspecification of the chosen model. If these more sophisticated methods fail to "solve" the problem, the researcher then conducts "specification" tests, hunting for an alternative specification that is "better," using age-old criteria such as correct signs, high R^2s, and significant t values on coefficients "known" to be nonzero. Thus in the AER approach the data ultimately do play a role in the specification, despite the researcher's initial attitude regarding the validity of the theoretical specification. This role may be characterized as proceeding from a simple model and "testing up" to a specific more general model.

(2)   TEST, TEST, TEST (TTT)

This approach uses econometrics to discover which models of the economy are tenable, and to test rival views. To begin, the initial specification is made more general than the researcher expects the specification ultimately chosen to be, and testing of various restrictions, such as sets of coefficients equal to the zero vector, is undertaken to simplify this general specification; this testing can be characterized as "testing down" from a general to a more specific model. Following this, the model is subjected to a battery of diagnostic, or misspecification, tests, hunting for signs that the model is misspecified. (Note the contrast with AER "specification" tests, which hunt for specific alternative specifications.) A significant diagnostic, such as a small DW value, is interpreted as pointing to a model misspecification rather than as pointing to a need for more sophisticated estimation methods. The model is continually respecified until a battery of diagnostic tests allows a researcher to conclude that the model is satisfactory on several specific criteria (discussed in the general notes), in which case it is said to be "congruent" with the evidence.

(3)   FRAGILITY ANALYSIS

The specification ultimately arrived at by the typical AER or TTT search may be inappropriate because its choice is sensitive to the initial specification investigated, the order in which tests were undertaken, type I and type II errors, and innumerable prior beliefs of researchers concerning the parameters that subtly influence decisions taken (through the exercise of innovation/imagination) throughout the specification process. It may, however, be the case that the different possible specifications that could have arisen from the AER or the TTT approaches would all lead to the same conclusion with respect to the purpose for which the study was undertaken, in which case why worry about the specification? This is the attitude towards specification adopted by the third approach. Suppose that the purpose of the study is to estimate the coefficients of some "key" variables. The first step of this approach, after identifying a general family of models, is to undertake an "extreme bounds analysis," in which the coefficients of the key variables are estimated using all combinations of included/excluded "doubtful" variables. If the resulting range of estimates is too wide for comfort, an attempt is made to narrow this range by conducting a "fragility analysis." A Bayesian method (see chapter 13) is used to incorporate non-sample information into the estimation, but in such a way as to allow for a range of this Bayesian information, corresponding to the range of such information that will surely characterize the many researchers interested in this estimation. This range of information will produce a range of estimates of the parameters of interest; a narrow range ("sturdy" estimates) implies that the data at hand yield useful information, but if this is not the case ("fragile" estimates), it must be concluded that inferences from these data are too fragile to be believed.

Which is the best of these three general approaches? There is no agreement that one of these methodologies is unequivocally the best to employ; each has faced criticism, a general summary of which is provided below.

(1) The AER is the most heavily criticized, perhaps because it reflects most accurately what researchers actually do. It is accused of using econometrics merely to illustrate assumed-known theories. The attitude that significant diagnostics reflect estimation problems rather than specification errors is viewed in an especially negative light, even by those defending this approach. "Testing up" is recognized as inappropriate, inviting type I errors through loss of control over the probability of a type I error. The *ad hoc* use of extraneous information, such as the "right" signs on coefficient estimates, is deplored, especially by those with a Bayesian bent. The use of statistics such as R^2, popular with those following this methodology, is frowned upon. Perhaps most frustrating to critics is the lack of a well-defined structure and set of criteria for this approach; there is never an adequate description of the path taken to the ultimate specification.

(2) The TTT methodology is also criticized for failing in practice to provide an adequate description of the path taken to the ultimate specification, reflecting an underlying suspicion that practitioners using this methodology find it necessary to use many of the *ad hoc* rules of thumb followed in the AER approach. This could in part be a reflection of the role played in specification by innovation/imagination, which cannot adequately be explained or defended, but is nonetheless unsettling. The heavy reliance on testing in this methodology raises fears of a proliferation of type I errors (creating pretest bias, discussed in section 12.4 of chapter 12), exacerbated by the small degrees of freedom due to the very general initial specification and by the fact that many of these tests have only asymptotic justification. When "testing up" the probability of a type I error is neither known nor controlled; using the "testing down" approach can allay these fears by the adoption of a lower α value for the tests, but this is not routinely done.

(3) Objections to fragility analysis usually come from those not comfortable with the Bayesian approach, even though care has been taken to make it palatable to non-Bayesians. Such objections are theological in nature and not likely to be resolved. There is vagueness regarding how large a range of parameter estimates has to be to conclude that it is fragile; attempts to formalize this lead to measures comparable to the test statistics this approach seeks to avoid. The methodology never does lead to the adoption of a specific specification, something that researchers find unsatisfactory. There is no scope for the general fami-

ly of models initially chosen to be changed in the light of what the data has to say. Many researchers find Bayesian prior formulation both difficult and alien. Some object that this analysis too often concludes that results are fragile.

5.3 GENERAL PRINCIPLES FOR SPECIFICATION

Although the controversy over econometric methodology has not yet been resolved, the debate has been fruitful in that some general principles have emerged to guide model specification.

(1) Although "letting the data speak for themselves" through econometric estimation and testing is an important part of model specification, economic theory should be the foundation of and guiding force in a specification search.

(2) Models whose residuals do not test as insignificantly different from white noise (random errors) should be initially viewed as containing a misspecification, not as needing a special estimation procedure, as too many researchers are prone to do.

(3) "Testing down" is more suitable than "testing up"; one should begin with a general, unrestricted model and then systematically simplify it in light of the sample evidence. In doing this a researcher should control the overall probability of a type I error by adjusting the α value used at each stage of the testing (as explained in the technical notes), something which too many researchers neglect to do. This approach, deliberate overfitting, involves a loss of efficiency (and thus loss of power) when compared to a search beginning with a correct simple model. But this simple model may not be correct, in which case the approach of beginning with a simple model and expanding as the data permit runs the danger of biased inference resulting from underspecification.

(4) Tests of misspecification are better undertaken by testing simultaneously for several misspecifications rather than testing one-by-one for these misspecifications. By such an "overtesting" technique one avoids the problem of one type of misspecification adversely affecting a test for some other type of misspecification. This approach helps to deflect the common criticism that such tests rely for their power on aspects of the maintained hypothesis about which little is known.

(5) Regardless of whether or not it is possible to test simultaneously for misspecifications, models should routinely be exposed to a battery of misspecification diagnostic tests before being accepted. A subset of the data should be set aside before model specification and estimation, so that these tests can include tests for predicting extra-sample observations.

(6) Researchers should be obliged to show that their model encompasses rival models, in the sense that it can predict what results would be obtained were one to run the regression suggested by a rival model. The chosen model

should be capable of explaining the data and of explaining the successes and failures of rival models in accounting for the same data.

(7)   Bounds on the range of results corresponding to different reasonable specifications should be reported, rather than just providing the results of the specification eventually adopted, and the path taken to the selection of this specification should be fully reported.

5.4   MISSPECIFICATION TESTS/DIAGNOSTICS

Despite the protestations of fragility analysis advocates, testing has come to play a more and more prominent role in econometric work. Thanks to the ingenuity of econometric theorists, and the power of asymptotic algebra, an extremely large number of tests have been developed, seemingly catering to practitioners' every possible need, but at the same time courting confusion because of unknown small-sample properties, suspicions of low power, and often-conflicting prescriptions. It is not possible in this book to discuss all or even a majority of these tests. The more prominent among them are discussed briefly in later chapters when it is relevant to do so; before moving on to these chapters, however, it may be useful to have an overview of tests used for specification purposes. They fall into several categories.

(1)   *Omitted variable (OV) tests* F and t tests for zero restrictions on (or, more generally, linear combinations of) the parameters, as discussed in chapter 4, are commonly used for specification purposes. Several more complicated tests, such as Hausman tests, can be reformulated as OV tests in an artificial regression, greatly simplifying testing.

(2)   *RESET tests*   RESET tests, discussed in chapter 6, are used to test for whether unknown variables have been omitted from a regression specification, and are not to be confused with OV tests that test for zero coefficients on known variables. They can also be used to detect a misspecified functional form.

(3)   *Tests for functional form*   Two types of tests for functional form are available, as discussed in chapter 6. The first type, such as tests based on recursive residuals and the rainbow test, does not specify a specific alternative functional form. For the second type, functional form is tested by testing a restriction on a more general functional form, such as a Box–Cox transformation.

(4)   *Tests for structural change*   In this category fall tests for parameter constancy, discussed in chapter 6, such as Chow tests, cusum and cusum-of-squares tests, and predictive failure (or post-sample prediction) tests.

(5)   *Tests for outliers*   These tests, among which are included tests for normality, are sometimes used as general tests for misspecification. Examples

are the Jarque–Bera test, the Shapiro–Wilk test, the Cook outlier test, and the use of the DFITS measure (discussed in chapter 18).

(6) *Tests for non-spherical errors* These are tests for various types of serial correlation and heteroskedasticity, discussed in chapter 8. Examples are the Durbin–Watson test, the Breusch–Godfrey test, Durbin's *h* and *m* tests, the Goldfeld–Quandt test, the Breusch–Pagan test and the White test.

(7) *Tests for exogeneity* These tests, often referred to as Hausman tests, test for contemporaneous correlation between regressors and the error. They are discussed in chapter 9 (testing for measurement error) and chapter 10 (testing for simultaneous equation bias).

(8) *Data transformation tests* These tests, which do not have any specific alternative hypothesis, are considered variants of the Hausman test. Examples are the grouping test and the differencing test.

(9) *Non-nested tests* When testing rival models that are not nested, as might arise when testing for encompassing, non-nested tests must be employed. Examples are the non-nested *F* test and the *J* test.

(10) *Conditional moment tests* These tests are based on a very general testing methodology which in special cases gives rise to most of the tests listed above. Beyond serving as a unifying framework for existing tests, the value of this testing methodology is that it suggests how specification tests can be undertaken in circumstances in which alternative tests are difficult to construct.

Categorizing tests in this way is awkward, for several reasons.

(1) Such a list will inevitably be incomplete. For example, it could be expanded to incorporate tests for specification encountered in more advanced work. Should there be categories for unit root and cointegration tests (see chapter 17), identification tests (see chapter 10), and selection bias tests (see chapter 16), for example? What about Bayesian "tests"?

(2) It is common for practitioners to use a selection criterion, such as the Akaike information criterion, or adjusted R^2, to aid in model specification, particularly for determining things like the number of lags to include. Should this methodology be classified as a test?

(3) These categories are not mutually exclusive. There are non-nested variants of tests for non-spherical errors and of functional form tests, some tests for functional form are just variants of tests for structural break, and the RESET test is a special case of an OV test, for example.

(4) Tests take different forms. Some are LM tests, some are LR tests, and some are W tests. Some use *F*-tables, some use *t*-tables, some use χ^2-tables, and some require their own special tables. Some are exact tests, whereas some rest on an asymptotic justification.

(5) Some tests are "specification" tests, involving a specific alternative, whereas others are "misspecification" tests, with no specific alternative.

This last distinction is particularly relevant for this chapter. A prominent feature of the list of general principles given earlier is the use of misspecification tests, the more common of which are often referred to as diagnostics. These tests are designed to detect an inadequate specification (as opposed to "specification" tests, which examine the validity of a specific alternative). There have been calls for researchers to submit their models to misspecification tests as a matter of course, and it is becoming common for computer packages automatically to print out selected diagnostics.

Of the tests listed above, several fall into the misspecification category. Possibly the most prominent are the non-spherical error tests. As stressed in chapter 8, a significant value for the DW statistic could be due to several misspecifications (an omitted variable, a dynamic misspecification, or an incorrect functional form), not just to autocorrelated errors, the usual conclusion drawn by those following the AER methodology. The same is true of tests for heteroskedasticity. As noted in chapter 6, significant values of RESET could be due to an incorrect functional form, and tests for structural break and the first type of functional form test statistic could be significant because of a structural break, an omitted variable or an incorrect functional form. So these tests should be viewed as misspecification tests. Outliers could arise from a variety of specification errors, so they also can be classified as misspecification tests.

It could be argued that the misspecification tests mentioned in the preceding paragraph are to some extent specification tests because they can be associated with one or more specific classes of alternatives that have inspired their construction. Because of this they are discussed in later chapters when that class of alternative is addressed. Three of the tests listed above, however, are sufficiently general in nature that there is no obvious alternative specification determining where they should appear in later chapters. These are data transformation tests, non-nested tests, and conditional moment tests.

Data transformation tests   The idea behind data transformation tests is that if the null hypothesis of a linear functional form with a set of specific explanatory variables is correct, then estimating with raw data should yield coefficient estimates very similar to those obtained from using linearly transformed data. If the two sets of estimated coefficients are not similar, one can conclude that the null hypothesis is not correct, but one cannot draw any conclusion about what dimension of that null hypothesis is incorrect, since many different misspecifications could have given rise to this discrepancy. Choosing a specific transformation, and formalizing what is meant by "very similar," produces a test statistic. Fortunately, as explained in the technical notes, data transformation tests have been shown to be equivalent to OV tests, greatly simplifying their application.

Non-nested tests   Two models are non-nested (or "separate") if one cannot be obtained from the other by imposing a restriction. The importance of this distinction is that in this circumstance it is not possible to follow the usual testing methodology, namely to employ a test of the restriction as a specification test. Non-nested hypothesis tests provide a means of testing the specification of one model by exploiting the supposed "falsity" of other models. A model chosen to play the role of the "other" model need not be an alternative model under consideration, but this is usually the case. If the null model is the "correct" model, then the "other" model should not be able to explain anything beyond that explained by the null model. Formalizing this, as explained in the technical notes, produces a non-nested hypothesis test, on the basis of which the null can be either rejected or not rejected/accepted. If the former is the case, then one cannot conclude that the "other" model should be accepted – the role of the "other" model in this exercise is simply to act as a standard against which to measure the performance of the null. (This is what makes this test a misspecification test, rather than a specification test.) If one wants to say something about the "other" model, then the roles of the two hypotheses must be reversed, with the "other" model becoming the null, and the test repeated. Note that in this testing procedure it is possible to reject both models or to accept both models.

Conditional moment tests   These tests are undertaken by selecting a function of the data and parameters that under a correct specification should be zero, computing this function for each observation (evaluated at the MLEs), taking the average over all the observations and testing this average against zero. The function used for this purpose is usually a moment or a conditional moment (such as the product of an exogenous variable and the residual), explaining why these tests are called *moment* (M) or *conditional moment* (CM) tests. The test would be formed by creating an estimate of the variance–covariance matrix of this average and using a Wald test formula. Its main appeal is that in some circumstances it is easier to formulate appropriate moment conditions than to derive alternative tests.

5.5 R^2 AGAIN

The coefficient of determination, R^2, is often used in specification searches and in undertaking hypothesis tests. Because it is so frequently abused by practitioners, an extension of our earlier (section 2.4) discussion of this statistic is warranted.

It is noted in the general notes to section 4.3 that the F test could be interpreted in terms of R^2 and changes in R^2. Whether or not a set of extra independent variables belongs in a relationship depends on whether or not, by adding the extra regressors, the R^2 statistic increases significantly. This suggests that, when one is trying to determine which independent variable should be included in a relationship, one should search for the highest R^2.

This rule would lead to the choice of a relationship with too many regressors (independent variables) in it, because the addition of a regressor cannot cause the R^2 statistic to fall (for the same reason that the addition of a regressor cannot cause the minimized sum of squared residuals to become larger – minimizing without the restriction that the extra regressor must be ignored gives at least as low a minimand as when the restriction is imposed). Correcting the R^2 statistic for degrees of freedom solves this problem. The R^2 statistic adjusted to account for degrees of freedom is called the "adjusted R^2" or "$\bar{R}^2$" and is now reported by most packaged computer regression programs, and by practically all researchers, in place of the unadjusted R^2.

Adding another regressor changes the degrees of freedom associated with the measures that make up the R^2 statistic. If an additional regressor accounts for very little of the unexplained variation in the dependent variable, $\bar{R}^2$ falls (whereas R^2 rises). Thus, only if $\bar{R}^2$ rises should an extra variable be seriously considered for inclusion in the set of independent variables. This suggests that econometricians should search for the "best" set of independent variables by determining which potential set of independent variables produces the highest $\bar{R}^2$. This procedure is valid only in the sense that the "correct set" of independent variables will produce, on average in repeated samples, a higher $\bar{R}^2$ than will any "incorrect" set of independent variables.

Another common use of the R^2 statistic is in the context of measuring the relative importance of different independent variables in determining the dependent variable. Textbooks present several ways of decomposing the R^2 statistic into component parts, each component being identified with one independent variable and used as a measure of the relative importance of that independent variable in the regression. Unfortunately, none of these partitions of R^2 is meaningful unless it happens that the independent variables are uncorrelated with one another in the sample at hand. (This happens only by experimental design or by extraordinary luck, economists almost never being in a position to effect either.) In the typical case in which the independent variables are correlated in the sample, these suggested partitionings are not meaningful because: (a) they can no longer be legitimately allocated to the independent variables; (b) they no longer add up to R^2; or (c) they do add up to R^2 but contain negative as well as positive terms.

The main reason for this can be explained as follows. Suppose there are only two independent variables, and they are correlated in the sample. Two correlated variables can be thought of as having, between them, three sorts of variation: variation unique to the first variable, variation unique to the second variable and variation common to both variables. (When the variables are uncorrelated, this third type of variation does not exist.) Each of the three types of variation in this set of two variables "explains" some of the variation in the dependent variable. The basic problem is that no one can agree how to divide the explanatory power of the common variation between the two independent variables. If the dependent variable is regressed on both independent variables, the resulting R^2 reflects the explanatory power of all three types of independent variable variation. If the dependent variable is regressed on only one independent variable, variation unique to the other variable is removed and the resulting R^2 reflects the explanatory power of the other two types of independent variable variation. Thus, if one independent variable is removed, the remaining variable gets credit for *all* of the common variation. If the second independent variable were reinstated and the resulting increase in R^2 were used to measure the influence of this second variable, this variable would get credit for *none* of the common variation. Thus it would be illegitimate to measure the influence of an independent variable either by its R^2 in a regression of the dependent variable on only that independent variable, or by the addition to R^2 when that independent variable is added to a set of regressors. This latter measure clearly depends on the order in which the independent variables are added. Such procedures, and others like them, can only be used when the independent variables are uncorrelated in the sample. The use of breakdowns of the R^2 statistic in this context should be avoided.

5.1 GENERAL NOTES

5.1 Introduction

- Economists' search for "truth" has over the years given rise to the view that economists are people searching in a dark room for a non-existent black cat; econometricians are regularly accused of finding one.
- The consensus reported in the second paragraph of this chapter may or may not exist. Some quotations reflecting views consistent with this interpretation are Pesaran (1988, p. 339), "econometric models are metaphors providing different windows on a complex and bewildering reality," and Poirier (1988, p. 139), " 'Truth' is really nothing more than a 'correspondence' with the facts, and an important role for econometrics is to articulate what constitutes a satisfactory degree of correspondence."
- That model specification requires creativity and cannot be taught is widely acknowledged. Consider, for example, the remarks of Pagan (1987, p. 20): "Constructing 'systematic theologies' for econometrics can well stifle creativity, and some evidence of this has already become apparent. Few would deny that in the hands of the masters the methodologies perform impressively, but in the hands of their disciples it is all much less convincing."
- Economists are often accused of never looking at their data – they seldom dirty their hands with primary data collection, using instead secondary data sources available in electronic form. Indeed, as noted by Reuter (1982, p. 137) "Economists are unique among social scientists in that they are trained only to analyse, not to collect, data. . . . One consequence is a lack of scepticism about the quality of data." Aigner (1988) stresses how dependent we are on data of unknown quality, generated by others for purposes that do not necessarily correspond with our own, and notes (p. 323) that "data generation is a dirty, time-consuming, expensive and non-glorious job." All this leads to an inexcusable lack of familiarity with the data, a source of many errors in econometric specification and analysis. This suggests that a possible route to finding better specifications is to focus on getting more and better data, and looking more carefully at these data, rather than on fancier techniques for dealing with existing data. Breuer and Wohar (1996) is an example in which knowing the institutional details of how the data were produced can aid an econometric analysis. Chatfield (1991) has some good examples of how empirical work can be greatly enhanced by being sensi-

tive to the context of the problem (the data-generating process) and knowing a lot about one's data.

EDA, exploratory data analysis, is an approach to statistics which emphasizes that a researcher should always begin by looking carefully at the data in a variety of imaginative ways. Exploratory data analysts use the *interocular trauma test*: keep looking at the data until the answer hits you between the eyes! For an exposition of EDA, see Hartwig and Dearing (1979), and for examples see L. S. Mayer (1980) and Denby and Pregibon (1987). Maddala (1988, pp. 55–7) presents a nice example from Anscombe (1973) in which four sets of data give rise to almost identical regression coefficients, but very different graphs. Leamer (1994, p. xiii) has an amusing graph in which the data spell out HELP. Unwin (1992) discusses how interactive graphics should revolutionize statistical practice. Perhaps econometric software should have built into it some means of preventing a user from running a regression until the data have been examined!

5.2   Three Methodologies

- Pagan (1987) has a good account of the wakening of the profession's interest in econometric methodology. Pagan (1995) is an update; Granger (1990) contains a selection of articles prominent in this controversy. Hendry et al. (1990) is an instructive informal discussion of these issues. In this context the word "methodology" refers to the principles of the procedures adopted in the testing and quantification of economic theories, in contrast to its more popular use as a synonym for econometric "technique" or "method." Nakamura et al. (1990) is a useful survey of methods of model specification. Readers should be warned that many econometricians do not view this debate over econometric methodology with favor; they prefer not to worry about such issues. This invariably means that they continue to use the approach to specification they have always used, the AER approach, albeit with more testing than in the past. Dharmapala and McAleer (1996) discuss econometric methodology in the context of the philosophy of science.
- The nomenclature AER (average economic regression) is taken from Gilbert (1986), which contains an extraordinarily clear exposition of the TTT (test, test, test) approach. Pagan (1987) has an excellent presentation of TTT and of fragility analysis, along with critiques of both. Pagan also identifies a fourth approach, the VAR methodology (discussed in chapter 10); it has not been included here because it cannot be interpreted as a general specification methodology (it applies only to time series data) and because it in effect makes no effort to seek or evaluate a traditional specification.
- The AER approach is defended by Darnell and Evans (1990), who refer to it as the "traditional" approach. They argue that if the traditional approach were modified to focus on finding specifications that exhibit non-spherical errors before undertaking tests, then it would be more palatable than TTT and fragility analysis, both of which they criticize.
- Johnston (1984, pp. 498–510) has a good description of how the AER approach ought to be implemented. He stresses the need for the researcher to talk with experts in the area being modeled, become familiar with the relevant institutions, actually look at the data, recognize the data limitations, avoid data mining, use economic theory, and, of utmost importance, exploit the judgement of an experienced critic. He gives an amus-

ing account of his experience on an energy research project; his specification search did not end until his experienced critic, Alex Cairncross, stated that he "wouldn't mind getting on a plane and taking this to Riyadh."

- The TTT approach is identified with David Hendry, the most prominent of its advocates. Hendry (1993) is a selection of papers tracing the evolution of this econometric methodology, of which Hansen (1996) is an interesting review and critique. Particularly useful are Hendry's Introduction (pp. 1–7), the introductions to each section, the preambles associated with each article, and the chapter 19 summary which also describes the PC-GIVE software designed for this type of specification work in the time series context. A well-known application is Davidson et al. (1978); a more recent application is Hendry and Ericsson (1991), with a critique by Friedman and Schwartz (1991). The nomenclature TTT was chosen with reference to an oft-cited quote from Hendry (1980, p. 403): "The three golden rules of econometrics are test, test, and test." This methodology has been developed in the context of a specific type of time series modeling, called autoregressive distributed lag models (discussed in chapter 17 under the heading "error-correction models"), but the general principles apply to other contexts.

- What does it mean to say, following TTT, that the model is "congruent" with the evidence? There are five main criteria.

(1) *Data-admissible* The model must not be capable of producing predictions that are not logically possible. For example, if the data to be explained are proportions, then the model should force all outcomes into the zero to one range.

(2) *Theory-consistent* The model must be consistent with the economic theory from which it is derived; it must make good economic sense. For example, if economic theory suggests that a certain long-run equilibrium should characterize a relationship, then the dynamic formulation of that relationship should be such that its equilibrium solution yields that long-run equilibrium.

(3) *Predictive validity* The model should be capable of adequately predicting observations not used in its estimation/specification. This is sometimes referred to as parameter constancy. This test is particularly important because it addresses the concern that exploring the data to develop a specification implies that those data cannot be used to test that specification.

(4) *Data coherency* The residuals from the model should be white noise (i.e., random), since otherwise some regularity has not yet been included in the specification. Many econometricians consider this requirement too strong because it rules out genuine autocorrelation or heteroskedasticity. A more realistic interpretation of this requirement is that if the errors are not white noise the researcher's first reaction should be to check the specification very carefully, not to adopt GLS.

(5) *Encompassing* The model should be able to encompass its rivals in the sense that it can explain other models' results, implying that these other models contain no information capable of improving the current model.

- The "fragility analysis" approach to specification is identified with Ed Leamer, its foremost proponent; the standard references are Leamer (1983a) and Leamer and Leonard (1983). An instructive critique is McAleer et al. (1985). For applications see Cooley and LeRoy (1981) and Leamer (1986). Fragility analysis can be undertaken using software called SEARCH, developed by Leamer. Caudill (1988) suggests that fragility analysis be reported by presenting a histogram reflecting the confidence intervals produced by running the range of regressions associated with that analysis. Leamer's view of the AER and TTT methodologies is reflected in the comments of Leamer and Leonard (1983, p. 306):

> Empirical results reported in economic journals are selected from a large set of estimated models. Journals, through their editorial policies, engage in some selection, which in turn stimulates extensive model searching and prescreening by prospective authors. Since this process is well known to professional readers, the reported results are widely regarded to overstate the precision of the estimates, and probably to distort them as well. As a consequence, statistical analyses are either greatly discounted or completely ignored.

- Leamer (1978, p. vi) is refreshingly frank in describing the wide gap between econometric theory and econometric practice:

> We comfortably divide ourselves into a celibate priesthood of statistical theorists, on the one hand, and a legion of inveterate sinner-data analysts, on the other. The priests are empowered to draw up lists of sins and are revered for the special talents they display. Sinners are not expected to avoid sins; they need only confess their errors openly.

His description (1978, p. vi) of how he was first led to this view, as a graduate student, is widely quoted:

> As it happens, the econometric modeling was done in the basement of the building and the econometric theory courses were taught on the top floor (the third). I was perplexed by the fact that the same language was used in both places. Even more amazing was the transmogrification of particular individuals who wantonly sinned in the basement and metamorphosed into the highest of high priests as they ascended to the third floor.

- Leamer (1978, pp. 5–13) contains an instructive taxonomy of specification searches, summarized in Darnell and Evans (1990).
- Using techniques that adopt specifications on the basis of searches for high R^2 or high t values, as practitioners of the AER approach are often accused of doing, is called data mining, fishing, grubbing or number-crunching. This methodology is described eloquently by Coase: "if you torture the data long enough, Nature will confess." Karni and Shapiro (1980) is an amusing account of data torturing. In reference to this unjustified (but unfortunately typical) means of specifying relationships, Leamer (1983a) is moved to comment: "There are two things you are better off not watching in the making: sausages and econometric estimates."
- Both searching for high R^2 and searching for high t values are known to be poor mechanisms for model choice; convincing arguments can be found in T. Mayer (1975, 1980), Peach and Webb (1983) and Lovell (1983). Mayer focuses on adjusted R^2, showing that it does a poor job of picking out the correct specification, mainly because it capitalizes on chance, choosing a specification because it is able to explain better the peculiarities of that particular data set. This underlines the importance of setting aside some data to use for extra-sample prediction testing after a tentative specification has been chosen and estimated (as urged by TTT). Peach and Webb fabricated 50 macroeconomic models at random and discovered that the majority of these models exhibited very high R^2 and t statistics. Lovell focuses on the search for significant t values, branding it data mining, and concludes that such searches will lead to

inappropriate specifications, mainly owing to a high probability of type I errors because of the many tests performed. Denton (1985) suggests that this phenomenon is not confined to individual researchers – that many independent researchers, working with the same data, will collectively be performing these many tests, ensuring that journals will tend to be full of type I errors. All this is summed up nicely by Lovell (1983, p. 10): "It is ironic that the data mining procedure that is most likely to produce regression results that appear impressive in terms of the customary criteria is also likely to be the most misleading in terms of what it asserts about the underlying process generating the data under study."

- It must be noted that the data mining methodology has one positive feature: sometimes such experimentation uncovers empirical regularities that point to errors in theoretical specifications. For example, through data mining one of my colleagues stumbled across a result that led him to re-examine the details of the British Columbia stumpage fee system. He discovered that he had overlooked some features of this tax that had an important bearing on the behavior of the forest industry. Because of this, he was able to develop a much more satisfactory theoretical specification, and thereby to produce better empirical results. I give John Maynard Keynes (1940, p. 155) the last word on the subject:

> It will be remembered that the seventy translators of the Septuagint were shut up in seventy separate rooms with the Hebrew text and brought out with them, when they emerged, seventy identical translations. Would the same miracle be vouchsafed if seventy multiple correlators were shut up with the same statistical material?

- One important dimension of TTT is that the data should be allowed to help to determine the specification, especially for model features such as lag lengths, about which economic theory offers little guidance. The earlier comments on data mining suggest, however, that letting the data speak for themselves can be dangerous. It may be necessary to have certain features in a model for logical consistency, even if a particular sample of data fails to reflect them, to avoid the common experience of an apparently well-fitting model performing poorly out-of-sample. Belsley (1986a) argues for the use of prior information in specification analysis; discussants of the Belsley paper wonder whether adoption of an incorrect model based on poor prior information is more dangerous than letting the data speak for themselves. Belsley (1988a) has a good general discussion of this issue in the context of forecasting. A balance must be found between letting the data help with the specification and not letting the data dominate the specification, which unfortunately returns us to the "specification is an art that cannot be taught" phenomenon.

5.3 General Principles for Specification

- That economic theory should be at the heart of a specification search is too often forgotten by practitioners. Belsley and Welsch (1988) provide a cogent example of the use of such *a priori* information and note (p. 447): "Don't try to model without understanding the nonstatistical aspects of the real-life system you are trying to subject to statistical analysis. Statistical analysis done in ignorance of the subject matter is just that – ignorant statistical analysis."

- Pagan (1987) calls for a greater integration of competing methodologies, in much the same spirit as that in which the general principles for guiding model specification were presented earlier. Since these principles may not be endorsed by all econometricians, some references may be warranted. On the issue of requiring white noise residuals see Darnell and Evans (1990, chapter 4), who defend the traditional (AER) approach providing it adopts this view. On "testing down" see Harvey (1990, pp. 185–7). On "overtesting" see Bera and Jarque (1982). On diagnostics and extrasample prediction see Harvey (1990, pp. 187–9). On encompassing see Mizon (1984). On the reporting of bounds and specification paths see Pagan (1987).

- Unusual observations can often be of particular value in specification, as they prompt researchers to develop their theoretical models more carefully to explain those observations. For discussion and examples see Zellner (1981). It should be noted that some robust estimation procedures (discussed in chapter 18) have a tendency to throw such "outliers" away, something that should not be done until they have been carefully examined.

- Koenker (1988) suggests that specification is affected by sample size, noting that as the sample size increases the number of explanatory variables in published studies tends to increase at a rate proportional to the sample size raised to the power one-quarter. Larger samples tempt researchers to ask new questions and refine old ones; implicitly, they are less and less willing to accept bias in the face of the extra precision brought by the larger sample size. Koenker notes (p. 139) an interesting implication for asymptotic theory, claiming that it rests on the following "willing suspension of disbelief": "Daily an extremely diligent research assistant arrives with buckets of (independent) new observations, but our imaginary colleague is so uninspired by curiosity and convinced of the validity of his original model, that each day he simply re-estimates his initial model – without alteration – employing ever-larger samples."

- Hogg (1988) suggests a useful rule of thumb for specification: compare the estimates from OLS and a robust method; if they disagree, take another hard look at both the data and the model. Note that this could be viewed as a (casual) variant of the Hausman specification testing method.

5.4   Misspecification Tests/Diagnostics

- Kramer and Sonnberger (1986) have a good exposition of many misspecification tests, along with examples of their application. Pagan (1984a) notes that most tests can be written in the form of an OV test, which he refers to as a variable addition test. McAleer (1994) tabulates (pp. 330, 331) possible causes of diagnostic failures. Beggs (1988) and McGuirk, Driscoll and Alway (1993) have good discussions for practitioners, with examples. MacKinnon (1992) is a very informative survey of the use of artificial regressions for calculating a wide variety of specification tests.

- Extensive use of diagnostic tests/checks is not universally applauded. Goldberger (1986) claims a recent empirical study reported more diagnostic test statistics than the number of observations in the data set; Oxley (1996, p. 229) opines that "we probably have more papers creating new test statistics than papers using them." Several complaints and warnings have been issued:

(1) their use may decrease the intensity with which researchers investigate their data and theoretical specifications;

(2) it may be replacing one kind of data mining with another;

(3) many tests are only valid in large samples, something often forgotten;

(4) inexperienced researchers frequently apply tests in contexts in which they are inappropriate;

(5) many tests are only valid if the model is "correctly specified";

(6) sequences of tests distort things like the probability of a type I error;

(7) most of the tests used are not independent of one another;

(8) the properties of pre-test estimators are not well understood.

These points suggest that some care should be taken in applying diagnostic tests, and that results should be viewed with a healthy degree of scepticism.

- That most researchers do not bother to subject their models to misspecification tests is illustrated convincingly by Kramer et al. (1985), who apply a battery of such tests to several empirical studies and find that these tests are failed with high frequency.

- Doran (1993) is a good exposition of non-nested testing. McAleer (1987) and MacKinnon (1983) are good surveys of the non-nested test literature; the commentary on the MacKinnon paper provides an interesting view of controversies in this area. The feature of non-nested tests that all models under consideration may be rejected (or accepted) is discussed by Dastoor (1981). Kennedy (1989) uses the Ballentine to exposit some of the non-nested tests and their common features.

- The non-nested F test is regarded as one of the best non-nested testing procedures, because of its computational ease and its relatively good performance in Monte Carlo studies. Suppose there are two theories, H_0 and H_1. According to H_0, the independent variables are X and Z; according to H_1, they are X and W. A general model with X, Z, and W as explanatory variables is formed (without any economic rationale!), called an artificial nesting model. To test H_0 the coefficients of W are tested against zero, using an F test, and to test H_1 the coefficients of Z are tested against zero, using an F test. Note that if neither H_0 nor H_1 is correct it is possible for both hypotheses to be rejected, and if one of H_0 and H_1 is correct, but X and Z happen to be highly collinear, it is possible for both to be accepted. It is often the case that degrees-of-freedom problems (the artificial nesting model could contain a lot of variables), collinearity problems or nonlinear functional forms make this test unattractive. There most popular alternatives are the J test and its variants.

- As is made clearer in the technical notes to this section, the J test is akin to the F test in that it stems from an artificial nesting model. To conduct this test, the dependent variable y is regressed on the explanatory variables of hypothesis H_0, together with $\hat{y}$, the estimated y from the regression associated with H_1. If $\hat{y}$ has some explanatory power beyond that contributed by the explanatory variables of H_0, then H_0 cannot be the "true" model. This question is addressed by using a t test to test if the coefficient of $\hat{y}$ is significantly different from zero: if it is, H_0 is rejected; otherwise, H_0 is accepted. The roles of H_0 and H_1 are reversed and the procedure is repeated to allow H_1 to be either accepted or rejected.

- Mizon and Richard (1986) exposit the encompassing principle and use it to unify several testing procedures. They show that the different non-nested tests all have different implicit null hypotheses. For example, the J test is a "variance" encompassing test – they test if a hypothesis can predict the estimated variance obtained by running the regression suggested by the other hypothesis. In contrast, the non-nested F test is a "mean" encompassing test – it tests if a hypothesis can predict the coefficient estimate obtained by running the regression suggested by the other hypothesis. This explains the different degrees of freedom of the J and non-nested F tests. A third type of encompassing test is a "forecast" encompassing test. Model 1 forecast encompasses model 2 if model 2 forecasts can be explained by model 1. The one-step-ahead forecast errors from model 2 are regressed on the difference between the one-step-ahead forecasts from models 1 and 2; a t test on the slope coefficient from this regression is used for the forecast encompassing test.

- Data transformation tests are said to be Hausman-type tests, because they are based on a principle popularized by Hausman (1978) in the context of testing for contemporaneous correlation between the regressor(s) and the error (discussed further in chapters 9 and 10). This principle is as follows: if the model specification is correct, estimates by any two consistent methods should be close to one another; if they are not close to one another, doubt is cast on the model.

- Several variants of the data transformation test exist, the more popular of which are Farebrother (1979), where the transformation groups the data; Davidson et al. (1985), where the transformation is first differencing; and Boothe and MacKinnon (1986), where the transformation is that usually employed for doing GLS. Breusch and Godfrey (1985) have a good discussion, as do Kramer and Sonnberger (1986, pp. 111–15). See the technical notes for discussion of how such tests can be operationalized as OV tests.

- For examples of situations in which conditional moment tests are easier to construct than alternatives, see Pagan and Vella (1989). Newey (1985) and Tauchen (1985) have developed a computationally attractive way of calculating CM tests by running an artificial regression. (Regress a column of ones on the moments and the first derivatives of the log-likelihood with respect to each parameter, and test the slopes of the moments against zero.) Unfortunately, this method relies on OPG (outer product of the gradient – see appendix B) estimates of variance–covariance matrices which cause the type I error (size) of tests to be far too large. For discussion of CM tests see Godfrey (1988, pp. 37–9), Greene (1997, pp. 534–6) and Davidson and MacKinnon (1993, pp. 571–8).

- Although most tests are such that their asymptotic distributions are not sensitive to the assumption of normal errors, in small samples this may be of some concern. Rank tests are robust in this respect; McCabe (1989) suggests several rank tests for use as misspecification tests and claims that they have good power.

5.5 R^2 Again

- $\bar{R}^2$, the adjusted R^2, is derived from an interpretation of R^2 as 1 minus the ratio of the variance of the disturbance term to the variance of the dependent variable (i.e., it is concerned with variances rather than variation). Estimation of these variances involves corrections for degrees of freedom, yielding (after manipulation) the expression

$$\bar{R}^2 = R^2 - \frac{K - 1}{T - K}(1 - R^2) \text{ or } 1 - \frac{T - 1}{T - K}(1 - R^2)$$

where K is the number of independent variables and T is the number of observations. Armstrong (1978, p. 324) discusses some alternative adjustments to R^2. It is interesting to note that, if the true R^2 is zero (i.e., if there is no relationship between the dependent and independent variables), then the expected value of the unadjusted R^2 is K/T, a value that could be quite large. See Montgomery and Morrison (1973) for the general formula when the true R^2 is not zero.

- Both R^2 and $\bar{R}^2$ are biased but consistent estimators of the "true" or "population" coefficient of determination. $\bar{R}^2$ has a smaller bias than R^2, though. An unbiased estimator of the population coefficient of determination has not been developed because the distributions of R^2 and $\bar{R}^2$ are intractable when this population coefficient is nonzero.
- The result that the "correct" set of independent variables produces a higher $\bar{R}^2$ on average in repeated samples was derived by Theil (1957).
- If adding an independent variable increases $\bar{R}^2$, its t value is greater than unity. See Edwards (1969). Thus the rule of maximizing $\bar{R}^2$ is quite different from the rule of keeping variables only if their t values are significant at the 5% level.
- It is worth reiterating that searching for a high R^2 or a high $\bar{R}^2$ runs the real danger of finding, through perseverance, an equation that fits the data well but is incorrect because it captures accidental features of the particular data set at hand (called "capitalizing on chance") rather than the true underlying relationship. This is illustrated in convincing fashion by Mayer (1975) and Bacon (1977).
- Aigner (1971, pp. 101–7) presents a good critical summary of measures used to capture the relative importance of independent variables in determining the dependent variable. He stresses the point that the relative strength of individual regressors should be discussed in a policy context, so that, for example, the impact on the dependent variable per dollar of policy action is what is relevant.
- Anderson-Sprecher (1994) offers an interpretation of the R^2 measure that clarifies many of the problems with its use.

TECHNICAL NOTES

5.2   Three Methodologies

- TTT was developed in the context of autoregressive distributed lag models, where the initial "more general" specification takes the form of a very generous lag length on all explanatory variables, as well as on the lagged dependent variable. This is done to reflect the fact that economic theory typically has very little to say about the nature of the dynamics of a relationship. Common sense is used to choose the initial lag lengths. For example, if quarterly data are being used, five lags might be initially specified, allowing for fourth-differences and first-differences of the fourth-differenced data. One of the problems this creates is a lack of degrees of freedom. There is a tendency to solve this problem by "cheating" a little on the general-to-specific methodology – by not including at first all explanatory variables under consideration (adding them in later after the initial over-parameterized model has been simplified).
- The main input to a fragility analysis is a Bayesian prior distribution, with its vari-

ance–covariance matrix indexed by a scale parameter. By varying this scale parameter to reflect different degrees of confidence in this prior held by different researchers, a range of parameter estimates is produced, the output of a fragility analysis. An alternative approach, suggested by Granger and Uhlig (1990), is to modify the extreme-bounds analysis by considering only specifications that produce R^2 values within 10 or 15% of the highest R^2.

- In "testing down," the size of the overall test (the overall probability of a type I error), α, can be determined/controlled from the result that $(1 - \alpha)$ is equal to the product over i of $(1 - \alpha_i)$, where α_i is the size of the ith individual test. For example, suppose we are conducting n tests during a testing down process and we want the overall type I error to be 5%. What common type I error α^* of the individual n tests will accomplish this? This is calculated from $0.95 = (1 - \alpha^*)^n$, yielding $\alpha^* = 1 - 0.95^{1/n}$ which becomes smaller and smaller as n grows.

- A sixth criterion is often found in the list of criteria used to determine data congruency, namely that the explanatory variables should be at least weakly exogenous (i.e., it is valid to condition on these regressors), since otherwise it will be necessary to model the regressand and the regressor jointly. This criterion is out of place in general application of the TTT methodology. What is meant is that exogeneity should be tested for, not that a model must be such that all its explanatory variables are exogenous, however convenient that may be. If an explanatory variable is found not to be exogenous, an alternative specification may be required, but not necessarily one in which that variable must be exogenous.

- There are three types of exogeneity. Suppose y is thought to be explained by x. The variable x is said to be weakly exogenous if current y does not also explain x. This implies that estimation and testing can be undertaken by conditioning on x. It is strongly exogenous if also the lagged value of y does not explain x (i.e., there is no "feedback" from y to x); strong exogeneity has implications mainly for using x to forecast y. The variable x is "super exogenous" if the x coefficients in the relationship determining y are not affected by changes in the x values or by the process generating the x values. This has relevance for policy; it reflects the "Lucas critique" (Lucas, 1976), which claims that a policy change will cause rational economic agents to change their behavior, and questions what meaning one can attach to the assumed-constant parameters estimated by econometrics. Maddala (1988, pp. 325–31) has a good textbook exposition of exogeneity.

5.4   Misspecification Tests/Diagnostics

- The rationale behind the J test is easily seen by structuring the artificial nesting model on which it rests. Suppose there are two competing linear hypotheses:

$$H_0: y = X\beta + \varepsilon_0, \text{ and}$$
$$H_1: y = Z\delta + \varepsilon_1.$$

The artificial nesting model

$$y = (1 - \lambda)X\beta + \lambda Z\delta + \varepsilon_2$$

is formed, combining H_0 and H_1 with weights $(1 - \lambda)$ and λ, respectively. Under the null hypothesis that H_0 is the correct specification, λ is zero, so a specification test of H_0 can be formed by testing $\lambda = 0$. Regressing y on X and Z will permit estimation of $(1 - \lambda)\beta$ and $\lambda\delta$, but not λ. Even this cannot be done if X and Z have a common variable. This dilemma is resolved by the following two-step procedure:

(1) regress y on Z, obtain δ^{OLS} and calculate $\hat{y}_1 = Z\delta^{OLS}$, the estimated y from this regression;
(2) regress y on X and $\hat{y}_1$ and test the (single) slope coefficient estimate $(\hat{\lambda})$ of $\hat{y}_1$ against zero by a t test.

This permits H_0 to be either accepted or rejected. The roles of H_0 and H_1 are then reversed and the procedure is repeated to allow H_1 to be either accepted or rejected. (Why not just test $\lambda = 1$ from the regression in (2)? The logic of the test described above is based on H_0 being the null; when H_1 is the null $\hat{\lambda} - 1$ divided by its standard error turns out not to be distributed as a t.)

In small samples the type I error of the J test tends to be too large; Fan and Li (1995) find that bootstrapping eliminates this problem. Bera et al. (1992) show how non-nested testing can be undertaken simultaneously with testing for other features of the specification. In nonlinear contexts $X\beta$ and/or $Z\delta$ above would be replaced with the relevant nonlinear function. If this creates computational difficulties the P test is employed. For an exposition see Davidson and MacKinnon (1993, pp. 382–3); Smith and Smyth (1990) is a good example.

- Suppose we have specified $y = X\beta + \varepsilon$ and have suggested the transformation matrix P for the purpose of constructing a data transformation test. Transforming the data produces $Py = PX\beta + P\varepsilon$ to which OLS is applied to obtain $\beta^* = (X'P'PX)^{-1}X'P'Py$. This must be compared to $\beta^{OLS} = (X'X)^{-1}X'y$. Now write y as $X\beta^{OLS} + \varepsilon^{OLS}$, where ε^{OLS} is the OLS residual vector, and substitute this in the expression for β^* to get $\beta^* = \beta^{OLS} + (X'P'PX)^{-1}X'P'P\varepsilon^{OLS}$ or $\beta^* - \beta^{OLS} = (X'P'PX)^{-1}X'P'P\varepsilon^{OLS}$. For this to be insignificantly different from zero, $P'PX$ must be uncorrelated (or nearly so) with ε^{OLS}. It turns out that this can be tested by using a familiar F test to test if the coefficient vector on $P'PX$ is zero when y is regressed on X and $P'PX$. (For an intuitive explanation of this, see the technical notes to section 9.2, where the Hausman test for measurement errors is explained.) Thus a data transformation test can be performed as an OV test, where the omitted variables are defined by $P'PX$. Any redundancies (a column of $P'PX$ equal to a column of X, for example) created in this way are handled by omitting the offending column of $P'PX$ and changing the degrees of freedom of the F test accordingly.

- An unusual variant of a Hausman-type misspecification test is White's information matrix test, in which two different estimates of the information matrix (the inverse of the variance–covariance matrix) are compared. If the model is correctly specified, these estimates are asymptotically equivalent. One estimate is based on the matrix of second derivatives of the log-likelihood (the Hessian form), while the other is obtained by adding up the outer products of the vector of first derivatives of the log-likelihood (the OPG, or outer product of the gradient form). Hall (1989) provides a computationally feasible way of calculating this test statistic.

6

VIOLATING ASSUMPTION ONE: WRONG REGRESSORS, NONLINEARITIES, AND PARAMETER INCONSTANCY

6.1   INTRODUCTION

The first assumption of the CLR model states that the conditional expectation of the dependent variable is an unchanging linear function of known independent variables. It is usually referred to as the "model specification." Chapter 5 discussed in general terms the question of how to go about finding a model specification that is in accord, or "congruent," with the data. The purpose of this chapter is to be more specific on this issue, examining the three major ways in which this first assumption can be violated. First is the case in which the specified set of independent variables omits relevant variables or includes irrelevant variables. Second is the case of a nonlinear functional form. And third is the case in which the parameters do not remain constant.

6.2   INCORRECT SET OF INDEPENDENT VARIABLES

The consequences of using an incorrect set of independent variables fall into two categories. Intuitive explanations for these results are given in the general notes to this section.

(1)   *Omission of a relevant independent variable*
    (a)   In general, the OLS estimator of the coefficients of the remaining variables is biased. If by luck (or experimental design, should the researcher be fortunate enough to have control over the data) the observations on the omitted variable(s) are uncorrelated in the sample with the observations on the other independent variables (i.e., if the

omitted variable is orthogonal to the included variables), the slope coefficient estimator will be unbiased; the intercept estimator will retain its bias unless the mean of the observations on the omitted variable is zero.

(b)　The variance–covariance matrix of β^{OLS} becomes smaller (unless the omitted variable is orthogonal to the included variables, in which case it remains unchanged). This result, in conjunction with the bias noted in (a) above, implies that omitting a relevant variable can either raise or lower an estimator's MSE, depending on the relative magnitudes of the variance reduction and the bias.

(c)　The estimator of the (now smaller) variance–covariance matrix of β^{OLS} is biased upward, because the estimator of σ^2, the variance of the error term, is biased upward. This causes inferences concerning these parameters to be inaccurate. This is the case even if the omitted variable is orthogonal to the others.

(2)　*Inclusion of an irrelevant variable*

(a)　β^{OLS} and the estimator of its variance–covariance matrix remain unbiased.

(b)　Unless the irrelevant variable is orthogonal to the other independent variables, the variance–covariance matrix β^{OLS} becomes larger; the OLS estimator is not as efficient. Thus in this case the MSE of the estimator is unequivocally raised.

At first glance a strategy of "throwing in everything but the kitchen sink as regressors" seems to be a good way of avoiding bias. This creates what is sometimes referred to as the "kitchen sink" dilemma – omitted variables, and the bias they cause, will be avoided, but the irrelevant variables that will inevitably be present will cause high variances.

There is no easy way out of this dilemma. The first and foremost ingredient in a search for the correct set of explanatory variables is economic theory. If economic theory cannot defend the use of a variable as an explanatory variable, it should not be included in the set of potential independent variables. Such theorizing should take place *before* any empirical testing of the appropriateness of potential independent variables; this guards against the adoption of an independent variable just because it happens to "explain" a significant portion of the variation in the dependent variable in the particular sample at hand. Unfortunately, there is a limit to the information that economic theory can provide in this respect. For example, economic theory can suggest that lagged values of an explanatory variable should be included, but will seldom suggest how many such variables should be included. Because of this, economic theory must be supplemented by some additional mechanism for determining the correct set of explanatory variables.

According to the TTT methodology discussed in chapter 5, this should be done by including more variables than thought necessary and then "testing down" to obtain a final specification. If this approach is followed, the question arises as to what critical value of the relevant t or F statistic should be employed to operationalize the testing procedure. An obvious possibility is the traditional 5% value, perhaps adjusted downwards if several tests are to be performed. An alternative, as mentioned in the general notes to section 4.5, is to use a critical value of unity, implying maximization of adjusted R^2. Several other suggestions for critical values correspond to maximization of alternative adjusted forms of R^2, with slightly different trade-offs between goodness of fit and parsimony (number of explanatory variables). These are usually formalized in terms of finding the set of explanatory variables that minimizes a specific function of the sum of squared errors and the number of explanatory variables. The more popular of these model selection criteria are the Akaike information criterion (AIC), Amemiya's prediction criterion (PC), and the Schwarz criterion (SC), which are discussed in the general notes.

Unfortunately there are no unequivocal means of testing for whether an unknown explanatory variable has been omitted, mainly because other misspecifications, such as incorrect functional form, affect available tests. Many of the misspecification tests discussed in chapter 5 are used to check for an omitted explanatory variable. Particularly popular in this regard are tests for serial correlation in the errors (discussed in chapter 8), since any cyclical movement in an omitted variable will be transmitted to the OLS residuals.

Also popular is the RESET test. When a relevant variable is omitted from a model, the "disturbance" term of the false model incorporates the influence of the omitted variable. If some variable or set of variables Z can be used as a proxy for the (unknown) omitted variable(s), a specification error test can be formed by examining Z's relationship to the false model's error term. The RESET (regression specification error test) does this by adding Z to the set of regressors and then testing Z's set of coefficient estimates against the zero vector by means of a traditional F test. There are two popular choices of Z: the squares, cubes and fourth powers of the predicted dependent variable, and the squares, cubes and fourth powers of the explanatory variables.

6.3 NONLINEARITY

The first assumption of the CLR model specifies that the functional form of the relationship to be estimated is linear. Running an OLS regression when this is not true is clearly unsatisfactory, since parameter estimates not only are biased but also are without meaning except in so far as the linear functional form can be interpreted as an approximation to a nonlinear functional form. Functional forms popular in applied econometric work are summarized in the technical notes to this section.

The OLS procedure must be revised to handle a nonlinear functional form. These revisions fall into two categories.

(1)   TRANSFORMATIONS

If by transforming one or more variables a nonlinear function can be translated into a linear function in the transformed variables, OLS estimation procedures can be applied to transformed data. These transformations are of two types.

(a) *Transforming only independent variables*   If, for example, the nonlinear functional form is

$$y = a + bx + cx^2 + \varepsilon$$

a linear function

$$y = a + bx + cz + \varepsilon$$

can be created by structuring a new independent variable z whose observations are the squares of the observations on x. This is an example of an equation non-linear in variables but linear in parameters. The dependent variable y can be regressed on the independent variables x and z using β^{OLS} to estimate the para-meters. The OLS estimator has its CLR model properties, the R^2 statistic retains its traditional properties, and the standard hypothesis tests are valid.

(b) *Transforming the entire equation*   When transforming only independent variables cannot create a linear functional form, it is sometimes possible to cre-ate a linear function in transformed variables by transforming the entire equa-tion. If, for example, the nonlinear function is the Cobb–Douglas production function (with a multiplicative disturbance)

$$Y = AK^{\alpha}L^{\gamma}\varepsilon$$

then transforming the entire equation by taking natural logarithms of both sides creates

$$\ln Y = \ln A + \alpha \ln K + \gamma \ln L + \ln \varepsilon$$

or

$$Y^* = A^* + \alpha K^* + \gamma L^* + \varepsilon^*,$$

a linear function in the transformed variables Y^*, K^* and L^*. If this new relation-ship meets the CLR model assumptions, which econometricians usually assume is the case, the OLS estimates from a regression using these transformed vari-ables have their traditional desirable properties.

(2) COMPUTER-ASSISTED NUMERICAL TECHNIQUES

Some nonlinear functions cannot be transformed into a linear form. The CES production function is an example of this, as is the Cobb–Douglas function with an additive, rather than a multiplicative, disturbance. In these cases econometricians turn to either nonlinear least squares or maximum likelihood methods, both of which require computer search procedures. In nonlinear least squares the computer uses an iterative technique to find those values of the parameters in the relationship that cause the sum of squared residuals to be minimized. It starts with approximate guesses of the parameter values and computes the residuals and then the sum of squared residuals; next, it changes one of the parameter values slightly, recomputes the residuals and sees if the sum of squared residuals becomes larger or smaller. It keeps changing parameter values in directions that lead to smaller sums of squared residuals until it finds the set of parameter values that, when changed slightly in any direction, causes the sum of squared residuals to rise. These parameter values are the least squares estimates in the nonlinear context. A good initial guess of the parameter values is necessary to ensure that the procedure reaches a global and not a local minimum for the sum of squared residuals. For maximum likelihood estimation a similar computer search technique is used to find parameter values that maximize the likelihood function. See the technical notes for a discussion of the way in which computer searches are structured, some of which have led to the development of new estimators.

In general, the desirable properties of the OLS estimator in the CLR model do not carry over to the nonlinear least squares estimator. For this reason the maximum likelihood estimator is usually chosen in preference to the nonlinear least squares estimator. The two techniques are identical whenever the dependent variable is determined by a nonlinear function of the independent variables plus a normally distributed, additive disturbance.

There are five main methods of testing for nonlinearity.

(1) *RESET* Although the Regression Equation Specification Error Test was designed to be used to test for missing regressors, it turns out to be powerful for detecting nonlinearities. This weakens its overall attractiveness, since rejection of a model could be due to either a nonlinearity or an omitted explanatory variable. (No test can discriminate between unknown omitted variables and unknown functional form; a strong case can be made that the RESET test can only test for functional form.)

(2) *Recursive residuals* The nth recursive residual is the error in predicting the nth observation using parameters estimated from a linear regression employing the first $n - 1$ observations. If the true functional form is nonlinear, then, if the data are ordered according to the variable entering nonlinearly, these residuals could become either all positive or all negative, a result that can be exploited to test for nonlinearity.

(3) *General functional forms* Some functional forms contain particular forms, such as linearity or log-linearity, as special cases corresponding to specific values of a parameter. These particular functional forms can then be tested by testing the estimate of this parameter against these specific values.

(4) *Non-nested tests* Variants of the non-nested testing methodology discussed in chapter 5 can be used to test functional form.

(5) *Structural change tests* Because a nonlinear function can be approximated by two or more linear segments, the structural change tests discussed in the next section can be interpreted as tests for nonlinearity.

6.4 CHANGING PARAMETER VALUES

A common criticism of econometricians concerns their assumption that the parameters are constants. In time series estimation, changing institutions and social mores have surely caused the parameter values characterizing the economy to change over time, and in cross-section estimation it is surely unrealistic to assume that the parameters for every individual or every region are exactly the same. Although most econometricians usually ignore these criticisms, maintaining that with small sample sizes they are forced to make these simplifying assumptions to obtain estimates of any sort, several techniques are available for addressing this problem.

(1) SWITCHING REGIMES

It may be known that at a particular point in time the economic structure changed. For example, the date of the Canada–USA auto pact might mark a change in parameter values associated with the Canadian or US auto industries. In such a case we need run only two regressions, one for each "regime." More often than not, however, the point in time at which the parameter values changed is unknown and must be estimated. If the error variances are the same for both regimes, this can be done by selecting several likely points of change, running pairs of regressions for each and then choosing among these points of change by determining which corresponds to the smallest total sum of squared residuals. (If the error variances cannot be assumed equal, a maximum likelihood technique must be used.) This approach has been extended in several directions:

(a) to accommodate more than two regimes;

(b) to permit continuous switching back and forth, either randomly or according to a critical value of an unknown function of some additional variables;

(c) to eliminate discontinuities, so that the function describing one regime blends into the function describing the next regime over an adjustment period.

(2) PARAMETERS DETERMINED BY OTHER VARIABLES

It could be that β is itself determined by variables outside the model. For example, the extent to which a firm reacts to demand changes may depend on government policy parameters such as tax rates. This problem is most easily resolved by substituting the relationship determining β directly into the originating estimating function. Thus if we have, for example,

$$y = \beta_1 + \beta_2 x_2 + \varepsilon$$

and β_2, say, is determined as

$$\beta_2 = \alpha_1 + \alpha_2 z_2,$$

we can combine these relationships to get

$$y = \beta_1 + \alpha_1 x_2 + \alpha_2(x_2 z_2) + \varepsilon$$

so that estimation should be undertaken by including the new variable $(x_2 z_2)$ as an additional regressor. If the relationship for β_2 includes an error term, the error term attached to the final estimating question is more complicated, and although the OLS estimator remains unbiased, a maximum likelihood estimating procedure is required for efficiency.

(3) RANDOM COEFFICIENTS

Instead of being determined by specific variables, the parameters may be random variables. This could be viewed as an alternative way of injecting a stochastic element into a relationship, or it could reflect specific recognition of the fact that the parameters being estimated are not the same for every observation. In this case the estimating equation can be rewritten, substituting for the random β its mean plus a disturbance term, to yield a new estimating equation, with a somewhat more complicated error term, in which the parameter to be estimated is the mean value of the random coefficient β. Although OLS estimation of the mean of β is unbiased, the more complicated nature of the error term requires a more sophisticated estimation procedure for efficiency (such as a maximum likelihood method or a weighted least squares technique: see chapter 8). This approach has been extended in two directions:

(a) β is allowed to "drift" according to a random walk (i.e., β is equated to its value in the previous time period, plus a disturbance);
(b) β is random and "drifts," but converges on an unknown fixed value.

Four types of test have become particularly popular for testing for structural change/parameter inconstancy.

(1) *The Chow test*, discussed in the technical notes to this section, is used to test whether or not a parameter or parameters are unchanged from one data set to another. Variants are required for special cases, such as if the variance of the error term has also changed.

(2) *Predictive failure tests*, also called extra-sample prediction tests, are tests for whether or not a new observation lies inside the forecast confidence interval. Most such tests are variants of the Chow test, as is the "rainbow" test, both of which can be interpreted as tests for structural change.

(3) *Tests based on recursive residuals* The cusum and cusum of squares tests, with the data ordered chronologically, rather than according to the value of an explanatory variable (as is done for a functional form test) can be used to test for structural stability.

(4) *Tests based on recursive parameter estimates* The methodology used to calculate recursive residuals can be used to estimate parameter estimates recursively. These estimates should not fluctuate too much (or their first differences should be close to zero) if the structure is stable.

GENERAL NOTES

6.1   Introduction

- A potential violation of the first assumption that is not mentioned in this chapter is the possibility that the stochastic ingredient of the relationship does not manifest itself as an additive error term. There are three main alternatives entertained in the literature. The case of a multiplicative disturbance can be reformulated as an additive heteroskedastic error, as discussed in chapter 8. The case of random coefficients is considered in this chapter. And the case of measurement error is discussed in chapter 9.

6.2   Incorrect Set of Independent Variables

- Kennedy (1981b) employs the Ballentine to exposit the consequences of omitting a relevant variable or adding an irrelevant variable. In figure 6.1 the real world is such that Y is determined by X and Z but the variable (or set of variables) Z is erroneously omitted from the regression. Several results can be noted.

  (a) Since Y is regressed on only X, the blue-plus-red area is used to estimate β_x. But the red area reflects variation in Y due to *both* X and Z, so the resulting estimate of β_x will be biased.

  (b) If Z has been included in the regression, only the blue area would have been used in estimating β_x. Omitting Z thus increases the information used to estimate β_x by the red area, implying that the resulting estimate, although biased, will have a smaller variance. Thus it is possible that by omitting Z the mean square error of the estimate of β_x may be reduced.

  (c) The magnitude of the yellow area reflects the magnitude of σ^2. But when Z is omitted, σ^2 is estimated using the yellow-plus-green area, resulting in an overes-

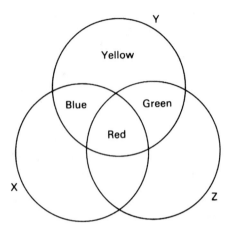

Figure 6.1 Omitting a relevant variable Z

timate of σ^2 (i.e., the green area influence of Z is erroneously attributed to the error term). This overestimate of σ^2 causes an overestimate of the variance–covariance matrix of the estimate of β_x.

(d) If Z is orthogonal to X the red area does not exist, so the bias noted above disappears.

● In figure 6.2 the real world is such that Y is determined by X but the irrelevant variable Z is erroneously added to the regression. The overlap of Z with Y comes about virtually entirely because of its collinearity with X; in this case the red area reflects variation in Y explained 100% by X and 0% by Z. The shaded area is negligible in size because only with finite degrees of freedom will Z be able to explain a small amount of variation in Y independently of X. Using the correct specification, Y is regressed on X and the blue-plus-red area is employed to create an unbiased estimate of β_x. Including Z in the regression implies that only the blue area is used to estimate β_x. Several results follow.

(a) The blue area reflects variation in Y due entirely to X, so this estimate of β_x is unbiased. Thus, adding an irrelevant variable does not bias coefficient estimates.
(b) Since the blue area is smaller than the blue-plus-red area, the variance of the estimate of β_x becomes larger; there is a loss of efficiency.
(c) The usual estimator of σ^2, using the yellow area, remains unbiased because the negligible shaded area is offset by the change in the degrees of freedom. Thus the usual estimator of the variance–covariance matrix of β_x remains unbiased. (It does become bigger, though, as noted in (b) above.)
(d) If Z is orthogonal to X, the red area disappears and there is no efficiency loss.

● Iterative techniques used to find the set of independent variables meeting some t test criterion are not always reliable. Consider the "forward selection" technique, for example. It augments the set of regressors one by one, by selecting the new variable with the highest t value, until no more variables with t values higher than the critical t value can be found. Unfortunately, a variable included in an early step may have its

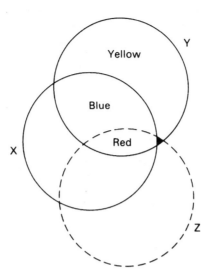

Figure 6.2   Adding an irrelevant variable Z

usefulness negated by the inclusion of new variables, whose *joint* influence is more effective in explaining the variation in the dependent variable that the variable included earlier had explained. Only if at each step the iterative procedure pauses and rechecks all the already included variables will this be caught. (Note that it will never be caught if the new variables, whose *joint* influence is more effective than an already included variable, are never included in the set of regressors because their individual *t* values are too low.) In summary, these methods tend to select sets of variables that are relatively uncorrelated, a result difficult to justify, particularly since, as noted above, omitting a correlated explanatory variable leads to bias in the estimation of the remaining parameters. For a summary discussion of this problem see Maddala (1977, pp. 124–7).

- When using a *t* or *F* criterion the "too-large" sample size phenomenon should be kept in mind.
- Of the several different ways of trading off goodness of fit and parsimony, adjusted R^2 has the least amount of adjustment for extra explanatory variables. The most popular alternatives are

AIC (Akaike information criterion), which minimizes $\ln (SSE/T) + 2K/T$
SC (Schwarz criterion), which minimizes $\ln (SSE/T) + (K \ln T)/T$ and
PC (Amemiya's prediction criterion), which minimizes $SSE(1 + K/T)/(T - K)$,

where T is the sample size and K is the number of regressors. Each is defended on the basis of the loss function on which its derivation rests. The SC, which is derived using Bayesian arguments, has performed well in Monte Carlo studies. Mills and Prasad (1992), for example, have examined several model selection criteria with an eye to seeing how well they stand up to complications such as non-normal errors and collinearity, and recommend the Schwarz criterion. Amemiya (1980) has an extensive discussion of these criteria, the relationships among them, and their relative merits. See also Judge et al. (1985, chapter 21). Having so many such criteria, differing by so little, creates a dilemma of choice, reflected by Amemiya's comment that "all the criteria considered are based on a somewhat arbitrary assumption which cannot be fully justified, and that by slightly varying the loss function and the decision strategy one can indefinitely go on inventing new criteria."

- Any method that selects regressors on the basis of a sample statistic such as R^2 is likely to "capitalize on chance" – to select a regressor because of an accidental feature of the particular sample at hand. *Cross-validation* is designed to overcome this problem. In this technique, half the sample is used to obtain parameter estimates that are used to forecast the other half of the sample, allowing computation of an R^2. If this R^2 is not too far below the R^2 from the first half of the sample, the specification is said to be satisfactory. Unfortunately, however, satisfactory methods for predicting the degree of shrinkage in R^2 when moving to the new data are not available, so that no formal statistical tests have been structured to formalize this technique; its use is subjective. (It should be noted, however, that all statistical testing is to some degree subjective, through the choice of such things as the significance level.) Uhl and Eisenberg (1970) examine shrinkage in R^2. Snee (1977) discusses the optimal way to split a sample for cross-validation. Because of these difficulties, this procedure should be operationalized by post-sample predictive tests, which are discussed in this chapter in the context of parameter stability, and mentioned in chapter 5 as one of the basic principles that should guide specification searches.

- Leamer (1983b) notes that one form of cross-validation via sample splitting is equivalent to minimizing the sum of squared errors with a penalty for coefficient instability. He suggests that a proper means of accommodating coefficient instability be employed instead. He also shows that cross-validation done by deleting one observation at a time (i.e., using all observations but one to estimate and then predict that missing observation) is inferior to the traditional $\bar{R}^2$ criterion.

- Thursby and Schmidt (1977) suggest that the best variant of RESET is one in which the additional regressors Z are the squares, cubes and fourth powers of the explanatory variables. Thursby (1979, 1981, 1982) has examined how RESET can be combined with a variety of other tests to aid in specification.

6.3   Nonlinearity

- Although the linear functional form is convenient, it should not be accepted unquestioningly, as is done too frequently. Hunderwasser (as quoted by Peitgen and Richter, 1986) has an extreme expression of this view:

> In 1953 I realized that the straight line leads to the downfall of mankind. The straight line has become an absolute tyranny. The straight line is something cowardly drawn with a rule, without thought or feeling; it is the line which does not exist in nature. And that line is the rotten foundation of our doomed civilization. Even if there are places where it is recognized that this line is rapidly leading to perdition, its course continues to be plotted.

- Lau (1986) has a useful survey of functional forms in econometrics. He suggests five criteria for choosing a functional form: theoretical consistency, domain of applicability, flexibility, computational facility, and factual conformity. Granger (1993) offers advice on modeling nonlinear time series.

- The properties of the OLS estimator applied to a situation in which the true functional form is nonlinear can be analysed in terms of omitted relevant variables. A nonlinear function can be restated, via a Taylor series expansion, as a polynomial. Estimating a linear function is in effect omitting the higher-order terms of this polynomial.

- Transforming an equation into a linear form sometimes creates an error term for that linear function that does not meet all of the CLR model assumptions. See chapter 7 for an example.

- A multiplicative error term for some nonlinear functional forms (such as the Cobb–Douglas production function) facilitates the transformation of the equation to a linear estimating form. It is not obvious, however, that this error term need necessarily be multiplicative. Leech (1975) addresses the problem of testing this error specification.

- A distinct danger in using the highest $\bar{R}^2$ criterion to choose the functional form is that, if the dependent variables are not the same, the R^2 is not directly comparable. For example, the R^2 from a regression of the logarithm of the dependent variable on the logarithms of the independent variables gives the proportion of the variation in the *logarithm* of the dependent variable explained, not the proportion of the variation in the dependent variable itself. Estimated values of the dependent variable must be used to construct a comparable R^2, or some transformation must be applied to the data to assure compatibility. (An example of such a transformation for a popular application is given in Rao and Miller, 1971, pp. 108–9.) Note, however, that Granger and Newbold (1976) suggest that under general conditions this entire problem of the comparability of the R^2s can be ignored. See Haessel (1978) on measuring goodness of fit in nonlinear models.

- Recursive residuals are standardized one-step-ahead prediction errors. Suppose the observations are ordered by the size of the explanatory variable and the true relationship is U-shaped. Use, say, the first ten observations to estimate via OLS a linear relationship. When this estimated relationship is employed to predict the eleventh observation, it will probably underpredict because of the U-shaped nonlinearity; the recursive residual for the eleventh observation is this (probably positive) prediction error, standardized by dividing by its variance. To obtain the twelfth recursive residual, the first eleven observations are used to estimate the linear relationship. Doing this will tilt the estimating line up a bit from what it was before, but not nearly by enough to prevent another underprediction; once again, the recursive residual, because of the nonlinearity, is likely to be positive. Thus a string of positive recursive residuals indicates a U-shaped nonlinearity and a string of negative recursive residuals indicates a hill-shaped nonlinearity. Harvey and Collier (1977) advocate the use of recursive residuals to test for nonlinearity, using the cusum (cumulative sum) and cusum-of-squares tests introduced by Brown et al. (1975).

- The cusum test is based on a plot of the sum of the recursive residuals. If this sum goes outside a critical bound, one concludes that there was a structural break at the point at which the sum began its movement toward the bound. Kramer et al. (1988) show that the cusum test can be used with lagged values of dependent variable as regressor. The cusum-of-squares test is similar to the cusum test, but plots the cumulative sum of squared recursive residuals, expressed as a fraction of these squared residuals summed over all observations. Edgerton and Wells (1994) provide critical values.

Practical experience has shown that cusum of squares is sensitive to outliers and severe non-normality.

- Unlike OLS residuals, recursive residuals are homoskedastic (because they are standardized) and are independent of one another (because a recursive residual's own observation is not involved in estimating the prediction line from which it is calculated). These attractive properties have made them a popular alternative to OLS residuals for use in calculating a variety of regression diagnostics. For a good review of their uses in this regard, see Galpin and Hawkins (1984). Because the behavior of recursive residuals in a misspecified model is very different from that of the OLS residuals, as should be evident from the discussion of the cusum test, test procedures based on recursive residuals should be viewed as complementary to tests based on OLS residuals.

- A related way of testing for linearity to break the data into sub-groups based on the magnitude of the independent variable being tested for nonlinearity and then run separate regressions for each sub-group. If these separate regressions are significantly different from one another, there is good reason to believe the functional form is not linear.

- The most popular general functional form used for testing nonlinearity is that associated with the Box–Cox transformation, in which a variable Z is transformed to $(Z^\lambda - 1)/\lambda$. Since the limit of this as λ approaches zero is $\ln Z$, it is defined to be $\ln Z$ when $\lambda = 0$. If all variables in a linear functional form are transformed in this way and then λ is estimated (in conjunction with the other parameters) via a maximum likelihood technique, significance tests can be performed on λ to check for special cases. If $\lambda = 0$, for example, the functional form becomes Cobb–Douglas in nature; if $\lambda = 1$ it is linear. Aigner (1971, pp. 166–9) and Johnston (1984, pp. 61–74) have good discussions of this approach. Spitzer (1982) is a particularly useful reference. Estimating the variance of a Box–Cox estimate can be a problem: see Spitzer (1984). Park 1990 suggests a means of testing for the appropriateness of the Box–Cox transformation. Although the Box–Cox transformation is very popular, it has the disadvantage that it breaks down when zero or negative values must be transformed. Burbridge, Magee and Robb (1988) note that the inverse hyperbolic sine function $\sinh^{-1}$ can circumvent this problem and has additional advantages over the Box–Cox transformation. $\sinh^{-1}(\theta y)/\theta$ transforms y to $\ln[\theta y + (\theta^2 y^2 + 1)^{0.5}]/\theta$ and to y when $\theta = 0$. See also MacKinnon and Magee (1990) and Wooldridge (1992).

- The Box–Cox technique has been generalized in several ways to permit testing of functional form simultaneously with testing for other violations of the CNLR model. All of these studies have concluded that there is much to gain (in terms of power) and little to lose from pursuing a policy of "overtesting" in this respect. For a survey of some of these studies, see Seaks and Layson (1983). The most general of these approaches is that of Bera and Jarque (1982), in which functional form, normality of the error term, heteroskedasticity, and autocorrelated errors are tested for simultaneously. Bera et al. (1992) extend this procedure to the context of testing non-tested models.

- The "rainbow" test, suggested by Utts (1982), can be used to test for nonlinearity. In this test "central" data points are used to estimate a linear relationship, which is used to predict the outlying data points. A Chow test (described in section 14.5 technical notes in chapter 14) is employed to test whether these predictions collectively lie within their confidence limits.

- Godfrey et al. (1988) have an excellent review of tests for linear versus log-linear functional form. On the basis of a Monte Carlo study they recommend the RESET test.
- Thursby (1989) finds that DW, RESET, Chow and differencing tests perform well against the specific alternative against which they were designed to perform well, but typically do not do well against general alternatives.
- Amemiya (1983) shows that OV tests for the nonlinear regression model of the form $y = f(X,\beta) + \varepsilon$ can be undertaken by regressing the residuals from this nonlinear regression on the matrix of observations on the partial derivatives of f with respect to β (evaluated at the nonlinear least-squares estimate), and the usual set of omitted variables, employing the usual F test for the significance of the OVs.
- In some contexts it is known that a differenced form of a time series should be estimated, but it is not clear whether the first difference form or the percentage change form is appropriate. For discussion and references see Seaks and Vines (1990).

6.4   Changing Parameter Values

- It has long been suspected that parameter values do not remain constant over time. For example, as quoted in Swamy et al. (1988a), in 1938 Keynes commented on a proof copy of Tinbergen's *Business Cycles in the United States of America* that "The coefficients arrived at are apparently assumed to be constant for 10 years or for a longer period. Yet, surely we know that they are not constant. There is no reason at all why they should not be different every year."
- Surveys of regime-switching can be found in Goldfeld and Quandt (1976, chapter 1) and Poirier (1976, chapter 7). In some cases it is reasonable to suppose that a regime change involves a transition period during which the relationship changes smoothly from the old to the new regime. Goldfeld and Quandt model this by using an S-curve (cumulative density) as do Lin and Terasvirta (1994); Wilton (1975) uses a polynomial in time. Disequilibrium models are popular examples of continuous regime-switching. If observations are generated by the minimum of the quantities supplied and demanded, for example, then some observations come from a supply curve (one regime) and the other observations come from a demand curve (the other regime). Estimation in this context exploits some kind of an indicator variable; for example, was the most recent price change positive or negative? Work in this area stems from Fair and Jaffee (1972). For surveys see Fomby et al. (1984, pp. 567–75), Quandt (1982), and Maddala (1986). Shaban (1980) and Hackl and Westlund (1989) are annotated bibliographies.
- Random parameter models create a regression equation with a nonspherical error term (chapter 8 discusses nonspherical errors). Estimation techniques begin by deriving the nature of this nonsphericalness, i.e., the variance–covariance matrix of the regression's error term. Then this is either built into a maximum likelihood estimation procedure or somehow estimated and employed as input to an EGLS estimator (see chapter 8). Tests for heteroskedasticity (see chapter 8) are often used to test for whether parameters are random. Maddala (1977, chapter 17) has a good textbook exposition of changing parameter models. Swamy and Tavlas (1995) survey random coefficient models. Raj and Ullah (1981) exposit the role of varying parameters in several econometric contexts.

- Machak et al. (1985) has a good discussion of time-varying random parameter models. Watson and Engle (1985) examine the case in which parameters follow an AR(1) structure. Flexible least squares allows the parameters to evolve slowly over time by minimizing a weighted sum of the sum of squared residuals and the sum of squared changes in the parameters over time. See Dorfman and Foster (1991) and Kalaha and Tesfatison (1989).
- Pesaran et al. (1985) is a good survey of variants of the Chow test and predictive failure tests. Ashley (1984) suggests an attractive generalization of the Chow test, along with a diagrammatic means of examining the model for structural change. Kramer and Sonnberger (1986, pp. 43–78) has a good review of tests using recursive residuals and recursive parameter estimates. Dufour (1982) suggests several extensions of the recursive methodology. Bleaney (1990) compares several tests for structural change, recommending that of Farley et al. (1975), which models each parameter as a linear function of time and then tests for whether the slope of this relationship is zero.
- An important application of random parameters, called the random effects model, is used in the context of panel data (a time series of cross-sectional data); it is discussed in chapter 14, where it is seen to be a competitor to a dummy variable formulation.
- Cadsby and Stengos (1986) and Hsu (1982) give examples of tests for structural stability that are robust to some other possible misspecifications. The former allows for autocorrelated errors; the latter is robust against departures from normality.
- *Spline theory*, an approach to the regime-switching problem in which functions are spliced together at points of structural change, is applied to economics by Poirier (1976). Suits et al. (1978) have a good exposition. Robb (1980) extends its application to seasonal data.

TECHNICAL NOTES

6.3   Nonlinearity

- Below is a summary of the more popular nonlinear functional forms. To be used for econometric purposes these equations must somehow incorporate an error term.

  (1) *Log-linear*, also called log-log, exponential, constant elasticity, and Cobb–Douglas: $\ln Y = \alpha + \beta \ln L + \gamma \ln K$. The parameters β and γ are elasticities, the elasticity of substitution is unity, and $\beta + \gamma$ is the returns-to-scale parameter.
  (2) *Semi-log*, with two forms:
      (a) $Y = \alpha + \beta \ln X$ Note β gives ΔY due to $\%\Delta X$. Popular for Engle curves.
      (b) In $Y = \alpha + \beta X$ Note β gives $\%\Delta Y$ due to ΔX, unless X is a dummy, in which case $\%\Delta Y$ is given by $e^\beta - 1$.
  (3) *Inverse*, also called reciprocal: $Y = \alpha + \beta X^{-1}$. Popular for Phillips curve estimation. One of many variants is $Y = \alpha + \beta(X + \delta)^{-1}$.
  (4) *Polynomial*: $Y = \alpha + \beta X + \gamma X^2$.
  (5) *CES*, constant elasticity of substitution:

  $$Y = \gamma[\delta K^{-\theta} + (1 - \delta)L^{-\theta}]^{-\phi/\theta}.$$

  The elasticity of substitution is $(1 + \theta)^{-1}$ and the scale parameter is ϕ.
  (6) *Transcendental*: $\ln Y = \alpha_0 + \alpha_1 \ln L + \alpha_2 \ln K + \alpha_3 L + \alpha_4 K$.

(7) *Translog*, transcendental logarithmic, considered the most flexible functional form for production function estimation:

$$Y = \alpha_0 + \alpha_1 \ln L + \alpha_2 \ln K + \alpha_3 \ln L \ln K + \alpha_4 (\ln L)^2 + \alpha_5 (\ln K)^2.$$

(8) *Box–Cox*: $(Y^\lambda - 1)/\lambda = \alpha + \beta X$. A similar transformation, with the same or a different λ, can be applied to X. Note that as λ approaches zero, the LHS approaches $\ln Y$, and as λ approaches one, the LHS approaches Y.

(9) *Logit*: $y = \dfrac{e^{\alpha + \beta x}}{1 + e^{\alpha + \beta x}}$. This functional form should be used whenever y is

constrained to lie in the zero-one interval, such as when it is a proportion.

With the exception of the CES, the Box–Cox, and the variant of the inverse, all of the above can be estimated by running a linear regression assuming an additive error term. Estimation for the logit is undertaken by transforming y to the log-odds ratio $\ln[y/(1 - y)] = \alpha + \beta x$ and adding an error.

- Computer search routines can sometimes be simplified by exploiting the fact that often if one parameter is known the others can be estimated by OLS. For example, suppose that $y = \alpha + \beta(x + \delta)^{-1}$. If δ were known, $w = (x + \delta)^{-1}$ could be calculated, implying that α and β could be estimated by regressing y on an intercept and w. This suggests simplifying the search process by looking for the δ value for which the *SSE* from the secondary regression is minimized.

- Most iterative schemes for minimizing a nonlinear function $F(\theta)$ with respect to the $k \times 1$ parameter vector θ are of the form

$$\theta^{**} = \theta^* + \lambda d(\theta^*)$$

where θ^{**} is the updated estimate of θ, θ^* is the estimate from the previous iteration, λ is a positive scalar called the step-length, and $d(\theta^*)$ is a $k \times 1$ direction vector. Once $d(\theta^*)$ has been chosen, the best value of λ can be found easily by searching over λ values to minimize $F[\theta^* + \lambda d(\theta^*)]$, so the real distinction between different iterative methods is the choice of $d(\theta^*)$.

A popular method is the Newton–Raphson, or Newton, method, which is based on approximating $F(\theta)$ by a quadratic function from a Taylor series expansion around the unknown value θ_m that maximizes F. For the case of θ a scalar we have

$$F(\theta) = F(\theta_m) + (\theta - \theta_m)g(\theta_m) + (1/2)(\theta - \theta_m)^2 H(\theta_m)$$

where $g(\theta_m)$ is the gradient, or first derivative of F evaluated at θ_m, and $H(\theta_m)$ is the second derivative, also evaluated at θ_m. Note that $g(\theta_m) = 0$, because θ_m is the point at which F is maximized, so the second term disappears. Differentiating this with respect to θ yields $g(\theta) = H(\theta_m)(\theta - \theta_m)$, which can be rearranged to give $\theta_m = \theta - H^{-1}(\theta_m)g(\theta)$, suggesting the iterative scheme $\theta^{**} = \theta^* - H^{-1}g$, where the step-length is one and the direction vector is $-H^{-1}g$, with H and g both evaluated at θ^*. Iteration continues until some convergence criterion, such as a sufficiently small change in F, a sufficiently small change in θ, or $g(\theta)$ sufficiently close to zero, is met. The choice of convergence criterion is made on the basis of what works well for the problem at hand.

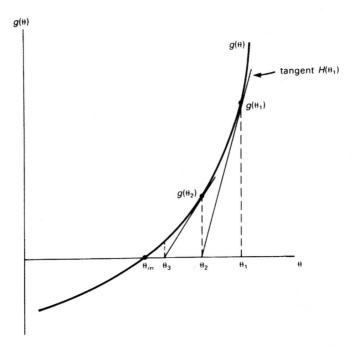

Figure 6.3   Illustrating the Newton Method

This is illustrated in figure 6.3 for the case of θ a scalar. The line g is the derivative of F, so the value of θ that we seek is θ_m, where g cuts the horizontal axis. Consider a starting value θ_1. The corresponding value of g is $g(\theta_1)$, at which the tangent line has slope $H(\theta_1)$. The updating formula creates θ_2 by extending the tangent down to the horizontal axis. Then we move in the next iteration to θ_3, eventually ending up at θ_m. Note that if F were a quadratic function, g would be linear and θ_m would be found in one iteration. Harvey (1990, chapter 4) and Greene (1997, pp. 198–218) are good discussions of nonlinear optimization. See also Judge et al. (1985, appendix B), Gallant (1975), and Quandt (1983).

When θ is a vector the Taylor series expansion is

$$F(\theta) = F(\theta_m) + (\theta - \theta_m)'g(\theta_m) + (1/2)(\theta - \theta_m)'H(\theta_m)(\theta - \theta_m)$$

with g the gradient vector and H the matrix of second derivatives, the Hessian.

- Whenever F is a log-likelihood function the expected value of the negative of the Hessian is the information matrix, and so sometimes alternative estimates of the information matrix are used in the updating formula in place of $-H$. One alternative is the method of scoring, which uses the formula for the expected value of the second derivative matrix. Another is BHHH, the method of Berndt, Hall, Hall and Hausman, which uses the OPG (outer product of the gradient) – the sum over all observations of gg', where g is the gradient of the log-likelihood.

- MacKinnon (1992) and Davidson and MacKinnon (1993, chapter 6) exposit the Gauss–Newton regression, an artificial OLS regression useful for computing a variety of results relating to nonlinear estimation, such as checks on satisfaction of first-order conditions, estimated covariance matrices, test statistics, one-step efficient estimates, and inputs to numerical optimization. Suppose that $y = G(X,\beta) + \varepsilon$ where $G(X,\beta)$ is a nonlinear function of parameters β and the explanatory variables X. Expanding in a Taylor series around β^* we get

$$y = G(X,\beta^*) + g(X,\beta^*)(\beta - \beta^*) + \text{ higher order terms } + \varepsilon$$

where $g(X,\beta^*)$ is the matrix of derivatives of G with respect to β, evaluated at β^*. This is rewritten as

$$y - G(X,\beta^*) = g(X,\beta^*)\delta + \text{residual}$$

to produce the Gauss–Newton regression: Regress the estimated errors using β^* on the estimated first derivatives to estimate δ, the extent to which β^* differs from β.

  To check your understanding of this, note that if G is linear and β^* is β^{OLS}, then g is X and δ should be estimated by the zero vector because the Gauss–Newton equation just reflects the first-order conditions for minimizing the sum of squared errors. Similarly, when G is nonlinear and β^* is the nonlinear least squares estimate of β, the Gauss–Newton equation also reflects the first-order conditions for minimizing the sum of squared errors and the resulting estimate of δ should be zero. Running the Gauss–Newton regression is therefore a useful check on whether these first-order conditions are satisfied by a particular β^*. It is also easily seen that the estimated variance–covariance matrix of δ from running the Gauss–Newton regression is an estimate of the variance–covariance matrix of β^*. The references cited earlier provide several examples of other uses of this regression, such as producing computationally convenient means of minimizing the sum of squared errors or producing two-step estimates for awkward maximum likelihood problems. An example of the latter appears in the general notes of section 9.4 in chapter 9.

6.4   Changing Parameter Values

- The Chow test is best undertaken by using dummy variables; an exposition of how this is done appears in chapter 14.
- In the Chow test σ^2 is assumed to be the same in both periods although its estimate is allowed to differ between periods in the unconstrained version; if σ^2 actually differs between the two periods, the Chow test is no longer suitable. Suppose b_1 and b_2 are the OLS estimates of the vector β from the first and second data sets, respectively, and $s_1^2(X_1'X_1)^{-1}$ and $s_2^2(X_2'X_2)^{-1}$ are their respective variance–covariance estimates. We wish to test $(b_1 - b_2)$ against the zero vector. A Wald test for this takes the form

$$W = (b_1 - b_2)'Q^{-1}(b_1 - b_2)$$

where Q is the variance–covariance matrix of $(b_1 - b_2)$. In this example Q is easily seen to be estimated by the sum of the estimated variance–covariance matrices of b_1

and b_2. Unfortunately, this test rejects the null more often than it should. Ohtani and Kobiyashi (1986) suggest a correction. Thursby (1992) finds that some alternatives to the Chow test perform much better than the Chow test when error variances are unequal, and only slightly worse than the Chow test when error variances are equal. A possible alternative to deal with this problem is to transform the data to eliminate the heteroskedasticity and then perform the Chow test.

7
VIOLATING ASSUMPTION TWO: NONZERO EXPECTED DISTURBANCE

The second assumption of the CLR model states that the population from which the disturbance or error term is drawn has mean zero. Violation of this assumption may or may not be of concern, depending on specific circumstances.

CONSTANT NONZERO MEAN

The disturbance may have a nonzero mean because of systematically positive or systematically negative errors of measurement in calculating the dependent variable. This problem is most easily analyzed if the estimating equation is rearranged by removing the nonzero mean from the error term and adding it to the intercept term. This creates an estimating equation obeying all the CLR model assumptions; in particular, the mean of the new error term is zero. The only problem is that OLS estimation gives an unbiased estimate of the *new* intercept, which is the sum of the original intercept and the mean of the original error term; it is therefore a *biased* estimate of the original intercept (the bias being exactly equal to the mean of the original error term). Thus the only implication of this violation of the second assumption of the CLR model is that the OLS estimate of the intercept is biased; the slope coefficient estimates are unaffected. This biased estimate is often welcomed by the econometrician since for prediction purposes he or she would want to incorporate the mean of the error term into the prediction.

ZERO INTERCEPT

Sometimes economic theory suggests that the intercept in a regression is zero. An example is transforming for heteroskedasticity (discussed in chapter 8) resulting in a regression on transformed variables without an intercept. Practitioners usually include an intercept, though, because it is possible that a relevant explanatory variable was omitted, creating bias which can be alleviated by including an intercept term. Furthermore, no bias is created by including an unnecessary intercept to guard against this.

LIMITED DEPENDENT VARIABLE

When the nonzero expected value of the error term is not constant, problems can arise. Consider, for example, the case of a limited dependent variable, discussed in chapter 16. Suppose an observation is included in the sample only if the dependent variable y is less than K. For example, data may have been gathered only on people whose income fell below some poverty level K. This means that the data will not contain errors large enough to cause the dependent variable to be greater than K. Thus in this example the right-hand tail of the distribution of the error terms is chopped off (the error comes from a "truncated" distribution), implying that the expected value of the error term is negative, rather than zero. But this negative expected value of the error term is not the same for all observations. People with characteristics such that their expected y values are greater than K cannot have positive errors – they are only included in the sample if their error terms are sufficiently negative, so for these observations the expected value of the error is a relatively high negative number. On the other hand, people whose characteristics are such that their expected y values are well below K will be included in the sample if their error terms are negative or positive numbers, excepting only very high positive errors, so for these observations the expected value of the error term is a low negative number.

This suggests that the expected value of the error term varies from observation to observation, and in a way that is affected by the values of the explanatory variables (characteristics of the individuals). The impact of this on the OLS estimator can be deduced by viewing the expected value of the error term as an omitted explanatory variable, discussed in chapter 6. Since this "omitted variable" is correlated with the other explanatory variables, the OLS estimator for all coefficients, not just the intercept, is biased.

FRONTIER PRODUCTION FUNCTION

In economic theory a frontier production function determines the maximum output that can be produced with given inputs. Firms could be less than fully efficient and thus produce inside the production frontier, but they cannot produce more than the output given by this frontier. This suggests that the error should be negative, or at best zero, causing its expected value to be negative.

Econometricians model this by specifying two error terms. The first of these error terms is a traditional error (with both positive and negative values) reflecting errors in measuring output or factors over which the firm has no control such as weather. When added to the frontier production function formula it creates a stochastic frontier production function, saying in effect that not all observations have exactly the same frontier production function. The second error is a nonpositive error reflecting the degree to which a firm is inside its stochastic frontier. The two errors together form a composite error which has a negative expected value. It is common to assume that the first error is distributed normally and the second error is distributed as a half-normal, allowing estimation to be undertaken with maximum likelihood.

LOGARITHMIC TRANSFORMATION

Estimation is often facilitated by performing a logarithmic transformation of variables to create a linear estimating equation. A popular example of this is the Cobb–Douglas functional form, which requires a multiplicative disturbance if the logarithmic transformation is to create a linear estimating form in transformed variables. Now if, as is traditional, the nonlinear function without the disturbance is to represent the expected value of the dependent variable given the independent variables, the expected value of this multiplicative disturbance must be unity. The logarithm of this disturbance, which is the "disturbance" associated with the linear estimating form, does not have a zero expectation. This means that the OLS estimator of the constant in the linear estimating equation (the logarithm of the original Cobb–Douglas constant) is biased.

GENERAL NOTES

- If a relevant explanatory variable is omitted from a regression, the "error" of the mis-specified equation will not have a constant, zero mean. This should be viewed as a violation of the first assumption of the CLR model, however, not the second.
- Since the OLS estimation procedure is such as automatically to create residuals whose mean is zero, the only way in which the assumption of zero expected disturbance can be tested is through theoretical means (such as that illustrated by the Cobb–Douglas example).
- Forsund et al. (1980) and Bauer (1990) are surveys of frontier production functions. LIMDEP can be used for estimation. DEA, data envelopment analysis, is an alternative to the econometric approach, popular in many other disciplines. It uses mathematical programming techniques with the advantage that no functional form is imposed on the data. In this approach all deviations from the frontier are attributed to firm inefficiency; an advantage of the econometric approach is that in fortuitous circumstances (a favorable error) firms can produce beyond the frontier, so that such errors do not dictate the frontier. See Charnes et al. (1995).
- The multiplicative error used for the Cobb–Douglas function is usually assumed to be distributed log-normally; this implies that the logarithm of this error is distributed normally. It is interesting to note that assuming that the logarithm of this multiplicative disturbance has zero mean implies that the Cobb–Douglas function without the disturbance represents the *median* (rather than the mean) value of the dependent variable given the independent variables. This example of the Cobb–Douglas production function is discussed at length in Goldberger (1968a).

8

VIOLATING ASSUMPTION THREE:
NONSPHERICAL DISTURBANCES

8.1 INTRODUCTION

The third assumption of the CLR model is that the disturbances are spherical: they have uniform variance and are not correlated with one another. These characteristics are usually described in terms of the variance–covariance matrix of the disturbance vector. Recall that the variance–covariance matrix of a vector $\hat{\beta}$ of parameter estimates is a matrix with the variances of the individual parameter estimates along the diagonal and the covariances between these individual estimates in the off-diagonal positions. The disturbance vector is simply a vector containing the (unobserved) disturbance terms for the given data set (i.e., if the sample is of size T, the disturbance vector is of length T, containing T "observations" on the disturbance term). The variance–covariance matrix of the disturbance vector is a matrix with T columns and T rows. The diagonal terms are the variances of the individual disturbances, and the off-diagonal terms are the covariances between them.

Each diagonal term gives the variance of the disturbance associated with one of the sample observations (i.e., the first diagonal term gives the variance of the disturbance associated with the first observation, and the last diagonal term gives the variance of the disturbance association with the Tth observation). If all these diagonal terms are the same, the disturbances are said to have uniform variance or to be *homoskedastic*. If the diagonal terms are not all the same, the disturbances are said to be *heteroskedastic*; the disturbance term is then thought of as being drawn from a different distribution for each observation. This case of heteroskedasticity is discussed in detail in section 8.3.

Each off-diagonal element of the variance–covariance matrix gives the covariance between the disturbances associated with two of the sample observations (i.e., the element in the second column and the fifth row gives the covariance between the disturbance associated with the second observation and the disturbance associated with the fifth observation). If all these off-diagonal terms are zero, the disturbances are said to be uncorrelated. This means that in repeated samples there is no tendency for the disturbance associated with one observation (corresponding, for example, to one time period or one individual) to be related to the disturbance associated with any other. If the off-diagonal terms are not all zero, the disturbances are said to be *autocorrelated*: the disturbance term for one observation is correlated with the disturbance term for another observation. This case of autocorrelated disturbances is discussed in detail in section 8.4.

If either heteroskedasticity or autocorrelated disturbances are present, assumption 3 of the CLR model is said to be violated. In mathematical terminology, if assumption 3 is satisfied, the variance–covariance matrix of the disturbance vector ε, written as $E\varepsilon\varepsilon'$, is given by $\sigma^2 I$ where σ^2 is the uniform variance of the individual disturbance terms and I is an identity matrix of size T (i.e., a matrix with T rows and T columns, with ones along the diagonal and zeros on the off-diagonal). When assumption 3 is violated, by either heteroskedasticity or autocorrelated errors, the variance–covariance matrix of the disturbance vector does not take this special form, and must be written as a general matrix G. The disturbances in this case are said to be *nonspherical*, and the CLR model in this context is referred to as the *generalized linear regression* model (GLR model).

8.2 CONSEQUENCES OF VIOLATION

If assumption 3 is violated and the variance–covariance matrix of the disturbance vector must be written as a general matrix G, the CLR model becomes the GLR model. There are three major consequences of this for the OLS estimator.

(1) *Efficiency* In the GLR model, although β^{OLS} remains unbiased, it no longer has minimum variance among all linear unbiased estimators. A different estimator, called the generalized least squares (GLS) estimator, and denoted β^{GLS}, can be shown to be the BLUE. This estimator involves the matrix G in its formulation; by explicitly recognizing the nonsphericalness of the disturbances, it is possible to produce a linear unbiased estimator with a "smaller" variance–covariance matrix (i.e., a more efficient estimator).

This is accomplished by making use of the information (in the heteroskedasticity case) that some disturbances are likely to be large because their variances are large or the information (in the autocorrelated disturbances case) that when, for example, one disturbance is large and positive then another disturbance is likely to be large and positive. Instead of minimizing the sum of squared residuals (OLS estimation), an appropriately *weighted* sum of squared residuals is minimized. Observations that are expected to have large residuals because the variances of their associated disturbances are known to be large are given a smaller weight. Observations whose residuals are expected to be large because other residuals are large (owing to correlation between the disturbances) are also given smaller weights. The GLS procedure thus produces a more efficient estimator by minimizing a weighted sum of squared residuals (hence the name "generalized least squares") where the weights are determined by the elements of the variance–covariance matrix G of the disturbance vector.

(2) *Inference* In the GLR model the usual formula for the variance–covariance matrix of β^{OLS} is incorrect and therefore the usual estimator of $V(\beta^{OLS})$ is biased. Thus, although β^{OLS} is unbiased in the GLR model, interval estimation and hypothesis testing using β^{OLS} can no longer be trusted in this context. The correct formula for $V(\beta^{OLS})$ in the GLR model involves the matrix G and is quite complicated. Only in some special cases, noted in the technical notes to this section, can it be determined whether the usual estimator of $V(\beta^{OLS})$ is biased upwards or downwards. It is this second problem that causes econometricians the most concern. Often it is difficult to tell whether the GLR model rather than the CLR model is applicable, so there is a distinct danger of faulty inference from using the OLS estimator. To address this problem, "heteroskedasticity-consistent" and "autocorrelation-consistent" variance–covariance matrix estimators for the OLS estimator have been developed, correcting for the influence of nonspherical errors and thereby allowing OLS to be employed for inference with more confidence.

(3) *Maximum likelihood* In the GLR model with the additional assumption that the disturbances are distributed joint-normally, β^{OLS} is not the maximum likelihood estimator (as it was in the CNLR model). β^{GLS} turns out to be the maximum likelihood estimator in this context.

These consequences of using β^{OLS} in the GLR model suggest that β^{GLS} should be used in this situation. The problem with this proposal is that to calculate β^{GLS} the matrix G must be *known* to a factor of proportionality. In actual estimating situations, of course, G is rarely known. Faced with this dilemma, it is tempting simply to forget about β^{GLS} and employ β^{OLS}. (After all, β^{OLS} is unbiased, produces the highest R^2 and has low computational cost.)

Econometricians have not done this, however. Instead they have used the data at hand to estimate G (by $\hat{G}$, say) and then have used $\hat{G}$ in place of the unknown G in the β^{GLS} formula. This creates a new estimator, called the EGLS (estimated GLS) or FGLS (feasible GLS) estimator, denoted here by β^{EGLS}. This new estimator is no longer linear or unbiased, but if $\hat{G}$ is a consistent estimator of G, it can be shown to have desirable asymptotic properties corresponding to the small-sample properties of β^{GLS}. Intuitively it would seem that because this new estimator at least tries to account for the nonsphericalness of the disturbances, it should produce a better estimate of β than does β^{OLS}. Monte Carlo studies have shown that β^{EGLS} is in many circumstances (described in the general notes to this section) superior to β^{OLS} on the criteria on which β^{GLS} can be shown mathematically to be superior to β^{OLS}. Thus econometricians often adopt β^{EGLS} as the appropriate estimator to employ in a GLR model estimating context.

There remains the problem of estimating G. This is not a trivial problem. The matrix G contains T^2 elements, $\frac{1}{2}T(T + 1)$ of which are conceptually different. (The off-diagonal elements below the diagonal are identical to those above the diagonal.) But there are only T observations, implying that it is impossible to estimate the matrix G in its general form. This dilemma is resolved by specifying (assuming) that the nonsphericalness of the disturbances takes a specific form within one of the general categories of heteroskedasticity or autocorrelated disturbances. This reduces the problem to one of finding the appropriate specific form, estimating the small number of parameters (usually only one) that characterize that specific form, and then using these estimates to produce the required estimate of G. This approach should become clear in the discussions below of heteroskedasticity and autocorrelated disturbances.

8.3 HETEROSKEDASTICITY

One way of resolving the problem of estimating G is to assume that the non-sphericalness is exclusively that of heteroskedasticity, and that this heteroskedasticity bears a particular relationship to a set of known variables, usually chosen to be a single independent variable. This means that the off-diagonal elements of the variance–covariance matrix of the disturbance term are assumed to be zero, but that the diagonal elements are not all equal, varying in size with an independent variable. This is not an unreasonable specification – often, the larger an independent variable, the larger the variance of the associated disturbance. For example, if consumption is a function of the level of income, at higher levels of income (the independent variable) there is a greater scope for the consumer to act on whims and deviate by larger amounts from the specified consumption relationship. In addition, it may also be the case that errors associated with measuring consumption are greater at higher levels of income.

Figure 8.1 illustrates how this type of heteroskedasticity affects the properties of the OLS estimator. The higher absolute values of the residuals to the right in this graph indicate that there is a positive relationship between the error variance and the independent variable. With this kind of error pattern, a few additional large positive errors near the right in this graph would tilt the OLS regression

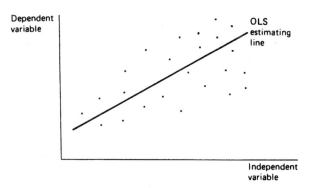

Figure 8.1   Illustrating heteroskedasticity

line considerably. A few additional large negative errors would tilt it in the opposite direction considerably. In repeated sampling these unusual cases would average out, leaving the OLS estimator unbiased, but the variation of the OLS regression line around its mean will be greater – i.e., the variance of β^{OLS} will be greater. The GLS technique pays less attention to the residuals associated with high-variance observations (by assigning them a low weight in the weighted sum of squared residuals it minimizes) since these observations give a less precise indication of where the true regression line lies. This avoids these large tilts, making the variance of β^{GLS} smaller than that of β^{OLS}.

The usual first step in attacking this problem is to determine whether or not heteroskedasticity actually exists. There are several tests for this, the more prominent of which are discussed below.

(1)   VISUAL INSPECTION OF RESIDUALS

The residuals are plotted on a graph against the independent variable to which it is suspected the disturbance variance is related. (Many econometric computer packages can produce this graph with simple instructions.) If it appears that the absolute magnitudes of the residuals are on average the same regardless of the values of the independent variables, then heteroskedasticity probably does not exist. However, if it appears that the absolute magnitude of the residuals is related to the independent variable (for example, if the residuals are quite small for low values of the independent variable, but noticeably larger for high values of the independent variable), then a more formal check for heteroskedasticity is in order.

(2)   THE GOLDFELD–QUANDT TEST

In this test the observations are ordered according to the magnitude of the independent variable thought to be related to the variance of the disturbances. A certain number of central observations are omitted, leaving two equal-sized groups of observations, one group corresponding to low values of the chosen independent variable and the other group corresponding to high values. Separate regressions are run for each of the two groups of observations and the ratio of their sums of squared residuals is formed. This ratio is an F statistic, which should be approximately unity if the disturbances are homoskedastic. A critical value from the F-distribution table can be used to test this hypothesis.

(3)   THE BREUSCH–PAGAN TEST

This test is relevant for a very wide class of alternative hypotheses, namely that the variance is some function of a linear combination of known variables. An LM test is employed, for which a computationally convenient means of calculation exists (see the technical notes). The generality of this test is both its strength (it does not require prior knowledge of the functional form involved) and its weakness (more powerful tests could be employed if this functional form were known). Tests utilizing specific functional forms are discussed in the general notes.

(4) THE WHITE TEST

This test examines whether the error variance is affected by any of the regressors, their squares or their cross-products. The strength of this test is that it tests specifically for whether or not any heteroskedasticity present causes the variance–covariance matrix of the OLS estimator to differ from its usual formula. It also has a computationally convenient formula (see the technical notes).

Once the presence of heteroskedasticity has been confirmed, steps must be taken to calculate β^{EGLS}. The first step in this process is to determine the specific form taken by the heteroskedasticity; i.e., to find the functional form of the relationship determining the variance. This relationship is then estimated and used to form an estimate of the variance of each disturbance term and thus an estimate of the variance–covariance matrix G of the disturbance term. Using this estimate $(\hat{G})$, the estimator β^{EGLS} can be calculated.

In most applications, however, $\hat{G}$ is not calculated. This is because using $\hat{G}$ to calculate β^{EGLS} is computationally difficult, owing primarily to the fact that $\hat{G}$ is usually such a large matrix. Instead, an alternative, and fully equivalent, way of calculating β^{EGLS} is employed. This alternative way involves transforming the original equation to create an estimating relationship, in transformed variables, that has spherical disturbances (i.e., the original disturbance, when transformed, is spherical). Then the OLS estimator is applied to the transformed data, producing the GLS estimator. In the case of heteroskedasticity, the appropriate transformation is obtained by dividing each observation (including the constant unit observation on the intercept term) by the square root of the estimated variance of the disturbance term. An example of this appears in the technical notes to this section.

8.4 AUTOCORRELATED DISTURBANCES

When the off-diagonal elements of the variance–covariance matrix G of the disturbance term are nonzero, the disturbances are said to be autocorrelated. This could arise for several reasons.

(1) *Spatial autocorrelation* In regional cross-section data, a random shock affecting economic activity in one region may cause economic activity in an adjacent region to change because of close economic ties between the regions. Shocks due to weather similarities might also tend to cause the error terms between adjacent regions to be related.

(2) *Prolonged influence of shocks* In time series data, random shocks (disturbances) have effects that often persist over more than one time period. An

earthquake, flood, strike or war, for example, will probably affect the economy's operation in periods following the period in which it occurs. Disturbances on a smaller scale could have similar effects.

(3) *Inertia* Owing to inertia or psychological conditioning, past actions often have a strong effect on current actions, so that a positive disturbance in one period is likely to influence activity in succeeding periods.

(4) *Data manipulation* Published data often undergo interpolation or smoothing, procedures that average true disturbances over successive time periods.

(5) *Misspecification* An omitted relevant independent variable that is autocorrelated will make the disturbance (associated with the misspecified model) autocorrelated. An incorrect functional form or a misspecification of the equation's dynamics could do the same. In these instances the appropriate procedure is to correct the misspecification; the methods proposed in this chapter cannot be justified if autocorrelated errors arise in this way.

Since autocorrelated errors arise most frequently in time series models, for ease of exposition the discussion in the rest of this chapter is couched in terms of time series data. Furthermore, throughout the rest of this chapter the correlation between the error terms is assumed, in line with most econometric work, to take a specific form called first-order autocorrelation. Econometricians make this assumption because it makes tractable the otherwise impossible task of estimating the very large number of off-diagonal elements of G, the variance–covariance matrix of the disturbance vector. First-order autocorrelation occurs when the disturbance in one time period is a proportion of the disturbance in the previous time period, plus a spherical disturbance. In mathematical terms, this is written as $\varepsilon_t = \rho\varepsilon_{t-1} + u_t$, where ρ (rho), a parameter less than 1 in absolute value, is called the autocorrelation coefficient and u_t is a traditional spherical disturbance.

The consequences for OLS estimation in a situation of positive (i.e., ρ positive) first-order autocorrelation are illustrated in figure 8.2. The first error term

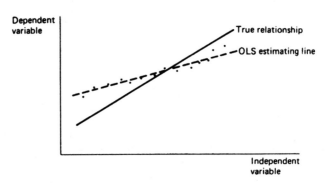

Figure 8.2   Illustrating positive autocorrelated errors

was arbitrarily chosen to be positive. With positive first-order autocorrelated errors this implies that several succeeding error terms are likely also to be positive, and once the error term becomes negative it is likely to remain negative for a while. Thus the data pattern portrayed is not atypical of the autocorrelated error case if the independent variable is growing over time. Fitting an OLS estimating line to these data clearly gives an estimate quite wide of the mark. In repeated samples these poor estimates will average out, since we are as likely to start with a negative error as with a positive one, leaving the OLS estimator unbiased, but the high variation in these estimates will cause the variance of β^{OLS} to be greater than it would have been had the errors been distributed randomly. The GLS technique pays less attention to large residuals that follow large residuals (by assigning them a low weight in the weighted sum of squared residuals it minimizes) since these residuals are likely to be large simply because the preceding residual is large. This causes the GLS estimator to miss the true value by less in situations such as that portrayed on the graph, making the variance of β^{GLS} smaller than that of β^{OLS}. Notice that the OLS estimating line gives a better fit to the data than the true relationship. This reveals why in this context R^2 is overestimated and σ^2 (and the variance of β^{OLS}) is underestimated.

The great appeal of the first-order autocorrelation assumption is that if the disturbance term takes this form all the off-diagonal elements of G can be expressed in terms of ρ so that estimation of a single parameter (ρ) permits estimation of G and allows calculation of β^{EGLS}. A "good" estimate of ρ may make β^{EGLS} superior to β^{OLS}; a "poor" estimate of ρ may do the opposite.

Before calculation of β^{EGLS}, however, it must first be determined that the disturbances actually are autocorrelated. There are several ways of doing this, the most popular of which, the Durbin–Watson test, is described below; some of the less common tests are described in the general notes to this section.

The Durbin–Watson (DW) test   Most packaged computer regression programs and most research reports provide the DW or d statistic in their output. This statistic is calculated from the residuals of an OLS regression and is used to test for first-order autocorrelation. When the parameter ρ of the first-order autocorrelation case is zero (reflecting no autocorrelation) the d statistic is approximately 2.0. The further away the d statistic is from 2.0, the less confident one can be that there is no autocorrelation in the disturbances. Unfortunately, the exact distribution of this d statistic, on the hypothesis of zero autocorrelation, depends on the particular observations on the independent variables (i.e., on the X matrix), so that a table giving critical values of the d statistic is not available. However, it turns out that the actual distribution of the d statistic can be shown to lie between two limiting distributions for which critical values have been tabulated. These limiting distributions, labeled "lower distribution" and "upper distribution," are shown in figure 8.3. The 95% critical levels are marked off for each distribution and denoted by A, B, C, and D. Now suppose the value of the d statistic lies to the left of A. Then, regardless of whether the d statistic for this case is distributed as the lower or upper distribution, or anywhere in between,

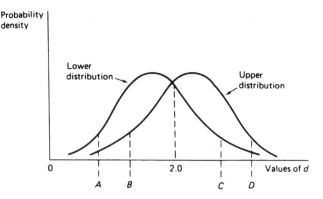

Figure 8.3   The Durbin–Watson statistic

the hypothesis of no autocorrelation will be rejected. Similarly, if the value of the d statistic lies to the right of D, the hypothesis of no autocorrelation will be rejected, regardless of the actual distribution of the d statistic for this particular estimating problem. Similar reasoning shows that, if the d statistic lies between B and C, the hypothesis of no autocorrelation will be accepted, regardless of the actual distribution of d. It is the cases in which the d statistic falls between A and B or between C and D that cause trouble. Suppose d falls between A and B. If the actual distribution of the d statistic for this problem were the lower distribution, the hypothesis of no autocorrelation would be accepted, but if the actual distribution were the upper distribution, it would be rejected. Since the actual distribution is unknown, the DW test in this case must be considered inconclusive. The existence of these two inconclusive regions is the most serious weakness of the DW test. (This weakness is disappearing as more computer routines automatically calculate the appropriate critical values for the data to hand.) Another weakness is that the test is biased towards acceptance of the hypothesis of no autocorrelation if a lagged value of the dependent variable is included among the regressors. (This case is discussed further in section 9.3.)

Suppose the DW test indicates autocorrelated errors. What then? It is typically concluded that estimation via EGLS is called for. This is not always appropriate, however, for reasons made clear in chapter 5: the significant value of the DW statistic could result from an omitted explanatory variable, an incorrect functional form, or a dynamic misspecification. Only if a researcher is satisfied that none of these phenomena are responsible for the significant DW should estimation via EGLS proceed.

Once the presence of first-order autocorrelation has been confirmed, attention is turned to the estimation of ρ. Once ρ has been estimated, an estimate $\hat{G}$ of G can be calculated and used to produce β^{EGLS}. However, as in the case of heteroskedastic disturbances, it is computationally far easier to transform the variables and apply OLS to obtain β^{EGLS} than to estimate G and employ this estimate in the β^{EGLS} formula. The estimating equation must be transformed so as to create a new estimating equation, in the transformed variables, whose disturbance vector is spherical (i.e., the original disturbance, when transformed, is spherical). Applications of OLS to the transformed variables then creates β^{EGLS}. The appropriate transformation in the context of first-order autocorrelation is to replace each observation by that observation minus the estimated value of ρ times the previous period's observation (i.e., replace x_t with $x_t - \hat{\rho}x_{t-1}$). To avoid losing one observation by this procedure, the first observation x_1 should be transformed to $\sqrt{(1 - \hat{\rho}^2)}x_1$. The rationale for this is discussed in the technical notes to this section.

There are several different techniques employed to produce β^{EGLS}, all of them following the method outlined above, essentially differing only in the way in which they estimate ρ. (Some methods do not bother to do the special transformation of the first observation, but should be revised to do so.) The most popular techniques used to produce β^{EGLS} are described briefly below; all appear frequently in packaged computer regression programs.

(1) COCHRANE–ORCUTT ITERATIVE LEAST SQUARES

Regressing the OLS residuals on themselves lagged one period provides an estimate of ρ. Using this estimate, the dependent and independent variables can be transformed as described earlier and an OLS regression on these transformed variables gives β^{EGLS}. Using this β^{EGLS}, new estimates of the original disturbances can be made, by substituting β^{EGLS} into the original (untransformed) relationship, which should be "better" than the OLS residuals (since β^{EGLS} is supposed to be "better" than β^{OLS} in this context). Regressing these new residuals on themselves lagged one period provides a new (and presumably "better") estimate of ρ. This procedure can be repeated until successive estimates of ρ are arbitrarily close.

(2) DURBIN'S TWO-STAGE METHOD

The dependent variable is regressed on itself lagged, all the independent variables and all the independent variables lagged. This estimating relationship results from mathematical manipulations designed to transform the original estimating form into one with a spherical disturbance. This is illustrated in the technical notes to this section. The estimated coefficient of the lagged dependent variable in this new relation provides an estimate of ρ. This estimate is then used to transform the variables, as described earlier, and an OLS regression on these transformed variables generates β^{EGLS}.

(3) HILDRETH–LU SEARCH PROCEDURE

For any particular value of ρ, the dependent and independent variables can be transformed as described earlier and an OLS regression on transformed variables will generate a β^{EGLS}. The sum of squared residuals from this regression on transformed variables will be different for different values of ρ. The Hildreth–Lu procedure searches for the particular value of ρ that minimizes the sum of these squared residuals and adopts its corresponding β^{EGLS} as the estimator of β.

(4) *MAXIMUM LIKELIHOOD*

If the spherical disturbance u (from $\varepsilon_t = \rho\varepsilon_{t-1} + u_t$) can be assumed to have a specific distribution (a normal distribution, for example), the maximum likelihood technique can be applied to estimate ρ and β simultaneously. When u is distributed normally, it turns out that all four of the methods discussed here are asymptotically equivalent.

Recent Monte Carlo evidence indicates that all of these estimators are markedly inferior to a Bayesian estimator; when this Bayesian estimator is available as an option in the popular computer software packages, it should become the estimator of choice. The basic difference between the Bayesian estimator and the estimators above is that each of the estimators above is calculated on the basis of a single estimated value of ρ, whereas the Bayesian estimator "hedges its bets" by taking a weighted average of the EGLS estimates corresponding to several values of ρ.

GENERAL NOTES

8.1 Introduction

- Many textbooks spell heteroskedasticity with a c in place of the k; McCulloch (1985) has shown that heteroskedasticity is the correct spelling.
- Applications of the GLS or EGLS estimating procedure are relevant in a variety of estimating contexts not discussed in this chapter, but covered in other parts of this book. Some examples are SURE (seemingly unrelated estimation, chapter 10), 3SLS (three stage least squares, chapter 10), mixed estimation (chapter 12), and random effects models (chapter 14).

8.2 Consequences of Violation

- The OLS estimator, by definition, maximizes R^2. The GLS estimator can be used to produce estimates of the dependent variables that can then be used to calculate an R^2 that must be less than the R^2 from OLS. In the context of the GLR model, however, since the GLS procedure minimizes a *generalized* sum of squared residuals, it is more appropriate to redefine the R^2 statistic so that it represents the proportion of the "generalized variation" of the dependent variable explained by the independent variables. Fortunately, in many instances (but not all) the GLS technique of regressing on transformed variables (discussed in sections 8.3 and 8.4) automatically produces this new R^2. See Buse (1973) for a discussion of this.

- Although GLS is BLUE in the GLR model, EGLS is not; in fact, EGLS is neither linear nor unbiased, and may have a higher variance than the OLS estimator if G is not much different from a constant times the identity matrix, or if a poor estimate of G is being employed. Monte Carlo studies, for example, indicate that for the case of a first-order autocorrelated error with coefficient ρ, for typical sample sizes, OLS is superior to EGLS for absolute values of ρ less than about 0.3. Grubb and Magee (1988) suggest some rules of thumb for determining when EGLS is likely to be superior to OLS.
- The true variance of β^{EGLS} is underestimated if the formula for the variance of β^{EGLS} is used with $\hat{G}$ in place of G. This is because the formula for the variance of β^{GLS} does not incorporate the additional variability of β^{EGLS} (in repeated samples) owing to $\hat{G}$ varying in repeated samples. This has implications for hypothesis testing using β^{EGLS}.
- Although the presence of heteroskedasticity or autocorrelated errors does not create bias in estimating β, whenever all other assumptions of the CLR model hold, interaction of nonspherical errors with other violations of the CLR model can cause problems. A classic example is autocorrelated errors in conjunction with the lagged value of the dependent variable serving as a regressor, as described in chapter 9. Examples for heteroskedasticity are models of qualitative and limited dependent variables, discussed in chapters 15 and 16, and estimation of frontier production functions (see chapter 7) and related measures such as firm-specific inefficiency, discussed by Caudill, Ford and Gropper (1995).

8.3   Heteroskedasticity

- Although it is usually the case that econometricians think in terms of error variances being positively related to independent variables, this is not necessarily the case. Error-learning models suggest that as time passes (and independent variables grow in size) errors will become smaller. Similarly, over time, data-collecting techniques improve so that errors from this source should decline in importance. In addition, it has been suggested that assuming an error-term variance that is declining over time could be useful since the correction procedure would explicitly give a heavier weight to recent data, which may more accurately reflect the world as it is today.
- Not all sources of heteroskedasticity can or should be captured via a relationship with an independent variable. For example, using grouped data leads to heteroskedasticity if the groups are not all the same size. In this case the error variances are proportional to the group sizes, so appropriate weighting factors can easily be deduced. However Dickens (1990) warns that errors in grouped data are likely to be correlated within groups so that weighting by the square root of group size may be inappropriate. Binkley (1992) assesses tests for grouped heteroskedasticity.
- Theory can sometimes suggest that an estimating relationship will be characterized by heteroskedasticity. The case of grouping data, noted earlier, is one example. As a second example, consider the case of a random coefficient. Suppose that $Y_t = \alpha + \beta_t X_t + \varepsilon_t$ where the random slope coefficient is given by $\beta_t = \beta + u_t$ with u_t an error with mean zero and variance σ_u^2. The estimating relationship becomes

$$Y_t = \alpha + \beta X_t + (\varepsilon_t + X_t u_t)$$

where the composite error term has variance $\sigma_\varepsilon^2 + X_t^2 \sigma_u^2$. As a third example, suppose the error term is multiplicative rather than additive. Suppose $Y_t = (\alpha + \beta X_t)\varepsilon_t$ where $\varepsilon_t = 1 + u_t$ and u_t has mean zero and variance σ_u^2. The estimating form

$$Y_t = \alpha + \beta X_t + (\alpha + \beta X_t)u_t$$

is such that the composite error term has variance $(\alpha + \beta X_t)^2 \sigma_u^2$.

- The Goldfeld–Quandt test is usually performed by omitting the middle third of the observations. Giles and Saxton (1993) find that the "omit one-third" rule is suitable for a sample size of about 20, but for larger sample sizes a smaller fraction of observations should be omitted. Since the common sense of this test is to split the observations into a group thought to have a relatively high error variance and a group thought to have a relatively low error variance, removing observations from the middle of the data set should not be a hard-and-fast rule. As usually employed, the Goldfeld–Quandt test allows the parameter vectors to differ between the two sub-data sets employed by the test. An LR version of the test can avoid this, as described in Zaman (1996, pp. 255–7).

- The tests for heteroskedasticity described in the body of this chapter are general in that they do not use a specific functional form for the relationship between the error variance and the variables thought to determine that variance. To construct β^{EGLS}, a specific functional form is required (although it should be noted that Monte Carlo studies suggest that precise knowledge of this functional form is not crucial). One popular way to be more specific is through the Glejser (1969) test. In this test the absolute values of the OLS residuals are regressed, using several functional forms, on the variable(s) to which the variance of the disturbance term is thought to be related. Whether or not heteroskedasticity exists depends on whether or not the coefficient(s) of these regressions tests significantly different from zero. A variant of this approach, the modified Glejser test, is to use the squared values of the OLS residuals, rather than their absolute values, as the dependent variable. Another popular functional form was suggested by Park (1966); see the technical notes. If the relevant functional form is known (from testing using the Glejser method, for example, or because theory has suggested a specific form), the maximum likelihood approach is possible. Here the parameters in the equation being estimated (i.e., β) and the parameter(s) in the relationship determining the error variances are estimated simultaneously. For elucidation, see Rutemiller and Bowers (1968). If the prerequisites for using the MLE approach are known to be valid (namely, knowledge of the distributional form of the error and the functional form of the relationship between the error variance and variable(s) determining that variance), this approach is attractive. Chapter 11 of Judge et al. (1985) is an extensive survey of heteroskedasticity.

- There is mounting evidence that Bayesian estimators for heteroskedasticity are superior to traditional EGLS estimators, as claimed for example by Ohtani (1982), Surekha and Griffiths (1984), and Kennedy and Adjibolosoo (1990). Their superiority comes from taking a weighted average of several EGLS estimators, each corresponding to a different value of the parameter representing the heteroskedasticity, rather than selecting a single EGLS estimate based on a single, poorly estimated value of that parameter.

- A popular form of heteroskedasticity for time series data is ARCH – autoregressive conditional heteroskedasticity – developed by Engle (1982). Engle noticed that in many time series, particularly those involving financial data, large and small residuals tend to come in clusters, suggesting that the variance of an error may depend on the size of the preceding error. This is formalized by writing the variance of ε_t, conditional on ε_{t-1}, as a linear function of the square of ε_{t-1}. The unconditional variance is constant, so OLS is BLUE, but because the conditional variance is heteroskedastic it is possible to find a nonlinear estimator, based on MLE considerations, that is more efficient. Greene (1993, pp. 438–40) has an exposition of the likelihood and of a simple method of creating an estimate that is asymptotically equivalent to the MLE. Despite this, many practitioners estimate by regressing the squared OLS residuals on themselves lagged to get a means of estimating G, and then apply EGLS. Bollerslev (1986) has generalized ARCH to form GARCH, in which the conditional variance is also a function of past conditional variances. The easiest test for ARCH is an LM test in which the square of the OLS residual is regressed on an intercept and its lagged values, with the sample size times the R^2 distributed as a chi-square with degrees of freedom equal to the number of lags. Engle et al. (1985) report some Monte Carlo results examining the small-sample properties of ARCH estimates and tests for ARCH. Bera and Higgins (1993) survey ARCH models: Enders (1995, pp. 162–5) and Darnell (1994, pp. 4–8) are good textbook expositions.

- Heteroskedasticity has been examined in conjunction with other violations of the CLR model. For example, Lahiri and Egy (1981) address the problem of nonlinear functional form and heteroskedasticity. Examples of its conjunction with autocorrelated errors are cited in the next section.
- Transforming an equation to correct for heteroskedasticity usually creates an estimating equation without an intercept term. Care must be taken in interpreting the R^2 from the resulting regression. Most researchers include an intercept anyway; this does little harm and avoids potential problems.
- Before correcting for heteroskedasticity, each variable should be examined for possible transformations (e.g., changing aggregate to per capita or changing nominal to real) that might be appropriate in the context of the relationship in question. This may uncover the source of the heteroskedasticity. More generally, the heteroskedasticity may be due to an omitted explanatory variable or an incorrect functional form; Thursby (1982) suggests a means of discriminating between heteroskedasticity and misspecification.

8.4 Autocorrelated Disturbances

- A first-order autocorrelated error is referred to as an AR(1) error; an AR(p) error is an error depending on the first p lagged values of that error. The most popular alternative to this type of autocorrelated error is the moving average error; an MA(1) error is written $\varepsilon_t = u_t + \theta u_{t-1}$ where u is a spherical error. An MA(q) error involves the first q lagged us. Combining the two types produces an ARMA(p,q) error; for further discussion see chapter 17.
- It was stressed in chapter 5 that misspecification can give rise to a significant DW statistic. Because of this it is important to check for misspecification before concluding that EGLS estimation is suitable. Godfrey (1987) suggests an appropriate test strategy for this, beginning with a RESET test using an autocorrelation-consistent estimate of the variance–covariance matrix, moving to a test of AR(1) versus AR(p) errors, and then to a test of independent versus AR(1) errors.

- If autocorrelated errors are thought to exist, an MA(1) error may be as *a priori* plausible as an AR(1) error, but is seldom employed in empirical work. This is because techniques for estimating with MA(1) errors are computationally burdensome relative to those available fro AR(1) errors. MacDonald and MacKinnon (1985) present a computationally attractive estimation technique for the context of an MA(1) error and argue that the common practice of ignoring the possibility of MA(1) errors cannot be justified. Choudhury et al. (1987) also present an attractive means of estimation in this context. Nicholls et al. (1975) give several arguments in favor of the use of MA(1) errors. Burke et al. (1990) suggest an attractive way of testing for MA(1) versus AR(1) errors. See also Sivapulle and King (1991).

- The DW test is by far the most popular test for autocorrelated errors, in spite of its inconclusive region. Many practitioners resolve the inconclusiveness by using the critical values associated with the upper distribution, since it is a good approximation to the actual distribution if, as is likely with economic time series, the regressors are changing slowly. The best way to deal with this problem, however, is to use a software package, such as SHAZAM, to calculate the appropriate critical value for the specific data set being employed. Maddala (1988, pp. 202–3) cites several sources providing extended DW tables suitable for cases of more explanatory variables, quarterly data, monthly data, etc. Strictly speaking the DW test is appropriate only if residuals from an OLS regression are used in its calculation. For discussion of its use in the context of nonlinear regression see White (1992).

- Several alternatives to the DW test exist (some of which are noted in the first edition of this book, pp. 87–8), but are seldom used. King (1987) is a survey of testing for autocorrelated errors. One attractive alternative is an LM test, due to Godfrey (1978) and Breusch (1978), for the case of an alternative hypothesis of either AR(p) or MA(p) errors. It can be calculated by re-running the regression using p lagged OLS residuals as extra explanatory variables, and testing their coefficients against the zero vector with an F test. Equivalent results are obtained using the OLS residual as the dependent variable, in which case F could be calculated as $[(T - K)/p] \times R^2$. In light of this F statistic's asymptotic justification, often pF, or TR^2, is used as a chi-square statistic with p degrees of freedom. See Maddala (1988, pp. 206–7) for a textbook exposition. One of its advantages is that it is appropriate even when a lagged value of the dependent variable serves as a regressor.

- The DW test is not reliable whenever a lagged value of the dependent variable appears as a regressor (or for any case in which the error is not uncorrelated with a regressor). The Durbin h test has traditionally been used in this context, but recent work, such as Inder (1984), has shown this to be unwise. The Breusch–Godfrey test described above, which for $p = 1$ is sometimes called the Durbin m test, is recommended. See Breusch and Godfrey (1981), Dezhbakhsh (1990) and Dezhbakhsh and Thursby (1994). Godfrey (1994) and Davidson and MacKinnon (1993, pp. 370–1) show how to modify the m test when using instrumental variable estimation. Rayner (1993) advocates using a bootstrap procedure to test for autocorrelated errors when lagged dependent variables serve as regressors.

- Estimating the variance–covariance matrix of the EGLS estimator for the case of autocorrelated errors is not easy; see for example Miyazaki and Griffiths (1984). There are further problems estimating this variance–covariance matrix whenever there are lagged values of the dependent variable appearing as regressors. Prescott and Stengos (1987) recommend the estimate suggested by Davidson and MacKinnon (1980).

- Many Monte Carlo studies have addressed the question of autocorrelated errors. A few general conclusions seem evident from these studies.

  (a) The possible gain from using EGLS rather than OLS can be considerable whereas the possible loss is small.
  (b) The special transformation for the first observation is important.
  (c) Standard errors for the EGLS estimator are usually underestimated.
  (d) The relative performance of estimating techniques is sensitive to the nature of the data matrix X.
  (e) Improvement in current techniques is most likely to be achieved through better estimates of the autocorrelation coefficient ρ.

  Chapter 8 of Judge et al. (1985) is an extensive textbook survey of autocorrelated errors. Beach and MacKinnon (1978a) present a convincing case for the MLE, noting that it retains the first observation and automatically incorporates the restriction that ρ be less than one in absolute value.

- Kennedy and Simons (1991) report on the basis of Monte Carlo studies that a Bayesian estimator for the case of AR(1) errors outperforms traditional EGLS estimators by a substantial margin. Their Bayesian estimator is operationalized as a weighted average of 40 GLS estimates corresponding to 40 values of ρ, equally spaced over the zero to one interval. The weights are the Bayesian probabilities that the true value of ρ is close to those values, obtained from the posterior distribution for ρ. The relative success of this estimator stems from the notoriously poor estimates of ρ that characterize estimation in this context. Chapter 13 discusses the Bayesian approach.

- Autocorrelated errors is one violation of the CLR that has been examined in conjunction with other violations. Epps and Epps (1977) investigate autocorrelation and heteroskedasticity together. Savin and White (1978) and Tse (1984) address autocorrelated errors and nonlinear functional forms. Bera and Jarque (1982) examine the conjunction of autocorrelated errors, heteroskedasticity nonlinearity and non-normality. Further examples are found in chapters 9 and 10.

- Most of the tests used to detect autocorrelation only test for first-order autocorrelation. This should not blind one to other possibilities. It is quite possible, for example, that in models using quarterly data the errors are correlated with themselves lagged four periods. On this see Wallis (1972). Although it might seem reasonable to suppose that treating the residuals as first-order autocorrelated, when they are in fact second-order autocorrelated, would be better than just applying OLS, this is not necessarily the case: see Engle (1974). Beach and MacKinnon (1978b) examine the MLE for second-order autocorrelation. Greene (1990, p. 440) has an exposition of the special transformations for the first two observations for this case.

- The case of positively autocorrelated errors usually leads to an upward bias in the R^2 statistic. A high R^2 in conjunction with a low DW statistic suggests that something funny is going on. See chapter 17.

TECHNICAL NOTES

8.1 Introduction

- The matrix G is usually normalized by rewriting it as $\sigma^2 G_N$ where σ^2 is chosen so as to make the trace of G_N (the sum of the diagonal elements of G_N) equal T. This makes it comparable to the CLR case in which the variance–covariance matrix of ε is $\sigma^2 I$, where I has trace T.

- The method of moments was introduced in the technical notes to section 2.11, but discussion there was confined to the case in which the number of moment conditions equalled the number of parameters to be estimated. Whenever the number of moment conditions exceeds the number of parameters to be estimated, it is not possible to find parameter values that cause all of the moment conditions to be satisfied by the data. For example, if there are six moment conditions and only four parameters, only four of these moment conditions can be satisfied. This could be dealt with by choosing which four of the six moment conditions to satisfy, but this is undesirable because it ignores information inherent in the two abandoned moment conditions – more efficient estimates can be produced by incorporating this information, and model specification testing can be enhanced by testing its validity. The alternative is to choose the four parameter values so as to minimize the "total extent" to which the six moment conditions are violated, even though this may mean that none of the six conditions is exactly satisfied. This approach is called the generalized method of moments (GMM).

  What is meant by "total extent" to which the moment conditions are violated? In the grand tradition of least squares this could be measured by the sum of the squares of the differences between each moment condition and its corresponding sample measure. Traditionally the ith moment condition is written as $m_i(\theta) = 0$ where θ is the vector of parameters, and all the moment conditions are placed together in a vector to form $m(\theta) = 0$. The parameter estimate θ^* could be chosen to minimize $m(\theta^*)'m(\theta^*)$. But this is a case in which the grand tradition of least squares can be improved upon. The individual $m_i(\theta^*)$ are random variables with unequal variances, so generalized least squares is appropriate, as we have learned in this chapter. In fact, because θ^* appears in each moment condition the covariances between the estimated moment conditions are non-zero, so the complete variance–covariance matrix V_m of $m(\theta^*)$ is relevant. In summary, the GMM procedure produces θ^* by minimizing $m(\theta^*)'V_m^{-1}m(\theta^*)$. In practice V_m is unknown so an estimate of it is employed.

  Notice that $m(\theta^*)'V_m^{-1}m(\theta^*)$ is in exactly the form of a chi-square statistic for testing if $m(\theta^*)$ is significantly different from zero, allowing a test of the overidentifying moment conditions, a natural general model specification test.

  GMM has several attractive features. First, it avoids having to specify a likelihood function; consistency depends only on correct specification of the residuals and the conditioning variables. Second, it provides a unifying framework for analysis of many familiar estimators such as OLS and IV. And third, it offers a convenient method of estimation for cases in which traditional estimation methods are computationally burdensome. For examples, such as nonlinear dynamic rational expectations models or Euler equation models, see Hall (1993).

8.2 Consequences of Violation

- The formula for β^{GLS} is given by $(X'G^{-1}X)^{-1}X'G^{-1}Y$ and the formula for its variance is given by $(X'G^{-1}X)$ or $\sigma^2(X'G_N^{-1}X)^{-1}$. This variance–covariance matrix is "smaller" than the variance–covariance matrix of β^{OLS}, given by the formula $\sigma^2(X'X)^{-1}(X'G_N X)(X'X)^{-1}$. Employing the usual formula $s^2(X'X)^{-1}$ to estimate this variance–covariance matrix of β^{OLS} gives a biased estimator, because the expected value of s^2 in the GLR model is no longer equal to σ^2, and because $(X'X)^{-1}$ does not equal $(X'X)^{-1}(X'G_N X)(X'X)^{-1}$. Goldberger (1964, pp. 239–42) traces through two special cases to show that in the case of only one independent variable (in addition to the constant term) the usual estimator is biased downward (a) if high variances correspond to high values of the independent variable, or (b) if the independent variable is positively serially correlated in the case of positive first-order autocorrelated errors (described in section 8.4).

  The "weighted" or "generalized" sum of squared errors minimized by the GLS technique is given by $\varepsilon'G^{-1}\varepsilon$. The GLS estimator of σ^2 is given by $\hat{\varepsilon}'G^{-1}\hat{\varepsilon}/(T-K)$ where $\hat{\varepsilon}$ is the GLS estimator of ε. The maximum likelihood estimate of σ^2, for joint-normally distributed errors, is given by $\hat{\varepsilon}'G^{-1}\hat{\varepsilon}/T$.

- The heteroskedasticity-consistent estimator of the variance–covariance matrix of the OLS estimator, due to White (1980), is recommended whenever OLS estimates are being used for inference in a situation in which heteroskedasticity is suspected but the researcher is not able to find an adequate transformation to purge the data of this heteroskedasticity. The variance–covariance matrix of OLS in the GLR model is $(X'X)^{-1}X'GX(X'X)^{-1}$. The heteroskedasticity-consistent estimator of this results from estimating G by a diagonal matrix with the squared OLS residuals along the diagonal. Leamer (1988) refers to this as "White-washing" heteroskedasticity. For computational considerations see Messer and White (1984); Erlat (1987) shows how to get heteroskedasticity-consistent test statistics for testing linear restrictions by using differences in SSEs. MacKinnon and White (1985) have proposed some alternative heteroskedasticity-consistent variance matrix estimators which have improved small-sample properties.

- The rationale behind the autocorrelation-consistent estimator of the variance–covariance matrix of the OLS estimator is similar to that described earlier for the heteroskedasticity case. It takes the general form $(X'X)^{-1}X'G^*X(X'X)^{-1}$ where G^* is an estimate of the unknown variance–covariance matrix of the error term. Newey and West (1987) provide a very general estimator (which is also heteroskedasticity-consistent); see Greene (1990, p. 493) for a textbook exposition. Godfrey (1987) uses a simpler version, available in the software package SHAZAM; it consists of filling in the diagonal of G^* with the squares of the residuals (rendering it heteroskedasticity-consistent as well), estimating the first few elements beside the diagonal with the products of the relevant residuals, and setting elements well-removed from the diagonal equal to zero. The Newey–West version is similar, but the off-diagonal elements are shrunk towards zero by a shrinking factor that grows with the distance from the diagonal. For computational simplifications see Wooldridge (1989).

8.3   Heteroskedasticity

- Breusch and Pagan (1979) show that their test statistic can be computed as one-half the regression (i.e., explained) sum of squares from a linear regression of $\hat{u}_t^2/\hat{\sigma}^2$ on a constant and the variables thought to affect the error variance. Here $\hat{u}_t$ is the OLS residual, $\hat{\sigma}^2$ is the average of the $\hat{u}_t^2$, and the statistic is distributed asymptotically as a chi-square with degrees of freedom equal to the number of variables thought to affect the error variance.

- The Breusch–Pagan test is a rare example of a test in which non-normality of the disturbances affects the asymptotic distribution of the test statistic. Koenker (1981) notes that the Breusch–Pagan test is sensitive in small samples to its assumption that the errors are distributed normally (because it uses the result that the variance of $\hat{u}_t^2$ is $2\sigma^4$; this is where the $\frac{1}{2}$ in this statistic comes from). He suggests replacing $2\hat{\sigma}^4$ by $\Sigma(\hat{u}_t^2 - \hat{\sigma}^2)^2/N$, where N is the sample size. The Breusch–Pagan statistic then becomes N times the R^2 in the regression of $\hat{u}_t^2$ on a constant and the variables thought to affect the error variance. In this form it is seen that the White test (see below) is a special case of this "studentized" Breusch–Pagan test, as noted by Waldman (1983).

- White (1980) shows that his test statistic can be computed as the sample size N times the R^2 from a regression of $\hat{u}_t^2$, the squares of the OLS residuals on a constant, the regressors from the equation being estimated, their squares and their cross-products. It is distributed asymptotically as a chi-square with degrees of freedom equal to the number of regressors (not counting the constant) in the regression used to obtain the statistic. This test is based on testing whether $V(\text{OLS}) = V(\text{GLS})$; it detects heteroskedasticity only if it affects the consistency of the usual estimator of the variance–covariance matrix of the OLS estimator. It is possible to have heteroskedasticity which does not affect this consistency but nonetheless causes OLS to be less efficient than GLS (or EGLS). This could happen if the heteroskedasticity were related to a variable orthogonal to the regressors, their squares and their cross-products.

- When the error variance is proportional to a variable, so that, for example, $\sigma_t^2 = KX_t$, it is not necessary to estimate K to calculate β^{EGLS}. In fact, if the heteroskedasticity does actually take that form, the appropriate transformation is to divide all observations by $\sqrt{X_t}$, yielding a transformed relationship whose error is homoskedastic with variance K. The actual value of K is not needed; in this case β^{EGLS} is β^{GLS}. One way in which this correction can be upset is if there is "mixed" heteroskedasticity so that $\sigma_t^2 = \gamma + KX_t$ where γ is some nonzero constant. Now the appropriate transformation is to divide by $\sqrt{(\gamma + KX_t)}$, so that it becomes necessary to estimate γ and K. But our estimates of γ and K are notoriously poor. This is because the "observation" for σ_t^2 is the squared OLS residual $\hat{\varepsilon}_t^2$ so that this observation on σ_t^2 is in effect an estimate of σ_t^2 from a sample size of one. If we have such poor estimates of γ and K, might we be better off ignoring the fact that γ is nonzero and continuing to use the transformation of division of $\sqrt{X_t}$? Kennedy (1985a) suggests that, as a rule of thumb, division by $\sqrt{X_t}$ should be employed unless γ exceeds 15% of the average variance of the error terms.

- A wide variety of functional forms for the relationship between the error variance and the relevant independent variable are used in the Glejser and maximum likelihood contexts. One popular general form was suggested by Park (1966). Assume that $\sigma^2 = kx^\alpha$ where σ^2 is the error variance, k is a constant and x is a relevant independent variable. This is estimated by adding a multiplicative disturbance term e^v, a log-normally distributed disturbance. Specific values of the parameter α correspond to specific relationships between the error variance and the independent variable. In particular, the case of $\alpha = 0$ corresponds to homoskedasticity.

8.4   Autocorrelated Disturbances

- In the simple model with only one independent variable and a first-order autocorrelated error term with autocorrelation coefficient ρ, the relative efficiency of β^{GLS} versus β^{OLS} (i.e., the ratio of the variance of β^{GLS} to that of β^{OLS}) is roughly $(1 - \rho^2)/(1 + \rho^2)$.
- The transformation of the dependent and independent variables used in obtaining the GLS estimates is derived as follows. Suppose the equation to be estimated is

$$y_t = \beta_1 + \beta_2 x_t + \varepsilon_t \text{ where } \varepsilon_t = \rho\varepsilon_{t-1} + u_t.$$

Lagging and multiplying through by ρ, we get

$$\rho y_{t-1} = \rho\beta_1 + \rho\beta_2 x_{t-1} + \rho\varepsilon_{t-1}.$$

Subtracting this second equation from the first, we get

$$y_t - \rho y_{t-1} = \beta_1(1 - \rho) + \beta_2(x_t - \rho x_{t-1}) + (\varepsilon_t - \rho\varepsilon_{t-1})$$

or

$$y_t^* = \beta_1^* + \beta_2 x_t^* + u_t.$$

This same technique can be used to derive the transformation required if the errors have a more complicated autocorrelation structure. For example, if the errors have a second-order autocorrelated structure so that $\varepsilon_t = \rho_1\varepsilon_{t-1} + \rho_2\varepsilon_{t-2} + u_t$, then x_t must be transformed to $x_t - \rho_1 x_{t-1} - \rho_2 x_{t-2}$.

- The special transformation for the first observation is deduced by noting that only if this transformation of the first observation is made will the general formula for β^{GLS} (in the context of first-order autocorrelation) correspond to the OLS regression in the transformed data. See Kadiyala (1968).
- The rationale behind Durbin's two-stage method is easily explained. Suppose that the equation being estimated is

$$y_t = \beta_1 + \beta_2 x_t + \varepsilon_t \text{ where } \varepsilon_t = \rho\varepsilon_{t-1} + u_t.$$

Lagging and multiplying through by ρ we get

$$\rho y_{t-1} = \beta_1\rho + \beta_2\rho x_{t-1} + \rho\varepsilon_{t-1}.$$

Subtracting the latter from the former we get

$$y_t - \rho y_{t-1} = \beta_1 - \rho\beta_1 + \beta_2 x_t - \beta_2\rho x_{t-1} + \varepsilon_t - \rho\varepsilon_{t-1}$$

which upon rearrangement becomes

$$y_t = \beta_1(1 - \rho) + \rho y_{t-1} + \beta_2 x_t - \beta_2 \rho x_{t-1} + u_t.$$

This is a linear estimating function with a spherical disturbance u. Although the estimate of the coefficient of y_{t-1} is a biased estimate of ρ (see section 9.3), it is consistent. It might be thought that this estimate could be improved by incorporating the knowledge that the coefficient of x_{t-1} is minus the product of the coefficient of y_{t-1} and the coefficient of x_t. Monte Carlo studies have shown that this is not worth while.

9
VIOLATING ASSUMPTION FOUR: MEASUREMENT ERRORS AND AUTOREGRESSION

9.1 INTRODUCTION

The fourth assumption of the CLR model specifies that the observations on the independent variables can be considered fixed in repeated samples. In many economic contexts the independent variables are themselves random (or stochastic) variables and thus could not have the same values in repeated samples. For example, suppose, as is common in econometric work, that a lagged value of the dependent variable appears as one of the independent variables. Because it is in part determined by the previous period's disturbance, it is stochastic and cannot be considered as fixed in repeated samples. (Recall that in repeated sampling new disturbance terms are drawn to create each repeated sample.)

This assumption of fixed regressors is made mainly for mathematical convenience; if the regressors can be considered to be fixed in repeated samples, the desirable properties of the OLS estimator can be derived quite straightforwardly. The essence of this assumption is that, if the regressors are nonstochastic, they are distributed independently of the disturbances. If this assumption is weakened to allow the explanatory variables to be stochastic but to be distributed independently of the error term, all the desirable properties of the OLS estimator are maintained; their algebraic derivation is more complicated, however, and their interpretation in some instances must be changed (for example, in this circumstance β^{OLS} is not, strictly speaking, a linear estimator). Even the maximum likelihood property of β^{OLS} is maintained if the disturbances are distributed normally and the distribution of the regressors does not involve either the parameter β or the variance of the disturbances, σ^2.

This fourth assumption can be further weakened at the expense of the small-sample properties of β^{OLS}. If the regressors are contemporaneously uncorrelated with the disturbance vector, the OLS estimator is biased but retains its desirable asymptotic properties. Contemporaneous uncorrelation in this context means that the nth observations on the regressors must be uncorrelated with the nth disturbance term, although they may be correlated with the disturbance terms

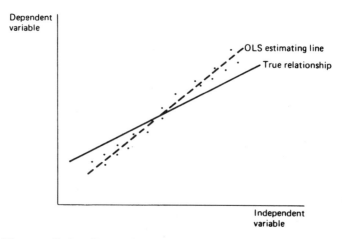

Figure 9.1   Positive contemporaneous correlation

associated with other regressor observations. In general, no alternative estimators are available with superior small-sample properties, so the OLS estimator is retained on the basis of its desirable asymptotic properties.

If the regressors are contemporaneously correlated with the error term, the OLS estimator is even asymptotically biased. This is because the OLS procedure, in assigning "credit" to regressors for explaining variation in the dependent variable, assigns, in error, some of the disturbance-generated variation of the dependent variable to the regressor with which that disturbance is contemporaneously correlated. Consider as an example the case in which the correlation between the regressor and the disturbance is positive. When the disturbance is higher the dependent variable is higher, and owing to the correlation between the disturbance and the regressor, the regressor is likely to be higher, implying that too much credit for making the dependent variable higher is likely to be assigned to the regressor. This is illustrated in figure 9.1. If the error term and the independent variable are positively correlated, negative values of the disturbance will tend to correspond to low values of the independent variable and positive values of the disturbance will tend to correspond to high values of the independent variable, creating data patterns similar to that shown in the diagram. The OLS estimating line clearly overestimates the slope of the true relationship. This result of overestimation with positive correlation between the disturbance and regressor does not necessarily hold when there is more than one explanatory variable, however. Note that the estimating line provides a much better fit to the sample data than does the true relationship; this causes the variance of the error term to be underestimated.

How does one know when there is contemporaneous correlation between the errors and the regressors? A testing methodology popularized by Hausman (1978) is used for this purpose. Consider an example of a regressor measured with error, which as discussed later gives rise to contemporaneous correlation between the error and this regressor. Two estimators are compared, one consistent (and efficient) under the null but inconsistent under the alternative, and the other consistent under both the null and the alternative. For example, OLS is consistent (and efficient) under the null of no measurement error, but is inconsistent in the presence of measurement error, whereas the consistency of an IV estimator (described later) is not affected by measurement error. This suggests that if the null hypothesis is true (no measurement error) both estimators should produce similar estimates, whereas if the null hypothesis is false (there is measurement error) these estimates should differ. The Hausman test is a test of equality of the estimates produced by these two estimators. See the technical notes for further discussion.

When there exists contemporaneous correlation between the disturbance and a regressor, alternative estimators with desirable small-sample properties cannot in general be found; as a consequence, the search for alternative estimators is conducted on the basis of their asymptotic properties. The most common estimator used in this context is the instrumental variable (IV) estimator.

9.2 INSTRUMENTAL VARIABLE ESTIMATION

The IV procedure produces a consistent estimator in a situation in which a regressor is contemporaneously correlated with the error, but as noted later, not without cost. To use the IV estimator one must first find an "instrument" for each regressor that is contemporaneously correlated with the error. This is a new independent variable which must have two characteristics. First, it must be contemporaneously uncorrelated with the error; and second, it must be correlated (preferably highly so) with the regressor for which it is to serve as an instrument. The IV estimator is then found using a formula involving both the original variables and the instrumental variables, as explained in the general notes.

Although it is sometimes difficult to find suitable instrumental variables, economic theory can be very helpful in this regard, as will become evident in later discussion of contexts in which IV estimation is common. The major drawback to IV estimation is that the variance–covariance matrix of the IV estimator is larger than that of the OLS estimator, by an amount that is inversely related to the correlation between the instrument and the regressor (this is why the "preferably highly so" was included earlier). This is the price paid for avoiding the asymptotic bias of OLS; the OLS estimator could be preferred on the MSE criterion.

Often there will exist more than one instrumental variable for a regressor. Suppose both x and w are suitable instruments for p. This embarrassment of choice is resolved by using a linear combination of x and w. Since both x and w

are uncorrelated with the error, any linear combination of them will be uncorrelated with the error. Since the variance of the IV estimator is smaller the higher is the correlation of the instrument with p, we should choose the linear combination of x and w that is most highly correlated with p. This is p^*, the estimated, or predicted, p obtained from regressing p on x and w. This procedure is called generalized instrumental variable estimation (GIVE).

The rest of this chapter discusses two major examples of contemporaneous correlation between the error and a regressor, the case of errors in measuring the regressors and the case of autocorrelated errors in conjunction with a lagged value of the dependent variable serving as a regressor. The next chapter examines a third major case, that of simultaneous equations.

9.3   ERRORS IN VARIABLES

Many economists feel that the greatest drawback to econometrics is the fact that the data with which econometricians must work are so poor. A well-known quotation expressing this feeling is due to Josiah Stamp:

> The Government are very keen on amassing statistics – they collect them, add them, raise them to the nth power, take the cube root and prepare wonderful diagrams. But what you must never forget is that every one of those figures comes in the first instance from the village watchman, who just puts down what he damn pleases. (1929, pp. 258–9)

The errors-in-variables problem is concerned with the implication of using incorrectly measured variables, whether these measurement errors arise from the whims of the village watchman or from the use by econometricians of a proxy variable in place of an unobservable variable suggested by economic theory.

Errors in measuring the dependent variables are incorporated in the disturbance term; their existence causes no problems. When there are errors in measuring an independent variable, however, the fourth assumption of the CLR model is violated, since these measurement errors make this independent variable stochastic; the seriousness of this depends on whether or not this regressor is distributed independently of the disturbance. The original estimating equation, with correctly measured regressors, has a disturbance term independent of the regressors. Replacing one of these regressors by its incorrectly measured counterpart creates a new disturbance term, which, as shown in the technical notes to this section, involves the measurement error embodied in the new regressor. Because this measurement error appears in both the new regressor (the incorrectly measured independent variable) and the new disturbance term, this new estimating equation has a disturbance that is contemporaneously correlated with a regressor; thus the OLS estimator is biased even asymptotically.

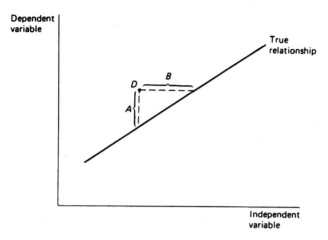

Figure 9.2   Illustrating weighted regression

There are three basic approaches to estimation in the presence of errors in variables.

(1)   WEIGHTED REGRESSION

The OLS procedure minimizes the sum of squared errors where these errors are measured in the vertical direction (the distance A in figure 9.2). But if we have errors in measuring the independent variable, there exist errors in the horizontal direction as well (i.e., the data point D in figure 9.2 could be off the true line either because of a traditional error A or because of an error of size B in measuring the independent variable – or, as is most likely, because of a combination of both these types of errors). The least squares procedure should be modified to incorporate these horizontal errors; the problem in doing this is how to weight these two types of errors. This weighting is usually determined on the basis of the ratio of the variances of the two errors. Several special cases arise:

(a)   If the variance of the vertical error is extremely large relative to the variance of the horizontal error, OLS is appropriate.

(b)   If the variance of the horizontal error is extremely large relative to the variance of the vertical error, inverse least squares (in which x is regressed on y and the inverse of the coefficient estimate for y is used as the estimate of β) is appropriate.

(c)   If the ratio of the variance of the vertical error to the variance of the horizontal error is equal to the ratio of the variances of the dependent and independent variables, we have the case of "diagonal" regression, in which a consistent estimate turns out to be the geometric mean of the OLS and inverse least squares estimators.

(d) If the ratio of these error variances is unity, we have the case of "orthogonal" regression, in which the sum of squared errors measured along a line perpendicular to the estimating line is minimized.

The great drawback of this procedure is that the ratio of the error variances is not usually known and cannot usually be estimated. This problem also characterizes the usually reliable maximum likelihood method. If the errors are all normally distributed (and independent of one another), the maximum likelihood estimates cannot be calculated without extra information (such as knowledge of the ratio of the error variances or knowledge of the variance of the measurement error).

(2) INSTRUMENTAL VARIABLES

There are several candidates for instrumental variables that are common in the context of measurement errors.

(a) It may be possible to use as an instrument the lagged value of the independent variable in question; it is usually correlated with the original independent variable, and, although it is correlated with the disturbance vector, because it is lagged it is not contemporaneously correlated with the disturbance (assuming the disturbance is not autocorrelated).

(b) The two-group method, in which the observations are split into two equal-sized groups on the basis of the size of the regressor and then the slope coefficient is estimated by the line joining the arithmetic means of the two groups, can be interpreted as an instrumental variables estimator with the instrumental variable taking the value -1 if the regressor value is below its median value and $+1$ if above its median value. The rationale behind this method is that by averaging the data in this way the measurement errors are also averaged, reducing their impact. This does not work well if the measurement error variance is large, causing the division into two groups not to correspond to a division based on the true values of the regressor. The three-group method is advanced to address this problem.

(c) The three-group method, a variation of the two-group method in which the middle third of the observations is ignored, corresponds to using an instrumental variable with values -1, 0 and $+1$.

(d) In the Durbin method the independent variable is ranked by size and an instrumental variable is defined as the rank order (i.e., with values $1, 2, 3, ... T$).

(3) LINEAR STRUCTURAL RELATIONS

Psychologists and sociologists often model using unobserved "latent" variables, equivalent to economists' unobserved "measured-with-error" variables. Their modeling procedure, called linear structural relations, avoids the asymptotic bias created by measurement error by incorporating additional information such as knowledge of the variance of a measurement error or zero covariance between latent variables. Estimation is undertaken by minimizing the difference between the actual covariance matrix of the observations and the covariance matrix implied by estimates of the unknowns. An example given in the technical notes illustrates how this is accomplished.

Economists do not use this estimation procedure much. One reason is that econometric software does not incorporate this modeling/estimation procedure. A second reason is that in many econometric contexts it is not reasonable to view variables as distributed normally as this analysis usually assumes. (This was particularly unsettling in older variants of linear structural relations in which dummy variables had to be treated just like continuous variables.) A third reason is that econometricians are seldom in the position of knowing the variance of the measurement error. This seems an odd objection given that econometricians so often are comfortable assuming it is zero! In the spirit of fragility analysis econometricians should report a range of estimates corresponding to a range of values of the measurement error variance.

9.4 AUTOREGRESSION

It is not uncommon in economics for a variable to be influenced by its own value in previous periods. For example, the habit-persistence theory of consumption suggests that consumption depends on the previous period's consumption, among other things. Whenever a lagged value of the dependent variable appears as a regressor in an estimating relationship, we have the case of *autoregression*. Because a lagged value of the dependent variable is stochastic (i.e., it was in part determined by a disturbance), using it as an independent variable (regressor) violates assumption 4 of the CLR model. The critical question is whether or not the lagged dependent variable is independent of the disturbance vector, or, failing that, contemporaneously independent of the disturbance.

The lagged dependent variable cannot be independent of the entire disturbance vector because the dependent variable is in part determined by the disturbance term. In particular, in the tth period the lagged dependent variable (i.e., the dependent variable value from the $(t-1)$th period) is correlated with the $(t-1)$th period's disturbance because this disturbance was one of the determinants of the dependent variable in that period. Furthermore, if this lagged dependent variable was in turn determined in part by the dependent variable value of the $(t-2)$th period, then it will be correlated with the disturbance of the $(t-2)$th period since that disturbance in part determined that period's dependent variable value. This reasoning can be extended to show that the lagged dependent variable is correlated with all of the past disturbances. However, it is *not* correlated with the current or future disturbances; thus, although the lagged dependent variable is not independent of the disturbance vector, it is contemporaneously independent of the disturbance. This means that, although β^{OLS} is a biased estimator of β, it is consistent and is on these grounds usually adopted as the most appropriate estimator.

It often happens that the autoregressive estimation problem arises not directly from specification of a habit-persistence theory, but indirectly through mathematical manipulations designed to transform an equation with estimation problems into a new estimating equation that is free of those problems. The following examples are typical of this.

(1) *Durbin two-stage method* The first stage of the Durbin two-stage method for dealing with autocorrelated errors (discussed in section 8.4 and its associated technical notes) transforms the original estimating equation into one with a lagged dependent variable as a regressor. The coefficient estimate of this lagged dependent variable produces an estimate of ρ, the error autocorrelation coefficient, which is used in the second stage. Although this estimate is biased, it is consistent.

(2) *Koyck distributed lag* Sometimes a dependent variable is determined by many or all past values of an independent variable, in addition to the current value of that independent variable. Estimating this *distributed lag* proves difficult, either because there are too many regressors relative to the number of observations (a degrees-of-freedom problem) or because the lagged values of the independent variable are collinear with one another (the multicollinearity problem – see chapter 11). To circumvent these estimating problems the distributed lag coefficients are usually assumed to follow some specific pattern. A popular specification is the Koyck distributed lag in which these coefficients decline geometrically. This relationship can be mathematically manipulated (see the technical notes) to produce an estimating relationship that contains as independent variables only the current value of the original independent variable and the lagged value of the dependent variable. Thus a large estimating equation has been transformed into a much smaller autoregressive equation.

(3) *The partial-adjustment model* Sometimes economic theory specifies that the desired rather than the actual value of the dependent variable is determined by the independent variable(s). This relationship cannot be estimated directly because the desired level of the dependent variable is unknown. This dilemma is usually resolved by specifying that the actual value of the dependent variable adjusts or is adjusted to the desired level according to some simple rule. In the *partial-adjustment* or *rigidity* model the actual adjusts by some constant fraction of the difference between the actual and desired values. This is justified by citing increasing costs associated with rapid change, or noting technological, institutional or psychological inertia. As shown in the technical notes, mathematical manipulation of these two relationships (one determining the desired level and the second determining the adjustment of the actual level) creates an estimating equation that is autoregressive.

(4) *Adaptive expectations model* Sometimes economic theory specifies that the dependent variable is determined by the anticipated or "expected" value of the independent variable rather than by the current value of the independent variable. This relationship cannot be estimated directly because the anticipated

values of the independent variables are unknown. This dilemma is usually resolved by specifying that the anticipated value of the independent variable is formed by some simple rule. In the *adaptive expectations* model the anticipated value of the independent variable is formed by taking the last period's anticipated value and adding to it a constant fraction of the difference between last period's anticipated and actual values. This is justified by appealing to uncertainty and claiming that current information is discounted. As shown in the technical notes, mathematical manipulation of these two relationships (one determining the dependent variable and the second determining how anticipations are formed) creates an estimating equation that is autoregressive.

In each of these examples the lagged value of the dependent variable became a regressor in an estimating relationship through mathematical manipulation. When an estimating equation is created in this way, it is important to ensure that the disturbance term is included in the mathematical manipulations so that the character of the disturbance term in this final estimating equation is known. Too often researchers ignore the original disturbance and simply tack a spherical disturbance on to the relationship derived for estimating purposes. This leads to the adoption of the OLS estimator, which may be inappropriate.

In the second and fourth examples given above it happens that the mathematical manipulations create a disturbance term for the ultimate estimating relationship that is autocorrelated. This creates an estimating problem in which two assumptions of the CLR model are violated simultaneously – autocorrelated errors and a lagged dependent variable as a regressor. Unfortunately, it is not the case that the problem of simultaneous violation of two assumptions of the CLR model can be treated as two separate problems. The interaction of these two violations produces new problems. In this case the OLS estimator, although unbiased in the presence of autocorrelated errors alone, and consistent in the presence of a lagged dependent variable as a regressor alone, is asymptotically biased in the presence of both together. This asymptotic bias results because the lagged dependent variable is contemporaneously correlated with the autocorrelated disturbance; the tth period's disturbance is determined in part by the $(t-1)$th period's disturbance and it in turn was one of the determinants of the lagged (i.e., $(t-1)$th period's) dependent variable.

In this case there is an obvious choice of an instrumental variable. The lagged value of an exogenous regressor appearing in this equation, say x_{t-1}, will not be correlated with the error (because x_{t-1} is an exogenous variable), but will be correlated with the lagged value of the dependent variable y_{t-1} (because x_{t-1} appears as an explanatory variable when the equation for y_t is lagged). If there is another exogenous variable appearing in the equation, say w, then there is a dilemma, since w_{t-1} also will be eligible to serve as an instrument for y_{t-1}. This embarrassment of choice is resolved by using y^*_{t-1}, the estimated y_{t-1} obtained from regressing y_{t-1} on x_{t-1} and w_{t-1}, as the instrument for y_{t-1}. This is the GIVE procedure described earlier.

The technique described in the preceding paragraph produces a consistent estimator via the instrumental variables methodology, but it lacks efficiency because it does not account for the autocorrelated error. Two-step linearized maximum likelihood estimators, described in the general notes, are used to improve efficiency.

GENERAL NOTES

9.1 Introduction

- Binkley and Abbott (1987) note that when the regressors are stochastic many of the standard results valid in the context of fixed regressors no longer hold. For example, when regressors are stochastic omission of a relevant regressor could increase the variance of estimates of the coefficients of remaining variables.

9.2 Instrumental Variable Estimation

- The Ballentine of figure 9.3 can be used to illustrate the rationale behind the instrumental variable (IV) estimator. Suppose that Y is determined by X and an error term ε (ignore the dashed circle Z for the moment), but that X and ε are not independent. The lack of independence between X and ε means that the yellow area (representing the influence of the error term) must now overlap with the X circle. This is represented by the red area. Variation in Y in the red area is due to the influence of *both* the error term and the explanatory variable X. If Y were regressed on X, the information in the red-plus-blue-plus-purple area would be used to estimate β_x. This estimate is biased

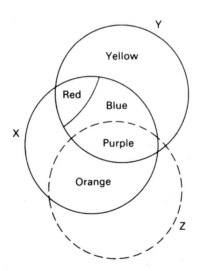

Figure 9.3   Using an instrumental variable Z

because the red area does not reflect variation in Y arising solely from variation in X. Some way must be found to get rid of the red area.

The circle Z represents an instrumental variable for X. It is drawn to reflect the two properties it must possess:

(1) It must be independent of the error term, so it is drawn such that it does not intersect the yellow or red areas.
(2) It must be as highly correlated as possible with X, so it is drawn with a large overlap with the X circle.

Suppose X is regressed on Z. The predicted X from this regression, $\hat{X}$, is represented by the purple-plus-orange area. Now regress Y on $\hat{X}$ to produce an estimate of β_x; this in fact defines the IV estimator. The overlap of the Y circle with the purple-plus-orange area is the purple area, so information in the purple area is used to form this estimate; since the purple area corresponds to variation in Y arising entirely from variation in X, the resulting estimate of β_x is unbiased (strictly speaking, asymptotically unbiased).

Notice that, in constructing this estimate, although the bias arising from the red area is eliminated, the information set used to estimate β_x has shrunk from the red-plus-blue-plus-purple area to just the purple area. This implies that the variance of the IV estimator will be considerably higher than the variance of the OLS estimator, a reason why many researchers prefer to stick with OLS in spite of its asymptotic bias. It should now be apparent why the instrumental variable should be as highly correlated with X as possible: this makes the purple area as large as possible (at the expense of the blue area), reducing the variance of the IV estimator.

It is tempting to use the purple area by regressing Y on Z. This would produce an estimate of the "coefficient" of Z rather than the coefficient of X which is desired. Suppose, for example, that $y = \beta x + \varepsilon$ and $x = \theta z + u$. Substituting the second equation into the first gives $y = \beta\theta z + \beta u + \varepsilon$ so that regressing y on z will produce an estimate of $\beta\theta$ rather than an estimate of β.

9.3   Errors in Variables

• Morgenstern (1963) wrote an entire book examining the accuracy of economic data. Some spectacular examples of data fudging by government agencies can be found in Streissler (1970, pp. 27–9). (Example: a large overstatement of housing starts in Austria was compensated for by deliberately understating several subsequent housing start figures.) Streissler claims that often the econometrician more or less completely misunderstands what the statistics he works with really mean. A joke popular with graduate students illustrates this. After running many regressions a professor had discovered that the nation's output of soybeans followed a semi-logarithmic production function. He had just finished writing up his paper when on a visit to the office of the bureaucrat in charge of soybean statistics he noticed a sign which read, "When in Doubt Use the Semi-Log." A more serious example of this is provided by Shourie (1972). He notes that value added by the construction industry in Sri Lanka is usually estimated by the national accounts statistician as a constant multiple of imports of construction materials, so that a regression postulating that imports of construction materials were linearly related to value added in the construction industry would fit quite well. As a last example consider Abraham's (1976) description of Ethiopia's figures for grain production, which are calculated as a base year figure extrapolated by an assumed rate of population growth. The base year figure was obtained from "a group of experts assembled by a planning minister many years ago and locked up in a room until they could agree on a set of estimates."

- Griliches (1985) offers four responses to Morgenstern: "1. The data are not that bad. 2. The data are lousy but it doesn't matter. 3. The data are bad but we have learned how to live with them and adjust for their foibles. 4. That is all there is – it is the only game in town and we have to make the best of it."

- Although the coefficient estimates are biased (even asymptotically) in the errors-in-variables case, OLS is still appropriate for predicting the expected value of y given the measured value of x.

- In some instances it could be argued that economic agents respond to the measured rather than the true variables, implying that the original estimating equation should be specified in terms of the measured rather than the true values of the regressors. This eliminates the errors-in-variables problem.

- In the case of a single explanatory variable, errors in measuring this variable lead to negative correlation between the error term and the incorrectly measured regressor, causing β^{OLS} to be biased downward. When there is more than one independent variable, the direction of bias is more difficult to determine. See Levi (1973).

- Inverse least squares, in which the dependent variable becomes a regressor and the incorrectly measured independent variable becomes the regressand, provides an unbiased estimate of the inverse of β when there is no error in the vertical direction. The inverse of this estimate is a biased but consistent estimate of β. (Recall the technical notes to section 2.8.)

- When both vertical and horizontal errors exist, in large samples the OLS and inverse least squares estimates contain the value of β between them. Levi (1977) discusses bounded estimates. When the interval between these two estimates of β is small, it can be concluded that measurement errors are not a serious problem.

- Kmenta (1986, pp. 352–6) discusses how estimation can be undertaken if the ratio of the two error variances is known, which includes orthogonal and diagonal least squares as special cases. Boggs et al. (1988) find in a Monte Carlo study that orthogonal least squares performs quite well relative to OLS.

- Feldstein (1974) suggests forming a weighted average of OLS and instrumental variable estimators to help reduce (at the expense of some bias) the inevitably large variance associated with instrumental variable estimation. Feldstein shows his estimator to be desirable on the mean square error criterion.

- For discussion of and references for the two- and three-group methods and the Durbin method, see Johnston (1984, pp. 430–2). All three methods produce consistent estimates under fairly general conditions; the two-group method is the least efficient of these, while the Durbin method is the most efficient. The intercept estimator for all these methods is found by passing a line with the estimated slope through the mean of all the observations.

- Often an explanatory variable is unobservable, but a proxy for it can be constructed. The proxy by definition contains measurement errors, and thus a biased estimate results. Forgoing the proxy and simply omitting the unobservable regressor also creates bias. McCallum (1972) and Wickens (1972) show that, on the criterion of asymptotic bias, using even a poor proxy is better than omitting the unobservable regressor.

Using the MSE criterion, Aigner (1974) shows that using the proxy is preferred in most, but not all, circumstances. Ohtani (1985) and Kakimoto and Ohtani (1985) show that it is better to include a proxy if interest focuses on testing. A popular proxy in econometric work is to use a forecast or an estimated error, both used frequently in empirical work on rational expectations. Pagan (1984b) investigates this. Oxley and McAleer (1993) is a survey of issues arising from using such generated regressors. A main conclusion is that variances are underestimated because they do not take into account the stochastic nature of the generated regressor. For examples of how to correct for this, see Murphy and Topel (1985), Gauger (1989) and Greene (1997, pp. 140–5). How strong does the correlation between a variable and its proxy need to be to ensure that the sign on the OLS coefficient estimate from using the proxy is correct? Krasker and Pratt (1986) address this question.

- The maximum likelihood technique breaks down in the errors-in-variables context, basically because each observation carries with it an extra unknown (the true value of the unobservable variable), referred to as an incidental parameter. Johnston (1984, pp. 432–5) discusses how extra information in the form of knowledge of a variance or of a ratio of variances can be used to salvage the maximum likelihood approach. For more on the MLE approach see Maddala (1977, pp. 294–6).

- Missing data can be viewed as an extreme form of measurement error. What should be done about missing data varies depending on why the data are missing. If there is a known reason for why they are missing, this must be built into the estimation procedure. Chapter 16 on limited dependent variables describes how analysis of missing dependent variable (y) values is undertaken to avoid selection bias. It is tempting to deal with missing explanatory variable (x) values by just omitting each observation for which one or more of the x values are missing. This is acceptable so long as these observations can be viewed as occurring randomly. If not, their omission causes sample selection bias, discussed in chapter 16. Even if these missing data occur randomly, however, a researcher may be reluctant to discard these observations because of a small sample size. A popular way of retaining these observations is to replace the missing x values with suitable proxy values and so allow the remaining information to improve estimation. The most defensible way of proxying a missing x value is to forecast this x value by regressing this variable on all the other independent variables. This technique leaves unaffected the coefficient estimate of the variable with missing observations, but can improve estimation of the remaining coefficients (because of the larger sample size) despite introducing some bias because of its measurement error. If this is done, however, it is wise to redo the estimation using a variety of forecasted x values from the hypothetical distribution of forecasts, to check for fragility and to produce suitable standard errors. Little (1992) surveys methods of dealing with missing x values. It is better not to replace missing y values with proxies.

9.4 Autoregression

- For the extremely simple case in which $y_t = \beta y_{t-1} + \varepsilon_t$, with ε a spherical disturbance, the bias of the OLS estimator is approximately $-2\beta/T$, which disappears as T becomes large. The presence of extra regressors in the model also decreases this bias. Several suggestions for correcting for this bias (such as using the estimator $[(T/(T-2)]\beta^{OLS})$) have been suggested, but the correction factors increase the variance of the estimator and run the danger of increasing the mean square error. A Monte Carlo study by Copas (1966) suggests that β^{OLS} is better than the suggested alternatives. When the model has an intercept so that $y_t = \alpha + \beta y_{t-1} + \varepsilon_t$, then the bias in β^{OLS} is given by $-(1 + 3\beta)/T$. A suggested corrected estimator is $(T\beta^{OLS} + 1)/(T - 3)$, which Orcutt and Winokur (1969), on the basis of a Monte Carlo study, claim is superior.

- It may well be the case that the real world is characterized by some combination of the partial adjustment and adaptive expectation models. Waud (1968) discusses the estimation problems associated with misspecification related to this possibility.

- The DW test is biased towards not finding autocorrelated errors whenever a lagged value of the dependent variable appears as a regressor. In the general notes to section 8.4 the Durbin m test was recommended for this case. McNown and Hunter (1980) have suggested an alternative test, which is easy to calculate, has desirable asymptotic properties and, on the basis of their Monte Carlo study, appears to perform well in small samples. See the technical notes.

- In the autoregressive model with first-order autocorrelated errors the asymptotic bias in β^{OLS} is positive if $\rho > 0$ and negative if $\rho < 0$. This bias becomes smaller if more regressors are involved. In the simple model in which $y_t = \beta y_{t-1} + \varepsilon_t$ and $\varepsilon_t = \rho \varepsilon_{t-1} + u_t$, the OLS bias in estimating β is exactly the negative of the OLS bias in estimating ρ. See Malinvaud (1966, pp. 459–65).

- A two-step Gauss–Newton estimator is suggested for the case of autocorrelated errors in conjunction with a lagged dependent variable serving as a regressor. For the case of AR(1) errors a convenient way of calculating this is via a method suggested by Hatanaka (1974). First, estimated by IV, obtain the residuals, and use them in the usual way to estimate the autocorrelation coefficient as ρ^*. Second, transform the variables in the usual way and regress on the transformed variables, but add as an extra regressor the lagged residual. The slope coefficient estimates from this regression are the two-step estimates; the two-step estimate of ρ is ρ^* plus the coefficient on the lagged residual. That this method is equivalent to one iteration of Gauss–Newton is shown by Harvey (1990, p. 271). The two-step Gauss–Newton estimator for the case of an MA(1) error is explained in Harvey (1990, p. 273).

TECHNICAL NOTES

9.1   Introduction

- The Hausman test appears in two forms. (Some of what follows rests on asymptotic arguments which are suppressed for expository purposes.) Suppose $Y = X\beta + \varepsilon$ and W is a set of instruments for X. Then $\beta^{IV} = (W'X)^{-1}W'Y = (W'X)^{-1}W'(X\beta^{OLS} + \varepsilon^{OLS}) = \beta^{OLS} + (W'X)^{-1}W'\varepsilon^{OLS}$ so that $\beta^{IV} - \beta^{OLS} = (W'X)^{-1}W'\varepsilon^{OLS}$. Straightforward algebra on this yields $V(\beta^{IV} - \beta^{OLS}) = V(\beta^{IV}) - V(\beta^{OLS})$. This suggests that a test of equality between β^{IV} and β^{OLS} could be formed by using the statistic

$$(\beta^{IV} - \beta^{OLS})'[V(\beta^{IV}) - V(\beta^{OLS})]^{-1}(\beta^{IV} - \beta^{OLS})$$

which is distributed as a chi-square with degrees of freedom equal to the number of elements in β. This is the original form of the Hausman test.

Unfortunately, there are two problems with this form of the Hausman test, one theoretical, the other practical. First, it turns out that in many cases $[V(\beta^{IV}) - V(\beta^{OLS})]$ cannot be inverted in the normal way. This arises, for example, when only one of the regressors is contemporaneously correlated with the error, so that we should really only be comparing its OLS and IV coefficient estimates, rather than the full vector of coefficient estimates. In this case we should only have one degree of freedom, and we should be using only a part of $[V(\beta^{IV}) - V(\beta^{OLS})]$. Second, the estimated $[V(\beta^{IV}) - V(\beta^{OLS})]$ often turns out to have incorrect signs (although in theory $V(\beta^{OLS})$ is "smaller" than $V(\beta^{IV})$, their estimates may not preserve this result). Both these problems are avoided with the second variant of the Hausman test.

From above we have that $\beta^{IV} - \beta^{OLS} = (W'X)^{-1}W'\varepsilon^{OLS}$. This will be zero if W and ε^{OLS} are uncorrelated, which suggests testing if W and ε^{OLS} are uncorrelated. This can be done by running the regression: $Y = X\beta + W\theta + \varepsilon$ and testing $\theta = 0$ with an F test.

The intuition behind this is straightforward. Without W the regression would produce residuals ε^{OLS}. If W is to have a nonzero coefficient, it will have to "steal" some explanatory power from ε^{OLS}. (Try drawing a Ballentine to see this.) So if W has a nonzero coefficient, it must be the case that W and ε^{OLS} are correlated. Thus a test of $\theta = 0$ is a test of W and ε^{OLS} being correlated which in turn is a test of $\beta^{IV} - \beta^{OLS} = 0$, which in turn is a test of contemporaneous correlation between the error and the regressors.

This is called the OV, or omitted variables, version of the Hausman test. It is computationally attractive, and there is no problem in figuring out the degrees of freedom because to run the OV regression W will have to be stripped of any variables that are serving as their own instruments (i.e., to avoid perfect multicollinearity if X and W have some elements in common). Equivalent forms of the OV version of this test use the errors from a regression of X on W, or the estimated X from this regression, as the omitted variable.

Because the Hausman test is sensitive to several types of misspecification, Godfrey and Hutton (1994) recommend testing for general misspecification before applying the Hausman test, and recommend a test for doing so. Wong (1996) finds that bootstrapping the Hausman test improves its performance.

9.2   Instrumental Variable Estimation

- Suppose $y = X\beta + \varepsilon$ where X contains K1 columns of observations on variables which are contemporaneously uncorrelated with ε, including a column of ones for the intercept, and K2 columns of observations on variables which are contemporaneously correlated with ε. The intercept and the variables contemporaneously uncorrelated with the error can serve as their own (perfect) instruments, K1 in number. New variables must be found to serve as instruments for the remaining explanatory variables. K3 ≥ K2 such variables are required for the instrumental variable technique to work, i.e., at least one instrument for each explanatory variable correlated with the error term. This produces K1 + K3 instruments which are gathered together in a matrix Z. By regressing each column of X on Z we get $\hat{X}$ the desired matrix of final instruments – the K1 columns of X that are contemporaneously uncorrelated with ε have themselves as their instruments (because variables in X that are also in Z will be predicted perfectly by the regression of X on Z), and the K2 columns of X that are contemporaneously correlated with ε have as instruments from this regression the best linear combination of all the possible instruments. Our earlier Ballentine discussion suggests that β^{IV} can be produced by regressing y on $\hat{X} = Z(Z'Z)^{-1}Z'X$ so that

$$\beta^{IV} = (\hat{X}'\hat{X})^{-1}\hat{X}'y = [(X'Z(Z'Z)^{-1}Z'X]^{-1}X'Z(Z'Z)^{-1}Z'y.$$

- If Z is the same dimension as X, so that there is one instrument for each variable in X, then algebraic manipulation of the formula above produces $\beta^{IV} = (Z'X)^{-1}Z'y$. Note that this is not (repeat, *not*) the same as $(Z'Z)^{-1}Z'y$ which is what many students want to use. (This same warning, with an example, was given at the end of the Ballentine discussion in the general notes.) This IV formula can also be derived as a method of moments estimator, using the moment conditions $Z'\varepsilon = Z'(y - X\beta) = 0$, just as the OLS estimator can be derived as a method of moments estimator using the moment conditions $X'\varepsilon = 0$.
- When Z has more columns than X because there are more than exactly enough instruments, the moments $Z'\varepsilon = 0$ are too numerous and so the GMM (generalized method of moments – see the technical notes to section 8.2) estimator must be used. This requires minimizing (with respect to β)

$$(Z'\varepsilon)'[V(Z'\varepsilon)]^{-1}Z'\varepsilon = (y - X\beta)'Z(Z'Z)^{-1}Z'(y - X\beta)/\sigma^2$$

because $V(Z'\varepsilon) = Z'V(\varepsilon)Z = \sigma^2 Z'Z$.
This minimization produces exactly the IV formula given earlier.

This result is of interest for two reasons. First, it suggests that in the GLS model when $V(\varepsilon) = \sigma^2\Omega$, with Ω known, the IV estimator can be found by minimizing

$$(y - X\beta)'Z(Z'\Omega Z)^{-1}Z'(y - X\beta)/\sigma^2.$$

And second, it suggests that when $y = f(X,\beta) + \varepsilon$ where f is a nonlinear function, the IV estimator can be found by minimizing

$$[y - f(X,\beta)]'Z(Z'Z)^{-1}Z'[y - f(X,\beta)]/\sigma^2.$$

Following Amemiya (1974), this is sometimes called nonlinear two-stage least squares, because if f is linear the estimator coincides with the two-stage least squares method of chapter 10. The choice of instruments is not clear here, as it is in the linear case, because the connection between instruments and explanatory variables may itself be nonlinear.

- The variance–covariance matrix of β^{IV} is estimated by

$$\hat{\sigma}^2(\hat{X}'\hat{X})^{-1} = \sigma^2[X'Z(Z'Z)^{-1}Z'X]^{-1}$$

which, when Z and X are of the same dimension, is written as

$$\hat{\sigma}^2(Z'X)^{-1}Z'Z(X'Z)^{-1}$$

It is tempting to estimate σ^2 by

$$s^2 = (y - \hat{X}\beta^{IV})'(y - \hat{X}\beta^{IV})/(N - K)$$

where K is the number of regressors. This is incorrect, however, because it is $y - X\beta^{IV}$ which estimates ε, not $y - \hat{X}\beta^{IV}$. Consequently, σ^2 is estimated using

$$\hat{\sigma}^2 = (y - X\beta^{IV})'(y - X\beta^{IV})/(N - K)$$

This has an important implication for F tests using the regression of y on $\hat{X}$. The numerator can continue to be the restricted minus unrestricted sums of squares divided by the number of restrictions, but now the denominator must be $\hat{\sigma}^2$ rather than s^2.

- How many instruments should be found? This turns out to be an awkward question. On the one hand, if the number of instruments (including variables that can serve as their own instrument) is just equal to the number of explanatory variables (i.e., one instrument for each explanatory variable) β^{IV} has neither mean nor variance so we would expect it in some cases to have poor properties in finite samples, as evidenced in Nelson and Startz (1990a, 1990b). Adding an extra instrument allows it to have a mean, and one more allows it to have a variance, so it would seem desirable to have at least two more instruments than explanatory variables. On the other hand, as we add more and more instruments, in small samples $\hat{X}$ becomes closer and closer to X and so begins to introduce the bias that the IV procedure is trying to eliminate.

  The use of extra instruments beyond the bare minimum of one for each explanatory variable should be tested. Davidson and MacKinnon (1993, pp. 232–7) suggest a means of doing so by testing the joint hypothesis that the model is correctly specified and that the instruments used are valid. This test statistic is calculated as N times the uncentered R^2 from regressing the IV residuals on all the instruments, and is distributed as a chi-square with degrees of freedom equal to the number of instruments in excess of the number of explanatory variables. (The uncentered R^2 is $1 - \Sigma e^2/\Sigma y^2$ instead of $1 - \Sigma e^2/\Sigma(y - \bar{y})^2$.)

- Bound et al. (1995) find that whenever there is weak correlation between the error and an explanatory variable, and also weak correlation between the instrument and this explanatory variable, OLS outperforms IV estimation, even when the sample size is very large. They recommend that the quality of the instrument be checked, for example by testing significance of the instrument in the first stage of IV estimation. Bartels (1991) reaches a related conclusion, noting that even if an instrument is not independent of the error it may be superior on the mean square error criterion to an instrument that is independent of the error.

9.3   Errors in Variables

- Suppose that the true relationship is

$$y = \beta_1 + \beta_2 x_2 + \varepsilon$$

but that x_2 is measured with error as z_2 where

$$z_2 = x_2 + u.$$

This implies that x_2 can be written as $z_2 - u$, and the first equation then becomes

$$y = \beta_1 + \beta_2(z_2 - u) + \varepsilon$$
$$y = \beta_1 + \beta_2 z_2 + (\varepsilon - \beta_2 u).$$

The new disturbance contains u, the error in measuring x_2, as does z_2. Notice that the correlation between z_2 and this new disturbance is negative, implying that β^{OLS} calculated by regressing y on z_2 will be biased downward.

● The linear structural relations modeling/estimation technique is best exposited via a simple example. Suppose the classical linear regression model applies to $y = \beta x + \varepsilon$, except that x is measured as $x^m = x + \varepsilon_x$ where ε_x is a measurement error. In the linear structural relations approach, the raw data (in this case the observations on y and x^m) are used to estimate the unique elements of the variance–covariance matrix of the vector of observed variables, namely $V(y)$, $V(x^m)$ and $C(y,x^m)$, which in theory can be written as

$$V(y) = \beta^2 V(x) + V(\varepsilon) + 2\beta C(x,\varepsilon),$$
$$V(x^m) = V(x) + V(\varepsilon_x) + 2C(x,\varepsilon_x) \text{ and}$$
$$C(y,x^m) = \beta V(x) + \beta C(x,\varepsilon_x) + C(x,\varepsilon) + C(\varepsilon,\varepsilon_x).$$

The left-hand sides of these equations are measured using the raw data, whereas the right-hand sides are functions of unknown parameters, variances and covariances. Invoking the usual assumptions that x and ε are independent, and that the measurement error is independent of x and ε, this becomes

$$V(y) = \beta^2 V(x) + V(\varepsilon),$$
$$V(x^m) = V(x) + V(\varepsilon_x) \text{ and}$$
$$C(y,x^m) = \beta V(x).$$

There are three equations in *four* unknowns β, $V(x)$, $V(\varepsilon)$ and $V(\varepsilon_x)$, suggesting that these unknowns cannot be estimated consistently. If the variance of the measurement error, $V(\varepsilon_x)$ is known, however, this problem is resolved and the resulting three equations in three unknowns can be used to produce a consistent estimate of the remaining unknowns, most notably β. If there were no measurement error so that $V(\varepsilon_x)$ were zero, these three equations would be solved to estimate β as $C(y,x)/V(x)$, the OLS formula i.e., OLS is a special case of linear structural relations in which measurement error is zero.

Extending this to multiple regression is straightforward: an extra explanatory variable w, measured without error, would create six equations in seven unknowns, one of which is $V(\varepsilon_x)$; if w were also measured with error there would be six equations in eight unknowns, the extra unknown being the variance of the w measurement error. The unknown "true" values of a variable are called latent variables, and their measured counterparts "indicators." In its general form, linear structural relations can model simultaneous or non-simultaneous sets of equations, with both dependent and independent variables measured with or without error, with multiple indicators for a single latent variable, with indicators being linear functions of several latent variables and with zero or non zero covariances between errors or between latent variables. In these more general forms it is possible for the parameters to be unidentified (more unknowns than equations, in which case no consistent estimates can be produced), just identified (the same number of unknowns as equations, in which case there is a unique way to use the covariance structure to produce parameter estimates) or overidentified (more equations than unknowns, in which case there is more than one way to produce coefficient estimates from the raw data covariance matrix).

In the overidentified case estimates of the unknowns are chosen to minimize the "distance" between the raw data covariance matrix (the left-hand sides of the equations above) and the covariance matrix calculated by plugging these estimates into the right-hand sides of these equations. Seen in this light this method can be interpreted as a GMM technique. Different ways of defining "distance" in this context give rise to different estimation procedures; the most popular is a maximum likelihood procedure assuming normally-distributed errors and normally-distributed latent variables. Because the linear structural relations estimation procedure involves "fitting" a covariance matrix, it is often referred to as *analysis of covariance structures*. This modeling/estimation technique was introduced to economists by Goldberger (1972). For textbook expositions see Hayduk (1987), Bollen (1989) and Mueller (1996); two attractive software packages exist for modeling and estimation, LISREL (Joreskog and Sorbom, 1993) and EQS (Bentler, 1992).

- Instrumental variable estimation is a special case of linear structural relations in which an instrument appears as an extra indicator of a variable measured with error. In the example above, suppose we have observations on $z = \delta x + \varepsilon_z$ where ε_z is independent of x, ε and ε_x. The linear structural relations estimate of β turns out to be the instrumental variable estimate of β using z as an instrument for x. In practice, this is what most econometricians do instead of using linear structural relations assuming knowledge of the variance of the measurement error.

9.4   Autoregression

- The Koyck distributed lag model may be written as

$$y_t = \beta x_t + \beta \lambda x_{t-1} + \beta \lambda^2 x_{t-2} + \beta \lambda^3 x_{t-3} + \ldots + \varepsilon_t$$

where $0 < \lambda < 1$ so that the influence of lagged values of the independent variable x declines geometrically. Lagging this equation one period and multiplying through by λ, we get

$$\lambda y_{t-1} = \beta \lambda x_{t-1} + \beta \lambda^2 x_{t-2} + \beta \lambda^3 x_{t-3} + \ldots + \lambda \varepsilon_{t-1}.$$

Subtracting the second equation from the first, we get

$$y_t = \lambda y_{t-1} + \beta x_t + (\varepsilon_t - \lambda \varepsilon_{t-1})$$

an estimating equation of the autogressive form, in which the number of regressors has shrunk to only two and there is an MA(1) error.

- In the partial adjustment model the desired level of the dependent variable y^*, is determined by x, so that

$$y_t^* = \beta_0 + \beta_1 x_t + \varepsilon_t$$

and the actual adjusts by some fraction of the difference between the desired and the actual so that

$$y_t - y_{t-1} = \alpha(y_t^* - y_{t-1}) + u_t.$$

Substituting y_t^* from the first equation into the second equation we get, after manipulation,

$$y_t = \alpha\beta_0 + (1 - \alpha)y_{t-1} + \alpha\beta_1 x_t + (\alpha\varepsilon_t + u_t),$$

an estimating equation of the autogressive form. In this case the error term is spherical.

- In the adaptive expectations model the dependent variable is determined by the anticipated value of the independent variable, x^*, so that

$$y_t = \beta_0 + \beta_1 x_t^* + \varepsilon_t.$$

The anticipated value is formed by updating last period's anticipated value by a fraction of its prediction error. Thus

$$x_t^* = x_{t-1}^* + \alpha(x_t - x_{t-1}^*) + u_t.$$

From the first equation $x_t^* = (y_t - \beta_0 - \varepsilon_t)/\beta_1$ and $x_{t-1}^* = (y_{t-1} - \beta_0 - \varepsilon_{t-1})/\beta_1$. Substituting these expressions into the second equation and simplifying, we get

$$y_t = \alpha\beta_0 + (1 - \alpha)y_{t-1} + \alpha\beta_1 x_t + [\varepsilon_t - (1 - \alpha)\varepsilon_{t-1} + \beta_1 u_t],$$

an estimating equation of the autoregressive form. In this case the error is of the moving-average type, similar to that found in the Koyck example.
- The test of McNown and Hunter is suggested through algebraic manipulation of $y_t = \beta y_{t-1} + \alpha x_t + \varepsilon_t$ with $\varepsilon_t = \rho\varepsilon_{t-1} + u_t$. If the y equation is lagged one period, multiplied through by ρ and then subtracted from the original relationship, the result can be rearranged to produce

$$y_t = (\beta + \rho)y_{t-1} + \alpha x_t - \rho\beta y_{t-2} - \rho\alpha x_{t-1} + u_t.$$

An OLS regression on this equation can be used to test against zero the coefficient of x_{t-1}. If $\alpha \neq 0$, this coefficient will be zero if $\rho = 0$.
- Construction of the likelihood function usually assumes that the y values are drawn independently of one another, which is clearly not the case when a lagged value of the dependent variable appears as a regressor. Because a joint density can be written as $p(y_2, y_1) = p(y_2|y_1)p(y_1)$, the likelihood function for an autoregression can be written as the product of the conditional densities of the last $T - 1$ observations times the unconditional density for the first observation y_1. Operationally, the term corresponding to this first observation is either omitted or approximated, simplifying the calculation of the MLE, usually in a way that does not affect its asymptotic properties. See Harvey (1990, pp. 104–11) for discussion and examples.

10

VIOLATING ASSUMPTION FOUR:
SIMULTANEOUS EQUATIONS

10.1 INTRODUCTION

In a system of simultaneous equations, all the endogenous variables are random variables – a change in any disturbance term changes *all* the endogenous variables since they are determined simultaneously. (An exception is a recursive system, discussed in the general notes.) Since the typical equation in a set of simultaneous equations has at least one endogenous variable as an independent variable, it does not fit the CLR mold: this endogenous variable cannot be considered as fixed in repeated samples. Assumption 4 of the CLR model is violated.

The character of the OLS estimator in this context depends on whether or not the endogenous variables used as regressors are distributed independently of the disturbance term in that equation. As noted above, though, when this disturbance term changes, the endogenous variable it determines directly changes, which in turn changes *all* of the other endogenous variables since they are determined simultaneously; this means that the endogenous variables used as regressors are contemporaneously correlated with the disturbance term in this equation (as well as with the disturbance term in all other equations). As a consequence, the OLS estimator is biased, even asymptotically, so that an alternative estimator is usually thought necessary.

A popular example used to illustrate this is a simple Keynesian system consisting of a consumption function

$$C = a + bY + \varepsilon$$

and an equilibrium condition

$$Y = C + I$$

where C (consumption) and Y (income) are endogenous variables and I (investment) is an exogenous variable. Consider the problem of estimating the consumption function, regressing consumption on income. Suppose the disturbance in the consumption function jumps up. This directly increases consumption, which through the equilibrium condition increases income. But income is the independent variable in the consumption function. Thus, the disturbance in the consumption function and the regressor are positively correlated. An increase in the disturbance term (directly implying an increase in consumption) is accompanied by an increase in income (also implying an increase in consumption). When estimating the influence of income on consumption, however, the OLS technique attributes *both* of these increases in consumption (instead of just the latter) to the accompanying increase in income. This implies that the OLS estimator of the marginal propensity to consume is biased upward, even asymptotically.

A natural response to this estimating problem is to suggest that the simultaneous system be solved and put into its reduced form. This means that every endogenous variable is expressed as a linear function of all the exogenous variables (and lagged endogenous variables, which are considered exogenous in this context). For the simple Keynesian example, the structural equations given above can be solved to give the reduced-form equations

$$Y = \frac{a}{1-b} + \frac{1}{1-b}I + \frac{1}{1-b}\varepsilon$$

$$C = \frac{a}{1-b} + \frac{b}{1-b}I + \frac{1}{1-b}\varepsilon$$

which can be rewritten in more general form as

$$Y = \pi_1 + \pi_2 I + v_1$$

$$C = \pi_3 + \pi_4 I + v_2$$

where the π are parameters that are (nonlinear) functions of the structural form parameters and the v are the reduced-form disturbances, functions of the structural form disturbances.

Because no endogenous variables appear as independent variables in these reduced-form equations, if each reduced-form equation is estimated by OLS, these estimators of the reduced-form parameters, the π, are consistent (and if no lagged endogenous variables appear among the exogenous variables, these estimators are unbiased). Economic theory tells us that these reduced-form parameters are the long-run multipliers associated with the model. If a researcher is only interested in predicting the endogenous variables, or only wishes to estimate the size of these multipliers, he can simply use these estimators. If, however, he is interested in estimating the parameter values of the original equations (the structural parameters), estimates of the reduced-form parameters are of help only if they can be used to derive estimates of the structural parameters (i.e., one suggested way of obtaining estimates of the structural parameters is to calculate them using estimates of the reduced-form parameters). Unfortunately, this is not always possible; this problem is one way of viewing the identification problem.

10.2 IDENTIFICATION

If you know that your estimate of a structural parameter is in fact an estimate of that parameter and not an estimate of something else, then that parameter is said to be identified: identification is knowing that something is what you say it is.

The identification problem is a mathematical (as opposed to statistical) problem associated with simultaneous equation systems. It is concerned with the question of the possibility or impossibility of obtaining meaningful estimates of the structural parameters. There are two basic ways of describing this problem.

(1) *Can the reduced-form parameters be used to deduce unique values of the structural parameters?* In general, different sets of structural parameter values can give rise to the same set of reduced-form parameters, so that knowledge of the reduced-form parameters does not allow the correct set of structural parameter values to be identified. (Hence the name "identification" problem.) The set of equations representing the simultaneous equation system can be multiplied through by a transformation matrix to form a new set of equations with the same variables but different (i.e., transformed) parameters and a transformed disturbance. Mathematical manipulation shows that the reduced form of this new set of simultaneous equations (i.e., with a new set of structural parameters) is *identical* to the reduced form of the old set. This means that, if the reduced-form parameters were known, it would be impossible to determine which of the two sets of structural parameters was the "true" set. Since in general a large number of possible transformations exists, it is usually impossible to identify the correct set of structural parameters given values of the reduced-form parameters.

(2) *Can one equation be distinguished from a linear combination of all equations in the simultaneous system?* If it is possible to form a linear combination of the system's equations that looks just like one of the equations in the system (in the sense that they both include and exclude the same variables), a researcher estimating that equation would not know if the parameters he or she estimates should be identified with the parameters of the equation he or she wishes to estimate, or with the parameters of the linear combination. Since in general it is possible to find such linear combinations, it is usually impossible to identify the correct set of structural parameters.

The identification problem can be resolved if economic theory and extraneous information can be used to place restrictions on the set of simultaneous equations. These restrictions can take a variety of forms (such as use of extraneous estimates of parameters, knowledge of exact relationships among parameters, knowledge of the relative variances of disturbances, knowledge of zero correlation between disturbances in different equations, etc.), but the restrictions usually employed, called *zero restrictions*, take the form of specifying that certain structural parameters are zero, i.e., that certain endogenous variables and certain exogenous variables do not appear in certain equations. Placing a restriction on the structural parameters makes it more difficult to find a transformation of the structural equations that corresponds to the same reduced form, since that trans-formation must maintain the restriction. Similarly, the existence of the restric-tion makes it more difficult to find a linear combination of the equations that is indistinguishable from an original equation. If the econometrician is fortunate, there will be enough of these restrictions to eliminate *all* of the possible transfor-mations and (what is equivalent) make it impossible to find one of those linear combinations. In this case the structural parameters are identified and can there-fore be estimated.

A favorite example used to illustrate the identification problem, originally analyzed by Working (1927), is the case of a supply and a demand curve for some good, each written in the normal fashion – quantity as a function of price. This, along with an equilibrium condition, represents a simultaneous system; observations on quantity and price reflect the intersection of these two curves in each observation period. The positions of the supply and demand curves in each period are determined by shifting the true supply and demand curves by the amount of their respective disturbances for that period. The observation points, then, are likely to be a cluster of points around the true equilibrium position, rep-resenting the intersections of the supply and demand curves as they jump around randomly in response to each period's disturbance terms. This is illustrated in figure 10.1. The scatter of data in figure 10.1(b) suggests that it is impossible to estimate either the supply or the demand curve.

The supply and demand curves have the same included and excluded vari-ables, so that regressing quantity on price generates estimates that could be esti-mates of the supply parameters, the demand parameters or, as is most likely, some combination of these sets of parameters.

Now suppose that an exogenous variable, say the level of income, is intro-duced as an independent variable in the demand function, and that it is postulat-ed that this variable does *not* appear in the supply function (i.e., the coefficient

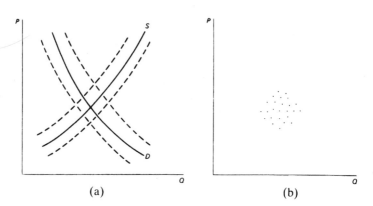

Figure 10.1   Neither supply nor demand identified

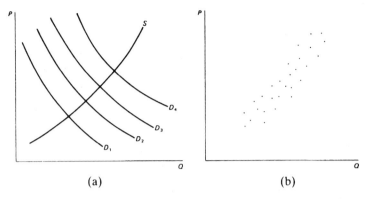

(a)   (b)

Figure 10.2 Supply curve identified

of this exogenous variable in the supply function is zero). It is now the case that the demand function shifts in response to changes in this exogenous variable (to form D_1, D_2, D_3, etc. in figure 10.2a) as well as to changes in the disturbance term. This creates a scatter of observations as illustrated in figure 10.2. This scatter of observations suggests that the supply curve can be estimated from the data (i.e., it is identified), but the demand curve cannot (i.e., it is unidentified). This is reflected in the fact that any linear combination of the supply and demand curves gives an equation that looks like the demand curve, but no combination can be found that looks like the supply curve. Note, however, that it is not necessarily the case that a scatter of observations like this corresponds to an identified case; it is possible, for example, that the supply curve could itself have shifted with changes in the exogenous variable income, as illustrated in figure 10.3. This emphasizes the role of the restriction that the exogenous variable must not affect the supply curve; in general, identification results only through an appropriate set of restrictions.

In a simple example such as the foregoing, it is easy to check for identification; in more complicated systems, however, it is not so easy. In general, how does an econometrician know whether or not his or her system of simultaneous equations contains enough restrictions to circumvent the identification problem? This task is made a little simpler by the fact that each equation in a system of simultaneous equations can be checked separately to see if its structural parameters are identified. Mathematical investigation has shown that in the case of zero restrictions on structural parameters each equation can be checked for identification by using a rule called the *rank condition*. It turns out, however, that this rule is quite awkward to employ (see the technical notes to this section for further discussion of this rule), and as a result a simpler rule, called the *order condition*, is used in its stead. This rule only requires counting included and excluded variables in each equation (see the general notes to this section). Unfortunately, this order condition is only a necessary condition, not a sufficient one, so that, tech-

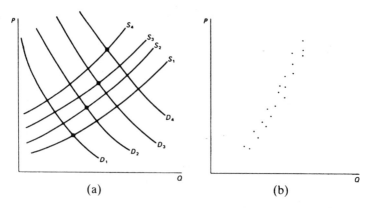

Figure 10.3 Neither supply nor demand identified

nically speaking, the rank condition must also be checked. Many econometricians do not bother doing this, however, gambling that the rank condition will be satisfied (as it usually is) if the order condition is satisfied. This procedure is not recommended.

If all equations in a system are identified, the system or model is said to be identified. If only some equations are identified, only the structural parameters associated with those equations can be estimated; structural parameters associated with unidentified equations cannot be estimated; i.e., there does not exist a meaningful way of estimating these parameters. The only way in which the structural parameters of these unidentified equations can be identified (and thus be capable of being estimated) is through imposition of further restrictions, or use of more extraneous information. Such restrictions, of course, must be imposed only if their validity can be defended.

If an equation is identified, it may be either "just-identified" or "over-identified." An equation is *just-identified* if the number of identifying restrictions placed on the model is the minimum needed to identify the equation; an equation is *over-identified* if there are some extra restrictions beyond the minimum necessary to identify the equation. The case of over-identification seems to be the most prevalent. The relevance of this distinction relates to the choice of estimator. In some cases, applying a complicated estimation technique to a just-identified equation is no different from applying a simpler (and thus less costly) estimation technique. One technique (the indirect least squares estimator) can be applied only to just-identified equations. Discussion of the various estimators used in the simultaneous equations context should clarify this.

10.3 SINGLE-EQUATION METHODS

The estimators described in this section are called "single-equation" methods because they are used to estimate a system of simultaneous equations by estimating each equation (provided it is identified) separately. The "systems" methods discussed in section 10.4 estimate all the (identified) equations in a system simultaneously; they are sometimes called "full information" methods because they incorporate knowledge of all the restrictions in the system when estimating each parameter. Single-equation methods are sometimes called "limited information" methods because they only utilize knowledge of the restrictions in the particular equation being estimated. Five single-equation methods are discussed in this section:

(1) Ordinary least squares (OLS).
(2) Indirect least squares (ILS).
(3) Instrumental variables (IV).
(4) Two-stage least squares (2SLS).
(5) Limited information, maximum likelihood (LI/ML).

Of all these methods, 2SLS is by far the most popular. The brief discussions of the other methods provide a useful perspective from which to view 2SLS and simultaneous equation estimation in general.

(1)   ORDINARY LEAST SQUARES (OLS)

It is possible to use the OLS estimator and simply accept its asymptotic bias. This can be defended in several ways.

(a) Although the OLS estimator is biased, in small samples so also are all alternative estimators. Furthermore, the OLS estimator has minimum variance among these alternative estimators. Thus it is quite possible that in small samples the OLS estimator has minimum mean square error. Monte Carlo studies have shown, however, that this is true only in very small samples.

(b) According to Monte Carlo studies, the properties of the OLS estimator are less sensitive than the alternative estimators to the presence of estimation problems such as multicollinearity, errors in variables or misspecifications, particularly in small samples.

(c) Predictions from simultaneous equation models estimated by OLS often compare quite favorably with predictions from the same models estimated by alternative means.

(d) OLS can be useful as a preliminary or exploratory estimator.

(e) If a simultaneous equation system is recursive (described in the general notes to section 10.1), OLS is no longer asymptotically biased and is unbiased if there are no lagged endogenous variables and no correlation between disturbances in different equations. This is discussed in the general notes to section 10.1.

(2) INDIRECT LEAST SQUARES (ILS)

Suppose we wish to estimate a structural equation containing, say, three endogenous variables. The first step of the ILS technique is to estimate the reduced-form equations for these three endogenous variables. If the structural equation in question is just identified, there will be only one way of calculating the desired estimates of the structural equation parameters from the reduced-form parameter estimates. The structural parameters are expressed in terms of the reduced-form parameters, and the OLS estimates of the reduced-form parameters are plugged in these expressions to produce estimates of the structural parameters. Because these expressions are nonlinear, however, unbiased estimates of the reduced-form parameters produce only consistent estimates of the structural parameters, not unbiased estimates (recall the discussion of this in the technical notes to section 2.8). If an equation is over-identified, the extra identifying restrictions provide additional ways of calculating the structural parameters from the reduced-form parameters, all of which are *supposed* to lead to the same values of the structural parameters. But because the estimates of the reduced-form parameters do not embody these extra restrictions, these different ways of calculating the structural parameters create different estimates of these parameters. (This is because unrestricted estimates rather than actual values of the parameters are being used for these calculations, as illustrated in the technical notes to this section.) Because there is no way of determining which of these different estimates is the most appropriate, ILS is not used for over-identified equations. The other simultaneous equation estimating techniques have been designed to estimate structural parameters in the over-identified case; many of these can be shown to be equivalent to ILS in the context of a just-identified equation, and to be weighted averages of the different estimates produced by ILS in the context of over-identified equations.

(3) INSTRUMENTAL VARIABLES (IV)

As seen in section 9.3, the instrumental variable technique is a general estimation procedure applicable to situations in which the independent variable is not independent of the disturbance. If an appropriate instrumental variable can be found for each endogenous variable that appears as a regressor in a simultaneous equation, the instrumental variable technique provides consistent estimates. The big problem with this approach, of course, is finding appropriate instrumental variables; exogenous variables in the system of simultaneous equations are considered the best candidates since they are correlated with the endogenous variables (through the interaction of the simultaneous system) and are uncorrelated with the disturbances (by the assumption of exogeneity).

(4) TWO-STAGE LEAST SQUARES (2SLS)

This technique is a special case of the instrumental variable technique in which the "best" instrumental variables are used. As noted above, the exogenous variables are all good candidates for instrumental variables; which is the best is difficult to determine. A natural suggestion is to combine all the exogenous variables to create a combined variable to act as a "best" instrumental variable. A good instrumental variable is one that is highly correlated with the regressor for which it is acting as an instrument. This suggests regressing each endogenous variable being used as a regressor on all the exogenous variables in the system and using the estimated values of these endogenous variables from this regression as the required instrumental variables. (Each estimated value is the "best" instrumental variable in the sense that, of all combinations of the exogenous variables, it has highest correlation with the endogenous variable.) This defines the 2SLS procedure:

Stage 1: regress each endogenous variable acting as a regressor in the equation being estimated on *all* the exogenous variables in the system of simultaneous equations (i.e., estimate the reduced form), and calculate the estimated values of these endogenous variables.

Stage 2: use these estimated values as instrumental variables for these endogenous variables *or* simply use these estimated values and the included exogenous variables as regressors in an OLS regression. (It happens that these two versions of the second stage give identical coefficient estimates.)

Because the 2SLS estimator is a legitimate instrumental variable estimator, we know that it is consistent. Monte Carlo studies have shown it to have small-sample properties superior on most criteria to all other estimators. They have also shown it to be quite robust (i.e., its desirable properties are insensitive to the presence of other estimating problems such as multicollinearity and specification errors). These results, combined with its low computational cost, have made the 2SLS estimator the most popular of all simultaneous equations estimators. Since it is equivalent to ILS in the just-identified case, 2SLS is usually applied uniformly to all identified equations in the system.

(5) LIMITED INFORMATION, MAXIMUM LIKELIHOOD (LI/ML)

In this technique, estimates of the reduced-form parameters are created by maximizing the likelihood function of the reduced-form disturbances *subject* to the zero restrictions on the structural parameters in the equation being estimated. (Only that part of the reduced form corresponding to the endogenous variables appearing in the structural equation in question need be estimated.) These estimates of the reduced-form parameters are then used, as in ILS, to create estimates of the structural parameters; because the zero restrictions have been built into the reduced-form estimates, the multiple ILS estimates of the over-identified case all turn out to be the same. In the just-identified case LI/ML is identical to ILS and 2SLS if the errors are distributed normally. An alternative (equivalent) way of viewing this procedure is as an application of instrumental variables: the reduced-form parameter estimates from this technique can be used to calculate estimated values of the endogenous variables included in the equation being estimated, and these can in turn be used as instrumental variables as in the 2SLS procedure. The LI/ML estimator is therefore consistent.

The usual assumption made is that the structural disturbances are distributed multivariate normally, implying that the reduced-form disturbances are also distributed multivariate normally. Under this condition the LI/ML is identical to the limited information, least generalized variance (LI/LGV) and the limited information, least variance ratio (LI/LVR) estimators, discussed in the technical notes to this section. Furthermore, these estimators, and the 2SLS estimator, which just happens to share the same asymptotic variance–covariance matrix, are at least as efficient asymptotically as any other estimator using the same amount of information. (This follows from maximum likelihood properties.)

10.4   SYSTEMS METHODS

Systems estimating procedures estimate *all* the identified structural equations together as a set, instead of estimating the structural parameters of each equation separately. These systems methods are also called "full information" methods because they utilize knowledge of *all* the zero restrictions in the entire system when estimating the structural parameters. Their major advantage is that, because they incorporate all of the available information into their estimates, they have a smaller asymptotic variance–covariance matrix than single-equation estimators. By the same token, however, if the system is misspecified (if an alleged zero restriction is incorrect, for example) the estimates of *all* the structural parameters are affected, rather than, in the case of single-equation estimation techniques, only the estimates of the structural parameters of one equation. This and their high computational costs are the major drawbacks of the systems methods. The two major systems methods are discussed briefly below.

(1)   THREE-STAGE LEAST SQUARES (3SLS)

This method is the systems counterpart of 2SLS. Its structure is based on an alternative interpretation of 2SLS: if a single equation is multiplied through (transformed) by the transpose of the matrix of observations on *all* the exogenous variables in the system, applying GLS to this new (transformed) relationship creates the 2SLS estimates. Now if all the equations to be estimated are transformed in this way, stacked one on top of the other, and then this stack is rewritten as a single, very large, equation, applying GLS to this giant equation should produce the 2SLS estimates of each of the component equations. Because the nonspherical disturbance of this giant equation can incorporate nonzero correlations between disturbances in different equations, however, these estimates can differ from the 2SLS estimates and are more efficient. This defines the 3SLS procedure.

The variance–covariance matrix of this giant equation's disturbance can be shown to involve the matrix of observations on all the exogenous variables in the system and the contemporaneous variance–covariance matrix of the structural equation's disturbances. (This matrix contains the variances of each equation's disturbances along the diagonal and the covariance between equations' disturbances in the off-diagonal positions.) The former matrix is known but the latter must be estimated (from estimates of the structural equations' disturbances). The 3SLS procedure can be summarized as follows:

Stage 1: calculate the 2SLS estimates of the identified equations.

Stage 2: use the 2SLS estimates to estimate the structural equations' errors, and then use these to estimate the contemporaneous variance–covariance matrix of the structural equations' errors.

Stage 3: apply GLS to the large equation representing all the identified equations of the system.

The 3SLS estimator is consistent and in general is asymptotically more efficient than the 2SLS estimator. If the disturbances in the different structural equations are uncorrelated, so that the contemporaneous variance–covariance matrix of the disturbances of the structural equations is diagonal, 3SLS reduces to 2SLS.

(2) FULL INFORMATION, MAXIMUM LIKELIHOOD (FI/ML)

This systems method corresponds to the single-equation technique LI/ML. In this technique estimates of *all* the reduced-form parameters (rather than just those corresponding to the endogenous variables included in a particular equation) are found by maximizing the likelihood function of the reduced-form disturbances, subject to the zero restirctions on *all* the structural parameters in the system. The usual assumption made is that the structural disturbances, and thus the reduced-form disturbances, are distributed multivariate normally. Under this condition the FI/ML estimator and the 3SLS estimator, which share the same asymptotic variance–covariance matrix, are at least as efficient asymptotically as any other estimator that uses the same amount of information. (This follows from maximum likelihood properties.)

10.5 VARs

Simultaneous equations models have been criticized on a number of grounds. Macroeconomic theory is not viewed with much confidence, the models are expensive to obtain and run, forecasts are often unreasonable, requiring judgemental adjustment, and confidence intervals seem unreasonably narrow. Further, many complain that the restrictions placed on a simultaneous equations model to identify it are "incredible" because in a general equilibrium analysis all economic variables will affect all other variables. This implies that all variables are endogenous and that the only equations that can be estimated are reduced-form equations in which the regressors/exogenous variables are all lagged values of the endogenous variables.

The alternative approach this argument suggests is called *vector autoregression*, or VAR; it postulates that all the variables in the system are endogenous and that each can be written as a linear function of its own lagged values and the lagged values of all the other variables in the system, where the number of lags is to be determined somehow. If all the variables are gathered into a single vector, this can be viewed as a vector autoregression – this vector is expressed as a linear function of its own lagged values (with several lags) plus an error vector. Estimation is undertaken by running a separate regression for each variable, regressing it on lags of itself and all other variables.

The VAR approach is controversial. Even more controversial, however, is the way the advocates of VAR have chosen to present and interpret their results. The vector autoregression equation is "solved" or "inverted" to express the vector of current values of the variables in terms purely of current and (an infinite number of) lagged values of the error vector (i.e., the lagged values of the vector of variables are algebraically eliminated from the vector autoregression), and then this representation is transformed into an "orthogonal" form in which the vector of current values of the variables is expressed as a linear function of current and lagged values of a vector of "orthogonal innovations" (errors whose current values are uncorrelated). The algebra of all of this is straightforward – the relationship between the orthogonal innovations and the vector of current values of the variables under study can be estimated using the estimates of the vector autoregression discussed above. What is controversial about these orthogonalized innovations is how they are interpreted – as an innovation in one variable that does not affect the current value of any other variable. What this means is not clear – how can a change in one variable have no effect on any other variable in a simultaneous system?

Despite all this controversy, VARs have come to be accepted as legitimate competitors to simultaneous equation systems for several purposes, the most prominent being forecasting. It should be noted, however, that some econometricians view VARs as no more than an evolutionary step along the road to more adequate dynamic modeling. See chapter 17 for further discussion.

GENERAL NOTES

10.1 Introduction

- Simultaneous equations used to be the "bread and butter" of econometrics – it was viewed as the main feature of econometrics that made it different from traditional statistics. This is no longer the case, perhaps because, in spite of its shortcomings, OLS still performs relatively well in this context, but more likely because the non-experimental data with which econometricians must work has given rise to so many other interesting problems. The decreased emphasis on simultaneous equation estimation problems is reflected in econometrics textbooks, as noted by Buse (1988): "This failure to be as thorough in the simultaneous equations context is perhaps an indication of the general decline of interest in the simultaneous equations model. The action, so to speak, is elsewhere, and textbook discussion of this model now appears to be more a matter of habit than of conviction."

- The Hausman test, a test for contemporaneous correlation between the error and regressors, is used to test for exogeneity/endogeneity of variables, as explained in the technical notes. Recall from the technical notes to section 5.3 that there are three different types of "exogeneity."

- Not all sets of equations are simultaneous. Several equations might be connected not because they interact, but because their error terms are related. For example, if these equations are demand functions, a shock affecting demand for one good may spill over and affect demand for other goods. In this case, estimating these equations as a set, using a single (large) regression, should improve efficiency. This technique, due to Zellner (1962) is called SURE (seemingly unrelated regression estimation); a description is given in the technical notes. A good example of its use is in estimating parameters of a general production function, such as the translog, via its associated set of interrelated input demand equations; Berndt (1991, chapter 9) is a good exposition of this example. Greene (1997, chapter 15) is an excellent textbook presentation of systems of regression equations, discussing many applications and expositing related tests.

- Lagged values of endogenous variables are treated as exogenous variables, because for determination of the current period's values of the endogenous variables they are given constants. For this reason the exogenous and lagged endogenous variables are often called *predetermined* variables. Their use as regressors creates reduced-form estimates that are biased but asymptotically unbiased (assuming the errors are not autocorrelated), as noted in section 9.3. This is not of concern in the context of structural simultaneous equation estimation, because all estimators used in this context are biased anyway; they are chosen on the basis of their asymptotic properties.

- Not all simultaneous equations systems suffer from the simultaneous equation estimation bias described in this chapter. A *recursive system* is one in which there is unidirectional dependency among the endogenous variables. The equations can be ordered such that the first endogenous variable is determined only by exogenous variables, the second determined only by the first endogenous variable and exogenous variables, the third by only the first two endogenous variables and exogenous variables, and so forth. There must be no feedback from an endogenous variable to one lower in the causal chain. In a recursive system, a change in the disturbance in the fourth equation, for example, affects directly the fourth endogenous variable, which in turn affects the higher-ordered endogenous variables in the system, but does *not* affect the lower-ordered endogenous variables. Because only lower-ordered variables appear as regressors in the fourth equation, there is no contemporaneous correlation between the disturbance and the regressors in the fourth equation. If there is no correlation between disturbances in different equations, OLS estimation is consistent, and if no lagged endogenous variables appear among the exogenous variables in the equation, it is unbiased.

- For an interesting discussion of problems associated with applying econometric techniques to the estimation of simultaneous equation systems, see Kmenta (1972). The application of simultaneous equation estimation with the highest profile is that of macroeconometric model-building; see Bodkin et al. (1991) for a history, and Intriligator et al. (1996, pp. 432–53) for a survey of US macroeconometric models.

10.2 Identification

- Goldberger (1964, pp. 312–13) and Greene (1997, p. 722) show how transforming structural parameters creates a new set of structural parameters with the same reduced-form parameters.
- Before the identification problem was recognized by economists, demand studies for agricultural products were undertaken using OLS. They gave good results, though, because the demand curve was relatively stable whereas the supply curve was quite erratic. This provides an example of how extraneous information could be used to identify an equation. If there is no exogenous variable in either the supply or the demand equation but the disturbance term in the supply equation is known to have a very high variance relative to the disturbance term in the demand equation, the data observations should trace out a demand curve in the same sense that a supply curve was traced out in figure 10.2. Thus, prior knowledge of the relative variances of the disturbances can aid in identification.
- The popularity of zero restrictions as a means of identifying equations probably stems from the fact that this method is easier to apply and has been given formal mathematical treatment. Other means do exist, however. Johnston (1984, pp. 463–6) and Maddala (1977, pp. 226–8) discuss the use of restrictions on the contemporaneous variance–covariance matrix of the simultaneous system. (This matrix contains the variance of the disturbance in each equation along the diagonal, and the contemporaneous covariances between equations' disturbances in the off-diagonal positions.) Christ (1966, pp. 334–43) discusses the use of restrictions on the range of an error term, knowledge of the ratio of two error term variances, and knowledge of the covariance between two equations' error terms. Maddala (1977, pp. 228–31) discusses non-homogeneous restrictions, nonlinearities and cross-equation restrictions. Greene (1997, pp. 724–34) has a good textbook exposition of several means of identification.
- Haynes and Stone (1985) claim that in many markets quantity tends to be demand-determined in the short run, but price tends to be supply-determined. They specify quantity as a function of lagged price (among other variables) for the demand curve, and price as a function of lagged quantity (among other variables) for the supply curve, creating a means of solving the identification problem for these types of markets. Leamer (1981) shows how knowledge of the sign of a coefficient in an unidentified equation, for example that the slope of price in the demand curve is negative, whereas in the supply curve it is positive, can be used in conjunction with reverse regression to estimate bounds for coefficient values, thereby "partially" identifying that equation.
- The order condition is written in many different (equivalent) ways in textbooks, all involving counting included and excluded variables of different types. The best of these ways is to check if there are enough exogenous (predetermined) variables excluded from the equation in question to provide an instrumental variable for each of the endogenous variables appearing as regressors in that equation. (The number of

excluded exogenous variables must be greater than or equal to the number of included endogenous variables less 1.) Maddala (1977, p. 234) gives some reasons why this way of checking the order condition is preferred to others. Maddala (1988, pp. 301–4) spells out an operational procedure for checking the rank condition; Harvey (1990, p. 328) notes that "the order condition is usually sufficient to ensure identifiability, and although it is important to be aware of the rank condition, a failure to verify it will rarely result in disaster."

- An equation is "just identified" if there are exactly enough exogenous variables excluded from the equation to act as instrumental variables for the endogenous variables appearing as regressors in that equation. It is over-identified if there are more than enough excluded exogenous variables.
- Over-identification can be thought of as a case in which the specification of the structural equation imposes restrictions on the reduced form.
- Identifying restrictions cannot be tested (because their validity must be assumed for meaningful estimation), but, as explained in the technical notes, over-identifying restrictions *can* be tested. Such tests, when undertaken, usually reject the over-identifying restrictions, casting doubt on the identifying restrictions since the over-identifying restrictions cannot be separated from the identifying restrictions. A skeptic might use this fact to explain why economists seldom undertake such tests. Hausman (1983, pp. 430–5) reviews available tests. Greene (1997, pp. 761–4) has a textbook exposition.

10.3   Single-equation Methods

- Little is known about the small-sample properties of simultaneous equation estimators. Several Monte Carlo studies exist, however; for a survey see Challen and Hagger (1983, pp. 117–21) or Johnston (1972, pp. 408–20). Unfortunately, the results from these studies are not clear-cut, mainly because the results are peculiar to the model specifications used in the Monte Carlo experiments. Furthermore, it turns out that many methods are not robust, in the sense that their performance on the usual estimating criteria is sensitive to things such as sample size, specification errors, the presence of multicollinearity, etc. This makes it difficult to draw general conclusions concerning the relative desirability of the many simultaneous equation estimators. These Monte Carlo studies have consistently ranked 2SLS quite highly, however, so that many econometricians recommend 2SLS for general use.
- Researchers use estimates of the asymptotic variances of simultaneous equation estimators to undertake hypothesis tests; although these estimates are usually underestimates of the true variances, alternative methods have not proved superior. See Maddala (1974).
- Autocorrelated errors in simultaneous equations cause inefficiency if there are no lagged endogenous variables, and inconsistency if there are lagged endogenous variables. In the former case estimation is done in two stages. In the first stage a consistent estimator, such as 2SLS, is used to get residuals that are used to estimate the autocorrelation coefficient, and in the second stage the variables are transformed and a consistent estimator is applied to the transformed variables. In the latter case, it is necessary to treat the lagged endogenous variables as though they were endogenous. Greene (1997, pp. 748–9) has a good text book exposition. Fair (1970) claims that for strong-

ly autocorrelated errors it is more important to correct for that problem than for the asymptotic bias due to simultaneity. Breusch and Godfrey (1981) is a good discussion of testing for autocorrelated errors in this context.

- In large econometric models it may be impossible to apply 2SLS because the total number of exogenous variables in the system exceeds the number of observations, making calculation of the reduced form (the first stage of 2SLS) impossible. This problem is usually solved by using, in the first stage of 2SLS, a small number of principal components in place of the exogenous variables excluded from the equation in question. See McCarthy (1971). A principal component is a linear combination of variables that captures as much of the variation in those variables as it is possible to capture via a linear combination of those variables (see section 11.4). If this procedure is followed the instrumental variable estimation of the second stage of 2SLS must be employed; the other variant of this second stage is no longer valid.

- Although the two versions of the second stage of 2SLS yield identical coefficient estimates, they do not produce the same estimates of the variance–covariance matrix. The version using estimated values of endogenous variables as regressors, rather than as instruments, produces incorrect estimates of the variance–covariance matrix. This happens because its estimate of the variance of the error term is computed using residuals calculated with estimated, rather than actual, values of these endogenous variables. For discussion of the use of F and LM tests in the context of 2SLS, see Wooldridge (1990). Hsu (1991) finds that a bootstrap test outperforms the F test in this context.

- When 2SLS is applied to an over-identified equation, a particular endogenous variable is chosen, from the set of endogenous variables included in that equation, to be the left-hand-side variable in that equation, and is given the coefficient 1. If the econometrician is uncertain of this specification, and a different endogenous variable is picked to play this role, the 2SLS procedure creates different estimates of the *same* parameters (i.e., after renormalizing to put a coefficient of 1 on the original variable chosen to be the left-hand-side variable). The LI/ML method does not suffer from this normalization problem; it creates a unique estimate that lies between the extremes of the different possible 2SLS estimates. The fact that 2SLS is sensitive to the normalization choice should not necessarily be viewed as a disadvantage, however. It could be claimed that this sensitivity allows economic theory (which usually suggests a specific normalization) to inject some extra information into the estimating procedure. The normalization problem does not exist for a just-identified equation. See Fisher (1976) for further discussion.

- Challen and Hagger (1983, chapter 6) contains an excellent discussion of practical reasons (such as nonlinearities, undersized samples, autocorrelated errors and computational cost) why most simultaneous equations systems are estimated by OLS, or some variant thereof, rather than by one of the more sophisticated estimating techniques introduced in this chapter.

10.4   Systems Methods

- The superiority of 3SLS is slight if the contemporaneous variance–covariance matrix of the structural equations' disturbances is only slightly different from a diagonal matrix or the sample size is small so that it cannot be well estimated. Unfortunately there is no easy rule to determine when 3SLS beats 2SLS. Belsey (1988b) suggests using the determinant, the smallest eigenvalue or the condition number of the contemporaneous correlation matrix between the equations' errors to index the potential superiority of 3SLS, but finds that threshold values of these measures depend on the circumstances of the problem, such as the sample size, the number of equations and the degree of overidentification (3SLS and 2SLS are identical if every equation is just identified). Some practitioners use a rule of thumb that 3SLS is superior if the estimated contemporaneous correlation between any two equations' errors exceeds one-third.

- 3SLS, like 2SLS, is not invariant to the choice of normalization.
- The 3SLS method can be iterated by using the original 3SLS estimates to create new estimates of the structural disturbances and repeating the rest of the 3SLS calculations. This "iterated 3SLS" estimator has the same asymptotic properties as the original 3SLS estimates. Monte Carlo studies have not shown it to be markedly superior to 3SLS.
- If there is extraneous information concerning the contemporaneous variance–covariance matrix of the structural equations' errors, or if there are lagged endogenous variables, FI/ML is asymptotically more efficient than 3SLS.
- The estimating techniques discussed in this chapter are designed to estimate the structural parameters. It may be, however, that the econometrician is only interested in the reduced-form parameters, in which case he or she could avoid estimating the structural parameters and simply estimate the reduced-form parameters by applying OLS to each of the reduced-form equations (i.e., regress each endogenous variable on all the endogenous variables in the system). If some structural equations are over-identified, however, more efficient estimates of the reduced-form parameters can be obtained by taking structural parameter estimates (that incorporate the over-identifying restrictions) and using them to estimate directly the reduced-form parameters. Although these "derived" reduced-form estimates are biased (whereas the OLS reduced-form estimates are not), they are consistent, and because they incorporate the over-identifying information, are asymptotically more efficient than the OLS reduced-form estimates. Monte Carlo studies have shown the derived reduced-form estimates to have desirable small-sample properties. Of course, if the over-identifying restrictions are untrue, the OLS reduced-form estimates will be superior; a suggested means of testing over-identifying restrictions is through comparison of predictions using OLS reduced-form estimates and derived reduced-form estimates.

10.5   VARs

- The VAR approach is due to Sims (1980). Pagan (1987) views VAR as a major methodological approach to econometrics, and in Pagan (1995) argues that it is evolving into a method more compatible with traditional simultaneous equations analysis. Cooley and LeRoy (1985) is an oft-cited critique of the VAR methodology. They claim that it is useful for forecasting, for describing various characteristics of the data, for searching for hypotheses worthy of interest, and for testing some types of theories, but argue that it is not suitable for testing exogeneity, that its concept of innovations (and the related impulse response function – a graph of the impact of an innovation over time) is not useful, and that it cannot be used for policy evaluation. Runkle (1987) and associated commentary is a good example of the controversy surrounding this methodology. Harvey (1997, p. 199) claims that VAR actually stands for "Very Awful Regression."

- A VAR is in essence a reduced form corresponding to a class of structural econometric models. Advocates of the VAR methodology have come to recognize that the interpretation of VAR estimation results is considerably enhanced by viewing them in terms of the restrictions they impose on the underlying class of structural models. Its value in econometric modeling stems from the empirical relationships (strong correlations in the data, lag lengths, list of included variables) it reveals that the structural model must be capable of explaining.

- The conclusions drawn from VAR analyses are sensitive to the choice of lag length and the number of included variables, for neither of which there is an agreed upon choice mechanism. Since VAR presumes that no variables are exogenous, and that all variables, each with multiple lags, appear in each equation, it usually faces severe degrees-of-freedom problems. This forces modelers to choose a small set of variables.

- Backus (1986) is a good example of an empirical application of the VAR methodology, along with commentary defending its use. Ambler (1989) is a good example of VAR in conjunction with testing for unit roots, searching for cointegration, and developing an ECM (all discussed in chapter 17). McNees (1986) has a concise comparison of VAR and the traditional approach in the context of its use and success in forecasting. The software package RATS (Regression Analysis of Time Series) is popular for estimating VARs.

- Although VARs are usually estimated without restrictions, to avoid the "incredible" restrictions placed on econometric structural models, studies have shown that imposing reasonable restrictions on VARs improves their performance. The usual methodology of either including or excluding a variable is thought to embody unreasonably weak prior information in the former case, or unreasonably strong prior information in the latter case. An appealing way of addressing this problem is through a Bayesian VAR approach, as discussed in Litterman (1986). One example of the kind of prior that is employed is a prior with mean zero for the coefficients of lagged variables, with the prior variance becoming smaller as the lag length grows.

TECHNICAL NOTES

10.1 Introduction

- The Hausman test for contemporaneous correlation between the error and a regressor was described in chapter 9. Its application in the context of this chapter is to test for endogeneity/exogeneity of regressors. Suppose $y = Y\delta + X\beta + \varepsilon$ and we wish to test all the variables in Y for exogeneity. This is done exactly as in chapter 9, via an OV version of the Hausman test. Estimated Y values, Y^*, are formed from the instruments (all the exogenous variables in the system), y is regressed on Y, X and Y^*, and the coefficient estimate of Y^* is tested against zero using an F test.

  This test becomes more complicated if only some of the elements of Y are to be tested for exogeneity. Suppose $y = Y_1\delta_1 + Y_2\delta_2 + X\beta + \varepsilon$ and it is desired to test Y_2 for exogeneity. This case is different from those examined earlier because rather than comparing OLS to IV, we are now comparing one IV to another IV. Spencer and Berk (1981) show that a regular Hausman test can be structured, to compare the 2SLS estimates with and without assuming Y_2 exogeneous. An OV form of this test is also available, and defended on asymptotic grounds: run the usual 2SLS second-stage regression that would be used if Y_2 were assumed to be exogenous, but add in the extra regressors Y_1^* and Y_2^*, the second-stage 2SLS regressors (corresponding to Y_1 and Y_2) that would be used if Y_2 were assumed to be endogenous, and test the coefficients of Y_1^* and Y_2^* jointly against zero.

- SURE consists of writing a set of individual equations as one giant equation. Suppose there are N equations $Y_1 = X_i\beta_i + \varepsilon_i$ where the subscript i refers to the ith equation. (Here each Y_i, β_i and ε_i are vectors; X_i is a data matrix.) These equations are written as

$$
\begin{bmatrix} Y_1 \\ Y_2 \\ \vdots \\ Y_n \end{bmatrix} = \begin{bmatrix} X_1 & & \\ & X_2 & O \\ & O & \ddots \\ & & X_n \end{bmatrix} \begin{bmatrix} \beta_1 \\ \beta_2 \\ \vdots \\ \beta_n \end{bmatrix} + \begin{bmatrix} \varepsilon_1 \\ \varepsilon_2 \\ \vdots \\ \varepsilon_n \end{bmatrix}
$$

or $Y^* = X^*\beta^* + \varepsilon^*$.

Now if we allow contemporaneous correlation between the error terms across equations, so that, for example, the tth error term in the ith equation is correlated with the tth error term in the jth equation, the variance–covariance matrix of ε^* will not be diagonal. Estimating these error correlations and the diagonal elements (by using the residuals from each equation estimated separately) should allow estimation of the variance–covariance matrix of ε^* and generation of EGLS estimates of β^*. Aigner (1971, pp. 197–204) has a good textbook exposition. No gains can be realized from this procedure (because SURE becomes identical to OLS) if either (a) the X_i are all the same, or (b) the variance–covariance matrix of ε^* is diagonal. Kmenta and Gilbert (1968) find that if the errors are distributed normally, iterating SURE (by re-estimating the variance–covariance matrix of ε^* using the most-recent SURE coefficient estimates) yields the MLE estimates.

Breusch and Pagan (1980) suggest an LM test for testing whether this variance–covariance matrix is diagonal. Estimate the correlation coefficient between the ith and jth residuals from OLS. The sample size times the sum of all these squared estimated correlations is distributed as a chi-square with degrees of freedom equal to the number of correlations. The comparable likelihood ratio statistic is the sample size times the difference between the sum of the logarithms of the OLS variance estimates and the logarithm of the determinant of the unrestricted maximum likelihood estimate of the contemporaneous variance–covariance matrix.

10.2 Identification

- The order condition for identification through the use of zero restrictions can be generalized in terms of homogenous linear restrictions: an equation is identified if there are $G - 1$ independent homogenous linear restrictions on the parameters of that equation, where G is the number of equations in the system. (A linear homogenous restriction equates to zero a linear combination of parameter values; for example, it may be specified that consumption is a function of disposable income so that the coefficient on income is equal in value but opposite in sign to the coefficient on taxes – their sum would be zero.) A similar generalization exists for the rank condition. See Fisher (1966, chapter 2).

- The "impossible to find a linear combination" view of identification can be used to check informally the rank condition for instances in which the order condition holds. A visual inspection of the pattern of included, and excluded, variables in a system of equations can often verify that:

  (a) it is not possible to form a linear combination of the equations in the system that looks like the equation being tested for identification;
  (b) it is obviously possible to do so; or
  (c) it is only possible to do so if the values of the parameters in the system bear a particular (and unlikely) relationship to one another.

Examples of these three cases are given below. If an econometrician is not confident that his visual inspection for the possibility of a linear combination was adequate, he can test the rank condition formally: the matrix of parameters (from all equations) associated with all the variables excluded from the equation in question must have rank equal to one less than the number of equations in the system.

- *Examples of case (a)*   Suppose we have the following two-equation model, where the y are endogenous variables, the x are exogenous variables and the θ are parameters. (For simplicity the constant terms, errors, and the normalization choice are ignored.)

$$y_1 + \theta_2 y_2 + \theta_3 x_1 \qquad\qquad = 0$$
$$y_1 + \theta_5 y_2 \qquad\qquad\qquad = 0$$

The second equation is identified by the order condition and there is clearly no way in which these equations can be combined to produce a new equation looking like the second equation; the rank condition must be satisfied. This is the example illustrated by figure 10.2.

- *Examples of case (b)*   Suppose a third equation is added to the previous example, introducing a new endogenous variable y_3 and a new exogenous variable x_2. The first equation now satisfies the order condition (because of the extra exogenous variable in the system). But the sum of the first and second equations yields an equation containing the same variables as the first equation, so the rank condition cannot be satisfied for this equation. In general, this problem arises whenever all the variables contained in one equation form a subset of variables in another equation; this is fairly easy to check visually.

Not all examples of case (b) are so easy to check, however. Consider the following four-equation example:

$$y_2 + \theta_2 y_3 \qquad\quad + \theta_3 x_1 \qquad\qquad\qquad = 0$$
$$y_1 + \theta_5 y_2 \qquad\quad + \theta_6 y_4 + \theta_7 x_1 \qquad\qquad = 0$$
$$y_1 \qquad\quad + \theta_9 y_3 \qquad\qquad + \theta_{10} x_2 + \theta_{11} x_3 = 0$$
$$y_1 \qquad\quad + \theta_{13} y_3 + \theta_{14} y_4 + \theta_{15} x_1 \qquad\qquad = 0$$

The second equation satisfies the order condition, but if θ_2 / θ_{13} times the fourth equation is subtracted from the first equation, a new equation is created that has the same included and excluded variables as the second equation, so the rank condition is not satisfied for this equation.

- *Examples of case (c)* Suppose we have the following three-equation model:

$$y_1 + \theta_2 y_2 \quad\quad + \theta_3 x_1 \quad\quad\quad\quad\quad = 0$$
$$y_1 \quad\quad + \theta_5 y_3 \quad\quad\quad + \theta_6 x_2 \quad\quad = 0$$
$$y_1 + \theta_8 y_2 + \theta_9 y_3 + \theta_{10} x_1 + \theta_{11} x_2 \quad = 0$$

The first equation is identified by the order condition. If it happens that $\theta_5 = k\theta_9$ and $\theta_6 = k\theta_{11}$, then the second equation minus k times the third equation (i.e., a particular linear combination of the second and third equations) will create an equation with the same included and excluded variables as the first equation; the rank condition is not met. In practice, the third case is usually ignored, since the probability is virtually zero that the true values of the parameters are related in this way.

- The easiest test for over-identifying restrictions for a single equation is an LM test. Obtain the residuals from an efficient single-equation estimator and regress them on all of the predetermined variables in the model. The sample size times the R^2 from this regression will be distributed asymptotically as a chi-square with degrees of freedom equal to the number of overidentifying restrictions (i.e., the number of predetermined variables outside that equation less the number of endogenous variables serving as regressors).

  The easiest test for over-identifying restrictions for an entire system of simultaneous equations is an LR test. Obtain the reduced-form residuals and the derived reduced-form residuals using an efficient systems estimation method. Use these residuals to estimate the respective contemporaneous variance–covariance matrices of the reduced-form errors. Then the sample size times the difference between the logarithms of the determinants of these estimated matrices is distributed as a chi-square with degrees of freedom equal to the total number of over-identifying restrictions. See Greene (1997, pp. 761–2) for discussion of both these tests.

10.3   Single-equation Methods

- Consider estimating by indirect least squares the just-identified supply equation corresponding to the example illustrated in figure 10.2. Ignoring constant terms for simplicity, suppose the demand equation can be written as $q = \beta p + \gamma y$ where q is quantity, p is price and y is income (exogenously determined). Write the supply function as $q = \delta p$. Solving these equations for the reduced form, we get

$$p = \frac{\gamma}{\delta - \beta} y = \pi_1 y$$

$$q = \frac{\gamma\delta}{\delta - \beta} y = \pi_2 y.$$

OLS estimation of these reduced-form equations yields unbiased estimates $\hat{\pi}_1$ and $\hat{\pi}_2$ of π_1 and π_2. Since $\pi_2/\pi_1 = \delta$, $\hat{\pi}_2/\hat{\pi}_1$ is the ILS estimate of δ; this estimate is not unbiased, since $\hat{\pi}_2/\hat{\pi}_1$ is a nonlinear function of $\hat{\pi}_1$ and $\hat{\pi}_2$, but it is consistent.

Now suppose that an additional exogenous variable, advertising, affects demand but not supply (e.g., an additional, over-identifying restriction, that the coefficient of advertising is zero in the supply equation, is imposed). The demand equation is now written as

$$q = \beta p + \gamma y + \theta a$$

where a is advertising. The reduced-form equations become

$$p = \frac{\gamma}{\delta - \beta} + \frac{\theta}{\delta - \beta} a = \pi_1 y + \pi_3 a$$

$$q = \frac{\gamma \delta}{\delta - \beta} y + \frac{\theta \delta}{\delta - \beta} a = \pi_2 y + \pi_4 a.$$

OLS estimation of these reduced-form equations yields unbiased estimates π_1^*, π_2^*, π_3^*, and π_4^* of π_1, π_2, π_3, and π_4. Since $\pi_2/\pi_1 = \delta$ and $\pi_4/\pi_3 = \delta$, there are two different ILS estimates of δ, namely π_2^*/π_1^* and π_4^*/π_3^*. Only if the estimation of π incorporates the zero restrictions will these two estimates of δ be the same.

In figure 10.2 we saw that identification was possible because shifts in the demand curve due to income changes traced out the supply curve. With the extra exogenous variable advertising, we now find that the supply curve is also traced out by shifts in the demand curve arising from changes in advertising expenditures. The indirect least squares procedure thus has two ways of estimating the supply curve: from variations in supply due to variations in income, or from variations in supply due to variations in advertising, illustrating the over-identification phenomenon.

- When the disturbances are distributed normally, the LI/ML method is identical to the *limited information, least variance ratio (LI/LVR)* method. In this technique the structural equation to be estimated is rewritten so that all the endogenous variables appearing in that equation are on the left-hand side and all the included exogenous variables and the disturbance are on the right-hand side. Suppose a particular set of values is chosen for the parameters of the included endogenous variables and a composite endogenous variable is calculated. This composite endogenous variable is a linear function of the included exogenous variables plus a disturbance term. Regressing this composite endogenous variable on the exogenous variables included in the equation should produce a sum of squared residuals only slightly larger than the sum of squared residuals obtained from regressing it on *all* the exogenous variables in the system, since the exogenous variables not included in the equation should have little explanatory power. The LI/LVR chooses the set of values of the (structural) parameters of the included endogenous variables so as to minimize the ratio of the former sum of squared residuals to the latter sum of squared residuals. This ratio is called the variance ratio; hence the name "least variance ratio." Econometricians have derived mathematically a means of doing this without having to search over all possible sets of parameter values of the included endogenous variables (see Wonnacott and Wonnacott, 1970, pp. 376–9). Once the parameter estimates of the included endogenous variables have been found, the composite endogenous variable is simply regressed on the included exogenous variables to find estimates of the (structural) parameters of the included exogenous variables. This technique can be shown to be identical to the limited information, least generalized variance method (discussed below) as well as to the LI/ML method. Computationally, however, the LI/LVR method is easier than the others, so it is the one employed in practice. Its computational cost is higher than that of 2SLS, however.

- It is interesting that 2SLS can be shown to minimize the difference between the numerator and the denominator of the least variance ratio.
- The least variance ratio should only slightly exceed 1 if the excluded exogenous variables do in fact all have zero coefficients. If some of the excluded variables should have been included, this ratio will exceed 1 by a significant amount. A test of over-identifying restrictions is based on this idea. An alternative test is based on the difference between the numerator and the denominator of this ratio. See Murphy (1973, pp. 476–80).
- When the disturbances are distributed normally the LI/ML method is also identical to the *limited information, least generalized variance (LI/LGV)* method. This technique, like LI/ML, is based on the idea that ILS could be applied to an over-identified equation if the reduced-form parameter estimates had built into them the zero restrictions on the structural parameters in that equation. To build these zero restrictions into the reduced-form parameter estimates, the reduced-form parameters must be estimated as a *set* of equations (including only those reduced-form equations corresponding to the endogenous variables appearing in the structural equation being estimated) instead of individually. When estimating a single equation the sum of squared residuals is usually minimized; when estimating an entire set of equations simultaneously, however, it is not obvious what should be minimized. The estimated *contemporaneous variance–covariance matrix* of the disturbances of the set of equations is used to resolve this problem. This matrix has the sum of squared residuals from each equation in the diagonal positions, and the sum of cross-products of disturbances from different equations in the off-diagonal positions, with each element divided by the sample size. The determinant of the contemporaneous variance–covariance matrix is called the generalized variance. The LI/LGV technique minimizes this generalized variance *subject to* the zero restrictions on the structural parameters in the equation being estimated. The estimates of the reduced-form parameters so obtained may be used to estimate the structural parameters; this can now be done in spite of the over-identification because the over-identifying restrictions are built into the estimates of the reduced-form parameters.
- It might seem more natural to minimize the trace (the sum of the diagonal elements) of the estimated contemporaneous variance–covariance matrix of the reduced-form disturbances rather than its determinant, since that corresponds more closely to the concept of minimizing the sum of squared residuals (i.e., minimizing the trace would minimize the sum of the sum of squared residuals in each equation). This approach has drawbacks, however, as noted in Wonnacott and Wonnacott (1970, pp. 365–71).
- Minimizing the generalized variance would be equivalent to minimizing the sum of squared residuals associated with each individual reduced-form equation (i.e., running OLS on each equation separately) were it not for the restrictions.
- Many simultaneous equation estimating techniques can be interpreted as using instrumental variables for the endogenous variables appearing as regressors. The OLS technique can be thought of as using the endogenous variables themselves as instrumental variables; the 2SLS technique uses as instrumental variables the calculated values of the endogenous variables from the reduced-form estimation. The *k-class estimator*

uses an instrumental variable calculated as a weighted average of the instrumental variables used by the OLS and the 2SLS techniques. The weighting factor is k; when $k = 1$ the k-class estimator is identical to 2SLS, and when $k = 0$ it is identical to OLS. When k is equal to the variance ratio from the LI/LVR estimator, the k-class estimator is identical to the LI/ML, LI/LVR and LI/LGV estimators. When the limit of k as the sample size goes to infinity is 1 (as is the variance ratio), the k-class estimator is consistent and has the same asymptotic variance–covariance matrix as the 2SLS, LI/ML, LI/LVR and LI/LGV estimators.

- The *fix-point* and *iterative instrumental variables* methods (see Dutta, 1975, pp. 317–26) are iterative procedures in which initial estimates of the structural parameters are used to create estimates of the endogenous variables, which in turn are used to generate, via an OLS or IV procedure, new estimates of the structural parameters. This process is repeated until convergence is attained. Extensions of these iterative techniques are discussed by Giles (1973, pp. 74–9). Such iterative techniques are of value in estimating very large systems of simultaneous equations.

10.4   Systems Methods

- The systems methods discussed in this chapter assume that disturbances in each individual structural equation are spherical, that disturbances in different time periods in different equations are independent, and that this contemporaneous variance–covariance matrix is the same in each time period. (For cross-sectional data, the reference to "time period" must be replaced by "individual" or "firm," or whatever is relevant.) Turkington (1989) generalizes the test of Breusch and Pagan (1980) to test for contemporaneous correlation of the errors in a simultaneous equations rather than a SURE context (i.e., to test for whether a full information estimation technique is warranted).
- When the errors are distributed normally, the FI/ML method is equivalent to the *full-information, least generalized variance (FI/LGV)* method, the systems counterpart of LI/LGV. In this method, all the reduced-form equations (rather than just those corresponding to the included endogenous variables in a particular equation) are estimated by minimizing the determinant of the estimated contemporaneous variance–covariance matrix of the reduced-form disturbances, subject to the zero restrictions from *all* the structural equations.

10.5   VARs

- Because each equation in a VAR has exactly the same explanatory variables (lagged values of all variables in the VAR) there is no benefit to using a SURE estimation procedure, as noted in the technical notes to section 10.1. Consequently, OLS is employed for estimation. Some effort must be made to pare down the large number of regressors, but because the regressors are bound to be highly collinear, t statistics are not used for this purpose. Instead, a series of F or associated chi-square test statistics are employed, with the level of significance of the individual tests adjusted (as explained in the technical notes to section 5.2) to achieve a desired overall significance level.

• Suppose for illustrative purposes we assume a one-period only lag for a VAR and for convenience set the intercept equal to zero. The "structural" form of this VAR can be written as

$$B_0 z_t = B_1 z_{t-1} + \varepsilon_t$$

where the errors in the error vector ε_t are assumed to be uncorrelated. The corresponding reduced form, the usual way in which a VAR appears in the literature, is

$$z_t = B_0^{-1} B_1 z_{t-1} + B_0^{-1} e_t = A z_{t-1} + u_t$$

By repeated substitution this can be written as

$$z_t = \Sigma A^i u_{t-i}$$

This is called the vector moving average representation of the VAR. Because of complicated feedbacks, VAR advocates claim that autoregressive systems like these are difficult to describe adequately by just looking at coefficient estimates or computing long-run equilibrium behavior, as is done by traditional econometric approaches. They recommend instead postulating a shock or "innovation" to one of the elements of u_t, and using this equation to trace out over time the response of the variables in the z vector, delivering what they believe is more useful information about interrelationships between variables.

Unfortunately, it is difficult to give meaning to a u error shock because it is a linear combination $(B_0^{-1} \varepsilon)$ of the structural errors. To deal with this those advocating the VAR methodology have resorted to a bit of technical wizardry. Estimation of VAR produces an estimate of the variance–covariance matrix Ω of u. This can be uniquely decomposed into PDP' where P is a lower triangular (i.e., all zeros above the diagonal) matrix with ones on the diagonal and D is a diagonal matrix. This means that $P^{-1}u = v$ has variance–covariance matrix D, a diagonal matrix, so the elements of v can be considered orthogonal errors. Rewriting the vector moving average form of the VAR in terms of v we get

$$z_t = \Sigma A^i P v_{t-1}$$

An innovation in an element of v_t is postulated and the resulting impact over time on an element of z is graphed to produce the orthogonalized *impulse response function*, a primary output of a VAR analysis.

At this stage critics of VAR analysis complain that although the mathematics of all this is straightforward, it is still not clear what meaning should be given to an innovation to an element of v. If v could be identified with ε, the impulse response function would have a clear interpretation – it would trace out the impact over time of a shock to one of the structural equations, which could in some cases be interpreted as a policy shock. But if v cannot be identified with ε, it is an artificial orthogonal shock without economic interpretation, rendering of questionable value the corresponding impulse response functions.

Under what circumstances could v be identified with ε? Because $u = B_0^{-1} \varepsilon$ and $v = P^{-1}u$, v is equal to ε if $P^{-1} = B_0$. Since P is triangular, this implies that B_0 must also be triangular. This in turn implies that the structural equation form of the VAR must be recursive. Indeed, if the system is recursive, the ε errors are uncorrelated, and B_0 is normalized to have ones down its diagonal, P^{-1} will equal B_0 (providing, of course, that the equations are arranged in the appropriate order). In this case the structural form of the VAR is identified because B_0 can be estimated by the estimate of P^{-1}. This leads to the awkward (for advocates of VARs) conclusion that the VAR impulse response functions make sense only when the structural equations are identified, exactly the situation the VAR advocates had scorned because of the "incredible" restrictions they required!

Recognition of this has caused VAR advocates to change their attitude toward the identification of structural forms of VARs. Meaningful impulse response functions can be produced so long as the associated structural VAR is identified, by whatever means. Identification can be accomplished by using economic information in the form of recursive structures, coefficient restrictions, variance or covariance restrictions, symmetry restrictions, or restrictions on long-run multiplier values. Enders (1995, pp. 320–42) has a good discussion. Pagan (1995) discusses this change in VAR methodology in a broader context. Hamilton (1995, pp. 291–340) has a good presentation of the technical details of VARs.

- The decomposition of Ω discussed above is sometimes undertaken using the Cholesky decomposition in which $\Omega = PD^{\frac{1}{2}}D^{\frac{1}{2}}P'$ with P in the analysis above being replaced by $PD^{\frac{1}{2}}$. The only difference this implies is that $PD^{1/2}$ has the standard deviation of u along its principal diagonal, so that a unit innovation in the orthogonal error now corresponds to a change of one standard deviation.

VIOLATING ASSUMPTION FIVE: MULTICOLLINEARITY

11.1 INTRODUCTION

The fifth assumption of the CLR model specifies that there are no exact linear relationships between the independent variables and that there are at least as many observations as independent variables. If either half of this assumption is violated, it is mechanically impossible to compute the OLS estimates; i.e., the estimating procedure simply breaks down for mathematical reasons, just as if someone tried to divide by zero.

Both of these phenomena are rare. Most economists recognize that it is impossible to estimate n parameter values with less than n numbers and so ensure that their sample size is larger than the number of parameters they are estimating. In fact, they usually seek out the largest available sample size to ensure that the difference between the sample size and the number of parameters being estimated (this difference is the degrees of freedom) is as large as possible, since the variances of their estimates are usually smaller the larger is the number of degrees of freedom. An exact linear relationship between the independent variables usually occurs only in data that have been constructed by the researcher (usually in cases involving dummy variables, an example of which is given in chapter 14); with care this can be avoided, or the regression problem can be reformulated when the computer rejects the regression run. To have an exact linear relationship in raw data is indeed a fluke.

It is quite possible, however, to have an *approximate* linear relationship among independent variables – in fact, such approximate relationships are very common among economic variables. It is often said in jest that, while one econometrician is regressing a dependent variable on several independent variables in the hopes of finding a strong relationship, another econometrician somewhere else in the world is probably regressing one of those independent variables on some of the other independent variables in the hope of showing *that* to be a strong linear relationship. Although the estimation procedure does not break down when the independent variables are highly correlated (i.e., approximately linearly related), severe estimation problems arise. *Multicollinearity* is the name given to this phenomenon. Although technically the fifth assumption of the CLR model is violated only in the case of *exact* multicollinearity (an *exact* linear relationship among some of the regressors), the presence of multi-collinearity (an *approximate* linear relationship among some of the regressors) leads to estimating problems important enough to warrant our treating it as a violation of the CLR model.

Multicollinearity does not depend on any theoretical or actual linear relation-ship among any of the regressors; it depends on the existence of an approximate linear relationship in the data set at hand. Unlike most other estimating prob-lems, this problem is caused by the particular sample available. Multicollinearity in the data could arise for several reasons. For example, the independent vari-ables may all share a common time trend, one independent variable might be the lagged value of another that follows a trend, some independent variables may have varied together because the data were not collected from a wide enough base, or there could in fact exist some kind of approximate relationship among some of the regressors. If economists could collect data from controlled experi-ments, the multicollinearity problem could be eliminated by proper experimental design – the observations on the independent variables would be constructed so as to be orthogonal (the opposite of collinear). Economists are almost never in the position of conducting controlled experiments, however, and thus often must worry about the effects of multicollinearity in their data.

11.2 CONSEQUENCES

The OLS estimator in the presence of multicollinearity remains unbiased and in fact is still the BLUE. The R^2 statistic is unaffected. In fact, since all the CLR assumptions are (*strictly* speaking) still met, the OLS estimator retains all its desirable properties, as noted in chapter 3. The major undesirable consequence of multicollinearity is that the variances of the OLS estimates of the parameters of the collinear variables are quite large. These high variances arise because in the presence of multicollinearity the OLS estimating procedure is not given enough independent variation in a variable to calculate with confidence the effect it has on the dependent variable. As a result, the consequences of this undesirable feature of the sample are indistinguishable from the consequences of inadequate variability of the regressors in a data set, an interpretation of multi-collinearity which has unfortunately not been well understood by practitioners.

Consider the case in which a dependent variable is being regressed on two highly correlated independent variables. Variation in the two regressors can be classified into three types: variation unique to the first regressor, variation unique to the second regressor, and variation common to both. In measuring the effect of the first regressor on the dependent variable (i.e., in estimating its coef-ficient) only variation in the first regressor unique to that regressor can be used; variation in the first regressor that is shared by the second regressor cannot be used because there would be no way of knowing whether the dependent variable variation was due to variation in the first or in the second variable. The OLS procedure uses *only* variation unique to the first regressor in calculating the OLS estimate of the coefficient of the first regressor; it uses only variation unique to the second regressor in calculating the coefficient estimate of the second regressor. For the purpose of calculating coefficient estimates, the common variation is ignored. (It is used, however, for prediction purposes and in calculating R^2.) When the regressors are highly correlated, most of their variation is common to both variables, leaving little variation unique to each variable. This means that the OLS procedure has little information to use in making its coefficient estimates, just as though it had a very small sample size, or a sample in which the independent variable did not vary much. Any estimate based on little information cannot be held with much confidence – it will have a high variance. The higher the correlation between the independent variables (the more severe the multicollinearity), the less information used by the OLS estimator to calculate the parameter estimates and thus the greater the variances.

As another way of looking at this, consider the information that was cast aside. It consists of variation in the dependent variable explained by common variation in the two regressors. If this common explanation were known to be due to one regressor rather than the other, the estimate of the two regressors' coefficients might have to be considerably changed. But the allocation of this common explanation between the two regressors is unknown. It is this uncertainty as to which variable deserves the credit for the jointly explained variation in the dependent variable that creates the uncertainty as to the true values of the coefficients being estimated and thus causes the higher variances of their estimates.

Having high variances means that the parameter estimates are not precise (they do not provide the researcher with reliable estimates of the parameters) and hypothesis testing is not powerful (diverse hypotheses about the parameter values cannot be rejected). As an example of this, consider the case illustrated in figure 11.1. The confidence ellipse (recall section 4.3) for the two parameter estimates is long, narrow and tilted, reflecting the collinearity in the regressors. If the influence on the dependent variable of the common variation is in fact due to the first regressor, β_1 will be large and β_2 small, implying a true parameter value set in the lower right of the ellipse. If it is due to the second regressor, β_2 will be large and β_1 small, implying a true parameter value set in the upper left of the confidence ellipse. There is a high (negative) covariance between the two estimators. In figure 11.1 the ellipse covers part of the vertical axis and part of the horizontal axis, implying that the individual hypothesis $\beta_1 = 0$ cannot be rejected and the individual hypothesis $\beta_2 = 0$ cannot be rejected. But the ellipse does not cover the origin, so that the joint hypothesis that both β_1 and β_2 are zero is rejected. Although the researcher knows that at least one of these variables is relevant, the correct specification is difficult to determine without sound guidance from economic theory. Thus a second consequence of multicollinearity is that it can easily lead to specification errors (which in this context is quite serious since the parameter estimates are very sensitive to the model specification).

11.3 DETECTING MULTICOLLINEARITY

Much controversy has surrounded the question of detecting the existence of multicollinearity, or, more correctly, the question of measuring the extent to which data are collinear. One reason for this is that many of the detection methods suggested are inadequate and have justifiably been criticized. But there exists a far more important reason. The only remedy for undesirably high variances is somehow to incorporate additional information in the estimating procedure. This remedy is the same regardless of whether these undesirably high variances were caused by multicollinearity or inadequate variation of the regressors in the data set. If it doesn't make any difference whether high variances of coefficient estimates are due to collinearity or to inadequate variability in the data, why bother trying to detect multicollinearity? This is an awkward question. The usual response is that, through efforts to detect the existence of multicollinearity, a researcher may be led to consider explicitly extra information that will be more likely (than other kinds of extra information) to reduce the variances in question. On the other hand, he or she for this same reason may be led more quickly to incorporate false information. This perspective is important to keep in mind whenever employing methods for detecting multicollinearity.

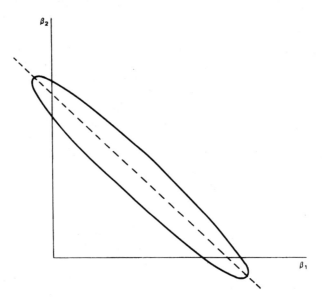

Figure 11.1   High negative covariance arising from collinearity

It is common for researchers to claim that multicollinearity is at work whenever their hypothesized signs are not found in the regression results, when variables that they know *a priori* to be important have insignificant *t* values, or when various regression results are changed substantively whenever an explanatory variable is deleted. Unfortunately, none of these conditions is either necessary or sufficient for the existence of collinearity, and furthermore none provides any useful suggestions as to what kind of extra information might be required to solve the estimation problem they represent.

Another popular means of detecting multicollinearity is through the use of the correlation matrix. Computer printouts of most regression packages include a matrix of simple correlation coefficients between all pairs of the independent variables. The off-diagonal elements contain the simple correlation coefficients for the given data set; the diagonal elements are all unity since each variable is perfectly correlated with itself. A high value (about 0.8 or 0.9 in absolute value) of one of these correlation coefficients indicates high correlation between the two independent variables to which it refers. This method does detect collinearity between two specific variables and thus can suggest what kind of extra information (e.g., that one of these variables' coefficients is zero) might be most useful in solving the problem; but it does not allow detection of a case in which three or more variables are collinear with no two taken alone exhibiting high correlation.

A less common, but more satisfactory, way of detecting multicollinearity is through the *condition index*, or number, of the data, the square root of the ratio of the largest to the smallest characteristic root of $X'X$. A high condition index reflects the presence of collinearity.

11.4 WHAT TO DO

There are two basic options for researchers faced with multicollinearity.

(1) DO NOTHING

The existence of multicollinearity in a data set does not necessarily mean that the coefficient estimates in which the researcher is interested have unacceptably high variances. The classic example of this is estimation of the Cobb–Douglas production function: the inputs capital and labor are highly collinear, but nonetheless good estimates are obtained. This has led to the rule of thumb, "Don't worry about multicollinearity if the R^2 from the regression exceeds the R^2 of any independent variable regressed on the other independent variables." Another rule of thumb sometimes used is "Don't worry about multicollinearity if the *t* statistics are all greater than 2."

A second reason for following a course of inaction can be illustrated by figure 11.1. It should be clear from this diagram that, although the variances of the estimates of β_1 and β_2 are high, the variance of an estimate of the linear combination of β_1 and β_2 given by the dashed line is low. Consequently, if the researcher's interest centers on this linear combination, the multicollinearity need not be of concern. This might happen, for example, if the estimated equation is to be used for prediction purposes and the multicollinearity pattern is expected to prevail in the situations to be predicted.

(2) INCORPORATE ADDITIONAL INFORMATION

There are several possibilities here, most of which should be considered even in the absence of multicollinearity.

(a) *Obtain more data*   Because the multicollinearity problem is essentially a data problem, additional data that do not contain the multicollinearity feature could solve the problem. Even getting additional data with the same multicollinearity character would help, since the larger sample size would provide some additional information, helping to reduce variances.

(b) *Formalize relationships among regressors*   If it is believed that the multicollinearity arises not from an unfortunate data set but from an actual approximate linear relationship among some of the regressors, this relationship could be formalized and the estimation could then proceed in the context of a simultaneous equation estimation problem.

(c) *Specify a relationship among some parameters*   Economic theory may suggest that two parameters should be equal, that the sum of several elasticities should be unity, or, in general, that there exists a specific relationship among some of the parameters in the estimating equation. Incorporation of this information, via methods discussed in chapter 12, will reduce the variances of the estimates. As an example, consider specifying that the coefficients of a lag structure take the form of a Koyck distributed lag (i.e., they decline geometrically), as discussed in section 9.3.

(d) *Drop a variable*   A popular means of avoiding the multicollinearity problem is by simply omitting one of the collinear variables. If the true coefficient of that variable in the equation being estimated is zero, this is a correct move. If the true coefficient of that variable is *not* zero, however, a specification error is created. As noted in section 6.2, omitting a relevant variable causes estimates of the parameters of the remaining variables to be biased (unless some of these remaining variables are uncorrelated with the omitted variable, in which case their parameter estimates remain unbiased). The real question here is whether, by dropping a variable, the econometrician can reduce the variance of the remaining estimates by enough to compensate for this bias introduced. This suggests the use of the MSE criterion in undertaking a decision to drop a variable. This approach should not be adopted cavalierly, since, as noted by Drèze (1983, p. 296), "setting a coefficient equal to zero because it is estimated with poor precision amounts to elevating ignorance to arrogance."

(e) *Incorporate estimates from other studies*   If an extraneous estimate of the coefficient of one of the variables involved in the multicollinearity is available, it can be used, via the mixed estimation technique described in chapter 12, to alleviate the high variance problem occasioned by the multicollinearity. If this is done, however, care must be taken to ensure that the extraneous estimate is relevant. For example, estimates from cross-sectional studies are often used to alleviate time series multicollinearity, but cross-section estimates relate to the long-run version of many parameters, rather than the short-run version relevant for time series studies.

(f) *Form a principal component* The variables that are collinear could be grouped together to form a composite index capable of representing this group of variables by itself. Such a composite variable should be created only if the variables included in the composite have some useful combined economic interpretation; otherwise the empirical results will have little meaning. For example, in undertaking a study of the effect of marketing activity on consumer demand, a researcher might find that variables representing different dimensions of marketing activity are highly collinear; some combination of these variables could readily be interpreted as a "marketing variable" and its use in the model would not confuse the meaning of the empirical results. The most popular way of constructing such a composite index is to use the first principal component of the variables in question.

(g) *Shrink the OLS estimates* By shrinking the OLS estimates towards the zero vector, a researcher may be able to reduce the risk (the sum of the MSEs of each individual parameter estimate) of the estimates. Implicitly, this is equivalent to incorporating the *ad hoc* stochastic prior information that the true β is close to the zero vector. The two most popular means of doing this are the ridge estimator and the Stein estimator.

GENERAL NOTES

11.2 Consequences

- Leamer (1983b, pp. 300–3) stresses the fact that collinearity as a cause of weak evidence (high variances) is indistinguishable from inadequate data variability as a cause of weak evidence. Goldberger (1989, p. 141) speculates that the reason practitioners seem not to understand this is because there is no fancy polysyllabic name for "small sample size." He suggests the term "micronumerosity" be used, and provides a very amusing account of how all of the ills and manifestations of multicollinearity can be described in terms of micronumerosity.

- The Ballentine portrays the multicollinearity phenomenon succinctly. Consider figure 3.2, in the general notes to chapter 3. Multicollinearity is reflected by a large overlap between the X and Z circles. This could create a large red area at the expense of the blue or green areas. These blue and green areas reflect the information used to estimate β_x and β_z; since less information is used, the variances of these parameter estimates are larger.

- In addition to creating high variances of coefficient estimates, multicollinearity is associated with the undesirable problem that calculations based on the data matrix are unstable in that slight variations in the data matrix, such as addition or deletion of an observation, lead to large changes in parameter estimates. An example of this is provided in Beaton et al. (1976), who perturb a set of collinear data by adding random numbers between -0.5 and $+0.5$ (i.e., they have added a rounding error beyond the last published digit). These small perturbations change drastically most parameter estimates. Incorporating additional information into the estimation procedure tends to stabilize estimates in this respect, as well as reducing variances.

11.3   Detecting Multicollinearity

- The use of condition indices for the detection of multicollinearity is advocated in persuasive fashion by Belsley et al. (1980, chapter 3). The data must be scaled before calculation of the condition index; see Belsley (1989). As a rule of thumb, a condition index greater than 30 indicates strong collinearity.
- The inverse of the correlation matrix is also used in detecting multicollinearity. The diagonal elements of this matrix are called variance inflation factors. VIF_i. They are given by $(1 - R_i^2)^{-1}$ where R_i^2 is the R^2 from regressing the ith independent variable on all the other independent variables. A high VIF indicates an R_i^2 near unity and hence suggests collinearity. As a rule of thumb, for standardized data a $VIF_i > 10$ indicates harmful collinearity.
- Multicollinearity detection methods suggested by Farrar and Glauber (1967) have become undeservedly popular. For a summary of the critiques of these methods, see Belsley et al. (1980, pp. 93–5).
- Belsley (1984b) notes that centering data (expressing them as deviations from their means) can produce meaningless and misleading collinearity diagnostics. See also Belsley (1986a).

11.4   What to Do

- A useful perspective on the "do nothing or incorporate additional information" approach to multicollinearity is offered by Blanchard (1987, p. 449):

> When students run their first ordinary least squares (OLS) regression, the first problem that they usually encounter is that of multicollinearity. Many of them conclude that there is something wrong with OLS; some resort to new and often creative techniques to get around the problem. But, we tell them, this is wrong. Multicollinearity is God's will, not a problem with OLS or statistical techniques in general. Only use of more economic theory in the form of additional restrictions may help alleviate the multicollinearity problem. One should not, however, expect miracles; multicollinearity is likely to prevent the data from speaking loudly on some issues, even when all of the resources of economic theory have been exhausted.

- The do-nothing approach is supported by Conlisk (1971), who shows that multicollinearity can be advantageous in several special circumstances. He gives examples of estimation of a linear combination of the parameters, estimation of the intercept, estimation in the presence of certain kinds of *a priori* information, estimation when there are unequal costs associated with different observations, and estimation in the context of autocorrelated residuals.

- It must be stressed that the incorporation-of-additional-information approach will "solve" the multicollinearity problem (in the sense of generating a lower MSE) only if the extra information is "close" to being correct. This is discussed at length in chapter 12.

- Silvey (1969) discusses the nature of additional data that would be most useful in resolving the multicollinearity problem.

- The discussion in the body of this chapter of solving multicollinearity by dropping a variable is a special case of the more general problem of testing any linear restriction to see whether or not adding that restriction will reduce MSE. See Toro-Vizcarrondo and Wallace (1968). It is a kind of pre-test estimator, discussed in chapter 12.

- Feldstein (1973) suggests using a weighted average of the estimates obtained with and without dropping a variable, where the weights, chosen to minimize MSE, involve the value of the t statistic used to test whether or not that variable's coefficient is significantly different from zero. This principle is similar to that underlying the Stein estimator, discussed in chapter 12.

- The problem of high variances could be solved by adding (rather than dropping) a variable. Adding a variable that was incorrectly excluded could markedly reduce the estimate of the error variance, which implies lower estimated variances of all coefficient estimates.

- Kuh and Mayer (1957) discuss problems associated with the use of extraneous estimates to avoid multicollinearity. See also Adams (1965) and Baltagi and Griffen (1984). Underspecification of dynamics, causing time series estimates to be underestimates of long-run effects, is the usual explanation offered for why time series and cross-section parameter estimates cannot be equated.

- The first principal component of a set of variables is a weighted average of the variables in which the weights are chosen to make the composite variable reflect the maximum possible proportion of the total variation in the set. Additional principal components can be calculated (i.e., the second principal component is orthogonal to the first and uses weights designed to incorporate within it the maximum possible proportion of the remaining variation in the original variables), but the first principal component usually captures enough of the variation in the set to be an adequate representative of that set on its own.

- The principal components technique as described in the body of this chapter is not the usual way in which it is advocated. If there are J explanatory variables, then J principal components can be constructed, each orthogonal to the others. If the regression is run on some of these J principal components, rather than on the original J variables, the results of this regression can be transformed to provide estimates $\hat{\beta}$ of the coefficients β of the original variables. If all J principal components are used, the resulting $\hat{\beta}$ is identical to the $\hat{\beta}$ obtained by regressing on the original, collinear data: nothing is gained. The rationale of the principal components method is not to include all of the principal components in the preliminary stage; by dropping some of the principal components, this method produces different estimates of β, with smaller variances. The reduction in variances occurs because implicitly this technique incorporates the extra information that the coefficients on the dropped principal components are zero. This in turn implies information on particular functions of the original coefficients, involving the weights used to form the principal components. For discussion see Judge et al. (1985, pp. 909–12). For an instructive example of an application of this technique, see Sanint (1982).

- The ridge estimator is given by the formula

$$(X'X + kI)^{-1}X'Y = (X'X + kI)^{-1}X'X\beta^{OLS}$$

where k is a non-negative number. For $k = 0$ the ridge estimator is identical to the OLS estimator. As k becomes more and more positive, β^{OLS} is shrunk more and more towards the zero vector. The rationale behind the ridge estimator is that there exists a number k such that the MSE of the ridge estimator is less than the MSE of β^{OLS}. Unfortunately, this k value is not known: it depends on the unknown parameters of the model in question. A wide variety of different methods of selecting k have been suggested, all using the sample data. This produces a stochastic k, implying that the existence of an MSE-reducing, non-stochastic k is no longer relevant. In particular, it is in the presence of multicollinearity that it is difficult to use the data to obtain an accurate estimate of k, implying that the ridge estimator is not likely to offer much improvement on β^{OLS} in the presence of multicollinearity. Fomby et al. (1984, pp. 300–2) have a concise exposition of this.
- There exists a plethora of Monte Carlo studies examining the relative merits of different ways of choosing k to operationalize the ridge estimator. For a critical review of many of these studies, see Draper and Van Nostrand (1979), who conclude (p. 464) that "The extended inference that ridge regression is 'always' better than least squares is, typically, completely unjustified." This conclusion is not shared by all, however – see for example Lin and Kmenta (1982). Ridge regression is in fact a topic of considerable debate. Vinod and Ullah (1981, chapter 7) are proponents, Draper and Van Nostrand (1979) are opponents, and Judge et al. (1980, pp. 471–87) fall in between. Smith and Campbell (1980, and ensuing discussion) illustrate some facets of this debate.
- The ridge estimator can be viewed as the OLS estimator incorporating the "stochastic" constraint that β is the zero vector. The extent of the shrinking towards the zero vector (the magnitude of k) depends on the "variance" of this additional information that β is "close" to the zero vector. In a Bayesian interpretation (see chapter 13) the extent of the shrinking depends on the confidence with which it is believed that β is the zero vector. Why should a researcher be prepared to incorporate this particular extra information? Vinod and Ullah (1981, p. 187) offer the justification that "In the absence of specific prior knowledge it is often scientifically conservative to shrink toward the zero vector." Chow (1983, p. 98) notes that econometricians scale their data so that a coefficient value of, say, 10,000 or larger is extremely unlikely, so that "Considering all the real numbers, . . . zero is not a bad guess." On the other hand, Maddala (1988, p. 236) opines that "in almost all economic problems, this sort of prior information (that the means of the β_i's are zero) is very unreasonable." Judge et al. (1980, p. 494) comment that "These estimators work by shrinking coefficients . . . towards zero. This is clearly a desperation measure."
- A concise exposition of the use of the Stein estimator in the context of multicollinearity can be found in Hill et al. (1981) and Mittelhammer and Young (1981). This estimator, discussed in chapter 12, is in essence a weighted average of the OLS estimates with and without extra information, where the weights are determined by the value of the F statistic used for testing the validity of the extra information. Although in some types of problems this guarantees an improvement in risk (MSE), in the regression context the Stein estimator dominates the OLS estimator only if

$tr(X'X)^{-1} > 2d_L$ where d_L is the largest characteristic root of $(X'X)^{-1}$. Unfortunately, the presence of multicollinearity is likely to cause this condition not to hold. For discussion see Hill and Ziemer (1982, 1984) and for examples with economic data see Aigner and Judge (1977).

- Like the ridge estimator, the Stein estimator can be given a Bayesian interpretation; if the stochastic prior for β is chosen to be the zero vector, the ridge and Stein estimators differ only in that implicitly they use different variance–covariance matrices for this prior vector. Unlike the ridge estimator, however, the Stein estimator is commonly used for problems not involving multicollinearity and so the choice of a nonzero prior vector is more readily considered. For example, a principal components estimate of β could be chosen as the extra information to serve as the prior vector.
- A drawback of addressing multicollinearity by using ridge, Stein or pre-test estimators is that these estimators have unknown distributions so that hypothesis testing cannot be undertaken.
- Fomby and Hill (1986) advocate a robust generalized Bayesian estimator which performs well in the face of multicollinearity.
- Creating multicollinear data for Monte Carlo studies is not easy. See Hill (1987).

TECHNICAL NOTES

- The estimated variance of a parameter estimate β_k^{OLS} is given by Stone (1945) as

$$\frac{1}{T-K} \frac{\sigma_y^2}{\sigma_k^2} \frac{1-R^2}{1-R_k^2}$$

where σ_y^2 is the estimated variance of the dependent variable, σ_k^2 is estimated variance of the kth independent variable and R_k^2 is the R^2 from a regression of the kth independent variable on all the other independent variables. This formula shows that

(a) the variance of β_k^{OLS} decreases as the kth independent variable ranges more widely (σ_k^2 higher);

(b) the variance of β_k^{OLS} increases as the independent variables become more collinear (R_k^2 higher) and becomes infinite in the case of exact multicollinearity;

(c) the variance of β_k^{OLS} decreases as R^2 rises, so that the effect of a high R_k^2 can be offset by a high R^2.

12 INCORPORATING EXTRANEOUS INFORMATION

12.1 INTRODUCTION

Economic data are not easy to deal with. For example, they are frequently characterized by multicollinearity. Because of problems like this, econometric estimates often lack efficiency. If extraneous (*a priori*) information, available from economic theory or previous studies, can be incorporated into the estimation procedure, efficiency can be improved. This is the case even if the extraneous information employed is incorrect (as it often is): more information cannot help but reduce variance. But incorrect extraneous information creates bias, so trading off variance and bias (usually through the MSE criterion) becomes a question of central importance in this context.

The purpose of this chapter is to describe a variety of ways in which extraneous information can play a role in improving parameter estimates. The discussion of this chapter is entirely in the classical mold. Bayesians claim that the most logical and consistent way of incorporating extraneous information is through the use of Bayes' theorem; the Bayesian approach is discussed at length in chapter 13.

12.2 EXACT RESTRICTIONS

The extraneous information might take the form of an exact restriction involving some of the parameters to be estimated. For example, economic theory might suggest that the sum of a number of propensities is equal to 1, or that the value of one parameter is twice the value of another. If this restriction is linear it can be used to eliminate mathematically one parameter, and a new estimating equation can be constructed with fewer parameters and fewer independent variables. (These new independent variables are linear combinations of the original independent variables.) The parameter estimates of the new estimating equation can be used to create estimates of the original parameters.

This method is analytically equivalent to restricted least squares, a technique in which the sum of squared error terms is minimized subject to the extraneous information restriction. The resulting estimator can be shown to be the BLUE in the CLR model extended to include the extraneous information. If the extraneous information restriction is nonlinear (for example, that the product of two parameters is equal to a third parameter), computer-assisted numerical techniques similar to those used for nonlinear least squares must be used to minimize the sum of squared residuals subject to the nonlinear constraint.

12.3 STOCHASTIC RESTRICTIONS

Another form of extraneous information is a stochastic restriction, the most common example of which is an estimate of a parameter from a previous study. Such restrictions must be written with an error term, so that, for example, an extraneous unbiased estimate $\hat{\beta}_k$ of β_k must be written as

$$\hat{\beta}_k = \beta_k + v$$

where v is an error term (with variance equal to the variance of $\hat{\beta}_k$). This information is incorporated into the estimation procedure by interpreting the stochastic restriction as an extra sample observation. In the example of $\hat{\beta}_k$, the extra observation consists of a value of 1 for the kth independent variable, zero values for all the other independent variables, and a value of $\hat{\beta}_k$ for the dependent variable. The variance of the error term (v) associated with this extra "observation" is the variance of $\hat{\beta}_k$ and is *not* equal to the variance of the error terms associated with the regular sample observations. Thus GLS, not OLS, should be applied to this "augmented" sample to produce an efficient estimate. This technique is called the *mixed estimator* because it mixes stochastic sample and stochastic prior information.

12.4 PRE-TEST ESTIMATORS

Our discussion of extraneous information so far has assumed that the information employed is correct when in general it is often the case that this is not known with certainty. In actual applications, a common practice is to test information for its validity, before estimation; if the hypothesis that the information/restriction is true is accepted, the restricted OLS estimator is used, and if this hypothesis is rejected, the unrestricted OLS estimator is used. This methodology defines what is called a pre-test estimator: an estimator of an unknown parameter is chosen on the basis of the outcome of a pre-test.

To illustrate the nature of pre-test estimators and their implications, consider the following popular example. Suppose a researcher is uncertain whether or not the variable z should be included as a regressor and consequently decides to include/exclude z on the basis of a t test at, say, the 5% level. Two cases must be examined.

(1) *z is in fact irrelevant* In this case the *t* test will correctly exclude *z* in repeated samples 95% of the time. But 5% of the time it will incorrectly be included, so that in 5% of the repeated samples the OLS estimator used will not have its desirable properties, implying that, *overall*, these desirable properties in repeated samples do not characterize the pre-test estimator. In this case, if *z* is not orthogonal to the other regressors, the variance of the pre-test estimator of the other slope coefficients will be higher than if *z* were omitted without testing. No bias is created.

(2) *z is in fact relevant* In this case the *t* test will correctly include *z* a percentage of times equal to the power *P* of the test, a percentage that becomes greater and greater as the slope coefficient of *z* becomes more and more different from zero. But $(100 - P)\%$ of the time *z* will be incorrectly excluded, so that in $(100 - P)\%$ of repeated samples the OLS estimator used will not have its desirable properties. Once again, *overall*, this pre-test estimator will not have the desirable properties of the appropriate OLS estimator. In this case the pre-test estimator exhibits bias.

This failure of the pre-test estimator to achieve the properties of the OLS estimator using the correct specification is called *pre-test bias* One of its major implications is that the traditional hypothesis-testing methodology, which depends on an estimator having certain properties in repeated samples, is now much more complicated; traditional formulas, such as the traditional formula for the standard error, cannot be used, and the correct measures are difficult to calculate.

The most dramatic implication of the pre-test bias phenomenon occurs when econometricians use sequential or "stepwise" testing procedures (sometimes called "data mining"), in which a large number of different hypotheses are tested to select a relatively small set of independent variables out of a much larger set of potential independent variables, greatly increasing the probability of adopting, by chance, an incorrect set of independent variables. This problem has been exacerbated by the advent of the computer. There is an unfortunate tendency among econometricians to do more computing than thinking when model-building; the pre-test bias phenomenon is sometimes described by the phrase, "Compute first and think afterwards."

Most econometricians ignore the pre-test bias problem; in fact, few even admit its existence. The main counter-argument to pre-test bias is that without pre-testing we must rely on an *assumption* concerning what variables are included in the set of independent variables. Is the probability that pre-testing yields an incorrect set of independent variables greater than or less than the probability that the econometrician has selected the "correct" assumption? Pre-testing is simply a means of providing additional evidence to aid the econometrician in selecting the appropriate set of independent variables. So long as the econometrician views this as evidence to be evaluated sensibly in light of other considerations (such as economic theory), rather than as a mechanical proce-

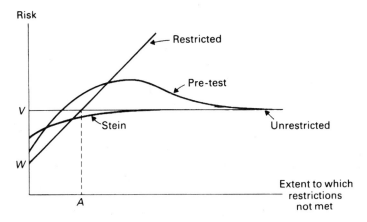

Figure 12.1 Risk functions for selected estimators

dure, pre-test bias should not be of great concern. A more cogent counter-argument is to note that an examination of the mean square error (MSE) properties of the pre-test estimator, relative to its competitors, needs to be undertaken to determine how serious this problem is. The next section examines this question.

12.5   EXTRANEOUS INFORMATION AND MSE

If extraneous information is incorrect, an estimator incorporating this information, or a pre-test estimator that sometimes (in repeated samples) incorporates this information, will be biased. This complicates the decision to incorporate extraneous information because the reduction in variance from its incorporation might be more than offset by the bias introduced. As is usual when faced with such a trade-off, econometricians turn to the mean square error (MSE) criterion.

Risk functions, portrayed in figure 12.1, can be used to show the MSE associated with relevant estimators in the context of some set of restrictions. The vertical axis measures *risk*, the sum of the MSEs of the estimators of each element of the parameter vector. The horizontal axis measures the extent to which the restrictions are *not* met, i.e., the degree of "falsity" of the extraneous information.

Recall that MSE can be broken into the sum of the variance and the square of the bias. The unrestricted OLS estimator has zero bias and a constant variance regardless of the truth of the restrictions, so its risk function is drawn as a horizontal line at V, where V is the sum of the variances of the unrestricted OLS estimators of the elements of the parameter vector. The restricted OLS estimator has a smaller variance than the unrestricted OLS estimator, and, when the restriction is true, also has no bias. Thus, when the restriction is true (i.e., at the vertical axis in figure 12.1), the risk of the restricted OLS estimator is lower than V, say W. As the restriction becomes more and more false, the restricted estimator retains its small variance but suffers a greater and greater bias; reflecting this, the risk function for the restricted OLS estimator slopes upward.

Consider now the pre-test estimator. When the restrictions are true it has no bias, and, being a mixture of the restricted and unrestricted OLS estimators, it has a variance between the variances of these two estimators. Thus its risk function cuts the vertical axis between V and W. When the restrictions are far from true, the pre-test estimator should almost always correctly reject the restrictions so that the risk of the pre-test estimator should be virtually the same as the risk of the unrestricted OLS estimator. This is shown in figure 12.1 by the risk function of the pre-test estimator approaching asymptotically the risk function of the unrestricted OLS estimator.

The pre-test estimator performs reasonably well when the restrictions are either very close to being met or quite far from being met. In between, however, as illustrated in figure 12.1, it does not do so well. The reason for this is that in this intermediate position the pre-test does not invariably accept or invariably reject; the percentage of times in repeated samples that it accepts the restrictions is substantial, as is the percentage of times that it rejects those restrictions. The estimates produced when it (correctly) rejects are distributed around the true unknown parameter value, but the estimates produced when it (incorrectly) accepts are biased and thus are distributed around some other unknown parameter value. Consequently, *overall*, both bias and a larger variance are created.

The explanation of the preceding paragraph suggests that the undesirable risk properties of the pre-test estimator stem from its dichotomous nature, namely the fact that it jumps between the unrestricted OLS formula and the restricted OLS formula. An ingenious alternative to the pre-test estimator that avoids this problem, yet still retains the flavor of the pre-test concept, is to use as an estimator a weighted average of the restricted and unrestricted OLS estimators, with the weights a function of the magnitude of the F statistic used to test the restrictions. This is the essence of the *Stein estimator*. The success of this principle is reflected in figure 12.1 by the risk function of the Stein estimator. Note that it lies everywhere below the risk function of the unrestricted OLS estimator (i.e., it dominates the unrestricted OLS estimator), a result which astounded the statistics world when it was first derived.

GENERAL NOTES

12.1   Introduction

- Not all forms of extraneous information are discussed here. For example, information concerning the variance–covariance matrix of the disturbance can clearly be incorporated directly into GLS estimation. The role of information in the form of identifying restrictions for simultaneous equations was discussed in chapter 10.

- As an example of how incorrect information can reduce variance, suppose the incorrect information that $\beta = 6.5$ is employed. Then $\hat{\beta}_R$, the estimate of β incorporating this information, is $\hat{\beta}_R = 6.5$, ignoring the data. The variance of this estimate is clearly zero, the smallest possible variance.

- It is an overstatement to claim that the introduction of extraneous information must reduce variance. It is possible to create examples in which this is not the case. Such examples rely on interaction of incorrect information with another incorrect feature of the analysis. For example, Taylor (1976) shows that extraneous information can worsen estimates if the econometrician assumes that the variance–covariance matrix of the disturbance is spherical when it in fact is not. Rothenberg (1973, p. 57) gives an example in which using the MSE criterion in conjunction with inequality constraints produces a worse estimate than if the constraints had been ignored.

- The problem of estimating *distributed lags* is one in which extraneous information plays a prominent role. For a variety of reasons (summarized nicely by Judge et al., 1980, pp. 623–9), economic relationships can be expected to be such that lagged values of the explanatory variable(s) appear as regressors. Although none of the CLR model assumptions is violated, so that OLS is an appropriate estimating procedure, invariably lagged values of an explanatory variable are highly collinear, causing the OLS estimates to have high variances. (If the lags are long, the resulting loss in degrees of freedom exacerbates this problem.) Any of the techniques suggested for addressing the multicollinearity problem (discussed in chapter 11) could be used here, but by far the most popular method employed in this context is the incorporation of extraneous information by specifying a *lag distribution*.

A lag distribution function gives the magnitude of the coefficient of a lagged explanatory variable, expressed as a function of the lag. By specifying that this function takes a particular form, extra information is injected into the estimation procedure. A wide variety of specifications have been suggested for this purpose, some examples of which are the arithmetic, inverted V, Almon, Shiller, harmonic, geometric, Pascal, rational, gamma and exponential. For a concise summary, see Judge et al. (1980, p. 631). A recently developed lag with attractive features is the polynomial inverse lag; see Mitchell and Speaker (1986).

Lag distributions are characterized as finite or infinite, depending on the time required for the lag effect to vanish completely. The most popular finite lag distribution is the *Almon polynomial lag distribution*. In this technique the n coefficients of the lagged explanatory variables are assumed to lie on a polynomial (i.e., a function of the lag length) of order r. This allows for a flexible lag structure with a reduction in the number of parameters that require estimation if $r + 1$ is less than n. It can be viewed as imposing a specific set of linear constraints on OLS estimation. *Shiller's distributed lag* is a variant of this in which these restrictions are stochastic, incorporated via the mixed estimation technique; the coefficients of the lagged explanatory variable lie close to, rather than on, a polynomial. The main problem with the Almon lag is determining n and r. Pre-testing is usually employed for this purpose, resulting in estimators with unknown properties.

The most popular infinite lag distribution is the *Koyck geometric distributed lag*. Earlier discussion of this technique (chapter 9) showed that it could be estimated by an autoregressive model with an autocorrelated error. One disadvantage of this lag structure is that the coefficients of the lagged explanatory variable(s) continually decline – they cannot first rise and then decline, a pattern thought by many to be *a priori* attractive and one which should not be ruled out of consideration. One way of addressing this problem is to allow unrestricted coefficients on the first few lagged variables and then to impose a geometric pattern.

Good textbook presentations of distributed lags and their associated estimation problems are Judge et al. (1985, chapters 9 and 10) and Maddala (1977, chapter 16). Zaman (1996, pp. 223–5) has complained that distributed lag estimation has assumed without justification that lagged values of the dependent variable do not appear as regressors in the original specification, violating one of the cornerstones of modern dynamic modeling.

12.2 Exact Restrictions

- An example can illustrate how a restricted least squares estimate is found when the restriction is linear. Suppose $y = \alpha + \beta x + \gamma z + \varepsilon$ and it is known that $3\beta + \gamma = 1$. Substituting $\gamma = 1 - 3\beta$ into this equation and rearranging produces the relationship $(y - z) = \alpha + \beta(x - 3z) + \varepsilon$. The restricted OLS estimates $\hat{\alpha}_R$ and $\hat{\beta}_R$ are found by regressing $(y - z)$ on a constant and $(x - 3z)$; then $\hat{\gamma}_R$ is computed as $1 - 3\hat{\beta}_R$. The sum of squared errors resulting from this regression is the restricted sum of squared errors. For discussion of a more general case, see Greene and Seaks (1991).

- An exact linear restriction is tested using the traditional F test, as expounded in chapter 4, in which the difference between the restricted and unrestricted sum of squared errors plays a prominent role.

- As an example of a nonlinear restriction, recall Durbin's two-stage method of dealing with autocorrelated errors. In the technical notes to section 8.2, the first-stage estimating relationship is shown to be such that one slope coefficient is the negative of the product of two other slope coefficients.

- Economic theory sometimes suggests inequality restrictions, such as that a parameter be negative or that it lie between zero and one. By minimizing the sum of squared errors subject to the inequality constraint(s), these restrictions can be incorporated. Unfortunately, it is not possible to accomplish this via a regression technique; a quadratic programming formulation of this problem is required. For an exposition, see Judge et al. (1985, pp. 62–4). For large samples, when the variance of the parameter estimates can be expected to be quite small, (correct) inequality constraints are invariably met, and thus little is lost by ignoring them. Geweke (1986) suggests an attractive way of handling inequality constraints using a Bayesian approach; see the general notes to section 13.3 for further comment.

12.3 Stochastic Restrictions

- The mixed estimation method was developed in its most general form by Theil and Goldberger (1961). They expressed the set of stochastic linear restrictions in the form $r = R\beta + u$ where r is a known vector and R a known matrix. This generalized the technique of Durbin (1953), in which r is a vector of parameter estimates from a previous study and R is an identity matrix. As makes intuitive sense, the mixed estimator approaches the restricted OLS estimator as the variance of u approaches zero, and approaches the unrestricted OLS estimator as the variance of u becomes very large. Srivastava (1980) is an annotated bibliography of estimation using stochastic constraints. Kennedy (1991a) shows how a certain kind of nonlinear stochastic information can be used by the mixed estimation technique.

- A popular way of incorporating a stochastic restriction is to assume that it is an exact restriction. Suppose for example that an extraneous estimate $\hat{\beta}_k$ of β_k is available. A common way of utilizing this information is to subtract $\hat{\beta}_k$ times the kth independent variable from the dependent variable and then regress this new dependent variable on the remaining independent variables. The obvious deficiency of this method is that it does not use the sample data to improve on the estimate of β_k. It is therefore not as efficient as the mixed estimator. This is explained in the technical notes to this section.

- The stochastic restrictions of the mixed estimator could be developed and interpreted in subjective fashion as is done in the Bayesian approach (see chapter 13). This creates a means of introducing subjective prior information into classical statistics, although, as should be clear from a reading of chapter 13, this requires a schizophrenic view of probability.

- The compatibility statistic developed by Theil (1963) is a means usually employed to test whether or not stochastic extraneous information is unbiased; i.e., it tests whether or not the stochastic restrictions are compatible with the data at hand. It is a straightforward application of the Wald statistic, very similar in form and interpretation to the Wald statistic discussed in the technical notes to section 6.4. There a Wald statistic was used to test for the equality of parameters in two data sets when the variance of the error term differed between the two data sets.

- When there is a large number of existing studies, a completely different way of making use of their results is through a technique called meta-regression, in which the estimates of a parameter of interest are themselves regressed on features of these studies thought to affect the estimates they produce. See Stanley and Jarrell (1989). One way of assessing if the evidence from several independent studies supports the hypothesis that a variable has an impact is to produce a consolidated t value by averaging the t values and dividing by the standard error of this average. Since the variance of a t statistic is close to unity, a rule of thumb for finding the consolidated t value is to multiply the average t value by the square root of the number of t values being averaged. See Christie (1990).

12.4   Pre-test Estimators

- Wallace and Ashar (1972) and Wallace (1977) are good expositions of pre-test bias. Giles and Giles (1993) is a recent survey of pre-test estimation and testing. Veall (1992) suggests dealing with pre-test bias in testing by bootstrapping the entire model selection process.

- A straightforward corollary of the pre-test bias phenomenon is the fact that researchers should not use the same sample evidence for both generating a hypothesis and testing it.

- The terminology "data mining" is often used in the context of pre-test bias. In particular, researchers often run a large number of different regressions on a body of data looking for significant t statistics (at, say, the 5% level). Using this approach invalidates traditional hypothesis-testing procedures because such data mining is likely by chance to uncover significant t statistics; i.e., the final results chosen are much more likely to embody a type I error than the claimed 5%. Lovell (1983) offers a rule of thumb for deflating the exaggerated claims of significance generated by such data-mining procedures: when a search has been conducted for the best k out of c candidate explanatory variables, a regression coefficient that appears to be significant at the level $\hat{\alpha}$ should be regarded as significant only at level $\alpha = (c/k)\,\hat{\alpha}$.

- The pre-testing phenomenon can arise in a variety of contexts. Some recent Monte Carlo studies are King and Giles (1984) and Griffiths and Beesley (1984), who examine pre-testing for autocorrelated errors, and Morey (1984), who examines pre-testing for specification error. Zaman (1984) conjectures that discontinuous functions of the data (such as pre-test estimators which jump from one estimator to another on the basis of a pre-test) are inadmissable, and that consequently shrinkage or weighted-average estimators like the Stein estimator are superior.

12.5   Extraneous Information and MSE

- Judge et al. (1985, pp. 72–90) and Fomby et al. (1984, chapter 7) have textbook discussions of pre-test and Stein estimators. Efron and Morris (1977) have an interesting elementary presentation of the Stein estimator. Judge and Bock (1978, pp. 309–11) has an excellent summary of the properties of pre-test and Stein rule estimators.

- Stein-type estimators do have disadvantages. They have unknown small-sample distributions and thus cannot be used to test hypotheses or construct confidence intervals, although this can be dealt with by bootstrapping, as shown by Yi (1991).

  Errors are assumed to be distributed normally. As noted in the general notes to chapter 11, in the regression context they dominate OLS only under certain circumstances, unlikely to be met by collinear data. And last, the loss function with respect to which they are superior is the sum of the MSEs of the estimators of the individual components of the parameter vector, and depends on there being at least three of these components. Nothing can be said about possible improvement of the MSE of the estimator of any individual component.

- The last point made above can be illustrated by an example from Efron and Morris (1977). Suppose we have data on the incidence of a disease in several regions of a small country. The unrestricted OLS estimate of the unknown true incidence for each region is given by the mean of the data for each region. But although the incidence of disease is likely to differ from region to region, the facts that these regions belong to the same country, and are or are close to being contiguous, suggest that these incidence parameters may all be very similar. A not unreasonable restriction to suggest in this context, then, is that all the incidences are identical. Using this restriction, a Stein estimate of the incidence for each region can be created, accomplished by "shrinking" each unrestricted OLS estimate above towards the overall mean of the data. Now suppose the national government plans to set up medical facilities in each region to combat this disease, and wants to use the estimates of regional disease incidence to determine how much of its budget it should allocate to each region. In this case the sum of the individual MSEs is the relevant criterion and the Stein estimates should be used for this purpose. If, however, a regional government is making a decision on how much money to spend on its own medical facility, only one MSE is relevant, and the Stein estimator may not be the best one to use.

- The Stein estimator can be interpreted as "shrinking" the unrestricted OLS estimator towards the restricted OLS estimator, where the extent of the shrinking depends on the magnitude of the F statistic used to test the restrictions. The formula used for the shrinking factor can sometimes shrink the unrestricted OLS estimator beyond the restricted OLS estimator. By truncating this shrinking factor so as to prevent this from happening, an estimator superior to the Stein estimator is created. It is called the Stein *positive rule* estimator. The name derives from the popular application to zero restrictions: the positive rule estimator prevents the sign of the Stein estimator from differing from that of the unrestricted OLS estimator.

TECHNICAL NOTES

12.3   Stochastic Restrictions

- Calculation of the mixed estimator can be illustrated by an example. Suppose we are estimating $y = \alpha + \beta x + \gamma z + \varepsilon$ for which we have T observations. Assume the CLR model assumptions hold with the variance of ε given by σ^2. Suppose from a previous study we have an estimate $\hat{\gamma}$ of γ with variance $V(\hat{\gamma})$. Thus we could write $\hat{\gamma} = \gamma + u$ where the variance of u is $V(\hat{\gamma})$. The estimating equation for the mixed estimator is given by $y^* = x^*\theta + \varepsilon^*$, where

$$y^* = \begin{bmatrix} y_1 \\ y_2 \\ \vdots \\ y_T \\ \hat{\gamma} \end{bmatrix}; x^* = \begin{bmatrix} 1 & x_1 & z_1 \\ 1 & x_2 & z_2 \\ \vdots & & \\ 1 & x_T & z_T \\ 0 & 0 & 1 \end{bmatrix}; \varepsilon^* = \begin{bmatrix} \varepsilon_1 \\ \varepsilon_2 \\ \vdots \\ \varepsilon_T \\ u \end{bmatrix}; \theta = \begin{bmatrix} \alpha \\ \beta \\ \gamma \end{bmatrix}$$

and the variance–covariance matrix of ε^* is given by

$$\begin{bmatrix} \sigma^2 & & & 0 \\ & \ddots & & \\ & & \sigma^2 & \\ 0 & & & V(\hat{\gamma}) \end{bmatrix}$$

- Consider the following two methods of estimating β in the relationship $y = \alpha + \beta x + \gamma z + \varepsilon$.

  (a) Ignore the estimate $\hat{\gamma}$ from a previous study and regress y on a constant, x, and z to obtain β^{OLS}.
  (b) Replace γ by $\hat{\gamma}$, rearrange to get $(y - \hat{\gamma}z) = \alpha + \beta x + \varepsilon$, and regress $(y - \hat{\gamma}z)$ on a constant and x to obtain β^*. (This is a popular means of incorporating stochastic information.)

  Notice that method (a) utilizes only the information about γ in the data at hand to help in estimating β, ignoring the information about γ from the previous study. In contrast, method (b) above utilizes only the information about γ from the previous study, ignoring the information about γ in the data at hand. The mixed estimator is superior to these two alternatives because it incorporates both sources of information about γ into the estimate of β.
- In the example above, the variance of β^{OLS} is smaller than the variance of β^* if the

variance of the OLS estimate of γ from method (a) is smaller than the variance of from the previous study. For a derivation see Goldberger (1964, pp. 258–9).

12.5   Extraneous Information and MSE

- The explanation of the risk function of the pre-test estimator in figure 12.1 was couched in terms of a type I error of 5%. It is easy to see that a type I error of 1% would create a different risk function, one lower on the left and higher on the right. This raises the question of what level of type I error is the optimum choice. Several criteria have been suggested in this regard. For example, the type I error could be chosen so as to minimize the maximum vertical distance in figure 12.1 between the risk function for the pre-test estimator and the minimum of the risk functions for the restricted and unrestricted OLS estimators. Wallace (1977) summarizes this literature.
- The usual measure of the extent to which the restrictions are not met – the horizontal axis of figure 12.1 – is the non-centrality parameter of the F statistic used to test the restrictions.
- In figure 12.1 the restricted OLS estimator is the best estimator if the case at hand lies to the left of point A, and the unrestricted OLS estimator is the best estimator if we are to the right of point A. This suggests that, rather than testing for the validity of the restrictions, we should test for whether or not the restrictions are close enough to being met that we are to the left of point A. This is the principle on which the tests of Toro-Vizcarrondo and Wallace (1968), Wallace and Toro-Vizcarrondo (1969), and Wallace (1972) are based. This pre-testing procedure is much more sophisticated than the usual pre-testing procedure.

13 THE BAYESIAN APPROACH

13.1 INTRODUCTION

There exist two very different approaches to statistics. The traditional "classical" or "frequentist" approach is what has been presented heretofore in this book; almost all econometrics textbooks exposit this approach, with little or no mention of its competitor, the Bayesian approach. One reason for this is the violent controversy among statisticians concerning the relative merits of the Bayesian and non-Bayesian methods, centering on the very different notions of probability they employ. This controversy notwithstanding, it seems that the main reason the Bayesian approach is used so seldom in econometrics is that there exist several practical difficulties with its application. In recent years, with the development of a variety of computer packages, these practical difficulties have for the most part been overcome; it therefore seems but a matter of time before Bayesian analyses become common in econometrics.

One purpose of this chapter is to explain the fundamentals of the Bayesian approach, with particular reference to the difference between Bayesian and non-Bayesian methods. A second purpose is to discuss the practical difficulties that, as alleged earlier, have prevented the adoption of the Bayesian approach. No effort is made to present the mechanics of Bayesian methods; textbook expositions are available for this purpose.

13.2 WHAT IS A BAYESIAN ANALYSIS?

Suppose that, for illustrative purposes, we are interested in estimating the value of an unknown parameter, β. Using the classical approach, the data are fed into an estimating formula $\hat{\beta}$ to produce a specific point estimate $\hat{\beta}_0$ of β. If $\hat{\beta}_0$ is the maximum likelihood estimate, it maximizes the likelihood function, shown in figure 13.1. Associated with $\hat{\beta}$ is a sampling distribution, also illustrated in figure 13.1, indicating the relative frequency of estimates $\hat{\beta}$ would produce in hypothetical repeated samples. This sampling distribution is drawn using a dashed line to stress that it is unknown. If the assumptions of the classical nor-

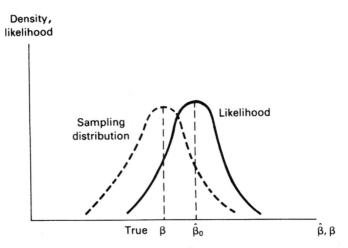

Figure 13.1   The classical sampling distribution

mal linear regression model hold, as is usually assumed to be the case, the MLE $\hat{\beta}$ is the OLS estimator and its sampling distribution is normal in form, with mean equal to the true (unknown) value of β. Any particular estimate $\hat{\beta}_0$ of β is viewed as a random drawing from this sampling distribution, and the use of $\hat{\beta}_0$ as a point estimate of β is defended by appealing to the "desirable" properties, such as unbiasedness, of the sampling distribution of $\hat{\beta}$. This summarizes the essentials of the classical, non-Bayesian approach.

The output from a Bayesian analysis is very different. Instead of producing a point estimate of β, a Bayesian analysis produces as its prime piece of output a density function for β called the "posterior" density function. This density function relates to β, not $\hat{\beta}$, so it most definitely is *not* a sampling distribution; it is interpreted as reflecting the odds the researcher would give when taking bets on the true value of β. For example, the researcher should be willing to bet three dollars, to win one dollar, that the true value of β is above the lower quartile of his or her posterior density for β. This "subjective" notion of probability is a conceptually different concept of probability from the "frequentist" or "objective" concept employed in the classical approach; this difference is the main bone of contention between the Bayesians and non-Bayesians.

Following this subjective notion of probability, it is easy to imagine that *before* looking at the data the researcher could have a "prior" density function of β, reflecting the odds that he or she would give, before looking at the data, if asked to take bets on the true value of β. This prior distribution, when combined with the data via Bayes' theorem, produces the posterior distribution referred to above. This posterior density function is in essence a weighted average of the

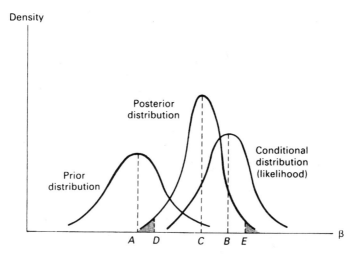

Figure 13.2 Obtaining the posterior distribution

prior density and the likelihood (or "conditional" density, conditional on the data), as illustrated in figure 13.2.

It may seem strange that the main output of the Bayesian analysis is a density function instead of a point estimate as in the classical analysis. The reason for this is that the posterior can be used as input to decision problems, only one example of which is the problem of choosing a point estimate. An illustration of how the posterior can be used in this way should clarify this. To begin, a loss function must be specified, giving the loss incurred, using a specific point estimate β_0^*, for every possible true value of β. The expected loss associated with using β_0^* can be calculated by taking the expectation over all possible values of β, using for this calculation the posterior density of β. Note that this expectation is *not* taken over repeated samples.

This is illustrated in figure 13.3, which is drawn for the case of β being estimated by the value β_2. The loss function shown in figure 13.3 is unique to this estimate β_2; note that it is smallest when $\beta = \beta_2$, as it should be. Different true values of β give rise to different losses that would be incurred if β were to be estimated by β_2, and, loosely speaking, the height of the posterior density function gives the probability of particular values of β being the true value of β. Thus, for the four β_i illustrated in figure 13.3, with probability p_i, the true value of β is β_i and the loss would be L_i.

The expected loss due to estimating β by β_2 is given as the weighted average of all possible L_i, with weights given by the corresponding p_i. *Note that this calculation gives the expected loss associated with only one estimate of* β, *namely* β_2. This calculation must now be repeated for all other possible estimates of β

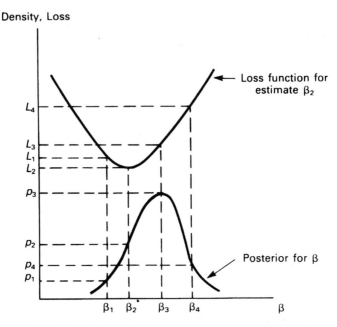

Figure 13.3   Finding the expected loss of the estimate ß₂

(in this example, an infinite number of alternative estimates) to find the expected losses associated with these alternative estimates. Figure 13.3 would look different for each of these alternative calculations – the loss function would move horizontally so as to have its minimum over the estimate for which the expected loss was being calculated. Once the expected losses associated with all alternative estimates have been calculated, the Bayesian point estimate for that loss function is chosen as the estimate whose expected loss is the smallest. (Algebraic means are employed to accomplish this – the expected losses are not actually all calculated for an example such as this where there are an infinite number of possible estimates.) In the example in figure 13.3, where the loss function is drawn as quadratic (i.e., proportional to the square of the difference between the estimate and the true value of β), the mean of the posterior distribution turns out to have minimum expected loss and will be chosen as the Bayesian point estimate.

To summarize, the Bayesian approach consists of three steps.

(1)   A prior distribution is formalized, reflecting the researcher's beliefs about the parameter(s) in question before looking at the data.

(2)   This prior is combined with the data, via Bayes' theorem, to produce the posterior distribution, the main output of a Bayesian analysis.

(3) This posterior is combined with a loss or utility function to allow a decision to be made on the basis of minimizing expected loss or maximizing expected utility. This third step is optional.

13.3 ADVANTAGES OF THE BAYESIAN APPROACH

The Bayesian approach claims several advantages over the classical approach, of which the following are some examples.

(1) The Bayesian approach is concerned with how information in data modifies a researcher's beliefs about parameter values and allows computation of probabilities associated with alternative hypotheses or models; this corresponds directly to the approach to these problems taken by most researchers.
(2) Extraneous information is routinely incorporated in a consistent fashion in the Bayesian method through the formulation of the prior; in the classical approach such information is more likely to be ignored, and when incorporated is usually done so in *ad hoc* ways.
(3) The Bayesian approach can tailor the estimate to the purpose of the study, through selection of the loss function; in general, its compatibility with decision analysis is a decided advantage.
(4) There is no need to justify the estimating procedure in terms of the awkward concept of the performance of the estimator in hypothetical repeated samples; the Bayesian approach is justified solely on the basis of the prior and the sample data.

A more complete, and more persuasive, listing of the advantages of the Bayesian approach can be found in Zellner (1974). The essence of the debate between the frequentists and the Bayesians rests on the acceptability of the subjectivist notion of probability. Once one is willing to view probability in this way, the advantages of the Bayesian approach are compelling. But most practitioners, even though they have no strong aversion to the subjectivist notion of probability, do not choose to adopt the Bayesian approach. The reasons are practical in nature.

(1) Formalizing prior beliefs into a prior distribution is not an easy task.
(2) The mechanics of finding the posterior distribution are formidable.
(3) Convincing others of the validity of Bayesian results is difficult because they view those results as being "contaminated" by personal (prior) beliefs.

In recent years these practical difficulties have been alleviated by the development of appropriate computer software. These problems are discussed in the next section.

13.4 OVERCOMING PRACTITIONERS' COMPLAINTS

(1) CHOOSING A PRIOR

In the words of Smith and Brainard (1976), a prior distribution tries to capture the "information which gives rise to that almost inevitable disappointment one feels when confronted with a straightforward estimation of one's preferred structural model." Non-Bayesians usually employ this information to lead them to add, drop or modify variables in an *ad hoc* search for a "better" result. Bayesians incorporate this information into their prior, exploiting it *ex ante* in an explicit, up-front fashion; they maintain that, since human judgement is inevitably an ingredient in statistical procedures, it should be incorporated in a formal, consistent manner.

Although non-Bayesian researchers do use such information implicitly in undertaking *ad hoc* specification searches, they are extremely reluctant to formalize this information in the form of a prior distribution or to believe that others are capable of doing so. Leamer (1983b, p. 298) has expressed this sentiment cogently: "It seems clear to me that the principal resistance to Bayesian methods is expressed in the incredulous grin which greets Bayesians when they make statements like: 'We need to begin with a multivariate prior distribution for the parameter vector β.'"

To those unaccustomed to the Bayesian approach, formulating a prior can be a daunting task. This prompts some researchers to employ an "ignorance" prior, which, as its name implies, reflects complete ignorance about the values of the parameters in question. In this circumstance the outcome of the Bayesian analysis is based on the data alone; it usually produces an answer identical, except for interpretation, to that of the classical approach. Cases in which a researcher can legitimately claim that he or she has absolutely no idea of the values of the parameters are rare, however; in most cases an "informative" prior must be formulated. There are three basic ways in which this can be done.

(a) *Using previous studies* A researcher can allow results from previous studies to define his or her prior. An earlier study, for example, may have produced an estimate of the parameter in question, along with an estimate of that estimate's variance. These numbers could be employed by the researcher as the mean and variance of his or her prior. (Notice that this changes dramatically the interpretation of these estimates.)

(b) *Placing hypothetical bets* Since the prior distribution reflects the odds the researcher would give, before looking at the data, when taking hypothetical bets on the value of the unknown parameter β, a natural way of determining the prior is to ask the researcher (or an expert in the area, since researchers often allow their prior to be determined by advice from experts) various questions relating to hypothetical bets. For example, via a series of questions a value β_0 may be determined for which the researcher would be indifferent to betting that the true value of β (1) lies above β_0, or (2) lies below β_0. As another example, a similar series of questions could determine the smallest interval that he or she would be willing to bet, at even odds, contains the true value of β. Information obtained in this way can be used to calculate the prior distribution.

(c) *Using predictive distributions*   One problem with method (b) above is that for many researchers, and particularly for experts whose opinions may be used to formulate the researcher's prior, it is difficult to think in terms of model parameters and to quantify information in terms of a distribution for those parameters. They may be more comfortable thinking in terms of the value of the dependent variable associated with given values of the independent variables. Given a particular combination of values of the independent variables, the expert is asked for his or her assessment of the corresponding value of the dependent variable (i.e., a prior is formed on the dependent variable, not the parameters). This distribution, called a "predictive" distribution, involves observable variables rather than unobservable parameters, and thus should relate more directly to the expert's knowledge and experience. By eliciting facts about an expert's predictive distributions at various settings of the independent variables, it is possible to infer the expert's associated (implicit) prior distribution concerning the parameters of the model.

For many researchers, even the use of these methods cannot allow them to feel comfortable with the prior developed. For these people the only way in which a Bayesian analysis can be undertaken is by structuring a range of prior distributions encompassing all prior distributions the researcher feels are reasonable. This approach is advocated under subsection (3) below as a necessary component of Bayesian analysis.

(2)   *FINDING THE POSTERIOR*

The algebra of Bayesian analyses is more difficult than that of classical analyses, especially in multidimensional problems. For example, the classical analysis of a multiple regression with normally distributed errors in the Bayesian context requires a multivariate normal-gamma prior which, when combined with a multivariate normal likelihood function, produces a multivariate normal-gamma posterior from which the posterior marginal distribution (marginal with respect to the unknown variance of the error term) of the vector of slope coefficients can be derived as a multivariate t distribution. This both sounds and is mathematically demanding.

From the practitioner's viewpoint, however, this mathematics is not necessary. Bayesian textbooks spell out the nature of the priors and likelihoods relevant to a wide variety of estimation problems, and discuss the form taken by the resulting output. Armed with this knowledge, the practitioner can call on several computer packages to perform the calculations required to produce the posterior distribution. And then when, say, the mean of the posterior distribution must be found to use as a point estimate, recently-developed computer techniques can be used to perform the required numerical integration. Despite all this, some econometricians complain that the Bayesian approach is messy, requiring numerical integration instead of producing analytical approximations, and has for this reason taken the fun out of statistics.

(3) CONVINCING OTHERS

The problem Bayesians have of convincing others of the validity of their results is captured neatly by Blyth (1972, p. 20):

> However meaningful and helpful such numbers [Bayesian results] are to the author, they are meaningless and irrelevant to his reader ... what the reader wants to know from the author is 'Leaving your opinions out of this, what does your experimental evidence say?'

One way of addressing this problem is to employ either an ignorance prior or a prior reflecting only results of earlier studies. But a better way of resolving this problem is to report a range of empirical results corresponding to a range of priors. This procedure has several advantages. First, it should alleviate any uncomfortable feeling the researcher may have with respect to his or her choice of prior. Second, a realistic range of priors should encompass the prior of an adversary, so that the range of results reported should include a result convincing to that adversary. Third, if the results are not too sensitive to the nature of the prior, a strong case can be made for the usefulness of these results. And fourth, if the results are sensitive to the prior, this should be made known so that the usefulness of such "fragile" results can be evaluated in that light.

GENERAL NOTES

13.1   Introduction

- Hey (1983) is a good reference for the Bayesian approach at the most elementary level. Novick and Jackson (1974) is invaluable at the intermediate level. Zellner (1971) is an excellent advanced reference, very comprehensive in its coverage of the Bayesian view of econometric problems. Judge et al. (1985, chapter 4) is a useful reference. Zellner and Richard (1973) is an instructive application. For references to Bayesian computer programs see Press (1989, pp. 86–100) and Koop (1994).
- Studying both Bayesian and non-Bayesian methods provides a much better understanding of statistics than that provided by studying only one approach. Weber (1973) examines the history of the Bayesian controversy; Qin (1996) is an historical account of the role of Bayesian methods in econometrics.
- Some recent references suitable for exploring the frequentist/Bayesian controversy are Efron (1986) and associated commentary, and Poirier (1988) and related discussion. Zellner (1983, 1988) provides reviews of the Bayesian approach in econometrics. Poirier (1989, 1992) reports on the Bayesian content of econometrics textbooks, and

Poirier (1991) cites examples of Bayesian applied studies. Koop (1994) is an excellent exposition of recent progress in applied Bayesian econometrics, with particular emphasis on computational considerations.

13.2 What is a Bayesian Analysis?

- It cannot be stressed too strongly that the main difference between Bayesians and non-Bayesians is the concept of probability employed. For the Bayesian probability is regarded as representing a degree of reasonable belief; numerical probabilities are associated with degrees of confidence that the researcher has in propositions about empirical phenomena. For the non-Bayesian (or "frequentist"), probability is regarded as representing the frequency with which an event would occur in repeated trials. This explains the gibe, "Bayesians do it with less frequency."
- The concept of a confidence interval can be used to illustrate the different concepts of probability employed by the Bayesians and non-Bayesians. In figure 13.2 the points D and E are placed such that 2.5% of the area under the posterior distribution appears in each tail; the interval DE can then be interpreted as being such that the probability that β falls in that interval is 95%. This is the way in which many clients of classical/frequentist statisticians want to and do interpret classical 95% confidence intervals, in spite of the fact that it is illegitimate to do so. The comparable classical confidence interval must be interpreted as either covering or not covering the true value of β, but being calculated in such a way that, if such intervals were calculated for a large number of repeated samples, then 95% of these intervals would cover the true value of β.
- In figure 13.2, the prior distribution is combined with the likelihood function (representing the data) to produce the posterior distribution, which is drawn as having the smallest variance because it incorporates information from the other two distributions. In many cases the mean C of the posterior distribution can be viewed as a weighted average of the mean A of the prior distribution and the mean B of the likelihood function, where the weights are the inverses of the variances (called the *precisions*) of the respective distributions. As the sample size becomes larger and larger, the likelihood function becomes narrower and narrower, and more and more closely centered over the true value of β. Since the variance of this conditional distribution becomes smaller and smaller (i.e., its precision becomes greater and greater), the role played by the prior becomes less and less. Asymptotically, the prior is completely swamped by the data, as it should be.
- When the decision problem is one of choosing a point estimate for β, the estimate chosen depends on the loss function employed. For example, if the loss function is quadratic, proportional to the square of the difference between the chosen point estimate and the true value of β, then the mean of the posterior distribution is chosen as the point estimate. If the loss is proportional to the absolute value of this difference, the median is chosen. A zero loss for a correct estimate and a constant loss for an incorrect estimate leads to the choice of the mode. The popularity of the squared error or quadratic loss function has led to the mean of the posterior distribution being referred to as the Bayesian point estimate. Note that, if the posterior distribution is symmetric with a unique global maximum, these three examples of loss functions lead to the same choice of estimate. For an example of an alternative loss function tailored

to a specific problem, see Varian (1974); for more discussion of this loss function, see Zellner (1986c).

- The ignorance prior is sometimes called a "diffuse," "uniform," "equiproportional," or "non-informative" prior. Its opposite is called an informative prior; an informative Bayesian analysis is one employing an informative prior. With a non-informative prior a Bayesian analysis often produces estimates identical to those of a classical analysis, with the all-important difference of interpretation (owing to the different concepts of probability). In the "empirical" Bayes approach a prior is constructed from the data themselves, and so can be viewed as incorporating a non-informative prior; Casella (1985) has an introductory discussion. The Stein estimator, discussed in chapter 12, can be viewed as an empirical Bayes estimator.

- If the disturbances are assumed to be distributed normally, if the prior distribution is uniform (reflecting ignorance), and if the loss function is symmetric (such as in the three examples given earlier), the Bayesian estimator is identical to the OLS estimator. If the prior distribution is uniform and if the loss function is of the third form described above, the Bayesian estimator is identical to the maximum likelihood estimator (MLE). Under general conditions the Bayesian estimator and the MLE coincide in large samples (although their interpretation differs), since in large samples the prior is swamped by the actual data.

- Although the Bayesian approach rejects the concept of repeated samples, it is possible to ask how the Bayesian estimator would perform on criteria utilizing hypothetical repeated samples. Under certain conditions, as noted in the preceding paragraph, it is identical to the OLS estimator or the MLE and thus would have the same properties in repeated samples as these estimators. When the uniform prior is not used, a normal prior is often employed. In this case the Bayesian estimate is biased in repeated samples (but asymptotically unbiased) unless by luck the mean of the prior is the true parameter value. The variance of the Bayesian estimator is in general smaller, however, because it incorporates more information (i.e., the prior itself is extra information) than the classical techniques. This is evidenced by the sharper interval estimates usually associated with the Bayesian technique.

- The Bayesian would object strenuously to being evaluated on the basis of hypothetical repeated samples because he or she does not believe that justification of an estimator on the basis of its properties in repeated samples is relevant. He or she would maintain that because the estimate is calculated from the data at hand it must be justified on the basis of those data. The Bayesian recognizes, however, that reliance on an estimate calculated from a single sample could be dangerous, particularly if the sample size is small. In the Bayesian view sample data should be tempered by subjective knowledge of what the researcher feels is most likely to be the true value of the parameter. In this way the influence of atypical samples (not unusual if the sample size is small) is moderated. The classical statistician, on the other hand, fears that calculations using typical samples will become contaminated with poor prior information.

13.3 Advantages of the Bayesian Approach

- Additional sample information is easily incorporated in a standard way via the Bayesian technique (the current posterior distribution is used as the prior in a new estimation using the additional data). Thus the Bayesian approach incorporates a formal and explicit learning model, corresponding directly with the learning process in research.

- The Bayesian approach is an attractive way of handling estimation subject to inequality constraints, a case that is troublesome in the classical approach. A truncated prior is employed, giving rise to a truncated posterior. In contrast to classical estimates, which are often on the inequality boundary, Bayesian point estimates are interior, moving closer and closer to the boundary as the data disagree more and more with the constraint; see Geweke (1986) and Griffiths (1988). Estimation using this technique can be done with SHAZAM.

13.4 Overcoming Practitioners' Complaints

- An important feature of the Bayesian approach is that prior information is incorporated in an explicit fashion. Bayesians view non-Bayesians as using prior information and *ad hoc* ways, as expressed for example by Zellner (1989, pp. 301–2):

> Non-Bayesians sit around thinking about restrictions on simultaneous equations models. That's prior information. Others think about what to assume about the error terms properties. That's many times prior information. Others sit around thinking about how to formulate a model for the observations. That involves a tremendous amount of prior information.

As another example, consider the remarks of Tukey, as quoted by Zellner (1984, p. 98):

> It is my impression that rather generally, not just in econometrics, it is considered decent to use judgement in choosing a functional form, but indecent to use judgement in choosing a coefficient. If judgement about important things is quite all right, why should it not be used for less important things as well? Perhaps the real purpose of Bayesian techniques is to let us do the indecent thing while modestly concealed behind a formal apparatus.

Non-Bayesians argue that one's prior beliefs are not always easily expressed in the form of a prior distribution and thus it may be better to incorporate such imprecise information in a thoughtful (*ad hoc*) fashion than to insist that it be forced into a formal prior. Many non-Bayesians view explicit incorporation of prior information as a straitjacket. Consider the disarming, and alarming, argument articulated by Goldberger (1989, p. 152):

> Well in a sense everybody's a Bayesian, we use information beyond the sample. The question is whether inclusion of prior information should be formalized. Formalizing may sound like a good idea, but maybe it's not a good idea. I like Manski's argument, which I will paraphrase. The objection to classical statistical inference is that it's nonsense. But everybody knows that. So if you follow the style I use, which would be classical statistical inference, you don't take it too seriously – you don't take it literally. If you use a Bayesian procedure. I get the impression you really have to believe the implications – you've already committed yourself to everything. You don't have the opportunity for waffling afterwards because you've already put everything in, and you have to take it literally from there on out.

- A Bayesian analysis employing a prior based on results from a previous study would produce estimates similar to those of the method of mixed estimation outlined in chapter 12, except of course for interpretation.
- Not all previous studies match up perfectly with the study at hand. Results from previous studies may relate to slightly different variables under slightly different circumstances so that they cannot be used directly as suggested in the body of this chapter. A researcher may have to assimilate subjectively a wide array of related empirical studies to formulate a prior; this would have to be done using one of the other two methods for formulating priors discussed earlier.
- Formulation of a prior using information gained from questions relating to hypothetical bets is straightforward if the functional form of that prior is specified. This functional form is usually chosen so as to facilitate calculation of the posterior for the problem at hand. For example, if we are attempting to estimate the parameter of a binomial distribution, the derivation of the posterior is much easier if the prior takes the form of a beta distribution. In this example the beta prior is a "natural conjugate prior" since it yields a posterior that also is a beta distribution. This choice of a natural conjugate form for the prior is innocuous: very few people have prior information so precise that it cannot be approximated adequately by a natural conjugate distribution. "Conjugate" may or may not be related to the adjective "conjugal": a conjugate distribution is a suitable mate for the model's distribution in that it produces offspring of its own kind.
- Given the distributional form of the prior, only answers to a small number of hypothetical betting questions are required to produce an actual prior. Additional betting questions are nonetheless asked, with their answers providing a check on the "coherence" of this prior; if answers to later questions are inconsistent with the fitted prior based on answers to earlier questions, this incoherence is used to prompt further thought on the nature of the prior beliefs in question. An iterative process ensues, leading eventually to the formulation of a coherent prior. Most undergraduate texts on Bayesian statistics have a section giving a detailed illustration of this process; for an example see Jones (1977, chapter 13). All this sounds like a lot of work. Thanks to Novick et al. (1983), however, there exists an interactive computer package (CADA) that relieves the analyst of almost all of the drudgery; the entire process is monitored by a computer-directed conversational dialogue, allowing priors to be formulated efficiently and painlessly. Examples of how CADA operates in this respect can be found in Novick and Jackson (1974, pp. 160–6, 217–23).
- Formulating priors by using predictive distributions is described and illustrated by Kadane et al. (1980), who also refer to a computer package implementing this approach. CADA includes a variant of this approach. One advantage of the predictive distribution approach is that it does not impose a specific model on the researcher/expert and thus the elicited information could allow detection of a nonlinearity in the implicit model. Kadane et al. (1980) discuss the relative merits of the predictive distribution method and the method of eliciting hypothetical bets, which they call the structural method.
- There exists considerable evidence that people can be inaccurate in their personal assessments of probabilities; for references see Hogarth (1975), Leamer (1978, chapter 10), Lindley et al. (1979), Wallsten and Budescu (1983), and Fishchoff and Beyth-Marom (1983). The existence of this phenomenon underlines the importance of reporting estimates for a range of priors.

- The suggestion of reporting the fragility of empirical estimates (for both Bayesian and non-Bayesian methods) is advanced in convincing fashion by Leamer and Leonard (1983). They illustrate graphically for a two-dimensional case how the set of possible coefficient estimates is affected by the nature of the prior information. In one case they examine, the set of possible estimates is bounded by estimates generated by regressions formed by omitting different combinations of variables thought *a priori* to have coefficients close to zero in value. This example illustrates the kind of Bayesian prior information corresponding to "information" employed by a classical statistician in a typical *ad hoc* specification search. To aid practitioners in reporting the fragility of their estimates, Leamer and Leonard have developed a computer package. SEARCH (Seeking Extreme and Average Regression Coefficient Hypotheses), which is capable of calculating the range of coefficient estimates associated with a range for the variance of the prior. Examples of this methodology can be found in Leamer and Leonard (1983) and Leamer (1983a, 1986). Ziemer (1984) speculates that fragility analysis will serve as a compromise between the *ad hoc* pre-test/search methods now in common use and the unfamiliar shrinkage/Bayesian methods advocated by theorists.

TECHNICAL NOTES

- Bayes' theorem is derived from the fact that the probability of obtaining the data and the parameters can be written either as:

$$\text{prob(data and parameters)} = \text{prob(data|parameters) prob(parameters)}$$

or:

$$\text{prob(data and parameters)} = \text{prob(parameters|data) prob(data)}$$

Equating these two expressions and rearranging, we get Bayes' theorem:

$$\text{prob(parameters|data)} = \frac{\text{prob(data|parameters) prob(parameters)}}{\text{prob(data)}}$$

The denominator can be calculated by integrating over all parameter values, so it becomes a normalization factor. The left-hand side of the expression is the *posterior* distribution, the prob(parameters) *after* the sample. The right half of the right-hand side is the *prior* distribution, the prob(parameters) *before* the sample. The left half of the right-hand side is the likelihood function. (Recall section 2.9 and its technical notes.) Thus, according to Bayes' theorem the posterior distribution is given by the product of the prior distribution, the likelihood function and a normalization factor.

- Bayesians undertake hypothesis testing by estimating the probability that the null hypothesis is true and comparing it to the probability that the alternative hypothesis is true. These two probabilities are used in conjunction with a loss function to decide whether to accept the null or the alternative. If the loss from accepting a false null is

Lossfalsenull and the loss from accepting a false alternative is Lossfalsealt, then the expected loss from accepting the null is

$$prob(alternative|data) \times Lossfalsenull$$

and the expected loss from accepting the alternative is

$$prob(null|data) \times Lossfalsealt.$$

Then the null would be accepted if

$$prob(null|data) \times Lossfalsealt \geq prob(alternative|data) \times Lossfalsenull$$

which can be rewritten as

$$\frac{prob(null|data)}{prob(alternative|data)} \geq \frac{Lossfalsenull}{Lossfalsealt}$$

The left-hand side of this is called the *posterior odds ratio*, whose calculation can be explained as follows. Bayes' rule can be used to deduce that

$$prob(null|data) = \frac{prob(null) \times prob(data|null)}{prob(data)} \quad \text{and that}$$

$$prob(alternative|data) = \frac{prob(alternative) \times prob(data|alternative)}{prob(data)}$$

so that the posterior odds ratio is given by

$$\frac{prob(null|data)}{prob(alternative|data)} = \frac{prob(null) \times prob(data|null)}{prob(alternative) \times prob(data|alternative)}$$

This in turn can be seen to be the prior odds, prob(null)/prob(alternative), times the *Bayes factor*, prob(data|null)/prob(data|alternative). The numerator of the Bayes factor is calculated as a weighted average of the likelihood functions for each possible parameter value where the weights are given by the posterior distribution of the parameters. (This is computed by integrating out the parameter values.) The denominator is computed in like fashion, using the likelihood and posterior associated with the alternative hypothesis. For the simple example in which the null is $\beta \geq 1$ and the alternative $\beta < 1$, the numerator is just the integral of the posterior distribution of β from one to infinity, and the denominator one minus the numerator.

We are now in a position to summarize the major differences between the classical and Bayesian hypothesis testing procedures:

(a) Bayesians "compare" rather than "test" hypotheses; they select one hypothesis in preference to the other, based on minimizing an expected loss function.

(b) Bayesians do not adopt an arbitrarily determined type I error rate, instead allowing this error rate to be whatever minimization of the expected loss function implies for the data at hand. One implication of this is that as the sample size grows the Bayesian allows both the type I and type II error rates to move towards zero whereas the classical statistician forces the type I error rate to be constant.

(c) Bayesians build prior beliefs explicitly into the hypothesis choice through the prior odds ratio.

(d) For Bayesians the Bayes factor is calculated by averaging likelihoods over all parameter values whereas in the comparable classical calculation the maximized likelihoods are used, producing the familiar likelihood ratio statistic.

For further discussion see Zellner (1984, pp. 275–305) or the textbook expositions cited earlier. Moulton (1991) is an example of how Bayesian techniques are used to select a model based on posterior odds and then combine inferences across potential models to incorporate uncertainty associated with the model specification.

- The joint density of a future y value and the parameter values is obtained by taking the product of the likelihood function of the future y value and the posterior density for the parameter values. By integrating out the parameter values the predictive density of the future y is produced. This in effect produces a y density which is a weighted average of y densities associated with different parameter values, where the weights are given by the posterior density of the parameter values. The predictive density can be used in different ways. It could be combined with a suitable loss function to make a prediction of the future y value, for example, or by integrating this density from the current y value to infinity, an estimate of the probability that the future y value will be higher than the current y value could be obtained.

- The Bayesian equivalent of the classical confidence interval is called the *highest posterior density* interval. If the integral of the posterior over this interval is 0.95, this interval is said to have 95 percent probability content. The shortest such interval is the 95 percent highest posterior density interval. With an ignorance prior this interval is usually the same magnitude as the classical 95 percent confidence interval, but the interpretation is completely different. The Bayesian interpretation is that there is a 95 percent probability that the true value of the parameter lies in this interval. The classical interpretation refuses to use this subjective definition of probability and so claims only that the true value either lies in this interval or it does not, but if repeated samples were taken an interval constructed in this way would cover the true parameter value in 95 percent of these repeated samples.

- Finding a non-informative prior is not as easy as it seems at first sight. If the parameter β for which we seek a prior can take any value from $-\infty$ to $+\infty$, then a uniform distribution, with $\text{prob}(\beta_0 \leq \beta \leq \beta_0 + d\beta) = d\beta$, is suitable. (The fact that the integral of this distribution is infinite rather than unity makes it an improper prior, but this is not of consequence in this context.) But suppose that we know that a parameter can take on only non-negative values, such as would be the case for the error variance σ, so that $0 \leq \sigma \leq \infty$. Then two problems arise if a uniform distribution is used as a prior for σ.

First, for any finite positive number a, $\text{prob}(\sigma \leq a)$ relative to $\text{prob}(\sigma > a)$ is zero, inconsistent with our belief that nothing is known about σ. Second, if we are ignorant about σ, we should also be ignorant about σ^2. But if we adopt a uniform prior for σ, so that $\text{prob}(\sigma_0 \leq \sigma \leq \sigma_0 + d\sigma) = d\sigma$, then it should also be the case that $\text{prob}[\sigma_0^n \leq \sigma^n \leq (\sigma_0 + d\sigma)^n]$ equals $d\sigma$, but instead it equals $d\sigma^n = \sigma^{n-1}d\sigma$. Both these problems are solved if $\text{prob}(\sigma_0 \leqslant \sigma \leqslant \sigma_0 + d\sigma) = d\sigma/\sigma$ so that the prior for σ is made proportional to σ^{-1} or, equivalently, $\ln\sigma$ is considered to have a uniform prior.

Consider now the problem of finding an ignorance prior for a parameter θ which is a proportion, so it is confined to lie in the zero to one interval. If we are ignorant about θ we should be equally ignorant about $\phi = \theta/(1 - \theta)$. Since ϕ lies between zero and infinity, we can apply the same solution to ϕ as for σ. This produces $d\phi/\phi = d\theta/\theta(1 - \theta)$ so the prior for θ is taken as proportional to $1/\theta(1 - \theta)$. Notice that the transformation of θ, in this example, that creates a variable lying between zero and infinity may not be unique, suggesting that there may be more than one ignorance prior relevant to a particular problem. This implies, in some special cases in which universal agreement on the appropriate ignorance prior cannot be reached, that there will be competing non-informative Bayesian estimators.

There is a common theme in the examples given above. The parameter is transformed so as to be capable of taking on all values on the real line and so can be given a uniform prior. Then the change-of-variable theorem is used to work backwards to find the corresponding density for the original parameter. A popular way of doing this is through Jeffrey's rule: choose the prior for the parameter vector as proportional to the square root of the determinant of the information matrix. For discussion see Berger (1985, pp. 82–90). An excellent discussion of the meaning and formulation of ignorance priors in an applied econometrics context (unit root testing) appears in Volume 6(4) of the *Journal of Applied Econometrics* where several discussants address issues raised by Phillips (1991). Kass and Wasserman (1996) is a good survey of problems in selecting an ignorance prior.

- It is instructive to discuss the Bayesian estimator for the case of a first-order autocorrelated error. Jeffrey's rule gives a prior for ρ proportional to $(1 - \rho^2)^{-\frac{1}{2}}$. Combining this with a prior for σ proportional to σ^{-1} and a uniform prior for the β coefficients gives rise to a straightforward expression for the posterior distribution of ρ, and an extremely complicated expression for the posterior distribution of β. Fortunately, though, the expected value of this distribution of β, the Bayesian estimator of β, can be seen to be the integral, over all values of ρ, of the GLS estimator (given ρ) times the posterior density of ρ. In other words, loosely speaking, the Bayesian estimator is a weighted average of an infinite number of GLS estimates, corresponding to an infinite number of different values of ρ, where the weights are given by the heights of the posterior distribution of ρ.

The algebra to calculate this is intractable, so it must be computed by numerical integration. To do this, the range of all possible values of ρ is divided into a large number of small subsets, say 500 of them. The area under the posterior distribution of ρ for each subset is calculated, the value of ρ in the middle of each subset is identified, and for each of these values of ρ the GLS estimator of β is calculated. The numerical integration then consists of taking a weighted average of each of these GLS estimates, with the weights given by the corresponding area under the posterior distribution of ρ. The greater is the number of subsets, the more closely will the numerical integration approximate the "true" Bayesian estimator. How many is enough? Kennedy and Simons (1991) suggest for this example that only 40 are required for this estimator to perform well. For a textbook exposition of these formulas, see Judge et al. (1985, pp. 291–3).

14
DUMMY VARIABLES

14.1   INTRODUCTION

Explanatory variables are often qualitative in nature (e.g., wartime versus peacetime, male versus female, east versus west versus south), so that some proxy must be constructed to represent them in a regression. Dummy variables are used for this purpose. A dummy variable is an artificial variable constructed such that it takes the value unity whenever the qualitative phenomenon it represents occurs, and zero otherwise. Once created, these proxies, or "dummies" as they are called, are used in the CLR model just like any other explanatory variable, yielding standard OLS results.

The exposition below is in terms of an example designed to illustrate the roles dummy variables can play, give insight to how their coefficients are estimated in a regression, and clarify the interpretation of these coefficient estimates.

Consider data on the incomes of doctors, professors and lawyers, exhibited in figure 14.1 (where the data have been ordered so as to group observations into the professions), and suppose it is postulated that an individual's income depends on his or her profession, a qualitative variable. We may write this model as

$$Y = \alpha_D D_D + \alpha_P D_P + \alpha_L D_L + \varepsilon \qquad (1)$$

where D_D is a dummy variable taking the value one whenever the observation in question is a doctor, and zero otherwise; D_P and D_L are dummy variables defined in like fashion for professors and lawyers. Notice that the equation in essence states that an individual's income is given by the coefficient of his or her related dummy variable plus an error term. (For a professor, for example, D_D and D_L are zero and D_P is one, so (1) becomes $Y = \alpha_P + \varepsilon$.)

From the structure of equation (1) and the configuration of figure 14.1, the logical estimate of α_D is the average of all doctors' incomes, of α_P the average of all professors' incomes, and of α_L the average of all lawyers' incomes. It is reassuring, then, that if Y is regressed on these three dummy variables, these are exactly the estimates that result.

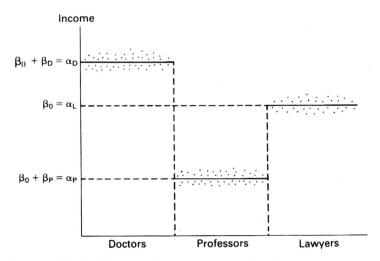

Figure 14.1 A step function example of using dummy variables

14.2 INTERPRETATION

Equation (1) as structured does not contain an intercept. If it did, perfect multi-collinearity would result (the intercept variable, a column of ones, would equal the sum of the three dummy variables) and the regression could not be run. Nonetheless, more often than not, equations with dummy variables do contain an intercept. This is accomplished by omitting one of the dummies to avoid perfect multi-collinearity.

Suppose D_L is dropped, for example, creating

$$Y = \beta_0 + \beta_D D_D + \beta_P D_P + \varepsilon. \qquad (2)$$

In this case, for a lawyer D_D and D_P are zero, so a lawyer's expected income is given by the intercept β_0. Thus the logical estimate of the intercept is the average of all lawyers' incomes. A doctor's expected income is given by equation (2) as $\beta_0 + \beta_D$; thus the logical estimate of β_D is the difference between the doctors' average income and the lawyers' average income. Similarly, the logical estimate of β_P is the difference between the professors' average income and the lawyers' average income. Once again, it is reassuring that, when regression (2) is undertaken (i.e., regressing Y on an intercept and the dummy variables D_D and D_P), exactly these results are obtained. The crucial difference is that with an intercept included the interpretation of the dummy variable coefficients changes dramatically.

With no intercept, the dummy variable coefficients reflect the expected income for the respective professions. With an intercept included, the omitted category (profession) becomes a base or benchmark to which the others are compared. The dummy variable coefficients for the remaining categories measure the extent to which they differ from this base. This base in the example above is the lawyer profession. Thus the coefficient B_D, for example, gives the *difference* between the expected income of a doctor and the expected income of a lawyer.

Most researchers find the equation with an intercept more convenient because it allows them to address more easily the questions in which they usually have the most interest, namely whether or not the categorization makes a difference and if so by how much. If the categorization does make a difference, by how much is measured directly by the dummy variable coefficient estimates. Testing whether or not the categorization is relevant can be done by running a t test of a dummy variable coefficient against zero (or, to be more general, an F test on the appropriate set of dummy variable coefficient estimates).

14.3 ADDING ANOTHER QUALITATIVE VARIABLE

Suppose now the data in figure 14.1 are rearranged slightly to form figure 14.2, from which it appears that gender may have a role to play in determining income. This issue is usually broached in one of two ways. The most common way is to include in equations (1) and (2) a new dummy variable D_F for gender to create

$$Y = \alpha_D^* D_D + \alpha_P^* D_P + \alpha_L^* D_L + \alpha_F^* D_F + \varepsilon \qquad (1^*)$$
$$Y = \beta_0^* + \beta_D^* D_D + \beta_P^* D_P + \beta_F^* D_F + \varepsilon \qquad (2^*)$$

where D_F takes the value 1 for a female and 0 for a male. Notice that no dummy variable D_M representing males is added; if such a dummy were added perfect multicollinearity would result, in equation (1^*) because $D_D + D_P + D_L = D_F + D_M$ and in equation (2^*) because $D_F + D_M$ is a column of ones, identical to the implicit intercept variable. The interpretation of both α_F^* and β_F^* is as the extent to which being female changes income, regardless of profession. α_D^*, α_P^* and α_L^* are interpreted as expected income of a male in the relevant profession; a similar reinterpretation is required for the coefficients of equation (2^*).

The second way of broaching this issue is to scrap the old dummy variables and create new dummy variables, one for each category illustrated in figure 14.2. This produces

$$Y = \alpha_{FD} D_{FD} + \alpha_{MD} D_{MD} + \alpha_{FP} D_{FP}$$
$$+ \alpha_{MP} D_{MP} + \alpha_{FL} D_{FL} + \alpha_{ML} D_{ML} + \varepsilon \qquad (1')$$

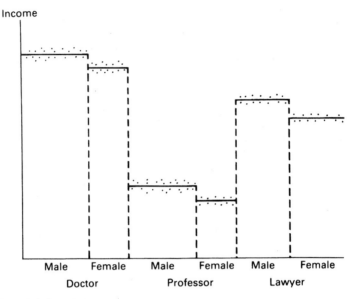

Income

Male Female Male Female Male Female

Doctor Professor Lawyer

Figure 14.2 Adding gender as an additional dummy variable

and

$$Y = \beta_0' + \beta_{FD} D_{FD} + \beta_{MD} D_{MD} + \beta_{FP} D_{FP}$$
$$+ \beta_{MP} D_{MP} + \beta_{FL} D_{FL} + \varepsilon. \qquad (2')$$

The interpretation of the coefficients is straightforward: α_{FD}, for example, is the expected income of a female doctor, and β_{FD} is the extent to which the expected income of a female doctor differs from that of a male lawyer.

The key difference between these two methods is that the former method forces the difference in income between male and female to be the same for all professions whereas the latter does not. The latter method allows for what are called interaction effects. In the former method a female doctor's expected income is the sum of two parts, one attributable to being a doctor and the other attributable to being a female; there is no role for any special effect that the combination or interaction of doctor and female might have.

14.4 INTERACTING WITH QUANTITATIVE VARIABLES

All the foregoing examples are somewhat unrealistic in that they are regressions in which all the regressors are dummy variables. In general, however, quantitative variables determine the dependent variable as well as qualitative variables. For example, income in an earlier example may also be determined by years of experience, E, so that we might have

$$Y = \gamma_0 + \gamma_D D_D + \gamma_P D_P + \gamma_E E + \varepsilon. \tag{3}$$

In this case the coefficient γ_D must be interpreted as reflecting the difference between doctors' and lawyers' expected incomes, taking account of years of experience (i.e., assuming equal years of experience).

Equation (3) is in essence a model in which income is expressed as a linear function of experience, with a different intercept for each profession. (On a graph of income against experience, this would be reflected by three parallel lines, one for each profession.) The most common use of dummy variables is to effect an intercept shift of this nature. But in many contexts it may be that the slope coefficient γ_E could differ for different professions, either in addition to or in place of a different intercept. (This is also viewed as an interaction effect.)

This case is handled by adding special dummies to account for slope differences. Equation (3) becomes

$$Y = \gamma_0^* + \gamma_D^* D_D + \gamma_P^* D_P + \gamma_E^* E + \gamma_{ED}^*(D_D E) + \gamma_{EP}^*(D_P E) + \varepsilon. \tag{4}$$

Here ($D_D E$ is a variable formed as the "product" of D_D and E; it consists of the value of E for each observation on a doctor, and 0 elsewhere. The special "product" dummy ($D_P E$) is formed in similar fashion. The expression (4) for observations on a lawyer is $\gamma_0^* + \gamma_E^* E + \varepsilon$, so γ_0^* and γ_E^* are the intercept and slope coefficients relevant to lawyers. The expression (4) for observations on a doctor is $\gamma_0^* + \gamma_D^* + (\gamma_E^* + \gamma_{ED}^*)E + \varepsilon$, so the interpretation of γ_D^* is as the difference between the doctors' and the lawyers' intercepts and the interpretation of γ_{ED}^* is as the difference between the doctors' and the lawyers' slope coefficients. Thus this special "product" dummy variable can allow for changes in slope coefficients from one data set to another and thereby capture a different kind of interaction effect.

Equation (4) is such that each profession has its own intercept and its own slope. (On a graph of income against experience, the three lines, one for each profession, need not be parallel.) Because of this there will be no difference between the estimates resulting from running this regression and the estimates resulting from running three separate regressions, each using just the data for a particular profession. Thus in this case using dummy variables is of no value. The dummy variable technique is of value whenever restrictions of some kind are imposed on the model in question. Equation (3) reflects such a restriction; the slope coefficient γ_E is postulated to be the same for all professions. By running equation (3) as a single regression, this restriction is imposed and more efficient estimates of all parameters result. As another example, suppose that years of education were also an explanatory variable but that it is known to have the same slope coefficient in each profession. Then adding the extra explanatory variable years of education to equation (4) and performing a single regression produces more efficient estimates of all parameters than would be the case if three separate regressions were run. (It should be noted that running a single, constrained regression incorporates the additional assumption of a common error variance.)

14.5 OBSERVATION-SPECIFIC DUMMIES

An observation-specific dummy is a dummy variable that takes on the value one for a specific observation and zero for all other observations. Since its use is mainly in time series data, it is called a period-specific dummy in the discussion below. When a regression is run with a period-specific dummy the computer can ignore the specific observation – the OLS estimates can be calculated using all the other observations and then the coefficient for the period-specific dummy is estimated as the value that makes that period's error equal to zero. In this way SSE is minimized. This has several useful implications:

(1) The coefficient estimate for the period-specific dummy is the forecast error for that period, and the estimated variance of this coefficient estimate is the estimate of the variance of the forecast error, an estimate that is otherwise quite awkward to calculate – see chapter 18.

(2) If the value of the dependent variable for the period in question is coded as zero instead of its actual value (which may not be known, if we are trying to forecast it) then the estimated coefficient of the period-specific dummy is the forecast of that period's dependent variable.

(3) By testing the estimated coefficient of the period-specific dummy against zero, using a t test, we can test whether or not that observation is "consistent" with the estimated relationship. An F test would be used to test if several observations could be considered consistent with the estimated equation. In this case each observation would have its own period-specific dummy. Such tests are sometimes called post-sample predictive tests. This is described in the technical notes as a variant of the Chow test. The "rainbow" test (general notes, section 6.3) is also a variant of this approach, as are some tests for outliers.

14.6 FIXED AND RANDOM EFFECTS MODELS

Dummy variables are sometimes used in the context of panel, or longitudinal, data – observations on a cross-section of individuals or firms, say, over time. In this context it is often assumed that the intercept varies across the N cross-sectional units and/or across the T time periods. In the general case $(N-1)+(T-1)$ dummies can be used for this, with computational short-cuts available to avoid having to run a regression with all these extra variables. This way of analyzing panel data is called the *fixed effects* model. The dummy variable coefficients reflect ignorance – they are inserted merely for the purpose of measuring shifts in the regression line arising from unknown variables. Some researchers feel that this type of ignorance should be treated in a fashion similar to the general ignorance represented by the error term, and have accordingly proposed the *random effects, variance components*, or *error components* model.

In the random effects model there is an overall intercept and an error term with two components: $\varepsilon_{it} + u_i$. The ε_{it} is the traditional error term unique to each observation. The u_i is an error term representing the extent to which the intercept of the ith cross-sectional unit differs from the overall intercept. (Sometimes a third error is included, representing the extent to which the tth time period's intercept differs from the overall intercept.) This composite error term is seen to have a particular type of nonsphericalness that can be estimated, allowing the use of EGLS for estimation. (EGLS is explained in chapter 8.)

Which of the fixed effects and the random effects models is better? This depends on the context of the data and for what the results are to be used. If the data exhaust the population (say observations on all firms producing automobiles), then the fixed effects approach, which produces results conditional on the units in the data set, is reasonable. If the data are a drawing of observations from a large population (say a thousand individuals in a city many times that size), and we wish to draw inferences regarding other members of that population, the fixed effects model is no longer reasonable; in this context, use of the random effects model has the advantage that it saves a lot of degrees of freedom.

The random effects model has a major drawback, however: it assumes that the random error associated with each cross-section unit is uncorrelated with the other regressors, something that is not likely to be the case. Suppose, for example, that wages are being regressed on schooling for a large set of individuals, and that a missing variable, ability, is thought to affect the intercept; since schooling and ability are likely to be correlated, modeling this as a random effect will create correlation between the error and the regressor schooling (whereas modeling it as a fixed effect will not). The result is bias in the coefficient estimates from the random effects model. This may explain why the slope estimates from the fixed and random effects models are often so different.

A Hausman test (discussed in chapters 9 and 10) for correlation between the error and the regressors can be used to check for whether the random effects model is appropriate. Under the null hypothesis of no correlation between the error and the regressors, the random effects model is applicable and its EGLS estimator is consistent and efficient. Under the alternative it is inconsistent. The OLS estimator of the fixed effects model is consistent under both the null and the alternative. Consequently, the difference between the variance–covariance matrices of the OLS and EGLS estimators is the variance–covariance matrix of the difference between the two estimators, allowing calculation of a chi-square test statistic to test this difference against zero.

GENERAL NOTES

14.1 Introduction

- The terminology "dummy variable" has invited irreverent remarks. One of the best is due to Machlup (1974, p. 892): "Let us remember the unfortunate econometrician who, in one of the major functions of his system, had to use a proxy for risk and a dummy for sex."

- Care must be taken in evaluating models containing dummy variables designed to capture structural shifts or seasonal factors, since these dummies could play a major role in generating a high R^2, hiding the fact that the independent variables have little explanatory power.

- Dummy variables representing more than two categories could represent categories that have no natural order (as in dummies for red, green and blue), but could represent those with some inherent order (as in low, medium and high income level). The latter are referred to as ordinal dummies; see Terza (1987) for a suggestion of how estimation can take account of the ordinal character of such dummies.

- Regressions using microeconomic data often include dummies representing aggregates, such as regional, industry or occupation dummies. Moulton (1990) notes that within these aggregates errors are likely to be correlated and that ignoring this leads to downward-biased standard errors.

- For the semi-logarithmic functional form $\ln Y = \alpha + \beta x + \delta D + \varepsilon$, the coefficient β is interpreted as the percentage impact on Y per unit change in x, but the coefficient δ cannot be interpreted as the percentage image on Y of a change in the dummy variable D from zero to one status. The correct expression for this percentage impact is $e^\delta - 1$. See Halvorsen and Palmquist (1980) and Kennedy (1981a).

- Dummy variable coefficients are interpreted as showing the extent to which behavior in one category deviates from some base (the "omitted" category). Whenever there exist more than two categories, the presentation of these results can be awkward, especially when laymen are involved; a more relevant, easily understood base might make the presentation of these results more effective. For example, suppose household energy consumption is determined by income and the region in which the household lives. Rather than, say, using the South as a base and comparing household energy consumption in the North East, North Central and West to consumption in the South, it may be more effective, as a means of presenting these results to laymen, to calculate dummy variable coefficients in such a way as to compare consumption in each region with the national average. A simple adjustment permits this. See Suits (1984) and Kennedy (1986).

- Goodman and Dubin (1990) note that alternative specifications containing different dummy variable specifications may not be nested, implying that a non-nested testing procedure should be employed to analyze their relative merits.

14.4   Interacting with Quantitative Variables

● Dummy variables play an important role in structuring Chow tests for testing if there
has been a change in a parameter value from one data set to another. Suppose Y is a
linear function of X and Z and the question at hand is whether the coefficients are the
same in period 1 as in period 2. A dummy variable D is formed such that D takes the
value zero for observations in period 1 and the value one for observations in period 2.
"Product" dummy variables DX and DZ are also formed (i.e., DX takes the value X in
period 2 and is 0 otherwise). Then the equation

$$Y = \beta_0 + \alpha_0 D + \beta_1 X + \alpha_1(DX) + \beta_2 Z + \alpha_2(DZ) + \varepsilon \qquad (1)$$

is formed.

Running regression (1) as is allows the intercept and slope coefficients to differ
from period 1 to period 2. This produces SSE unrestricted. Running regression (1)
forcing α_0, α_1, and α_2 to be 0 forces the intercept and slope-coefficients to be identical
in both periods. An F test, structured in the usual way, can be used to test whether or
not the vector with elements α_0, α_1, and α_2 is equal to the zero vector. The resulting F
statistic is

$$\frac{[SSE(\text{constrained}) - SSE(\text{unconstrained})]/K}{SSE(\text{unconstrained})/(T_1 + T_2 - 2K)}$$

where K is the number of parameters, T_1 is the number of observations in the first period and T_2 is the number of observations in the second period. If there were more than
two periods and we wished to test for equality across all periods, this methodology
can be generalized by adding extra dummies in the obvious way.

Whenever the entire set of parameters is being tested for equality between two data
sets the SSE unconstrained can be obtained by summing the SSEs from the two separate regressions and the SSE constrained can be obtained from a single regression
using all the data; the Chow test often appears in textbooks in this guise. In general,
including dummy variables to allow the intercept and all slopes to differ between two
data sets produces the same coefficient estimates as those obtained by running separate regressions, but estimated variances differ because the former method constrains
the estimated variance to be the same in both equations.

● The advantage of the dummy varaible variant of the Chow test is that it can easily be
modified to test subsets of the coefficients. Suppose, for example, that it is known that,
in equation (1) above, β_2 changed from period 1 to period 2 and that it is desired to
test whether or not the other parameters (β_0 and β_1) changed. Running regression (1)
as is gives the unrestricted SSE for the required F statistic, and running (1) without D
and DX gives the restricted SSE. The required degrees of freedom are 2 for the numerator and $T - 6$ for the denominator, where T is the total number of observations.

Notice that a slightly different form of this test must be used if, instead of knowing
(or assuming) that β_2 had changed from period 1 to period 2, we knew (or assumed)
that it had *not* changed. Then running regression (1) without DZ gives the unrestricted
SSE and running regression (2) without D, DX and DZ gives the restricted SSE. The
degrees of freedom are 2 for the numerator and $T - 5$ for the denominator.

- Using dummies to capture a change in intercept or slope coefficients, as described above, allows the line being estimated to be discontinuous. (Try drawing a graph of the curve – at the point of change it "jumps.") Forcing continuity creates what is called a *piecewise linear model*; dummy variables can be used to force this continuity, as explained, for example, in Pindyck and Rubinfeld (1981, pp. 126–7). This model is a special case of a *spline function*, in which the linearity assumption is dropped. For an exposition see Suits et al. (1978). Poirier (1976) has an extended discussion of this technique and its applications in economics.

- A popular use of dummy variables is for seasonal adjustment. Setting dummies up to represent the seasons and then including these variables along with the other regressors eliminates seasonal influences in so far as, in a linear model, these seasonal influences affect the intercept term (or, in a log-linear model, these seasonal influences can be captured as seasonal percentage impacts on the dependent variable). Should the slope coefficients be affected by seasonal factors, a more extensive de-seasonalizing procedure would be required, employing "product" dummy variables. Johnston (1984, pp. 234–9) has a good discussion of using dummies to de-seasonalize. It must be noted that much more elaborate methods of de-seasonalizing data exist. For a survey see Pierce (1980). See also Raveh (1984) and Bell and Hillmer (1984). Robb (1980) and Gersovitz and MacKinnon (1978) suggest innovative approaches to seasonal factors. See also Judge et al. (1985, pp. 258–62) and Darnell (1994, pp. 359–63) for discussion of the issues involved.

14.5 Observation-specific Dummies

- Salkever (1976) introduced the use of observation-specific dummies for facilitating estimation; see Kennedy (1990) for an exposition. Pagan and Nicholls (1984) suggest several extensions, for example to the context of autocorrelated errors.

- The Chow test as described earlier cannot be performed whenever there are too few observations in one of the data sets to run a regression. In this case an alternative (and less-powerful) version of the Chow test is employed, involving the use of observation-specific dummies. Suppose that the number of observations T_2 in the second time period is too small to run a regression. T_2 observation-specific dummy variables are formed, one for each observation in the second period. Each dummy has a value of 1 for its particular observation and 0 elsewhere. Regressing on the K independent variables plus the T_2 dummies over the $T_1 + T_2$ observations gives the unrestricted regression, identical to the regression using the K independent variables and T_1 observations. (This identity arises because the coefficient of each dummy variable takes on whatever value is necessary to create a perfect fit, and thus a zero residual, for that observation.)

  The restricted version comes from restricting each of the T_2 dummy variable coefficients to be zero, yielding a regression identical to one using the K independent variables and $T_1 + T_2$ observations. The F statistic thus becomes:

$$\frac{[SSE(\text{constrained}) - SSE(\text{unconstrained})]/T_2}{SSE(\text{unconstrained})/(T_1 - K)}$$

This statistic can be shown to be equivalent to testing whether or not the second period's set of observations falls within the prediction confidence interval formed by using the regression from the first period's observations. This dummy-variable approach, introduced in the first edition of this book, has been formalized by Dufour (1980).

14.6 Fixed and Random Effects Models

- Baltagi (1995, pp. 1–7) is an excellent reference for the econometrics of panel data, offering descriptions of major panel data sets such as the Panel Study of Income Dynamics (PSID) and the National Longitudinal Surveys of Labor Market Experience (NLS), and discussion of the benefits and limitations/problems of panel data. Estimation with panel data allows us to control for individual heterogeneity, alleviate aggregation bias, improve efficiency by using data with more variability and less collinearity, estimate and test more complicated behavioral models, and examine adjustment dynamics. Furthermore, this type of data allows examination of some issues that otherwise could not be broached. For example, in a specific cross-section a high percentage of people may be unemployed, but from that alone we cannot tell if this percentage is an average or if the same people are unemployed in every period. As a second example, consider the problem of separating economies of scale from technological change. Cross-sectional data provide information on the former, while time series data mix the two. In both these examples, panel data allow the researcher to resolve these issues.

- Fixed and random effects models are usually employed when the number of cross-sectional units is large and the number of time periods over which those units are observed is small. When the reverse is the case, several alternative models are common, differing in the assumptions they make regarding the error variance–covariance matrix. The simplest case assumes that each cross-section unit has an error with a different variance, so a simple correction for heteroskedasticity is employed. A slightly more complicated case is to assume also contemporaneous correlation between the errors of different cross-section units. A further complication would be to allow for errors to be autocorrelated across time in some way. All these models require EGLS estimation, which Beck and Katz (1995) find in practice performs very poorly in this context because the error variance–covariance matrix is poorly estimated. They recommend using OLS with its variance–covariance matrix estimated by $(X'X)^{-1}X'WX(X'X)^{-1}$ where W is an estimate of the error variance–covariance matrix. Baltagi (1986) uses a Monte Carlo study to compare these types of estimators to random effects estimators, concluding that the loss in efficiency is less severe when employing incorrectly the random effects estimator than when the alternatives are employed incorrectly.

- Greene (1997, chapter 14) has an excellent textbook exposition of estimation with panel data, including examples, computational simplifications, relationships among various estimators, and relevant test statistics. Baltagi and Griffin (1984) have a good discussion of the issues. Judge et al. (1985) and Dielman (1983) also have useful surveys.

- Gumpertz and Pantula (1989) suggest using the mean of the parameter estimates from OLS estimation (on each cross-sectional unit separately) for inference in the random effects model.

- Robertson and Symons (1992) suggest that if the slope parameters are not the same for all observations in panel data estimation, but estimation forces equality, serious bias problems arise. If one is not certain whether the coefficients are identical, Maddala (1991) recommends shrinking the separate estimates towards some common estimate.

TECHNICAL NOTES

- *Analysis of variance* is a statistical technique designed to determine whether or not a particular classification of the data is meaningful. The total variation in the dependent variable (the sum of squared differences between each observation and the overall mean) can be expressed as the sum of the variation between classes (the sum of the squared differences between the mean of each class and the overall mean, each times the number of observations in that class) and the variation within each class (the sum of the squared difference between each observation and its class mean). This decomposition is used to structure an F test to test the hypothesis that the between-class variation is large relative to the within-class variation, which implies that the classification is meaningful, i.e., that there is a significant variation in the dependent variable between classes.

  If dummy variables are used to capture these classifications and a regression is run, the dummy variable coefficients turn out to be the class means, the between-class variation is the regression's "explained" variation, the within-class variation is the regression's "unexplained" variation, and the analysis of variance F test is equivalent to testing whether or not the dummy variable coefficients are significantly different from one another. The main advantage of the dummy variable regression approach is that it provides estimates of the magnitudes of class variation influences on the dependent variables (as well as testing whether the classification is meaningful).

  Analysis of covariance is an extension of analysis of variance to handle cases in which there are some uncontrolled variables that could not be standardized between classes. These cases can be analyzed by using dummy variables to capture the classifications and regressing the dependent variable on these dummies and the uncontrollable variables. The analysis of covariance F tests are equivalent to testing whether the coefficients of the dummies are significantly different from one another. These tests can be interpreted in terms of changes in the residual sums of squares caused by adding the dummy variables. Johnston (1972, pp. 192–207) has a good discussion.

  In light of the above, it can be concluded that anyone comfortable with regression analysis and dummy variables can eschew analysis of variance and covariance techniques.

15
QUALITATIVE DEPENDENT VARIABLES

15.1 DICHOTOMOUS DEPENDENT VARIABLES

When the dependent variable is qualitative in nature and must be represented by a dummy variable, special estimating problems arise. Examples are the problem of explaining whether or not an individual will buy a car, whether an individual will be in or out of the labor force, whether an individual will use public transportation or drive to work, or whether an individual will vote yes or no on a referendum.

If the dependent variable is set up as a 0–1 dummy variable (for example, the dependent variable is set equal to 1 for those buying cars and equal to 0 for those not buying cars) and regressed on the explanatory variables, we would expect the predicted values of the dependent variable to fall mainly within the interval between 0 and 1, as illustrated in figure 15.1. This suggests that the predicted value of the dependent variable could be interpreted as the probability that that individual will buy a car, given that individual's characteristics (i.e., the values of the explanatory variables). This is in fact the accepted convention. In figure 15.1 the dots represent the sample observations; most of the high values of the explanatory variable x correspond to a dependent dummy variable value of unity (implying that a car was bought), whereas most of the low values of x correspond to a dependent dummy variable value of zero (implying that no car was bought). Notice that for extremely low values of x the regression line yields a negative estimated probability of buying a car, while for extremely high values of x the estimated probability is greater than 1. As should be clear from this diagram, R^2 is likely to be very low for this kind of regression, suggesting that R^2 should not be used as an estimation criterion in this context.

An obvious drawback to this approach is that it is quite possible, as illustrated in figure 15.1, to have estimated probabilities outside the 0–1 range. This embarrassment could be avoided by converting estimated probabilities lying outside the 0–1 range to either 0 or 1 as appropriate. This defines the *linear probability model*. Although this model is often used because of its computational ease,

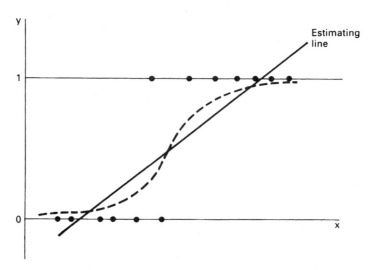

Figure 15.1   The linear probability model

many researchers feel uncomfortable with it because outcomes are sometimes predicted with certainty when it is quite possible that they may not occur.

What is needed is some means of squeezing the estimated probabilities inside the 0–1 interval without actually creating probability estimates of 0 or 1, as shown by the dashed line in figure 15.1. Many possible functions of this nature are available, the two most popular being the cumulative normal function and the logistic function. Using the cumulative normal function for this purpose creates the *probit* model; using the logistic function creates the *logit* model. These two functions are very similar, and in today's software environment the choice between them is a matter of taste because both are so easy to estimate. Logit is more common, perhaps for historical reasons – its lower computational cost made it more common before modern software eliminated this advantage.

A novel feature of these models, relative to the traditional regression model, is that the stochastic ingredient is no longer represented by an error term. This is because the stochastic element in this model is inherent in the modeling itself – the logit equation, for example, provides the expression for the probability that an event will occur. For each observation the occurrence or non-occurrence of that event comes about through a chance mechanism determined by this probability, rather than by a draw from a bowl of error terms.

Estimation is almost always undertaken by maximum likelihood. For the logit case, for example, the logit function provides the probability that the event will occur and one minus this function provides the probability that it will not occur. The likelihood is thus the product of logit functions for all observations for which the event occurred multiplied by the product of one-minus-the-logit-functions for all observations for which the event did not occur. This is formalized in the technical notes.

15.2 POLYCHOTOMOUS DEPENDENT VARIABLES

The preceding section addressed the problem of binary, or dichotomous, variables, for which there are only two choice categories. Categorical variables that can be classified into many categories are called polychotomous variables. For example, a commuter may be presented with a choice of commuting to work by subway, by bus or by private car, so there are three choices. Estimation in this context is undertaken by means of a generalization of the logit or probit models, called, respectively, the multinomial logit and the multinomial probit models. These generalizations are motivated by employing the random utility model.

In the random utility model the utility to a consumer of an alternative is specified as a linear function of the characteristics of the consumer and the attributes of the alternative, plus an error term. The probability that a particular consumer will choose a particular alternative is given by the probability that the utility of that alternative to that consumer is greater than the utility to that consumer of all other available alternatives. This makes good sense to an economist. The consumer picks the alternative that maximizes his or her utility. The multinomial logit and multinomial probit models follow from assumptions made concerning the nature of the error term in this random utility model.

If the random utility error terms are assumed to be independently and identically distributed as a log Weibull distribution, the *multinomial logit* model results. The great advantage of this model is its computational ease; the probability of an individual selecting a given alternative is easily expressed (as described in the technical notes), and a likelihood function can be formed and maximized in straightforward fashion. The disadvantage of this model is that it is characterized by what is called the *independence of irrelevant alternatives* property. Suppose a new alternative, almost identical to an existing alternative, is added to the set of choices. One would expect that as a result the probability from this model of choosing the duplicated alternative would be cut in half and the probabilities of choosing the other alternatives would be unaffected. Unfortunately, this is not the case, implying that the multinomial logit model will be inappropriate whenever two or more of the alternatives are close substitutes.

If the random utility error terms are assumed to be distributed multivariate-normally, the *multinomial probit* model results. This model allows the error terms to be correlated across alternatives, thereby permitting it to circumvent the independence of irrelevant alternatives dilemma. Its disadvantage is its high computational cost, which becomes prohibitively high when there are more than four alternatives.

15.3 ORDERED LOGIT/PROBIT

For some polychotomous dependent variables there is a natural order. Bond ratings, for example, are expressed in terms of categories (triple A, double A, etc.) which could be viewed as resulting from a continuous, unobserved measure called "creditworthiness"; students' letter grades for an economics course may be generated by their instructor's assessment of their "level of understanding" of the course material; the reaction of patients to a drug dose could be categorized as no reaction, slight reaction, severe reaction, and death, corresponding to a conceptual continuous measure called "degree of allergic reaction."

For these examples, using multinomial probit or logit would not be efficient because no account would be taken of the extra information implicit in the ordinal nature of the dependent variable. Nor would ordinary least squares be appropriate, because the coding of the dependent variable in these cases, usually as 0, 1, 2, 3, etc., reflects only a ranking: the difference between a 1 and a 2 cannot be treated as equivalent to the difference between a 2 and a 3, for example.

The *ordered logit* or *probit* model is used for this case. Consider the example of bond ratings, for which the unobserved continuous measure, creditworthiness, is specified to be a linear function (with parameter vector β, say) of explanatory variables. Each bond rating corresponds to a specific range of the creditworthiness index, with higher ratings corresponding to a higher range of creditworthiness values. Suppose, for example, that a firm's current bond rating is A. If its creditworthiness were to grow, it would eventually exceed the creditworthiness value that marks the boundary between the A and double A categories, and the firm would then experience an increase in its bond rating. Estimation is undertaken by maximum likelihood, with β being estimated in conjunction with estimation of the unknown boundary values defining the ranges of the creditworthiness index. For further discussion see the technical notes.

15.4 COUNT DATA

Very often data take the form of non-negative integer values such as number of children, recreational trips, bankruptcies, or patents. To exploit this feature of the data, estimation is undertaken using a count-data model, the most common example of which is a Poisson model. In this model the Poisson distribution provides the probability of the number of event occurrences and the Poisson parameter corresponding to the expected number of occurrences is modeled as a function of explanatory variables. Estimation is undertaken by maximum likelihood.

The Poisson model embodies some strong assumptions, such as that the probability of an occurrence is constant at any point in time and that the variance of the number of occurrences equals the expected number of occurrences. Both are thought to be unreasonable since contagious processes typically cause occurrences to influence the probability of future occurrences, and the variance of the number of occurrences usually exceeds the expected number of occurrences. Generalizations of the Poisson model, discussed in the technical notes, are employed to deal with these shortcomings.

GENERAL NOTES

- Maddala (1993) is an extensive reference on qualitative dependent variables and modelling options. Amemiya (1981) is a classic survey article for qualitative choice. Fry et al. (1993) discuss economic motivations for models with qualitative dependent variables. Winkelmann and Zimmermann (1995) is a good survey of count-data modeling; Winkelmann (1997) is a comprehensive reference. LIMDEP is the software of choice for estimating models discussed in this chapter.

15.1 Dichotomous Dependent Variables

- Although estimation of the dichotomous or binary dependent variable is almost always by maximum likelihood, on occasion one sees an alternative procedure, popular before computer software made maximum likelihood so simple to perform. This case occurs when there is a very large data set, large enough that observations can be grouped into sets of several observations on identical individuals. If there are enough observations in each group, a reliable estimate of the probability of an observation in that group experiencing the event can be produced by calculating the percentage of observations in that group experiencing the event. (Alternatively, the data may be available only in aggregated form.) This estimated probability can be used in two ways to provide estimates. First, it can be used as the dependent variable in a regression on the group characteristics to estimate a linear probability model. Second, the log of the ratio of this probability to one minus this probability (the log-odds ratio) can be used as the dependent variable in a regression on the group characteristics to estimate a logit function. (The technical notes show how this comes about.) In both cases there is heteroskedasticity that should be adjusted for.
- The role of the error term in qualitative dependent variable models is not obvious. In traditional regression models the dependent variable is written as a linear function of several explanatory variables plus an error, so that for example we have $y = X\beta + \varepsilon$. For qualitative dependent variables, however, the probability of obtaining the dependent variable value is written as a logit or probit function of these explanatory variables, without an error term appearing, so that for example

$$\text{prob}(y = 1) = \text{logit}(X\beta) = \frac{e^{X\beta}}{1 + e^{X\beta}}.$$

An error term is not necessary to provide a stochastic ingredient for this model because for each observation the value of the dependent variable is generated via a chance mechanism embodying the probability provided by the logit equation.

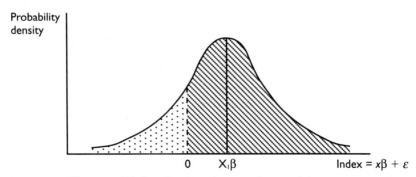

Figure 15.2 Explaining probit and logit

Despite this, most researchers conceptualize an underlying model that does contain an error term. An unobserved (latent) index is specified as a linear function of explanatory variables plus an error term (i.e., $X\beta + \varepsilon$). If this index exceeds a critical value (normalized to be zero, assuming an intercept appears in $X\beta$) then $y = 1$, otherwise $y = 0$. More formally,

$$\text{prob}(y = 1) = \text{prob}(X\beta + \varepsilon > 0) = \text{prob}(\varepsilon > -X\beta)$$

which is a cumulative density. If ε is distributed normally this is the cumulative density of a normal distribution (normalized to have variance one, which scales the coefficient estimates) and we have the probit model; if ε is distributed such that its cumulative density is a logistic function, we have the logit model.

Thinking of this model in terms of its underlying latent index can be advantageous for several reasons. First, it provides a means of interpreting outcomes in terms of the theoretically attractive random utility model, as described later in the technical notes. Second, it facilitates the exposition of ordered logit/probit, discussed later in this chapter. Third, it is consistent with the modeling of sample selection problems, presented in chapter 16. And fourth, it allows the development of R^2 measures applicable to this context.

- Figure 15.2 illustrates the exposition given above. Suppose we are modeling the decision to buy a car, so that the latent index $X\beta + \varepsilon$ is referred to as a "buying index," and if an individual's buying index exceeds zero, he or she buys. An individual with characteristics given by the row vector X_1 has buying index $X_1\beta + \varepsilon$, so the density of buying indices for such people is shown in figure 15.2 centered at $X_1\beta$. Some such individuals need little encouragement to buy a car and so have high, positive error terms producing high index values, whereas other seemingly identical individuals hate buying cars and so have large, negative error terms producing low index values. The probability that such a person buys is the probability that his or her index value exceeds zero, given by the lined area to the right of zero. If ε is distributed normally this is the cumulative density of ε from minus $X_1\beta$ to infinity, equal to the cumulative density from minus infinity to plus $X_1\beta$. This is just the probit model. For the logit model this area/probability is given by $\dfrac{e^{X_1\beta}}{1 + e^{X_1\beta}}$.

For an individual with a different row vector of characteristics the lined area would be of a different size. The likelihood function is formed by multiplying together expressions for the probability of each individual in the sample doing what he or she did (buy or not buy). Expressions measuring the lined area are used for buyers and expressions for the dotted area (one minus the expression for the lined area) are used for those not buying.

- Cameron (1988) shows how to undertake logit estimation in the context of "referendum" survey data when people are asked to answer yes or no to a choice question, such as willingness to pay for a project, with the payment varying across respondents.

- An estimated β value in a logit or a probit does not estimate the change in the probability of $y = 1$ due to a unit change in the relevant explanatory variable. This probability change is given by the partial derivative of the expression for prob($y = 1$) with respect to β, which is not equal to β. For the logit, for example, it is [prob($y = 1$)][1 − prob($y = 1$)]β, which is usually reported by estimating it at the mean values of the explanatory variables. It should be noted that this formula can give misleading estimates of probability changes in contexts in which an explanatory variable is postulated to change by an amount that is not infinitesimal. Estimation using the difference between the estimated prob($y = 1$) before and after the change is safer. See Caudill and Jackson (1989).

- There is no universally-accepted goodness-of-fit measure (pseudo-R^2) for probit, logit, or count-data models. Veall and Zimmermann (1996) is a good survey of alternative measures and their relative attributes. They recommend the measure of McKelvey and Zavoina (1975), a pseudo-R^2 which is close to what the OLS R^2 would be using the underlying latent index implicit in the model. Most computer packages provide a table giving the number of $y = 1$ values correctly and incorrectly predicted, and the number of $y = 0$ values correctly and incorrectly predicted, where an observation is predicted as $y = 1$ if the estimated prob($y = 1$) exceeds one-half. It is tempting to use the percentage of correct predictions as a measure of goodness of fit. This temptation should be resisted: a naive predictor, for example that every $y = 1$, could do well on this criterion. A better measure along these lines is the sum of the fraction of zeros correctly predicted plus the fraction of ones correctly predicted, a number which should exceed unity if the prediction method is of value. See McIntosh and Dorfman (1992). It should be noted that a feature of logit is that the number of $y = 1$ predictions it makes is equal to the number of $y = 1$ observations in the data.

- One use of logit models is to classify observations. Suppose a logit analysis has been done on the dichotomous choice of public versus private transportation. Given the characteristics of a new individual, the probabilities that he or she will choose public or private transportation are estimated from the estimated logit function, and he or she is classified to whichever transportation mode has the higher estimated probability.

  The main competitor to logit for classification is *discriminant analysis*. In this technique it is assumed that the individual's characteristics can be viewed as being distributed multivariate-normally, with a different mean vector (but the same variance–covariance matrix) associated with the two transportation modes. The original data are used to estimate the two mean vectors and the joint variance–covariance matrix. Given a new individual's characteristics these estimates can be used to estimate the height of the density function for each transportation mode; the new observation is classified to the transportation mode with the higher estimated density (since it is "more likely" to have come from that category).

Most studies, such as Press and Wilson (1978), have concluded that logit is superior to discriminant analysis for classification, primarily because the assumption of multi-variate-normally distributed characteristics is not reasonable, especially when some characteristics are qualitative in nature (i.e., they are represented by dummy variables). Recently, linear programming techniques for classification have been providing strong competition for logit. See Freed and Glover (1982). Kennedy (1991b) provides a graphical comparison of these three classification techniques.

- By adding an error to the traditional logit or probit specifications so that, for example,

$$\text{prob}(y = 1) = \frac{e^{X\beta + \varepsilon}}{1 + e^{X\beta + \varepsilon}},$$

it is possible to model unobserved differences between individuals beyond those captured by the error in the latent index. Although this unobserved heterogeneity, as it is called, is important in some contexts, such as count-data models or duration models, Allison (1987) finds that in logit and probit models it is a problem only in special cases.

- Unfortunately, logit and probit models are sensitive to misspecifications. In particular, in contrast to OLS in the CLR model, estimators will be inconsistent if an explanatory variable (even an orthogonal variable) is omitted or if there is heteroskedasticity. Davidson and MacKinnon (1993, pp. 523–8) suggest a computationally attractive way of using a modified Gauss-Newton regression to test for various specification errors. Murphy (1994) shows how a heteroskedasticity test of Davidson and MacKinnon (1984) can be applied to the multinomial case. Landwehr et al. (1984) suggest some graphical means of assessing logit models. Grogger (1990) exposits a Hausman-type specification test for exogeneity in probit, logit and Poisson regression models. Lechner (1991) is a good exposition of specification testing in the context of logit models. Pagan and Vella (1989) is a classic paper showing that many difficult-to-derive LM tests for specification in qualitative and limited dependent variable models can more easily be undertaken as conditional moment tests. Greene, Knapp and Seaks (1995) show how a Box–Cox transformation can be used to allow a more flexible functional form for the independent variables in a probit model. Fader, Lattin and Little (1992) address the problem of estimating nonlinearities within the multinomial logit model.

15.2 Polychotomous Dependent Variables

- There are three ways of structuring the deterministic part of the random utility model.

(1) Specify that the utility of an alternative to an individual is a linear function of that individual's n characteristics, with a different set of parameters for each alternative. In this case n coefficients must be estimated for each of the alternatives (less one – as shown in the example in the technical notes, one alternative serves as a base). Given characteristics of an individual – say, income, sex, and geographic location – with this specification one could estimate the probabilities of that individual choosing, say, each type of commuter mode.

(2) Specify that the utility of an alternative to an individual is a linear function of the m attributes of that alternative, as seen through the eyes of that individual. In this case, m coefficients, identical for all individuals, must be estimated. Given how the characteristics of an alternative relate to an individual – say, commuting time, cost, and convenience – it would be possible to estimate the probabilities of that individual choosing each type of commuter mode. If the researcher wanted to capture inherent differences between the alternatives that are the same for all individuals, dummy variables for all but one alternative would be included.

(3) Specify a combination of (1) and (2) above, namely a linear function of both the attributes of the alternatives as they affect the individuals and the characteristics of the individuals, with a different set of parameters for the individuals' characteristics for each alternative (less one) plus one set of parameters for the alternatives' attributes.

Specification (1) above is called the multinomial logit/probit, specification (2) is called the conditional logit/probit, and specification (3) is called the mixed logit/probit model. Frequently, as is the case in this book, the multinomial terminology is used to refer to all three.

- The independence-of-irrelevant-alternatives problem arises from the fact that in the multinomial logit model the *relative* probability of choosing two existing alternatives is unaffected by the presence of additional alternatives. As an example, suppose a commuter is twice as likely to commute by subway as by bus and three times as likely to commute by private car as by bus, so that the probabilities of commuting by bus, subway and private car are 1/6, 2/6 and 3/6, respectively. Now suppose an extra bus service is added, differing from the existing bus service only in the color of the buses. One would expect the probabilities of commuting by new bus, old bus, subway and private car to be 1/12, 1/12, 2/6 and 3/6, respectively. Instead, the multinomial logit model produces probabilities 1/7, 1/7, 2/7 and 3/7, to preserve the relative probabilities.

- One way of circumventing the independence of irrelevant alternatives problem is to estimate using a sequential logit/probit model. In this model people are assumed to make decisions sequentially. For example, rather than choosing between an imported car, an imported truck, a domestic car and a domestic truck, which creates an IIA problem, people are assumed first to make a decision between a car and a truck and then, conditional on that decision, to choose between an imported and a domestic model. Van Ophem and Schram (1997) examine a model that nests sequential and multinomial logit models and so allows testing one against the other.

- Hausman and McFadden (1984) develop tests for the independence of irrelevant alternatives (IIA) assumption. One test is based on the idea that if a category is dropped then if the IIA assumption is true the estimated coefficients should not change. A second test is based on the fact that under IIA a multinomial logit is a special case of a sequential logit. Zhang and Hoffman (1993) have a good exposition of these methods of testing for IIA, recommending a procedure due to Small and Hsiao (1985).

- A flexibility of the multinomial probit model is that the coefficients of the individual characteristics in the random utility model can be stochastic, varying (normally) over individuals to reflect individual's different tastes. This can be incorporated in the multinomial probit model through the covariances of the error terms; it cannot be made part of the multinomial logit model because the covariance between the error terms must be zero. This restriction of the multinomial logit model is what gives rise to the IIA problem. Using the multinomial probit to circumvent this problem involves very high computational cost, however, because multiple (one less than the number of categories) integrals must be calculated, which is why the multinomial logit is used so often despite the IIA problem. Chintagunta (1992) has introduced a computationally feasible means of estimation for the multinomial probit model. Keane (1992) discusses the computational problems associated with calculating the multinomial probit. He notes that although exclusion restrictions (some explanatory variables do not affect the utility of some options) are not required for estimation, in practice estimation is questionable without them.

15.3   Ordered Logit/Probit

- Surveys often ask respondents to select a range rather than provide a specific value, for example indicating that income lies in one of several specified ranges. Is the measurement error avoided by asking respondents to select categories worth the loss in information associated with foregoing a continuous measure? By comparing OLS and ordered logit with a unique data set, Dunn (1993) concludes that it is better to avoid gathering categorical data. Stewart (1983), Stern (1991), Caudill and Jackson (1993) and Bhat (1994) suggest ways of estimating in this context.
- Murphy (1996) suggests an artificial regression for testing for omitted variables, heteroskedasticity, functional form and asymmetry in ordered logit models.

15.4   Count Data

- Many individual decisions are made in a two-stage process in which first a decision is made to, say, purchase a good, and then a decision is made on the number of purchases. This can lead to more or fewer zeros in the data than that predicted by the Poisson model. The hurdle Poisson model is used to deal with this problem, in which a dichotomous model capturing the first stage is combined with a Poisson model for the second stage. This approach has been extended by Terza and Wilson (1990) to allow a choice of several different types of trips, say, in conjunction with choice of number of trips.
- In some applications zero values are unobserved because, for example, only people at a recreational site were interviewed about the number of trips they made per year to that site. In this case a truncated count-data model is employed in which the formula for the Poisson distribution is rescaled by dividing by one minus the probability of zero occurrences. Interestingly, the logit model results from truncating above one to produce two categories, zero and one. Caudill and Mixon (1995) examine the related case in which observations are censored (i.e., the explanatory variables are observed but the count is known only to be beyond some limit) rather than truncated (no observations at all beyond the limit).

TECHNICAL NOTES

15.1   Dichotomous Dependent Variables

- If the linear probability model is formulated as $Y = X\beta + \varepsilon$ where Y is interpreted as the probability of buying a car, the heteroskedastic nature of the error term is easily derived by noting that if the individual buys a car (probability $X\beta$) the error term takes the value $(1 - X\beta)$ and that if the individual does not buy a car (probability $(1 - X\beta)$) the error term takes the value $-X\beta$.
- The logistic function is given as $f(\theta) = e^\theta/(1 + e^\theta)$. It varies from zero to one as θ varies from $-\infty$ to $+\infty$, and looks very much like the cumulative normal distribution. Note that it is much easier to calculate than the cumulative normal, which requires evaluating an integral. Suppose θ is replaced with an index $x\beta$, a linear function of (for example) several characteristics of a potential buyer. Then the logistic model specifies that the probability of buying is given by

$$\text{prob(buy)} = \frac{e^{x\beta}}{1 + e^{x\beta}}.$$

This in turn implies that the probability of not buying is

$$\text{prob(not buy)} = 1 - \text{prob(buy)} = \frac{1}{1 + e^{x\beta}}.$$

The likelihood function is formed as

$$L = \prod_i \frac{e^{x_i\beta}}{1 + e^{x_i\beta}} \prod_j \frac{1}{1 + e^{x_j\beta}}$$

where i refers to those who bought and j refers to those who did not buy.

Maximizing this likelihood with respect to the vector β produces the MLE of β. For the nth individual, then, the probability of buying is estimated as

$$\frac{e^{x_n\beta^{\text{MLE}}}}{1 + e^{x_n\beta^{\text{MLE}}}}$$

The formulae given above for the logit model imply that

$$\frac{\text{prob(buy)}}{\text{prob(not buy)}} = e^{x\beta}$$

so that the log-odds ratio is

$$\ln\left[\frac{\text{prob(buy)}}{\text{prob(not buy)}}\right] = x\beta.$$

This is the rationale behind the grouping method described earlier.

- The logic of discriminant analysis described earlier is formalized by the *linear discriminant rule*, namely classify an individual with characteristics given by the vector x to category 1 if

$$(\mu_1 - \mu_2)'\Sigma^{-1}x > (1/2)(\mu_1 - \mu_2)'\Sigma^{-1}(\mu_1 + \mu_2)$$

where the μ_i are the estimated mean vectors of the characteristics vectors of individuals in category i, and Σ is their estimated common variance–covariance matrix. This is easily derived from the formula for the multivariate normal distribution. This rule can be modified for cases in which the prior probabilities are unequal or the misclassification costs are unequal. For example, if the cost of erroneously classifying an observation to category 1 were three times the cost of erroneously classifying an observation to category 2, the 1/2 in the linear discriminant rule would be replaced by 3/2.

15.2   Polychotomous Dependent Variables

- The log Weibull distribution, also known as the type I extreme-value distribution, has the convenient property that the cumulative density of the difference between any two random variables with this distribution is given by the logistic function. Suppose, for example, that the utility of option A to an individual with a row vector of characteristics x_0 is $x_0\beta_A + \varepsilon_A$ and of option B is $x_0\beta_B + \varepsilon_B$ where ε_A and ε_B are drawn independently from a log Weibull distribution. This individual will choose option A if

$$x_0\beta_B + \varepsilon_B < x_0\beta_A + \varepsilon_A$$

or, alternatively, if

$$\varepsilon_B - \varepsilon_A < x_0(\beta_A - \beta_B).$$

The probability that this is the case is given by the cumulative density of $\varepsilon_B - \varepsilon_A$ to the point $x_0(\beta_A - \beta_B)$. Since the cumulative density of $\varepsilon_B - \varepsilon_A$ is given by the logistic function we have

$$\text{prob(choose option A)} = \frac{e^{x_0(\beta_A - \beta_B)}}{1 + e^{x_0(\beta_A - \beta_B)}}.$$

This shows, for the binary case, the relationship between the random utility function and the logit model. A similar result for the polychotomous case can be derived (see Maddala, 1993, pp. 59–61), producing the multinomial logit model, a generalization of the binary logit. Notice that both β_A and β_B cannot be estimated; one category serves as a base and the estimated coefficients $(\beta_A - \beta_B)$ reflect the difference between their utility function coefficients.

- The type I extreme-value (or log Weibull) distribution has density $f(x) = \exp(-x - e^{-x})$, with cumulative density $F(x < a) = \exp(-e^{-a})$. Its mode is at zero, but its mean is 0.577. Consider the random utility model with the utility of the ith option to the jth individual given by $U_i = X_j\beta_i + \varepsilon_i (i = 1, 2)$ with the ε_i distributed as independent log Weibulls. The probability that the jth individual chooses option 1 is

$$\text{prob}[\varepsilon_2 < \varepsilon_1 + X_j(\beta_1 - \beta_2)] = \int \text{prob}(\varepsilon_1)\text{prob}[\varepsilon_2 < \varepsilon_1 + X_j(\beta_1 - \beta_2)|\varepsilon_1]d\varepsilon_1.$$

By exploiting the fact that the integral of the density above is unity, this can be shown to be the logit $\{1 + \exp[X_j(\beta_2 - \beta_1)]\}^{-1}$.

● A proper derivation of the multinomial logit is based on the random utility model. The resulting generalization of the binary logit can be illustrated in less rigorous fashion by specifying that the ratio of the probability of taking the kth alternative to the probability of taking some "base" alternative is given by $e^{x\beta_k}$ where β_k is a vector of parameters relevant for the kth alternative. This is a direct generalization of the earlier result that prob(buy)/prob(not buy) = $e^{x\beta}$. Note that this ratio is unaffected by the presence of other alternatives; this reflects the independence of irrelevant alternatives phenomenon. Note also that the coefficient estimates change if the "base" alternative is changed (as they should, because they estimate something different); if different computer packages normalize differently in this respect, they will not produce identical estimates.

As an example of how this generalization operates, suppose there are three alternatives A, B and C, representing commuting alone (A), by bus (B), and by carpool (C). The model is specified as

$$\frac{\text{prob(A)}}{\text{prob(C)}} = e^{x\beta_A} \text{ and } \frac{\text{prob(B)}}{\text{prob(C)}} = e^{x\beta_B}$$

Here carpooling is chosen as the "standard" or base alternative; only two such ratios are necessary since the remaining ratio, prob(A)/prob(B), can be derived from the other two. Using the fact that the sum of the probabilities of the three alternatives must be unity, a little algebra reveals that

$$\text{prob(A)} = \frac{e^{x\beta_A}}{1 + e^{x\beta_A} + e^{x\beta_B}}$$

$$\text{prob(B)} = \frac{e^{x\beta_B}}{1 + e^{x\beta_A} + e^{x\beta_B}}$$

$$\text{prob(C)} = \frac{1}{1 + e^{x\beta_A} + e^{x\beta_B}}.$$

The likelihood function then becomes

$$L = \prod_i \frac{e^{x_i\beta_A}}{1 + e^{x_i\beta_A} + e^{x_i\beta_B}} \prod_j \frac{e^{x_j\beta_B}}{1 + e^{x_j\beta_A} + e^{x_j\beta_B}} \prod_k \frac{1}{1 + e^{x_k\beta_A} + e^{x_k\beta_B}}$$

where the subscripts i, j, and k refer to those commuting alone, by bus and by carpool, respectively. This expression, when maximized with respect to β_A and β_B, yields β_A^{MLE} and β_B^{MLE}. For any particular individual, his or her characteristics can be used, along with β_A^{MLE} and β_B^{MLE}, to estimate prob(A), the probability that that person will commute to work alone, prob(B), the probability that that person will commute to work by bus, and prob(C), the probability that he or she will carpool it. Extension of this procedure to more than three alternatives is straightforward.

- The commuter example can be used to describe more fully the independence-of-irrelevant-alternatives phenomenon. Suppose we were to use the same data to estimate a logit model expanded to discriminate between commuting on a red bus (RB) versus commuting on a blue bus (BB). In the original example these two alternatives had been lumped together. Now there are four alternatives, A, RB, BB and C. Assuming everyone is indifferent between blue and red buses, it would seem logical that, when estimated, the expanded model should be such that for any individual each of the estimated probabilities of commuting alone, taking the bus (either red or blue) and carpooling it should remain unchanged, with the probability of riding the bus broken in half to estimate each of the two bus line alternatives. Unfortunately, this is not the case: adding an irrelevant alternative changes the probabilities assigned to all categories.

The key to understanding why this comes about is to recognize that the number of people in the data set who commute by bus, relative to the number of people in the data set who, say, carpool it, is irrelevant from the point of view of calculating the estimate of β_B. It is the differences in these people's characteristics that determine the estimate of β_B. If the people riding the bus are now arbitrarily divided into two categories, those riding red buses and those riding blue buses, there will be a change in the number of people in a bus category relative to the carpool category, but there will be no change in the nature of the differences in the characteristics of people in the bus categories versus people in the carpool category. Consequently, the estimate of β_{RB} (where prob(RB)/prob(C) = $e^{x\beta_{RB}}$) will be virtually the same as the original estimate of β_B, as will the estimate of β_{BB}.

For the nth individual, before the introduction of the irrelevant alternative, the probability of commuting alone is estimated as

$$\text{prob(A)} = \frac{e^{x_n \beta_A^{MLE}}}{1 + e^{x_n \beta_A^{MLE}} + e^{x_n \beta_B^{MLE}}}$$

a probability we would hope would remain unchanged when the irrelevant alternative is introduced. But it does change; by setting $\beta_B^{MLE} = \beta_{RB}^{MLE} = \beta_{BB}^{MLE}$ it becomes approximately

$$\text{prob(A)} = \frac{e^{x_n \beta_A^{MLE}}}{1 + 2e^{x_n \beta_A^{MLE}} + e^{x_n \beta_B^{MLE}}}.$$

Because of this problem, the multivariate logit methodology can be used only when the categories involved are all quite different from one another.

15.3 Ordered Logit/Probit

- Ordered probit specifies that, for example, $y^* = \alpha + \beta x + \varepsilon$ is an unobservable index of "creditworthiness," and we observe $y = B$ if $y^* \leq \delta_1$, $y = A$ if $\delta_1 \leq y^* \leq \delta_2$, $y = AA$ if $\delta_2 \leq y^* \leq \delta_3$ and $y = AAA$ if $\delta_3 \leq y^*$. The δs are unknown "threshold" parameters that must be estimated along with α and β. If an intercept is included in the equation for y^*, as it is here, it is customary to normalize by setting δ_1 equal to zero.

  Estimation proceeds by maximum likelihood. The probability of obtaining an observation with $y = AA$, for example, is equal to

$$\text{prob}(\delta_2 \leq y^* = \alpha + \beta x + \varepsilon \leq \delta_3)$$
$$= \text{prob}(\delta_2 - \alpha - \beta x \leq \varepsilon \leq \delta_3 - \alpha - \beta x).$$

A likelihood function can be formed, and thus estimation undertaken, once a density for ε is known. The ordered probit model results from assuming that ε is distributed normally. (The ordered logit model results from assuming that the cumulative density of ε is the logistic function; in practice the two formulations yield very similar results.) The usual normalization is that ε has mean zero and variance one; selecting a variance of four, say, would simply double the estimated values of the coefficients.

Application of ordered probit has become more frequent since it has been built into computer packages, such as LIMDEP. Greene (1990, pp. 703–6) has a good textbook presentation; Becker and Kennedy (1992) have a graphical exposition. Note that if a change in an x value increases the creditworthiness index, the probability of having rating AAA definitely increases, the probability of having rating B definitely decreases, but the probabilities of being in the intermediate categories could move in either direction.

15.4 Count Data

- In the Poisson model the probability of y number of occurrences of an event is given by $e^{-\lambda}\lambda^y/y!$ for y a non-negative integer. The mean and variance of this distribution are both λ, typically specified to be $\lambda = \exp(x\beta)$ where x is a row vector of explanatory variables. Choosing the exponential function has the advantage that it assures non-negativity.
- Like the logit and probit models, in the Poisson model the formula for the probability of an occurrence is a deterministic function of the explanatory variables – it is not allowed to differ between otherwise-identical individuals. In the case of logit and probit, relaxation of this assumption can be achieved by introducing "unobserved heterogeneity" in the form of an error term, adding an extra stochastic ingredient. Unlike the case of logit and probit, however, in the Poisson model this addition makes a substantive difference to the model, allowing the variance of the number of occurrences to exceed the expected number of occurrences, thereby creating a model consistent with the almost universal tendency to observe such overdispersion.

  A popular way of introducing unobserved heterogeneity into the Poisson model is to specify λ as $\exp(x\beta + \varepsilon)$ where ε is an error distributed as a gamma distribution.

This leads to a negative binomial distribution for the number of occurrences, with mean λ and variance $\lambda + \alpha^{-1}\lambda^2$ where α is the common parameter of the gamma distribution. By assuming α to be different functions of λ, different generalizations of this compound Poisson model are created.

An alternative way of modeling count data to produce overdispersion is to relax the assumption of the Poisson model that the probability of an occurrence is constant at any moment of time and instead allow this probability to vary with the time since the last occurrence. See Winkelmann (1995) and Butler and Worrall (1991).

16 LIMITED DEPENDENT VARIABLES

16.1 INTRODUCTION

Dependent variables are sometimes limited in their range. For example, data from the negative income tax experiment are such that income lies at or below some threshold level for all observations. As another example, data on household expenditure on automobiles has a lot of observations at 0, corresponding to households who choose not to buy a car. As a last example, data on wage rates may be obtainable only for those for whom their wage exceeds their reservation wage, others choosing not to work. If the dependent variable is limited in some way, OLS estimates are biased, even asymptotically.

The upper half of figure 16.1 illustrates why this is the case (ignore for now the lower half of this diagram). The relationship $y = \alpha + \beta x + \varepsilon$ is being estimated, where ε is a normally distributed error and observations with y values greater than k are not known. This could happen because y is the demand for tickets to hockey games and the arena on some occasions is sold out so that for these games all we know is that the demand for tickets is greater than k, the capacity of the arena. These unknown y values are denoted by small circles to distinguish them from known data points, designated by dots. Notice that for high values of x the known (dotted) observations below the (unconditional) expectation $E(y) = \alpha + \beta x$ are not fully balanced off by observations above $E(y) = \alpha + \beta x$, because some of these observations (the circled ones) are missing. This causes the resulting OLS regression line to be too flat, as shown by the dashed line.

Samples with limited dependent variables are classified into two general categories, censored and truncated regression models, depending on whether or not the values of x for the missing y data are known.

(1) *Censored sample* In this case some observations on the dependent variable, corresponding to known values of the independent variable(s), are not observable. In figure 16.1, for example, the y values corresponding to the circled data points are not known, but their corresponding x values are known. In a study of the determinants of wages, for example, you may have data on the explanatory variables for people who were not working, as

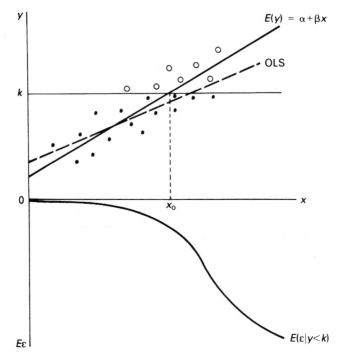

Figure 16.1   A limited dependent variable model

well as for those who were working, but for the former there is no observed wage.

(2) *Truncated sample*   In this case values of the independent variable(s) are known only when the dependent variable is observed. In the example of the negative income tax experiment noted earlier, no data of any kind are available for those above the income threshold; they were not part of the sample.

The dependent variable can be limited in a variety of different ways, giving rise to several alternative models. The easiest of these models is the Tobit model for censored data.

16.2   THE TOBIT MODEL

A common feature of microeconomic data is that observations on the dependent variable that lie in a certain range are translated into (or reported as) a single variable. In the demand for hockey game tickets example all demands above the capacity of the arena are translated into k, the arena capacity. This problem is analyzed using a Tobit model, named after James Tobin who was the first to analyze this type of data in a regression context.

How should estimation be undertaken? Our discussion earlier indicated that omitting the limit observations creates bias. Ignoring these observations would in any case be throwing away information, which is not advisable. How should they be included? It should be obvious from inspection of figure 16.1 that including the limit observations as though they were ordinary observations also creates bias. The solution to this dilemma is to employ maximum likelihood estimation.

The likelihood consists of the product of expressions for the "probability" of obtaining each observation. For each non-limit observation this expression is just the height of the appropriate density function representing the probability of getting that particular observation. For each limit observation, however, all we know is that the actual observation is above k. The probability for a limit observation therefore must be the probability of getting an observation above k, which would be the integral above k of the appropriate density function. In Tobin's original article (Tobin, 1958) durable goods purchases as a fraction of disposable income were modeled as a function of age and the ratio of liquid assets to disposable income. There were several limit observations at zero, corresponding to people who bought no durable goods, which entered the likelihood function as integrals from minus infinity to zero. The bottom line here is that the likelihood function becomes a mixture of densities and cumulative densities; fortunately, modern computer packages handle this with ease.

This estimation procedure for the Tobit model applies to the case of censored data. If the data are truncated, so that for example the limit observations are missing completely, the Tobit model no longer applies and an alternative maximum likelihood estimation procedure must be employed, described in the technical notes.

16.3   SAMPLE SELECTION

The Tobit model is a special case of a more general model incorporating what is called *sample selection*. In these models there is a second equation, called the selection equation, which determines whether an observation makes it into the sample. This causes the sample to be non-random, drawn from a subpopulation of a wider population. For example, observations on hours worked are available only on those for whom their wage exceeds their reservation wage. The main problem here is that often the researcher wishes to draw conclusions about the wider population, not just the subpopulation from which the data is taken. If this is the case, to avoid *sample selection bias* estimation must take the sample selection phenomenon into account.

In the Tobit model, the sample selection equation is the same as the equation being estimated, with a fixed, known limit determining what observations get into the sample. Many cases do not fit this sample mold. For example, the decision to purchase a consumer durable may in part depend on whether desired expenditure exceeds a threshold value equal to the cost of the cheapest acceptable durable available. This threshold value will be unique to each individual, depending on each individual's characteristics, and will incorporate a random error. In this case the limit is unknown, varies from person to person, and is stochastic.

Unlike the Tobit model, these extended models have likelihood functions that are difficult to derive and are not always found in push-button form in econometrics packages. Consequently, practitioners are eager to find a practical alternative to maximum likelihood. The Heckman two-step estimation procedure, a second-best alternative to maximum likelihood, is very popular in this context.

The rationale of the Heckman method can be explained with the help of figure 16.1. Consider the value x_0. For the corresponding y to be observed, the related error must be zero or negative, since if it were positive y would exceed k and would therefore be unobserved. This implies that for x_0 the expected value of the error term is negative. Now consider values of x less than x_0. For y to be observed the error can take on small positive values, in addition to being negative or zero, so the expected value of the error becomes less negative. When x is greater than x_0 the opposite occurs. As x becomes larger and larger, for y to be observed the error must lie below a larger and larger negative number. The expected value of the error term becomes more and more negative, as shown in the bottom half of figure 16.1.

The implication of this is that the error term is correlated with the explanatory variable, causing bias even asymptotically. If the expected value of the error term were known it could be included in the regression as an extra explanatory variable, removing that part of the error which is correlated with the explanatory variables and thereby avoiding the bias. The first stage of the Heckman procedure estimates the expected value of the error and the second stage reruns the regression with the estimated expected error as an extra explanatory variable. The details of finding estimates of the expected value of the error term are explained in the technical notes. It requires observations on the explanatory variables for the limit observations, so the Heckman procedure only works with censored data.

16.4 DURATION MODELS

Economic analysis often focuses on the length of time a person or firm stays in a specific state before leaving that state. A popular example is the state of unemployment – what determines the duration of unemployment spells? Duration models are used to investigate empirically this issue.

Typically the data available for duration analysis consists of two types of observations. For the first type, the length of the unemployment spell is known (an individual found work after five weeks, for example). For the second type, the length of the unemployment spell is unknown because at the time of gathering data the individual was in the middle of an unemployment spell (an individual was still looking for work after five weeks, for example). In the latter case the observations are censored, implying that an estimation technique similar to that used for limited dependent variables should be employed.

Models in this context are formalized by specifying a probability density function for the duration of the unemployment spell. This is a function of time t (measured from when the individual first became unemployed) providing the "probability" that an unemployment spell will be of length/duration t. Explanatory variables such as age, education, gender, and unemployment insurance eligibility, are included in this formula as well, to incorporate additional determinants of this probability. Maximum likelihood estimation can be used. The likelihood ingredient for each completed unemployment spell in the data is given by this duration density formula. The likelihood ingredient for each uncompleted unemployment spell in the data is given by an appropriate cumulation of this duration density giving the probability of getting an observation at least as great as the observed uncompleted spell. Thus the likelihood function becomes a mixture of densities and cumulative densities, just as in the Tobit analysis earlier.

Although the duration density function introduced above is the essential ingredient in duration models in that it is used to produce the likelihood function, discussion of duration models usually is undertaken in terms of a different function, the hazard function. This function gives the probability of leaving unemployment at time t given that the unemployment spell has lasted to time t; it is a conditional rather than an unconditional density function. The hazard function is the basis for discussion because it is usually the phenomenon of most interest to economists: What is the probability that someone who is unemployed will leave that state during this week?

The hazard function can be derived mathematically from the duration density function, so introduction of the hazard function does not change the nature of the model. But because interest and economic theory focus on the hazard function, it makes sense to choose a duration density specification that produces a hazard function that behaves as we believe it should. This explains why the duration densities used in duration models do not take a familiar form such as the normal distribution – they must be chosen so as to produce suitable hazard functions.

Some special cases of hazard functions are illustrated in Figure 16.2. The flat hazard, associated with the exponential duration density, says that the probability of leaving the unemployment state is the same, no matter how long one has been unemployed. The rising and falling hazards, associated with Weibull duration densities (with different Weibull parameter values giving rise to these two different hazards), says that the probability of leaving the unemployment state

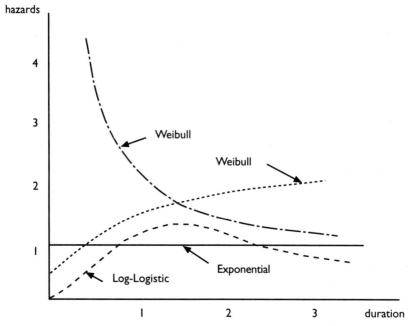

Figure 16.2   Examples of hazard functions associated with
different duration densities

increases or decreases, respectively, as the unemployment spell lengthens. The
hazard associated with the log-logistic duration density at first rises and then
falls.

Explanatory variables such as age and gender enter by affecting the level
and/or shape of these basic hazard functions. Estimation is simplified if a change
in an explanatory variable simply shifts the basic hazard up or down. As
explained in the technical notes, this produces what is called a proportional hazards model.

GENERAL NOTES

16.1   Introduction

- Maddala (1983) is an extensive reference on limited dependent variables and modeling options. Amemiya (1984) is a classic survey article. LIMDEP is the software of
  choice for estimation. Limited dependent variable modeling is prominent in the analysis of disequilibrium and switching phenomena; Maddala (1986) is a survey.
- A major problem with limited dependent variable models is that estimation is quite
  sensitive to specification errors such as omission of a relevant explanatory variable

(even if orthogonal), heteroskedasticity, and non-normal errors. Maddala (1995) is a survey of specification tests in this context. Pagan and Vella (1989) have advocated use of conditional moment tests in this context; Greene (1997, pp. 972–4) is a good textbook exposition. Selection bias can be tested by performing the Heckman two-stage procedure and testing against zero the coefficient of the expected error term. Greene (1997, p. 970) exposits a test for Tobit versus the more general model in which a second equation determines whether y is observed. Volume 34 (1,2) of the *Journal of Econometrics* is devoted to specification tests in limited dependent variable models. Because of this sensitivity to specification errors, attention has focused recently on the development of robust estimators for this context. (Robust estimation is discussed in chapter 19.) Volume 32 (1) of the *Journal of Econometrics* is devoted to robust methods for limited dependent variables.

- Heteroskedasticity of known form can be dealt with by building it into the likelihood function. Izadi (1992) suggests dealing with non-normal errors by assuming the errors come from the Pearson family of distributions of which the normal is a special case. These solutions require dealing with awkward likelihood functions, some of which are programmed into LIMDEP. Greene (1997, pp. 968–9) shows how an LM test can avoid this difficulty.

16.2 The Tobit Model

- The Tobit model was introduced by Tobin (1958) to model a limit of zero expenditure. Garcia and Labeaga (1996) survey alternative approaches to modeling zero expenditures. Veall and Zimmermann (1996) survey goodness-of-fit measures (pseudo-R^2s) for Tobit and duration models. Lankford and Wyckoff (1991) show how the Tobit model can be generalized to incorporate a Box–Cox functional form. Greene (1981) finds that the Tobit maximum likelihood estimates can be approximated quite well by dividing the OLS estimates by the proportion of nonlimit observations in the sample.

- The estimated coefficients from censored and truncated models must be interpreted with care. Suppose we are estimating an equation explaining desired expenditure but that whenever it is negative we observe zero expenditure. McDonald and Moffit (1980) show that although the expected change in desired expenditure due to a unit change in an explanatory variable is the coefficient of that explanatory variable, the expected change in actual expenditure is not; for the latter the required calculation must account for the probability of being above the limit and changes therein. To be specific, they show that the expected actual change is the change in expected expenditure of those above the limit times the probability of being above the limit, plus the expected expenditure of those above the limit times the change in the probability of being above the limit. Note that this illustrates how Tobit contains the elements of regression (expected expenditure, and changes therein, of those above the limit) and the elements of probit (the probability, and changes therein, of being above the limit). They discuss and illustrate the implications of this for the use and interpretation of results of studies employing this type of model. For example, we could be interested in how much of the work disincentive of a negative income tax takes the form of a reduction in the probability of working versus a reduction in hours worked. In other cases, however, interest may focus on the untruncated population, in which case the

Tobit coefficients themselves are the relevant results since the Tobit index reflects the underlying population.

16.3 Sample Selection

- The Heckman two-stage estimator was introduced in Heckman (1976). It is inferior to maximum likelihood because although it is consistent it is inefficient. Further, in "solving" the omitted variable problem the Heckman procedure introduces a measurement error problem, since an estimate of the expected value of the error term is employed in the second stage. In small samples it is not clear that the Heckman procedure is to be recommended. Monte Carlo studies such as Stolzenberg and Relles (1990), Hartman (1991), Zuehlke and Zeman (1991) and Nawata (1993) find that on a MSE criterion, relative to subsample OLS the Heckman procedure does not perform well when the errors are not distributed normally, the sample size is small, the amount of censoring is small, the correlation between the errors of the regression and selection equations is small, and the degree of collinearity between the explanatory variables in the regression and selection equations is high. It appears that the Heckman procedure can often do more harm than good, and that subsample OLS is surprisingly efficient, and more robust to non-normality. Nawata (1994) and Nawata and Hagase (1996) recommend using maximum likelihood, and discuss computational considerations.
- Limited dependent variable models can arise in a variety of forms. Suppose for example that we have

$$y = \alpha + \beta x + \varepsilon$$
$$p = \gamma + \delta z + u$$

with y being observed only if $y \geq p$. The likelihood function for this model is discussed by Maddala (1983, pp. 174–7). For example, suppose y represents wages of females and p represents the reservation wage. Consider individuals with high ε values, so that their actual wage happens to be particularly high. Their reservation wage is more likely to be exceeded and such people are likely to be employed. Individuals with low ε values, on the other hand, are more likely to have actual wage below reservation wage and such people are likely not to be employed. Thus using a sample of employed women to estimate the wage function will contain a disproportionate number of observations with high ε values, biasing the estimators.
- The preceding example is only one of several possible variants. One alternative is to specify that instead of y being observed when $y \geq p$, it is observed when $p \geq 0$. Bias arises in this case from the fact that often the two errors, ε and u, are correlated; see Maddala (1983, p. 231) for the likelihood function for this case. Suppose, for example, that y represents earnings and p represents the decision to emigrate. There may be an unobservable element of u, call it "energy," that also affects earnings, i.e. energy is also an element of ε, so that u and ε are correlated. Immigrants as a group will have a disproportionate number of people with high energy, so using observations on immigrants to estimate the earnings function creates biased estimators of the earnings function relevant to the population at large, or relevant to the population of the country from which they emigrated.
- An important variant of this last example is a context in which a researcher is interest-

ed in the impact of a treatment or program of some kind. Greene (1993, pp. 713–14) has a good example of an equation determining earnings as a function of several explanatory variables plus a dummy representing whether or not an individual has a college education. An estimation problem arises because individuals self-select them-selves into the college education category on the basis of the expected benefit to them of a college education, biasing upward the coefficient estimate for this dummy. A selection equation must be recognized, with an error term correlated with the error term in the earnings equation.

16.4   Duration Models

- Duration modeling goes by many different names in the literature. To biologists it is *survival* analysis because it was originally developed to analyze time until death. Engineers, interested in the breakdown of machines, call it *reliability* or *failure time* analysis. Sociologists refer to it as *event history analysis*. The literature in this area can be quite technical, a notable exception being Allison (1984). Kiefer (1988) and Lancaster (1990) are expositions aimed at economists, the latter quite advanced. Goldstein et al. (1989) review software; the econometrics package with the most extensive duration model estimating routines is LIMDEP.
- The exposition earlier was couched in terms of a *continuous-time* analysis in which knowledge of the exact time of duration was available. Although this may be reason-able for some types of economic data, for example strike durations measured in days, often this knowledge is not available. Unemployment duration, for example, is fre-quently measured in weeks, with no knowledge of when during the week of departure a particular individual left the unemployment state. In this case all those leaving the unemployment state during that week are grouped into a single discrete-time measure. Whenever the length of time of these discrete units of measurement is relatively large, analysis is undertaken via a *discrete-time* duration model, sometimes called a *grouped-data* duration model. For a variety of reasons, explained in the technical notes, estimation via a discrete-time duration model is a very attractive alternative to estimation using a continuous-time duration model, and so is becoming more and more the method of choice amongst economists.

TECHNICAL NOTES

16.1   Introduction

- The likelihood functions for censored and truncated samples are quite different. This can be illustrated with the help of figure 16.3, which graphs the density function of the error ε from figure 16.1. Consider a particular value x_3 of x. For y_3 to be observable, ε_3 must lie to the left of $k - \alpha - \beta x_3$; for y_3 unobservable, ε_3 must lie to the right of $k - \alpha - \beta x_3$. This result follows from the discussion of $E\varepsilon$ above.

  Suppose first we have a censored sample. If x_3 corresponds to an observable y, then there will be a specific ε_3 and the likelihood for that observation is given by L_3 in fig-ure 16.3, the height of the density function for ε at ε_3. But if x_3 corresponds to an unobservable (i.e., missing) value of y, we have no specific ε_3; all we know is that ε_3

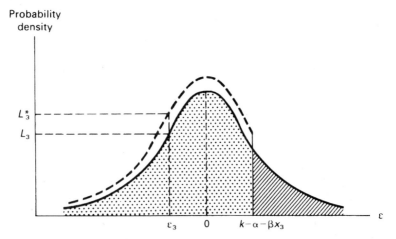

Figure 16.3 Explaining the likelihood for censored and truncated models

must lie to the right of $k - \alpha - \beta x_3$. The likelihood of this observation is thus the probability that ε_3 exceeds $k - \alpha - \beta x_3$, given by the lined area in figure 16.3, and calculated as 1 minus the density function cumulated to the point $k - \alpha - \beta x_3$. The likelihood for each observation in the sample may be calculated in one of these two ways, depending on whether the y value is observed or unobserved. Multiplying together all of these likelihood expressions, some of which are densities and some of which are cumulative densities, creates the likelihood for the censored sample.

Suppose now we have a truncated sample. For every possible value of x_3 in the sample the associated error must come from the left of $k - \alpha - \beta x_3$ in figure 16.3. Consequently the lined area should not be viewed as part of the density of ε_3. Because of this, ε_3 can be viewed as being drawn from the truncated normal distribution given by the dashed curve in figure 16.3. This dashed curve is obtained by dividing the height of the original normal distribution by the dotted area, forcing the area under the dashed curve to equal 1. Thus the likelihood of the observation y_3 is given in figure 16.3 by L_3^*. Note that L_3^* is a complicated function of the data, consisting of the height of the normal density function at the observation (y_3, x_3), divided by that density function cumulated to the point $k - \alpha - \beta x_3$. Each observation will give rise to a different dashed curve from which the likelihood of that observation can be calculated. Multiplying together all these likelihood expressions creates the likelihood function for the entire sample.

16.3 Sample Selection

● How does one go about estimating Eε to implement the Heckman two-step procedure? Consider once again the example of figure 16.1 as reflected in its supplementary graph figure 16.3. For any value x_3 of x, the corresponding error term ε_3 for an observed y_3 has in effect been drawn from the truncated normal distribution shown in figure 16.3 as the dashed curve, cut off at the point $k - \alpha - \beta x_3$. Thus $E\varepsilon$ is the expected value of this truncated normal distribution. A standard formula for the calculation of $E\varepsilon$ can be used if it is known how many standard deviations $k - \alpha - \beta x_3$ represents. Estimation of $(k - \alpha - \beta x_3)/\sigma$, where σ^2 is the variance of the normal untrucated distribution, therefore allows estimation of $E\varepsilon$.

In a censored sample the data on y can be interpreted as dichotomous, with y taking the value 1 if observed and 0 if unobserved. Then a probit analysis can be done on these data, generating for x_3, say, an estimate of the probability that y_3 is observed. (Note: this cannot be done for a truncated sample, since the x values for the unobserved y values are also missing – this explains why the Heckman two-step method can be used only with censored samples.) Given an estimate of this probability, the dotted area in figure 16.3, it is easy to find the corresponding number of standard deviations of the standard normal giving rise to that probability, yielding the required estimate of $(k - \alpha - \beta x_3)/\sigma$.

The standard formula for the expected value of a truncated distribution is $E(\varepsilon|\varepsilon \leq a) = \mu + \sigma\lambda(\theta)$ where θ is the number of standard deviations, $(a - \mu)/\sigma$, of a from the mean μ of ε, and $\lambda(\theta)$ is $-\phi(\theta)/\Phi(\theta)$, the inverse of the "Mills ratio," where ϕ is the density function for the standard normal and Φ is its cumulative density function. Here μ is zero and the estimate of $(k - \alpha - \beta x_3)/\sigma$ is an estimate of θ; the inverse of the Mills ratio is estimated and used as an extra regressor, reducing the bias (and eliminating it asymptotically). For discussion of the interpretation of this extra regressor's coefficient estimate see Dolton and Makepeace (1987).

For this example, maximum likelihood estimation is not costly, so the two-step method is not used. However, the principles illustrated are employed to generate an estimate of the expected value of the error for more difficult cases such as the immigration example discussed earlier in the general notes to section 16.3. In this example the expected value of the error ε in the earnings equation is nonzero because it is correlated with the error u that determines the decision to emigrate. The expected value of ε is $\rho\sigma\lambda(\theta)$ where ρ is the correlation between ε and u. Consequently, when the inverse Mills ratio $\lambda(\theta)$ is added as a regressor for the second step of the Heckman method, its coefficient estimator estimates $\rho\sigma$.

16.4   Duration Models

- Often the first step in undertaking estimation in a continuous-time duration model is to plot a preliminary version of the hazard function by calculating the fraction of observations leaving the unemployment state during successive discrete time intervals. The measure for the fifth week, for example, is the number of observations leaving unemployment during the fifth week divided by the number of observations which could have left unemployment during that week. This picture can sometimes help determine the basic shape of the hazard function, facilitating the development of an appropriate specification. The two most popular ways of calculating this preliminary sketch of the hazard (or related survivor) function are called the life table and Kaplan–Meier methods.
- A popular continuous-time duration model specification is the *proportional hazards* model. In this model the hazard function is composed of two separate parts, multiplied together. The first part is exclusively a function of duration time. It is called the *baseline hazard* and is usually written as $\lambda_0(t)$. The second part is a function of explanatory

variables other than time and is traditionally chosen to take the form $\exp(x'\beta)$ where x is a vector of observations on an individual's characteristics (which may vary with time) and β is a parameter vector. The hazard function is then written as

$$\lambda(t) = \lambda_0(t)\exp(x'\beta)$$

The key thing is that time itself is separated from the explanatory variables so that the hazard is obtained simply by shifting the baseline hazard as the explanatory variables change (i.e., for all individuals the hazard function is proportional to the baseline hazard function). The reason for its popularity is that estimation can be undertaken by maximizing a much simpler function, called the "partial likelihood," instead of the full likelihood, with little loss in estimation efficiency. Furthermore, it happens that the baseline hazard cancels out of the partial likelihood formula, so that this estimation method has the tremendous advantage of being insensitive to the specification of the baseline hazard. This advantage is offset by the fact that the baseline hazard and thus the full hazard function is not estimated. This disadvantage is not of consequence if interest focuses exclusively on the influence of the explanatory variables, as it often does.

- Two ways of testing for the appropriateness of the proportional hazard model are popular. First, different categories of the explanatory variables should give rise to hazard functions that are proportional, so plotting an estimated hazard function for males, say, should produce a function roughly parallel to the estimated hazard function for females. In the second method, an extra explanatory variable, measured as an interaction of time with one of the existing explanatory variables, is added to the specification. Upon estimation this variable should have an estimated coefficient insignificantly different from zero if the proportional hazards specification is correct. An LR test can be used.

- To obtain a sense of the algebra of continuous-time duration models, suppose $f(t)$ is the duration density, reflecting the probability that a spell of unemployment has duration t. The hazard function is then $\lambda(t) = f(t)/[1 - F(t)]$ where $F(t)$ is the cumulative density of t. The expression $[1 - F(t)]$ is called the survivor function since it gives the probability of an individual surviving in the unemployment state at least to time t. Each observation on a completed spell is entered into the likelihood function as $f(t)$ and each observation on an uncompleted spell is entered as $[1 - F(t)]$.

A popular density function to use for $f(t)$ is the exponential $f(t) = \delta e^{-\delta t}$ where the parameter δ is greater than zero. For this case $F(t) = 1 - e^{-\delta t}$ and the hazard function is a constant $\lambda(t) = \delta$. Other distributions for $f(t)$ give rise to hazard functions that are functions of t. For example, the Weibull distribution is a generalization of the exponential with

$$f(t) = \gamma\alpha t^{\alpha-1}\exp(-\gamma t^\alpha)$$

and corresponding hazard

$$\lambda(t) = \gamma\alpha t^{\alpha-1}$$

where the two Weibull parameters γ and α are positive. Note that if $\alpha = 1$ this distribution becomes the exponential. If $\alpha > 1$ the hazard function is increasing, and if $\alpha < 1$ it is decreasing. These were illustrated in figure 16.2.

Explanatory variables are incorporated into duration models by specifying how they affect the hazard function, usually introduced in ways that are computationally tractable. For the exponential distribution, for example, the parameter δ is modeled as $e^{x'\beta}$. Since δ^{-1} in this model is the mean duration, this is specifying that the mean duration is determined by explanatory variables according to the formula $e^{-x'\beta}$. In the likelihood function δ is replaced by $e^{-x'\beta}$ and maximization is done with respect to the β vector.

- Duration models assume that individuals with identical values of the explanatory variables have exactly the same probability of leaving the state of unemployment, in the same way that probit and logit models assume that probabilities are deterministic. But we know that observationally similar people differ because of unobserved characteristics or just plain randomness; this is the reason why specifications of behavior in OLS regressions include an error term. This unobserved difference among individuals causes problems for duration models. Suppose there are two types of people with an unobservable difference in their "spunk." Those with a lot of spunk are very active in seeking a job and so spend less time in the unemployment state than those with less spunk. Consequently, over time those with less spunk come to be over-represented in the set of those still unemployed, biasing downward the hazard function. This *unobserved heterogeneity* problem is addressed by adding a multiplicative error term with mean unity to the hazard function, complicating still further the likelihood function (this error must be integrated out of the likelihood expression). A computationally tractable, and thus frequently employed density for this error is the gamma density. Heckman and Singer (1984) contend that a discrete error distribution with only a few possible values for this error works well and facilitates computation.

- Estimation in a discrete-time model is much simpler because a complicated likelihood maximization problem is replaced with a familiar logit estimation problem for which standard software programs are available. This is accomplished by viewing each individual as contributing not one but several observations to a giant logit likelihood function. In the first time period each individual either stays or leaves the state of unemployment, so a logit likelihood could be structured, with appropriate explanatory variables, to capture this. Now consider all the individuals who have not yet left the unemployment state and who have not become censored, namely all the individuals for whom it is possible to leave the unemployment state during the second time period. In the second time period each of these individuals either stays or leaves the state of unemployment, so a second logit likelihood, with the same explanatory variables (whose values could be different if they vary with time), can be structured to capture this. Similar logit likelihoods can be formulated for each of the remaining time periods, with the number of observations contributing to these likelihoods diminishing as individuals are censored or leave the unemployment state. A giant likelihood can then be formed by multiplying together all these separate-period likelihoods. Each individual contributes several terms to this giant likelihood, one term for each time period for which that individual was at risk of leaving the unemployment state.

A baseline hazard can be built into this specification by including a function of time among the explanatory variables. Alternatively, we could allow the intercept in each of the separate-period logit formulations to be different. If there are a total of k time periods, k dummy variables, one for each period (taking the value one for that period and zero for all other periods) are entered as additional explanatory variables in the logit specification in place of the intercept. These dummy variables allow each duration length to contribute to the intercept of the logit specification separately, thereby modeling a completely unrestricted baseline hazard.

This discrete-time estimation procedure for duration models has become popular for several reasons. First, although most economic decisions are not made at discrete times, the data we have available usually report events as having occurred during some discrete time period rather than at a specific time. Second, the partial likelihood approach becomes quite difficult whenever more than one observation experiences the event during a measurement period, a common phenomenon in economic data. Third, it avoids having to deduce and program a complicated likelihood function. Not all specifications have software available for their estimation. Fourth, it permits an easy nonparametric way of estimating the baseline hazard. And fifth, it provides a good approximation to continuous-time duration models. For a good economist-oriented exposition of discrete-time estimation see Jenkins (1995). This does not mean that more complicated maximum likelihood estimation is not employed; a popular proportional hazards approach that allows the baseline hazard to be flexible is that of Meyer (1990).

17 TIME SERIES ECONOMETRICS

17.1 INTRODUCTION

Until not so long ago econometricians analyzed time series data in a way that was quite different from the methods employed by time series analysts (statisticians specializing in time series analysis). Econometricians tended to formulate a traditional regression model to represent the behavior of time series data, and to worry about things like simultaneity and autocorrelated errors, paying little attention to the specification of the dynamic structure of the time series. Furthermore, they assumed that the fact that most time series economic data are "non-stationary" (because they grow over time and so do not have a fixed, "stationary" mean) did not affect their empirical analyses. Time series analysts, on the other hand, tended to ignore the role of econometric "explanatory variables," and modeled time series behavior in terms of a sophisticated extrapolation mechanism. They circumvented the stationarity problem by working with data that were differenced a sufficient number of times to render them stationary.

Neither group paid much attention to the other until the appearance of two types of disquieting (for econometricians) studies. The first set of studies claimed that forecasts using the econometricians' methodology were inferior to those made using the time series analysts' approach; the second type claimed that running regressions on non-stationary data can give rise to misleading (or "spurious") values of R^2, DW and t statistics, causing economists erroneously to conclude that a meaningful relationship exists among the regression variables. Although technically none of the CLR model assumptions is violated, inference using OLS is invalid, causing erroneous specifications to be adopted. These revelations caused econometricians to look very hard at what they were doing, leading to extensive research activity, still ongoing, that has markedly changed and improved the way in which econometricians analyze time series data. The purpose of this chapter is to provide an overview of this activity, summarizing various topics that reflect what the terminology "time series analysis" has come to mean to econometricians.

17.2 ARIMA MODELS

The terminology "time series analysis" at one time referred to the *Box–Jenkins* approach to modeling time series, a technique developed by Box and Jenkins (1970) in the context of forecasting. This method abandoned the econometric modeling approach of using explanatory variables suggested by economic theory to explain/forecast, choosing instead to rely only on the past behavior of the variable being modeled/forecast. Thus in essence it is a sophisticated method of extrapolation.

Suppose Y is the variable to be modeled/forecast. Box–Jenkins analysis begins by transforming Y to ensure that it is *stationary*, namely that its stochastic properties are invariant with respect to time (i.e., that the mean of Y_t, its variance, and its covariance with other Y values, say Y_{t-k}, do not depend on t). This is checked in a rather casual way, by visual inspection of the estimated *correlogram*, a graph that plots the estimated kth-order autocorrelation coefficient, ρ_k, as a function of k. (ρ_k is the covariance between Y_t and Y_{t-k}, normalized by dividing it by the variance of Y). For a stationary variable the correlogram should show autocorrelations that die out fairly quickly as k becomes large.

Although many scientific time series data are stationary, most economic time series data are trending (i.e., the mean changes over time) and thus clearly cannot be stationary. Box and Jenkins claimed that most economic time series data could be made stationary by differencing (perhaps after taking logs to remove heteroskedasticity), and found that usually only one or two differencing operations are required. This creates a new data series, Y^*, which becomes the input for the Box–Jenkins analysis.

The general model for Y^* is written as

$$Y_t^* = \phi_1 Y_{t-1}^* + \phi_2 Y_{t-2}^* + \ldots + \phi_P Y_{t-p}^* + \varepsilon_t + \theta_1 \varepsilon_{t-1} + \theta_2 \varepsilon_{t-2} + \ldots + \theta_q \varepsilon_{t-q}$$

where the ϕ and θ are unknown parameters and the ε are independent and identically distributed normal errors with zero mean. Note that this model expresses Y^* in terms only of its own past values along with current and past errors; there are no explanatory variables as there would be in a traditional econometric model. This general model is called an ARIMA(p,d,q) model for Y. Here p is the number of lagged values of Y^*, representing the order of the *autoregressive* (AR) dimension of the model, d is the number of times Y is differenced to produce Y^*, and q is the number of lagged values of the error term, representing the order of the *moving average* (MA) dimension of the model. The acryonym ARIMA stands for *autoregressive integrated moving average*. The "integrated" means that to obtain a forecast for Y from this model it is necessary to integrate over (sum up) the forecast Y^* because the Y^* are differenced values of Y.

There are three basic steps to the development of an ARIMA model:

(1) *Identification/model selection* The values of p, d and q must be deter-

mined. The principle of parsimony is adopted; most stationary time series can be modeled using very low values of p and q.

(2) *Estimation* The θ and ϕ parameters must be estimated, usually by employing a least squares approximation to the maximum likelihood estimator.

(3) *Diagnostic checking* The estimated model must be checked for its adequacy and revised if necessary, implying that this entire process may have to be repeated until a satisfactory model is found.

The most crucial of these steps is identification, or model selection. This step requires the researcher to use his or her personal judgement to interpret some selected statistics, in conjunction with a plot of the correlogram, to determine which model the data suggest is the appropriate one to employ. In this respect the Box–Jenkins method is an art form, requiring considerable experience for a researcher to be able to select the correct model.

17.3 SEMTSA

At first econometricians ignored the Box–Jenkins approach, although it was not uncommon for the residuals in an econometric model to be modeled as an ARIMA process. In the early 1970s however, econometricians were forced to pay more attention to this approach by studies showing that Box–Jenkins forecasting equations were out-performing econometric forecasting models. At about the time that these studies were appearing the Box–Jenkins methodology was being extended to incorporate more than a single variable, the most extensive generalization being *multivariate Box–Jenkins*, in which an entire vector of variables is modeled as an ARIMA process. Some even claimed that the econometric approach would be wiped off the map whenever it had to compete against forecasts from multivariate Box–Jenkins models.

Econometricians responded to this slight by developing a (long overdue) synthesis of econometric modeling and the Box–Jenkins/time series methodologies. This synthesis, referred to as the *structural econometric time series approach*, or SEMTSA, is based on the observation that dynamic structural equation econometric models are special cases of multivariate time series (Box–Jenkins) processes in which *a priori* restrictions suggested by economic theory have been imposed on the parameters. Furthermore, if the exogenous variables in the econometric model can be viewed as being generated by a multiple time series (ARIMA) process, then each of the individual endogenous variables in the econometric model can be expressed as a univariate Box–Jenkins ARIMA process.

Assumptions about the properties of the structural econometric model, such as variable exogeneity and identifying restrictions, imply restrictions on the parameters of these ARIMA equations that can (and should) be tested. Since

ARIMA models are estimated without imposing any restrictions, it seems reasonable to conclude that the reason they out-forecast the econometric method is that the econometric approach has imposed inappropriate restrictions, i.e., it is not the econometric method that is at fault, but rather the way in which it has been operationalized.

In the SEMTSA approach a traditional econometric structural model is developed, incorporating the usual input from economic theory. The implied properties of the corresponding ARIMA equations are derived. Time series methods are then used to estimate the ARIMA equations and they are checked for consistency with the restrictions implied by the econometric model. Inconsistencies should prompt a reappraisal of the econometric model; SEMTSA is thus a procedure for discovering and repairing defects in proposed structural econometric models.

Box–Jenkins ARIMA modeling is atheoretical. Econometricians acknowledge that ARIMA models are efficient summaries of the time dependencies in the data, and that they are useful as benchmarks for forecasting, but do not consider them satisfactory with regard to explaining or understanding how the economy functions. They uncover facts that realistic models must explain and in so doing aid the formulation of such models; as such they can be viewed as complements to, not substitutes for, traditional structural modeling.

17.4   ERROR-CORRECTION MODELS

One reason for the relative success of ARIMA models is that traditional econometric structural models were too static – their dynamic specifications were not flexible enough to allow them adequately to represent an economy which when observed is more frequently out of equilibrium (going through a transition stage) than it is in equilibrium. This lack of attention to the dynamics of models was a natural outcome of the fact that economic theory has some ability to identify long-run relationships between economic variables, as created by equilibrium forces, but is of little help regarding the specification of time lags and dynamic adjustments. There is a paucity of dynamic theory. Viewed from this perspective, ARIMA models were seen to have two notable characteristics: they were very flexible in their specification of the dynamic structure of the time series, and they ignored completely the information that economic theory could offer concerning the role of long-run equilibria.

In light of this it seemed reasonable to structure econometric models to incorporate information from economic theory about long-run equilibrium forces and at the same time to allow for a very flexible lag structure, permitting the data to play a strong role in the specification of the model's dynamic structure. Providing the economic theory is correct, this approach should be superior to the ARIMA methodology. This line of thinking does not manifest itself in a new variant of the traditional simultaneous equation model, however; instead, the variable to be explained/forecast is modeled via a single equation. The only concession to the possibility of simultaneity is that if an explanatory variable fails a test for exogeneity, estimation is undertaken by an instrumental variables technique.

Economic theory plays two roles in the development of this equation. First, it suggests explanatory variables for inclusion in this equation; and second, it identifies long-run equilibrium relationships among economic variables, which if not exactly satisfied will set in motion economic forces affecting the variable being explained. The equation is developed in two stages. First, a traditional econometric equation is specified, with a generous lag structure (which is later pared down by testing procedures) on all the explanatory variables, including lagged values of the dependent variable. Second, this equation is manipulated to reformulate it in terms that are more easily interpreted, producing a term representing the extent to which the long-run equilibrium is not met. This last term, one of the unique features of this approach, is called an error-correction term since it reflects the current "error" in achieving long-run equilibrium. A distinctive feature of these models is that the long-run equilibrium position is not embodied in an explicit associated set of simultaneous equations but instead is captured by one or more error-correction terms. This type of model has consequently come to be known as an *error-correction model*, or ECM.

As a simple example of this consider the relationship

$$y_t = \beta_0 + \beta_1 x_t + \beta_2 x_{t-1} + \beta_3 y_{t-1} + \varepsilon_t$$

where y and x are measured in logarithms, with economic theory suggesting that in the long run y and x will grow at the same rate, so that in equilibrium $(y - x)$ will be a constant, save for the error. This relationship can be manipulated (see the technical notes) to produce

$$\Delta y_t = \beta_0 + \beta_1 \Delta x_t + (\beta_3 - 1)(y_{t-1} - x_{x-1}) + \varepsilon_t.$$

This is the ECM representation of the original specification; the last term is the error-correction term, interpreted as reflecting disequilibrium responses. The terminology can be explained as follows: if in error y grows too quickly, the last term becomes bigger, and since its coefficient is negative ($\beta_3 < 1$ for stationarity), Δy_t is reduced, correcting this error. In actual applications, more explanatory variables will appear, with many more lags.

Notice that this ECM equation turns out to be in terms of differenced variables, with the error-correction component measured in terms of levels variables. This is what is supposed to give it an edge over ARIMA models, since in ARIMA models the variables are all differenced, with no use made of the long-run information provided by the levels data. But this mixing of differenced and levels data does raise questions concerning the legitimacy of having these two very different types of variables both appearing in the same equation, much as one would be concerned about mixing stocks and flows, or the proverbial apples and oranges. This turns out to be an extremely important issue, identified with the concept of *cointegration*, discussed in section 17.6.

17.5 TESTING FOR UNIT ROOTS

The Box–Jenkins approach is only valid if the variable being modeled is stationary. Although there are màny different ways in which data can be nonstationary, Box and Jenkins assumed that the nature of economic time series data is such that any nonstationarity can be removed by differencing. This explains why, as noted above, the Box–Jenkins approach deals mainly with differenced data. This concern of time series analysts about differencing to achieve stationarity was for the most part ignored by econometricians, for two reasons. First, it was generally believed that although economic time series data looked nonstationary, this was only because of an underlying trend, which could be explained by exogenous factors such as population growth, and if the trend were removed, the data would be stationary. And second, it was thought that the validity of traditional econometric analyses was not adversely affected by nonstationarity of the variables being analyzed.

It came as a bit of a shock to econometricians, then, when studies appeared claiming that most macroeconomic data are nonstationary, because they are characterized by a "random walk" (this period's value equal to last period's value plus a random error), even after a deterministic trend has been removed. It was a further shock when additional studies showed that statistics such as the *t* and DW statistics, and measures such as R^2, did not retain their traditional characteristics in the presence of nonstationary data: running regressions with such data could produce spurious results (i.e., results which erroneously indicate, through misleading values of R^2, DW and t statistics, that a meaningful relationship among the regression variables exists). One consequence of these discoveries is that it has become very important when working with economic time series data to test for nonstationarity before proceeding with estimation. This has forever changed the character of all empirical work in macroeconomics.

How does one test for nonstationarity? It turns out that this is not an easy thing to do. Box and Jenkins use a casual means (inspection of the correlogram) to determine whether or not a series is stationary. A key ingredient of their methodology, an ingredient adopted by econometricians (without any justification based on economic theory), is their assumption that the nonstationarity is such that differencing will create stationarity. This concept is what is meant by the term *integrated*: a variable is said to be integrated of order *d*, written $I(d)$, if it must be differenced *d* times to be made stationary. Thus a stationary variable is integrated of order zero, written $I(0)$, a variable which must be differenced once to become stationary is said to be $I(1)$, integrated of order one, and so on. Economic variables are seldom integrated of order greater than two, and if nonstationary are usually $I(1)$. For ease of exposition what follows is couched in terms of $I(0)$ and $I(1)$ variables.

Consider for illustrative purposes the simplest example of an $I(1)$ variable, a random walk. (Random walks have become prominent in the macroeconomics literature since the development of rational expectations; they are implications, for example, of the efficient market hypothesis for real stock market prices, of hysteresis models of unemployment, and of the permanent income hypothesis of consumption.) Let $y_t = y_{t-1} + \varepsilon_t$, where ε is a stationary error term, i.e., ε is $I(0)$. Here y can be seen to be $I(1)$ because $\Delta y_t = \varepsilon_t$, which is $I(0)$. Now let this relationship be expressed in a slightly more general form as $y_t = \alpha y_{t-1} + \varepsilon_t$. If $|\alpha| < 1$, then y is $I(0)$, i.e., stationary, but if $\alpha = 1$ then y is $I(1)$, i.e., nonstationary. Thus formal tests of stationarity are tests for $\alpha = 1$, and because of this are referred to as tests for a *unit root*. (The case of $|\alpha| > 1$ is ruled out as being unreasonable because it would cause the series y_t to explode.) A wide variety of unit root tests have been developed recently; most require the use of special critical values, even when the test statistic itself takes a familiar form. A major problem is that none is very powerful.

17.6 COINTEGRATION

If the data are shown to be nonstationary, on the basis of an appropriate unit root test, it is tempting to do as Box and Jenkins did, namely purge the non-stationarity by differencing and estimate using only differenced variables. But this would mean that valuable information from economic theory concerning the long-run equilibrium properties of the data would be lost, as was stressed by those developing the error-correction model approach. On the other hand, the ECM approach involved mixing data in levels and differences in the same equation, which, if the levels data are $I(1)$, means that the ECM estimating equation could be producing spurious results.

Fortunately, econometricians have discovered a way out of this dilemma. Recall that the levels variables in the ECM entered the estimating equation in a special way: they entered combined into a single entity that captured the extent to which the system is out of equilibrium. It could be that even though these levels variables are individually $I(1)$, this special combination of them is $I(0)$. If this is the case, their entry into the estimating equation will not create spurious results.

This possibility does not seem unreasonable. A nonstationary variable tends to wander extensively (that is what makes it nonstationary), but some pairs of nonstationary variables can be expected to wander in such a way that they do not drift too far apart, thanks to disequilibrium forces that tend to keep them together. Some examples are short- and long-term interest rates, prices and wages, household income and expenditures, imports and exports, spot and future prices of a commodity, and exchange rates determined in different markets. Such variables are said to be *cointegrated*: although individually they are $I(1)$, a particular linear combination of them is $I(0)$. The cointegrating combination is interpreted as an equilibrium relationship, since it can be shown that variables in the error-correction term in an ECM must be cointegrated, and vice versa, that co-integrated variables must have an ECM representation. This is why economists have shown such interest in the concept of cointegration – it provides a formal framework for testing for and estimating long-run (equilibrium) relationships among economic variables.

One important implication of all this is that differencing is not the only means of eliminating unit roots. Consequently, if the data are found to have unit roots, before differencing (and thereby losing all the long-run information in the data) a researcher should test for cointegration; if a cointegrating relationship can be found, this should be exploited by undertaking estimation in an ECM frame-work. If a set of $I(1)$ variables are cointegrated, then regressing one on the others should produce residuals that are $I(0)$; most tests for cointegration therefore take the form of a unit root test applied to the residuals resulting from estimation of the cointegrating (long-run equilibrium) relationship.

These results suggest the following methodology for practitioners. First, use unit root tests to determine the order of integration of the raw data series. Second, run the cointegrating regression suggested by economic theory. Third, apply an appropriate unit root test to the residuals from this regression to test for cointegration. Fourth, if cointegration is accepted, use the lagged residuals from the cointegrating regression as an error correction term in an ECM. Unfortunately, Monte Carlo studies have shown that estimates of the cointegrating regression have considerable small-sample bias, in spite of excel-lent large-sample properties ("superconsistency"), and have suggested that the fourth step above be replaced by estimation of the full ECM equation, i.e., it is better to estimate the long-run relationship jointly with the short-run dynamics rather than to estimate it separately.

Two major problems exist with the methodology sketched above. First, using a single-equation representation is implicitly assuming that all the explanatory variables are exogenous, which may not be the case. And second, if there are more than two variables involved in the equation being estimated, there could be more than one cointegrating relationship, which unfortunately renders traditional estimation procedures inappropriate. In light of this, it has become common not to begin by using a single-equation model, but rather by adopting a more general simultaneous-equation formulation in which each variable is modeled in terms of lagged values of all the other variables. When written in vector notation this becomes a vector autoregressive model, or VAR, discussed in chapter 10. Within this more general framework testing is undertaken to determine the num-ber of cointegrating relationships and the exogeneity of the variables. This is accomplished by means of the Johansen procedure, discussed further in the gen-eral and technical notes.

GENERAL NOTES

17.1 Introduction

- Time series analysis does not have a twin "cross-section analysis," although the terminology "microeconometrics," referring to the econometric analysis of large sets of observations on microeconomic units, is becoming common. Problems peculiar to cross-section data are treated elsewhere in this book under various titles, some examples of which are error component models, logit analysis, limited dependent variables, panel data, duration models and self-selection bias. At one stage the expression "time series analysis" was used synonomously with "Box–Jenkins analysis," but now it has a much broader meaning to econometricians, as the contents of this chapter explain. Gilbert (1989) discusses several facets of the historical development of this modern view of time series econometrics.

- Nonstationary time series and cointegration has been a major growth industry in econometrics recently, as noted by Phillips (1995) who opines that "It is probably fair to say that the subject of nonstationary time series has brought together a wider group of participants and has excited more interest than any subject in econometrics since the development of simultaneous equations theory." He has a good discussion of this dramatic growth, reasons for econometricians' interest, themes for future research, criticisms and controversies. Granger (1997) is another good overall perspective on research in this area. Harvey (1997) is a very interesting critique of the entire direction taken by time series analysts, arguing that a better approach is to formulate a structural model in levels in which the parameter values are time-varying.

17.2 ARIMA Models

- Granger (1982) claims that ARIMA should really have been called IARMA, and that a key reason for the success of the Box–Jenkins methodology is the pronounceability of their choice of acronym. It should also be noted that ARIMA has been known to replace MARIA in the well-known West Side Story song, allowing it to play a starring role in graduate student skits!

- Pankratz (1983) and Hoff (1983) are introductory texts for the Box–Jenkins approach. Pindyck and Rubinfeld (1991, part 3) also have a good exposition. Newbold (1983) has a good overview. Mills (1990) is a comprehensive reference with lots of examples. Mills (1991) surveys extensions to incorporate nonlinearities. For a survey of checks of model adequacy in this context, see Godfrey and Tremayne (1988).

- Mills (1990, chapters 2–4) stresses that data should be "explored" by graphical means before formal analysis. All ARIMA modeling uses the data to determine the specification, which means that one should not use the same data to test the specification.

- In econometric models, economic theory usually provides a model and then it is imposed on the data. In contrast, ARIMA models allow the data to determine the model. In allowing the data to do this, however, parsimony, in the form of small p and q values, is a guiding principle. Because a nonzero p value implies a model with an infinite q value, and a nonzero q value implies a model with an infinite p value, a combination of small p and q values can capture an amazingly wide variety of time series structures.

- An ARIMA model in which no differencing is required is called an ARMA model. An AR model is an ARMA model with q equal to zero; an MA model is an ARMA model with p equal to zero. Thus, for example, a first-order autocorrelated error has an AR(1) structure. A purely random error is often called white noise; its ARIMA structure has $p = d = q = 0$.

- A modification of an ARIMA model, called a *transfer* model, allows an explanatory variable to play a role in the general ARIMA formulation. A variant of this is an *intervention* model, in which a large shock to a time series is modeled by using a dummy variable. Mills (1990, chapters 12 and 13) has a good exposition.

- Although a true Box–Jenkins analysis requires judgemental input at the identification/model selection stage, there do exist some computer-directed automatic model-selection methods, cited for example in Hill and Fildes (1984) and Libert (1984).

- Inference based on the autocorrelation function, as in the Box–Jenkins methodology, is often called analysis in the time domain. An analytically equivalent way of viewing the data is to transform the autocorrelation function into the frequency domain, in which the data are analyzed in terms of their cyclical properties. This approach to time series is called *spectral* analysis. These two forms of data analysis permit different insights into the properties of the time series and so are complementary, rather than competitive. Spectral analysis has been particularly helpful in analyzing seasonal factors and evaluating deseasonalizing procedures. It has not proved useful in model selection/identification, but it is hoped that it will be of value in testing for and interpreting cointegration. A brief introduction to this technically difficult area is presented in the technical notes.

17.3   SEMTSA

- Granger and Newbold (1986, pp. 287–92) have an excellent survey and discussion of the studies claiming that Box–Jenkins out-forecasts econometric models.

- Jenkins (1979, pp. 88–94) has a good comparison of Box–Jenkins and econometric forecasting methods, stressing the advantages of the former. Granger and Newbold (1986, pp. 292–4) also have a good discussion. On the synthesis between the two approaches, see Anderson et al. (1983). Zellner (1979, pp. 636–40) has a good exposition of the SEMTSA approach. Harvey (1997) presents a strong case for the structural time series approach and a persuasive argument for why the recent emphasis on unit roots, autoregressions and cointegration is misplaced.

- The VAR methodology, discussed in chapter 10, could be viewed as a variant of multivariate Box–Jenkins.

- Multivariate Box–Jenkins, or vector ARMA models, are not easy to specify; see Mills (1990, chapter 14). Riise and Tjosthein (1984) suggest that they are not worth the extra computational cost. For an effort to simplify this problem, see Tsay (1989).

17.4   Error-correction Models

- Davidson *et al* (1978) popularized the ECM approach; it is a good example of its application. Malley (1990) is a good, short exposition of ECMs, written for practitioners. Alogoskoufis and Smith (1991) have a good survey of its history, noting that there exist several different interpretations of ECMs. For example, although error-correction models are usually interpreted as reflecting partial adjustment of one variable to another, Campbell and Shiller (1988) note that they could arise because one variable forecasts another. Empirical work with ECMs tends to be undertaken by modeling the time series relationships in the data and then, ex post, interpreting the results, rather than by using economic theory to derive relationships and imposing an error correction mechanism as an auxiliary adjustment mechanism when estimating. One problem with this traditional ECM approach, as stressed by Alogoskoufis and Smith, is that parameterizations with quite different theoretical interpretations are observationally equivalent, so that the interpretation of estimated parameters must be qualified, something that is not always recognized. For example, it may be that estimated long-run coefficients involve a mixture of partial adjustment and expectations coefficients, inhibiting proper interpretation.

- Although economic theory gives little guidance regarding the nature of dynamics, it does offer reasons for why economies may often be out of long-run equilibrium. For a good summary and discussion, see Hendry, Pagan and Sargan (1984, pp. 1037–40).

- In its initial formulation an ECM is sometimes referred to as an "autoregressive distributed lag" – there are lagged values of the dependent variable appearing as explanatory variables (the "autoregressive" part), and the other explanatory variables all have several lags (the "distributed lag" part). As noted in chapter 5, the "test, test, test" methodology is typically employed to specify this model, in particular to pare it down to a smaller number of right-hand-side variables. This makes many practitioners nervous, since the presence of lagged dependent variables invalidates many tests, as stressed by Kiviet (1985). In an extensive Monte Carlo study, Kiviet (1986) concludes that testing for autocorrelated errors in this type of model is best done by using an F test to test the coefficients of lagged OLS residuals in a regression of the OLS residuals on the lagged OLS residuals and the original regressors (i.e., Durbin's m test). For a post-sample prediction test the (small-sample) Chow F test is recommended. Dezhbakhsh (1990) also recommends Durbin's m test, finding that it outperforms Durbin's h test. Note that the Box–Pierce and Ljung–Box tests are inappropriate because they are not valid whenever there exist regressors other than lagged dependent variables.

- One way of paring down the number of explanatory variables in an ECM is by exploiting the fact that certain parameter restrictions imply that a dynamic specification can be written with fewer lags but an autocorrelated error, which may facilitate estimation. These parameter restrictions are called common factors; COMFAC analysis is used to test the validity of the relevant parameter restrictions (explained in more detail in the technical notes). Note the implication that the finding of autocorrelated residuals corresponds to a dynamic misspecification rather than an inherently autocorrelated error. Hendry and Mizon (1978) have a good exposition of COMFAC.

- The fact that an ECM can be viewed as an ARIMA model incorporating additional information can be of use in specification. For example, if the ARIMA model fits better, it suggests that the ECM is misspecified in some way.

17.5 Testing for Unit Roots

- There are several fundamental differences between a stationary and an integrated (nonstationary) series. A stationary series has a mean and there is a tendency for the series to return to that mean, whereas an integrated series tends to wander widely. Stationary series tend to be erratic, whereas integrated series tend to exhibit smooth behavior. A stationary series has a finite variance, shocks are transitory, and its auto-correlations ρ_k die out as k grows, whereas an integrated series has an infinite variance (it grows over time), shocks are permanent, and its autocorrelations tend to one. These differences suggest some casual means of testing for stationarity. For stationary data a plot of the series against time should cross the horizontal axis frequently, and the autocorrelations should decrease steadily for large enough lags. For nonstationary data the estimated variance should become larger as the time series is extended, it should not cross the horizontal axis often, and the autocorrelations should tend not to die out.
- By repeated substitution, a random walk $y_t = y_{t-1} + \varepsilon_t$ can be written as $y_t = y_0 + \Sigma \varepsilon_{t-i}$, from which it can be seen that the impact of an error on an $I(1)$ variable does not die out – it is permanent, implying that the $I(1)$ variable has an infinite variance. (Note that the y variable is obtained by summing up, or integrating, the errors; this is the rationale for the "integrated variable" terminology.) On the other hand, the stationary process $y_t = \alpha y_{t-1} + \varepsilon_t$, where $|\alpha| < 1$, can by repeated substitution be written as $y_t = \alpha^t y_0 + \Sigma \alpha^i \varepsilon_{t-i}$, from which it can be seen that the influence of an error has a transitory effect, dying out as time passes.
- Consider a random walk with drift, $y_t = \mu + y_{t-1} + \varepsilon_t$ where μ is a constant. By repeated substitution, this can be written as $y_t = y_0 + \mu t + \Sigma \varepsilon_{t-i}$, which is clearly a "trending" variable, but a trending variable very different from one that is "stationary about a deterministic trend." Nelson and Plosser (1982) is a seminal study claiming that macroeconomic data are better characterized as random walks with drift than as stationary with a time trend.
- For cogent critiques of the role of unit roots in econometrics see Sims (1988), Christiano and Eichenbaum (1990) including comment by Stock, Cochrane (1991) and comments by Cochrane and by Miron on Campbell and Perron (1991), Campbell and Perron (1991) and Blough (1992) note that in finite samples any trend-stationary process can be approximated arbitrarily well by a unit root process and vice-versa, so that any test of the one against the other must have power no greater than size. Fortunately, it seems that the consequences of making an error in this regard are not severe. For example, if the autoregressive parameter is close to one its estimate should have a normal asymptotic distribution, but in fact the unit root asymptotic distribution provides a better finite-sample approximation, so erring by concluding there is a unit root would be fortuitous. Similarly, near unit root variables are better forecast using unit-root models than using stationary models.
- Some computer packages, such as SHAZAM, PC-GIVE and RATS, provide basic tests for determining the order of integration of variables.

17.6 Cointegration

- Engle and Granger (1987) is the seminal paper on cointegration. An early summary is Hendry (1986). Stock and Watson (1988a) is a useful overview. There exist several survey papers discussing both cointegration and unit root testing. Examples are

Dolado *et al.* (1990), McDermott (1990) and Muscatelli and Hurn (1992). Holden and Thompson (1992) is a good introductory survey, and good textbook expositions can be found in Harris (1995) and Enders (1995). Banerjee et al. (1993) is a more advanced reference, but their chapter introductions provide good summaries of the elements of econometric analysis of nonstationary data. Murray (1994) presents an amusing and instructive example of a drunk and her dog to illustrate cointegration.

- Most tests for cointegration are based on looking for unit roots in the cointegration regression residuals. (Finding a unit root means no cointegration.) Because these residuals have been produced by a process which makes them as small as possible, applying a DF or ADF test to these residuals would be biased toward finding cointegration. This problem is resolved by using special critical values, tabulated for some combinations of sample size and number of cointegrating variables in Engle and Granger (1987) and Engle and Yoo (1987). For other cases MacKinnon (1991) provides a response surface to estimate critical values.
- The essence of cointegration is that the cointegrated variables share a common trend which is removed when producing the cointegrating regression residuals. Because of the common trend there may be strong multicollinearity, tempting a researcher to drop a variable. This would be disastrous – the cointegration would be lost.
- The error correction influence may not be linear. To capture this the error correction term can be entered as a quadratic or in some other nonlinear form.
- The superconsistency of the estimates of the cointegrating relationship parameters comes about because a parameter value different from the true parameter value will give rise to an $I(1)$ error term, which will have an infinite variance and therefore produce a very high sum of squared errors; the true parameter value, on the other hand, gives rise to an $I(0)$ error term, whose variance is finite, and thus should produce a markedly smaller sum of squared errors. So a procedure that minimizes the sum of squared errors should quickly zero in on the true parameter value as the sample size grows, even in the presence of problems such as simultaneous equations bias. Unfortunately, Monte Carlo studies, such as Banerjee et al. (1986), have shown that this superconsistency does not manifest itself in small samples. It is not obvious what is the most appropriate way of estimating, but there is some concensus that the long-run cointegrating relationship is best estimated as a by-product of estimating the full error-correction model (with a generous lag length). Banerjee et al. (1986) and Inder (1993) recommend doing this with OLS. Note that it is not necessary that the cointe-grated variables be isolated in an error correction term for estimation – mixing levels and differences regressors is acceptable because the cointegrated variables automatically combine during estimation to resolve the dilemma of mixed orders of integration. When there is more than one cointegrating relationship (see below), Gonzalo (1994) recommends estimating with the Johansen maximum likelihood procedure. On the other hand, Hargreaves (1994) finds that the Johansen procedure only beats OLS if one can be sure there is more than one cointegrating relationship.
- Whenever more than two variables appear in a cointegrating relationship new problems arise. First, to run the cointegrating regression, one of the variables must be chosen to be the regressand, and thus have a coefficient of·unity. It turns out that OLS estimation of the cointegrating parameters is sensitive to this choice of normalization. Second, with more than two variables in the cointegrating relationship it is possible that there is more than one set of cointegrating parameters. If this is so, running the usual cointegrating regression will not yield consistent estimates of any of these

multiple sets of cointegrating parameters (mainly because estimation in general produces estimates of a linear combination of these multiple sets of cointegrating parameters), and will of course not alert one to the existence of these additional cointegrating relationships. The methods of Johansen (1988) and Stock and Watson (1988b) can be used in this context, the former of which appears to have become the method of choice, perhaps due to the availability of software. Ho and Sorensen (1996) review the literature, provide an illustration and emphasize the importance of determining the correct lag length.

In the Johansen method all the variables are viewed as endogenous, with each expressed as a linear function of lagged values of itself and all other variables. This set of equations is expressed mathematically in the form of a single vector autoregressive equation, a VAR. Manipulation of this vector equation produces a vector error correction equation in which differenced vector terms are explained as lagged differenced vector terms plus a lagged levels term which represents the error correction phenomenon. It turns out that the number of cointegrating vectors is equal to the rank of the matrix of coefficients associated with the levels variables in the vector ECM equation. The first step of the Johansen method consists of a test for the rank of this matrix. Following this the parameters of this system are estimated simultaneously via maximum likelihood.

The Johansen method has several advantages.

(a) First, it deals automatically with the problem of choosing a normalization. None is imposed on the estimation procedure, implying that afterwards an appropriate normalization must be applied to render the cointegration results meaningful. This may require no more than dividing through all the estimated cointegrating parameters by the estimated parameter of the variable chosen to have coefficient unity. But it may also require finding a linear combination of the multiple cointegrating vectors that makes economic sense: interpretation of multiple cointegrating vectors can be frustrating. For example, some empirical studies of the demand for money have found that one cointegrating vector represents the equilibrium relationship between money demand and money supply and a second, puzzling cointegrating vector represents the equilibrium relationship between two interest rates included in the specification. Some researchers deal with this problem by ignoring those cointegrating vectors that seem not to make good economic sense. This is akin to imposing slightly false restrictions to improve mean square error. The bottom line here is that because of the difficulty of interpreting estimates of the coinetegrating vectors, it is important that economic arguments form the basis for imposing restrictions. In general more than one cointegrating relationship does not mean that there is more than one long-run equilibrium position. More likely it means that there is one long-run equilibrium which has embodied within it several sectoral equilibria, or cointegrated subsets of variables as illustrated by the money demand example above.

(b) Second, one guards against inconsistent estimation of the cointegrating relationships by incorporating knowledge that there is more than one cointegrating vector.

(c) Third, estimation (by maximum likelihood) of the short-run dynamics is undertaken simultaneously, increasing the efficiency of estimation.

(d) Fourth, estimation of the parameters in any single equation incorporates information about what is happening in other equations in the system. This advantage is of course offset by the fact that specification errors in other parts of the system affect estimation of the parameters in all equations.

(e) Fifth, the Johansen method allows testing of restrictions on the cointegrating vectors.

● Harris (1994, 1995 Appendix) evaluates software for undertaking the Johansen procedure. Cheung and Lai (1993) point to several finite-sample shortcomings of the Johansen test for cointegration. Pagan (1995) discusses the relationship between the traditional error correction model and the VAR model associated with the Johansen procedure, noting that the latter is estimating a reduced form whereas the former, thanks to assumptions about exogeneity, is estimating a structural form. He notes that problems in interpreting cointegration relationships may stem from the fact that because the Johansen method is estimating a reduced form, the usual interpretation of the cointegrating vector as a structural-form relationship depends on the identification status of the structural form.

● Note that when testing for cointegration if a relevant variable has been omitted the test should fail to find cointegration; thus it is important that testing be undertaken by beginning with the most general specification and testing down.

TECHNICAL NOTES

17.1 Introduction

● The *state space* model is a generalization of the linear regression model that provides a unifying framework for all dynamic linear models used in econometrics. This model originated in the engineering literature, where interest focuses on estimating the "state" of a system, such as the location of a satellite, using noisy measurements. The *Kalman filter* is used to create an optimal estimate of the state, given knowledge of the parameters. In economics, however, these parameters are unknown, and interest focuses on finding estimates for them. Econometricians have used this state space framework to reformulate existing time series models, allowing the powerful Kalman filter to facilitate estimation. In these models the unobserved states have a variety of interpretations of interest to economists, the most prominent of which is as time-varying parameters. For example, an observed variable y_t is specified as a linear function of observed x_t values with a time-varying parameter vector β_t (the "state" variable) plus an error term. The vector β_t is in turn determined by a transition equation in which β_t is a linear combination of itself lagged, plus an error term. A rich variety of overall error specifications for this model can be created by altering the specification of these two error terms. For discussion and illustrations see Engle and Watson (1987) and Harvey (1987). Hall, Cuthbertson and Taylor (1992, pp. 199–217) and Darnell (1994, pp. 211–14) have good textbook expositions. Diderrich (1985) and Welch (1987) note an instructive connection between the state space estimation procedure and the mixed estimation procedure of chapter 12.

17.2 ARIMA Models

● A time series variable y is said to be *strictly stationary* if the properties (e.g., mean, variance, etc.) of its elements do not depend on t. The word stationary usually refers to *weak stationarity*, however, which requires only that the first two moments of the y_t process do not depend on t. This requires that the mean and variance of y_t are constant over time, and that the autocovariances depend only on the lag (or time difference), not on t. Strict stationarity and weak stationarity are equivalent if the y_t are distributed joint normally.

- Stationarity for the AR process $Y_t = \phi_1 Y_{t-1} + \phi_2 Y_{t-2} + \ldots + \phi_p Y_{t-p} + \varepsilon_t$ requires that the roots of $1 - \phi_1 x - \phi_2 x^2 - \ldots - \phi_p x^p = 0$ lie outside the unit circle, or, equivalently, that the roots of $x^p - \phi_1 x^{p-1} - \phi_2 x^{p-2} - \ldots - \phi_p = 0$ are all less than one in absolute value. Stationarity of an ARMA process depends on the stationarity of its AR part. The MA process $Y_t = \varepsilon_t + \theta_1 \varepsilon_{t-1} + \theta_2 \varepsilon_{t-2} + \ldots + \theta_q \varepsilon_{t-q}$ can be written as an AR process if it is *invertible*, namely if the roots of $1 + \theta_1 x + \theta_2 x^2 + \ldots + \theta_q x^q$ lie outside the unit circle.

- The correlogram is a plot of the autocorrelation function – the autocorrelation coefficient ρ_k as a function of the lag, k. An estimate of the correlogram is used as a visual aid for identification in Box–Jenkins modeling. First, it should fall off to numbers insignificantly different from zero if the series is stationary. Second, a rough 95% confidence band can be drawn at $\pm 2/\sqrt{N}$, allowing the significance of the estimated ρ_k to be determined at a glance. (Note, though, that at the 95% level, for every 20 estimates of ρ_k plotted, we would expect, on the null hypothesis that all the ρ_k are zero, that one of the estimated ρ_k would lie outside this band.) Third, theoretical derivations of the autocorrelation function show that certain patterns of the correlogram should correspond to specific types of ARMA models. An experienced modeler should be able to look at the estimated correlogram and on the basis of what he or she perceives to be the pattern revealed there suggest a particular ARMA model; it is at this stage that "ARMA modeling is an art form" enters.

- Some of the standard patterns may be easy to identify. A correlogram with one estimated ρ_k that is significantly different from zero, followed by what appears to be a random series of estimated ρ_k that are insignificantly different from zero, corresponds to an MA(1) model. An MA(2) model will have the first two estimated ρ_k significantly different from zero, with the rest random and insignificantly different from zero. If the correlogram seems to be declining geometrically, an AR(1) model is suggested, although it could also be an AR(2) (or higher) model. If it declines geometrically, but reverses sign at each increment of k, an AR(1) with a negative coefficient is suggested. If the first estimated ρ_k is significant but inconsistent with the geometrically declining pattern, an ARMA(1,1) is suggested. If the correlogram looks like a damped sine wave, an AR(2) or higher is suggested.

- A significant ρ_k at every twelfth value of k, say, suggests a seasonal influence. But if the seasonal influence appears in conjunction with, say, an AR(1) formulation, then the seasonal pattern will show up in unusual ways (e.g., at lag 12 and lag 13, rather than just lag 12), inhibiting the interpretation of the correlogram; because of this the seasonality is usually removed before analysis. If the spike in the correlogram at every twelfth value of k does not appear to die out as k grows, the Box–Jenkins approach deals with this seasonality by taking a seasonal difference, in this example by transforming y_t to $(y_t - y_{t-12})$, and fitting an ARMA model to the resulting data.

- The order of an MA model can be determined from the correlogram: for an MA(q) model ρ_k is nonzero for $k \leq q$ and is zero thereafter. For an AR(p) model, however, the value of p cannot be determined from looking at the correlogram, because different values of p give rise to similar-looking correlograms. A second diagram, the partial autocorrelation function, is often used to determine the order of an AR process. This is a plot of the estimate of the pth coefficient, assuming an AR(p) model, against p. The order of the AR process is the value of p beyond which the partial autocorrelations are insignificantly different from zero (i.e., if an AR(3) process has generated the data, then if we assume an AR(4) process and estimate the fourth lag coefficient, it should be insignificantly different from zero). The 95% confidence band for the partial autocorrelation function is also $\pm 2/\sqrt{N}$. Some researchers use a model selection criterion such as Akaike's AIC to help in the selection of the magnitudes of p and q; see Mills (1990, pp. 138–9), who recommends the Schwarz and Hannan criteria.

- Use of these visual identification techniques is a prominent feature of the Box–Jenkins technique, but must be supplemented, after estimation, by diagnostic checks, of which there are two main types.

  (1) *Overfitting* This model is re-estimated for a value of p or q one greater than that used for the selected model. The coefficient on this extra lag should test as insignificantly different from zero; the MA test of Godfrey (1979) is often employed.

  (2) *Portmanteau tests for white noise errors* If the selected model is correct, the residuals from estimating the model should be "white noise," implying that their autocorrelations should be zero for all lags (k). The Box–Pierce statistic and Ljung–Box statistic are often used for this purpose but, as stressed by the survey of Godfrey and Tremayne (1988), are not to be recommended.

- Hall and McAleer (1989) use a Monte Carlo study to compare several statistics used for determining the values of p and q, also concluding that the Box–Pierce and Ljung–Box statistics cannot be recommended. They suggest using instead the separate, or non-nested, test given by McAleer et al. (1988).

- Spectral analysis focuses on the cyclical components of a time series, and tries to determine which cyclical frequencies play important roles in explaining the variance of the time series. A single cycle is written as $A\cos(wt + p)$ where A is the amplitude of the cycle, w is its frequency (in terms of radians per unit time), and p is its phase. A is a crucial variable in spectral analysis because it determines how widely the cycle ranges and thus determines the variance of observations generated by that cycle. p is of little interest because it simply determines the lateral position of the cycle with respect to the origin. Now suppose a time series y_t can be written as the sum of a large number of cycles, each of different frequency, so that we can write

$$y_t = \Sigma A_i \cos(w_i t + p_i) + \varepsilon_t.$$

Spectral analysis tries to estimate how much contribution to the overall variance of the time series is made by the cycle corresponding to each frequency. In loose terms, this is exposited by drawing a graph relating frequency w_i on the horizontal axis to the corresponding amplitude A_i on the vertical axis. The discussion below provides an overview of how this is done, and introduces some of the terminology used in this area of time series analysis.

Suppose that every frequency in the range $(0,\pi)$ contributes to the y series, so that in effect y is the sum of an infinite number of cycles. It can be shown that $\gamma(k)$, the autocovariances of y, can be written as

$$\gamma(k) = \int \cos wk \, dF(w),$$

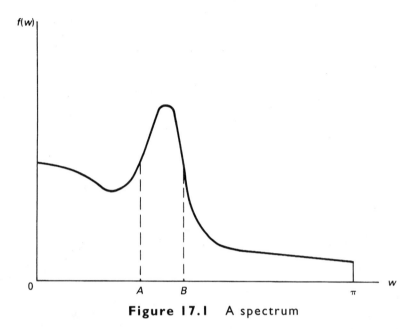

Figure 17.1 A spectrum

where $F(w)$ is a monotonically increasing function. (Notice that both A and p have disappeared.) This property of F allows $dF(w)$ to be written as $f(w)dw$ where $f(w)$ is positive. Attention focuses on the variance of y, which is $\gamma(0)$; since the cosine of zero is unity, this becomes

$$V(y) = \gamma(0) = \int f(w)dw$$

so that $f(w)dw$ can be interpreted as the contribution to the variance of cycles with frequencies in the range $(w, w + dw)$. Because of the obvious analogy to a density function, when normalized $f(w)$ is called the spectral density function, but when graphed against w it is usually referred to as the variance spectrum, the power spectrum, or just the *spectrum*.

In figure 17.1 the relatively high values of $f(w)$ in between A and B mean that of the infinite number of cosine terms added to yield y, those with frequencies in the range between A and B have particularly large amplitudes relative to other cosine terms, and thus make a relatively larger contribution to the overall variance of y. If $f(w)$ were flat, there would be no cyclical elements (regularities) in y, suggesting that y is white noise. A typical spectrum for an economic time series is high at low frequencies, falls steeply, and becomes flat at high frequencies, with an occasional peak at seasonal frequencies.

We saw earlier that there is a relationship between the autocovariances and the spectrum, namely

$$\gamma(k) = \int \cos wk\, f(w)dw.$$

This relationship can be inverted by using the *Fourier transform* to give the spectrum in terms of the autocovariances, namely

$$f(w) = \pi^{-1}\Sigma\gamma(k)e^{-wk} = \pi^{-1}[\gamma(0) + 2\Sigma\gamma(k)\cos wk],$$

where the first summation is over all integer values of k, both positive and negative, and the second is over all positive integer values of k. The spectrum is thus the Fourier transform of the autocovariance function, explaining why spectral analysis is sometimes called Fourier analysis, and also explaining why analysis in the time domain and analysis in the frequency domain are simply two different ways of looking at the data that are analytically equivalent.

The formula above suggests an obvious way of estimating: just use the $\gamma(k)$ estimates in this formula. (These estimates must be of a time series from which trend and seasonal elements have been removed.) This produces an estimate of the spectrum called the *periodogram*. Unfortunately, although the periodogram is an asymptotically unbiased estimate of the spectrum, it is not consistent, basically because of the infinite summation (as k becomes very large the estimate of $\gamma(k)$ is based on fewer and fewer observations and becomes unreliable). This problem is circumvented by "smoothing" the periodogram.

This smoothing is accomplished by taking, for each frequency, a weighted average of periodogram values for that and adjacent frequencies, with the weights given by what is called the *spectral window*, or kernel, which can be viewed as comparable to the kernel used in non-parametric estimation. The window terminology arises from the fact that the weighting system determines what part of the periodogram is "seen" (i.e., has non-negligible weights) by the estimator. The width of the spectral window, which is comparable to the class interval when constructing a histogram, is referred to as the *bandwidth*. It must be chosen with some care, since too small a bandwidth implies a large variance, producing a choppy-looking estimated spectrum, and too large a bandwidth may smooth out interesting features of the spectrum, such as peaks. The *fast Fourier transform* is a method of performing this calculation efficiently.

- The literature on spectral analysis is very technical, made worse by the fact that notation is not uniform. (For example, the spectrum is sometimes measured in autocorrelations rather than autocovariances, and the frequency is sometimes measured in cycles per unit time.) There is no easy reference on spectral analysis; Chatfield (1984) is at a relatively introductory level. For a more advanced look, concentrating on applications in econometrics, see Granger and Engle (1984).

17.4 Error-correction Models

- Nine different types of dynamic specifications can be formulated from the equation $y_t = \beta_1 x_t + \beta_2 x_{t-1} + \beta_3 y_{t-1} + \varepsilon_t$ by selecting particular values of the three coefficients. For example, $\beta_2 = \beta_3 = 0$ yields a static regression, $\beta_1 = \beta_2 = 0$ yields a univariate time series model, $\beta_3 = 0$ yields a finite distributed lag, $\beta_2 = 0$ yields a partial adjustment model, $\beta_1\beta_3 + \beta_2 = 0$ yields an autoregressive error model, and $\beta_1 + \beta_2 + \beta_3 = 1$ yields an error-correction model. See Hendry et al. (1984, pp. 1040–9) and Hendry (1995, chapter 7) for discussion.

- Suppose $y_t = \beta_0 + \beta_1 x_t + \beta_2 x_{t-1} + \beta_3 y_{t-1} + \varepsilon_t$ where y and x are measured in logarithms, with economic theory suggesting that in the long run y and x will grow at the same rate, so that in equilibrium $(y - x)$ will be a constant. By setting $y_t = y_{t-1}$ and $x_t = x_{t-1}$ to solve for the long-run equilibrium it is seen that this requires that $\beta_1 + \beta_2 + \beta_3 = 1$. Using this result, the original relationship can be manipulated (subtract y_{t-1} from each side, add and subtract both $\beta_1 x_{t-1}$ and $(\beta_3 - 1)x_{t-1}$ on the RHS) to produce $\Delta y_t = \beta_0 + \beta_1 \Delta x_t + (\beta_3 - 1)(y_{t-1} - x_{t-1}) + \varepsilon_t$. This is the ECM representation of the original specification; the last term is the error-correction term, interpreted as reflecting disequilibrium responses, and the $\beta_1 \Delta x_t$ term is interpreted as reflecting equilibrium responses. An added feature is that estimation of the parameters is enhanced by the fact that Δx_t and $(y_{t-1} - x_{t-1})$ are closer to being orthogonal than are the variables in the original relationship. In actual applications there are more explanatory variables, and many more lags, but the manipulations used to produce the ECM form are the same. Suppose in this example that y and x are integrated of order one. If the equilibrium specification is correct the levels variables are cointegrated (with cointegrating parameter unity) rendering $(y_{t-1} - x_{t-1})$ integrated of order zero, consistent with the differenced variables.

- In addition to the basic parameters of the ECM model, a researcher may be interested in estimating combinations of these parameters, such as the long-run elasticity $(\beta_1 + \beta_2)/(1 - \beta_3)$ in the example above. (This elasticity is calculated by setting $y_t = y_{t-1}$ and $x_t = x_{t-1}$ and solving for y_t.) Manipulation of the ECM can produce equations facilitating the estimation of such combinations. (In the example above, subtract $\beta_3 y_t$ from both sides, add and subtract $\beta_2 x_{t-1}$ on the RHS, and rearrange to show that regressing y_t on an intercept, Δx_t, Δy_t and x_{t-1} allows estimation of the long-run elasticity as an instrumental variable estimate of the coefficient on x_{t-1}.) For examples and discussion see Bewley (1979), Wickens and Breusch (1988), Bardsen (1989), and Banerjee et al. (1990). Gurney (1989) is a good example of an empirical implementation of one of these suggested transformation procedures.

- A crucial ingredient in the estimation of an ECM is the assumption that the term capturing the disequilibrium effect is correctly specified. If estimation of the ECM does not produce residuals that are stationary, it may be because the levels variables are not cointegrated, and this in turn may be because a levels variable has inadvertently been omitted. For example, an ECM explaining consumer prices could be developed with an equilibrium specified in terms of prices and wages growing in the long run at the same rate. But it may be that in the long run the ratio of wages to prices is trending upward rather than constant, implying that a time trend term should appear as one of the cointegrated levels variables in the error-correction term. For a good exposition and example of this see Hall and Brooks (1986).

- COMFAC analysis is best explained via a simple dynamic model

$$y_t = \alpha y_{t-1} + \beta x_t + \delta x_{t-1} + \varepsilon_t$$

which, using the lag operator L (where $Lx_t = x_{t-1}$), can be written as

$$(1 - \alpha L)y_t + \beta[1 + (\delta/\beta)L]x_t + \varepsilon_t.$$

If $\alpha = -\delta/\beta$ (or, equivalently, $\alpha\beta + \delta = 0$) the polynomials in L multiplying y_t and x_t have a common root of α and the terms involving y_t and x_t have a common factor of $(1 - \alpha L)$. Dividing through by this common factor produces

$$y_t = \beta x_t + u_t, \text{ where } u_t = \alpha u_{t-1} + \varepsilon_t.$$

In general, each common factor reduces the lag structure by one, so that, for example, if there were four explanatory variables appearing with extensive lags, and two common factors were found, eight variables could be dropped, at a cost of having to estimate with a correction for a second-order autocorrelated error. A Wald test is used to test the common factor restriction $\alpha\beta + \delta = 0$. MacKinnon (1992, pp. 112–13) suggests a simpler and more powerful test for this type of dynamic specification, based on a Gauss–Newton regression.

17.5   Testing for Unit Roots

- Suppose two unrelated series each contain a trend, and thus are nonstationary. As the sample size grows, the trend will dominate, causing the R^2 between the two series to approach unity. (This is basically because the total sum of squares, *SST*, will become infinite, causing R^2, as calculated by $1 - SSE/SST$ to approach one.) Consider now the DW statistic, which is approximately equal to $2 - 2\rho^*$, where ρ^* is an estimate of ρ. It will approach zero, because an $I(1)$ error term has $\rho = 1$. And last consider the t statistic; it will blow up, basically because of the high R^2. These observations reflect the problem of spurious regression results: unrelated $I(1)$ series appear to be related, using conventional methods. (Note that these phenomena suggest some diagnostics for this, for example a high R^2 in conjunction with a low DW.) Granger and Newbold (1974) was one of the first papers bringing this to the attention of econometricians; Hendry (1980) has a nice example of cumulative rainfall explaining the price level. These and other results, such as those of Nelson and Kang (1984), have been shown, by recent theoretical studies, to be predictable consequences of regression using integrated variables. In general, standard asymptotic distribution theory does not apply to integrated variables and is a poor approximation to finite sample results.
- Consider for illustrative purposes the simplest case of a possibly integrated variable, namely $y_t = \alpha y_{t-1} + \varepsilon_t$, where y is $I(1)$ if $\alpha = 1$. By subtracting y_{t-1} from each side this becomes $\Delta y_t = (\alpha - 1)y_{t-1} + \varepsilon_t$, suggesting that if Δy_t were regressed on y_{t-1} the t statistic on the slope coefficient could be used to test $\alpha = 1$, with a sufficiently large negative t statistic leading to rejection of the unit root null hypothesis. Several tests for unit roots take this general form, namely a t statistic calculated from running an auxiliary regression. Unfortunately, two problems arise with this general procedure. First, under the null hypothesis of a unit root this t statistic does not have a t distribution (and, in particular, is not asymptotically normally distributed), so that special critical values are required. And second, the special critical values are different depending on what kind of $I(1)$ process is being specified by the null hypothesis. The auxiliary regression above might, for example, be $\Delta y_t = \mu + (\alpha - 1)y_{t-1} + \varepsilon_t$ if the $I(1)$ process is specified to be a random walk with drift, rather than a pure random walk. Including a time trend in the original specification is another possibility; this would imply an auxiliary regression $\Delta y_t = \mu + \beta t + (\alpha - 1)y_{t-1} + \varepsilon_t$ where t is time, usually expressed as a deviation from its sample mean.
- The special critical values for the t statistic from the auxiliary regressions noted above have been tabulated for several cases, many of which appear in Fuller (1976) and Dickey and Fuller (1981), *inter alia*, and are referred to as DF, or Dickey–Fuller tests. Other tabulations, for additional sample sizes, or for additional special cases, are appearing regularly, as for example in Guilkey and Schmidt (1989) and Schmidt

(1990). The cases in question relate to various combinations of zero versus nonzero values of μ and β (e.g., $\mu = \beta = 0$, only $\mu = 0$, only $\beta = 0$, and neither equal zero) assumed in the auxiliary regression, as well as (possibly different) values of these parameters assumed in the data-generating process. This leads to a complicated testing strategy, beginning with the most general auxiliary regression and working down, moving from one set of critical values to another, as described, for example, by Dolado et al. (1990, p. 255). Good textbook expositions of this procedure can be found in Enders (1995, pp. 256–8) and Holden and Perman (1994, pp. 63–6).

- If the data-generating process has more than one lagged value of y on the right-hand side (i.e., if it is autoregressive of higher order than one) the ADF, or augmented Dickey–Fuller, test is employed. In this case the auxiliary regression is adjusted by adding an appropriate number of lagged Δy's to become $\Delta y_t = \mu + \beta t + (\theta - 1)y_{t-1} + \Sigma \delta_i \Delta y_{t-i} + \varepsilon_t$ and the critical values are the same as those which would be relevant if the lagged Δy's were not needed. Here θ is the sum of all the coefficients on the lagged dependent variables. To see how this comes about, consider the simplest case:

$$y_t = \alpha_1 y_{t-1} + \alpha_2 y_{t-2} + \varepsilon_t.$$

Subtract y_{t-1} from each side, and add and subtract $\alpha_2 y_{t-1}$ on the right-hand side to get

$$\Delta y_t = (\alpha_1 + \alpha_2 - 1)y_{t-1} - \alpha_2 \Delta y_{t-1} + \varepsilon_t.$$

A pth-order autocorrelated error in the original specification gives rise to an estimating equation with p lagged values of y serving as regressors. (This was exposited in section 8.4 of the technical notes to chapter 8 when describing the rationale of the Durbin two-stage procedure.) Thus the ADF test is also employed to protect against the possibility of an autocorrelated error. An alternative way of modifying the DF test to deal with autocorrelated errors is due to Phillips and Perron (1988) who adjust the DF statistic before consulting the appropriate critical values. This avoids the loss of degrees of freedom caused by the extra regressors used in the ADF test. Both this and the ADF test are unaffected by heteroskedasticity.

The ADF test seems to be the most popular unit root test, because of its simplicity and also because Monte Carlo studies such as Haug (1993, 1996) have found that it performs well. Harris (1992) finds that the size and power properties of the ADF test are enhanced if a generous lag is employed. He recommends the lag $12(N/100)^{0.25}$ as suggested by Schwert (1989). On the basis of an extensive Monte Carlo study Dods and Giles (1995) recommend the default method in the Shazam econometrics package, based on testing for the highest significant lag in the autocorrelation and partial autocorrelation functions of first-differenced data. Cheung and Lai (1995) find that the small-sample critical values for the ADF test depend on the lag order; they provide a response surface equation to determine critical values.

- A completely different test procedure is based on testing the DW statistic equal to zero. Special critical values are required; see Bhargava (1986). It is not as popular, however, because there is an indeterminant region, and because the nature of the data-generating process assumed is more restrictive. New ideas for testing for unit roots appear regularly. Hansen (1995) shows that unit root tests can be much more powerful when additional explanatory variables are included in the testing regression. Mocan

(1994) allows for a more flexible trend than the linear time trend. Yi et al. (1995) find promising results by filtering the data before performing the test. Leybourne (1994) bases a test on the fact that an $I(0)$ variable is likely to have its first negative autocorrelation appear at a lower lag level than an $I(1)$ variable. Leybourne (1995) finds that power can be increased by using the maximum of two Dickey–Fuller test statistics, one using the original data and one using these data in reverse order. Sims and Uhlig (1991) argue that unit roots is a situation in which Bayesian and classical probability statements cannot be reconciled, the latter requiring modification. Volume 6 (4) of the *Journal of Applied Econometrics* (1991) has an extensive and very interesting discussion of unit root testing by Bayesian means.

- The vast majority of unit root tests have non-stationarity, i.e., a unit root, as the null hypothesis. (Note that when testing for cointegration this implies that the null is no cointegration because it is no cointegration that corresponds to a unit root!) Because the traditional classical testing methodology accepts the null unless there is strong evidence against it, unit root tests usually conclude that there is a unit root. This problem is exacerbated by the fact that unit root tests generally have low power. Kwiatkowski et al. (1992) introduced a test for unit roots which adopts stationarity as the null hypothesis. They do this by modeling a time series as a sum of a deterministic trend, a random walk and a stationary error, and then testing for the random walk having zero variance. Unsurprisingly, they frequently draw conclusions opposite to those of the traditional unit root tests. Critical values for this KPSS test can be found in Sephton (1995). This result supports results from other renegade testing methods, such as Bayesian methods. See Kwiatkowski et al. for references. Leybourne and McCabe (1994) extends the KPSS test.
- All unit root tests have difficulty discriminating between an $I(1)$ process and an $I(0)$ process with a shift in its mean, as noted by Rappoport and Reichlin (1989), among others. To see why, picture a stationary series bumping along at a low level and then jumping to a higher level where it continues to bump along. A trend line fitted through these data will have an upward slope, causing unit root tests to be fooled by this structural break. As an example, consider the possibility that output growth is trend stationary over extended periods but is subject to major shocks such as the Great Depression or a productivity slowdown. Enders (1995, pp. 243–8) has a good exposition of unit root tests in the context of structural breaks. Gregory and Hansen (1996a,b) suggest using the smallest (i.e., largest negative) of ADF t values calculated for different structural break points. Banerjee, Lumsdaine and Stock (1992) suggest some alternative tests.
- The power of unit root tests depends much more on the span of the data, ceteris paribus, than on the number of observations i.e., for macroeconomic data where long business cycles are of importance, a long span of annual data would be preferred to a shorter span with, say, monthly data, even though the latter case may have more observations. (A caveat is that the longer span has a greater chance of containing a structural break.) This does not mean that one should throw monthly observations away if available because extra observations of any form are of value. Rossana and Seater (1995) find that temporal aggregation of economic time series, such as converting monthly data to annual data, creates substantial losses in information and can cause misleading results in empirical analysis. In particular, they find that long-run business-cycle variation present in monthly data disappears when these data are aggregated to annual data. They recommend using quarterly data which are not as

plagued by measurement error as monthly data, and do not suffer severely from temporal aggregation problems. Osborn (1990) finds that seasonal unit roots are rare and that economic time series are typically integrated of order one with a deterministic seasonal pattern imposed. Cointegration could appear as a seasonal phenomenon; see Ilmakunnas (1990) or Hurn (1993) for good examples of how this can be handled.

- ADF tests are sensitive to nonlinear transformations of the data, such as when a variable is found to be non-stationary in levels but stationary in logarithms. Franses and McAleer (1997) propose a means of testing if the data have been adequately transformed in this respect.

- An alternative way of testing for nonstationarity models the underlying process using the concept of *fractional* integration. The traditional analysis examines $(1 - \alpha L)y_t$, with nonstationarity corresponding to $\alpha \geq 1$. In contrast, we could adopt a different model and examine $(1 - L)^d y_t$, where $d \geq 0.5$ corresponds to nonstationarity. For this to be viable we must allow d to take on non-integer values, hence the name fractional integration. Although there are higher computational costs, modeling in terms of fractional integration has several advantages. It allows a continuous transition from non-unit root behavior to a unit root, it is better suited to capturing low frequency (long memory) behavior and so is able more adequately to model long-term persistence, and it nests both difference stationary and trend stationary models. In short, it provides a more flexible alternative against which to test unit roots, and because of this empirical studies using this approach tend to reject a unit root. See Sowell (1992) and Crato and Rothman (1994). In this context ARIMA becomes ARFIMA, autoregressive fractionally-integrated moving average.

17.6 Cointegration

- The "superconsistency" result arises because as the sample size increases, the "denominator" $(X'X)^{-1}$ of the expression for the bias of the OLS estimate increases much more quickly than usual, since the X data do not hover around a constant level. This overwhelms the "numerator," eliminating the asymptotic bias that would otherwise characterize this estimate in the presence of contemporaneous correlation between the error and the regressors due to simultaneity. This creates the consistency. In addition it can be shown that this bias disappears at a rate proportional to T rather than, as is usual, at a rate proportional to $\sqrt{T}$; this is why the super prefix is used.

- The logic of the Johansen procedure can be exposited by drawing a crude parallel with the simplest version of the single-equation case. Suppose $y_t = \alpha y_{t-1} + \varepsilon_t$ which by subtracting y_{t-1} from each side can be rewritten as $\Delta y_t = (\alpha - 1)y_{t-1} + \varepsilon_t$. This is the traditional form in which a unit root test is undertaken, consisting of testing for $\alpha - 1$ equal to zero. (This can be generalized by adding additional lags of y and other explanatory variables in current or lagged form.) Think of this as saying that the only context in which it is legitimate to regress differenced y on levels y is when the coefficient on levels y is zero or levels y is stationary.

Now consider a similar equation, but this time in terms of an $N \times 1$ vector z where the elements of z are individual time series connected by the general vector equation

$$z_t = A z_{t-1} + \varepsilon_t$$

where A is an $N \times N$ matrix of coefficients. (This would be generalized by adding additional lags of z; readers should recognize this from chapter 10 as a VAR.) The first row of A for example, consists of the N coefficients associated with expressing the first element of z_t as a linear function of the N elements of z_{t-1}. Subtracting z_{t-1} from each side we get

$$\Delta z_t = (A - I)z_{t-1} + \varepsilon_t$$

a multivariate version of the equation used above to test for unit roots. Now think of this as saying that the only context in which it makes sense to regress a differenced element of z on all its levels elements is when a row of A–I when multiplied down the levels elements creates zero or creates a stationary variable. The number of rows of A–I that do not create zero when multiplied down a vector is equal to the rank of A–I, so testing for the rank of $A-I$ can be interpreted as testing for the number of cointegrating vectors. Further, the rank of $A-I$ is equal to the number of its nonzero characteristic roots (eigenvalues). Johansen's λ_{trace} and λ_{max} test statistics for the number of cointegrating vectors are based on estimates of the characteristic roots.

By normalizing A–I to put a coefficient of unity on a chosen variable, A–I can be rewritten as $\theta\beta$ where β is a matrix of normalized cointegrating row vectors and θ is a matrix containing the speed-of-adjustment parameters associated with the error-correction terms corresponding to each of the coinegrating vectors. The first row of θ, for example, contains the speed-of-adjustment parameters for each of the error-correction (cointegrating relationships) terms in the first equation. Suppose for example there are only two cointegrating relationships, the parameters of which appear in the first two rows of β. Then only the first two columns of θ will have non-zero values – the number of cointegrating relationships is equal to the number of non-zero columns of θ. The Johansen procedure tests for the rank of A–I (equal to the number of non-zero columns of θ) and then uses maximum likelihood, sometimes referred to as reduced rank regression in this context, to estimate θ and β. Hypotheses about the parameters are tested by checking to see if imposing restrictions reduces the number of cointegrating vectors.

Suppose the nth row of θ consists entirely of zeros. This means that the error-correction terms do not enter into the equation determining the nth variable, implying that this variable is (weakly) exogenous to the system. Tests for exogeneity exploit this.

FORECASTING

18.1 INTRODUCTION

Although the creation of good parameter estimates is often viewed as the primary goal of econometrics, to many a goal of equal importance is the production of good economic forecasts. The preceding chapter on time series econometrics makes this evident: some time series techniques were developed solely for the purpose of forecasting. The purpose of this chapter is to provide a brief overview of economic forecasting; no effort is made to describe forecasting methods, since textbooks doing this abound.

Economic forecasting methods can be classified into two very broad categories.

(1) *Causal forecasting/econometric models* Once estimates of the parameters of an economic model are available, the model can be employed to forecast the dependent variable if the associated values of the independent variables are given. It is this forecasting method, relying on the causal interpretation of the economic model in question, that is usually meant by the terminology "econometric forecast." The model used can range in sophistication from a single equation with one or two explanatory variables to a large simultaneous-equation model with scores of variables.

(2) *Time series models* Time series can be characterized as consisting of a time trend, a seasonal factor, a cyclical element and an error term. A wide variety of techniques is available to break up a time series into these components and thereby to generate a means of forecasting behavior of the series. These methods are based on the supposition that history provides some guide as to what to expect in the future. The most sophisticated of these time series techniques is Box–Jenkins analysis; it has become so common in economic forecasting that it is usually what is referred to when economists (as opposed to business forecasters) talk about the time series method. (See chapter 17.)

18.2 CAUSAL FORECASTING/ECONOMETRIC MODELS

Suppose the model $Y_t = \alpha + \beta x_t + \varepsilon_t$ is assumed to satisfy the CLR model assumptions, and data for T periods are used to estimate α and β using OLS. If the value of X in time period $T + 1$ is given as X_{T+1}, then Y_{T+1} is forecast as $\hat{Y}_{T+1} = \alpha^{\text{OLS}} + \beta^{\text{OLS}} X_{T+1}$. Four potential sources of error exist when using $\hat{Y}_{T+1}$ to forecast Y_{T+1}.

(1) *Specification error* It may not be true that the assumptions of the CLR model are met, in particular that all the relevant explanatory variables are included, that the functional form is correct, and that there has been no change in regime.

(2) *Conditioning error* The value of X_{T+1}, on which the forecast is conditioned, may be inaccurate.

(3) *Sampling error* The estimates α^{OLS} and β^{OLS}, rather than the true (unknown) values of α and β, are used in calculating $\hat{Y}_{T+1}$.

(4) *Random error* The calculation of $\hat{Y}_{T+1}$ implicitly estimates ε_{T+1} as zero when its true value may differ considerably from zero.

Although each of these four sources of error plays a role in making $\hat{Y}_{T+1}$ diverge from Y_{T+1}, only sources (3) and (4) above are used to derive the forecast interval, shown in figure 18.1. This interval covers the actual value being fore-

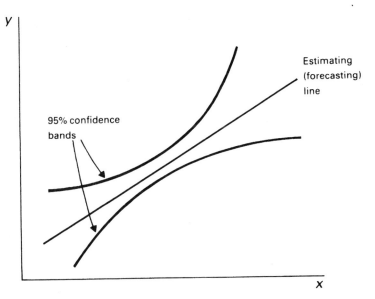

Figure 18.1 Confidence intervals for forecasting

cast in, say, 95% of repeated samples (assuming no specification or conditioning errors); in figure 18.1 it is given for each value of X as the vertical distance between the two 95% confidence bands. The interval is smallest at the average value of the given data set used to estimate α and β; as predictions are made for values of X further and further away from this average, these intervals become larger and larger. Inside the X data set we have information on the behavior of Y and so can be fairly confident about our forecasts; outside the data set the opposite is the case.

If error sources (1) and (2), the specification and conditioning errors, are absent, $\hat{Y}_{T+1}$ is the best linear unbiased forecast and the forecast interval in figure 18.1 is "tighter" than that of any alternative linear unbiased forecast. This is because in that circumstance α^{OLS} and β^{OLS} are BLUE. From this it should be clear that the two main objectives of econometrics – obtaining good parameter estimates and generating good forecasts – are tied closely together, at least in so far as the error sources (1) and (2) above can be ignored. The influence of these specification and conditioning errors, particularly the former, prompts many econometricians to adjust estimates from their models in light of information about factors in the economy whose influences are not incorporated in their model. In fact, this "judgemental modification" of econometric models, consisting of a blend of qualitative information and the forecaster's experience (and often referred to as "tender loving care"), is viewed as an essential ingredient of the process of forecasting from an econometric model. Examples are forecast modifications undertaken in light of a major strike, an application of moral suasion by a policy authority, or the announcement of a future oil price increase.

18.3 TIME SERIES ANALYSIS

The main competitors to econometric models for forecasting purposes are Box–Jenkins, or ARIMA models, explained in some detail in chapter 17. Univariate Box–Jenkins models are sophisticated extrapolation methods, using only past values of the variable being forecast to generate forecasts; they ignore the many explanatory variables which form the foundation of econometric models. There are several reasons why forecasters should be interested in these naive models: thanks to improved computer software, they are easy and cheap to produce; the extra information required to estimate a proper econometric model may be expensive to obtain; forecasts from such models can serve as a useful benchmark for comparison purposes; forecasts from this process can be combined with other forecasts to produce improved forecasts; and they are useful as a preliminary step for further modeling – they clarify the nature of the data and make clear what behavior patterns require explanation.

During the 1970s controversy raged over the relative forecasting merits of econometric models and ARIMA models, prompted by studies claiming the superiority of the ARIMA models. As noted in chapter 17, this led to a synthesis of the two approaches, and prompted the development of models, such as ECMs, that paid more attention to dynamics. In retrospect, the reason why econometric models performed so poorly in these comparisons was because of misspecification errors in the econometric models, primarily with respect to their dynamic structure. It is generally acknowledged that whenever specification or conditioning errors render econometric models impractical (which some claim is most of the time), the Box–Jenkins approach has considerable merit for forecasting. It is also recognized that if an econometric model is outperformed by an ARIMA model, this is evidence that the econometric model is misspecified.

18.4 FORECASTING ACCURACY

There are several ways of measuring forecasting accuracy and thereby comparing one forecasting method to another. In all of the methods mentioned below, the forecasts and forecast errors referred to are errors in forecasting extra-sample observations.

(1) *Mean absolute deviation (MAD)* This is the average of the absolute values of the forecast errors. It is appropriate when the cost of forecast errors is proportional to the absolute size of the forecast error. This criterion is also called MAE (mean absolute error).

(2) *Root mean square error (RMSE)* This is the square root of the average of the squared values of the forecast errors. This measure implicitly weights large forecast errors more heavily than small ones and is appropriate to situations in which the cost of an error increases as the square of that error. This "quadratic loss function" is the most popular in use.

(3) *Mean absolute percentage error (MAPE)* This is the average of the absolute values of the percentage errors; it has the advantage of being dimensionless. It is more appropriate when the cost of the forecast error is more closely related to the percentage error than to the numerical size of the error.

(4) *Correlation of forecasts with actual values* For this measure actual changes (not the levels) of the variable being forecast are regressed on the forecasts of these changes and the resulting R^2 is used as a measure of forecasting accuracy.

(5) *Percentage of turning points forecast* This criterion is relevant if prediction of turning points, rather than numerical accuracy of forecasts, determines the payoff from forecasting.

(6) *Conditional efficiency* A forecast A is said to be conditionally efficient relative to forecast B if B possesses no useful information beyond that contained in A. One way of determining this is to combine A and B into a best combination forecast and see if the variance of the resulting forecast error is significantly smaller than that resulting from forecasting with A alone.

There is some agreement in the literature that the "best" forecasting method, overall, is a "combined" forecast, formed as a weighted average of a variety of forecasts, each generated by a different technique. If the principles on which these different forecasts are based are sufficiently different from one another, this average should prove superior to any single forecasting technique because the errors in the separate forecasts will tend to cancel one another. In the context of model specification problems, this suggests that good forecasts do not come from using a single, favorite model specification, but rather come from combining results from a variety of reasonable models. The weights for the combined forecast are found by regressing the actual values on all the competing forecasts (including an intercept). There are many variants of this combined forecasting methodology.

GENERAL NOTES

18.1 Introduction

- When estimating parameter values, the failures of econometrics are shielded from public view by the fact that the true parameter values are unknown and thus cannot be compared with their estimated values. This protection does not exist when econometrics is used for forecasting – eventually predicted and actual values can be directly compared. Unfortunately for econometricians, most such comparisons have not shown their forecasts to be particularly accurate. This has prompted jokes from critics, such as "If an economist is someone who guesses wrong about the economy, an econometrician is someone who uses a computer to guess wrong about the economy." Economists reply with "We only forecast to show the world that we have a sense of humour."

    Joking aside, economists' forecasting record is not good. Martin Feldstein, chairman of the US Council of Economic Advisors, was quoted (*Time*, August 27, 1984, p. 46) as saying "One of the great mistakes of the past 30 years of economic policy has been an excessive belief in the ability to forecast." Nobel prize-winner Wassily Leontief (1971, p. 3) noted that "in no other field of empirical enquiry has so massive and sophisticated a statistical machinery been used with such indifferent results." Non-economists are much blunter in their assessment, as evidenced by US Treasury Secretary Donald Regan's statement (*Time*, August 27, 1984, p. 46) that, "If you believe them, then you also believe in the tooth fairy."

    One way of defending economic forecasts is to appeal to Alice-in-Wonderland logic: " '... how can you possibly award prizes when everybody missed the target?' said Alice. 'Well,' said the Queen, 'Some missed by more than others, and we have a fine normal distribution of misses, which means we can forget the target.' "

    Even if forecasts are poor, there are none better, and perhaps a poor forecast is better than none at all. Not everyone believes that economic forecasts are as poor as they are made out to be, however, or that the quality of what some claim to be poor forecasts is so bad that they cannot be useful. Klein (1984) has a good exposition of how forecasts are used and examples of their success in this regard. Armstrong et al. (1978) is a source of interesting debate on this subject. Simon (1994) argues that

although economic forecasting is notoriously bad in the short run, it is quite good in the long run, primarily because economic laws tend to dominate over long periods of time.
- Not all forecasting methods can be neatly classified into one of the two categories structured here. A prominent example is the leading indicator approach; Klein and Moore (1983) have a good survey of its use.
- The discussion of this chapter is couched entirely in terms of forecasting time series data. For forecasting cross-sectional data, only the econometric approach can be used. In this context, Gencay and Yang (1996) find that nonparametric methods (discussed in chapter 19) outperform methods that rely on a parametric functional form.
- Faulhaber and Baumol (1988, pp. 591–2) is a concise history of the modern economic forecasting industry in the United States.

18.2   Causal Forecasting/Econometric Models

- A variant of causal forecasting is *simulation*. The impact on the economy of a policy change is simulated by using the econometric model to forecast into the future. Challen and Hagger (1983) have a good discussion.
- For further discussion of the role played by the conditioning error, see Johnston (1984, pp. 198–200), Ashley (1983), and Feldstein (1971).
- Forecasting unknown values is called *ex ante* forecasting; forecasting known values is called *ex post* forecasting.
- Many critics of econometric forecasting claim that, for example, the model and parameter estimates used relate to the 1980s, for which data are available, but not to the 1990s, for which forecasts are required. Streissler (1970) even goes so far as to define econometrics as dealing with predictions of the economic past. Both Streissler (1970) and Rubner (1970) severely criticize economic forecasting. In the macroeconomic context the problem of regime changes is particularly nettlesome, as noted by Lucas (1976), since the behavior of rational individuals should change whenever the policy environment within which they live changes. This "Lucas critique", as it has come to be known, is largely ignored by econometricians, mainly because it does not appear to be of substantive magnitude, as argued by Doan et al. (1984) and Favero and Hendry (1992). For a contrary view see Miller and Roberds (1991).
- Forecast intervals are sometimes used to test the specification of a model – if the actual value falls within the forecast interval, the model specification is confirmed. In the context of testing the specification of a dynamic model (such as an ECM), it is often referred to as a post-sample predictive test. As noted earlier, this test is equivalent to the variant of the Chow test employing period-specific dummy variables.
- Fair (1984, chapter 8) explains a method of measuring the influence on prediction of model misspecification. Simulation is used to obtain the forecast error variance due to conditioning error, sampling error and random error. The difference between this variance and the actual forecast error variance is attributed to specification error.
- An intuitive explanation for why the confidence interval widens as X moves further away from its average value in the data set in figure 18.1 is as follows. Suppose the error term for one of the data points were slightly different. This would change slightly the estimates of α and β. If this is visualized in figure 18.1, it should be clear that the predicted value of Y at the mid-point of the data set will change by a small

amount, because the new estimating line will cut the old near that point. It will diverge markedly from the old the further one goes beyond the bounds of the data set.

- The best linear unbiased forecast in the context of the GLS model differs from that of the CLR model in two ways. First, the GLS estimates are used instead of the OLS estimates, and second, if the errors are autocorrelated, the estimated values of past errors can be used to help predict future errors. For example, if $\varepsilon_t = \rho \varepsilon_{t-1} + u_t$, then the error in the $(T + 1)$th time period would be predicted as $\hat{\rho} \hat{\varepsilon}_T$, rather than 0. See Goldberger (1962). Many econometricians claim that failure to account for autocorrelated errors (characteristic of simultaneous equation model estimation) is a significant factor leading to poor forecasts.

- Young (1982) and Challen and Hagger (1983, pp. 184–90) have good discussions of judgemental modification/tender loving care. See also Howrey et al. (1974) and Evans et al. (1972).

- Belsley (1984a) has a good discussion of the impact of multicollinearity on forecasting.

18.3   Time Series Analysis

- Makridakis (1976, 1978) and Anderson (1977) provide an extensive survey of time series methods (not just Box–Jenkins). For a useful perspective on the future of time series forecasting, see Chatfield (1988).

- Fildes and Makridakis (1995) note that empirical findings on time series forecasting accuracy have identified several anomalies which have been ignored by theoretical time series analysts who seem not to be interested in the out-of-sample forecasting performance of their techniques. Even if time series analysts are more interested in parameter estimation and testing, they should be testing their specifications by evaluating their out-of-sample forecasting performance.

- As should be evident from the discussion of nonstationarity in chapter 17, forecasting with $I(1)$ variables is not reliable – a random walk can appear to give reasonable predictions of another random walk, for example.

- An excellent summary of the controversy concerning the relative merits of Box–Jenkins and econometric models for forecasting can be found in Granger and Newbold (1986, pp. 287–92). Nelson (1972) is an early study favoring Box–Jenkins; McNees (1982) presents a convincing case for econometric models. Dorfman and McIntosh (1990) report a forecasting contest in which an econometric forecasting method which exploits knowledge of the true data-generating process does not dominate competing forecasting methods. Misspecifying an econometric model by omitting a relevant explanatory variable need not spell disaster. If the omitted explanatory variable A is correlated with an included explanatory variable B, ordinary least squares produces a biased coefficient estimate for B that ensures unbiased forecasts for situations in which the historical correlation between A and B continues.

- The VAR methodology (discussed in chapter 10), which can be viewed as a variant of multivariate Box–Jenkins, is often used for forecasting. As shown by Hafer and Sheehan (1989), its forecasting accuracy varies dramatically over alternative lag structures. The use of modest lag lengths is recommended. On the other hand, as noted in the general notes to section 10.5 of chapter 10, imposing reasonable restrictions on VARs, such as those advocated by the Bayesians to temper the influence of lagged variables, improves their performance markedly. Shoesmith (1995) finds that combining a Bayesian VAR with an error correction model (see chapter 17) improves forecasting. He warns that addition of error correction terms corresponding to cointegrating vectors which do not test significantly different from zero harms forecasts.

- When using the Box–Jenkins methodology to forecast a constructed variable, for example (*GNP/P*), it is not clear whether it is better to forecast *GNP* and *P* separately to produce the forecast, or to forecast (*GNP/P*) directly. Kang (1986) suggests that the former approach is better.

18.4   Forecasting Accuracy

- Granger (1996) offers several suggestions for how forecasters might improve accuracy: use more up-to-date information as input; make better use of past forecast errors, leading indicators and expected values; incorporate lagged error correction terms; correct for the tendency for change to be underforecast; and be quicker to recognize structural breaks, temporarily switching to an adaptive model such as a random walk.
- Criteria for selecting a forecasting method are discussed in Dhrymes et al. (1972) and Granger and Newbold (1973). See also Maddala (1977, pp. 343–7) and Granger and Newbold (1986, pp. 276–87). For a survey of characteristics of various measures of forecasting accuracy, see Armstrong (1978, pp. 319–29).
- Leitch and Tanner (1995) argue that failure of high-priced forecasters to outperform simple methods on the basis of measures like mean square forecast error is not relevant because profitability from using forecasts comes from success in directional forecasting. They claim that measured on this criterion professional forecasters outperform simple forecasting methods. Directional forecasting is an example of classification analysis, discussed in chapter 15. Kamstra and Kennedy (1997) discuss how combining of such "qualitative" forecasts might be undertaken.
- Mahmoud (1984) is an excellent survey of studies on accuracy in forecasting. His general conclusions are that quantitative methods outperform qualitative (subjectively oriented) methods so long as there are adequate data and no obvious regime changes have taken place; that simple methods are as accurate as sophisticated methods; and that amalgamating forecasts offers an improvement over the best of the individual forecasting methods.
- A popular method of evaluating a predictor is to regress the actual changes on the predicted changes and a constant. If the intercept estimate tests insignificantly different from 0 and the slope coefficient tests insignificantly different from 1, the predictor is said to be a good one. (More than one predictor may satisfy his criterion, however, in which case some additional criterion must be introduced; see Granger and Newbold, 1973.)
- Armstrong (1978, p. 86) presents a graph reflecting his findings that a small amount of forecasting expertise dramatically improves the accuracy of forecasts but thereafter further expertise does not improve (and may even worsen) forecasts. He concludes that for forecasting the cheapest expert should be hired. Why then is it the case that the most expensive forecasters using the most complex forecasting methods tend to be hired? His explanation for this (p. 399) is the "rain dance theory":

> The rain dance has something for everyone. The dancer gets paid. The clients get to watch a good dance. The decision-maker gets to shift the problem onto someone else in a socially acceptable way. (Who can blame him? He hired the best dancer in the business.)

- The term "conditional efficiency" was introduced by Granger and Newbold (1973). A similar concept was used by Nelson (1972), who suggested formulating the variable to be forecast, y, as a linear combination of the two forecasts A and B, to get $y_t = kA_t + (1 - k)B_t + \varepsilon_t$ and estimating k by regressing $(y - B)$ on $(A - B)$. A test of $k = 1$ can be used to test for the conditional efficiency of A. This methodology has been extended to include an intercept and additional forecasts. It is suggested that all econometric model forecasts be automatically tested in this way against an ARIMA model. Fair and Shiller (1989) introduce a similar concept.

- In the evaluation of forecasting mechanisms and the testing of rational expectations, much has been made of the necessity for forecasts to be unbiased. Zellner (1986a) notes that this assumption of unbiased forecasts may not be warranted; its validity depends on the loss function employed by those forecasting. In general, estimation of parameters to be used for forecasting should incorporate the loss function/criterion used to evaluate the forecasts.

- Clemens (1989) is an excellent survey of the combining forecasts literature. When forecasting by using the combining forecasts methodology, one is always on the look-out for forecasts to include in the combining. Two obvious cases are sometimes overlooked. If a series is stationary, then the mean is a potential (albeit inefficient) forecast warranting inclusion. (This explains the result of Granger and Ramanathan (1984) that including an intercept in the combining regression improves the results.) If the series is integrated of order one, then its most recent value is a good forecast and so worthy of inclusion.

- Spiro (1989) notes that forecasters tend to be conservative, causing the combining methodology to underpredict change. He suggests correcting for this bias by regressing the actual values A on the group average forecasts F and $F - A_{t-1}$ and using the result to modify future Fs.

- Makridakis et al. (1982) report the results of a forecasting competition known as the M-competition, in which 1,001 time series were forecast using a wide variety of competing forecasting methods. Zellner (1986b) notes that in this competition the Bayesian forecasting procedure produced the lowest overall average MSE forecast. He also notes that it is unfair to expect the Bayesian estimator to perform well on other criteria unless the loss function used to produce the Bayesian forecast is modified to reflect the criteria being used for evaluation. For a response see Fildes and Makridakis (1988).

- "Normative forecasting" is an approach to forecasting in which evaluation of a forecast in terms of its accuracy becomes less important than its utility in producing "good" decisions or policies. For example, a deliberately exaggerated forecast of pollution would score well on this criterion if it induced people to take the appropriate measures to solve the actual problem.

TECHNICAL NOTES

18.2   Causal Forecasting/Econometric Models

● The variance of the forecast error, from which the confidence interval is constructed, is given by the formula $\sigma^2 + \sigma^2 X'_0 (X'X)^{-1} X_0$ where X_0 is a vector of regressor observations corresponding to the value of the dependent variable that is to be forecast. The first term in this expression results from estimating the error term as zero; the second term results from the use of OLS estimates rather than the true parameter values. (Notice that the variance–covariance matrix of the OLS estimator, $\sigma^2 (X'X)^{-1}$, appears in this second term.) Salkever (1976) presents a computationally attractive way of calculating this variance, as well as the forecasts themselves, using period-specific dummy variables; see section 14.5.

18.4   Forecasting Accuracy

● The mean square error of a predictor can be broken down into three parts. The first, called the *bias proportion*, corresponds to that part of the MSE resulting from a tendency to forecast too high or too low, reflected by the extent to which the intercept term in the regression of actual changes on predicted changes is nonzero. The second, called the *regression proportion*, corresponds to that part of the MSE resulting from other systematic influences, reflected by the extent to which the slope coefficient in this regression differs from 1. The third, called the *disturbance proportion*, measures that part of the MSE resulting from an unpredictable error (measured by the variance of the residuals from this regression). This decomposition (see Theil, 1966, pp. 26–36) provides useful information to someone attempting to evaluate a forecasting method. (An alternative decomposition, also due to Theil, into bias, variance and covariance proportions has been shown by Granger and Newbold (1973) to have questionable meaning.)

● A common statistic found in the forecasting context is Theil's inequality (or "U") statistic (see Theil, 1966, pp. 26–36), given as the square root of the ratio of the mean square error of the predicted change to the average squared actual change. For a perfect forecaster, the statistic is zero; a value of unity corresponds to a forecast of "no change." (Note that an earlier version of this statistic has been shown to be defective; see Bliemel, 1973.)

19

ROBUST ESTIMATION

19.1 INTRODUCTION

Estimators designed to be the "best" estimator for a particular estimating problem owe their attractive properties to the fact that their derivation has exploited special features of the process generating the data, features that are assumed known by the econometrician. Knowledge that the CLR model assumptions hold, for example, allows derivation of the OLS estimator as one possessing several desirable properties. Unfortunately, because these "best" estimators have been designed to exploit these assumptions, violations of the assumptions affect them much more than they do other, sub-optimal estimators. Because researchers are not in a position of knowing with certainty that the assumptions used to justify their choice of estimator are met, it is tempting to protect oneself against violations of these assumptions by using an estimator whose properties, while not quite "best," are not sensitive to violations of those assumptions. Such estimators are referred to as *robust* estimators.

We have on occasion encountered such estimators. An example is the heteroskedasticity-consistent estimator of the variance–covariance matrix of the OLS estimator. This estimator reduces the sensitivity of inference using OLS to erroneous assumptions made about the variance of the error term. The OLS estimator can itself in some contexts be viewed as a robust estimator – it was noted in chapter 10 that in the context of simultaneous equation estimation the OLS estimator is not as sensitive as its competitors to problems such as multicollinearity and errors in variables.

Although generically a robust estimator is one that is insensitive to violations of any of the assumptions made about the way in which the data are generated, in practice most robust estimators have been designed to be resistant to erroneous assumptions regarding the distribution of the errors. The next two sections discuss this type of robustness; the final section of this chapter discusses an estimation procedure designed to be robust to a wider variety of erroneous modeling assumptions. The topic of robustness has become quite popular recently in econometrics, as researchers have become aware of the extreme sensitivity of some of their estimation procedures, such as Tobit estimation, to non-normality of the error term.

19.2 OUTLIERS AND INFLUENTIAL OBSERVATIONS

When the errors are distributed normally, the OLS estimator in the CLR model is best unbiased, meaning that among all unbiased estimators it has the smallest variance. Whenever the errors are not distributed normally, a weaker result holds, namely that the OLS estimator is best linear unbiased (BLUE), meaning that among all linear unbiased estimators it has the smallest variance. If the distribution of the errors is "fat-tailed," in that it frequently produces relatively large errors, it turns out that linearity is unduly restrictive: in the presence of fat-tailed error distributions, although the OLS estimator is BLUE, it is markedly inferior to some nonlinear unbiased estimators. These nonlinear estimators, called robust estimators, are preferred to the OLS estimator whenever there may be reason to believe that the error distribution is fat-tailed.

Observations that have large residuals associated with them are thought to reflect the presence of a fat-tailed error distribution, so a search for such "outliers" is usually the first step in addressing this potential problem. An easy way to look for outliers is to plot the OLS residuals and see if any observations are relatively large. This is not a good method; a large error when squared becomes very large, so when minimizing the sum of squared errors OLS gives a high weight to this observation, causing the OLS estimating line to swing towards this observation, masking the fact that it is an outlier. (The fact that the OLS line swings so much in response to a single observation is why OLS performs poorly in the presence of fat-tailed error distributions.) A better method is to investigate the ith observation, say, by running the regression without the ith observation and seeing if the prediction error for the ith observation is significantly large. This is repeated to check all observations.

The rationale for looking for outliers is that they may have a strong influence on the estimates produced by OLS, an influence that may not be desirable. The type of outlier discussed above, an observation with an unusually large error, is only one of two kinds of outlying observations that can have a strong influence on OLS estimates. The second type of outlier is an observation with an unusual value of an explanatory variable, referred to as a leverage point. Consider a graph of the dependent variable plotted against a single explanatory variable, with a group of observations clustered in a small area, and a single observation with a markedly different value of the explanatory variable; this single observation will have a strong influence on the OLS estimates, so much so that it is as worthy of special attention as are the outliers discussed earlier.

It should now be evident that what one should be looking for is not just "outliers," of whatever type, but observations that have a strong influence on the OLS estimates; such observations are called *influential observations*. Measures for the detection of influential observations are based on comparing OLS coefficient (or error) estimates calculated using the entire data set, to OLS estimates calculated using the entire data set less one observation. Any observation which, when dropped, causes the OLS estimates to change markedly is identified as an influential observation.

19.3   ROBUST ESTIMATORS

Once influential observations have been identified it is tempting just to throw them away. This would be a major mistake. Often influential observations are the most valuable observations in a data set; if for years interest rates or relative energy prices do not change much, when they do change the new observations are exactly what is needed to produce good estimates. Furthermore, outliers may be reflecting some unusual fact that could lead to an improvement in the model's specification.

The first thing that should be done after influential observations have been identified is to examine these observations very carefully to see if there is some obvious reason why they are outliers. There may have been an error in measuring or classifying the data, or the data may have been entered into the computer erroneously, for example, in which case remedying these mistakes is the best solution; if a mistake cannot be remedied, then throwing an observation away is justified. There may be an unusual circumstance associated with an observation, such as an earthquake or an accountant's "extraordinary item," in which case some thought should be given to modifying the model to allow incorporation of this observation.

If influential observations remain after this examination, it is not obvious what should be done. If as a result of this examination the researcher is convinced that these observations are bona fide and therefore valuable, OLS should not necessarily be abandoned, but if some suspicion remains that the data may have errors from a fat-tailed disribution, then a robust estimator could be used. Five general types of robust estimators are discussed below.

(1) *M estimators*   The sum of squared error terms can be viewed as a weighted average of the absolute values of the errors, where the weights are their own values. From this point of view, OLS minimizes a weighted sum of absolute error values, where the weights are the magnitudes of the absolute error values. The idea behind an M estimator is to use different weights, in particular to use weights that do not continue to grow in magnitude as the absolute value of the error term grows. Some examples should clarify this:

(a)   Make every weight one, in which case this estimator would minimize the sum of absolute errors.

(b)   Let the weight be the absolute value of the error until it reaches some arbitrarily determined value, say b, at which point the weight stays at b for all absolute error values greater than b.

(c)   Follow the previous option, but when the value of the absolute error reaches an arbitrarily determined value c, have the weights decrease (as a linear function of the absolute value of the error) until they become zero (at value d, say), after which point they stay zero. This would throw away all observations for which the absolute value of the associated residual is greater than d.

(d)   Option (c) above could be approximated by a sine curve.

(2) *Lp estimators*   This estimator results from minimizing the sum of the absolute values of the errors each raised to the pth power, where p is usually a value between one and two. When $p = 2$, the OLS estimator results; when $p = 1$, this estimator minimizes the sum of absolute errors. The value chosen for p should be lower the fatter are the tails of the error distribution, but beyond this vague guidance, the choice of p, unfortunately, is arbitrary.

(3) *L estimators*   These estimators are linear combinations of sample order statistics, the most attractive of which are *regression quantiles*. A regression quantile is an estimate of a coefficient that results from minimizing a weighted sum of the absolute values of the errors, with positive errors weighted differently from negative errors. The 0.25 regression quantile, for example, results from using the weight 0.25 for positive errors and the weight 0.75 for negative errors. The θth regression quantile is the coefficient estimate that results from minimizing the weighted sum of absolute values of the errors, using the weight θ for positive errors and the weight $(1 - \theta)$ for negative errors. Note that when $\theta = 0.5$ this becomes identical to the estimator that minimizes the sum of absolute values of the errors. L estimators are calculated by taking a weighted average of several of these regression quantile estimates, with the quantiles and weights chosen for this purpose determined arbitrarily. Two popular versions are the Gatswirth, in which the one-third, one-half and two-thirds regression quantiles are weighted 0.3, 0.4 and 0.3, respectively, and the trimean, in which the one-quarter, one-half and three-quarters regression quantiles are weighted 0.25, 0.5 and 0.25, respectively.

(4) *Trimmed least squares*   This is basically a method for throwing away some observations. The 0.05 and the 0.95 regression quantiles, say, are calculated, and observations with negative residuals from the former, and positive residuals from the latter, are thrown away. This should eliminate about 10% of the observations. OLS is used on the remaining observations to produce the α-trimmed least-squares estimate, where in this example α is 10%.

(5) *Bounded influence estimators*   The OLS estimator has an unbounded influence function, meaning that the influence of an aberrant observation on the coefficient estimate grows steadily as that observation becomes more and more aberrant. A bounded influence estimator, or BIF, is designed to limit, or bound, the influence an aberrant observation can have on the coefficient estimate. This is accomplished by minimizing a weighted sum of squared errors, where the weight for each observation is chosen so as to limit, or bound, that observation's influence on the estimation result. Influential observations are downweighted; other observations retain their weight of unity. Such estimators are operational-

ized by defining what is meant by "influence" and choosing a bound. The bound is usually chosen such that the efficiency of BIF would not be too much lower, say 5% lower, than that of OLS were the data suitable for OLS. This in effect would mean that one would be paying 5% insurance premium for protection against the possibility of data unsuitable for OLS.

19.4 NON-PARAMETRIC ESTIMATION

A completely different alternative to the robust methods discussed above allows the data to determine the shape of the functional form without any guidance/constraints from theory. Since this involves the use of techniques which have no meaningful associated parameters, they are called non-parametric procedures. The distribution of the error term, for example, is not viewed as taking a specific functional form, ruling out maximum likelihood estimation, and the relationship between the dependent and independent variables is not forced into a constraining parametric structure. Because the specification is unconstrained, conclusions drawn from non-parametric procedures are robust to erroneous assumptions that might have been made had the estimating problem been parameterized in the usual way. Two types of non-parametric analysis are popular: Artificial neural network models allow the data to dictate the specification via an extremely flexible functional form without economic meaning, and kernel estimation allows the data to determine a specification using no functional form at all.

ARTIFICIAL NEURAL NETWORKS

Artificial neural networks, called neural nets for short, model the unknown function by expressing it as a weighted sum of several sigmoids, usually chosen to be logit curves, each of which is a function of all the relevant explanatory variables. An example is given in the technical notes. This amounts to nothing more than an extremely flexible functional form for which estimation requires a non-linear-least-squares iterative search algorithm based on gradients. (See the technical notes to section 6.3 for a discussion of such algorithms.)

This unusual flexible functional form comes from the vast artificial neural network literature developed by scholars investigating how the brain (composed of networks of neurons) works and how that process can be mimicked on a computer. Unfortunately, econometricians have retained the terminology of this literature, making it difficult for practitioners to understand the essence of this modeling process. For example, this literature speaks of an input layer, a hidden layer and an output layer, each containing "nodes." Each node in the input layer takes a piece of information and feeds it to the brain where several hidden nodes (inside the brain) each process all this information and then each pass on one piece of processed information to the output layer where a node uses all these pieces of processed information to compute the value of an output variable. In econometricians' terms the nodes in the input layer are just the explanatory variables, the nodes in the hidden layer each take all the explanatory variable values and calculate a different logit function, and the node in the output layer takes a weighted average of these logit results to produce the dependent variable estimate. A natural generalization is to have more than one node in the output layer, permitting simultaneous estimation of more than one dependent variable.

This functional form is remarkably flexible and for that reason is very appealing. In fact, it is too flexible in that it can twist and turn to fit peculiarities of the data and thereby mislead regarding the underlying specification of the functional form. As described in the technical notes, estimation requires that care be taken to ensure that such overfitting is avoided.

KERNEL ESTIMATION

A popular alternative to neural nets is to specify $y = m(x) + \varepsilon$ where $m(x)$ is the conditional expectation of y with no parametric form whatsoever, and the density of the error ε is completely unspecified. The N observations y_i and x_i are used to estimate a joint density function for y and x. The density at a point (y_0, x_0) is estimated by seeing what proportion of the N observations are "close to" (y_0, x_0). As explained in the technical notes, this procedure involves using a formula called a kernel to weight nearby observations, explaining why this non-parametric procedure is called kernel estimation. Once the joint distribution has been estimated it is possible to find the marginal distribution of x (by integrating the joint density over y) and then the conditional distribution of y given x (by taking the ratio of these joint and marginal distributions). It is important to note that these distributions are not "found" in the sense that a formula is identified for them in the usual parametric way. What is meant is that for a given value of x, the height of the conditional density, say, can be estimated.

This conditional distribution can be used to find several items of interest. The conditional expectation of y given x, namely $m(x)$, could be estimated, and the equivalent of a "regression coefficient" could be estimated by estimating the change in $m(x)$ resulting from a unit change in x. The conditional variance of y could be estimated, yielding an estimate of the variance of the error term.

If the variance of the error term is not the same for all values of x, there is heteroskedasticity. For each observation this non-parametric methodology could be used to estimate the variance of the error term. If $m(x)$ were known to be linear, these estimates of the variance could be employed as input to a standard EGLS estimation procedure to produce estimates of the coefficients of $m(x)$. This would in effect be combining non-parametric and parametric methods, a procedure called *semi-parametric* estimation, which is applicable in contexts in which a researcher is comfortable parameterizing some parts of the specification, but not others.

GENERAL NOTES

19.1 Introduction

- Stigler (1973, p. 872) explains some of the history of the word robust: "In the eighteenth century, the word 'robust' was used to refer to someone who was strong, yet boistrous, crude, and vulgar. By 1953 when Box first gave the word its statistical meaning, the evolution of language had eliminated the negative connotation: robust meant simply strong, healthy, sufficiently tough to withstand life's adversities."
- Robust estimation methods can play a role in model specification. For example, should OLS differ markedly from a robust estimate, one should take a fresh, hard look at one's data and model specification. Janson (1988), and especially the associated commentary, is a useful perspective on this dimension of robust estimation. See also Belsley (1986a) and associated commentary.

  Zellner (1981) has stressed that outliers can be of particular value in specification – unusual and surprising facts can generate major advances as generalizations are sought to explain them. On the other hand, care must be taken because an outlier could cause adoption of a data-specific specification. Franses and Biessen (1992) suggest a method of checking if outliers have led to the inclusion of an explanatory variable in a specification.
- A drawback of robust estimation methods is that they usually require that errors be distributed symmetrically and be independent of the regressors, assumptions that may not be appropriate in some econometric problems. Godfrey and Orme (1991) discuss testing for skewness of the residuals.

19.2 Outliers and Influential Observations

- As a prelude to looking for outliers or influential observations, many researchers test for non-normality of errors. Most such tests, strictly speaking, require observations on the actual errors, but White and McDonald (1980) suggest that these tests remain viable if OLS residuals are used instead. Maddala (1977, pp. 305–8) reviews such tests, recommending the Shapiro–Wilk test. Poirier et al. (1986) suggest a new test statistic with attractive properties. Among econometricians the Jarque-Bera test (see the technical notes) is very popular.

  The presence of non-normal errors does not necessarily imply that one of the robust estimators described earlier should be employed. Butler et al. (1990) model the distribution of the errors as a generalized t distribution and estimate its parameters along with the regression parameters. This allows the estimation procedure automatically to adapt to the error distribution. Similar results concerning the benefits of making the estimation procedure such that it adapts to the nature of the residuals it finds were found using different methods by McDonald and White (1993).
- Testing for an outlier due to a large error can be accomplished most easily by using an observation-specific dummy, as discussed in chapter 14. To investigate the ith observation, say, run the regression with an observation-specific dummy for the ith observation; the t statistic for the coefficient on this dummy tests for whether this observation is an outlier. This is repeated for all N observations; since in effect one would be looking at the maximum over all observations, the appropriate critical value

should be that associated with an $\alpha/2$ level divided by N. This t statistic is a normalized prediction error, sometimes called the *studentized residual*.

- There are two main statistics popular for checking for whether the ith observation is influential. One is DFFITS, the (normalized) change in the OLS estimate of the ith value of the dependent variable resulting from omitting the ith observation when calculating the OLS coefficient estimates. The other is DFBETA, the (normalized) change in an OLS coefficient estimate resulting from omitting the ith observation. Belsley et al. (1980) discuss these measures and their extensions.
- All of the methods of searching for outliers and influential observations that were discussed earlier involve looking at summary statistics; a natural alternative to this is to look at the data themselves through graphical means. Numerical summaries focus on expected values whereas graphical summaries focus on unexpected values. Exploratory data analysis (EDA, discussed in the general notes to section 5.1 of chapter 5) is an approach to statistics which emphasizes that a researcher should begin his or her analyses by looking at the data, on the grounds that the more familiar one is with one's data the more effectively they can be used to develop, test and refine theory. This should be viewed as an ingredient of robust estimation.

19.3   Robust Estimators

- Judge et al. (1985, pp. 829–39) discuss M estimators, L estimators, and trimmed least squares, including how hypothesis testing can be undertaken with them, along with appropriate references. The regression quantile was introduced by Koenker and Bassett (1978). Krasker et al. (1983) give a good description of BIF. Koenker (1982) is a more advanced survey of robust methods in econometrics.
- The estimator minimizing the sum of the absolute values of the errors is a special case of the M estimator, the L_p estimator, and the L estimator. It is called the LAR (least absolute residual), LAE (least absolute error) or MAD (minimum absolute deviation) estimator. Estimation can be undertaken by solving a linear programming problem. An alternative is to divide each observation by the square root of the absolute value of the OLS residual (from raw data) and run OLS on the transformed data; when iterated this may converge on the LAR estimator. Taylor (1974) and Narula and Wellington (1982) have good surveys of LAR estimation. See also Dielman and Pfaffenberger (1982).
- The name M estimator stands for "maximum-likelihood-type" estimator. If normally distributed errors are assumed, maximizing the likelihood function produces a set of first-order conditions with a certain generic structure. An M estimator is estimated by replacing a key function in this generic structure with an alternative functional form.
- Bounded-influence estimation is computationally awkward. Welsch (1980) uses an approximation, minimizing a weighted sum of squared residuals, with weight unity for every observation for which the absolute value of DFFITS is less than 0.34 and for other observations a weight 0.34 times the inverse of the absolute value of that observation's DFFITS. This makes it look a lot like an M estimator.
- Zaman (1996, chap. 5) has a good discussion of recent advances in robust regression, such as estimating by minimizing the sum of the T/2 smallest squared errors and identifying bad influential observations by noting if they have high residuals associated with robust estimates.

19.4   Non-parametric Estimation

- For interpretation of neural nets modeling it is useful to know that the iterative process of searching for the best fitting equation is likened to the system (brain) "learning," or being "trained" via "examples" (observations). This process is called "backpropagation" because at each iteration ("epoch") the residual is fed "backwards" through the equation to determine the gradient needed to change optimally the parameter values for the next iteration. Smith (1993) is an unusually clear exposition of neural networks for statistical modeling, spelling out these parallels, describing a variety of estimation procedures, and offering practical advice on technical details such as what starting values should be used for the iterative minimization procedure. See also Warner and Misra (1996).
- Hardle (1990) and Pagan and Ullah (1997) are comprehensive surveys of non-parametric estimation; Ullah (1988) and Robinson (1986) are brief surveys. Robinson surveys semi-parametric estimation. Using a flexible functional form is an alternative to nonparametric estimation, but with the exception of a totally unconstrained flexible form such a neural nets, is only satisfactory over limited ranges of explanatory variables. A major drawback to the nonparametric procedure is that it requires a large sample size. In parametric problems the speed at which estimated parameters tend to the true value is typically proportional to $n^{-\frac{1}{2}}$, but is usually much slower in the nonparametric context.
- Econometricians are hoping that semi-parametric methods will be successful in dealing with censored data, because conventional estimation in this context has been shown to be quite sensitive to the error specification. See Horowitz and Neumann (1989) and Moon (1989).
- Cleveland, Devlin and Grosse (1988) suggest an alternative nonparametric method called loess, "regression by local fitting." For each value x_0 of an explanatory variable vector a specified number of observations in the data set that are "closest" to x_0 are selected. These observations are used to predict the associated y_0 value using a regression minimizing a weighted average of squared residuals, where the weights vary inversely with the distance of each x observation from x_0.

TECHNICAL NOTES

19.3   Robust Estimators

- The Jarque–Bera test, introduced by Jarque and Bera (1980) has become popular because it is easy to compute, asymptotically independent of other common diagnostic checks on regression residuals, and intuitively appealing because it combines testing asymmetry and kurtosis. Because it does not perform well in small samples, Urzua (1996) suggests a small-sample adjustment, and Deb and Sefton (1996) provide small-sample critical values.

   When the errors are distributed normally their third moment should be zero and their fourth moment should be three times their second moment (variance). The Jarque–Bera test is a joint test of these two phenomena. Using the residuals, the estimated third moment divided by an estimate of its standard deviation should in large samples be distributed as a standard normal. And the estimated fourth moment minus three times the estimated variance, divided by an estimate of its standard deviation should also in large samples be distributed as a standard normal. Since these standard normals turn out to be independent of one another, the sum of their squares, the Jarque–Bera statistic, is distributed as a chi-square with two degrees of freedom.

- It can be shown that LAR is more efficient than OLS whenever the error distribution is such that the sample median is a better (more efficient) measure of location (estimate of the mean of the distribution) than is the sample mean. The LAR estimator is the MLE is the error has a double-exponential (Laplace) distribution: $f(\varepsilon) = (1/2\lambda)\exp(-|\varepsilon|/\lambda)$, and so is best unbiased, with a variance half that of the OLS estimator, as shown by Harvey (1990, pp. 117–18). OLS is still BLUE, though; LAR is not linear.

19.4 Non-parametric Estimation

- The most popular version of the neural nets functional form is based on using logits. It is written as

$$y = \alpha + \sum_{i=1}^{k} \beta_i \frac{e^{\theta_i}}{1 + e^{\theta_i}} + \varepsilon$$

where k is the number of logits averaged, the β_i are the weights used in averaging the logits, and the θ_i are linear functions of the explanatory variables.

Figure 19.1 illustrates this for a simple case in which there is only one explanatory variable x and four logits are averaged. In the lower part of this figure are drawn four logit functions which are weighted and summed to produce the nonlinear function shown in the upper part of figure 19.1. In this example there are thirteen unknown parameters: the intercept α; the four β_i weights for taking the weighted average of the four logits; and the slope and intercept parameters of each logit. Even with only four logits this functional form is very flexible. It is easy to capture dramatic jumps or drops by introducing a very steep logit which moves rapidly from near zero to near one (or vice versa) at the point where the change occurs. The shape can be influenced by changing the β values as well as by changing the parameters of the individual logits. In addition, it is possible to append traditional terms to the function for y above, so that, for example, we could add a linear term in x.

- By choosing a large number of logits to average a modeler can fit literally any functional form. A healthy number of logits should be chosen to ensure that the minimization-of-squared-errors process avoids local minima, but doing so runs the very real danger of overfitting – matching the data so well that the neural net reflects peculiarities of this data set rather than the general underlying specification. To guard against overfitting, as the search process iterates to find parameter values periodic cross-validations are conducted – checking to see if an estimated specification performs well on data that have not been used in estimation, usually chosen to be about a third of the data. Whenever the sum of squared errors of this out-of-sample data starts to rise, overfitting has begun. If it never rises there are not enough logits to create overfitting which means there are probably not enough logits to capture the underlying functional form, so more logits should be added.

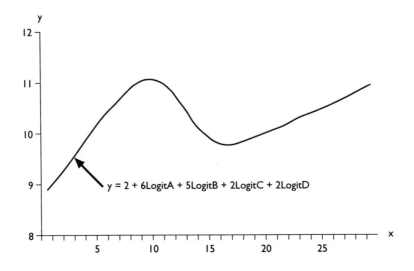

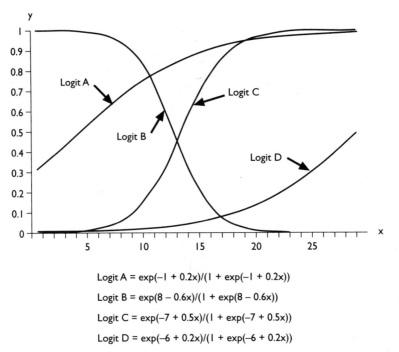

Logit A = exp(−1 + 0.2x)/(1 + exp(−1 + 0.2x))

Logit B = exp(8 − 0.6x)/(1 + exp(8 − 0.6x))

Logit C = exp(−7 + 0.5x)/(1 + exp(−7 + 0.5x))

Logit D = exp(−6 + 0.2x)/(1 + exp(−6 + 0.2x))

Figure 19.1 Illustrating neural net modeling

- To use neural nets for qualitative dependent variables the neural nets function is written as the logit of the y function given earlier and the qualitative dependent variable is coded 0.1 and 0.9 rather than zero and one. (This is done because minimizing the sum of squared errors will otherwise lead the output y value to be pushed out to plus or minus infinity in an effort to estimate one or zero.) A logit transformation of the y variable is typically used for quantitative variables as well, because it enhances the estimation procedure; the minimum value of the dependent variable is set to 0.1 and the maximum to 0.9, with the other values interpolated appropriately.
- Estimation of density functions is crucial to kernel estimation. Suppose N observations on a variable x are available to estimate a density function for x. If a normal functional form could be assumed, one would just use the observations to estimate the two parameters of this functional form, the mean and variance, and then the density for any value x could be estimated using estimates of these parameters plugged into the formula for the normal density. The whole point of non-parametric analysis is to avoid making any assumptions about the functional form of the density, so a completely different approach must be taken.

  A possible method of estimating the density of x is to construct a histogram. This is unsatisfactory for at least three reasons. First, it is not smooth – it has little jumps as one moves from interval to interval. Second, it is affected by how the intervals have been defined – if intervals of unit length were defined as, say, from 1.0 to 2.0 to 3.0, etc., rather than as 1.5 to 2.5 to 3.5, etc., it is possible that a quite different picture of the density would emerge. And third, it is sensitive to the length of the interval chosen. One way of addressing these problems is to use a *local histogram* approach – employ a moving interval to calculate the histogram heights.

  Figure 19.2 shows a blow-up of a section of possible x values. The little Os represent observations on x. Consider the height of the density for the value $x = 18.0$.

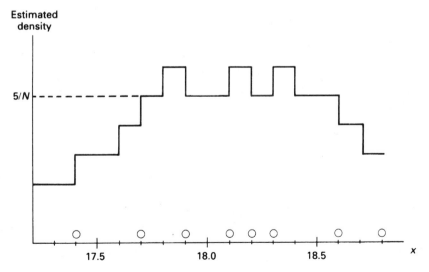

Figure 19.2 Explaining local histogram variation

Following the logic of a histogram, it is planned to measure the height of this density by the fraction of the total number of observations that are found in an interval centered on $x = 18.0$. If we choose this interval to be of unit length, it will stretch from 17.5 to 18.5, as shown in figure 19.2. There are five observations in this interval, so the height of the density function at $x = 18.0$ is measured as $5/N$. If we slide this interval a small distance to the right, say, there will be no change in the number of observations in this interval, so the same height, $5/N$, corresponds to values of x just above 18.0. Once this interval has slid far enough that its right-hand edge captures the observation at $x = 18.6$, though, the interval will contain six observations, and so starting at 18.1 (the current mid-point of the interval) the height of the estimated density jumps to $6/N$. This estimatd height stays at $6/N$ until the interval center has moved to 18.2, at which point the interval loses the observation at 17.7 and so the estimated height jumps down to $5/N$. For values of x between 18.2 and 18.3 the estimated density remains at $5/N$, but it then jumps back up to $6/N$ because the sliding interval will pick up the observation 18.8.

If the interval is slid to the left from its original position (centered over 18.0), there is no change in the number of observations in the interval until the left-hand edge of the interval reaches 17.4, so the estimated density stays at $5/N$ until x falls to 17.9, at which point it jumps to $6/N$. It stays at this level until x falls to 17.8, where it jumps down to $5/N$. At $x = 17.7$ it drops to $4/N$, and so on.

Although the local histogram methodology has removed the arbitrariness associated with the choice of interval break points, the other two problems mentioned earlier still exist, namely the discontinuity and the sensitivity to choice of interval length. The first of these problems is resolved by using a generalization of a local histogram estimator, which is best explained through a reinterpretation of the local histogram methodology.

The local histogram approach estimates the density of x at a particular point x_0 as the fraction of the total number of x observations that are "close to" x_0, where "close to" is defined by the choice of interval width, arbitrarily set equal to one in the example above. This could be interpreted as the sum over all observations of $1/N$ times a weight for each observation, where the weight is one for each observation in the interval and zero for each observation outside the interval. This interpretation is extremely useful, because it makes evident the following two phenomena. (a) The discontinuity in the estimated density function is caused by the discontinuity in these weights – as an observation moves into or out of the interval, its weight takes a discontinuous jump, causing the estimated density to jump. (b) All observations in the interval, no matter what their proximity to x_0, have the same weight; it would seem reasonable to put a bigger weight on observations closer to x_0.

With this perspective, it seems reasonable to devise a weighting system for this estimating procedure that is continuous and weights observations closer to x_0 more heavily. A favorite weighting function used for this purpose is a standard normal density function, expressed as a function of the distance from x_0 to an x observation. Note that in addition to continuity, it puts a nonzero weight on all observations, with observations close to x_0 having high weights (heights of the standard normal density near its mean) and observations far away from x_0 having negligible weights (heights of the standard normal density out in its tails).

To recapitulate, using N observations $x_1, \ldots, x_N$, the density function for x is now being estimated at a point $x = x_0$ as a weighted sum over all observations of $1/N$, where the weight for the ith observation x_i is given by the height of the standard normal density function evaluated at $(x_i - x_0)$. The "weighting function" role being played here by the standard normal density could be played by any positive function of $(x_i - x_0)$ that integrates to unity. Such a function is referred to as a *kernel* and the resulting density estimator for x is called a *kernel estimator*.

Although the introduction of the kernel has resolved the problems noted earlier, there remains an issue – how is the kernel chosen? Clearly the kernel should be symmetric and centered at zero. It turns out, in practice, that the functional form of the kernel is not important (so the choice of the normal distribution is uncontroversial), but that the choice of variance for the kernel is very important. This suggests that an appropriate kernel could be of the form $N(0,h^2)$, where the standard deviation h is chosen with some care. A small value of h means that the kernel puts non-negligible weight only on observations very close to x_0; thus the choice of h is analogous to the choice of interval width introduced earlier. Because the magnitude of h determines which observations are "looked at" (given non-negligible weight), h is sometimes called the *window width*.

Evaluating $N(0,h^2)$ at $(x_i - x_0)$ yields the same value as h^{-1} times $N(0,1)$ evaluated at $(x_i - x_0)/h$, so the standard normal could be retained as the kernel if the latter approach to calculation of the kernel estimator is employed. This is in fact what is done, giving rise to the following formula for the kernel estimator:

$$f(x) = (1/hN)\Sigma K[(x_i - x)/h], \text{ where } K \text{ is the kernel function.}$$

- Unfortunately there is no agreed method of selecting the window width. If it is chosen to be "too small," too few observations will have a non-negligible weight and the resulting density estimate will appear rough (or "undersmoothed" – this is why h is sometimes also called the *smoothing parameter*). If it is chosen to be "too large," too many observations will have a non-negligible weight, "oversmoothing" the density. (For example, it could estimate a bimodal density by a unimodal density.) This introduces extra bias into the estimation procedure, because observations not extremely close to the x value for which the density is being calculated do not "belong." Thus there is a trade-off between variance and bias – a high value of h reduces the variance of the density estimate (because it causes more observations to be used) but introduces more bias.

The logic of all this suggests that h should decrease as the sample size increases, and in fact it can be shown that the optimal value of h is proportional to the inverse of the fifth root of the sample size. Unfortunately, there is no agreed method for selecting the factor of proportionality. A further problem is that a value of h that is suitable for estimation of the main body of the density of x may not be large enough for estimation of the tails of that distribution (because there are fewer observations in the tails), suggesting that some method of allowing h to vary might be appropriate; doing so creates variable-window-width estimators. Despite these problems, there is some agreement that cross-validation should be used to aid in selecting the window width. Set some data aside before estimation; if the average squared error of these data begins to rise, the window width has become too small.

The choice of smoothing parameter can also depend on the purpose of the analysis. One might deliberately oversmooth for presentation purposes or help in selecting an appropriate parametric model, for example, or undersmooth to examine more carefully a local structure.

- Estimation of a multivariate density function is a straightforward generalization of the kernel estimator. Suppose we wish to estimate $f(y,x)$, the joint density of y and x; the kernel estimator is changed in only two regards. First, the kernel function $K^*(y,x)$ must be a bivariate density function, and second, the h in $1/hN$ now becomes h^2. To estimate the marginal density of x this expression is integrated over y to produce an estimator that takes the form of a kernel estimator with kernel function K equal to the integral of $K^*(y,x)$ over y. What is important here is that now the conditional distribution of y given x, $f(y|x)$, can be estimated as the ratio of the joint density to the marginal density of x, and can be used to obtain things like the conditional mean of y given x.
- In the relationship $y = m(x) + \varepsilon$, where m is a function of unknown form, $m(x)$ is the conditional expectation of y, and can be calculated as $E(y|x) = \int yf(y|x)dy$. Performing this calculation using for $f(y|x)$ the estimate of it that results from the discussion above produces, after some algebra,

$$m^*(x) = \Sigma y_i K[(x_i - x)/h]/\Sigma K[(x_i - x)/h]$$

where the summations run over all observations. This could be calculated for several values of x, producing an empirical representation of the unknown functional form m. This formula can be exploited to produce an estimate of the conditional mean of any function of x, simply by replacing y_i by the relevant function of x; an example given later is the conditional variance.

For a particular $x = x_0$, this formula can be viewed as taking a weighted average of observations "close to" x_0, where "close to" is determined by the window width h, and the weights are defined by the kernel function K. If x were discrete, and we had several observations on y at $x = x_0$, then the average of these y values would be the usual estimate of the conditional expectation of y at x_0. This is exactly what would be produced by the formula given above for a sufficiently small value of h and a weighting function that is of the zero/one discontinuous type discussed earlier.

- The "regression coefficient" in the context of non-parametric estimation is the partial derivative of m with respect to x. One way of estimating it is to estimate $m(x)$ for $x = x_0$ and then for $x = x_0 + \delta$; the difference between these two estimated m values, divided by δ, is the estimate of the regression coefficient. Unless m is linear, it will vary with x.
- The variance of the error term is the variance of y conditional on x. For a homoskedastic error this would be the same for all values of x. In general terms, this variance is given by

$$V(y|x) = \sigma^2(x) = E(y^2|x) - [E(y|x)]^2,$$

the second term of which can be estimated by the square of $m^*(x)$ given earlier, and the first term of which can be estimated by using the formula for $m^*(x)$ with y_i replaced by y_i^2. A more general formula results from estimating ε_i by $y_i - m^*(x_i)$ and then using the formula for $m^*(x)$ with y_i replaced by the square of this estimated ε_i.

- A partial linear model $y = X\beta + m(z) + \varepsilon$ is an example of a semi-parametric analysis. Estimation proceeds by fitting y and X nonparametrically as a function of z. Then the resulting residualized y is regressed on residualized X to get β^{OLS} and $m(z)$ is obtained by fitting $y - X\beta^{OLS}$ nonparametrically with z.

APPENDIX A: SAMPLING DISTRIBUTIONS, THE FOUNDATION OF STATISTICS

It cannot be stressed too strongly how important it is for students to understand the concept of a sampling distribution. This concept provides a unifying logic which permits econometrics' algebraic manipulations to be seen in context, making clear what econometricians are trying to accomplish with all their proofs, formulas and algebraic derivations. The purpose of this appendix is to provide an exposition of this concept and the implications it has for the study of econometrics.

I An Example

Suppose that you have 45 observations on variables x and y and you know that y has been produced from x by using the formula $y = \beta x + \varepsilon$ where ε is an error with mean zero and variance σ^2. Note that there is no intercept in this linear relationship, so there is only one unknown parameter, β, the slope of x. This specification means that y_1, the first observation on y, was created by multiplying x_1, the first observation on x, by the unknown number β and then adding ε_1, the first error, obtained randomly from a bowl of errors with mean zero and variance σ^2. The other 44 observations on y were created in similar fashion.

You are interested in estimating the unknown parameter β. Suppose the formula $\beta^* = \Sigma y / \Sigma x$ has been suggested, where the subscripts have been omitted for convenience. This suggestion just involves putting the data into an algebraic formula to produce a single number that is proposed as the estimate of β. Suppose this is done using your data, producing $\beta^* = 2.34$. Is this a good estimate of the unknown β?

Since $y = \beta x + \varepsilon$ you can substitute this into the formula to get

$$\beta^* = \Sigma(\beta x + \varepsilon)/\Sigma x = \beta + \Sigma\varepsilon/\Sigma x$$

From this it is apparent that this formula is such that it is equal to β plus an expression that involves the unknown ε values. Because the ε values are positive about half the time and negative about half the time, it looks as though this expression involving the errors is probably going to be fairly close to zero, suggesting that this formula is reasonable in that it appears to be creating a suitable estimate of β.

Consider the estimate $\beta^* = 2.34$. How close 2.34 is to β clearly depends on the particular set of 45 error terms that were drawn out of the bowl of errors to produce the y observations. If in obtaining the data, mostly large positive errors were drawn, β^* would substantially overestimate β (assuming Σx is positive). If mostly large negative errors were drawn, β^* would substantially underestimate β. If a more typical set of errors were drawn, β^* would produce an estimate fairly close to β. The point here is that the set of 45 unknown error terms drawn determines the estimate produced by the β^* formula and so there is no way of knowing how close the particular estimate 2.34 is to the true β value.

This problem is addressed via the concept of the sampling distribution. Suppose for a moment that you know the true value of β. Visualize obtaining 45 error terms, calculating y using β, the x values and these errors, computing β^*, and recording the result. Mentally do this a million times, each time grabbing 45 new error terms. This produces a million hypothetical β^* values, each produced by mimicking exactly the process thought to be generating the actual y data. These million β^* values can be used to construct a histogram of possible β^* values. This histogram should show that very high values of β^* will be relatively rare because such a β^* value would require an unusual draw of 45 error terms. Similarly, very low values of β^* will also be rare. Values of β^* closer to the true β value will be more common because they would result from more typical draws of 45 errors. This histogram estimates a distribution of β^* values, providing a picture of the relative probabilities of obtaining different β^* values during this conceptual *repeated sampling* procedure. This distribution is called the *sampling distribution* of β^*. The sampling distribution of a statistic tells us the relative frequency with which values of that statistic would occur if we repeatedly drew new sets of errors.

2   Implications for Studying Econometrics

The logic of the sampling distribution is the foundation of classical statistics, with several important implications. If these implications are understood, the study of econometrics becomes much easier.

(1) Using β^* to produce an estimate of β can be conceptualized as the econometrician shutting his or her eyes and obtaining an estimate of β by reaching blindly into the sampling distribution of β^* to obtain a single number.

(2) Because of 1 above, choosing between β^* and a competing formula β^{**} comes down to the following: Would you prefer to produce your estimate of β by reaching blindly into the sampling distribution of β^* or by reaching blindly into the sampling distribution of β^{**}?

(3) Because of 2 above, desirable properties of an estimator β^* are defined in terms of its sampling distribution. For example, β^* is unbiased if the mean of its sampling distribution equals the number β being estimated. These properties are discussed in sections 2.5, 2.6 and 2.7 of chapter 2.

(4) The properties of the sampling distribution of an estimator β^* depend on the process generating the data, so an estimator can be a good one in one context but a bad one in another. Much of econometric theory is concerned with finding for a particular data-generating process the estimator with the most attractive sampling distribution; the OLS estimator, for example, has an attractive sampling distribution in some applications, but a less attractive sampling distribution in others, such as when the error is correlated with an explanatory variable.

(5) The properties of the sampling distribution also depend on the sample size. A larger sample size means that there is more information used in producing a parameter

estimate and so the variance of its sampling distribution is smaller, and in some cases bias diminishes as the sample size grows. This is discussed in section 2.8 of chapter 2.

(6) Most algebraic derivations in econometrics are trying to find the characteristics of the sampling distribution of a statistic. Since interest focuses almost exclusively on the mean and variance of the sampling distribution, students must become expert at finding means and variances of distributions.

(7) All statistics, not just parameter estimates, have sampling distributions. An F value, for example, is a test statistic rather than a parameter estimate. Hypothesis testing is undertaken by seeing if the value of a test statistic is unusual relative to the sampling distribution of that test statistic calculated assuming the null hypothesis is true. Suppose it is stated that under the null a statistic is distributed as an F, for example. This means that if the null hypothesis is true the sampling distribution of this statistic is described by the numbers in the F table found in most statistics textbooks. Econometricians work hard to find test statistics which have sampling distributions described by familiar statistical tables.

3 Calculating Sampling Distributions

There are three basic techniques employed to learn the properties of a statistic's sampling distribution.

(1) For simple problems algebraic derivations can be undertaken to deduce the properties of a sampling distribution, such as in the following examples.

   (i) In the example above where $y = \beta x + \varepsilon$, the mean and variance of the sampling distribution of β^* can easily be calculated to be β and $45\sigma^2/(\Sigma x)^2$, respectively. If there had been a nonzero intercept so that $y = \alpha + \beta x + \varepsilon$, the mean of the sampling distribution of β^* would be $\beta + 45\alpha/\Sigma x$, illustrating how the sampling distribution depends on the data-generating process.

   (ii) As described in chapter 3, when the data have been generated by the CLR model with $y = X\beta + \varepsilon$ and $V(\varepsilon) = \sigma^2 I$, the mean of the sampling distribution of β^{OLS} is β and its variance is $\sigma^2(X'X)^{-1}$. If in addition ε is distributed normally (the CNLR model), this sampling distribution is also normal in shape, and the OLS estimate of a parameter divided by its estimated standard error has a sampling distribution described by the t table provided in most statistics texts.

   (iii) When N values of x are drawn randomly from a distribution with mean μ and variance σ^2, the sampling distribution of $\bar{x}$ has mean μ and variance σ^2/N. This is a result all students are expected to "remember" from introductory statistics. A central limit theorem is usually invoked to conclude that when N is of reasonable size this sampling distribution is normal in shape.

(2) When the algebra is too difficult to derive the properties of a sampling distribution, as is often the case, two alternative techniques are used. The first of these is to perform the algebra allowing the sample size to become very large. This simplifies the algebra (as explained in the technical notes to section 2.8), allowing "asymptotic" or "large-sample" properties (see appendix C) of the sampling distribution of the estimator or test statistic to be derived. This asymptotic distribution is often a remarkably good proxy for the sampling distribution when the sample is of only modest size. Consider the following examples.

    (i)   Nonlinear functions of parameter estimates have complicated small-sample distributions whose asymptotic properties can usually easily be derived. An example is steady-state parameter estimates calculated as nonlinear functions of short-run parameter estimates.

   (ii) Whenever the error is correlated with an explanatory variable, the sampling distribution of OLS exhibits undesirable properties and is often replaced by an instrumental variable (IV) estimator, as discussed in section 9.2 of chapter 9. The IV estimator has an intractable small-sample sampling distribution but its asymptotic distribution can be derived straightforwardly.

  (iii) W, LR and LM tests, described in section 4.5 of chapter 4, have very complicated small-sample distributions, but asymptotically are each distributed as a chi-square.

(3) The second method of determining the properties of a sampling distribution when the algebra is too difficult is to perform a Monte Carlo study, discussed in section 2.10 of chapter 2. In a Monte Carlo study typical parameter values are selected, observations on non-stochastic variables are chosen, and a computer is used to draw error terms. The computer is then programmed to create hypothetical data according to the process thought to be generating the actual data. These data are used to calculate a value for the statistic under investigation. Then the computer creates new error terms and uses them to produce a new hypothetical data set, allowing calculation of a second value of the statistic. This process is repeated until a large number, say 5,000, of hypothetical values of the statistic are created. These 5,000 values are used via a histogram to picture the sampling distribution, or more likely, to estimate the relevant properties (such as its mean, variance or values cutting off 5% tails) of this statistic's sampling distribution. Below is a description of how a Monte Carlo study would be conducted to examine the sampling distribution of β^* for our earlier example. (Other examples appear in several of the exercises of appendix D).

   (a) Choose 45 values for x, either by using the x values from an actual empirical study or by using the computer to generate 45 values in some way.

   (b) Choose values for the unknown parameters, say $\alpha = 1$, $\beta = 2$ and $\sigma^2 = 4$.

   (c) Have the computer draw 45 error terms (ε) randomly from a distribution with mean zero and variance 4.

   (d) Calculate 45 y values as $1 + 2x + \varepsilon$.

   (e) Calculate β^* and save it. (If comparing to another estimator, one would also at this stage calculate the competing estimate and save it.)

   (f) Return to step (c) and repeat this procedure until you have, say, 5,000 β^* estimates.

   (g) Use the 5,000 β^* values to draw a histogram representing the sampling distribution of β^*. Since usually the sampling distribution is characterized by only three measures, its mean, its variance, and its MSE these 5,000 values would be used to estimate these properties, as explained in section 2.10 of chapter 2.

APPENDIX B: ALL ABOUT VARIANCE

The purpose of this appendix is to gather together the basic formulas used to compute and estimate variances in econometrics. Because these formulas are discussed in textbooks, no proofs, and only a few examples, are provided. It is strongly recommended that students become intimately familiar with these results, as much attention is paid in econometrics to efficiency, requiring assessment of estimators' variances.

I   Definition

Suppose x is a scalar random variable with probability density function $f(x)$; to make the discussion below more relevant x can be thought of as a coefficient estimate $\hat{\beta}$ and thus $f(\hat{\beta})$ would be its sampling distribution. The variance of x is defined as

$$V(x) = E(x - Ex)^2 = \int(x - Ex)^2 f(x)\mathrm{d}x.$$

In words, if you were randomly to draw an x value and square the difference between this value and the mean of x to get a number Q, what is the average value of Q you would get if you were to repeat this experiment an infinite number of times? Most derivations in econometrics are done using the expected value notation rather than the integral notation, so the latter is not seen much.

The covariance between two variables, x and y, is defined as

$$C(x,y) = E(x - Ex)(y - Ey) = \iint(x - Ex)(y - Ey)f(x,y)\mathrm{d}x\mathrm{d}y$$

where $f(x,y)$ is the joint density function for x and y. In words, if you were randomly to draw a pair of x and y values, subtract their means from each and multiply them together to get a number Q, what is the average value of Q you would get if you were to repeat this experiment an infinite number of times? Notice how the expected value notation avoids the messiness of the double integral notation.

If x is a vector of length k, its variance–covariance matrix is defined as the k by k matrix

$$V(x) = E(x - Ex)(x - Ex)'$$

described in the technical notes of section 2.6. It has the variances of the individual elements of x down the diagonal, and the covariances between these elements in the off-diagonal positions.

2   Estimation

The definitions given above refer to the *actual*, or theoretical, variance, not to be confused with an *estimate* of $V(x)$, which can be calculated if some data are available. Consider the following examples:

(a) For x a scalar, if we have N observations on x, say x_i through x_N, then $V(x)$ is usually estimated by $s^2 = \Sigma(x_i - \bar{x})^2/(N - 1)$.

(b) If we have N corresponding observations on y, say y_i through y_N, then $C(x,y)$ is usually estimated by $s_{xy} = \Sigma(x_i - \bar{x})(y_i - \bar{y})/(N - 1)$.

(c) If x is the error in a regression model with K explanatory variables (including the intercept), then $V(x)$ is usually estimated by $s^2 = SSE/(N - K)$.

(d) When x is a vector, its variance–covariance matrix is estimated using the estimating formulas given in (a) and (b) above to fill in the individual elements of this matrix.

3   Well-known Formulas

Variances for several special cases are so well known that they should probably be memorized, even though their derivations are easy:

(a) The variance of $\bar{x}$, the sample mean of N randomly drawn observations on a variable x: $V(\bar{x}) = V(x)/N$.

(b) The variance of a linear function of x, say $w = a + bx$ where a and b are constants: $V(w) = b^2V(x)$.

(c) The variance of the sum or difference of two random variables, say $w = z \pm y$: $V(w) = V(z) + V(y) \pm 2C(z,y)$.

4   More-general Formulas

The following are some more-general formulas, of which the well-known results given above are special cases.

(a) The variance–covariance matrix of β^{OLS} in the CLR model $y = X\beta + \varepsilon$: $V(\beta^{OLS}) = V(\varepsilon)(X'X)^{-1} = \sigma^2(X'X)^{-1}$. If there is only an intercept in this regression, so that X is a column of ones, $\beta^{OLS} = \bar{y}$. Furthermore, in this case $V(\varepsilon) = V(y)$, so that this formula yields $V(\beta^{OLS}) = V(\bar{y}) = V(y)/N$, exactly the formula of 3(a) above.

(b) Nonlinear function $g(x)$ of a scalar x: asymptotically, $V(g(x)) = (\partial g/\partial x)^2V(x)$. The rationale behind this formula is explained in the technical notes to section 2.8. If $g(x) = a + bx$, a linear function, then $V(g(x)) = b^2V(x)$, exactly the formula of 3(b) above.

(c) Univariate linear function $w = a'x$ of a vector x, where a is a vector of constants: $V(a'x) = a'V(x)a$.

If $x = (z, y)'$ and $a = (1,1)'$ then $w = z + y$ and $V(w) = (1,1)V(x)\begin{pmatrix} 1 \\ 1 \end{pmatrix}$

which when multiplied out yields $V(w) = V(z) + V(y) + 2C(z,y)$, exactly the formula of 3(c) above.

(d) Univariate nonlinear function $g(x)$ of a vector x: asymptotically, $V(g(x)) = (\partial g/\partial x)'V(x)(\partial g/\partial x)$ where $\partial g/\partial x$ is a vector whose ith element is the partial of g with respect to the $i$the element of x. Note that this is the same as the previous formula with $\partial g/\partial x$ replacing the vector a.

(e) Multivariate linear function $w = Ax$ of a vector x, where A is a matrix of constants (so that w is now a vector, each element of which is a linear combination of the elements of x): $V(w) = AV(x)A'$. The asymptotic formula for a multivariate nonlinear function is the same as this, using the matrix of partial derivatives for the matrix A.

5 Examples of the More-general Formulas

(a) Example for 4(b) variance of the nonlinear function of a scalar. Suppose we regress logs on logs and produce a forecast f of $\ln y$ which has variance $V(f)$, and we wish to forecast y by $\hat{y} = e^f$. Then asymptotically $V(\hat{y}) = (\partial \hat{y}/\partial f)^2 V(f) = e^{2f}V(f)$.

(b) Example for 4(c), univariate linear function of a vector. Suppose α^{OLS} and β^{OLS} have variances $V(\alpha^{OLS})$ and $V(\beta^{OLS})$, and covariance $C(\alpha^{OLS}, \beta^{OLS})$. Consider $Q = 2\alpha^{OLS} + 3\beta^{OLS}$. Then by definition

$$\begin{aligned} V(Q) &= E[(2\alpha^{OLS} + 3\beta^{OLS}) - E(2\alpha^{OLS} + 3\beta^{OLS})]^2 \\ &= E[2(\alpha^{OLS} - E\alpha^{OLS}) + 3(\beta^{OLS} - E\beta^{OLS})]^2 \\ &= 4E(\alpha^{OLS} - E\alpha^{OLS})^2 + 9E(\beta^{OLS} - E\beta^{OLS})^2 \\ &\quad + 12E(\alpha^{OLS} - E\alpha^{OLS})(\beta^{OLS} - E\beta^{OLS}) \\ &= 4V(\alpha^{OLS}) + 9V(\beta^{OLS}) + 12C(\alpha^{OLS}, \beta^{OLS}). \end{aligned}$$

Or, using the formula from 4(c), we have $Q = (2,3)\begin{pmatrix} \alpha^{OLS} \\ \beta^{OLS} \end{pmatrix}$ and so

$$V(Q) = (2,3)\begin{bmatrix} V(\alpha^{OLS}) & C(\alpha^{OLS}, \beta^{OLS}) \\ C(\alpha^{OLS}, \beta^{OLS}) & V(\beta^{OLS}) \end{bmatrix}\begin{pmatrix} 2 \\ 3 \end{pmatrix}$$

which when multiplied out produces exactly the same answer.

(c) Second example for 4(c), univariate linear function of a vector. Suppose $y = X\beta + \varepsilon = \alpha + \delta w + \theta q + \varepsilon$ and we have used the data to estimate $\beta^{OLS} = (X'X)^{-1}X'y$, so $V(\beta^{OLS}) = \sigma^2(X'X)^{-1}$.

Given the values w_0 and q_0, we forecast y_0 by

$$\begin{aligned} \hat{y}_0 &= \alpha^{OLS} + \delta^{OLS}w_0 + \theta^{OLS}q_0 \\ &= (1, w_0, q_0)\beta^{OLS} \\ &= x_0'\beta^{OLS}. \end{aligned}$$

The variance of this forecast is $V(\hat{y}_0) = \sigma^2 x_0'(X'X)^{-1}x_0$.

Continuing with this example, the forecast error is

$$fe = y_0 - \hat{y}_0 = \alpha + \delta w_0 + \theta q_0 + \varepsilon_0 - \hat{y}_0.$$

The first three terms are constants, so the variance of the forecast error is the same as the variance of $\varepsilon_0 - \hat{y}_0$, which using the formula for the variance of the difference between two random variables gives

$$
\begin{aligned}
V(fe) &= V(\varepsilon_0) + V(\hat{y}_0) - 2C(\varepsilon_0, \hat{y}_0) \\
&= \sigma^2 + \sigma^2 x_0'(X'X)^{-1}x_0 \\
&= \sigma^2[1 + x_0'(X'X)^{-1}x_0].
\end{aligned}
$$

The covariance is zero since ε_0 is in no way connected to the ingredients of $\hat{y}_0$.

(d) Example for 4(d), univariate nonlinear function of a vector. Suppose

$$\ln y_t = \beta_0 + \beta_1 \ln y_{t-1} + \beta_2 \ln x_t + \varepsilon_t.$$

The long-run, or equilibrium, elasticity of y with respect to x is $\theta = \beta_2/(1 - \beta_1)$, estimated as $\hat{\theta} = \beta_2^{OLS}/(1 - \beta_1^{OLS})$. Then from 4(d) above:

$$V(\hat{\theta}) = (\partial\hat{\theta}/\partial\beta^{OLS})'V(\beta^{OLS})(\partial\hat{\theta}/\partial\beta^{OLS})$$

$$= \sigma^2[0,\beta_2^{OLS}(1 - \beta_1^{OLS})^{-2}, (1 - \beta_1^{OLS})^{-1}](X'X)^{-1}\begin{bmatrix} 0 \\ \beta_2^{OLS}(1 - \beta_1^{OLS})^{-2} \\ (1 - \beta_1^{OLS})^{-1} \end{bmatrix}$$

Because of the zero in the first element of the derivative vector, we could have truncated this vector and combined it with the corresponding (lower right) block of $V(\beta^{OLS})$.

(e) Example for 4(e), multivariate linear function of a vector. Suppose

$$y_t = \alpha + \beta_0 x_t + \beta_1 x_{t-1} + \beta_2 x_{t-2} + \beta_3 x_{t-3} + \varepsilon_t$$

and we specify that the β values are determined as a polynomial distributed lag of the form

$$\beta_i = \delta_0 + \delta_1 i + \delta_2 i^2 \text{ where } i \text{ is the lag length.}$$

This implies that

$$
\begin{aligned}
\beta_0 &= \delta_0 \\
\beta_1 &= \delta_0 + \delta_1 + \delta_2 \\
\beta_2 &= \delta_0 + 2\delta_1 + 4\delta_2 \text{ and} \\
\beta_3 &= \delta_0 + 3\delta_1 + 9\delta_2
\end{aligned}
$$

which can be written as $\beta = A\delta$, with the 4 by 3 matrix A containing the numbers 1, 1, 1, 1 in the first column, 0, 1, 2, 3 in the second column, and 0, 1, 4, 9 in the third column.

The δ vector can be estimated by running an OLS regression on transformed data (explained in any textbook discussion of the polynomial, or Almon, distributed lag) to obtain δ^{OLS} and an estimate of its variance $V(\delta^{OLS})$. To estimate the β vector, the estimator $\hat{\beta} = A\delta^{OLS}$ is used, with $V(\hat{\beta}) = AV(\delta^{OLS})A'$.

6 Cramer–Rao Lower Bound

No asymptotically unbiased estimator has a variance–covariance matrix smaller than the Cramer–Rao lower bound. Since if this bound is attained it is attained by the maximum likelihood estimator, it is customary to consider the Cramer–Rao lower bound to be the variance of the MLE, and to estimate the variance of the MLE by an estimate of the Cramer–Rao lower bound.

The Cramer–Rao lower bound is the inverse of the information matrix, which is the expected value of the negative of the matrix of second partial derivatives of the log-likelihood with respect to the parameters being estimated:

$$\text{information matrix} = -E(\partial^2 \ln L/\partial\theta^2]$$

where θ is the vector of parameters to be estimated. In the CNLR model θ would consist of β and σ^2. This calculation yields the formula for the information matrix, the inverse of which is the variance–covariance matrix of θ^{MLE}; an estimate of this produces the estimated variance–covariance matrix.

There are three different ways of estimating the information matrix. First, the information matrix itself can be evaluated at the MLE. This involves finding the formula for the expected value of the negative of the Hessian (the matrix of second derivatives) of the log-likelihood function, something that may be computationally difficult. Second, the negative of the Hessian of the log-likelihood could be used. This avoids having to find expected values, but still requires taking second derivatives. Third, the outer product of the gradient (OPG) could be used, exploiting a theoretical result that the expected value of the OPG is equal to the information matrix. Let g be the gradient (first derivative vector) of the component of the log-likelihood corresponding to a single observation. The OPG estimate of the information matrix is the sum over all observations of gg'. For an exposition of why this result holds, see Darnell (1994, pp. 254–5). This is computationally attractive because it requires only taking first derivatives. Unfortunately, studies such as Davidson and MacKinnon (1983) have shown that it is not reliable.

NOTES

- The presence of an additive constant has no impact on variance; when the mean is subtracted out before squaring, additive constants are eliminated.
- Another well-known variance formula: the variance of $\hat{p}$, the sample proportion of successes, say, in N random observations from a population with a true fraction p of successes, is $V(\hat{p}) = p(1-p)/N$. Note that the number of successes is $N\hat{p}$. Using 3(b) above, $V(N\hat{p}) = N^2 V(\hat{p})$, yielding $V(N\hat{p}) = Np(1-p)$.
- Knowing that the variance of a chi-square is twice its degrees of freedom can sometimes be useful.

APPENDIX C: A PRIMER ON ASYMPTOTICS

The rationale behind asymptotic distribution theory, and the reasons for econometricians' interest in it, are presented in chapter 2. The purpose of this appendix is to provide an overview of the technical details of asymptotics. Readers are warned that to keep this presentation readable, many not-quite-correct statements appear; for those interested in mastering the details, several recent advanced textbooks have good presentations, for example Greene (1997, pp. 115–29, 270–99) and Judge et al. (1985, ch. 5). A good advanced reference is Greenberg and Webster (1983, ch. 1). White (1984) is very advanced, Kmenta (1986, pp. 163–72) and Darnell (1994, pp. 45–9, 290–3, 217–22) have good expositions at the beginner level.

Asymptotic distribution theory is concerned with what happens to a statistic, say $\hat{\beta}$, as the sample size T becomes very large. To emphasize the role of the sample size, $\hat{\beta}$ is sometimes written as $\hat{\beta}_T$. In particular, interest focuses on two things:

(a) Does the distribution of $\hat{\beta}_T$ collapse on a particular value (i.e., become heavily concentrated in the neighborhood of that value) as the sample size becomes very large? This leads to the large-sample concept of consistency.

(b) Does the distribution of $\hat{\beta}_T$ approximate a known form (e.g., the normal distribution) as the sample size becomes very large? This allows the development of large-sample hypothesis testing procedures.

To address these questions, two concepts of convergence are employed. Convergence in probability is used for (a) above, and convergence in distribution is used for (b).

I Convergence in Probability

Suppose that as the sample size becomes very large the distribution of $\hat{\beta}_T$ collapses on the value k. Then $\hat{\beta}_T$ is said to *converge in probability* to k, or has *probability limit k*, written as plim $\hat{\beta} = k$. If k equals β, the number that $\hat{\beta}$ is estimating, $\hat{\beta}$ is said to be *consistent*; $k - \beta$ is called the *asymptotic bias* of $\hat{\beta}$ as an estimator of β.

A popular means of showing consistency is to show that the bias and the variance of $\hat{\beta}_T$ both approach zero as the sample size becomes very large. This is called *convergence in quadratic mean* or *convergence in mean square*; it is a sufficient condition for convergence in probability. Consider, for example, the sample mean statistic from a sample drawn randomly from a distribution with mean μ and variance σ^2. Because the sample mean is unbiased in small samples, it has zero bias also in large samples, and because its variance is σ^2/T, its variance approaches zero as the sample size becomes very large. Thus the sample mean converges in quadratic mean and therefore is a consistent estimator of μ.

A major reason for using asymptotic distribution theory is that the algebra associated with finding (small-sample) expected values can become formidable whenever nonlinearities are involved. In particular, the expected value of a nonlinear function of $\hat{\beta}$, say, is not equal to the nonlinear function of the expected value of $\hat{\beta}$. Why this happens is explained in the technical notes to section 2.8. This problem disappears when using asymptotics, however, because the plim of a nonlinear (continuous) function of $\hat{\beta}$ is the nonlinear function of the plim of $\hat{\beta}$. This is referred to as *Slutsky's theorem*; the reason for this is also explained in the technical notes to section 2.8. As an example, suppose you have an unbiased estimator π^* of the multiplier $\pi = 1/(1 - \beta)$ but you wish to estimate β. Now $\beta = 1 - \pi^{-1}$ so it is natural to suggest using $1 - (\pi^*)^{-1}$ to estimate β. Since this is a nonlinear function of the unbiased estimate π^* it will be biased, but, thanks to Slutsky's theorem, asymptotically unbiased.

Consider now the task of showing the consistency of the OLS estimator in the CLR model $y = X\beta + \varepsilon$. Since β^{OLS} can be written as $\beta + (X'X)^{-1}X'\varepsilon$ we have plim $\beta^{OLS} = \beta + \text{plim}(X'X)^{-1}X'\varepsilon$. It is instructive to spell out fully the logic of the remainder of the argument.

(a) $(X'X)^{-1}X'\varepsilon$ is multiplied and divided by T, producing $(X'X/T)^{-1}(X'\varepsilon/T)$.

(b) Slutsky's theorem is used to break the plim into two halves, namely

$$\text{plim}(X'X)^{-1}X'\varepsilon = \text{plim}(X'X/T)^{-1}\text{plim}(X'\varepsilon/T)$$

and then is used again to bring the first plim inside the inverse sign, producing

$$[\text{plim}(X'X/T)]^{-1}\text{plim}(X'\varepsilon/T).$$

(c) It should now be evident why the Ts were inserted. $X'X$ is a matrix consisting of sums, with each extra observation adding something to each of these sums. As T becomes very large some of these sums will undoubtedly become infinite. (All the diagonal elements are sums of squares; if there is an intercept, the upper left corner of this matrix is equal to T.) Consequently it would not make much sense to find plim$(X'X)$. In contrast, by examining plim$(X'X/T)$ we are in effect looking at the average values of the elements of the $X'X$ matrix, and these are finite under a fairly broad set of assumptions as the sample size becomes very large.

(d) To proceed further it is necessary to make some assumption about how extra observations on the independent variables are obtained as the sample size grows. The standard assumption made is that these extra observations are such that plim$(X'X/T)$ is equal to a finite, invertible matrix Q. Loosely speaking, Q can be thought of as the expected value of the $X'X$ matrix for a sample of size one. Theoretical results are often expressed in terms of Q; it must be remembered that, operationally, Q will be estimated by $X'X/T$.

(e) We now have that plim $\beta^{OLS} = \beta + Q^{-1}\text{plim}(X'\varepsilon/T)$. It is tempting at this stage to use Slutsky's theorem once again to break plim$(X'\varepsilon)$ into plimX'plimε. This would not make sense, however. Both X and ε have dimension T, so as the sample size grows X becomes a bigger and bigger matrix and ε a longer and longer vector.

(f) What does a typical element of $X'\varepsilon/T$ look like? Suppose the ith explanatory variable is w. Then the ith element of $X'\varepsilon/T$ is $\Sigma w_t \varepsilon_t/T$. In the CLR model the w are fixed in repeated samples, and the expected value of ε is zero, so the expected value of $\Sigma w_t \varepsilon_t/T$ is zero. What about the variance of $\Sigma w_t \varepsilon_t/T$? It is equal to $\sigma^2 \Sigma w_t^2/T^2 = (\sigma^2/T)\Sigma w_t^2/T$, which approaches zero as the sample size becomes very large (since the term $\Sigma w_t^2/T$ is finite, approaching the ith diagonal element of Q). Thus because the expected value and variance both approach zero as the sample size becomes very large (i.e., convergence in quadratic mean) the plim of $X'\varepsilon/T$ is the zero vector, and thus plim $\beta^{OLS} = \beta$; β^{OLS} is consistent in the CLR model.

(g) A more straightforward way of obtaining convergence in quadratic mean for this case, and thus consistency, is to note that because β^{OLS} is unbiased in small samples it is also unbiased in large samples, and that the variance of β^{OLS} can be written as $\sigma^2(X'X)^{-1} = (\sigma^2/T)(X'X/T)^{-1}$ which approaches zero as the sample size becomes very large.

(h) The observant reader will have noticed that the assumption that plim$(X'X/T)$ equals a finite invertible matrix rules out a very common case, namely a regressor following a growth trend. If the regressor values grow as the sample size grows, plim$(X'X/T)$ will become infinite. Fortunately, this does not cause insurmountable problems, mainly because if this becomes infinite its inverse becomes zero. Look again at the argument in (g) above. The key is that $(\sigma^2/T)(X'X/T)^{-1}$ converges to zero as the sample size becomes very large; this comes about because (σ^2/T) approaches zero while $(X'X/T)^{-1}$ is assumed to approach a finite value. In the case of a trending regressor this latter term also approaches zero, aiding the convergence of $(\sigma^2/T)(X'X/T)^{-1}$ to zero.

(i) A key element in (f) above is that the expected value of $\Sigma w_t \varepsilon_t/T$ is zero. If w is stochastic, rather than fixed in repeated samples, this will happen if w is contemporaneously independent of the error term. This reveals why it is only contemporaneous dependence between a regressor and the error term that leads to asymptotic bias.

2   Convergence in Distribution

Suppose that as the sample size becomes very large the distribution f_T of $\hat{\beta}_T$ becomes virtually identical to a specific distribution f. Then $\hat{\beta}_T$ is said to *converge in distribution* to f (sometimes expressed as converging in distribution to a variable whose distribution is f). The distribution f is called the *limiting distribution* of $\hat{\beta}_T$; the intention is to use this limiting distribution as an approximation for the unknown (or intractable) small-sample distribution of $\hat{\beta}$. Two difficulties are apparent.

First, we saw earlier that in most applications the distribution of $\hat{\beta}_T$ collapses to a spike, so it doesn't make sense to use it to approximate the small-sample distribution of $\hat{\beta}_T$. This difficulty is overcome by transforming/normalizing $\hat{\beta}_T$ to prevent its distribution from collapsing. The most common way of accomplishing this is to focus attention on the distribution of $\sqrt{T}(\hat{\beta}_T - \beta)$. For the example of β^{OLS} in the CLR model, it is easy to see that as the sample size becomes very large the mean of $\sqrt{T}(\beta^{OLS} - \beta)$ is zero and its variance is $\sigma^2 Q^{-1}$.

Second, how are we going to know what form (e.g., normal distribution) the distribution of $\sqrt{T}(\hat{\beta}_T - \beta)$ takes as the sample size becomes very large? This problem is solved by appealing to a *central limit theorem*. Central limit theorems in effect say that the sample mean statistic is distributed normally when the sample size becomes very large, i.e., that the limiting distribution of $\sqrt{T}(\hat{\theta}_T - \theta)$ is a normal distribution if $\hat{\theta}_T$ is a sample average. It is remarkable that so many statistics can be shown to be functions of a sample mean statistic, allowing a central limit theorem to be exploited to derive limiting distributions of known form.

To illustrate this consider once again β^{OLS} in the CLR model. If the errors were distributed normally, β^{OLS} would be normally distributed with mean β and variance $\sigma^2(X'X)^{-1}$. If the errors are not distributed normally, the distribution of β^{OLS} is difficult to describe and to utilize for hypothesis testing. Instead of trying to derive the exact distribution of β^{OLS} in this circumstance, what is usually done is to approximate this exact distribution with what is called the *asymptotic distribution* of β^{OLS}.

3 Asymptotic Distributions

The first step in finding this asymptotic distribution is to find the limiting distribution of $\sqrt{T}(\beta_T^{OLS} - \beta) = (X'X/T)^{-1}(X'\varepsilon/\sqrt{T})$. Look first at $(X'\varepsilon/\sqrt{T})$, which can be rewritten as $\sqrt{T}(X'\varepsilon/T)$. Following our earlier discussion, suppose the ith explanatory variable is w. Then the ith element of $\sqrt{T}(X'\varepsilon/T)$ is $\sqrt{T}(\Sigma w_t \varepsilon_t/T)$. Notice that $\Sigma w_t \varepsilon_t/T$ is a sample average of the $w_t\varepsilon_t$s, and that the common mean of the $w_t\varepsilon_t$s is zero. Consequently a central limit theorem can be applied to show that the limiting distribution of $\sqrt{T}(X'\varepsilon/T)$ is normal with mean zero. The variance can be derived as $\sigma^2 Q$.

We can now apply a very useful theorem concerning the interaction between plims and limiting distributions: if one variable has a plim and another variable has a limiting distribution, then when dealing with their product the first variable can be treated as a constant in so far as the limiting distribution of that product is concerned. Thus, for example, suppose plim $a_T = a$ and the limiting distribution of b_T is normal with mean μ and variance σ^2. Then the limiting distribution of $a_T b_T$ is normal with mean $a\mu$ and variance $a^2\sigma^2$. To be even more specific, suppose $\sqrt{T}(\bar{x} - \mu)$ has limiting distribution $N(0, \sigma^2)$, and plim $s^2 = \sigma^2$; then the limiting distribution of $\sqrt{T}(\bar{x} - \mu)/s = (\bar{x} - \mu)/(s/\sqrt{T})$ is $N(0, 1)$.

We wish to use this theorem to find the limiting distribution of $\sqrt{T}(\beta_T^{OLS} - \beta) = (X'X/T)^{-1}(X'\varepsilon/\sqrt{T})$. Since $\text{plim}(X'X/T)^{-1} = Q^{-1}$ and the limiting distribution of $(X'\varepsilon/\sqrt{T})$ is $N(0, \sigma^2 Q)$, the limiting distribution of $(X'X/T)^{-1}(X'\varepsilon/\sqrt{T})$ is $N(0, Q^{-1}\sigma^2 QQ^{-1}) = N(0, \sigma^2 Q^{-1})$.

It is customary, although not technically correct, to use the expression "the asymptotic distribution of β^{OLS} is $N(\beta, (\sigma^2/T)Q^{-1})$" to refer to this result. This distribution is used as an approximation to the unknown (or intractable) small-sample distribution of β^{OLS}; in this example, β^{OLS} is said to be *asymptotically normally distributed* with mean β and asymptotic variance $(\sigma^2/T)Q^{-1}$. On the assumption that the sample size is large enough for this distribution to be a good approximation (it is remarkable that such approximations are typically quite accurate for samples of modest size), hypothesis testing proceeds in the usual fashion, in spite of the errors not being normally distributed. Since Q is estimated by $X'X/T$, operationally the variance $(\sigma^2/T)Q^{-1}$ is estimated by the familiar $s^2(X'X)^{-1}$.

Joint hypotheses are tested via the usual $F(J, T - K)$ statistic, or, in its asymptotic incarnation, J times this F statistic, which is distributed asymptotically as $\chi(J)$. This is justified by appealing to another extremely useful theorem: if a statistic converges in distribution to x, then a continuous function g of that statistic converges in distribution to

$g(x)$. For example, if the limiting distribution of θ^* is $N(0, 1)$, then the limiting distribution of $(\theta^*)^2$ is $\chi(1)$.

Another way of dealing with nonlinearities is to appeal to the result that if a statistic $\hat{\beta}$ is distributed asymptotically normally then a continuous function g of that statistic is distributed asymptotically normally with mean $g(\text{plim}\hat{\beta})$ and variance equal to the variance of $\hat{\beta}$ times the square of the first derivative of g with respect to $\hat{\beta}$, as described in appendix A and the technical notes to chapter 2.

NOTES

- The terminology $\xrightarrow{p}$ is used to express convergence in probability, so $a_T \xrightarrow{p} a$ means that a_T converges in probability to a. The terminology $\xrightarrow{d}$ is used to express convergence in distribution, so $\sqrt{T}(a_T - a) \xrightarrow{d} x$ means that the limiting distribution of a_T is the distribution of x. If the distribution of x is known to be $N(0, 1)$, for example, this is often written as $\sqrt{T}(a_T - a) \xrightarrow{d} N(0, 1)$.

- A formal definition of consistency is as follows: an estimator $\hat{\beta}$ of β is consistent if the probability that $\hat{\beta}$ differs in absolute value from β by less than some preassigned positive number δ (however small) can be made as close to one as desired by choosing a suitably large sample size. This is usually written as

$$\text{plim } \hat{\beta} = k \text{ if } \lim_{T \to \infty} \text{prob} (|\hat{\beta} - k| < \delta) = 1$$

where δ is any arbitrarily small positive number.

- The discussion above has on occasion referred to the plim as the *asymptotic expectation*. Unfortunately, there is some confusion in the literature concerning this: some people define the asymptotic expectation to be the plim, but most define it to be the limit of the expected value, which is not the same thing. Although in virtually all practical applications the two are identical, which explains why most people treat them as being equivalent, it is possible to find cases in which they differ. It is instructive to look at some examples.

  (1) Suppose $\text{prob}(\hat{\beta} = \beta) = 1 - 1/T$ and $\text{prob}(\hat{\beta} = T) = 1/T$ where T is the sample size. The plim is β, but the asymptotic expectation is $\beta + 1$.

  (2) Suppose we have a sample on x of size T and estimate the population mean μ by $\mu^* = x_1/2 + \Sigma x_i/2(T - 1)$ where the summation runs from 2 to T. The asymptotic expectation is μ, but the plim is $x_1/2 + \mu/2$.

  (3) Consider the inverse of the sample mean statistic as an estimate of a nonzero population mean μ. Its plim is μ^{-1}, but its asymptotic expectation does not exist (because of the possibility that the sample mean is zero).

  The plim and the asymptotic expectation will be the same whenever they both exist and the variance goes to zero as the sample size goes to infinity.

- The above examples illustrate why convergence in quadratic mean is not a necessary condition for consistency.

- A stronger form of convergence in probability, called *almost sure convergence*, is sometimes encountered. The former allows some erratic behavior in the converging sequence, whereas the latter does not.

- The order of a statistic is sometimes encountered when dealing with asymptotics. A statistic θ^* is said to be at most of order T^k if plim θ^*/T^k is a nonzero constant. For example, since $X'X/T$ converges to Q, $X'X$ is at most of order T. The big O notation, $X'X = O(T)$ is used to denote this. The little o notation $\theta = o(T^k)$ means the statistic θ is of smaller order than T^k, implying that plim $\theta/T^k = 0$. Typically, for coefficient estimators that are biased, but consistent, the order of their bias is $1/\sqrt{T}$, meaning that this bias disappears at a rate proportional to the square root of the sample size: plim $\sqrt{T}$(bias) is a constant. For the OLS estimator of the cointegrating vector, discussed in chapter 17, the bias disappears at a rate proportional to T, explaining why this estimator is called "superconsistent." In this example, the usual transformation $\sqrt{T}(\hat{\beta}_T - \beta)$ suggested earlier is inappropriate; the transformation $T(\hat{\beta}_T - \beta)$ must be used for this case.

- Note that although strictly speaking the limiting/asymptotic distribution of β^{OLS} is a degenerate spike at β, many econometricians speak of the asymptotic distribution of β^{OLS} as normal with mean β and asymptotic variance $(\sigma^2/T)Q^{-1}$. This should be interpreted as meaning that the limiting distribution of $\sqrt{T}(\beta^{OLS} - \beta)$ is normal with mean zero and variance $\sigma^2 Q^{-1}$.

- Continuing to speak loosely, an estimator's asymptotic variance cannot be calculated by taking the limit of that estimator's variance as the sample size becomes very large, because usually that limit is zero. In practice it is common for it to be calculated as

$$\text{Asy. Var } \hat{\beta} = (1/T) \lim_{T \to \infty} TV(\hat{\beta}).$$

- There exist several central limit theorems, which are applicable in differing circumstances. Their general flavor is captured by the following: if $\bar{x}$ is the average of T random drawings from probability distributions with common finite mean μ and (differing) finite variances, then the limiting distribution of $\sqrt{T}(\bar{x} - \mu)$ is normal with mean zero and variance the limit of the average of the variances.

- A consistent estimator is said to be *asymptotically efficient* if its asymptotic variance is smaller than the asymptotic variance of any other consistent estimator. Sometimes this refers only to estimators that are distributed asymptotically normally. The maximum likelihood estimator, whose asymptotic variance is given by the Cramer–Rao lower bound, is asymptotically efficient, and therefore is used as a benchmark in this regard.

APPENDIX D: EXERCISES

This appendix contains exercises on a variety of topics. Several points should be noted.

(1) Why is a set of exercises included in this book? Problem sets found in textbooks range widely in quality and level. Since this book is designed to supplement econometrics texts, it seemed appropriate to include a set of problems offering instructors an alternative.

(2) What I have provided may not be suitable for all students and instructors. For the most part these problems focus on an understanding of the material, rather than on numerical calculation or mathematical manipulation; in this respect they reflect the flavor of the book. The questions are designed for students at intermediate levels of study – beyond the rank beginner and below the advanced graduate student. In my experience, students (at whatever level) who understand what is going on find these questions easy, whereas students who do not, find them difficult. In particular, students who do not understand the material very well have difficulty in figuring out what the questions are asking and why. Instructors should use judgement in selecting problems suitable for their students. Asterisked problems require more difficult algebraic manipulations. Answers to the even-numbered questions appear in appendix E.

(3) I believe that students do not fully understand an issue if they cannot describe clearly how to conduct a Monte Carlo study to investigate that issue. This is why so many Monte Carlo questions appear in this appendix. Some of these questions provide the structure of a Monte Carlo study and ask students to anticipate the results; these questions should be attempted first, because they help students learn how to structure their own Monte Carlo studies. Kennedy (1998) offers advice on using Monte Carlo questions with students.

(4) Two notable shortcomings of this set of problems are that there are no case studies (problems dealing with real numbers, showing how actual empirical problems are handled) and no computer exercises. Both these types of questions are valuable and should be a prominent part of econometrics courses. Lott and Ray (1992) address this need by providing the data for and questions on 50 economics journal articles. Berndt (1991) is an applied econometrics text full of computer-oriented questions.

(5) Most of these problems have been classroom tested, but some have not. Regardless of how often they have been tested, I am amazed at how frequently I must rewrite, either to correct mistakes or to clarify. I have no doubt that this appendix will be full of shortcomings; I would be grateful for suggestions for improvement, or ideas for questions for inclusion in a future edition.

(6) Exercises have been grouped into several categories, listed below for reference purposes:

A	Monte Carlo: General
B	Calculating Expected Values and Variances
C	Best Unbiasedness
D	Mean Square Error
E	Applications of Expected Values in Economic Theory
F	OLS: Monte Carlo
G	OLS: General
H	OLS: Numerical Examples
I	Transforming Variables
J	OLS: Estimating Variances
K	OLS with Restrictions
L	Theoretical Results for Multivariate Regression
M	Pooling Data and Missing Observations
N	Multicollinearity
O	Dummy Variables: Interpretation
P	Dummy Variables: Estimation
Q	Dummy Variables: Hypothesis Testing
R	Dummy Variables: Modeling Structural Breaks
S	Maximum Likelihood: General Principles
T	Maximum Likelihood: Examples
U	Bayesian: General
V	Bayesian: Priors
W	Hypothesis Testing: Monte Carlo
X	Hypothesis Testing: Fundamentals
Y	Hypothesis Testing: Power
Z	Hypothesis Testing: Examples
AA	Hypothesis Testing: Numerical Examples
BB	Test Statistics
CC	Hypothesis Testing: Theoretical Derivations
DD	Pre-test Estimators
EE	Non-nested Hypothesis Tests
FF	Nonspherical Errors: Monte Carlo
GG	Nonspherical Errors: General
HH	Heteroskedasticity: General
II	Autocorrelated Errors: General
JJ	Heteroskedasticity: Testing
KK	Heteroskedasticity: Numerical Examples
LL	Autocorrelated Errors: Numerical Examples
MM	SURE: Numerical Examples
NN	Stochastic Extraneous Information
OO	Nonspherical Errors: Theoretical Results
PP	Heteroskedasticity: Theoretical Results
QQ	Autocorrelated Errors: Theoretical Results
RR	Dynamics
SS	Stochastic Regressors: Monte Carlo
TT	Measurement Error

UU   Instrumental Variables
VV   Simultaneous Equations
WW Hausman Tests
XX   Qualitative and Limited Dependent Variables: Monte Carlo
YY   Qualitative Dependent Variables
ZZ   Limited Dependent Variables
AB   Duration Models

A   Monte Carlo: General

1   Suppose you have programmed a computer to do the following:
   i.   Draw randomly 25 values from a standard normal distribution.
   ii.   Multiply each of these values by 3 and add 2.
   iii.   Take their average and call it A1.
   iv.   Repeat this procedure to obtain 500 averages A1 through A500.
   v.   Compute the average of these 500 A values. Call it Abar.
   vi.   Compute the variance of these 500 A values. Call it Avar.
   (a) What is this Monte Carlo study designed to investigate?
   (b) What number should Abar be close to? Explain your logic.
   (c) What number should Avar be close to? Explain your logic.

2   Suppose you have programmed a computer to do the following:
   i.   Draw randomly 100 values from a standard normal distribution.
   ii.   Multiply each of these values by 5 and add 1.
   iii.   Average the resulting 100 values.
   iv.   Call the average A1 and save it.
   v.   Repeat the procedure above to produce 2000 averages A1 through A2000.
   vi.   Order these 2000 values from the smallest to the largest.
   (a) What is your best guess of the 1900th ordered value? Explain your logic.
   (b) How many of these values should be negative? Explain your logic.

3   Suppose you have programmed a computer to do the following:
   i.   Draw 50 x values from a distribution uniform between 10 and 20.
   ii.   Count the number g of x values greater than 18.
   iii.   Divide g by 50 to get h1.
   iv.   Calculate $w1 = h1(1 - h1)/50$.
   v.   Repeat this procedure to get 5000 h values h1 to h5000 and 5000 w values w1 to w5000.
   vi.   Calculate the average hav and the variance hvar of the h values, and the average wav of the w values.
   (a) What is this Monte Carlo study designed to investigate?
   (b) What number should hav be close to? Explain your logic.
   (c) What number should hvar be close to? Explain your logic.
   (d) What number should wav be close to? Explain your logic.

4   Suppose you have programmed a computer to do the following:
   i.   Draw 60 x values from a distribution uniform between 0 and 100.
   ii.   Count the number g of x values less than 20.
   iii.   Repeat this procedure to get 5000 g values g1 to g5000.
   iv.   Calculate the average gav and the variance gvar of the g values.

(a) What is this Monte Carlo study designed to investigate?
(b) What number should gav be close to? Explain your logic.
(c) What number should gvar be close to? Explain your logic.

5 Explain how to perform a Monte Carlo study to investigate the relative merits (bias and variance) of the sample mean and the sample median as estimates of the true mean when data with sample size 44 have come from a normal distribution with mean 6 and variance 4.

6 Suppose we have 20 observations from $N(\mu, \sigma^2)$.
(a) Explain how to perform a Monte Carlo study to check if the sample variance is an unbiased estimate of σ^2.
(b) The variance of the sample variance is $2\sigma^4/(N - 1)$ where N is the sample size. Explain how to perform a Monte Carlo study to confirm this.

7 Suppose x is distributed uniformly between a and b. From a sample size 25 you wish to estimate the mean of the distribution of $1/x^2$. Student A suggests using the formula $(1/\bar{x})^2$, and student B suggests using the formula $\Sigma(1/x^2)/25$. Explain in detail how you would use a Monte Carlo study to evaluate these two suggestions. *Hint*: Be careful choosing a and b. *Second hint*: You need somehow to find the mean of the distribution of $1/x^2$. Work it out algebraically, or explain how to find it using a Monte Carlo study.

8 Consider the case of N independent observations on a random variable x which has mean μ and variance σ^2.
(a) Explain in detail how you would conduct a Monte Carlo study to verify that the variance of the sample mean statistic is σ^2/N.
(b) What is the usual estimator of the variance of the sample mean statistic for this case?
(c) Explain in detail how you would conduct a Monte Carlo study to verify that this estimator is unbiased as an estimate of the variance of the sample mean statistic.

9 Suppose you have conducted a Monte Carlo study to investigate, for sample size 25, the bias of an estimator β^* of the slope coefficient in the relationship $y = 2 + 3x + \varepsilon$ where you drew 400 repeated samples of errors (ε) from a normal distribution with mean zero and variance 9.0. Your study estimates the bias of β^* as 0.04 and the variance of β^* as 0.01. You are not sure whether 0.04 is small enough to be considered zero.
(a) From the information provided, test the null hypothesis that β^* is unbiased.
(b) Explain how, if given the 400 β^* values, you could perform this test without calculating a test statistic.

10 Explain how to conduct a Monte Carlo study to examine the relative merits of the sample mean and the sample median, for sample size 25, when each observation comes with probability 95% and 5% from $N(50,4)$ and $N(50,100)$, respectively.

*11 Suppose you have 27 random observations on a variable x which you know is distributed normally with mean μ and variance 6. You wish to estimate $\theta = \mu^3$, and propose using $\theta^* = (\bar{x})^3$.
(a) Explain in a sentence why θ^* is biased in small samples but not in large samples.
(b) What formula would you use to estimate the variance of θ^*?
(c) Explain in detail how you would undertake a Monte Carlo study to examine how well your formula in (b) does in estimating the actual variance of θ^* for a sample size of 27.
  Hint: View θ^* as a nonlinear function of $\bar{x}$. *Second hint*: You will have to estimate the actual variance of θ^* in your Monte Carlo study.

12 Suppose you program a computer to draw 800 errors from a standard normal distribution and then you multiply them by 2, add 6 and square them. Next you take their average and call it A. Of what number should A be an estimate?

13 Suppose you have programmed a computer to do the following:
   i.   Draw 20 x values from a standard normal distribution.
   ii.   Multiply each x value by 2 and add 8 to produce 20 w values.
   iii.   Subtract the average of the w values from each w value to obtain 20 y values.
   iv.   Square the y values and add them to obtain s.
   v.   Divide s by 19 to get a1, divide s by 20 to get b1 and divide s by 21 to get c1.
   vi.   Repeat this procedure to get 4000 a, b, and c values.
   vii.   Compute the averages and variances of the 4000 a, b and c values.
   viii. Subtract four from each a, b and c value, square the result and then average each set of 4000 squared values to produce A, B and C.

   (a) Which of the three averages computed in step vii should be closest to four? Explain why.
   (b) Which of the three variances in computed in step vii should be the smallest? Explain why.
   (c) What is the purpose of step viii? Which of A, B and C should be the smallest? *Hint:* Check the technical notes to section 2.9 of chapter 2.

14 Consider observations from a production line in which the proportion of defectives is θ. For a sample of size 60, say, the usual estimate θ is $\theta^* = k/60$ where k is the number of defectives in the sample. From elementary statistics, the variance of θ^* is $v = \theta(1 - \theta)/60$, estimated by $v^* = \theta^*(1 - \theta^*)/60$.
   (a) Explain how to perform a Monte Carlo study to verify that v^* is an unbiased estimate of v.
   (b) How would you test that the bias is zero?

B Calculating Expected Values and Variances

1 Suppose the *pdf* of x is given by $f(x) = kx(2 - x)$ for $0 \leqslant x \leqslant 2$ and zero otherwise. Find $E(x)$ and $V(x)$. *Hint:* Your answer should be two numbers.

2 For a fee of $2 you toss three fair coins and are paid $(x^2 - x)$ where x is the number of heads thrown. What is your expected profit from playing?

3 Suppose the *pdf* of the monthly demand x for a perishable product is given by $f(x)$, with only six possible demand quantities:

x	100	200	300	400	500	600
f(x)	0.05	0.10	0.25	0.35	0.15	0.10

Production costs are $10 per unit and the fixed price is $15, so that for each unit sold profit is $5 and for each unit left unsold a loss of $10 is suffered. Assuming you produce to maximize expected profit, what is your expected profit and the variance of your profit? *Hint:* Use "trial and error" by trying various supplies.

4 Suppose x is distributed uniformly between a and b. Derive the textbook formulas for Ex and $V(x)$, in terms of a and b. Explain your calculations.

5 Suppose there is an infinite number of stores, half charging $1 and half charging $2.

You decide to check three stores randomly and buy from a store which has the minimum of the three prices checked. What is the expected value of the price you will pay?

6 Suppose x and y are iid (independently and identically distributed), each with probability distribution $p(2) = 0.5$ and $p(3) = 0.5$. Is $E(x/y)$ smaller than, greater than or equal to $(Ex)/(Ey)$? Be explicit.

7 Suppose $E\alpha^* = \alpha$ and $V(\alpha^*) = 4\alpha/T + 16\alpha^2/T^2$, where T is the sample size. Answer each of the following true, false, or uncertain, and explain.
(a) α^* is asymptotically unbiased as an estimator of α.
(b) The asymptotic variance of α^* is zero.
(c) α^* is consistent.
(d) α^* is asymptotically efficient.

8 Suppose you have a sample of size 25 from a distribution with nonzero mean μ and variance 50. The mean of your sample is 2. Consider estimating the inverse of μ by the inverse of the sample mean. Although the expected value of this statistic does not exist, it is nonetheless consistent.
(a) Explain in one sentence how consistency can be deduced.
(b) What estimate would you use for the variance of this statistic?

9 Consider three stocks, A, B and C, each costing $10, with their returns distributed independently, each with mean 5% and variance 6.
(a) What are the relative merits (mean and variance of returns) of portfolio 1, consisting of 30 shares of A, and portfolio 2, consisting of 10 shares of each of A, B and C?
(b) Suppose that the returns from A and B have correlation coefficient -0.5 (so that their covariance is -3) but they are uncorrelated with returns from C. How are the properties of portfolios 1 and 2 affected?
(c) "If stocks tend to move together so that their returns are positively correlated with one another, then diversification will not reduce risk." True, false, or uncertain? Explain.
(d) "If stocks A and B are perfectly negatively correlated, then a portfolio with 50% A and 50% B has a zero expected return and zero variance." True, false, or uncertain? Explain.

10 Suppose you have T observations from the density $f(x) = \lambda x^{\lambda-1}$ for $0 \leqslant x \leqslant 1$. Find a method of moments estimator for λ.

11 Suppose you have N observations on x, where x is distributed uniformly between 10 and an unknown parameter λ.
(a) Derive a method of moments estimator for λ.
(b) What is its variance? *Hint:* For $x \sim U(a,b)$, $Ex = (b - a)/2$ and $V(x) = (b - a)^2/12$.

12 Sample variances of x are usually calculated by dividing the sum of x minus xbar squared by N $-$ 1 which "corrects for degrees of freedom." What does this correction accomplish?

C   Best Unbiasedness

1 Suppose $y = \beta x + \varepsilon$ where the xs are non-stochastic and the εs are iid with mean zero and variance σ^2. Consider estimating β by the slope of a line drawn between the origin and one of the plotted observations.

(a) What is the bias of this estimator?
(b) What is its variance?
(c) Which of the observations would you choose to calculate this estimate? Why?
(d) Does this estimator possess the usual desirable asymptotic properties? Explain in one sentence why or why not.

2 Suppose $y = \alpha + \beta x + \varepsilon$ where the εs are iid with mean zero and variance σ^2. Suppose the data are divided evenly into two groups denoted by the subscripts a and b, and β is estimated by $\beta^* = (y_a - y_b)/(x_a - x_b)$ where y_a is the *average* of all the y observations in group a, etc.
(a) Find the expected value and variance of β^*.
(b) How would you allocate observations into the two groups? Why?

3 A professor asked two students to come up with the best possible estimate of a parameter β by searching the literature. Student A found a study with an unbiased estimate $\beta^* = 5.0$, with variance 8.0, from a regression with an R^2 of 0.86. Student B found a completely different study with an unbiased estimate $\beta^{**} = 6.0$, with variance 4.0, from a regression with an R^2 of 0.43. They could not agree on what to report to the professor, so they asked a friend for advice. Not wishing to offend either student, the friend elected to be diplomatic, and advised them to report $b^{***} = 5.5$, the average of the two estimates.
(a) Which of these three estimates do you prefer? Explain why. Be explicit.
(b) What would you have told these students had they come to you for advice? Explain.
(c) Kmenta (1986, p. 257) has a similar question in which the two students are each running the same regression but with different data sets. How would your answer to part (b) change in this case in which the two data sets are available?

4 Suppose the independent random variables x and y have variances 4 and 16, respectively. You wish to estimate the difference between their means, and can afford to take a total of 30 observations. How many should you draw on x and how many on y?

5 Two independent samples drawn from the same population resulted in unbiased estimates b^* and b^{**}, with variances Vb^* and Vb^{**}. Consider estimating with the linear combination $b^{***} = ab^* + (1 - a)b^{**}$.
(a) What value of a would you choose?
(b) Explain the common sense of your answer to part (a) (for example, does it give sensible answers for the obvious special cases?).

6 Suppose $y = \alpha + \beta x + \varepsilon$ where the CLR model assumptions hold and you have N observations. A friend suggests estimating β with

$$\frac{1}{N - 1} \sum_{i=2}^{N} \frac{y_i - y_1}{x_i - x_1}$$

In what sense is your friend's suggestion good and in what sense is it not so good?

D   Mean Square Error

1 Suppose x is distributed with mean μ and variance σ^2. Given a sample of T independent observations on x, under what condition would estimating μ by $\beta^* = 0$ (i.e.,

ignore the data and estimate by zero) be superior, on the MSE criterion, to using $\beta^{**} = \bar{x}$?

2 Suppose we have the sample x_1, x_2, and x_3, drawn randomly from a distribution with mean 4 and variance 9.

(a) Does $\mu^* = (x_1 + x_2 + x_3)/3$ or $\mu^{**} = (x_1 + x_2 + x_3)/4$ have the smaller MSE as an estimator of $\beta = 4$?

(b) Can you draw any general conclusion from this example? If so, what? If not, why not?

3 Suppose β^* is an unbiased estimator of β. Let $\beta^{**} = a\beta^*$ where a is some number. Find the value of a (in terms of β and $V\beta^*$) that minimizes the MSE of β^{**}. Why is this estimator not used more often? *Hint*: Use the result that MSE = var + bias^2.

*4 A generalization of the MSE criterion is to weight the squared bias and the variance differently, minimizing $(wB^2 + V)$, where w is a positive weighting factor. Suppose x has nonzero mean μ and variance σ^2 and we have a random sample of size T. It can be shown that the "minimum weighted MSE linear" estimator of μ is $\mu^* = \Sigma x/[T + (\sigma^2/w\mu^2)]$.

(a) Derive this result. *Hints*: Express your estimator as $\Sigma a_i x_i$, express x as $x_i = \mu + \varepsilon_i$, and notice that the normal equations are symmetric in the as and so can be solved via one equation by equating the as.

(b) Is the minimum MSE linear estimator smaller or larger in absolute value than the BLUE?

(c) Suppose as our criterion that we want to minimize the sum of the relative bias (bias of the estimator relative to the population mean) squared and the relative variance (variance of the estimator relative to the variance of the population). Express the resulting estimator as a "shrinking factor" times the BLUE.

E   Applications of Expected Values in Economic Theory

*1 Suppose there is an infinite number of stores, with prices distributed uniformly over the $1 to $2 interval.

(a) Calculate the expected minimum price found by randomly entering two stores. (The answer can be found in Stigler, 1961, p. 213). *Hint*: Find the distribution of the minimum price by finding the probability that a given p is the minimum price.

(b) Explain how to conduct a Monte Carlo study to verify your answer.

*2 Suppose we know that the overall price level P is distributed normally with mean μ and variance σ_p^2, and that p_k, the price of the kth good, deviates randomly from P by an amount d which is distributed normally with mean zero and variance σ_k^2. Given knowledge of p_k, the "rational expectations" value of P is the mean of the distribution of P conditional on p_k. Express this rational expectation in terms of p_k, μ, σ_k^2 and σ_p^2. *Hint*: The probability of getting a particular P, given p_k, is proportional to prob$(P) \times$ prob$(d = p_k - P)$, and so the conditional density is normal, and thus symmetric, so that the mean can be found by maximizing with respect to P. The answer can be found in Lucas (1973, p. 326).

F   OLS: Monte Carlo

1 Suppose you have programmed a computer to do the following:

    i.   Draw 20 x values from a distribution uniform between 2 and 8.
    ii.   Draw 20 z values from a standard normal distribution.
    iii.   Compute 20 w values as $5 + 2x + 9z$.
    iv.   Draw 20 ε values from a standard normal distribution.
    v.   Compute 20 y values as $1 + 4x + 3\varepsilon$.
    vi.   Regress y on x and save the R^2 value, q1, and the adjusted R^2 value aq1.
    vii. Regress y on x and w and save the R^2 value, s1, and the adjusted R^2 value as1.
    viii. Repeat this procedure from iv to get 3000 q, aq, s and as values.
    ix.   Compute the averages of these sets of 3000 values to get Q, AQ, S and AS, respectively.
(a) What should be the relative magnitudes of Q and S? Explain your reasoning.
(b) What should be the relative magnitudes of AQ and AS? Explain your reasoning.

2   Suppose you have programmed a computer to do the following:
    i.   Draw 50 x values from a distribution uniform between 3 and 12.
    ii.   Draw 50 z values from a standard normal distribution.
    iii.   Compute 50 w values as $4 - 3x + 8z$.
    iv.   Draw 50 ε values from a standard normal distribution.
    v.   Compute 50 y values as $2 + 3x + 4\varepsilon$.
    vi.   Regress y on x and save the x slope coefficient estimate b1.
    vii. Regress y on x and w and save the x slope coefficient bb1.
    viii. Repeat this procedure from iv to get 1000 b and bb values.
    ix.   Compute the averages of these sets of 1000 values to get B and BB, respectively.
    x.   Compute the variances of these sets of 1000 values to get VB and VBB, respectively.
(a) Should B or BB be closer to three?
(b) Should VB or VBB be closer to zero?

3   Suppose the classical linear regression model applies to the money demand function $m = \alpha + \beta y + \delta r + \varepsilon$ and you have 25 observations on income y and on the nominal interest rate r, which in your data are negatively correlated. You wish to compare the OLS β estimates including versus omitting the relevant explanatory variable r.
(a) Explain in detail how to do this with a Monte Carlo study.
(b) What results do you expect to get? Why?
(c) How would you expect your results to differ if y and r are positively correlated in your data?
(d) How would you expect your results to differ if y and r are uncorrelated in your data?

*4 Suppose $y = \beta x + \varepsilon$ and you have two observations on (y, x), namely $(6, 1)$ and $(7, 2)$. You estimate β by OLS and wish to do a bootstrap to estimate its variance. What estimate for the variance of β^{OLS} do you expect to get (your answer should be a specific number), and how does it compare to the usual OLS estimate of this variance? *Hint*: Don't forget the small-sample adjustment – see the technical notes to section 4.6.

5   Suppose the CLR model applies to $y = \alpha_0 + \alpha_1 x + \alpha_2 q + \alpha_3 w + \varepsilon$ where the observations on the explanatory variables are not orthogonal and you are concerned about estimating α_3. You wish to undertake a Monte Carlo study to examine the payoff of incorporating (true) extraneous information of the form $\alpha_1 + \alpha_2 = 1$.

(a) What is meant by "payoff" in this context?

(b) Explain in detail how you would conduct this study.

(c) What results do you expect to get?

(d) If "true" in parentheses above had been "false," how would your answer to part (c) differ?

G OLS: General

1 For observations on investment y and profits x of each of 100 firms, it is known that $y = \alpha + \beta x + \varepsilon$ and it is proposed to estimate α and β by OLS.

(a) Suppose every firm in the sample had the same profits. What, if any, problem would this create?

(b) If the distribution of profits over the firms were not normal, we would not be able to apply the CNLR model. True, false, or uncertain? Explain.

(c) If the conditional variance of investment (given profits) were not the same for all firms, we would be unable to rely on the CLR model to justify our estimates. True, false, or uncertain? Explain.

(d) If the CLR model is applicable, then we should use the OLS estimator of β because it is the BLUE. True, false, or uncertain? Explain.

2 If the errors in the CLR model are not normally distributed, although the OLS estimator is no longer BLUE, it is still unbiased. True, false, or uncertain?

3 Suppose the CLR model applies to $y = \alpha_0 + \alpha_1 x + \alpha_2 w + \varepsilon$. If the data are cross-sectional at a point in time and w does not vary in the cross-section, should you include w anyway to avoid bias in your estimate of α_1? Explain.

4 Suppose the CLR model applies to $y = \beta x + \varepsilon$. The slope coefficient in the regression of x on y is just the inverse of the slope from the regression of y on x. True, false, or uncertain? Explain.

5 Suppose you regress family weekly food expenditure (E) on family income (Y) and get a negative slope coefficient estimate. Omission of the explanatory variable family size (F) may have caused this unexpected sign. What would have to be true about F for this to be the case? Explain your reasoning. *Hint*: Write F as an approximate linear function of family income.

6 Suppose income $= \alpha + \beta(\text{experience}) + \delta(\text{education}) + \gamma(\text{sex}) + \theta(\text{age}) + \varepsilon$.

(a) What would you speculate the direction of the bias of the estimate of β to be if age were omitted from the regression?

(b) If the dummy for sex were omitted? Explain your reasoning.

7 Suppose the CNLR model applies to $y = \alpha + \beta x + \varepsilon$. Your sample has only positive x values, producing $\beta^{\text{OLS}} = 3$, which you are told is an overestimate. Is your intercept estimate more likely to be an overestimate or an underestimate, or are they equally likely? Explain your reasoning, and illustrate the common sense of your answer on a diagram showing the true regression line.

8 How would you interpret the estimated intercept resulting from a production-function regression of $\Delta \ln y$ on $\Delta \ln L$ and $\Delta \ln K$?

9 Consider applying OLS to a consumption function $C = \alpha + \beta Y$ and to the corresponding saving function $S = \gamma + \delta Y$ where for all observations $Y = C + S$.

(a) Show that $\delta^{\text{OLS}} = 1 - \beta^{\text{OLS}}$.

(b) The sum of squared residuals is the same for each regression. True, false, or uncertain? Explain.

(c) The R^2s are the same for each regression. True, false, or uncertain? Explain.

10 Suppose $y + \alpha + \beta(x + \delta)^{-1} + \varepsilon$. Suggest a search procedure, using OLS regression, to find the least squares estimates. *Hint*: Search over δ.

11 Suppose we have T observations from a CLR model $y = \alpha + \beta x + \varepsilon$. Let β^* result from regressing y on x and an intercept. Suppose we have extraneous information that the intercept α is zero. In this context, some have suggested using the "raw moment estimator" $\beta^{**} = \Sigma xy/\Sigma x^2$, or the "ratio estimator" $\beta^{***} = \Sigma y/\Sigma x$, or the "mean of the slopes" estimator $b^{****} = \Sigma(y/x)/T$ instead of β^*. Assuming that α is in fact zero:

(a) Find the expected value and variance of each of these three estimators.

(b) Which estimator would you choose? Why? *Hint*: Which one is BLUE?

12 Consider an estimate β^* of the slope of x, which results from regressing y on an intercept and x, and β^{**} which results from regressing y on an intercept, x and w. Explain in a single sentence for each the circumstances in which

(a) $\beta^* = \beta^{**}$.

(b) β^* tests significantly different from zero but β^{**} does not.

(c) β^{**} tests significantly different from zero but β^* does not.

13 Suppose the CLR model applies to $y = \beta x + \varepsilon$ and we have T observations. We wish to estimate the value of y at the sample mean of the x values. Compare the following two estimates: $\bar{y}$ and $\beta^{OLS}\bar{x}$.

14 As the sample size grows, R^2 should fall. True, false, or uncertain? Explain.

15 Suppose the CNLR model applies and you obtain the OLS result yhat $= 1.2 + 0.73x$ where the standard error for the slope estimate is 0.2. Because in this case the estimates are unbiased, the sampling distribution of the slope estimator is distributed around 0.73 with standard error 0.2. True, false or uncertain? Explain your reasoning.

H   OLS: Numerical Examples

1 Suppose the CLR model applies to $y = 3x + \varepsilon$ where ε takes values of -1, 0, and $+1$ with probabilities 1/4, 1/2, 1/4 respectively. Suppose you have a data set in which x takes on the values 0, 1, 2, 3, and 4. What are the mean and variance of the slope estimate from:

(a) Regressing y on a constant and x, and

(b) Regressing y on just x.

2 Suppose the CLR model applies to $y = \alpha + \beta x + \varepsilon$. The sample size is 25, $\sigma^2 = 9$, $\Sigma x = 5$, and $\Sigma x^2 = 10$. A researcher erroneously assumes that α is zero, estimating β by $\Sigma xy/\Sigma x^2$.

(a) What is the mean square error of this estimator?

(b) How small would α have to be to allow this researcher to claim that his estimator beats the usual estimator (i.e., OLS including an intercept) on the MSE criterion?

3 An article examining the allocation of corporate profits (P) between dividends (D) and retained earnings (R), where $P = R + D$ by definition, estimates the equation

$$D_t = \underline{\quad} P_t + \underline{\quad} D_{t-1} + \underline{\quad} P_{t-1} \qquad R^2 = \underline{\quad} d = \underline{\quad}$$

but does not report the results because the coefficient on P_{t-1} was insignificant. The data are re-analyzed, with dividends rather than retained earnings viewed as a residual, yielding

$$R_t = 0.891P_t + 0.654R_{t-1} - 0.622P_{t-1} \quad R^2 = 0.99 \; d = 2.23$$

$$(0.027) \quad (0.092) \quad (0.078)$$

    (a) Fill in four of the five blanks above and explain why you are unable to fill in the fifth blank.

    (b) Provide, with explanation, numbers for the standard errors of two of the three coefficient estimates in the first equation, and explain what information is required to calculate the third standard error.

*4 Suppose the CLR model applies to $y = 2 + 3x + \varepsilon$ with $\sigma^2 = 4$. A sample of size 10 yields $\Sigma x = 20$ and $\Sigma x^2 = 50$. What is the expected value of $(\beta^{OLS})'(\beta^{OLS})$? *Hint:* Express β^{OLS} as $\beta + (X'X)^{-1}X'\varepsilon$, and use what you know about the trace.

5 Suppose you have the following data from 100 observations on the CLR model $y = \alpha + \beta x + \varepsilon : \Sigma x = 200, \Sigma y = 100, \Sigma xy = 400, \Sigma x^2 = 500$, and $\Sigma y^2 = 10,300$. A number z is calculated as $2\alpha + 9\beta$. A number q is formed by throwing 10 true dice and adding the total number of spots appearing. A contest is being held to guess $W = z + q$ with contestants being rewarded (or penalized) according to the formula $P = 60 - (W - W^*)^2$ dollars where W^* is the contestant's guess.

    (a) What would your guess be if you wanted to make the expected value of your guess equal to the expected value of W?

    (b) What is the expected payoff of this guess?

    (c) What is your estimate of this expected payoff? *Hint:* $\Sigma \hat{y}^2 = (\beta^{OLS})'X'y$.

I Transforming Variables

1 Use the Ballentine to answer the following two questions.

    (a) In time series regression, we obtain the same regression coefficients when working on data from which linear time trends have been removed as when we keep the trends and include time, t, in the set of regressors. True, false, or uncertain? Explain. Note: *All* the data are to be detrended.

    (b) Suppose we replace the phrase "regression coefficients" above by "coefficient of determination." Would the new statement be true, false, or uncertain? Explain. *Hint:* The time trend is removed from w when w is replaced with the residuals from a regression of w on t.

2 Suppose the dependent variable, but not the independent variable, is expressed as deviations from its mean. What implications does this have for the bias of the OLS estimates?

3 Suppose you are regressing the logarithm of the current dollar value of a house ($\ln y$) on an intercept and distance from city center (x), using 1981 data. You have a new sample of 1985 data and you wish to investigate whether the coefficients have changed in value since 1981. You know that the overall increase in housing prices due to inflation since 1981 is 20%. If you do not scale the new data to express them in 1981 dollars, what will be the implication for the interpretation of your estimates?

4 Suppose your data produce the regression result $y = 5 + 2x$. Consider scaling the data to express them in a different base year dollar, by multiplying observations by 0.8.
   (a) If both y and x are scaled, what regression results would you obtain?
   (b) If y is scaled but x is not (because y is measured in dollars and x is measured in physical units, for example), what regression results would you obtain?
   (c) If x is scaled but y is not, what regression results would you obtain?
   (d) In part (c) suppose you perform a t test to test whether or not the slope coefficient is zero. Is this t statistic larger, smaller, or the same as the comparable t statistic calculated on unscaled data? Explain.

5 Suppose we have the regression results (standard errors in parentheses):

$$y = 300 + 6.0w \quad R^2 = 0.85$$

$$(25) \quad (1.1)$$

where $w_t = (x_t/x_{t-1})$. Suppose the regression is rerun with w expressed in percentages, so that now the regressor is $w^* = 100(x_t - x_{t-1})/x_{t-1}$. What results should be obtained?

6 Suppose you wish to estimate the βs in $\ln Y = \beta_1 + \beta_2 \ln W + \beta_3 Q + \varepsilon$. The results from regressing $\ln(Y/W)$ on $\ln W$ and Q are available.
   (a) How would you use these results to estimate the βs?
   (b) Their standard errors?

7 Suppose the CLR model applies to $y = \alpha + \beta x + \varepsilon$. A prankster multiplies all your x values by 3. If the old y were regressed on the new x, what can you say about the expected values of your estimates of α and β?

8 The classical linear regression model applies to $y = \alpha + \beta x + \varepsilon$ where ε is a random error with mean zero and variance 4. A prankster multiplies all your y values by 3.
   (a) Conditional on x, what is the variance of the new y? Explain your logic.
   (b) If the new y were regressed on the old x, what should be the expected values of your OLS estimates of α and β? Explain your logic.

J   OLS: Estimating Variances

1 If an extra explanatory variable is added to a regression, the estimate of σ^2 will remain the same or fall. True, false, or uncertain?

2 The estimator of the variance–covariance matrix of the OLS estimator becomes smaller when a relevant explanatory variable is omitted. True, false, or uncertain? Explain.

3 Suppose y is determined by x and w. The coefficient of x is estimated by b^* from a regression of y on x and by b^{**} from a regression of y on x and w. What, if anything, can you say about the relative magnitudes of the estimates of the variances of b^* and b^{**}?

4 Suppose the CLR model applies to $y = \alpha + \beta x + \delta w + \varepsilon$ and it is known that α, β and δ are all positive. Then the variance of $(\beta^{OLS} + \delta^{OLS})$ is greater than the variance of $(\beta^{OLS} - \delta^{OLS})$. True, false, or uncertain? Explain.

5 Suppose the CLR model applies to $y = \alpha + \beta x + \varepsilon$, with $\sigma^2 = 30$. A sample of size 10 yields $\Sigma x = 20$ and $\Sigma x^2 = 50$. You must produce an unbiased estimate θ^* of $\theta = \alpha + \beta$, for which you will be paid $[10 - (\theta^* - \theta)^2]$ dollars. What is your expected pay?

K OLS with Restrictions

1 Imposing a linear constraint on a regression will raise R^2 if the constraint is true and lower R^2 if it is false. True, false, or uncertain? Explain.

2 Suppose $y = \alpha + \beta x + \theta z + \delta w + \varepsilon$ where the CLR model assumptions hold. If you know that $\theta + \delta = 1$ and $\beta = 2\delta$, what regression would you run to produce your parameter estimates?

3 Suppose you have observations 3, 4 and 5 on a dependent variable y and corresponding observations 6, 7 and 8 on explanatory variable x and 7, 9, and 11 on explanatory variable w. Suppose you know that the intercept is zero and the sum of the two slope coefficients is 2. What are your estimates of the slope coefficients?

4 Suppose $\beta^{OLS} = (2, 1)'$, the diagonal elements of the estimated variance–covariance matrix are 3 and 2, respectively, and the off-diagonal elements are both ones. What is your estimate of β if you believe that $\beta_1 + \beta_2 = 4$? *Hint*: Use the matrix formula for restricted β^{OLS}.

5 Suppose the CLR model applies to $y = \alpha + \beta x + \delta w + \theta z + \varepsilon$.
   (a) Explain what regression to run to find the OLS estimates which incorporate the (true) information that $\beta = 2\delta$.
   (b) Will the R^2 from this regression be larger than, smaller than or equal to that of the unconstrained regression?
   (c) Will your estimate of θ remain unbiased?
   (d) Will the variance of the θ estimate be larger, smaller or unchanged as a result of incorporating this constraint? Explain intuitively.
   (e) If in fact $\beta \neq 2\delta$, in what way would your answers to parts (b), (c), and (d) above be different?

6 Suppose the CLR model is applicable to $y = \alpha + \beta x + \delta w + \varepsilon$ with $V(\varepsilon) = 5$. From the data, $\Sigma x^2 = 3$, $\Sigma w^2 = 2$, and $\Sigma xw = -1$, where observations are expressed as deviations about their means. Consider the restriction that $\beta + \delta = 1$. How much smaller is the variance of the restricted estimate of β than the variance of the unrestricted estimate of β? Explain fully how you obtained your answer.

7 Suppose we wish to estimate $y_t = \alpha + \beta_0 x_t + \beta_1 x_{t-1} + \beta_2 x_{t-2} + \beta_3 x_{t-3} + \varepsilon_t$ by assuming a polynomial distributed lag of order 2, so that $\beta_i = \delta_0 + \delta_1 i + \delta_2 i^2$ where i is the lag length.
   (a) What regression would we run to obtain estimates of the δs?
   (b) Suppose our estimates of δ_0, δ_1 and δ_2 are 4, 2, and -1, respectively. What are the estimates of the βs?
   (c) Suppose the estimated variance–covariance matrix for the δ estimates is the 3×3 matrix V. How would you estimate the 4×4 variance–covariance matrix of the β estimates? Be explicit.

8 Suppose you have the observations 0, 0, 4, 4 and 0, 4, 0, 4 on x and y, respectively, from the CLR model $y = \alpha + \beta x + \varepsilon$.
   (a) Graph these observations and draw in the OLS estimating line.
   (b) Draw in the OLS estimating line that incorporates the constraint that $\alpha = 0$.
   (c) Calculate the R^2s associated with both these estimating lines, using $R^2 = 1 - SSE/SST$.
   (d) Calculate these R^2s using $R^2 = SSR/SST$.
   (e) What is the lesson here?

L   Theoretical Results for Multivariate Regression

1   Estimation of the mean of a univariate population can be viewed as a special case of classical linear regression. Given a random sample of size T, namely $y_1, \ldots, y_T$ from a population with $Ey = \mu$ and $V(y) = \sigma^2$, we can write $y_t = \mu + \varepsilon_t$ or $y_t = \beta_0 + \varepsilon_t$ where $\beta_0 = \mu$. Express each of the following CLR concepts explicitly (i.e., algebraically) for this special case: X, $X'X$, $(X'X)^{-1}$, $X'y$, β^{OLS}, $\beta^{OLS} - \beta = (X'X)^{-1}X'\varepsilon$, $V(\beta^{OLS})$. Which two of these could you have guessed? Why?

*2   Suppose $y = X\beta + \varepsilon$ is broken into $y = X_1\beta_1 + X_2\beta_2 + \varepsilon$. By minimizing the sum of squared errors with respect to β_1 and β_2 simultaneously, show that $\beta_1^{OLS} = (X_1'M_2X_1)^{-1}X_1'M_2y$ where $M_2 = I - X_2(X_2'X_2)^{-1}X_2'$.

3   Suppose the CLR model applies to $y = X\beta + \varepsilon$ and we estimate β by minimizing the sum of squared errors subject to the *erroneous* restriction that $R\beta = r$.
   (a) Find the bias of this estimator.
   (b) Show that the variance–covariance matrix of this estimator is smaller than that of the unrestricted OLS estimator.

4   Suppose the CLR model is applicable to $Y = X\beta + \varepsilon$ and the J linear constraints $R\beta = r$ are known to hold. Find an unbiased estimator for σ^2 that incorporates the constraints. *Hint*: Guess and check for unbiasedness.

*5   Suppose you have data on the CLR model $y = X\beta + \varepsilon$ (which includes an intercept), and you are asked to forecast y_0 given a row vector x_0 of observations on the explanatory variables (with first element unity).
   (a) Explain in words how you would show that $x_0\beta^{OLS}$ is the BLUE of $x_0\beta$.
   (b) What is your forecast error if y_0 is forecast by $x_0\beta^{OLS}$?
   (c) What is the variance of this forecast error?
   (d) By minimizing this variance subject to the first element unity constraint, show that the forecast variance is minimized when x_0 is the average of the x values in the data. *Hint*: Use matrix terminology.

6   Suppose the CLR model applies to $y = X\beta + \varepsilon$ and you have decided to estimate β by a constant θ times β^{OLS}. Further, you wish to choose θ so that it minimizes the sum of the MSEs of the elements of $\theta\beta^{OLS}$.
   (a) Explain why this value of θ is the one that minimizes $(\theta - 1)^2\beta'\beta + \theta^2\sigma^2 tr(X'X)^{-1}$.
   (b) Find the optimal value of θ.
   (c) Why might this estimator be referred to as a "shrinkage" estimator?
   (d) Why is this estimator not used more often?

7   Suppose the CLR assumptions apply to $y = X\beta + \varepsilon$ and that we are interested in finding the BLUE of $\theta = c'\beta$ where c is a vector of known constants. Call our proposed BLUE $\theta^* = a'y$ where a is to be determined.
   (a) What condition must hold for θ^* to be unbiased?
   (b) What is the variance of θ^*?
   (c) By minimizing the variance of θ^* subject to the constraint in (a), show that the BLUE of θ is $c'\beta^{OLS}$.
   (d) How would you use this result to claim that β^{OLS} is the BLUE of β?
   (e) Of what relevance is this result to forecasting?

*8   Suppose $y = X_1\beta_1 + X_2\beta_2 + \varepsilon$ and the data are such that $X_2'y = 0$. Then a regression of y on X_1 and X_2 will estimate β_2 by the zero vector. T, F or uncertain? Explain.

*9   Consider estimating σ^2 in the CLNR model by a constant θ times *SSE*. Find the value of θ that minimizes the MSE of this estimator. *Hint*: Recall that *SSE* is distributed as σ^2 times a chi-square with $(T - K)$ degrees of freedom, and that the mean and variance of a chi-square are equal to its degree of freedom and twice its degrees of freedom, respectively.

M   Pooling Data and Missing Observations

1   Suppose $y = X\beta + \varepsilon$ and you have two data sets, subscripted 1 and 2.
   (a) Show that the OLS estimate using all of the data is a "matrix" weighted average of the OLS estimates that result from using the data sets separately. *Hint*: Use a partitioned matrix approach.
   (b) Suppose there is only one regressor, and no intercept. What are the weights from part (a) for this case, and why do they make sense?
2   Suppose the CLR model applies to $Y = X\beta + \varepsilon$ and data are measured as deviations about their means.
   (a) Suppose X_2, the last N observations on X, is missing, and is replaced by its mean, a zero vector. Does β^{OLS} remain unbiased?
   (b) Suppose Y_2, a subset of the data on Y, is missing, and is replaced by its mean, a zero vector. Does β^{OLS} remain unbiased?
3   Researcher A runs an OLS regression on his data to estimate α and β as 4 and 4, with estimated variances 12 and 9, respectively, estimated covariance -6, and estimated error variance 3. Researcher B runs an OLS regression on her data to estimate α and β as 4 and 2, with estimated variances 6 and 6, respectively, estimated covariance -2, and estimated error variance 2. What estimates of α and β would have been obtained if the data had been pooled? *Hint*: Get the "pooled" formula first.
*4   Suppose the CLR model applies to $Y = X\beta + \varepsilon$ but that Y_2, a subset of the data on Y, is missing. Consider addressing this "missing data" problem by obtaining $Y_2^* = X_2\beta^{OLS}$ where β^{OLS} results from regressing Y_1 on the corresponding X observations X_1, and then doing a full regression using Y_2^* for the missing data. Show that the resulting estimate of β is identical to β^{OLS}. *Hint*: Exploit the answer to M(1a).

N   Multicollinearity

1   Explain in what sense dropping a variable can be a "solution" for multicollinearity.
2   Since x^2 is an exact function of x, we will be faced with exact multicollinearity if we attempt to use both x and x^2 as regressors. True, false, or uncertain? Explain.
3   If the regressors are correlated, although OLS estimates remain unbiased, t statistics tend to be too small. True, false or uncertain? Explain. *Hint*: Be sure to specify what is meant by "too" small.
4   In the CLR model, multicollinearity leads to bias, not in the estimation of the regression coefficients themselves, but rather in the estimation of their variances. True, false, or uncertain? Explain.
5   The value of R^2 in a multiple regression cannot be high if all the estimates of the regression slopes are shown to be insignificantly different from zero on the basis of t tests of significance, since in that case most of the variation in the regressand must be unexplained and hence the value of R^2 must be low. True, false, or uncertain? Explain.
6   Suppose the CLR model applies to $y = \alpha + \beta x + \delta w + \varepsilon$. Most samples are such

that x and w are correlated, but by luck you observe a sample in which they are uncorrelated. You regress y on x and an intercept, producing β^*.

(a) Is β^* unbiased?

(b) Is your estimate of the variance of β^* unbiased?

7   Comment on the following proposal for reducing multicollinearity. "Suppose that $y = \beta_0 + \beta_1 x_1 + \beta_2 x_2 + \varepsilon$ where x_1 and x_2 are highly correlated. Regress x_2 on x_1 obtaining residuals x_2^*. Then regress y on x_1 and x_2^* together. We are guaranteed that x_1 is uncorrelated with x_2^*; this reduction in multicollinearity should yield estimates of the β_i with smaller variances."

8   In the relationship $y = \beta_1 + \beta_2 x + \beta_3 z + \beta_4 w + \beta_5 (x - z) + \varepsilon$ the information implicit in the last regressor improves the estimation of the other βs, in comparison to what would be the case without this regressor. True, false, or uncertain? Explain.

9   Suppose you have annual data on C (average grams of coffee consumed per capita), YD (real per capita disposable income), PC (price index for coffee), PT (price index for tea), and POP (population in millions). You regress C on $\ln YD$, PC, PT, and POP, obtaining a reasonable R^2 but no significant t statistics. What do you suspect is the problem here, and how would you remedy it?

10   Suppose that the CLR model is applicable to $y = \alpha x + \beta w + \varepsilon$. Let α^{OLS} and β^{OLS} denote the OLS estimates from regressing y on x and w together, and α^* the estimate of α from regressing y on x alone. It can be shown that $MSE(\alpha^*) \leqslant MSE(\alpha^{OLS})$ provided $\beta^2 \leqslant V(\beta^{OLS})$.

(a)   Discuss/improve upon the following proposal. Since in the presence of high multicollinearity it is quite possible that $\beta^2 \leqslant V(\beta^{OLS})$, under the MSE criterion we should estimate α with α^* rather than α^{OLS}.

*(b)   Derive the condition given above. *Hint*: Use regular algebra, not matrix algebra.

*11   Consider the special case $y = \beta x + \varepsilon$, where the variance of ε is σ^2.

(a) What is the formula for the ridge estimator $\beta^* = (X'X + kI)^{-1} X'Y$?

(b) The ridge estimator is viewed as "shrinking" the OLS vector towards the zero vector. For this special case, what is the "shrinking factor"?

(c) Call the shrinking factor θ. By finding the "optimal" value for θ, find the "optimal" value for k for this special case.

(d) What problem do you see in using this optimal value of k in actual applications?

12   Assume the CLR model $Y = X\beta + \varepsilon$. Consider $\beta^* = (X'X + kI)^{-1} X'Y$, where $0 \leqslant k \leqslant \infty$, the "ridge" estimator proposed for high multicollinearity.

*(a)   Show that $V(\beta^*)$ is "smaller" than $V(\beta^{OLS})$. *Hint*: If $A - B$ is nnd, then so is $B^{-1} - A^{-1}$. *Second hint*: Multiply out the relevant $B^{-1} - A^{-1}$.

(b)   Does this mean that β^{OLS} is not BLUE in cases of high multicollinearity? Explain.

13   Suppose the CLR model applies to $Y = X\beta + \varepsilon$ but we have perfect multicollinearity. Suppose, however, that we wish to estimate $a'\beta$ rather than β, where $a = X'X\lambda$ with λ a column vector, so that a is a vector which is a linear combination of the columns of $X'X$.

(a) Show that although we cannot estimate β, we can estimate $a'\beta$.

(b) Show that your estimator is unbiased and find its variance–covariance matrix.

O   Dummy Variables: Interpretation

1 Suppose we have estimated $y = 10 + 2x + 3D$ where y is earnings, x is experience and D is zero for females and one for males.
   (a) If we were to rerun this regression with the dummy redefined as one for females and two for males, what results would we get?
   (b) If it were defined as minus one for females and plus one for males, what results would we get?

2 Suppose we have obtained the following regression results:

$$\hat{y} = 10 + 5x + 4\text{sex} + 3\text{region} + 2\text{sexregion}$$

   where sex is one for males and zero for females, region is one for north and zero otherwise (south) and sexregion is the product of sex and region. What coefficient estimates would we get if we regressed y on an intercept, x, NM, NF and SF, where NM is one for northern males, zero otherwise, NF is one for northern females, zero otherwise, and SF is one for southern females, zero otherwise?

3 A friend has added regional dummies to a regression, including dummies for all regions and regressing using a no intercept option. Using t tests, each dummy coefficient estimate tests significantly different from zero, so she concludes that region is important.
   (a) Why would she have used a no intercept option when regressing?
   (b) Has she used an appropriate means of testing whether region is important? If not, how would you have tested?

4 Suppose $y = \alpha + \beta x + \delta D + \varepsilon$ where D is a dummy for sex. Suppose we know that the fraction of males in the sample is twice the fraction of males in the population. What modification, if any, would you suggest?

5 Suppose you are regressing money on income, the interest rate, and a set of quarterly dummies, where the first three variables are expressed in natural logarithms. Because the economy is growing, the seasonal influence should be growing. What, if anything, should be done to capture this?

6 Suppose a sample of adults is classified into groups 1, 2 and 3 on the basis of whether their education stopped in (or at the end of) elementary school, high school, or university, respectively. The relationship $y = \beta_1 + \beta_2 D_2 + \beta_3 D_3 + \varepsilon$ is specified, where y is income, $D_i = 1$ for those in group i and zero for all others.
   (a) In terms of the parameters of the model, what is the expected income of those whose education stopped in university?
   (b) In terms of the parameters of the model, what is the null hypothesis that going on to university after high school makes no contribution to adult income?
   (c) Can the specified model be expressed in a simpler, equivalent form $y = \alpha_0 + \alpha_1 x + \varepsilon$, where x is years of education completed? Explain.
   (d) Suppose that the dummy variables had been defined as $D_4 = 1$ if attended high school, zero otherwise; $D_5 = 1$ if attended university, zero otherwise and $y = \alpha_3 + \alpha_4 D_4 + \alpha_5 D_5 + \varepsilon$ was estimated. Answer parts (a) and (b) above for this case.

7 Suppose two researchers, with the same data, have run similar regressions

$$y = \alpha_0 + \alpha_1 x + \alpha_2 \text{sex} + \alpha_3 \text{region} + \alpha_4 \text{sexregion}, \text{ for researcher A, and}$$
$$y = \beta_0 + \beta_1 x + \beta_2 \text{sex} + \beta_3 \text{region} + \beta_4 \text{sexregion}, \text{ for researcher B,}$$

where sexregion is an interaction dummy, the product of the sex and region dummies. Both researchers have defined sex as one for males and zero for females, but researcher A has defined region as one for north and zero for south whereas researcher B has defined it the other way – zero for north and one for south. Researcher A gets an insignificant t value on the sex coefficient, but researcher B does not.

(a) In terms of the interpretation of the model, what hypothesis is A implicitly testing when looking at the significance of his t value?

(b) In terms of the interpretation of the model, what hypothesis is B implicitly testing when looking at the significance of her t value?

(c) In terms of the parameters of her model, what null hypothesis would B have to test in order to produce a test of A's hypothesis?

(d) What is the lesson here?

8 Suppose you have specified $C = \alpha + \beta Y + \delta P + \theta N + \eta H + \varepsilon$, where C is number of long-distance calls, Y is per capita income, P is an index of the price of calling long distance relative to the price of alternative means of communication. N is number of phones in existence, and $H = 1$ for statutory holidays, zero otherwise. You have daily data extending over several years.

(a) Explain how to alter this specification to recognize that most businesses close on weekends.

(b) If there are more phones, more calls should be made on holidays. Is this incorporated in your specification? If so, how? If not, how would you do it?

9 Suppose the CLR model applies to $\ln y = \alpha + \beta K + \delta D + \varepsilon$ where D is a dummy for sex.

(a) Verify that 100β can be interpreted as the $\%\Delta y$ due to ΔK.

(b) Show that $\theta = 100(e^{\delta} - 1)$ is the $\%\Delta y$ due to sex. (The answer can be found in Halvorsen and Palmquist, 1980, p. 474.)

(c) Explain why putting δ^{OLS} into the expression in part (b) creates a biased estimate of θ.

*(d) If ε is distributed normally, show explicitly how to reduce this bias. *Hint*: If $\varepsilon \sim N(\mu, \sigma^2)$ then $\exp(\varepsilon) \sim$ log-normally with mean $\exp(\mu + 0.5\sigma^2)$. (The answer is in Kennedy, 1981a, p. 802.)

*(e) If ε is not distributed normally, show explicitly how to reduce this bias. *Hint*: You need to use a Taylor series expansion.

10 Advise the editor what to do with this dispute.

Comment by B: "In a recent issue of this journal A published a paper in which he reported a regression $y = 4 + 5x + 2D$ where y is expenditure, x is income and D is zero for males and one for females. The sample average x value is reported as higher for females (xf) than for males (xm) but the sample average y value is reported as higher for males. This is inconsistent with the results."

Reply by A: "B's logic is incorrect. The average female expenditure is $yf = 6 + 5xf + ef$, and the average male expenditure is $ym = 4 + 5xm + em$, where ef (em) is the average female (male) residual. Their difference is $2 + 5(xf - xm) + ef - em$. Although OLS causes the average residual to be zero, so that $ef + em = 0$, the difference between ef and em could be sufficiently negative to make $yf - ym$ negative. There is no inconsistency in the results."

P   Dummy Variables: Estimation

1 Suppose $y = \beta_0 + \beta_1 D + \varepsilon$ where D is a dummy for sex (male = 1). The average y value for the 20 males is 3, and for the 30 females is 2, and you know that ε is distributed as $N(0, 10)$.
   (a) What are the OLS estimates of the βs?
   (b) What is the value of the test statistic for testing $3\beta_0 + 2\beta_1 = 3$?
   (c) How is this statistic distributed?
2 Suppose $y = \beta_0 + \beta_1 D + \varepsilon$ where $D = 0$ for the first 20 observations, $D = 1$ for the 25 remaining observations, and the variance of ε is 100.
   (a) Interpreting this regression as a way of calculating the means of the two sets of observations, what are your *a priori* guesses of the variance of β_0^{OLS} and the variance of $\beta_0^{OLS} + \beta_1^{OLS}$?
   (b) Verify your answer by using the $\sigma^2(X'X)^{-1}$ formula.
   (c) Further verify by using the relevant matrix formula to calculate the variance of the predicted y when $D = 1$.
3 Consider the regression results (standard errors in parentheses)

$$y = 3.0x + 4.0DM + 10.0DF$$
$$(1.1) \quad (1.0) \quad \quad (2.0)$$

where DM and DF are dummies for males and females, respectively. The covariance between the estimates of the coefficients on x and DM is 0.8, on x and DF is 0.6, and on DM and DF is 0.5. What would be the t statistic on DM if the regression were run including an intercept and excluding DF?
4 Suppose $\ln y = \alpha + \beta \ln x + \varepsilon$.
   (a) Show that if the x data are scaled by multiplying each observation by, say, 100, the same estimate of the coefficient β (the elasticity) results.
   (b) Now suppose there is a slope dummy in this relationship, taking the value zero for, say, the first half of the observations, and the value $\ln x$ for the remaining observations. Explain why scaling the x data in this context will change the β estimate, and suggest a means of avoiding this problem. (The answer is in Giordano and Veall, 1989, p. 95.)

Q   Dummy Variables: Hypothesis Testing

1 Suppose that demand for your product is a linear function of income, relative price, and the quarter of the year. Explain in detail exactly how you would test the hypothesis that *ceteris paribus* the demand for your product is identical in spring, summer and fall.
2 Suppose x and y are iid normal variables except that they may have different means. We have 6 observations on x and 10 observations on y. Explain how to use regression results to test the null hypothesis that x and y have the same mean.
3 You have run the regression $Y = X\beta + \varepsilon$ with the CLR model in effect. A critic claims that by omitting one observation the coefficient estimates change dramatically, but you feel that these coefficient differences are not significant. Explain how to defend your view with a statistical test.

4 Suppose the amount per week a student spends on alcohol can be explained (linearly) by income, age, sex, and whether the student is an undergraduate, an MA student or a PhD student. You feel certain that the impact of sex is wholly on the intercept and the impact of level of studies is wholly on the slope of income. Given a sample of size 75, explain in detail how you would test whether or not level of studies has any effect.

5 Suppose $S = \alpha + \beta Ed + \phi IQ + \eta Ex + \lambda Sex + \delta DF + \theta DE + \varepsilon$ where S is salary, Ed is years of education, IQ is IQ level, Ex is years of on-the-job experience, Sex is one for males and zero for females, DF is one for French-only speakers and zero otherwise, DE is one for English-only speakers and zero otherwise. Given a sample of N individuals who speak only French, only English or are bilingual:

(a) Explain how you would test for discrimination against females (in the sense that *ceteris paribus* females earn less than males).

(b) Explain how you would measure the payoff to someone of becoming bilingual given that his or her mother tongue is (i) French, (ii) English.

(c) Explain how you would test the hypothesis that the two payoffs of the preceding question are equal.

(d) Explain how you would test the hypothesis that a French-only male earns as much as an English-only female.

(e) Explain how you would test if the influence of on-the-job experience is greater for males than for females.

6 Suppose you are estimating the demand for new automobiles, with quarterly data, as a linear function of income, a price index for new autos (inclusive of tax), and a set of quarterly dummies. Suppose that on January 1, in the middle of your data set, the government announced that on April 1 of that year the sales tax on new autos would increase. You believe that as a result of this many people who would have bought a new car in the second quarter instead bought it in the first quarter.

(a) Explain how to structure a dummy variable to capture this "expenditure switching" hypothesis.

(b) Explain how you would test this hypothesis, against the alternative that although expenditure was higher than normal in the first quarter, and lower than normal in the second, the changes were unequal.

7 Suppose household demand for gasoline (G) is thought to be a linear function of household income (Y) but that the intercept depends on region, namely Maritime, Quebec, Ontario, and the West. Researcher A regresses G on an intercept, Y and dummy variables for the Maritimes, Ontario and the West. Researcher B regresses G on Y and dummies for all regions.

(a) How would you estimate the difference between the intercepts for Quebec and Ontario using (i) A's results and (ii) B's results? Which estimated difference would you expect to be larger (or would you expect them to be the same) and why?

(b) How would you test the hypothesis that the intercepts for Quebec and Ontario are the same using (i) A's results and (ii) B's results? Be explicit.

(c) Suppose that researcher C believes that the intercept for Quebec is identical to that of Ontario but that the slope for Quebec differs from the common slope of the other regions. Explain how C would estimate to incorporate these beliefs.

(d) Suppose that researcher D believes that each region has a unique slope and a unique intercept. Explain in detail how D would test the belief of C.

8 Suppose $y = \alpha + \beta x + \varepsilon$ and your 47 observations are divided into three groups: those

related to the lowest five x values, those related to the highest five x values, and the remaining 37 observations. The "rainbow" test for specification uses the middle 37 observations to estimate this relationship and then tests for whether or not the remaining observations lie within their forecast confidence intervals. Explain in detail the easiest way to do this test.

9 You have data on exam score S, an intelligence measure IQ, a dummy D for gender, study time ST and a categorical variable CAT that takes the value 1 for "I hate this course," 2 for "I don't like this course," 3 for "I am indifferent to this course," 4 for "I like this course" and 5 for "I love this course." You regress S on IQ, D, ST and CAT. A friend points out to you that you are imposing a special set of restrictions, namely that the influence of loving the course is exactly five times the influence of hating the course, five-thirds the influence of being indifferent to the course, etc. Explain what regressions to run to get the restricted and unrestricted sums of squared errors, and find the degrees of freedom for the appropriate F test.

R   Dummy Variables: Modeling Structural Breaks

1 Suppose you believe that the relationship between x and y changes at the known value x^* and can be represented by two linear segments that intersect at x^*, and thus is continuous.
  (a) How would you estimate this relationship?
  (b) How would you test the hypothesis of continuity?

2 Suppose we have data for 1950–80, and we know that a change took place in early 1964 that affected the intercept. A dummy variable DD is structured with zeroes for years prior to 1964, one in 1964, two in 1965, three in 1966, and four for all remaining years.
  (a) Interpret the meaning of this setup as contrasted with a traditional dummy variable equal to zero prior to 1964 and one thereafter. Of what is the coefficient of DD a measure?
  (b) In the context of this specification, if we want the coefficient of DD to measure the difference between the intercepts before 1964 and after 1966, how should we define DD?

*3 Suppose the CLR model applies to $y = \alpha + \beta x + \varepsilon$ and you have annual data from 1956 to 1976. In 1965 an institutional change occurred which changed the intercept, but the intercept changed over a five-year transition period rather than abruptly.
  (a) Explain how to use traditional dummy variables to model this. How many parameters are you estimating?
  (b) Assume that the value of the intercept during the transition period can be modeled as a cubic function of the time since the institutional change (i.e., where 1965 = 0). How many parameters are you estimating now?
  (c) Explain how to estimate. *Hint*: Structure a special explanatory variable for each of the new parameters.
The answer is in Wilton (1975, p. 423).

S   Maximum Likelihood: General Principles

1   Comment on the following: The method of least squares does not require an assumption about the distribution of the error, whereas maximum likelihood does; thus, OLS estimates are preferred to MLEs.

2   Suppose you have annual data from 1950 to 1984 on a CNLR relationship which sometime during 1964–9 switched from $Y = \beta_0 + \beta_1 X$ to $Y = \alpha_0 + \alpha_1 X$. You wish to estimate when the switch occurred. An adviser suggests using a maximum likelihood approach in which you choose the switching point by finding the maximum of the relevant maximum likelihoods. Explain how you would do this, and how you would then estimate the parameters.

3   Suppose that an IQ test score is the sum of a true IQ (distributed normally in the population with mean 100 and variance 400) and an independent testing error (distributed normally with mean 0 and variance 40). What is your best guess of the true IQ of someone who scores 140 on the test?

4   Heights are normally distributed with means 70 inches (males) and 64 inches (females) and common variance 6 inches. Is it more likely that a sample has been drawn from the male population if (i) the sample consists of a single person with height 70 inches, or (ii) the sample consists of six persons with average height 68 inches? Explain your reasoning.

5   Suppose that $y = \alpha + \beta x + \varepsilon$ where the εs are iid with pdf $f(\varepsilon) = \lambda \varepsilon^{-(\lambda+1)}$ where $\lambda > 2$ and $1 \leqslant \varepsilon \leqslant \infty$.
   (a) Are the OLS estimators of α and β BLUE?
   (b) Would prior knowledge of λ help in estimating α and β? Why or why not?
   (c) Would prior knowledge of λ be of help in estimating the variance of the OLS estimates of α and β? Explain how or why not.
   (d) For λ unknown, explain what you would do to estimate α, β and λ.

6   Suppose $w \sim N(\mu, \sigma^2)$. Use the change of variable technique to find the density function of $Q = a + bw$.

*7   Suppose a $K \times 1$ observation vector x from group i comes from $N(\mu_i, \Sigma)$, where $i = 1, 2$. Note that Σ has no i subscript. It makes sense to assign an observation to group i if it is "more likely" to have come from that group.
   (a) Assuming equal prior probabilities and equal misclassification costs, show that when formalized this gives rise to the linear discriminant rule, namely classify x to group 1 if $(\mu_1 - \mu_2)'\Sigma^{-1}x > (1/2)(\mu_1 - \mu_2)'\Sigma^{-1}(\mu_1 + \mu_2)$. *Hint*: Exploit the formula for the *pdf* of a multivariate normal distribution.
   (b) How would this have to be modified if the prior probabilities were unequal and the misclassification costs were unequal?

*8   The information matrix, $-E[\partial^2 \ln L/\partial\theta^2]$ can be shown to equal $E[(\partial \ln L/\partial\theta)(\partial \ln L/\partial\theta)']$, a result that is frequently exploited when calculating the Cramer–Rao lower bound. Verify this result for T random observations from $N(\mu, 1)$.

9   Suppose you wish to generate observations x from the distribution $f(x) = 3e^{-3x}$ for $0 \leqslant x$. Explain how to do so given a computer which can generate observations w distributed uniformly between zero and one. *Hint*: Exploit the change-of-variable theorem.

10   Suppose x is distributed uniformly between zero and one. For θ positive, what is the *pdf* of $y = -(1/\theta)\ln x$?

T   Maximum Likelihood: Examples

1   Suppose we have T observations on a random variable x which is distributed normally with mean μ and variance σ^2.
   (a) What is the MLE of μ?
   (b) Find the variance of this MLE by finding the Cramer–Rao lower bound.

2   Suppose you wish to estimate the proportion α of defective widgets coming off a production line and to this end draw a random sample of size T, observing N defectives.
   (a) Find the MLE of α.
   (b) Show that the Cramer–Rao lower bound gives the traditional formula for the variance of this estimator.

3   Suppose x is a random variable with $pdf\ f(x) = k\, e^{-kx}$ for $x \geq 0$. Given a sample of size N, find the MLE of k and use the Cramer–Rao lower bound to find the variance of this estimator.

4   Suppose income y is distributed as a Pareto distribution: $f(y) = \alpha y^{-(\alpha+1)}$ for $1 \leq y$, with $\alpha > 1$. Your sample of size N is drawn from the population of incomes greater than or equal to $\$9,000$.
   (a) What is the MLE of α? *Hint*: The density must be adjusted.
   (b) What is the variance of the MLE of α?
   (c) Suppose you believe that the mean of the Pareto distribution out of which you draw an observation is affected linearly by a variable w. Given the w observation corresponding to each x observation, explain how you would estimate the parameters of this linear relationship. *Hint*: Find the mean of this Pareto distribution.

5   Suppose you have 100 observations drawn from a population of incomes following the Pareto distribution $f(y) = \alpha y^{-(\alpha+1)}$ for $y \geq 1$ and $\alpha > 1$ but that your sample was actually drawn so that income was greater than or equal to $\$9,000$ i.e., you are drawing your observations out of a truncated distribution. The average of the natural logs of your income observations is 9.62 and $\ln 9000 = 9.10$.
   (a) What is the MLE of α?
   (b) Test the hypothesis that $\alpha = 2$ against the alternative $\alpha < 2$.

6   Consider the Poisson distribution

$$f(n) = e^{-\lambda}\lambda^n/n!$$

where n is the number of oil spills at a well and you have observations on N wells. Unfortunately, you are missing the data on wells with no oil spills. What is the likelihood you would maximize to find the MLE of λ?

7   Suppose T observations on x are drawn randomly from a Poisson distribution: $f(x) = \lambda^x e^{-\lambda}/(x!)$. The mean and also the variance equal λ.
   (a) Find the MLE of λ.
   (b) Find the asymptotic variance of this MLE by finding the Cramer–Rao lower bound.

8   Suppose that $y = \alpha + \beta x + \varepsilon$ where the εs are iid with the double exponential *pdf* $f(\varepsilon) = [2\theta e^{|\varepsilon/\theta|}]^{-1}$. Show that the MLEs of α and β result from minimizing the sum of the absolute values of the errors rather than the sum of the squares of the errors.

9   Suppose x is a random variable with $pdf\ f(x) = \lambda x^{\lambda-1}$ for $0 \leq x \leq 1$ and zero other-

wise, where λ is positive. Suppose we have drawn a sample of size T, denoted by $x_1, x_2, \ldots, x_T$.

(a) Find the expected value of x, denoted by μ, and the variance of x, $V(x)$.

(b) Find the MLE of λ, denoted by λ^{MLE}.

(c) Using the fact that the MLE of a nonlinear function is the nonlinear function of the MLE, find the MLE of μ, denoted by μ^{MLE}.

(d) Find the asymptotic variance of λ^{MLE} by using the Cramer–Rao lower bound.

(e) Find the asymptotic variance of μ^{MLE}.

(f) Find the expected value and variance of the sample mean.

(g) Which has the smaller asymptotic variance, the sample mean or μ^{MLE}?

(h) Which estimator, the sample mean or μ^{MLE}, do you prefer? Why?

10 Suppose x and y are random variables taking on values of zero or one, with probability distribution defined by

$$
\begin{aligned}
p(x = 1) &= \alpha \\
p(y = 1|x) &= e^{\beta x}/(1 + e^{\beta x})
\end{aligned}
$$

(a) Given a random sample of size N on (y,x), find the MLE of α and β.

(b) Suppose that in your sample of the observations with $x = 1$, half have $y = 1$. What is your estimated prob$(y = 1|x = 1)$?

11 Subjects spin a special roulette wheel out of your sight. If the wheel stops on blue they are to answer yes or no to the question "Do you cheat on your taxes?" If it stops on green they are to answer yes, and if it stops on red they are to answer no.

(a) Explain how you would estimate the probability that an individual cheats.

(b) Suppose you know the subjects' income levels and believe that the probability of cheating on taxes is a function of gender and income level. Explain how you would estimate the parameters of this relationship.

*12 Suppose we have the N-equation simultaneous equation model $Y\Gamma + XB = E$ where the contemporaneous covariance matrix of the errors is Φ. Then for a single time period, period t, we have

$$
f(\varepsilon_t) = (2\pi)^{-N/2}(\det\Phi)^{-1/2}\exp\{-\varepsilon_t'\Phi^{-1}\varepsilon_t/2\}
$$

where ε_t is the tth row of E expressed as a vector. What is the log-likelihood for the entire sample, size T, needed to calculate the FIML estimates? *Hint*: Express $\varepsilon_t = \Gamma'y_t + B'x_t$ where y_t and x_t are the tth rows of Y and X expressed as vectors. Don't forget the Jacobian!

13 Suppose you wish to estimate

$$
y^\delta = \alpha + \beta x + \varepsilon
$$

where ε is distributed $N(0, \sigma^2)$. What is the log-likelihood function you would maximize to create your estimates of α, β, δ and σ^2?

*14 (a) Suppose that $y = \alpha + \beta x + \varepsilon$ and that $\varepsilon_t = \rho\varepsilon_{t-1} + u_t$, where the *us* are iid $N(0,\sigma^2)$. Given data on x and y, what is the likelihood function? *Hint*: Find the relationship between the *ys* and the *us* through the Prais–Winsten transformation matrix, and then make use of the (multivariate) change-of-variable theorem. (The answer is in Beach and MacKinnon, 1978a, p. 52).

(b) Given data on x and y, find the likelihood function for $(y^\lambda - 1)/\lambda = \alpha + \beta x + \varepsilon$ (i.e., a Box–Cox transformation) where the εs are iid $N(0, \sigma^2)$.

(c) Suppose that $(y^\lambda - 1)/\lambda = \alpha + \beta x + \varepsilon$ *and* that $\varepsilon_t = \rho \varepsilon_{t-1} + u_t$ where the us are iid $N(0, \sigma^2)$. Given data on x and y, what is the likelihood function?

(d) Explain how in this context you would test for linearity assuming (i) spherical errors, and (ii) autocorrelated errors. (Answer to all parts are in Savin and White, 1978, p. 1.)

15 Suppose, following Hausman et al. (1984, p. 909), that the Poisson distribution captures the distribution of patents granted in a year, so that if P is the number of patents granted then $f(P) = \theta^P e^{-\theta}/(P!)$.

*(a) Show that $EP = \theta$.

(b) Suppose you believe that $EP = \exp(\alpha + \beta x)$, where x is expenditure on R&D. Given T observations on P and x, find the log-likelihood function needed to calculate the MLE estimates of α and β.

U Bayesian: General

1 Suppose the mean β^* of your posterior distribution is your point estimate of β. This estimate is calculated by a formula that could conceptually be recalculated for repeated samples, so that the repeated sample properties of β^* could be examined even though it results from a Bayesian analysis. For the CNLR model, compare the sampling distribution properties of β^* with those of β^{OLS}, for both large and small samples, for the case of an informative prior.

2 Suppose your posterior distribution of a parameter β is proportional to β for $0 \le \beta \le 2$ and zero otherwise. Given the loss function $(\beta - \beta^*)^2$, what number would you choose as your point estimate β^*?

3 Your posterior distribution for β is given by 2β, where $0 \le \beta \le 1$. Let β^* denote an estimate of β. Suppose your loss function is $(\beta - \beta^*)$ if β^* is less than β, and is $2(\beta^* - \beta)$ otherwise. What is the Bayesian point estimate? Explain your calculation.

4 Consider the CNLR model $y = \beta x + \varepsilon$. With a uniform prior for β the posterior distribution looks exactly like the likelihood function, so that the classical and Bayesian point estimate of β are the same (using the mean of the posterior as the Bayesian point estimate). Now suppose β satisfies the inequality constraint $\beta \ge 3$.

(a) What is the logical prior to employ now?

(b) What does the posterior look like?

(c) Explain the difference that now arises between the classical and Bayesian point estimates, with particular reference to cases in which the peak of the likelihood function corresponds to a β value less than 3.

(d) How would a Bayesian calculate the probability that the inequality constraint is true? (The answer is in Geweke, 1986, p. 127.)

5 Suppose the net cost to a firm of undertaking a venture is $1,800 if $\beta \le 1$ and its net profit is $Q if $\beta > 1$. You have a large data set for which the CNLR model is applicable and you produce $\beta^{OLS} = 2.28$ with estimate variance $V^*(\beta^{OLS}) = 1.0$.

(a) Would a classical statistician reject the hypothesis that $\beta = 1$ against the alternative $\beta > 1$ at the 5% significance level, and therefore undertake this venture?

(b) Assuming an ignorance prior, describe a Bayesian statistician's posterior distribution.

(c) What are the Bayesian's posterior odds in favor of the hypothesis that $\beta > 1$?

(d) How small does Q need to be to induce the Bayesian to make the same decision as the classical statistician?

6 Suppose the CNLR model applies to $y = \beta x + \varepsilon$ where the variance of ε is known to be 13. A Bayesian analysis of your data has produced the posterior distribution of β as normal with mean 6 and variance 4. You are interested in predicting y for the value $x = 3$.

(a) Describe the "predictive density" of this y value.

(b) What is the probability that this y value is greater than 25?

7 Suppose $y = \alpha + \beta x + \varepsilon$ and you have data on periods 1 through T. Assume that $y_T > y_{T-1}$. Given x_{T+1}, explain how a Bayesian would estimate the probability of a turning point in period $T + 1$, i.e., $y_{r+1} < y_T$.

8 Suppose x is distributed as a Poisson, so that $f(x) = e^{-\lambda}\lambda^x(x!)^{-1}$ and you have a random sample of size 7 yielding $\Sigma x = 35$.

(a) What is λ^{MLE}?

(b) What is your estimate of the variance of λ^{MLE}?

(c) Suppose you are a Bayesian with gamma prior $f(\lambda) \propto \lambda^{\alpha-1}e^{-\beta\lambda}$ with $\alpha = 4.2$ and $\beta = 0.7$, so that the prior has mean $\alpha/\beta = 6$. What is your Bayesian point estimate of λ, assuming a quadratic loss function?

9 The beta distribution with parameters α and β, $f(x) \propto x^{\alpha-1}(1 - x)^{\beta-1}$ has mean $\alpha/(\alpha + \beta)$ and variance $\alpha\beta(\alpha + \beta)^{-2}(\alpha + \beta + 1)^{-1}$. It is a conjugate prior for a binomial likelihood such as is the case for estimation of the proportion θ of defectives coming off a production line. Suppose your prior is a beta distribution with parameters $\alpha = 1.5$ and $\beta = 4.5$ and you draw 100 observations, observing 5 defectives. If your loss function is $(\theta - \theta^*)^2$ what is your point estimate θ^*?

V   Bayesian: Priors

1 The beta distribution given by $f(x) \propto x^{\theta-1}(1 - x)^{\phi-1}$, is a popular form for a prior distribution when $0 \leq x \leq 1$. It has mean $\theta/(\theta + \phi)$ and variance $\theta\phi(\theta + \phi)^{-2}(\theta + \phi + 1)^{-1}$. Consider estimation of the Cobb–Douglas production function $\ln y = \ln A + \alpha \ln L + \beta \ln K + \varepsilon = \ln A + \alpha(\ln L - \ln K) + \eta \ln K + \varepsilon$, where $\eta = \alpha + \beta$ is the returns to scale parameter. A suggestion for a prior distribution on (α,η) is $p(\alpha,\eta) = g_1(\alpha|\eta)g_2(\eta)$, where

$$g_1(\alpha|\eta) \propto (\alpha/\eta)^{3.2}(1 - \alpha/\eta)^{0.05} \qquad \text{with } 0 < \alpha/\eta < 1$$
$$g_2(\eta) \propto \eta^{0.5}(2 - \eta)^{0.5} \qquad \text{with } 0 < \eta < 2.$$

(a) What are the mean and variance of g_1?

(b) What are the mean and variance of g_2?

(c) Explain in words the rationale behind this prior.

Answers are in Zellner and Richard (1973, p. 112).

2 Suppose that before opening your ice cream store you surveyed 45 people and found that 15 preferred soft ice cream products and 30 preferred hard products.

(a) What is the maximum likelihood estimate of θ, the probability that a customer will want a soft product?

(b) Using a uniform prior what is your posterior distribution for θ?

(c) What is the mean of this distribution? *Hint:* The beta distribution given by $f(x) \propto x^{\theta-1}(1 - x)^{\phi-1}$, has mean $\theta/(\theta + \phi)$.

(d) What prior would be required to make the posterior mean equal to the maximum likelihood estimate?

(e) What prior results from using Jeffrey's rule? (Prior proportional to the square root of the determinant of the information matrix.)

(f) Assuming your ignorance prior is the prior of part (d), what is the mean of your updated posterior distribution if during the first week of business 75 of your 200 customers ordered soft products?

3 Suppose a parameter can take on some but not all real values, but that a transformation of this parameter exists which can take on all real values. A uniform prior can be used as an ignorance prior for the transformation, and change-of-variable theorem can be used to find the corresponding ignorance prior for the original parameter. Use this approach to find an ignorance prior for

(a) σ, where $0 \leq \sigma$, with transformation $\ln\sigma$;

(b) θ, where $0 \leq \theta \leq 1$, with transformation $\ln[\theta/(1 - \theta)]$;

(c) ρ, where $-1 \leq \rho \leq 1$, with transformation $\ln[\rho^2/(1 - \rho^2)]$.

4 Suppose x is distributed as a Poisson, so that $f(x) = e^{-\lambda}\lambda^x(x!)^{-1}$ and you have a random sample of size 7 yielding $\Sigma x = 35$.

(a) Find an ignorance prior for λ for this case by using Jeffrey's rule (prior proportional to the square root of the determinant of the information matrix).

(b) What ignorance prior is required to make the mean of the posterior distribution equal the MLE? *Hint:* Read part (c) below.

(c) Suppose the prior for λ takes the form of a gamma distribution: prior$(\lambda) \propto \lambda^{\alpha-1}e^{-\beta\lambda}$ with $\alpha = 4.2$ and $\beta = 0.7$, so that the prior has mean $\alpha/\beta = 6$ and variance $\alpha/\beta^2 = 8.6$. What form does the posterior take? What does this tell you about this prior?

(d) What are the posterior mean and variance? Do they change in the right direction, as compared to your answer to part (b) above? Explain.

5 Suppose $-1 \leq \rho \leq 1$ so that $0 \leq \rho^2 \leq 1$ and thus a possible ignorance prior for ρ^2, following question (2e) above, is the beta distribution with parameters one-half and one-half. What ignorance prior for ρ does this imply?

W Hypothesis Testing: Monte Carlo

1 Suppose you have programmed a computer to do the following.

i. Draw 20 x values from a distribution uniform between 2 and 8.

ii. Draw 20 z values from a normal distribution with mean 12 and variance 2.

iii. Draw 20 e values from a standard normal distribution.

iv. Create 20 y values using the formula $y = 2 + 3x + 4z + 5e$.

v. Regress y on x and z, obtaining the estimate bz of the coefficient of z and the estimate sebz of its standard error.

vi. Subtract 4 from bz, divide this by sebz and call it w1.

vii. Repeat the process described above from step iii until 5,000 w values have been created, w1 through w5000.

viii. Order the five thousand w values from smallest to largest.

What is your best guess of the 4750th of these values? Explain your reasoning.

2 Suppose you have programmed a computer to do the following.
   - i.   Draw 50 x values from a distribution uniform between 2 and 22.
   - ii.   Draw 50 e values from a standard normal distribution.
   - iii. Create 50 y values using the formula y = 2 + 3x + 4e.
   - iv.   Regress y on x obtaining the sum of squared residuals SSE1.
   - v.   Regress y on x for the first 20 observations, obtaining SSE2.
   - vi.   Regress y on x for the last 30 observations, obtaining SSE3.
   - vii. Add SSE2 and SSE3 to get SSE4.
   - viii. Calculate w1 = (SSE1 − SSE4)/SSE4.
   - ix.   Repeat the process described above beginning with step ii until 3,000 w values have been created, w1 through w3000.
   - x.   Order the three thousand w values from smallest to largest.

What is your best guess of the 2970th of these values? Explain your reasoning.

3 Suppose you have programmed a computer to do the following.
   - i.   Draw 6 x values from a standard normal distribution.
   - ii.   Square these x values and compute the sum w of the first three squared values and the sum y of the last three squared values.
   - iii. Compute r1, the ratio of w to y.
   - iv.   Repeat this process to produce 2000 r values, r1 through r2000.
   - v.   Order the 2,000 r values from smallest to largest.

What is your best guess of the 20th of these numbers? Explain your reasoning.

4 Suppose you have programmed a computer to do the following.
   - i.   Draw 8 x values from a standard normal distribution.
   - ii.   Square these x values and compute their sum w1.
   - iii. Repeat this process to produce 3,000 w values, w1 through w3000.
   - iv.   Compute the average A and the variance V of these 3,000 values.
   - v.   Order the 3,000 w values from smallest to largest.
   - vi.   Compute AA, the 2,850th value.

What are your best gueses of A, VA and AA?

5 Suppose the classical normal linear regression model applies to the money demand function m = θ + βy + δr + ε and you have 25 observations on income y and on the nominal interest rate r which in your data are negatively correlated. You regress m on y (erroneously omitting r) and use a t test to test the true null β = 1 against the alternative β > 1 at the α = 5% significance level.
   - (a) Explain in detail how to conduct a Monte Carlo study to find the type 1 error of this t test.
   - (b) What results do you expect to get? Explain.

6 Suppose you have programmed a computer to do the following.
   - i.   Draw 25 x values from a distribution uniform between 4 and 44.
   - ii.   Set ctr = 0
   - iii. Draw 25 e values from a distribution uniform between 0 and 10.
   - iv.   Compute 25 y values as 3 + 2x + e.
   - v.   Regress y on x, saving the intercept estimate as int, the slope estimate as b, the standard error of b as se and the residuals as a vector res.
   - vi.   Compute t# = (b − 2)/se and save it.
   - vii. Compute 25 y values as int + 2x + 1.087be where be is drawn randomly with replacement from the elements of res.

viii.   Regress y on x and compute bt1 $= (b - 2)/se$ where b is the slope coefficient estimate and se is its standard error.

ix.   Repeat from vii to obtain 1,000 bt values.

x.   Order these bt values from smallest to largest.

xi.   Add one to ctr if t# is greater than the 950th of the ordered bt values.

xii.   Repeat from iii to obtain 3,000 t# values.

xiii.   Divide ctr by . . . and compare to . . .

Explain what this program is designed to do, and complete the instructions.

7 Suppose you run a regression using 30 observations and obtain the result $y = 2 + 3x + 4z + res$. You wish to test the hypothesis that the z slope is 5, but because you suspect that the error term in this specification is not normally distributed you decide to undertake the following bootstrapping procedure.

i.   Create 30 y values as $2 + 3x + 5z + e$ where e is drawn with replacement from the residuals res.

ii.   Regress y on x and z and save the z slope estimate.

iii.   Repeat from i to produce 1,000 slope estimates.

Explain how to use these results to perform the desired test.

8 Suppose the CNLR model applies to $y = \alpha + \beta x + \theta z + \delta p + \varepsilon$ where x, z and p are not orthogonal in the data. Researcher A has unwittingly omitted regressor p and has done an asymptotic t test to test the null $\beta(1 - \theta) = 1$.

(a) Explain *in detail* how to conduct a Monte Carlo study to investigate the type I error of A's test.

(b) What results do you expect to get?

(c) How would you guess these results would differ from the type I error of a Wald test of this same hypothesis? Explain your reasoning.

9 Consider the *t* statistic printed out by regression packages for each coefficient estimate. Explain in detail how you would conduct a Monte Carlo study to verify that this statistic actually has a *t* distribution when the null hypothesis is true.

10 The power of a test is one minus the probability of a type II error. The power curve graphs how this number varies with the extent to which the null hypothesis is false. Suppose $y = \alpha + \beta x + \varepsilon$ and you propose using a traditional *t* test to test the null hypothesis that $\beta = 1.0$. Explain in detail how to conduct a Monte Carlo study to produce a rough picture of the power curve for this test statistic. Assume that neither you nor the computer have access to statistical tables.

11 Suppose you have just completed a Monte Carlo study in which you have generated data according to the CNLR model $y = \alpha + \beta x + \varepsilon$ for sample size 25 and have run 2,000 regressions, creating 2,000 estimates (call them β*s) of β (which you had set equal to 3.0 for the Monte Carlo study) along with the corresponding 2,000 estimates (call them V*s) of the variance of these estimates. Suppose you take each β*, subtract 3 from it, square the result, and then divide this result by its corresponding V*. Take the resulting 2,000 numbers and get the computer to order them from smallest to largest. What is your guess of the value of 1,900th of these numbers? Explain your reasoning.

12 Explain how you would undertake a Monte Carlo study to graph the risk function of a pre-test estimator when the pre-test is for a coefficient equal to zero.

13 Suppose $y = \alpha + \beta x + \varepsilon$ where ε is distributed uniformly between -1 and 1.

(a) Explain how to undertake a Monte Carlo study to estimate the type I error of a t-test for $\beta = 1$ using the 5% critical value from the t table.

(b) Explain how you would test (at the 1% significance level) the hypothesis that the type I error of your test is significantly different from 5%.

14 Suppose you are examining the relative merit of using the LM or the W statistic to test $\beta_1 = \beta_2^{-1}$ in the relationship $y = \beta_0 + \beta_1 x + \beta_2 w + \varepsilon$. Although both statistics are distributed asymptotically as a chi-square (with one degree of freedom), in small samples this is only approximately true, so that in small samples one test could be "better" than the other.

(a) Which test in this example will have the lower computational cost? Explain why.

(b) One criterion for determining which of these two statistics is "better" is the extent to which the appropriate critical value (say, for the 5% level) from the chi-square table is the "correct" critical value. Explain concisely how you would undertake a Monte Carlo study to examine this. (You do not need to explain how the test statistics are calculated.)

(c) How would you estimate the "correct" critical values in part (b)? (These are called empirically determined critical values.)

(d) Another relevant criterion here is relative power. Explain concisely how you would undertake a Monte Carlo study to examine the relative power of these two tests in this context.

(e) Explain how misleading results could arise if you did not employ empirically determined critical values in part (d).

X   Hypothesis Testing: Fundamentals

1 Using a preliminary sample, your hypothesis that the average income in a city equals $10,000 (with alternative hypothesis that it exceeds $10,000) is barely rejected at the 5% significance level. Suppose you take a new sample, of the same size. What is your best guess of the probability that it will also reject this null hypothesis?

2 For which of the following cases are you more confident about rejecting your null hypothesis, or are you equally confident?
(a) The null is rejected at the 5% level, sample size 20.
(b) The null is rejected at the 5% level, sample size 100.

3 From sample size 15, A gets a t value of 2.2 (5% critical value is 2.1). B replicates A's experiment with 15 new subjects, gets a t value of 1.7 (one-tailed 5% critical value is 1.75), and claims that since A's result has not been replicated, it should not be accepted. Do you agree? Explain. (The answer is in Busche and Kennedy, 1984).

4 Hypothesis tests of the least squares slope are based on the t distribution, which requires that the sampling distribution of β^{OLS} be distributed normally. True, false, or uncertain? Explain.

5 I am running a regression using a cross-section sample of 2,000 families. The F statistic is very significant and the t values are all high, but R^2 is only 0.15. How can that be?

6 A random sample of size 4 is drawn from a normal population of x values with variance 9 and mean μ either 25 or 30. Draw a diagram showing the sampling distributions of $\bar{x}$ under the null hypothesis that $\mu = 25$ and under the alternative hypothesis that $\mu = 30$.
(a) Consider a testing procedure which accepts H_0 if $\bar{x}$ is less than 27.5. What logic lies behind this methodology?
(b) What are the approximate probabilities of type I and type II errors for this test?

(c) Use your diagram to explain what happens to these probabilities as the sample size increases.

(d) How does your answer to part (c) differ from what would happen using the traditional testing methodology, as the sample size increased?

(e) What is the lesson here?

7   As the sample size grows, t statistics should increase. True, false, or uncertain? Explain.

*8 Suppose you are dealing with a specification $y = \alpha + \beta x + \varepsilon$ and a friend suggests a test statistic based on

$$r = (1/N)\Sigma x_i(e_i^2 - s^2),$$

where e is the OLS residual.

(a) What would this test be testing?

(b) What generic name would be given to it?

9   Is an F test a one-sided or a two-sided test? Explain.

Y   Hypothesis Testing: Power

1   Suppose the CNLR model applies to $y = \alpha + \beta x + \varepsilon$ and you are testing the hypothesis $\beta = 1$. If the variance of ε becomes larger, then *ceteris paribus* the power of your test increases. True, false, or uncertain? Explain.

2   What happens to the power of a one-sided t test as its size (type I error) increases from 5% to 10%? Explain. *Hint*: Use a diagram.

3   Suppose x is distributed uniformly between 5 and θ and you wish to test the hypothesis Ho: $\theta = 10$ against Ha: $\theta = 25$ by means of a single observed value of x. What are the size and power of your test if you choose your rejection region as $x \geqslant 9.5$? *Hint*: Use a diagram.

4   Suppose the CNLR model applies to $x = \alpha + \beta x + \varepsilon$ with $\sigma^2 = 40$. A sample of size 10 yields $\Sigma x = 20$ and $\Sigma x^2 = 50$. You plan to test the hypothesis that $\beta = 1$, at the 5% significance level, against the alternative $\beta > 1$. If the true value of β is 4.0, what is the probability that you will correctly reject your null hypothesis?

5   A random sample of size 64 is to be used to test the null hypothesis that the mean of a normal population (with variance 256) is 40 against the alternative hypothesis that it is greater than 40. Suppose the null is to be rejected if and only if the mean of the sample exceeds 43.

(a) Find the probability of a type I error.

(b) Sketch the power curve by finding the power when the true mean is 41, 43, 45, and 47.

6   Suppose the classical normal linear regression model applies, with sample size 200, and you have run a regression estimating a slope coefficient as 0.1 with a t value of 2. If the true value of this slope coefficient is 0.06, explain how with the help of statistical tables you would estimate the power of a t test (at 5% significance level) of this slope equal to zero against the alternative that it is greater than zero.

Z   Hypothesis Testing: Examples

1   Evaluate the following proposal for testing the assumption that $E\varepsilon = 0$: "Since the residuals from the OLS regression are BLUE estimates of the disturbances, the aver-

age of the residuals will be a good estimate of the expectation of the disturbance. Therefore, after fitting the OLS regression, compute the average residual and reject the null hypothesis (that $E\varepsilon = 0$) if it is significantly different from zero."

2 Suppose the population regression function is specified to be $C = \beta_0 + \beta_1 Y + \beta_2 A + \beta_3 YA + \varepsilon$ where C is consumption, Y income, and A age. Explain how you would test the hypothesis that the marginal propensity to consume does not depend on age.

3 Suppose we have run the following two regressions:

$$y^* = \alpha_0^* + \alpha_1^* x + \alpha_2^* (r - p)$$
$$y^* = \beta_0^* + \beta_1^* x + \beta_2^* r + \beta_3^* p$$

where y is loans, x is sales, r is the nominal rate of interest and p is a measure of the expected rate of inflation. Asterisks denote estimates. Suppose that you are certain that borrowers respond to the real rate of interest, rather than responding separately to its components.

(a) Which equation will have the higher R^2, or will they be the same? Explain.
(b) Which estimate of the effect of the real interest rate do you prefer: α_2^*, β_2^* or $-\beta_3^*$, or are you indifferent among them? Explain why.
(c) How would you use the results of these regressions to test the hypothesis that borrowers look only at the real rate of interest rather than paying separate attention to its components, using a t test?
(d) As (c), but using an F test?

4 Suppose you believe that the CNLR model applies to $y = \beta_0 + \beta_1 x + \varepsilon$, but you suspect that the impact of x on y depends on the value of another explanatory variable, w. Explain how you would test for this.

5 Suppose you are estimating the cost function $\ln C = \beta_0 + \beta_1 \ln Q + \beta_2 (\ln Q)^2 + \varepsilon$. Explain how to test the hypothesis that the elasticity of cost (of C) with respect to output (Q) is unity. Be explicit.

6 Consider the "translog" production function given by

$$\ln y = \beta_0 + \beta_1 \ln L + \beta_2 \ln K + \beta_3 \ln^2 L + \beta_4 \ln^2 K + \beta_5 \ln L \ln K + \varepsilon$$

(a) Comment on the statement: "Obtaining a negative coefficient estimate for $\ln K$ casts doubt on the applicability of this production function because it should possess a positive elasticity with respect to capital."
(b) How would you test for this functional form versus the Cobb–Douglas?

7 Consider the "transcendental production function" $Y = AL^\alpha K^\beta e^{(\theta L + \delta K)}$. How would you test this for this functional form versus the Cobb–Douglas?

8 Suppose $Y_t = \beta E_{t-1} M_t + \varepsilon_t$, where $E_{t-1} M_t$ denotes the rational expectation of M_t made at time $t - 1$. Assume that M is determined by

$$M_t = \theta_1 x_{t-1} + \theta_2 w_{t-1} + u_t, \text{ so that } E_{t-1} M_t = \theta_1 x_{t-1} + \theta_2 w_{t-1}.$$

Suppose we are interested in testing whether expectations are rational. Consider the two equations

$$M_t = \theta_1 x_{t-1} + \theta_2 w_{t-1} + u_t, \text{ and}$$
$$Y_t = \lambda_1 x_{t-1} + \lambda_2 w_{t-1} + v_t.$$

(a) What cross-equations restriction reflects the rational expectations hypothesis?

(b) Explain in detail how you would use a Wald test to test this restriction. Be explicit. (The answer is in Hoffman and Schmidt, 1981, p. 265.)

9 Suppose $y_t = \alpha + \beta_0 x_t + \beta_1 x_{t-1} + \beta_2 x_{t-2} + \beta_3 x_{t-3} + \beta_4 x_{t-4} + \varepsilon_t$ and we wish to estimate by assuming a polynomial distributed lag of order 2, so that $\beta_i = \delta_0 + \delta_1 i + \delta_2 i^2$, where i is the lag length. Explain how you would test the hypothesis that the β_i lie on a second-order polynomial. *Hint*: Structure a standard F test, calculated by running restricted and unrestricted regressions.

10 Suppose that output is given by the Cobb–Douglas function $Y = AK^\alpha L^\beta \varepsilon$ where K is capital, L is labor, A, α and β are parameters, and ε is an error distributed lognormally with mean one.

(a) What does ε distributed log-normally mean? Why might we want it distributed log-normally? Why would we specify it to have mean one?

(b) Show that testing for constant returns to scale implies testing that $\alpha + \beta = 1$. How would you test this hypothesis?

11 Suppose the CNLR model applies to $y = \alpha + \beta x + \theta w + \varepsilon$ but that your data covers three distinct periods. Explain how to test the hypothesis that β and θ (but not α) were unchanged across the three periods, against the alternative that all parameters were different in all three periods.

12 Suppose you have estimated the relationship

$$\ln y_t = \beta_0 + \beta_1 \ln y_{t-1} + \beta_2 \ln x_t + \beta_3 \ln x_{t-1} + \varepsilon.$$

(a) How would you test the hypothesis that the long-run (steady state) elasticity of y with respect to x is unity?

(b) Explain how you would calculate a 90% confidence interval for this elasticity.

13 Suppose you have observations on average cost C and total output Y for 45 firms. You run a linear regression of C on Y and it looks pretty good, but a friend suggests doing a diagnostic check on functional form. You decide to do a RESET test followed by a rainbow test. Explain how you would do these two tests.

AA   Hypothesis Testing: Numerical Examples

1 A wage/price equation with an intercept and four explanatory variables was estimated for (a) 39 quarters in which no incomes policy was in place, (b) 37 quarters in which an incomes policy was in place, and (c) the combined data. The respective estimates of the variance of the error term are 0.605, 0.788 and 0.815. Can we conclude that the parameters are unchanged in the presence of incomes policy?

2 Suppose you have cross-section data on income y and electricity consumption x for three regions and you have regressed $\ln x$ on $\ln y$ for each region and for the full sample, obtaining (standard errors in parentheses):

	$\hat{\beta}$		SSE	T
Region A	1.1	(0.05)	45	92
Region B	0.90	(0.1)	32	82
Region C	0.85	(0.08)	11	32
All regions	0.88	(0.05)	100	206

where $\hat{\beta}$ is the slope coefficient estimate.

(a) Test that this equation is the same for all regions.

(b) Assuming that these equations are the same, test that the common elasticity is unity.

(c) Suppose that in parts (a) and (b) you wished to assume that the intercepts were definitely different (and so in part (a) were only testing for all the slopes being the same, and in part (b) were only assuming that the slope coefficients were the same). Explain what you would have to do to enable you to answer parts (a) and (b).

3 Suppose you have 24 observations from $y = \alpha + \beta x + \varepsilon$, which satisfies the CNLR model. You wish to test the hypothesis that there was a structural break between the 20th and 21st observations. To this end, you run three regressions, one using all the data ($SSE = 130$), one using only the first 20 observations ($SSE = 80$), and one using only the last four observations ($SSE = 20$).

(a) Calculate the F statistic for the traditional Chow test.

(b) Calculate the F statistic for the Chow test usually employed only when the number of observations in the second period is "too small."

(c) Explain how to do a Monte Carlo study to examine the question of which F test is more powerful.

4 Suppose you draw the observations 1, 2, 3, 4, 5 from a normal distribution with unknown mean m and unknown variance v.

(a) Test the null m $= 4$ against the alternative m > 4 at the 5% significance level.

(b) Suppose you are told that v $= 0.36$. Would your testing procedure differ? If so, how? If not, why not?

5 Suppose the classical normal linear regression model applies and we regress log output on an intercept, log labor and log capital to get estimates of 6.0, 0.75 and 0.40 for the intercept, slope of log labor and slope of log capital, respectively. The estimated variance–covariance matrix has 0.015 in each diagonal position, 0.005 beside the diagonal and zeroes elsewhere. Test the hypothesis that there is constant returns to scale, i.e., that the two slopes sum to unity. Explain how you performed this test.

6 Suppose the CLR model applies to $y = \alpha + \beta x + \varepsilon$ and your regression yields estimates of α and β of 1 and 2, with estimated variances 3 and 2, respectively, estimated covariance -1, and estimated error variance 4. A new observation, $y = 17$ and $x = 3$, appears. Calculate the F statistic for testing if this new observation is consistent with the earlier data. *Hint*: Do not try to calculate the sum of squared errors.

7 Suppose $y = \beta_0 + \beta_1 x + \beta_2 w + \varepsilon$ and you have obtained the regression results $\beta_1^{OLS} = 4.0$, $\beta_2^{OLS} = 0.2$, with estimated variances 2.0 and 0.06, and estimated covariance 0.05. You wish to test the hypothesis that β_1 is the inverse of β_2. Calculate the relevant test statistic, explaining your calculations.

8 Suppose $y = \theta + \beta(x + \alpha)^{-1} + \varepsilon$ and you have the observations 1, 1/2, 1/3, and 1/4 on x, and the corresponding observations 1, 5, 7, and 7 on y. What is the LM test statistic for testing $\alpha = 0$? (The answer is in Breusch and Pagan, 1980, p. 243.) *Hint*: Use a computer package for the final step.

9 Suppose $y = \alpha + \beta x + \varepsilon$ and $\varepsilon_t = \rho\varepsilon_{t-1} + u_t$. In the Durbin two-stage estimation procedure, the first stage estimates the equation

$$y_t = \alpha(1 - \rho) + \beta x_t + \rho y_{t-1} - \rho\beta x_{t-1} + u_t,$$

which can be rewritten as

$$y_t = \theta_0 + \theta_1 x_t + \theta_2 y_{t-1} + \theta_3 x_{t-1} + u_t.$$

(a) What restriction, in terms of the θs, should be imposed when running this regression?

(b) Suppose you run the unrestricted regression, obtaining estimates 8, 3, 0.5, and -2 of θ_0, θ_1, θ_2, and θ_3, respectively, and estimated variance–covariance matrix V^*. What formula, in terms of V^*, would you use to calculate the Wald statistic to test this restriction?

BB   Test Statistics

1 If the CNLR model applies to $y = X\beta + \varepsilon$ with T observations and K explanatory variables, it can be shown that SSE/σ^2, the sum of squared OLS residuals divided by the variance of the error term, is distributed as a chi-square with $T - K$ degrees of freedom. It is well known that the mean and variance of a chi-square distribution are equal to its degrees of freedom and twice its degrees of freedom, respectively. Use these facts to find the expected value and variance of $s^2 = SSE/(T - K)$.

2 A normally distributed variable has skewness zero and kurtosis three. One way of testing for normality is to refer the statistic $N\text{skew}^2/6 + N(\text{kurt} - 3)^2/24$ to a chi-square distribution with 2 degrees of freedom, where N is the sample size, skew is a measure of skewness, and kurt is a measure of kurtosis. Explain what must be the logic of this and thereby deduce where the 6 and 24 must have come from.

3 Suppose the CNLR model applies to $y = X\beta + \varepsilon$. Consider the statistic

$$\theta = [(T - k - 1)^{-1}\Sigma(e_t - \bar{e})^2]^{-1/2}(T - k)^{-1/2}\Sigma e_t$$

where T is the sample size, e_t are the recursive residuals, k is the number of explanatory variables in the regression, and the summation is from $t = k + 1$ to T. Harvey (1981, p. 156) notes that when the model is correctly specified, θ has a t distribution with $T - k - 1$ degrees of freedom, a result which follows immediately from the properties of the recursive residuals.

(a) Explain the logic of why this statistic has a t distribution.

(b) What are the key properties of the recursive residuals that are relevant here?

(c) Will this test work with OLS residuals in place of recursive residuals? Why, or why not?

4 Suppose the CNLR model is applicable to $Y = X\beta + \varepsilon$ and we wish to test the J *stochastic* restrictions that $Er = R\beta$ or $r = R\beta + u$, where u is distributed normally with mean zero and variance–covariance matrix Q. The statistic

$$(r - R\beta^{\text{OLS}})'[R(X'X)^{-1}R' + Q/s^2]^{-1}(r - R\beta^{\text{OLS}})/Js^2$$

is suggested in this context. Explain the intuitive sense of this statistic. *Hint*: This is called Theil's "compatibility" statistic.

5 Suppose you wish to use a Chow test to test for whether the entire parameter vector is unchanged in going from period one to period two, but as part of both the null and the alternative hypotheses you wish to allow the variances of the error terms in the two periods to differ. The statistic

$$(\beta_1^{\text{OLS}} - \beta_2^{\text{OLS}})'[s_1^2(X_1'X_1)^{-1} + s_2^2(X_2'X_2)^{-1}]^{-1}(\beta_1^{\text{OLS}} - \beta_2^{\text{OLS}})$$

is suggested in this context. Explain the intuitive sense of this statistic.

6 Suppose $y_t = g(x_t, \beta) + \varepsilon_t$ where g is a nonlinear function and ε_t is distributed normally. Then it can be shown that the LM statistic for testing a restriction can be written as $LM = e'Z(Z'Z)^{-1}Z'e/(s^2)$ where e is the residual vector that results from restricted nonlinear least squares, Z is a matrix, each column of which contains T observations on the partial of g with respect to an element of β, and s^2 is the usual MLE estimate of σ^2, namely SSE divided by the sample size T. Suppose g includes an intercept.
   (a) Show that $LM = TR^2$ where R^2 is the coefficient of determination from regressing e on Z.
   (b) Why was it necessary to specify that g included an intercept?

7 (a) The NR^2 for an LM test of the hypothesis that $\theta = \delta = 0$ when $y = \alpha + \beta x + \theta w + \delta z + \varepsilon$ comes from running what regression?
   (b) How would you adjust the NR^2 figure if you wanted to use an F-table rather than a chi-square table to implement the test? Explain your logic.

8 Suppose $y = \alpha + \beta x + \varepsilon$ where $\varepsilon_t = \rho \varepsilon_{t-1} + u_t$.
   (a) What regression would you run to get the NR^2 for an LM test of the hypothesis that $\rho = 0$? *Hint*: Ignore the first y observation, write the relationship in terms of the error u, and note that one of the derivative terms turns out to be the estimated ε_{t-1}.
   (b) Explain the logic behind the following statement. The LM test for a first-order autocorrelated error boils down to testing the usual $\hat\rho$ against zero.

9 Suppose the CNLR model applies to $y = \alpha + \beta x + \delta w + \varepsilon$. Explain how to test $\beta = \delta^2$ using:
   (a) an "asymptotic" t test.
   (b) a W test.

10 Suppose we have T observations from the Poisson $f(x) = \lambda^x e^{-\lambda}/x!$ What are the LR, LM and W statistics for testing the null that $\lambda = \lambda_0$? *Hint*: $Ex = \lambda$.

11 Suppose we have T observations from the exponential $f(x) = \theta e^{-\theta x}$. Show that the W and LM tests for the hypothesis $\theta = \theta_0$ are identical.

12 Suppose $y = \alpha + \beta x + \delta w + \varepsilon$ and you wish to test $\beta = 0$.
   (a) Show that LR is the sample size times the log of the ratio of the restricted SSE to the unrestricted SSE.
   (b) What is the relationship between the W and t test statistics?
   (c) What regression would you run to get NR^2 to calculate LM?

CC   Hypothesis Testing: Theoretical Derivations

1 Suppose x is distributed normally with mean μ and known variance σ^2. Given T randomly drawn observations on x, the usual way of testing the null hypothesis that $\mu = \mu_0$ is to divide $(\bar{x} - \mu_0)$ by its standard deviation, creating a standard normal.
   (a) Show that this formula results from applying the LR test.
   (b) Show that this same formula can be interpreted as a Wald test.
   (c) By finding the partial of the log-likelihood with respect to μ, show that the LM testing procedure also gives rise to this formula.

*2 Suppose the CNLR model is applicable to $Y = X\beta + \varepsilon$ and we wish to test the set of J restrictions $R\beta = r$. Suppose further that σ^2 is *known*. Show that the W, LM and LR statistics are identical by using the following hints:

i.   Derive the LR test in terms of SSE_R and SSE_U, then use the textbook formula $SSE_R - SSE_U = \varepsilon'X(X'X)^{-1}[R(X'X)^{-1}R']^{-1}(X'X)^{-1}X'\varepsilon/\sigma^2$.

ii. Calculate W by using $z'V^{-1}z$, where z is $N(0,V)$, and write it in terms of ε.

iii. Calculate LM by applying this formula to test the Lagrange multiplier $\lambda = 0$ (get the expression for λ from the constrained maximization that yielded SSE_R). Alternatively, apply the LM formula directly (more difficult).

*3 Suppose that x_1 and x_2 are bivariate normally distributed with expectations zero, variances unity, and covariance zero. Let $w_1 = x_1 - x_2$ and $w_2 = x_1 + x_2$; let $y_1 = w_1^2/2$ and $y_2 = w_2^2/2$; and let $u = y_1/y_2$. Use a matrix formulation to show that the *pdf* of u is $F(1,1)$.

4   Suppose that $Y = X\beta + \varepsilon$ and the CNLR model assumptions are satisfied with σ^2 unknown, and that you are interested in testing J linear restrictions. Show that the likelihood ratio λ is a monotonic function of the F statistic. *Hint*: Use SSE_R and SSE_U notation instead of algebraic formulas.

*5 Show that if the adjusted R^2 increases when a set of J explanatory variables is deleted from a regression, then the F statistic for testing the significance of these J variables is less than one. *Hint*: Define adjusted R^2 as $1 - (SSE/df)/v$ where v is the variance of the dependent variable, and work exclusively with these terms. (The answer is in Edwards, 1969, p. 28.)

*6 Explain how the "rainbow test" of Utts (1982, p. 1801) is just a variant of the Chow test.

DD   Pre-test Estimators

1   Explain in detail how to conduct a Monte Carlo study to graph the risk function of a pre-test estimator.

*2 Suppose y is distributed uniformly between zero and β for $0 \leq \beta \leq 4$, so that $f(y) = 1/\beta$ on the relevant interval. We suspect that $\beta = 4$ and decide to estimate β as 4 if our single observation $y \geq 2$. Otherwise we estimate β as $2y$. *Hint*: If x is distributed $U(a,b)$ then $V(x) = (b - a)^2/12$.

(a) What is the MSE of the restricted estimator $\beta^* = 4$?

(b) What is the MSE of the unrestricted estimator $\beta^{**} = 2y$?

(c) What is the MSE of the pre-test estimator for $\beta \leq 2$?

(d) What is the mean of the pre-test estimator for $\beta \geq 2$?

(e) What is the variance of the pre-test estimator for $\beta \geq 2$?

3   Evaluate the following suggestion for dealing with pretest bias: Break the sample into two parts, use the first part to perform the pretest and the second part to estimate.

EE   Non-nested Hypothesis Tests

1   The degree to which an initial stock offering is underpriced is thought by one strand of the literature to be a linear function of risk, the degree of asymmetry of information between the underwriters and the issuers, and the underwriter's reputation. A second strand of the literature suggests that it is a linear function of risk, the degree of asymmetry of information between issuers and investors, and the proportion of the offering

retained by the issuers. Assuming you have appropriate data, explain in detail how you would assess the truth of these two theories.

2 Suppose researcher A believes $y = \beta x + \varepsilon$ and researcher B believes $y = \theta w + v$ where in both cases the CNLR model applies. You have four observations on (y, x, w), namely $(4, 1, 2)$, $(3, 2, 1)$, $(-6, -3, -2)$ and $(-1, 0, -1)$.

(a) Perform a non-nested F test or a J test, whichever is easier.

(b) Explain how the other test would be performed.

3 A colleague feels that for current firm sizes in a certain industry marginal product mp decreases with firm size N according to

$$mp = \alpha - \beta \ln(N)$$

but you believe that it varies according to

$$mp = \theta + \phi e^{-\delta N}.$$

You have 34 observations on several comparisons that have been made between pairs of firms. Each observation reports the small firm size (Ns), the large firm size (Nl) and the difference (diff) between their marginal products. Explain how to use these data to address this dispute between you and your colleague.

FF Nonspherical Errors: Monte Carlo

1 Explain in detail how to conduct a Monte Carlo study to show that inference is "biased" when using OLS when the data has been generated by a GLR model.

2 Explain in detail how to undertake a Monte Carlo study to examine the relative merits of OLS and EGLS when $y_t = \beta_0 + \beta_1 x_t + \varepsilon_t$ and the variance of ε_t is known to take the multiplicative form Kx_t^q. Note: comparing EGLS, not GLS.

3 Explain in detail how to conduct a Monte Carlo study to examine the relative merits of the OLS and EGLS estimates of β when $Y = \alpha + \beta X + u$ and the CNLR assumptions hold except that the variance of u jumps to a higher level halfway through the data set.

4 Explain very briefly how to conduct a Monte Carlo study to investigate the relative power of the Goldfeld–Quandt and the Breusch–Pagan tests for a specific case of heteroskedasticity.

5 Explain how you would generate 25 observations on an AR(1) error for use in a Monte Carlo study.

6 Explain briefly but clearly how to do a Monte Carlo study to examine the difference between the risk functions of the OLS estimator, a relevant EGLS estimator, and a relevant pre-test estimator for a case in which the CLR model holds except that we *may* have a first-order autocorrelated error.

7 You believe the CLR model assumptions apply to $y = \alpha + \beta x + \varepsilon$ except that you fear that the error variance is larger for the last half of the data than for the first half. You also fear that the error is not distributed normally, so that the Goldfeld–Quandt test will not have an F distribution. Explain how to bootstrap the Goldfeld–Quandt statistic to test the null that the error variances are the same.

8 Suppose you have estimated cost share equations assuming a translog production function homogeneous of degree one, using a SURE estimation procedure imposing sym-

metry constraints. You estimate substitution and price elasticities using formidable-looking formulas and wish to produce confidence intervals for these elasticity estimates. Explain in detail how to bootstrap to produce the confidence intervals.

GG   Nonspherical Errors: General

1 Because it provides a better fit to the sample data, the GLS estimator is considered more desirable than the OLS estimator in the GLR model. True, false, or uncertain? Explain.

2 In the absence of lagged dependent variables serving as regressors, the problems caused by autocorrelated errors concern efficiency, not consistency. True, false, or uncertain? Explain.

3 Suppose it is suspected that the error term in a CLR model has as variance–covariance matrix a known matrix Ω. It is suggested that this could be tested by setting up a test statistic based on the difference between the GLS and the OLS estimators of the coefficient vector. Comment on this proposal.

4 Suppose we have data from a GLR model and run OLS. Then we learn the *true* error variance–covariance matrix and so run GLS. We note from the computer output that for some of the coefficients the standard errors in the second regression are larger than in the first regression. Is this possible? Explain why or why not.

5 Negative autocorrelation in the disturbances can reduce the variance of the OLS estimator below what it would be in the absence of autocorrelation. Is it possible that it could make the variance less than that of the GLS estimator? Explain intuitively why or why not.

6 If the presence of nonspherical errors causes our variance estimates of the OLS coefficients to be overestimated, then the probability of making a type I error increases. True, false, or uncertain? Explain.

HH   Heteroskedasticity: General

1 Suppose the CLR model applies to $y = \alpha + \beta x + \theta w + \varepsilon$. A researcher mistakenly believes that the error variance is proportional to the square of x and so divides all the data through by x before running OLS. If x and w are positively correlated in the data, what can you say about the bias of the resulting estimate of θ? Explain.

2 If the variance of the disturbance is proportional to x, we should run a regression with all data divided by x. True, false, or uncertain? Explain.

3 The "solution" to heteroskedasticity involves multiplying through the estimating equation by a "correcting factor." Doing so will build spurious correlation into our estimating equation, rendering our ultimate regression results unmeaningful. True, false, or uncertain? Explain. *Hint:* Spurious correlation causes the R^2 to be higher than otherwise.

4 Suppose $y = \beta x + \varepsilon$ where the CLR assumptions hold except that the variance of the error term ε is a constant K times x^2. Then the BLUE is the average of the y values divided by the average of the x values. True, false, or uncertain? Explain.

5 Suppose the CLR model assumptions hold for both of the relationships $y = \beta x + \varepsilon$ and $w = \alpha x + u$, where ε and u are error terms with different variances. Your data

produce the two estimates β^{OLS} and α^{OLS}. Then although regressing $(y + w)$ on x produces an unbiased estimate of $(\beta + \alpha)$, it is not as efficient as $(\beta^{OLS} + \alpha^{OLS})$, because it does not allow for heteroskedasticity. True, false, or uncertain? Explain.

6 Suppose income is the dependent variable in a regression and contains errors of measurement (a) caused by people rounding their income to the nearest \$100, or (b) caused by people not knowing their exact income but always guessing within 5% of the true value. How do these alternative specifications affect the properties of the OLS estimator?

7 Suppose that all individuals have exactly the same consumption function $C_i = \beta_0 + \beta_1 Y_i + \varepsilon_i$ and suppose that the CLR model applies with the variance of ε denoted by σ^2. Now suppose that we have time series observations on *aggregate* data with varying numbers N_t of individuals. Assuming that β_0, β_1, and σ^2 are constant from time period to time period, and that the errors are time-independent, how would you estimate β_0 and β_1? *Hint*: Figure out how the aggregate data have been generated.

8 Suppose $y = (\alpha + \beta x)\varepsilon$ where the multiplicative error term ε is spherical with $E(\varepsilon) = 1$.
   (a) How would you estimate α and β? *Hint*: Express ε as one plus a new error.
   (b) How would you estimate α and β if in addition you knew that ε was distributed normally? Be explicit.

9 Suppose we have *two* equations, each satisfying the CLR model:

$$y = \alpha_0 + \alpha_1 x + \alpha_2 z + \varepsilon$$

$$p = \beta_0 + \beta_1 w + \beta_2 q + \beta_3 z + \varphi$$

Suppose you know that $\alpha_1 + \beta_1 = 1$, $\alpha_2 = \beta_3$ and $V(\varepsilon) = 2V(\varphi)$. Explain how you would estimate.

10 Suppose you have N observations on a variable with constant mean μ but a heteroskedastic disturbance. What is the heteroskedasticity-consistent estimate of the variance of the sample mean? How does it compare to the usual estimate of this variance that ignores the heteroskedasticity?

11 Comment on the following statement: "If the errors are characterized by an ARCH process OLS is BLUE and therefore should be the estimator of choice."

12 Suppose that we have the model $w = \alpha + \beta x + \varepsilon$ and the CLR model applies except that w is a Box–Cox transformation of y and the variance of the error term is δx^θ.
   (a) Write out the log-likelihood for N observations on y and x.
   (b) Explain how you would test jointly for a linear functional form and homoskedasticity.
   (c) Suppose the test in (b) is rejected. Explain how you would test for linear functional form assuming heteroskedasticity. (The answer is in Lahiri and Egy, 1981.)

13 A friend is investigating the determinants of per capita demand for lamb in the 50 U.S. states. She shows you the following preliminary report. "Data were available for 1991 in current dollars. I regressed per capita lamb expenditure on state GDP, the state's 1991 average price of lamb, and state advertising on lamb during 1991. A Breusch–Pagan test suggests there is heteroskedasticity associated with GDP, so I divided all the data through by GDP and reran the regression. The coefficient on advertising is significantly positive suggesting that advertising should be increased." What advice would you offer your friend?

II   Autocorrelated Errors: General

1 The CLR model is applicable to the *weekly* relationship $y_t = \alpha + \beta x_t + \varepsilon_t$.
   (a) If you have aggregate data on (non-overlapping) two-week periods, how would you estimate?
   (b) If you have weekly moving-average data, with each observation being one-third of the sum of the actual data for the previous, current and following weeks, how would you estimate?
   Hint: Exploit the weekly relationship given above to determine the relationship relevant for your data. Example: For part (a), add the relationships for weeks 1 and 2 to get the relationship relevant for the first observation on the aggregate data.
2 While neither autocorrelated errors nor the presence of a lagged value of the regressand among the regressors introduces bias into OLS estimation, the combination of the two does. True, false, or uncertain? Explain.
3 Suppose $y_t = \alpha_1 + \alpha_2 y_{t-1} + \alpha_3 x_t + \alpha_4 x_{t-1} + \varepsilon_t$ and that $\alpha_2 \alpha_3 + \alpha_4 = 0$.
   (a) Explain how you would test this restriction.
   (b) How would you estimate, assuming the restriction is true?
   (c) Assuming the restriction is true, what kind of error would be associated with a regression on y on x? *Hint:* Use a lag operator.
   (d) What is the lesson here?
4 It is sometimes suggested that the DW statistic be used to test for nonlinearity. Provide an intuitive rationale for this.
5 Suppose in the report given in question HH13 your friend had stated that the DW statistic was close to two and concluded that autocorrelated errors was not a problem. What comment would you have made on this?

JJ   Heteroskedasticity: Testing

1 Suppose $y = \alpha + \beta x + \gamma D + \varepsilon$ where D is a dummy for sex. Explain how you would test that the variance of ε is the same for males as for females.
2 Suppose casual examination of residuals from a regression run on quarterly data suggests that the variance of the error term for the fourth quarter may be bigger than for the other quarters. Explain how you would test this.
3 The regression $y = \alpha + \beta x + \delta w$ produced $SSE = 14$ using annual data for 1961–70, and $SSE = 45$ using data for 1971–88. Use these results to calculate a Goldfeld–Quandt test for a change in error variance starting in 1971.
*4 Suppose the CLR model applies to $y = \beta x + \varepsilon$ except that heteroskedasticity is suspected. You have the observations 1, 2, −3, 0 on x, and corresponding observations 4, 3, −6 and −1 on y.
   (a) What is the usual estimate of the variance of the OLS *ESTIMATOR*?
   (b) What is White's heteroskedasticity-consistent estimate of the variance of the OLS estimator?
   (c) What is the value of White's test statistic for heteroskedasticity?
   (d) Suppose you suspected that there was heteroskedasticity of the form $\sigma^2 = g(\alpha + \delta x^2)$ where g is some unknown function. What is the value of the studentized Breusch–Pagan statistic?

5 From a sample of 25 observations, each representing a group of households (taken from a prominent family expenditure survey), the result

$$y = 10 + 0.14x \quad DW = 0.4 \quad R^2 = 0.6 \quad \chi^2 = 7.8$$

was obtained, where y is expenditure on food and x is total expenditure. The χ^2 refers to the Breusch–Pagan test of homogeneity versus $\sigma^2 = \exp(\alpha_1 + \alpha_2 \ln x + \alpha_3 \ln z)$ where z is the reciprocal of the number of households in each group. What suggestions would you offer?

KK   Heteroskedasticity: Numerical Examples

1 Suppose we have observations $y_1 = 1$, $y_2 = 3$ and $y_3 = 5$ from the GLR model $y = \beta + \varepsilon$ (i.e., only an intercept) with $V(\varepsilon)$ diagonal with diagonal elements 1.0, 0.5 and 0.2. Calculate:
   (a) β^{OLS} and β^{GLS};
   (b) $V(\beta^{OLS})$ and $V(\beta^{GLS})$;
   (c) the traditional estimate of $V(\beta^{OLS})$, namely $s^2(X'X)^{-1}$;
   (d) the estimate of $V(\beta^{GLS})$, assuming you only know that $V(\varepsilon)$ is proportional to the variance–covariance matrix specified above.
2 Suppose x, y and w are, respectively, 1, 6 and 12, and that you know that $x = \theta + \varepsilon_1$, $y = 2\theta + \varepsilon_2$ and $w = 3\theta + \varepsilon_3$ where the ε_i are independent with zero expectations and variances 1, 4, and 9, respectively. What is your estimate of θ?
3 Suppose the CLR model holds for $y = \beta x + \varepsilon$ except that σ_t^2 is proportional to x. You have observations 3, 10, and 15 on y, and corresponding observations 1, 4, and 9 on x.
   (a) Find the GLS estimate of β, and its estimated variance, using the GLS formula.
   (b) Find the GLS estimate of β, and its estimated variance, by applying OLS to transformed data.
   (c) How much more efficient is this estimate than OLS?
4 Suppose the CLR model holds for $y = \alpha + \beta x + \varepsilon$ except that you suspect that the variance of the error term for the first 22 observations is not the same as for the other 32 observations. For the first 22 observations the data (expressed as deviations about their means) yield $\Sigma xy = 100$, $\Sigma x^2 = 10$, and $\Sigma y^2 = 1,040$. For the remaining observations the data yield $\Sigma xy = 216$, $\Sigma x^2 = 16$, and $\Sigma y^2 = 3,156$.
   (a) Perform a Goldfeld–Quandt test at the 5% significance level to test whether the error variances are the same in both periods.
   (b) Assuming that the error variances differ between the two periods, what is β^{EGLS}?
   (c) What estimate of the variance of β^{OLS} would you use if you believed that the error variances differ between the two periods? *Hint*: Recall that $SSR = \beta^{OLS'}X'y$.

LL   Autocorrelated Errors: Numerical Examples

1 Suppose we have four observations on y produced as follows: $y_t = K + \varepsilon_t$, $t = 1,2,3,4$ where K is a constant. Suppose further that $\varepsilon_t = u_t + u_{t-1} + u_{t-2}$ where the u_t are iid with mean zero and variance 1/3. Let K^* be the sample mean of the ys and let K^{**} be the average of the first and last observations on y. Which of these two estimators do you prefer? Why?

2 Suppose $y_t = K + \varepsilon_t$ where $\varepsilon_t = u_t + u_{t-1}$ with the u_t independent $N(0,\sigma^2)$ variables. If you have three observations $y_1 = 4$, $y_2 = 5$, and $y_3 = 3$, what is your estimate of K?

3 Suppose the CLR model applies to $y = \beta x + \varepsilon$ except that ε is first-order auto-correlated with autocorrelation coefficient $\rho = 0.5$ and variance 9. You have two observations on x and y; the first observations are $x = 1$ and $y = 4$, and the second observations are $x = 2$ and $y = 10$.
   (a) What is the OLS estimate of β?
   (b) What is the GLS estimate of β?
   (c) What are the variances of these two estimates?

4 Suppose the CLR model applies to $y = \beta x + \varepsilon$ where there are only two observations, with $x_1 = 1$ and $y_2 = 2$, except that the error vector has the distribution $p(1,1) = 0.1$, $p(1,-1) = 0.4$, $p(-1,1) = 0.4$, and $p(-1,-1) = 0.1$.
   (a) What is the bias of β^{OLS}?
   (b) What is its variance?
   (c) What is the variance of the BLUE?

MM   SURE: Numerical Examples

1 Suppose $y_1 = \beta + \varepsilon_1$ and $y_2 = \varepsilon_2$ where the ε_i have variance 2 and covariance 1. What formula would you use to estimate β given T corresponding observations on the ys?

2 Suppose $y_1 = \mu_1 + \varepsilon_1$ and $y_2 = \mu_2 + \varepsilon_2$ where the εs have variances 2 and 3, respectively, and covariance 1.
   (a) Given 20 observations with $\Sigma y_1 = 60$ and $\Sigma y_2 = 100$ what are your estimates of the μs?
   (b) If in addition you knew that $\mu_2 = 2\mu_1$, what are your estimates of the μs?

3 Suppose $y = \alpha x + u$ and $q = \beta w + v$ where u and v are serially independent errors with zero means, $V(u) = 2$, $V(v) = 3$, and $E(u_t v_r) = 1$ for $t = r$ and zero otherwise. Data are expressed as deviations from means. Using the sample moment matrix

		y	q	x	w
x		3	6	4	2
w		1	1	2	1

   (a) Find the BLUEs of α and β.
   (b) Test $\beta = 2\alpha$.
   (c) Suppose you had not been told the values for $V(u) = 2$, $V(v) = 3$, and $E(u_t, v_r)$. If the sample size is 11, $\Sigma y^2 = 25$, $\Sigma q^2 = 33$, and $\Sigma yq = 15$, what estimates would you use in their stead?

NN   Stochastic Extraneous Information

1 In the CLR model $y = \alpha + \beta x + \delta w + \varepsilon$, if an extraneous unbiased estimator of β, say β^*, is available, then regressing $y - \beta^* x$ on w will provide a better estimate of δ than is obtainable from the regression of y on x and w. True, false, or uncertain? Explain intuitively.

*2 Suppose the CLR model applies to $Y = X_1\beta_1 + X_2\beta_2 + \varepsilon$ so that β_2^{OLS} is given by $(X_2'M_1X_2)^{-1}X_2'M_1Y$. Suppose β_2^* is an unbiased estimate of β_2 from a previous study, with variance–covariance matrix V_2^*.

(a) What are the variance–covariance matrices of β_1^{OLS} and β_2^{OLS}? Call them V_1 and V_2.

(b) Show that regressing $Y - X_2\beta_2^*$ on X_1 produces an unbiased estimate β_1^* of β_1.

(c) What is the variance–covariance matrix of β_1^*? Call in W.

(d) Show that W is smaller than V_1 if $V_2 - V_2^*$ is nnd.

(e) What is the common sense of this result?

Hint: For part (d) use the result (from partitioned matrix inversion) that $(X_1'M_2X_1)^{-1} = (X_1'X_1)^{-1} + (X_1'X_1)^{-1}X_1'X_2(X_2'M_1X_2)^{-1}X_2'X_1(X_1'X_1)^{-1}$. (The answer is Goldberger, 1964, pp. 258–9.)

3 Suppose $y = \beta x + \varepsilon$ and the CLR model assumptions hold with the variance of ε known to be 16. Suppose you have data on y and on x, with $\Sigma xy = 186$ and $\Sigma x^2 = 26$. Suppose that β was estimated unbiasedly in a previous study to be 6, with a variance of 4.

(a) What is your estimate of β? Explain your reasoning, as well as producing an actual number for your estimate.

(b) What is the variance of your estimate? How much lower is it than the variance of the estimate that does not incorporate the information from the previous study?

4 Suppose β in $y = \beta x + \varepsilon$ was estimated unbiasedly in a previous study to be 3, with an estimated variance of 4. Suppose you have 21 observations, for which the CLR model holds, with $\Sigma xy = 20$, $\Sigma y^2 = 360$ and $\Sigma x^2 = 10$.

(a) What is your estimate of β? *Hint*: Use SSE = SST − SSR = $\Sigma y^2 - (\beta^{OLS})^2\Sigma x^2$

(b) What is the approximate efficiency gain over $\beta^{OLS} = 2$?

5 Suppose you have 22 annual observations on output Y, capital K and labor L and you plan to estimate a Cobb–Douglas production function. You suspect that there is approximately constant returns to scale and so wish to build this information into your estimation procedure. Your uncertainty is captured by a variance of 0.01 attached to your "guestimate" of constant returns to scale. Explain how you would estimate.

6 You have 75 observations on a dependent variable y and two independent variables x and w, for which the CLR model assumptions hold. You give your data to your research assistant, foolishly not keeping a copy, and instruct him to run the appropriate OLS regression. Unfortunately he is shortly thereafter killed in a tragic accident. You hire a replacement. She cannot find either the data or the regression results in her predecessor's files, but she is very industrious and finds a new, comparable sample with 95 observations. She reports to you the regression results using these new data.

(a) Suppose she finds the missing regression results. What instructions would you give her? Be explicit.

(b) Suppose she finds the lost data. Would you change your instructions of part (a)? If yes, what are your new instructions?

OO Nonspherical Errors: Theoretical Results

1 Suppose the GLR model holds. Derive the formula for the GLS estimator incorporating extraneous information in the form of a set of J linear restraints $R\beta = r$.

*2 Suppose $Y = X\beta + \varepsilon$ and the GLR model holds with var(ε) = Ω. Suppose further that $\Omega = I + XVX'$ with V any symmetric positive definite matrix.

(a) By repeated application of the theorem

$$(A + BCB')^{-1} = A^{-1} - A^{-1}B(B'A^{-1}B + C^{-1})^{-1}B'A^{-1}$$

show that the OLS and GLS estimators are identical in this special case.

(b) What implication does this result have for Monte Carlo studies relating to non-spherical errors? *Hints*: Three applications of the theorem are necessary. Interpret a negative sign on the LHS as a negative sign on C.

*3 Show that the seemingly unrelated estimator

$$\text{SURE} = [W'(\Sigma^{-1} \otimes I)W]^{-1}W'(\Sigma^{-1} \otimes I)y$$

yields the same result as OLS applied to the individual equations for the cases in which
(a) the Σ matrix is diagonal; or
(b) the X matrix is the same in all equations. *Hint*: Make use of $(A \otimes B)^{-1} = A^{-1} \otimes B^{-1}$ and then $(A \otimes B)(C \otimes D) = AC \otimes BD$.

PP Heteroskedasticity: Theoretical Results

*1 The Breusch–Pagan statistic can be written as $w'Z(Z'Z)^{-1}Z'w/2s^{*4}$, where w_t is $e_t^2 - s^{*2}$ and s^{*2} is the average of the e_t^2, the squared OLS residuals. Here Z is a matrix of observations on variables thought to affect the variance of the error term, with the first column a column of ones. It is claimed that this is equivalent to one-half the regression sum of squares from a regression of e_t^2/s^{*2} on Z. Explain why this is so.

*2 Suppose the CNLR model applies to $y = \beta x + \varepsilon$ except that the variance of ε_t is $\exp(\alpha w_t)$. Find the Cramer–Rao lower bound for the variance of the estimate of α.

3 A popular general form of heteroskedasticity is $\sigma_t^2 = \exp(\alpha'x_t)$ where α is a vector of parameters, and x_t is a vector of observations on variables influencing the variance. The first element of x_t is set equal to unity.
(a) Why is the first element of x_t set equal to one?
(b) What is the null hypothesis of homoskedasticity in terms of the parameters?
(c) Show how the form $\sigma^2 = kw^\theta$, where k and θ are parameters, and w an exogenous variable, is a special case of this general form.

*4 Suppose the CLR model holds for $y = X\beta + \varepsilon$ except that $\sigma_t^2 = \sigma^2 x_t^\alpha$. Show that the LR test statistic for testing $\alpha = 0$ is LR $= T\ln(\sigma^2)^* - \Sigma\ln(\sigma_t^2)^{**}$ where T is the sample size, $(\sigma^2)^*$ is the restricted MLE of σ_t^2 and $(\sigma_t^2)^{**}$ is the unrestricted MLE of σ_t^2. (The answer is in Harvey, 1981, p. 164.)

*5 Suppose $y = X\beta + \varepsilon$ and you wish to calculate the heteroskedasticity-consistent estimate of the variance of the OLS estimator. Define a transformation matrix P with the inverses of the OLS residuals on the diagonal and zeros elsewhere. Transform y and X to obtain $y^* = Py$ and $X^* = PX$, and create $W = P^{-1}X$.
(a) Show that the IV estimator of y^* regressed on X^*, using W as a set of instruments for X^*, is just β^{OLS}.
(b) Use the formula for the variance of the IV estimator assuming a spherical error to find the estimated variance–covariance matrix of this estimator.
(c) Explain what relationship this bears to White's heteroskedasticity consistent estimate of the variance of the OLS estimator. (The answer is in Messer and White, 1984, pp. 182–3.)

6 Suppose the probability P of owning a VCR is given by the logit formulation $P = (1 + \exp{-(\alpha + \beta x)})^{-1}$ where x is income implying that $Q = \ln[P/(1 - P)] = \alpha + \beta x$. You group the data (on the basis of x) to calculate for each group $Q^* = \ln(P^*/1 - P^*)$ where P^* is the proportion of households in that group owning

a VCR. Consider now $Q^* = \alpha + \beta x + \varepsilon$ where ε arises entirely from the fact that Q^* is estimated. Estimation of this equation incorporates a correction for heteroskedasticity based on the variance of ε_i being given by $[N_i P_i (1 - P_i)]^{-1}$, where N_i is the number of households in the ith group. Show how this variance is derived. *Hint*: Q^* is a (nonlinear) function of P^* and the variance of P^* you know.

QQ   Autocorrelated Errors: Theoretical Results

1 Suppose you are regressing using observations on N households for two consecutive time periods. Assume the errors are cross-sectionally uncorrelated, but timewise autocorrelated with common ρ.
   (a) What does the variance–covariance matrix of the errors look like?
   (b) Devise a transformation matrix that enables you to use OLS for estimation purposes. *Hint*: Work it out for $N = 2$.

*2 For what values of the first-order autocorrelation coefficient will first differencing reduce the degree of first-order autocorrelation? *Hint*: Let $\varepsilon_t = \rho \varepsilon_{t-1} + u_t$ so that first differencing creates an error $v_t = \varepsilon_t - \varepsilon_{t-1}$. Find the values of ρ for which the absolute value of the autocorrelation between v_t and v_{t-1} is less than $|\rho|$.

*3 Suppose $y_t = \beta y_{t-1} + \varepsilon_t$ and that $\varepsilon_t = u_t + u_{t-1}$ where the us are iid with zero mean and variance σ^2. Derive an expression for the asymptotic bias of β^{OLS} in terms of β and σ^2.

*4 Suppose the CLR model applies to $y = X\beta + \varepsilon$ except that $\varepsilon_t = \rho \varepsilon_{t-2} + u_t$, as might be the case, for example, for semi-annual data. Suppose you have five observations, the variance of u is σ^2, and ρ is known.
   (a) What is the appropriate transformation to use to compute the GLS estimator? *Hint*: Make a guess, based on what you know about first-order autocorrelated errors.
   (b) Confirm your answer by showing explicitly that the 5×5 transformation matrix P that it implies is such that $P'P = \Omega^{-1}$, where Ω is the variance–covariance matrix of ε, to a factor of proportionality.

RR   Dynamics

1 Suppose a firm selects the value of y_t to minimize the cost function $\alpha_1(y_t - y_t^*)^2 + \alpha_2(y_t - y_{t-1})^2$ consisting of a weighted sum of "disequilibrium" and "adjustment" costs (y^* is the desired level of y). Show that this leads to a traditional partial adjustment estimation model.

2 Consider the "adaptive expectations" model

$$y_t = \beta_1 x_t^e$$
$$x_t^e = \delta x_t + (1 - \delta) x_{t-1}^e$$

where one of these two equations must have an error term added to it to provide a stochastic element. Regardless of which equation has the error term, the resulting estimating equation will have a nonspherical error. True, false, or uncertain? Explain.

3 Consider the consumption function $C_t = \beta Y P_t + \alpha(L_{t-1} - L_t^*) + \varepsilon_t$ where L_{t-1} is

liquid assets at the beginning of the current period and L_t^* is the desired level of such assets during the current period, given as a proportion θ of permanent income YP. Permanent income is determined by an adaptive expectations process $YP_t = YP_{t-1} + \lambda(Y_t - YP_{t-1})$.

(a) Show that the relevant estimating equation has C_{t-1}, L_{t-1}, L_{t-2} and Y_t as explanatory variables.

(b) Comment on the estimation problems of this estimating equation.

4 Consider the "partial adjustment" model

$$y_t^* = \beta_1 x_t + \beta_2 w_t$$
$$y_t - y_{t-1} = \delta(y_t^* - y_{t-1}) + \varepsilon_t$$

and the "adaptive expectations" model

$$y_t = \beta_1 x_t^e + \beta_2 w_t + \varepsilon_t$$
$$x_t^e = \delta x_t + (1 - \delta)x_{t-1}^e$$

(a) How would you discriminate between these two models?

(b) How would your answer to (a) be affected if $\beta_2 = 0$?

5 Consider an accelerator model in which the actual capital stock K moves towards the desired K^* according to a partial adjustment process $K_t - K_{t-1} = \lambda(K_t^* - K_{t-1})$. Assume a constant capital/output ratio to justify K^* as a fraction θ of output Y, and assume a depreciation rate δ so that gross investment I is $I_t = K_t - K_{t-1} + \delta K_{t-1}$.

(a) Derive an estimating relationship in which I_t is regressed on Y_t and K_{t-1} and discuss its identification properties.

(b) Suppose you do not have data on K. Eliminate K and then discuss the identification properties of the resulting estimating equation. *Hint*: Solve for K using the lag operator.

(c) What is the long-run impact of a sustained unit change in Y? Does your answer make economic sense? Explain.

6 Suppose p is determined linearly by p^e and two other explanatory variables x and w, with p^e determined adaptively as $p_t^e = p_{t-1}^e + \lambda(p_{t-1} - p_{t-1}^e)$.

(a) Derive the estimating equation and discuss its estimating problems.

(b) Consider the following two ways of estimating this equation, both of which assume a spherical error term: (i) OLS; and (ii) OLS in conjunction with a "search" over λ. Will these estimates be essentially the same? If not, which would you prefer, and why?

(c) How is your answer to (b) affected if the coefficient on w is known to be zero?

7 Consider the dynamic model (1): $y_t = \eta + \alpha y_{t-1} + \beta_0 x_t + \beta_1 x_{t-1} + \varepsilon_t$. The long-run equilibrium is $y = \theta x$ where θ, the long-run multiplier, is $(\beta_0 + \beta_1)/(1 - \alpha)$, which can be estimated by running OLS on equation (1) and plugging the OLS estimates into the formula for θ. The variance of this estimate can be estimated by using the formula for the variance of a nonlinear function of a vector.

(a) Show how equation (1) can be rewritten to allow direct estimation of θ and its variance by regressing y on x, Δy and Δx. *Hint*: Begin by subtracting αy_t from both sides.

(b) Most dynamic models can be rewritten as "error-correction models," expressing this period's change in y as a linear function of (among other things) the extent to which the system was in disequilibrium in the previous period. What is the "error-correction" form for equation (1)? *Hint*: Start by subtracting y_{t-1} from both sides.

(c) In some empirical work the y and the x in the preceding are variables expressed in logarithms, and the error-correction term (i.e., the extent to which the system was in disequilibrium) is expressed as ($\ln y_{t-1} - \ln x_{t-1}$). What, in words, does this imply about the nature of the equilibrium relationship assumed between y and x?

8 Suppose Ey is influenced by both x and z, each having its impact distributed according to a Koyck distributed lag, but with different parameters, so that

$$y_t = \alpha + \beta(1 - \lambda L)^{-1}x_t + \theta(1 - \delta L)^{-1}z_t$$

where L is the lag operator.

(a) Find the relevant estimating equation and explain why it is overidentified. How many overidentifying restrictions are there?

(b) Assuming a random error added onto the estimating equation, explain how you would test each of the overidentifying restrictions separately using a t test. Does the error need to be distributed normally? Why or why not?

(c) Explain how you would test these restrictions jointly.

SS Stochastic Regressors: Monte Carlo

1 Explain how to undertake a Monte Carlo study to examine the relative merits of OLS and 2SLS in the simultaneous equation system

$$D: Q = \alpha_0 + \alpha_1 P + \alpha_2 Y + \alpha_3 A + \varepsilon_1 \quad S: Q = \beta_0 + \beta_1 P + \varepsilon_2$$

2 Explain how to conduct a Monte Carlo study to compare OLS and IV estimators in the context of measurement errors.

TT Measurement Error

1 In the "permanent income" model $c^* = \beta y^*$, in which the asterisked variables are observed with error, the sample mean ratio (the mean of c divided by the mean of y) is a more desirable estimator of β than is β^{OLS}. True, false, or uncertain? Explain in one sentence.

2 Measurement errors in a dependent variable create bias in OLS estimates and increase their variance. True, false, or uncertain? Explain.

3 The argument that inflation stimulates growth has been discredited by regressing (across countries in a given year) y, the rate of growth in real income, on x, the rate of inflation. However, inflation and real income measures are notoriously subject to error. Suppose that there is in reality an exact linear relation between y^*, the true rate of growth in real income, and x^*, the true rate of inflation. Their sum, $w^* = x^* + y^*$, the true rate of growth in *money* income, is correctly measured, but x^* is erroneously measured as $x = x^* + \varepsilon$ where ε is an independent random error, and y^* is measured as $y = w^* - x$.

(a) Derive a useful expression for the asymptotic bias of the OLS estimator.

(b) What implication can be drawn regarding the discreditation mentioned above?

4   Consider $y = \beta x + \varepsilon$ where x is measured with error. (Note no intercept.) Show explicitly that the two-group method produces the same estimate as using an instrumental variable with -1 and $+1$ values.

5   Suppose the CLR model applies to $y = \alpha_0 + \alpha_1 x + \alpha_2 w + \varepsilon$ except that estimated values of w have been employed, and w has been overestimated in your sample.

(a) If the measured w is the true w plus 2, what are the implications for your estimates of the α_i?

(b) If the measured w is 1.15 times the true w?

(c) If the measured w is the true w plus a random error distributed uniformly between zero and four?

*6 For the special case of $y = \beta x + \varepsilon$, where x is measured with error, show that the OLS and reverse regression estimates of β can be interpreted as providing bounds on β.

UU   Instrumental Variables

1   Suppose $y = X\beta + \varepsilon$ and a set of instrumental variables Z is available for X.

(a) Show that β^{IV} can be obtained by regressing y on W, the predicted values of X resulting from a regression of X on Z.

(b) Use the result of (a) to suggest a formula for the variance–covariance matrix of the instrumental variable estimator.

2   Suppose $y_t = \alpha_t + \beta x_t + \gamma z_t + \theta y_{t-1} + \varepsilon_t + \phi \varepsilon_{t-1}$ so that the regressor y_{t-1} and the error are contemporaneously correlated. What would you choose as an instrumental variable to produce the IV estimator? Be explicit.

3   Suppose the CLR model applies to $y = \beta x + \varepsilon$ but you choose to estimate β by using the instrumental variable estimator that results from using the fixed regressor w as an instrument for x. You have three observations on the triple (y, x, w): $(-21, -1, 1)$, $(14, 1, 2)$, and $(21, 2, 3)$.

(a) What is the ratio of the MSE of β^{OLS} to the MSE of β^{IV}?

(b) What t statistic value would you use to test $\beta = 12$, assuming estimation using β^{IV}?

4   Suppose the CLR model applies to $y = X\beta + \varepsilon$ except that $V(\varepsilon) = \sigma^2\Omega$ and X is contemporaneously correlated with ε. Assume that a set of instrumental variables W is available for X and you know the transformation matrix P such that $P'P = \Omega^{-1}$. Using intuition, formulate an IV estimator that has been "modified" to correct for nonspherical errors and suggest how you would estimate its variance–covariance matrix. Explain the logic of your intuition.

5   Consider $m = \beta i + \varepsilon$ where m is the money supply and i is the interest rate, and for simplicity we have ignored the usual income variable and omitted the intercept. Suppose that the money supply is determined exogenously by the monetary authorities, so that ε relates to i, not m.

(a) Show explicitly that using m as an instrument for i produces the same estimate as inverse least squares.

(b) Suppose you know that for certain observations m was determined exogenously by the monetary authorities and for the other observations i was determined exogenously. How would you estimate? *Hint*: Use the result in (a). (The answer is in Kohli, 1989, p. 283.)

6 Suppose $y = \beta x + \varepsilon$ where there is no intercept and one explanatory variable.
  (a) Show that using the moment condition $\Sigma x\varepsilon = 0$ results in OLS.
  (b) Show that using the moment condition $\Sigma z\varepsilon = 0$ results in IV.
  (c) Spell out what you would do to produce the GMM estimate here. Be explicit.

7 You have observations on y, i, and h. You wish to estimate $y = \alpha + \beta i + \theta h + \varepsilon$ but suspect that h is measured with error. Suppose also that you have in your data file two legitimate instruments for h, namely w and z.
  (a) Explain how you would test for this measurement error.
  (b) Assuming measurement error, explain how you would estimate.

VV   Simultaneous Equations

1   The main reason that we seldom use OLS to estimate the coefficients of a structural equation in a simultaneous equation model is that other methods of estimation are available which yield better-fitting equations. True, false, or uncertain? Explain.

2   If the equation is not identified, the OLS estimator cannot be calculated. True, false, or uncertain? Explain.

3   Suppose you wish to estimate the equation $y = \alpha_0 + \alpha_1 x + \alpha_2 w + \varepsilon$ and there is another equation $x = \delta_0 + \delta_1 y + v$. You want to ignore this other equation and use OLS, but a colleague advises you instead to regress x on w, get predicted values x^* and then regress y on x^* and w.
  (a) What is the rationale behind this advice?
  (b) Is it good advice?

4   Suppose $y_1 = \alpha_0 + \alpha_1 y_2 + \alpha_2 x + \varepsilon_1$ and $y_2 = \beta_0 + \beta_1 y_1 + \varepsilon_2$, and the reduced form estimates are $y_1 = 2 + 4x$ and $y_2 = 1 + 8x$.
  (a) Estimate the identified structural coefficients.
  (b) Assume that $\alpha_1 = 0$ and estimate the identified structural coefficients.
  (c) Assume that $\alpha_0 = 0$ and estimate the identified structural coefficients.

5   Consider the simultaneous equation model $Q = \alpha P + \delta x + \varepsilon$ and $Q = \beta P + u$ where x is exogenous. Your data yield $\Sigma Q^2 = 110$, $\Sigma P^2 = 50$, $\Sigma x^2 = 80$, $\Sigma PQ = 100$, $\Sigma Qx = 90$, and $\Sigma Px = 30$.
  (a) What is the OLS estimate of β? The 2SLS estimate? The indirect least squares estimate?
  (b) Which estimation method would you choose to estimate α and δ?

6   Consider the simultaneous equation model

$$y_1 = \alpha_1 y_2 + \varepsilon_1$$
$$y_2 = \alpha_2 y_1 + \beta_1 x_1 + \beta_2 x_2 + \varepsilon_2$$

$$\text{with } X'X = \begin{bmatrix} 1 & 0 \\ 0 & 1 \end{bmatrix} \quad X'Y = \begin{bmatrix} 2 & 3 \\ 3 & 4 \end{bmatrix}$$

What are the 2SLS estimates of the identified parameter(s)?

7   Consider the following simultaneous equation model, where the errors are not independent: $y_1 = \beta x + u_1$ and $y_2 = \alpha y_1 + u_2$.
   (a) How would you estimate β?
   (b) Show that the ILS and 2SLS estimators of α are identical. Call it α^*.
   (c) What is it about this example that makes them identical?
   (d) Evaluate the use of α^* as opposed to α^{OLS}.
   (e) On the basis of this example, what general conclusion would you draw about estimation in the context of recursive simultaneous equations?

8   When estimating the reduced form of a system of simultaneous equations, we do not incorporate the fact that the reduced form disturbances are correlated across equations. Should we, to obtain more efficient estimates? Why or why not?

9   Consider a cobweb model in which demand is $Q_t = \alpha_0 + \alpha_1 P_t$ and supply is $Q_t = \beta_0 + \beta_1 w$ where w is (a) P_{t-1}, (b) an adaptive expectation of P_t using the adaptive expectations mechanism $P_t^e = \theta P_{t-1}^e + (1 - \theta)P_{t-1}$, or (c) the rational expectation of P_t. Given time series data on P and Q, explain how you would choose among these three specifications.

*10   Suppose S: $q = \alpha p + u$ and D: $q = \beta p + v$ are two relations operating simultaneously, where the errors u and v have zero covariance and q and p are quantity and price measured in logs.
   (a) Show that the plim of the least squares regression coefficient of q on p is equal to a weighted average of α and β, the weights being the variances of u and v, respectively.
   (b) Show why this estimate could be interpreted as a lower limit on the absolute values of the supply and demand elasticities.
   (c) If $\sigma_v^2 = k\sigma_u^2$ where k is a known constant, show how α and β can be estimated. *Hint*: Two regressions are needed.
   (d) What does this question illustrate about identification?

WW   Hausman Tests

1   Comment on the following test for contemporaneous correlation between X and ε. Run OLS on the original equation, then regress the estimated errors on X and test the resulting coefficient vector against zero, using an F test.

2   Suppose the CLR model applies to $y = \alpha_0 + \alpha_1 x + \alpha_2 w + \varepsilon$ except that you suspect that w contains measurement error. Fortunately an instrument is available for w and you are able to conduct a Hausman test. Because only the w variable is suspect, the degrees of freedom for the Hausman chi-square test statistic is one. True, false, or uncertain? Explain.

3   Suppose $y = X\beta + \varepsilon$ and on the null hypothesis satisfies the CNLR model assumptions. Let Z be an instrumental variable for X (where Z also is fixed in repeated samples). Consider $q = \beta^{OLS} - \beta^{IV}$.
   (a) What is the expected value of q?
   (b) Find the covariance between β^{OLS} and q by calculating $E(\beta^{OLS} - E\beta^{OLS})(q - Eq)'$.
   (c) Use the result of (b) to find $V(q)$ in terms of $V(\beta^{OLS})$ and $V(\beta^{IV})$.
   (d) What test statistic could be employed to test the vector $q = 0$?
   (e) Explain in words what conclusion it would be reasonable to draw if q tested significantly different from zero (i.e., what are the null and alternative hypotheses of this test?). (The answer is in Hausman, 1978, p. 1253.)

4 Suppose $y = X\beta + \varepsilon$ and on the null hypothesis satisfies the CLR model assumptions. Let Z be an instrumental variable for X (where Z also is fixed in repeated samples).
(a) By inserting $y = X\beta^{OLS} + \varepsilon^{OLS}$ into the formula for the IV estimator, express $\beta^{IV} - \beta^{OLS}$ as a function of ε^{OLS}.
(b) Use this result to calculate the formula for the variance–covariance matrix of $\beta^{IV} - \beta^{OLS}$ in terms of $V(\beta^{IV})$ and $V(\beta^{OLS})$.

5 Suppose $y = \beta x + \varepsilon$, where you know that $V(\varepsilon) = 100$, and you have observations 20, 30, -50, 60, -60 on y, corresponding observations 3, 7, -4, 5, -11 on x and corresponding observations 1, 2, -2, 4, -5 on z, an instrument for x.
(a) Perform a Hausman test directly by calculating the OLS and IV estimators and taking their difference, etc.
(b) What is the OV version of this Hausman test? Calculate the square of the relevant statistic.
(c) An alternative way of conducting the OV version is as follows. Calculate the predicted x values, w, from a regression of x on z. Regress y on x and w and perform a Hausman test indirectly by testing the coefficient on w against zero. Show that this produces the same test statistic as in (b).

6 Suppose it is believed that $y = \alpha + \beta x + \varepsilon$. Student A has run OLS to obtain $\alpha^{OLS} = 12$ and $\beta^{OLS} = 21$ with $V(\alpha^{OLS})$, $V(\beta^{OLS})$ and $C(\alpha^{OLS}, \beta^{OLS})$ estimated as 2, 4 and -1, respectively. Student B believes that this equation is part of a simultaneous equation system and has run 2SLS to obtain $\alpha^{2SLS} = 14$ and $\beta^{2SLS} = 20$ with $V(\alpha^{2SLS})$, $V(\beta^{2SLS})$ and $C(\alpha^{2SLS}, \beta^{2SLS})$ estimated as 3, 6 and -2, respectively. Use these results to test student B's belief that x is an endogenous variable.

7 Suppose we have a single equation from a system of simultaneous equations, namely $Q = \alpha_0 + \alpha_1 P + \alpha_2 Y + \alpha_3 A + \varepsilon$ where Q and P are thought to be endogenous, A is thought to be exogenous, and there is some dispute over whether Y is endogenous or exogenous. Researcher A has applied 2SLS assuming that Y is endogenous, producing estimates α^* with estimated covariance matrix $V(\alpha^*)$. Researcher B has applied 2SLS assuming that Y is exogenous, producing estimates α^{**} with estimated covariance matrix $V(\alpha^{**})$. Explain how you would use these results to test whether or not Y is endogenous. (The answer is in Spencer and Berk, 1981, p. 1079.)

XX   Qualitative and Limited Dependent Variables: Monte Carlo

1 Suppose observations on a dichotomous dependent variable have been generated by a logit model with a single explanatory variable x. The OLS estimator of the slope of x from a linear probability model could be used to estimate the effect of a change in x on the probability of the dependent variable equaling one. Explain how to conduct a Monte Carlo study to examine the bias of this estimator when x takes on its mean value.

2 Explain how to conduct a Monte Carlo study to compare the bias of the OLS estimator to that of the Tobit estimator, in the context of a censored sample.

3 Suppose you are estimating the fraction f of income spent on transportation as a function of several characteristics. You have data on f and several characteristics of 900 individuals. You estimate using the traditional $y = X\beta + \varepsilon$ but a friend suggests using a logistic functional form instead.
(a) Explain the easiest way to do this.

(b) Explain in detail how you would conduct a Monte Carlo study to investigate the relative merits of your and your friend's estimation of the influence of an explanatory variable on f, assuming that your friend's specification is correct.

(c) Explain how to bootstrap to find the variance of your friend's influence estimates.

4 You wish to estimate a salary equation $\ln y = \alpha + \beta x + \varepsilon$. You have observations on y, x and w for several individuals, but for those individuals for whom $\delta + \theta w + u$ is less than zero the observation on y is coded zero (u is an unobserved error). Explain how to conduct a Monte Carlo study to investigate the relative merits of OLS and the Heckman two-stage estimator.

YY Qualitative Dependent Variables

1 Suppose the probability of getting a student loan is determined by a student's grade point average (GPA), age, sex, and level of study – undergraduate, MA, or PhD student.

(a) Explain how to use the logit model to represent this.

(b) Given data on 45 students, 25 of whom were offered a loan, explain how to estimate the parameters of your model.

(c) How would you estimate the probability that a 23-year-old, male, undergraduate student, with a GPA of 3.2, will obtain a loan? Be explicit.

(d) Suppose you wish to test $\beta = 0$. Is an LM, LR or W test easiest? Explain why.

(e) Explain in detail how to use the test of part (d) to test for whether or not level of study has any influence on the probability of getting a loan.

2 Suppose the probability that a person is a smoker is given by the logit model, namely $e^{\alpha + \beta x}(1 + e^{\alpha - \beta x})^{-1}$ where x is a dummy variable taking the value one for males and zero for females. We have 100 observations, of which 10 are smoking males, 15 are smoking females, and 35 are nonsmoking males.

(a) What is the MLE of the probability that a person is a smoker, under the null that $\beta = 0$?

(b) What are the MLEs of α and β?

(c) What is the MLE of the probability that a male is a smoker, and of the probability that a female is a smoker? Compare these answers to those obtained by estimating the probability by the fraction of smokers in the data in the relevant category.

(d) Explain what calculations are needed to test the hypothesis that $\beta = 0$ using an LR test.

3 Unemployment insurance tax rates paid by firms vary, but there is an upper limit. Suppose you believe that the probability of being at this limit is affected by firm size, but that this influence of firm size varies across three identifiable industry types.

(a) How would you estimate?

(b) How would you test the hypothesis that this influence does not vary across industry type? Be explicit.

4 For a large sample of full-time salaried workers you have data on years of education, years of work experience, gender, race, occupational category and annual salary. Unfortunately, for reasons to do with the way the data were collected you only know the salary range, namely less than 20 thousand, between 20 and 30 thousand, between 30 and 40 thousand, etc., up to above 80 thousand. You wish to test jointly if (a) gender affects annual salary through the intercept, and (b) if gender affects the influence of experience on annual salary. Explain how you would perform the test.

5 Suppose you are surveying people to see how much they are willing to pay to create a park. You follow the advice of the contingency valuation literature and ask people a yes or no question – are you willing to pay $w?, where w is an amount that you vary from person to person. You specify that individuals value the park according to $v = X\beta + \varepsilon$ where X is a matrix of observations on individuals' characterisitcs, so that if $v_i \geq w_i$ individual i is willing to pay $w_i. Explain in detail how you would estimate β. The answer is in Cameron (1988).

6 The outcome of a new policy applied in all 50 US states was viewed as very successful, moderately successful or unsuccessful. Suppose the ith state's unobserved index of success is $y^*_i = \alpha + \beta x_i + \varepsilon_i$ and we wish to use an ordered logit model to estimate. What is the likelihood function?

ZZ Limited Dependent Variables

1 The average length of life for 900 US male professors was 73 years, compared to the US male life expectancy of 70 years. Can we conclude that professors live longer?

2 Suppose you wish to estimate the demand curve for tickets to hockey games. You believe that demand is determined linearly by a variety of variables, such as ticket prices, the relative standings of the home and visiting teams, home city income and population, etc. You have data for ten years, during which time some rinks were on several occasions sold out. What do you recommend doing with the data for the sold-out games?

3 We wish to estimate the hedonic prices of various characteristics of rental units by regressing rent on these characteristics. Some of our data are on rental units to which rent controls apply, so that the rent for these units (which can be identified) is below the free market price. Explain how to estimate.

4 Suppose the price of a stock is determined by $p = \alpha + \beta x + \varepsilon$ where ε is distributed normally with mean zero and variance σ^2. On some days the stock does not trade, so the bid and ask prices (P_b and P_a, respectively) are reported instead of the actual price (which if it were to have been determined, would lie between the bid and ask prices). Given a year's worth of daily data, including days on which the stock did not trade, explain how you would estimate.

*5 Suppose you are estimating the determinants of income assuming a CNLR model. To protect privacy all individuals with income greater than $100,000 were assigned the income value $100,000. Further, all those with income less than $5,000 were deleted from the sample. Explain how you would estimate.

6 Due to transactions costs, small changes in an independent variable will have no effect on the decision variable. Suppose the desired change in asset holdings, y^*, is determined by the change in yield, x, but that actual asset holdings, y, do not change for small changes in y^*. Suppose this is formalized through the following "friction" model:

$$\Delta y^* = \beta \Delta x + \varepsilon \text{ where } \varepsilon \sim N(0, \sigma^2)$$
$$\Delta y = \Delta y^* \text{ if } \Delta y^* < a_1 < 0$$
$$\Delta y = 0 \text{ if } a_1 \leq \Delta y^* \leq a_2$$
$$\Delta y = \Delta y^* \text{ if } \Delta y^* > a_2 > 0.$$

(a) Draw a graph of this in Δy^*, Δy space.

(b) What is the likelihood function for this model?

AB   Duration Models

1   Suppose you have a random sample of workers, from several localities, who have recently suffered, or are suffering, unemployment. For those currently employed, the unemployment duration is recorded as x_i. For those still unemployed, the duration is recorded as y_i, the duration to date. Assume that unemployment duration w is distributed exponentially with $pdf\, \lambda e^{-\lambda w}$ for $0 < w < \infty$.

(a) Find the MLE of λ. *Hint*: Find the cumulative distribution of w.

(b) How would you estimate the variance of this estimator?

(c) Suppose the average duration of unemployment depends on local conditions. How would you model this and estimate the parameters? *Hint*: Calculate the average duration of unemployment in terms of λ.

*2   Suppose you have data from an insurance company on auto accident claims. You can deduce the market value of all the autos in the data set, but unfortunately the cost-of-repair figure is not available for "write-offs." Suppose that auto value p and cost-of-repair x are distributed independently exponentially as $\alpha e^{-\alpha p}$ and $\beta e^{-\beta x}$, respectively, and that an auto is "written off" if its cost-of-repair exceeds its value.

(a) Find the MLEs of α and β. *Hint*: Find the cumulative distribution of the exponential.

(b) Suppose you learn from the Motor Vehicle Department that of all autos the fraction scrapped annually because of accidents is 2%. How would you use this information, in conjunction with your estimates from part (a) above, to estimate the probability of having an accident? *Hint*: Use the expression for the probability of being scrapped.

APPENDIX E: ANSWERS TO EVEN-NUMBERED QUESTIONS

A2 (a) Numbers are being drawn from a normal distribution with mean 1 and variance 25. The average of 100 such numbers has a sampling distribution that is normal with mean 1 and variance $25/100 = 0.25$ (standard deviation 0.5). The 1900th ordered value should cut off 5% of the tail of this distribution. From the normal tables a value 1.645 standard deviations above the mean should do this, so a good guess is $1 + 1.645 \times 0.5 = 1.82$.

(b) To be negative an average would have to be more than two standard deviations below the mean. From the normal tables the probability of this happening is 0.0228%, so we would expect $0.0228 \times 2000 = 45$ or 46 of these values to be negative.

A4 (a) This procedure examines the sampling distribution of the number of successes occurring in 60 draws where the probability of success is 20%.

(b) In each draw of 60 numbers we expect 20 percent to be successes, so gav should be approximately 12.

(c) From introductory statistics, the variance of this sampling distribution is Npq where N is the number of draws, p is the probability of success and q is $1 - p$. So gvar should be close to $60(0.2)(0.8) = 9.6$.

A6 (a) (i) Choose μ and σ^2 equal to 2 and 4, say. (ii) Draw 20 x observations from N(2, 4). (iii) Calculate the sample variance $s^2 = \Sigma(x - \text{xbar})^2/19$. (iv) Repeat from (ii) to get 500 estimates of s^2. (v) Average the 500 s^2 estimates and see if it is close to 4.

(b) Calculate the variance of the 500 s^2 estimates (as $\Sigma(s^2 - s^2\text{bar})^2/499$) and see if it is close to $32/19 = 1.68$.

A8 (a) (i) Choose values for N, μ and σ^2. (ii) Get the computer to produce N values of a random variable with mean μ and variance σ^2 (say from a normal distribution). (iii) Calculate $\bar{x}$, the average of these N values, and save it. (iv) Repeat from (ii), say 2,000 times, yielding 2,000 $\bar{x}$ values. (v) Compute the sample variance of these 2,000 values and compare to σ^2/N.

(b) s^2/N where $s^2 = \Sigma(x - \bar{x})^2/(N - 1)$.

(c) At stage (iii) above, also calculate s^2/N and save it. Then at stage (v) also calculate the mean of these 2,000 s^2/N values and compare to σ^2/N.

A10 (i) Get the computer to choose a value from a uniform distribution, say between 0 and 1. (ii) If this value is less than 0.95, get the computer to select a value of x from $N(50,4)$, otherwise from $N(50,100)$. (iii) Repeat from (i) 25 times. (iv) Calculate the mean and the median of the 25 x values, call them $\bar{x}$ and x_{med}, and save them. (v) Repeat from (i), say 2,000 times. (vi) Calculate the sample mean and the sample variance of the 2,000 $\bar{x}$ and of the 2,000 x_{med}. Compare these two sample means to 50, and the two sample variances to each other.

A12 A is an estimate of the mean of the sampling distribution of $(6 + 2x)^2$ where x is a standard normal. This is 36 plus 4 times the expected value of the square of a standard normal. The square of a standard normal is distributed as a chi-square with one degree of freedom. The expected value of a chi-square is equal to its degrees of freedom, so A is an estimate of 40.

A14 **(a)** (i) Choose $\theta = 0.1$ so that $v = .09/60 = 0.0015$. (ii) Draw 60 observations from a distribution uniform between zero and one, and count the number k of these observations less than 0.1. (iii) Calculate $\theta^* = k/60$ and $v^* = \theta^*(1 - \theta^*)/60$. (iv) Repeat from (ii) above to obtain 2,000 v^* values. (v) Find the mean mv^* of the v^* values and compare to 0.0015.
(b) Calculate the variance of the 2,000 v^* values as $vv^* = \Sigma(v^* - mv^*)^2/1999$. Then sev^*, the estimated standard error of mv^*, can be estimated by the square root of $vv^*/2000$. The test statistic $(mv^* - 0.0015)/sev^*$ is distributed as a standard normal.

B2 There are four possible outcomes, $x = 0, 1, 2,$ and 3, yielding four possible net payoffs, $-2, -2, 0,$ and 4, respectively. The probabilities of these events are 1/8, 3/8, 3/8, and 1/8, respectively, allowing calculation of the expected net payoff as a loss of 50 cents.

B4 $f(x) = 1/(b - a)$ for x between a and b, zero otherwise. $Ex = $ integral from a to b of $x/(b - a) = (a + b)/2$. $V(x) = E(x - Ex)^2$. The easiest way to calculate is as $Ex^2 - (Ex)^2$, producing $(b - a)^2/12$.

B6 x/y is a nonlinear function, so $E(x/y) \neq Ex/Ey$. Since both Ex and Ey are 2.5, $Ex/Ey = 1$. Possible values of x/y are 2/3, 1, and 3/2, with probabilities 1/4, 1/2, and 1/4, respectively. $E(x/y)$ can therefore be calculated as 25/24.

B8 **(a)** The plim of the sample mean is μ, and because the plim of a nonlinear function is the nonlinear function of the plim, it follows that the plim of the inverse of the sample mean is $1/\mu$.
(b) The asymptotic variance of a nonlinear function of an estimator is the square of the first derivative times the variance of the estimator. The square of the first derivative of $\bar{x}^{-1}$ with respect to $\bar{x}$ is $\bar{x}^{-4}$, estimated by 1/16. The variance of $\bar{x}$ is 50/25 = 2, so the variance of $\bar{x}^{-1} = 1/8$.

B10 The expected value of x is $\lambda/(\lambda + 1)$; setting this equal to the mean of the observations $\bar{x}$ we get $\lambda^{mm} = \bar{x}/(1 - \bar{x})$.

B12 This correction makes the formula an unbiased estimator of the true variance.

C2 **(a)** The expected value of β^* is β, and the variance is $2\sigma^2/T(x_a - x_b)^2$, where the sample size is T, with T/2 observations in each group.
(b) Allocate observations to make $x_a - x_b$ as large as possible – this makes the variance of β^* as small as possible.

C4 Your estimator is the difference between the sample means, which is unbiased with variance $4/T + 16/(30 - T)$ where T is the number of observations drawn on x. Choose $T = 10$ to minimize this variance.

C6 This estimator is unbiased, so in that sense it is good. But it is not efficient – there exist other estimators, such as OLS, that are unbiased but have a smaller variance.

D2 **(a)** $E\mu^* = 4$, so bias $= 0$. $V(\mu^*) = 3$, so MSE $= 3$. $E\mu^{**} = 3$, so bias $= 1$. $V(\mu^{**}) = 27/16$, so MSE $= 2.7$.

(b) It is tempting to conclude that μ^{**} is better than μ^* on the MSE criterion, but this is not true for all values of (the usually unknown) μ.

D4 **(b)** Smaller. The BLUE is $\Sigma x/T$ which is larger because the denominator of μ^* is bigger.

(c) In this case $w = \sigma^2/\mu^2$, so that $\mu^* = \Sigma x/(T + 1) = [T/(T + 1)]$BLUE.

E2 Prob(P) is proportional to $(2\pi\sigma_p^2)^{-1/2}\exp[-(P - \mu)^2/2\sigma_p^2]$ $(2\pi\sigma_k^2)^{-1/2}\exp[-(p_k - P)^2/2\sigma_k^2]$. Maximizing ln of this with respect to P yields $EP = (\mu\sigma_k^2 + p_k\sigma_p^2)/(\sigma_k^2 + \sigma_p^2)$.

F2 **(a)** This procedure is comparing the sampling distribution of the OLS slope estimator b using a correct specification to the sampling distribution of the OLS estimator bb which results from adding an irrelevant explanatory variable w. Since adding an irrelevant regressor does not create bias, B and BB should be roughly equally close to 3.

(b) Since by construction the irrelevant explanatory variable w is correlated with the relevant explanatory variable x, including w will increase the variance of the slope coefficient estimator of x, so VB should be smaller than VBB.

F4 The OLS estimate of β is 4, yielding two estimated errors, 2 and -1. For bootstrapping purposes these errors must be multiplied by 1.414, the square root of 2, for the small sample adjustment. The usual estimate of the variance of the OLS estimator is $s^2/\Sigma x^2 = 1.0$. In the bootstrap Monte Carlo study, there are four possible β estimates occurring with equal probability, namely 4.0, 5.7, 3.2 and 4.85, corresponding to the four different error vector drawings. The variance of these estimates is 0.8.

G2 The result that the OLS estimator is BLUE in the CLR model does not require that the errors are distributed normally.

G4 The slope estimate from regressing y on x is $\Sigma xy/\Sigma x^2$, whereas the inverse of the reverse regression is $\Sigma y^2/\Sigma xy$. They are not the same.

G6 **(a)** Write age as an approximate linear function of experience, with slope coefficient λ. Substituting out age yields a slope coefficient on experience of $\beta + \lambda\theta$. Since λ and θ are both likely to be positive in this context, the resulting estimate of β should have positive bias.

(b) Since sex should not be correlated with age, the coefficient comparable to λ of part (a) is likely to be zero, so there should be no bias.

G8 Such an intercept would arise from a time trend, interpreted in this context as representing technological change.

G10 Pick a reasonable value for δ and use it to calculate T values of $w = (x + \delta)^{-1}$ using the T observations on x. Now regress y on an intercept and w, noting the sum of squared errors that results. Now choose a slightly different value for δ and repeat. Continue in this way until the smallest value of the sum of squared errors is found.

G12 **(a)** x and w are orthogonal.

(b) x and w are highly collinear.

(c) A lot of the variation in y is uniquely due to w, so that including w eliminates a large upward bias in the estimator of the variance of the error term (and thus also in the estimator of the variance of β^*).

G14 True because R^2 has no correction for degrees of freedom. A regression with N explanatory variables fits perfectly a sample with N observations. As N increases the fit deteriorates because the perfect fit to the first N observations has a smaller and smaller influence on the overall fit.

H2   **(a)** $E\beta^* = \beta + \alpha\Sigma x/\Sigma x^2$, so bias is $\alpha/2$; $V(\beta^*) = \sigma^2/\Sigma x^2 = 9/10$. Thus MSE is $\alpha^2/4 + 9/10$.
      (b) The MSE of the usual estimator is $V(\beta^{OLS}) = \sigma^2/\Sigma(x - \bar{x})^2 = \sigma^2/[\Sigma x^2 - T\bar{x}^2] = 1$. $\mathrm{MSE}(\beta^*) < \mathrm{MSE}(\beta^{OLS})$ if $\alpha^2 < 0.4$.

H4 $E(\beta^{OLS})'(\beta^{OLS}) = \beta'\beta + E\varepsilon'X(X'X)^{-1}(X'X)^{-1}X'\varepsilon$ and since this is a scalar it is equal to its trace, so that it can be written as $\beta'\beta + \mathrm{tr}[E\varepsilon'X(X'X)^{-1}(X'X)^{-1}X'\varepsilon] = \beta'\beta + \mathrm{tr}[EX\varepsilon\varepsilon'X(X'X)^{-1}(X'X)^{-1}] = \beta'\beta + \mathrm{tr}[\sigma^2(X'X)^{-1}] = 15.4$.

I2   Subtract the mean of y, say θ, from both sides to get $y - \theta = \alpha - \theta + \beta x + \varepsilon$, showing unbiased estimate of β but biased estimate of α.

I4   **(a)** $0.8y = 4 + 2(0.8x)$.
      (b) $0.8y = 4 + 1.6x$.
      (c) $y = 5 + 2.5(0.8x)$.
      (d) The t statistic is unchanged. The new slope coefficient estimate is the old divided by 0.8, and its variance is the original variance divided by the square of 0.8, so when constructing the new t statistic the 0.8s cancel out, leaving the original t statistic.

I6   **(a)** $\ln(Y/W) = a_1 + a_2\ln W + a_3 Q$ implies that $\ln Y - \ln W = a_1 + a_2\ln W + a_3 Q$ so that $\ln Y = a_1 + (a_2 + 1)\ln W + a_3 Q$. Thus a_1, $(a_2 + 1)$, and a_3 are estimates of β_1, β_2, and β_3, respectively.
      (b) The standard errors are those of a_1, a_2 and a_3.

I8   **(a)** The relationship in the new data is $3y = 3\alpha + (3\beta)x + 3\varepsilon$, so the variance of the new error term is 36, 9 times the variance of ε.
      (b) The α and β estimators are now unbiased estimators of 3α and 3β, respectively.

J2   The variance–covariance matrix becomes smaller, but its estimate is an overestimate, because σ^2 is overestimated; the net effect is uncertain.

J4   Uncertain, because we cannot deduce the sign of the covariance between β^{OLS} and δ^{OLS}.

K2   Regress $y - z$ on an intercept and $(2x - z + w)$ to get slope estimate δ^* and then use δ^* to get $\beta^* = 2\delta^*$ and $\theta^* = 1 - \delta^*$.

K4   Restricted $\mathrm{OLS} = \beta^{OLS} + (X'X)^{-1}R'[R(X'X)^{-1}R']^{-1}(r - R\beta^{OLS})$ where the restriction is written as $R\beta = r$. For this example $R = (1, 1)$ and $r = 4$. Note that although $(X'X)^{-1}$ is not known, it is known up to a factor of proportionality which cancels out. Substitution of numerical values yields restricted $\mathrm{OLS} = (18/7, 10/7)'$.

K6   Since the observations are in deviation form, α can be considered zero. The variance of the unrestricted estimate of β is found from the upper left element of $\sigma^2(X'X)^{-1}$, which is 2. The restricted estimate is calculated by regressing $(y - w)$ on $(x - w)$, so its variance is $\sigma^2/\Sigma(x - w)^2 = 5/7$.

K8   **(a)** The OLS estimating line is horizontal at $y = 2$.
      (b) The line must pass through the origin, implying that the residuals of the first two observations must be 0 and 4. The sum of squared errors is minimized by equating the other two residuals, passing the OLS line through the point (4, 2), creating residuals of -2 and 2 for the last two observations. The estimating line is thus $y = 0.5x$. This could be calculated using the formula $\Sigma xy/\Sigma x^2$ for the slope estimate.
      (c) R^2 for the unrestricted line is zero. For the restricted line it is

$1 - 24/16 = -0.5$.

(d) R^2 for the unrestricted line is zero. For the restricted line it is $-8/16$ or $+4/16$, the former resulting if the average of the estimated ys is calculated as equal to the mean of the ys.

(e) R^2 can be misleading when a regression is restricted.

L2 Set the partial derivative of the sum of squared errors with respect to β_1 equal to zero, repeat for β_2, and then solve these two equations.

L4 Find the expected value of the sum of squared errors associated with the restricted OLS estimator; this will reveal the required adjustment for degrees of freedom.

L6 **(a)** The expected value of $\theta\beta^{OLS}$ is $\theta\beta$, so its bias is $(\theta - 1)\beta$. the sum of the squared biases of the elements of $\theta\beta^{OLS}$ is thus $(\theta - 1)^2\beta'\beta$. The variance–covariance matrix of $\theta\beta^{OLS}$ is $\theta^2\sigma^2(X'X)^{-1}$, so the sum of the variances of the elements of $\theta\beta^{OLS}$ is $\theta^2\sigma^2\text{tr}(X'X)^{-1}$.

(b) $\beta'\beta/[\beta'\beta + \sigma^2\text{tr}(X'X)^{-1}]$.

(c) The OLS estimator is multiplied by a value θ that is less than unity, shrinking it towards zero.

(d) The optimal θ depends on the unknown parameter β.

L8 False. OLS estimate of β_2 is $(X_2'M_1X_2)^{-1}X_2'M_1y$
$= (X_2'M_1X_2)^{-1}X_2'(I - X_1(X_1'X_1)^{-1}X_1')y$
$= (X_2'M_1X_2)^{-1}X_2'X_1(X_1'X_1)^{-1}X_1')y$
which is not necessarily zero. This is an example of a situation in which the Ballentine lets us down. Although y and X_2 are orthogonal, y and X_2-residualized-for-X_1 may not be orthogonal.

M2 **(a)** Yes. The OLS formula ignores the observations corresponding to the zero x values because they offer no information regarding how y varies as x varies. This can be seen formally by noting that the pooled formula collapses to the OLS estimate on the first subset of data, an unbiased estimate.

(b) No. It is biased towards the zero vector because the OLS formula incorporates the information that for these observations when x varies there is no corresponding variation in y. This can be seen formally from the pooled formula.

M4 The pooling formula from question M1(a) is $[X_1'X_1 + X_2'X_2]^{-1}$ $[X_1'X_1\beta_1^{OLS} + X_2'X_2\beta_2^{OLS}]$ where the subscripts refer to the first and second subsets of the data. Substituting $X_2\beta_1^{OLS}$ for Y_2 we get $[X_1'X_1 + X_2'X_2]^{-1}[X_1'X_1\beta_1^{OLS} + X_2'X_2(X_2'X_2)^{-1}X_2'X_2\beta_1^{OLS}] = \beta_1^{OLS}$.

N2 False. x^2 is not a linear function of x.

N4 False. The variances become bigger, but so also do their estimates.

N6 **(a)** Yes, because x and w are uncorrelated.

(b) No, because the estimate of σ^2 is biased upward owing to omitted w.

N8 False. Inclusion of this regressor creates perfect multicollinearity.

N10 **(a)** There is no way of knowing a priori whether or not this condition is satisfied. A more reasonable suggestion might be to test for whether this condition is met and choose one's estimator accordingly.

(b) The variance, and thus the MSE, of α^{OLS} is $\sigma^2\Sigma w^2/[\Sigma x^2\Sigma w^2 - (\Sigma xw)^2]$. The bias of α^* is $\beta\Sigma xw/\Sigma x^2$ and its variance is $\sigma^2/\Sigma x^2$ so its MSE is $\beta^2(\Sigma xw)^2/(\Sigma x^2)^2 + \sigma^2/\Sigma x^2$. The condition for the latter to be smaller than the former is that $\beta^2 < \sigma^2\Sigma x^2/[\Sigma x^2\Sigma w^2 - (\Sigma xw)^2] = V(\beta^{OLS})$.

N12   **(a)** $V(\beta^{\text{OLS}}) = \sigma^2(X'X)^{-1}$ and $V(\beta^*) = \sigma^2(X'X + kI)^{-1}X'X(X'X + kI)^{-1}$ so we wish to show that $(X'X)^{-1} - (X'X + kI)^{-1}X'X(X'X + kI)^{-1}$ is nnd, or, alternatively, that $(X'X + kI)(X'X)^{-1}(X'X + kI) - X'X$ is nnd. Multiplying this out requires that $2kI + k^2(X'X)^{-1}$ is nnd, true for $k \geqslant 0$.
   (b) No, because β^* is biased.

O2 $y = 14 + 5x + 5NM - NF - 4SF$, obtained by working out the intercept for each of the four categories.

O4   None. This information has no implication for the parameter values.

O6   **(a)** $\beta_1 + \beta_3$.
   (b) $\beta_2 = \beta_3$.
   (c) No, because the original specification does not specify that income increases as the number of years completed within a category increases.
   (d) The part (a) answer becomes $\alpha_3 + \alpha_4 + \alpha_5$. The part (b) answer becomes $\alpha_5 = 0$.

O8   **(a)** Add a dummy for weekends.
   (b) Add an interaction dummy, the product of N and H.

O10   B is correct. The dummy variable coefficient estimate of 2 results from normal equations forcing ef and em to be zero, in the same way that the intercept estimate causes the sum of the residuals to equal zero.

P2   **(a)** β_0^{OLS} should be the mean of the first 20 observations, so its variance should be $100/20 = 5$. $(\beta_0^{\text{OLS}} + \beta_1^{\text{OLS}})$ should be the mean of the second 25 observations, so its variance should be $100/25 = 4$.
   (b) The $\sigma^2(X'X)^{-1}$ formula yields variances 5 and 9 for the OLS estimates of β_0 and β_1, respectively, and -5 as their covariance. This implies that the variance of $(\beta_0^{\text{OLS}} + \beta_1^{\text{OLS}})$ is $5 + 9 - 10 = 4$.
   (c) The relevant formula is $\sigma^2(1,1)(X'X)^{-1}(1,1)'$, which yields 4.

P4   **(a)** $\ln y = \alpha + \beta \ln(100x/100) + \varepsilon = \alpha - \beta \ln(100) + \beta \ln(100x) + \varepsilon$, so regressing $\ln y$ on an intercept and $\ln(100x)$ should produce the same estimate of β but a different (biased) estimate of α.
   (b) $\ln y = \alpha + \beta \ln(100x/100) + \delta D \ln(100x/100) + \varepsilon$
   $= \alpha - \beta \ln(100) - \delta D \ln(100) + \beta \ln(100x) + \delta D \ln(100x) + \varepsilon$,

implying that an intercept dummy is required to capture this specification – its omission will affect the β estimate. Including an intercept dummy will avoid this problem.

Q2   Arrange all the observations into a single vector w, say. Regress w on an intercept and a dummy taking value 1 for observations on y and 0 for observations on x. Use the traditional t statistic to test the hypothesis that the coefficient of this dummy is zero.

Q4   Alcohol $= \alpha + \beta$income $+ \delta$age $+ \lambda$sex $+ \theta$MAincome $+ \eta$PhDincome,   where sex is a zero/one dummy for sex, MAincome takes the value income for MA students and zero otherwise, and PhDincome takes the value income for PhD students and zero otherwise. Use an F test to test the hypothesis that $\theta = \eta = 0$. SSE unrestricted is obtained by running the regression above; SSE restricted is obtained by running this regression without the regressors MAincome and PhDincome. The numerator degrees of freedom is 2; the denominator degrees of freedom is 69.

Q6   **(a)** The variable takes value one in the quarter in which the sales tax was announced, minus one in the following quarter, and zero otherwise.

(b) An F test with restricted SSE from regression of part (a), unrestricted regression replacing the dummy of part (a) with two observation-specific dummies, one for each of the two periods in question. There is one restriction, that the coefficients of these two observataion-specific dummies are the negative of each other.

Q8 Set up observation-specific dummies for all ten of the lowest and highest observations. Use an F test to test if their coefficients are all zero.

R2 **(a)** This setup allows the intercept to move gradually over four years to its new level instead of taking a sudden jump in 1964. The coefficient of DD is a measure of one-quarter of the eventual change in the intercept. It is the change that occurs in each of the four transition years.

(b) Define DD as 0.25 in 1964, 0.5 in 1965, 0.75 in 1966 and one for all remaining years.

S2 Assume the change occurred in 1964 and calculate the maximum likelihood estimates, noting the value of the likelihood. Repeat for the other years through to 1969. Choose the switching point on the basis of which year assumed for the switch gave rise to the highest maximized likelihood; the MLE estimates from estimation based on this switching year are the required parameter estimates.

S4 Evaluate for height 5'10" the formula for the normal distribution using the male parameters. Repeat using the female parameters, and take the ratio of the former to the latter. This yields e^3. Perform the same calculation for height 5'8" but with variance $6/6 = 1$. This yields e^6, a considerably *higher* relative odds.

S6 $f(w) = (2\pi\sigma^2)^{-1/2}\exp[-(w - \mu)^2/2\sigma^2]$
$f(Q) = f(w)|dw/dQ|$
where $w = (Q - a)/b$ and $|dw/dQ| = 1/b$ for b positive
$= (2\pi\sigma^2)^{-1/2}\exp[-((Q - a)/b - \mu)^2/2\sigma^2](1/b)$
$= (2\pi b^2\sigma^2)^{-1/2}\exp[-(Q - (a + b\mu))^2/2b^2\sigma^2]$
so $Q \sim N(a + b\mu, b^2\sigma^2)$.

S8 Log-likelihood $= -(T/2)\ln 2\pi - (1/2)\Sigma(x - \mu)^2$. First partial $= \Sigma(x - \mu)$ and second partial $= -T$. Minus expected value of second partial $= T$. Expected value of first partial squared $= E[\Sigma(x - \mu)]^2 = TV(x) = T$.

S10 $f(y) = f(x)|dx/dy|$ where $x = e^{-\theta y}$
so $f(y) = \theta e^{\theta y}$

T2 **(a)** The likelihood is proportional to $\alpha^N(1 - \alpha)^{T-N}$, the log-likelihood of which is $N\ln\alpha + (T - N)\ln(1 - \alpha)$. The first partial is $N/\alpha - (T - N)/(1 - \alpha)$ which is zero when $\alpha = N/T$, so the MLE of α is N/T.

(b) The second partial of the log-likelihood is $-N/\alpha^2 - (T - N)/(1 - \alpha)^2$, the expected value of which is $-T/\alpha - T(1 - \alpha)$. Minus the inverse of this is $\alpha(1 - \alpha)/T$, the traditional formula.

T4 **(a)** Adjust the original distribution by dividing it by the area to the right of 9000, yielding $f(y) = \alpha 9000^\alpha y^{-(\alpha+1)}$ for $y \geqslant 9000$. The log-likelihood is $T\ln\alpha + T\alpha\ln 9000 - (\alpha + 1)\Sigma\ln y$. The first partial is $T/\alpha + T\ln 9000 - \Sigma\ln y$ so that α^{MLE} is $T(\Sigma\ln y - T\ln 9000)^{-1}$.

(b) The second partial is $-T/\alpha^2$ so that the Cramer–Rao lower bound is α^2/T. Estimate the variance by substituting α^{MLE} for α in this expression.

(c) The mean of this distribution is $9000\alpha/(\alpha - 1)$. Setting this equal to $\theta + \beta w$ we get that $\alpha = (\theta + \beta w)/(\theta + \beta w - 9000)$. Substituting this into the likelihood allows estimation of θ and β by MLE.

T6 The Poisson density must be adjusted to represent the density conditional on n being greater than zero. This is done by dividing $f(n)$ by the probability that $n > 0$, given by $1 - f(0) = 1 - e^{-\lambda}$. The likelihood then is proportional to $(1 - e^{-\lambda})^{-N} e^{-N\lambda} \lambda^{\Sigma n}$.

T8 The likelihood is $(2\theta)^{-T} \exp[-\Sigma|(y - \alpha - \beta x)/\theta|]$ so the log-likelihood is $-T\ln 2\theta - \Sigma|(y - \alpha - \beta x)/\theta|$. For any given value of θ, maximization of this requires minimization of $\Sigma|y - \alpha - \beta x|$, the sum of the absolute errors.

T10 **(a)** $\text{prob}(1,1) = \alpha e^{\beta}/(1 + e^{\beta})$; $\text{prob}(0,1) = \alpha/(1 + e^{\beta})$; $\text{prob}(1,0) = (1 - \alpha)/2$ and $\text{prob}(0,0) = (1 - \alpha)/2$. The likelihood is $\alpha^{Nx}(1 - \alpha)^{N - Nx}(1/2)^{N - Nx} e^{\beta Nxy}(1 + e^{\beta})^{-Nx}$ where Nx is the number of observations with $x = 1$ and Nxy is the number of observations with both $x = 1$ and $y = 1$. The first partial of the log-likelihood with respect to α is $Nx/\alpha - (N - Nx)/(1 - \alpha)$, which yields the MLE of α as Nx/N. The first partial of the log-likelihood with respect to β is $Nxy - Nx(1 + e^{\beta})^{-1}e^{\beta}$ which yields the MLE of β as $\ln[Nxy/(Nx - Nxy)]$.
(b) If of the observations with $x = 1$, half have $y = 1$, the MLE of $\beta = 0$ so that the estimated $\text{prob}(y = 1|x = 1) = 1/2$.

T12 $f(y_t) = f(\varepsilon_t)|d\varepsilon_t/dy_t|$
$f(y_t) = (2\pi)^{-N/2}(\det\Phi)^{-1/2}\exp(-(\Gamma'y_t + B'x_t)'\Phi^{-1}(\Gamma'y_t + B'x_t)/2)\det\Gamma$
likelihood $= (2\pi)^{-NT/2}(\det\Phi)^{-T/2}(\det\Gamma)^T$
$\exp(-\Sigma(\Gamma'y_t + B'x_t)'\Phi^{-1}(\Gamma'y_t + B'x_t)/2)$

T14 **(a)** The density of u is the usual one, but we need the density of the observed y. The Jacobian of the transformation from ε to y is unity, so we need the Jacobian of transformation from u to ε, which is $(1 - \rho^2)^{1/2}$.
(b) The density for ε is the usual one, but we need the density of the observed y. The Jacobian of the transformation from ε to $(y^\lambda - 1)/\lambda$ is unity, so we need the Jacobian of the transformation from $(y^\lambda - 1)/\lambda$ to the observed y, which is the product of the $y^{\lambda - 1}$.
(c) We need both Jacobians.
(d) (i) Use an LR test in which the restricted likelihood is calculated restricting $\lambda = 1$ and $\rho = 0$ and the unrestricted likelihood is calculated restricting $\rho = 0$.
(ii) Use an LR test in which the restricted likelihood is calculated restricting $\lambda = 1$ and the unrestricted likelihood is calculated with no restrictions.

U2 Find the expected loss, the integral from zero to two of the loss function times the posterior, then minimize it with respect to β^*. The answer is $4/3$. Alternatively, because the loss function is quadratic, just find the mean of the posterior distribution.

U4 **(a)** Use the same uniform prior but with height reduced to zero for all $\beta < 3$.
(b) Like a truncated normal distribution, with value zero for $\beta < 3$.
(c) The classical point estimate is the peak of the likelihood function (identical to the untruncated posterior distribution) or 3, whichever is larger. The Bayesian point estimate is the mean of the posterior distribution. When the peak of the likelihood function corresponds to a β value less than 3 the classical estimate is always 3, but the Bayesian estimate is larger than 3, getting closer and closer to 3 as the peak of the likelihood function moves further and further from 3.
(d) By calculating the area under the "untruncated" posterior lying to the right of $\beta = 3$.

U6 **(a)** The predictive density is the density of $y = 3\beta + \varepsilon$ where 3β and ε are distributed independently as $N(18,36)$ and $N(0,13)$, respectively. This is $N(18,49)$.

(b) $\text{prob}(y > 25) = \text{prob}(z > 1)$ where $z \sim N(0,1)$.

U8 **(a)** Likelihood $\propto e^{-7\lambda}\lambda^{35}$, which is maximized at $\lambda = 5$. Cramer–Rao lower bound is $\lambda/7$ (see answer to V4(a)), estimated as 5/7, posterior $\propto e^{-7\lambda}\lambda^{35}\lambda^{3.2}e^{-0.7\lambda} = \lambda^{38.2}e^{-7.7\lambda}$ the mean of which is $39.2/7.7 = 5.1$.

V2 **(a)** The likelihood is proportional to $\theta^{15}(1 - \theta)^{30}$ which yields the MLE of $\theta = 1/3$.

(b) The posterior is proportional to $\theta^{15}(1 - \theta)^{30}$.

(c) The posterior mean is 16/47.

(d) The prior required is $\theta^{-1}(1 - \theta)^{-1}$.

(e) The second partial of the log-likelihood is $-N/\theta^2 - (T - N)/(1 - \theta)^2$ where T is sample size and N is number of successes. The expected value of this is $-T/\theta - T/(1 - \theta)$, so the information matrix is the scalar $T/\theta(1 - \theta)$ and the prior is proportional to $\theta^{-1/2}(1 - \theta)^{-1/2}$.

(f) The posterior is $\theta^{14}(1 - \theta)^{29}$; the updated posterior is $\theta^{89}(1 - \theta)^{154}$ with mean 90/245.

V4 **(a)** The likelihood for a sample size T is proportional to $e^{-\lambda T}\lambda^{\Sigma x}$. The second partial of the log-likelihood is $-\Sigma x/\lambda^2$, the expected value of which is $-T/\lambda$ (which follows from calculating $Ex = \lambda$), so the information matrix is the scalar T/λ. Thus the ignorance prior is proportional to $\lambda^{-1/2}$.

(b) If the prior is λ^{-1} the posterior is proportional to $e^{-7\lambda}\lambda^{34}$ with mean $35/7 = 5$, equal to the MLE.

(c) The posterior takes the form of a gamma distribution, implying that this prior is a conjugate prior.

(d) The posterior is proportional to $e^{-7.7\lambda}\lambda^{38.2}$ with mean $39.2/7.7 = 5.1$, which has moved slightly towards the prior, as it should, and variance $5.1/7.7 = 0.66$, which is smaller than the variance of $5/7 = 0.71$ characterizing the case of an ignorance prior, as it should be.

W2 This Monte Carlo procedure creates 3,000 values which except for a degrees of freedom correction (dividing the numerator by 2 and the denominator by 46) are F statistics for testing the true null that the $y = 2 + 3x$ relationship is the same for the first 20 observations as for the last 30 observations. If it had the degrees of freedom correction, the 2970th value would cut off the top one percent of values from an F distribution with 2 and 46 degrees of freedom, which from an F table is 5.1. So $46/2 = 23$ times this 2970th value should be close to 5.1. The 2970th value therefore should be close to $5.1/23 = 0.22$.

W4 This Monte Carlo procedure computes 3,000 chi-square values with degrees of freedom 8. Since the mean of a chi-square is equal to its degrees of freedom, and its variance is twice its degrees of freedom, then A should be about 8 and VA about 16. The 2850th value cuts off the top 5 percent of these values. From the chi-square tables this value is about 15.5.

W6 This Monte Carlo study is checking to see if a bootstrap testing procedure when errors are distributed uniformly has an appropriate type I error. The instructions are completed with "Divide ctr by 3,000 and compare to 0.05."

W8 **(a)** (i) Select parameter values, say $\alpha = 1$, $\beta = 2$, $\theta = 0.5$, $\delta = 4$, $\sigma^2 = 5$, ensuring that $\beta(1 - \theta) = 1$, and choose sample size 50, say. (ii) Find or create 50 x, z and p values that are not orthogonal. (iii) Set ctr = 0. (iv) Draw 50 e values from $N(0,5)$. (v) Create 50 y values as $1 + 2x + 0.5z + 4p + e$. (vi) Regress y on x and z to obtain estimates β^* and θ^*, estimated variances $V\beta^*$ and $V\theta^*$

and estimated covariance C*. (vii) Calculate the asymptotic t statistic numerator $n = \beta^*(1 - \theta^*) - 1$ and denominator d the square root of $(1 - \theta^*)2V\beta^* - 2\beta^*(1 - \theta^*)C^* + \beta^*2V(\theta^*)$. (viii) Calculate n/d and add one to ctr if it exceeds the 5% critical value from the t table. (ix) Repeat from step (iv) to obtain 5,000 t values. (x) Compare ctr/5,000 to .05.

(b) Because of the omitted explanatory variable we expect the coefficient estimates to be biased and so the type I error will be far from 5%.

(c) The Wald test statistic is the same as the asymptotic t statistic and so the results should be identical.

W10 (i) Select values for α, the variance of ε, and the sample size T. Set β slightly larger than one. (ii) Select T values for x. (iii) Have the computer obtain T errors and use to calculate T y values. (iv) Run the regression, calculate the t statistic, and accept or reject the null hypothesis using the appropriate critical value for, say, $\alpha = 0.05$. Save whether accepted or rejected. (v) Repeat from (iii) 1,000 times, say, to obtain 1,000 decisions on whether to accept or reject. (vi) Estimate the power as the number of rejects as a percentage of 1,000. (vii) Repeat from (iii) for a selected number of slightly larger β values. (viii) Plot the estimated power against the selected β values.

W12 The following is for graphing the risk of θ^*, the estimated coefficient of x in the equation $y = 5 + 3x + \beta w + \varepsilon$ where $\varepsilon \sim N(0,4)$, say, and a sample size of 30, say. Select 30 values of x and w so they are modestly collinear. Begin with $\beta = 0$. (i) Have the computer obtain 30 errors and use to calculate 30 y values. (ii) Regress y on intercept, x and w and test for $\beta = 0$ using a standard t test. (iii) If the null is rejected save the estimated coefficient of x and go to (iv) below; if the null is accepted, regress y on the intercept and x, save the estimated coefficient of x and go to (iv) below. (iv) Repeat from (i) 1,000 times, say. (v) Use the resulting 1,000 estimates of the x coefficient to estimate MSE in the usual way and graph against the β value. (vi) Repeat from (i) for a selected number of larger β values.

W14 **(a)** The W statistic because the LM test requires estimation incorporating the nonlinear restriction whereas the W statistic requires only unrestricted estimation.

(b) (i) Choose values for σ^2 and the β_i, ensuring that $\beta_1 = \beta_2^{-1}$. (ii) Set sample size = 25, say, and select 25 values for x and w. (iii) Get computer to generate 25 errors from $N(0, \sigma^2)$ and calculate the corresponding 25 y values. (iv) Calculate the W and the LM test statistics and save them. (v) Repeat from (iii) until you have, say, 5,000 sets of W and LM statistics. (vi) Order the W statistics from smallest to largest, and do the same for the LM statistics. (vii) Find the number of W values that exceed the 5% critical value 3.84 and express it as a percentage of 5,000. Do the same for LM. (viii) The statistic whose % is closer to 5% is better.

(c) For W use value 4,750 in the list of 5,000 W values. For LM use value 4,750 in the list of LM values.

(d) Answer same as part (b) above, with following changes. In part (i), choose the β values such that β_1 does not equal β_2^{-1}. Call the extent to which this equality is violated d. In part (vii) use the relevant empirically-determined critical values (from part (b)) in place of 3.84. In part (viii) the statistic with the higher percentage is better since this percentage measures power. The study should be repeated for different values of d to investigate how relative power varies with the extent to which the null is false.

(e) If 3.84 were used instead of the relevant empirically determined critical value, then the statistic with the higher type I error probability will have an advantage. For infinitesimal value of d the power is equal to the probability of a type one error, growing larger as d grows.

X2 In theory one should be equally confident, since both tests were conducted at the same significance level. In practice, however, the phenomenon of the too-large-sample-size may play a role here. Since all point null hypotheses are likely to be false, all nulls can be rejected if the sample size is allowed to become large enough. Viewed in this light, one may wish to place more confidence in the rejection of part (a).

X4 True. The t statistic is a ratio in the numerator of which is a normally distributed variable.

X6 The diagram will have two normal curves, both with variance 9/4, one centered at 25 and the other centered at 30, intersecting at 27.5.

(a) If $\bar{x}$ is less than 27.5, the height of the sampling distribution under the hypothesis $\mu = 25$ is higher than that of the alternative hypothesis, so the probability is greater that the data came from the sampling distribution associated with the former hypothesis. It is "more likely" that the former hypothesis is true.

(b) prob(type I error) = prob($\bar{x} > 27.5$ | null true) = prob($z > 2.5/1.5$) = approximately 5%. prob(type II error) = prob($\bar{x} < 27.5$ | alternative true) = prob($z < -2.5/1.5$) = same as probability of type I error. These probabilities are given as the area under the null sampling distribution to the right of 27.5, for the former, and the area under the alternative sampling distribution to the left of 27.5 for the latter.

(c) As the sample size increases the two sampling distributions grow taller and narrower, causing the two areas described above to shrink toward zero; both type I and type II errors fall towards zero.

(d) Using the traditional testing methodology, the type I error would be held constant at some arbitrary level, such as 5%, so as the sample size grew the critical value would shrink towards 25, keeping the type I error constant as the type II error falls towards zero.

(e) The traditional testing methodology has some peculiar characteristics.

X8 (a) Testing r against zero would be testing if x and the square of the residual are correlated, so it is a test for heteroskedasticity.

(b) A conditional moment test.

Y2 The power increases. This is easiest to explain by using a diagram with a point null and a point alternative; moving the critical value to create a 10% size will increase the power.

Y4 Using $\sigma^2(X'X)^{-1}$ the variance of β^{OLS} is found to be 4. The test statistic used will be $(\beta^{OLS} - 1)/2$ with critical value 1.645, which implies that the null hypothesis will be rejected if $\beta^{OLS} > 4.290$. prob($\beta^{OLS} > 4.290$ | $\beta = 4$) = prob[$z > 0.145$] = 0.442.

Y6 The standard error of the slope coefficient estimator is estimated to be $0.1/2 = 0.05$. The critical value for the test is 1.645, but because the true value of the slope is 0.06 (which is 1.2 standard errors), this critical value represents only

0.445 standard errors. From the normal tables, the power can be estimated as the probability of getting a z value 0.445 standard errors or greater above the mean, about 33%.

Z2 MPC $= \beta_1 + \beta_3 A$, so test $\beta_3 = 0$ using a traditional t test.

Z4 Define a new variable xw as the product of x and w. Include this variable as a regressor and test its coefficient against zero using a traditional t test.

Z6 (a) The partial of $\ln y$ with respect to $\ln K$ is $\beta_2 + 2\beta_4\ln K + \beta_5\ln L$, which should be positive for a positive elasticity, not β_2 by itself.

(b) Do an F test for $\beta_3 = \beta_4 = \beta_5 = 0$.

Z8 (a) $\theta_1/\lambda_1 = \theta_2/\lambda_2$ or $\theta_1\lambda_2 = \theta_2\lambda_1$.

(b) Run both equations unrestricted to obtain estimates of the four parameters. Estimate $(\theta_1\lambda_2 - \theta_2\lambda_1)$ by plugging in these estimates and use the square of this as the numerator for the eventual chi-square (with one degree of freedom) test statistic. The denominator is the estimated variance of this numerator, say $\delta'V\delta$. Here V is the 4×4 variance–covariance matrix of the unrestricted estimates of the parameters, obtained using the two 2×2 variance–covariance matrix estimates from the two unrestricted regressions. δ is the 4×1 vector of first derivatives of $(\theta_1\lambda_2 - \theta_2\lambda_1)$ evaluated at the unrestricted estimates.

Z10 (a) ε distributed log-normally means that $\ln\varepsilon$ is distributed normally. If estimation is undertaken by regressing logs on logs, the relevant error term is $\ln\varepsilon$, which if it is distributed normally implies that the OLS estimator is the MLE (with attendant desirable properties) and facilitates inference. If it is specified to have mean one, $AK^\alpha L^\beta$ is the expected value of Y given K and L, the usual meaning attached to the functional specification.

(b) Multiply both inputs by a constant w and note that output is multiplied by $w^{\alpha+\beta}$ so that constant returns will obtain if $\alpha + \beta = 1$. The easiest test is an F test, regressing logs on logs restricted and unrestricted. For restricted regress $(\ln Y - \ln L)$ on a constant and $(\ln K - \ln L)$.

Z12 (a) By setting y_t equal to y_{t-1} and x_t equal to x_{t-1} and solving for y_t, the long-run elasticity can be estimated as $(\beta_2 + \beta_3)/(1 - \beta_1)$. To test this equal to one we can test $\beta_1 + \beta_2 + \beta_3 = 1$ which can easily be done with an F test.

(b) The confidence interval is more difficult to estimate because it requires finding the standard error of $(\beta_2^* + \beta_3^*)/(1 - \beta_1^*)$, a non-linear function of the vector of parameter estimates. This can be estimated as the square root of $d'Vd$ where V is the estimated variance–covariance matrix of the vector $(\beta_1^*, \beta_2^*, \beta_3^*)$ and d is the estimate of the first derivative of the long-run elasticity, namely $[(\beta_2^* + \beta_3^*)(1 - \beta_1^*)^{-2}, (1 - \beta_1^*)^{-1}, (1 - \beta_1^*)^{-1}]'$.

AA2 (a) SSE restricted is 100, SSE unrestricted is 88, and there are 4 restrictions, so the numerator of the F test is 3. Degrees of freedom for the denominator are 200, so the denominator is $1/2$. The F statistic is thus 6, which exceeds the $(\alpha = 0.05)$ critical value of 2.37 for the F with 4 and 200 degrees of freedom, so the null hypothesis is rejected.

(b) Do a t test to see if 0.88 differs significantly from unity. The test statistic is $0.12/0.05 = 2.4$, which exceeds the $(\alpha = 0.05)$ critical value of 1.96 for the t with 204 degrees of freedom, so the null is rejected.

(c) For part (a) one would have to obtain the SSE restricted by including two dummies, one for each of two regions. There would only be 2 rather than 4 restrictions, changing the degrees of freedom for the numerator. For part (b) the coefficient estimate to be tested against one must come from the new restricted regression; the degrees of freedom for the t test are now 202.

AA4 **(a)** m is estimated by the mean of the data, 3, and v is estimated by the sample variance, 2.5. The estimated variance of the sample mean is thus $2.5/5 = 0.5$, the square root of which is about 0.7. The t statistic to test m = 4 is $1/0.7 = 1.43$ which must be compared to the critical value 2.015.
(b) A z statistic, calculated as $1/0.6 = 1.667$ must be compared to the critical value 1.645.

AA6 The prediction error is 10. The required F statistic is the square of the t statistic used to test if this number is significantly different from zero. The variance of the prediction error, calculated using $s^2[1 + x'(X'X)^{-1}x]$, is 64. The required F statistic is thus 100/64.

AA8 Under the null hypothesis, the OLS estimate of β is 2, producing errors -1, 1, 1 and -1. The partials of y with respect to the parameters, evaluated at the restricted estimates, are proportional to x^{-1} and x^{-2}. The LM statistic can be calculated as the sample size times the R^2 from regressing the errors above on a constant and these partials.

BB2 On the null hypothesis skew and (kurt $-$ 3) must be independently and normally distributed with mean zero, so that when adjusted to have unit variance the sum of their squares is distributed as a chi-square. Thus the variance of skew and kurt must be $6/N$ and $24/N$, respectively.

BB4 This is an F statistic, with J and $T - K$ degrees of freedom, calculated as the ratio of two independent chi-squares, each divided by their degrees of freedom. Visualize the numerator as $(r - R\beta^{OLS})'V^{-1}(r - R\beta^{OLS})/J$ and the denominator as $s^2/\sigma^2 = (SSE/\sigma^2)/(T - K)$ where V is the variance–covariance matrix of $(r - R\beta^{OLS})$, namely $[\sigma^2 R(X'X)^{-1}R' + Q]$. The unknown σ^2 in this last expression is pulled out to cancel the σ^2 in the denominator, leaving an element Q/σ^2 which is estimated by Q/s^2.

BB6 **(a)** $TR^2 = T\hat{e}'\hat{e}/e'e = [Z(Z'Z)^{-1}Z'e]'[Z(Z'Z)^{-1}Z'e]/(e'e/T) = e'Z(Z'Z)^{-1}Z'e/s^2$.
(b) If g did not include an intercept, the means of the es and the ês would not be zero, so the formula for R^2 would have the square of these means subtracted from both numerator and denominator, upsetting the result given above.

BB8 **(a)** Following the hint we get y, a linear function of lagged y, x, and lagged x. Of the three derivatives, the partial with respect to ρ evaluated at the restricted estimator is the lagged OLS residual from regressing y on x. To get NR^2 regress the OLS residual on an intercept, x, and the lagged OLS residual.
(b) x by itself has no explanatory power regarding the OLS residual, because x and this residual are uncorrelated. Consequently, a large R^2 results only if the lagged OLS residual has some explanatory power, implying that its slope coefficient when regressed on the OLS residual (the usual $\hat{\rho}$) is significantly different from zero.

BB10 The log-likelihood is $(\ln\lambda)\Sigma x - T\lambda - \Sigma\ln x!$, the first partial is $\Sigma x/\lambda - T$, and the second partial is $-(\Sigma x)/\lambda^2$ so that $\lambda^{MLE} = \bar{x}$ and the Cramer–Rao lower bound is λ/T (using the hint that $Ex = \lambda$). LR is $2[(\ln\bar{x})\Sigma x - \Sigma x - (\ln\lambda_0)\Sigma x + T\lambda_0]$. LM is $(\Sigma x/\lambda_0 - T)^2(\lambda_0/T)$. W is $(\bar{x} - \lambda_0)^2(T/\bar{x})$.

BB12 **(a)** The restricted log-likelihood is $-(T/2)\ln2\pi - (T/2)\ln(SSE_R/T) - T/2$ and the unrestricted log-likelihood is $-(T/2)\ln2\pi - (T/2)\ln(SSE_U/T) - T/2$, so LR is $-2[(T/2)\ln(SSE_U/T) - (T/2)\ln(SSE_R/T)]$, equal to $T\ln(SSE_R/SSE_U)$.

(b) W is the square of the t statistic for testing $\beta = 0$.

(c) Regress the residuals from the restricted regression on 1, x and w.

CC2 By calculating $-2\ln\lambda$, where λ is the ratio of the restricted maximized likelihood to the unrestricted maximized likelihood, LR can be shown to be $(SSE_R - SSE_U)/\sigma^2 = \varepsilon'X(X'X)^{-1}[R(X'X)^{-1}R']^{-1}(X'X)^{-1}X'\varepsilon/\sigma^2$. The W test statistic is $(R\beta^{OLS} - r)'[V(R\beta^{OLS} - r)]^{-1}(R\beta^{OLS} - r)$, which reduces to the same thing. For the LM statistic, λ is estimated by $\lambda^* = [R(X'X)^{-1}R']^{-1}(R\beta^{OLS} - r)$ and LM $= \lambda^{*'}[V(\lambda^*)]^{-1}\lambda^*$ reduces to the same formula.

CC4 The likelihood ratio becomes $(2\pi SSE_R/T)^{-T/2}/(2\pi SSE_U/T)^{-T/2} = (SSE_R/SSE_U)^{-T/2} = [JF/(T - K) - 1]^{-T/2}$.

CC6 The Chow test, applied to the case in which there are not enough observations in one subset to run a regression, tests for whether or not these observations lie inside a forecast confidence region. It can be formulated in terms of observation-specific dummies. This formula is identical to the formula for the rainbow test, which tests whether several observations, at the beginning and at the end of the data set, lie within a forecast confidence region.

DD2 **(a)** $(4 - \beta)^2$.

(b) $4\beta^2/12$.

(c) When $\beta < 2$ the pre-test eliminator is identical to the unrestricted estimator, so its MSE is $4\beta^2/12$.

(d) $(2/\beta) \times 2 + [(\beta - 2)/\beta] \times 4 = 4(\beta - 1)/\beta$.

(e) It is easiest to use the formula that variance equals the expected value of the square minus the square of the expected value. This gives $(2/\beta)$ times the integral from zero to 2 of y^2, plus $[(\beta - 2)/\beta] \times 16$, minus the square of the mean above.

EE2 **(a)** Regressing y on x and w yields coefficient estimates 1.0 and 0.9, with $s^2 = 1.45$ and estimated variances 0.36 and 0.51. The non-nested F test treating A's model as the null is the square of the t statistic on the estimated coefficient 0.9. This is 2.48. For B's model as the null it is the square of the t statistic on estimated coefficient 1.0. This is 1.96. Both are less than the 5% critical value of 18.5, so both nulls are accepted.

(b) Regressing y on x yields estimate $\beta^* = 2$ and residuals 2, -1, 0, and -1. To test B's model as the null using the J test, regress y on w and these residuals and do a t test on the residuals' coefficient. Regressing y on x yields estimate $\theta^* = 2.4$ and residuals 1.6, -1.8, 1.2, and -1. To test A's model as the null regress y on x and these residuals and do a t test on the residuals' coefficient.

FF2 (i) Choose values for the four parameters, select a sample size, say 25, and get 25 x values. (ii) Have the computer produce 25 errors from a normal distribution with mean zero and variance one. Transform all errors by multiplying the tth error by the square root of Kx_t^α. (iii) Calculate the corresponding 25 y values. (iv) Regress y on an intercept and x to get the OLS estimate. Save it. (v) Regress the logarithm of the squared OLS residuals on an intercept and $\ln x$ to get slope coefficient estimate a^*. Divide y, x and 1 (the intercept term) by the square root of $x_t^{a^*}$. (vi) Regress the transformed y on the transformed x and the transformed intercept term to get the EGLS estimate. Save it. (vii) Repeat from (ii) to obtain, say, 2,000 sets of estimates. (viii) Use the 2,000 OLS estimates to estimate the mean of the OLS estimator (and thus its bias), its variance and its MSE. Do the same for EGLS, using the 2,000 EGLS estimates, and compare.

FF4 Select form of heteroskedasticity, parameter values, sample size, and x values.

Draw $N(0,1)$ errors and transform to create heteroskedasticity. Calculate y values. Run OLS regression. Perform Goldfeld–Quandt test and note if heteroskedasticity detected; repeat for Breusch–Pagan test. Draw new errors and repeat above 1,000 times, say. Power is compared by comparing number of times each test detected heteroskedasticity. For a more effective comparison run a Monte Carlo study to determine for each test what critical values create the proper type I error, and then use these critical values in the Monte Carlo power study.

FF6 Select parameter values, sample size, and x values. Draw $N(0, \sigma^2)$ errors and transform to create autocorrelation. Calculate y values. Run OLS regression and save OLS estimate. Calculate EGLS estimate and save it. Perform test of autocorrelated errors. If null of zero autocorrelation is accepted, set pre-test (PT) estimate equal to OLS estimate, otherwise set PT estimate equal to EGLS estimate. Save this PT estimate. Draw new errors and repeat the above to obtain, say, 2,000 OLS, EGLS and PT estimates. For each estimate MSE. Repeat the above for several different values of the autocorrelation coefficient ρ and graph the estimated MSE of each of the three estimators against ρ.

FF8 Suppose there are N cost share equations and T observations on each. Estimate using SURE but do not impose the constraints. Save the T resulting sets of N errors, call them EN. Use the resulting parameter estimates as the "true" parameter values to produce new dependent variable values along with T drawings with replacement from the set of EN error vectors. Estimate with SURE, imposing the restrictions, and calculate the elasticity estimates. Repeat to obtain 2,000 such estimates. By finding the distance from the mean of these estimates to the values that cut off the appropriate tail percentages, compute the required confidence intervals as your original elasticity estimates minus and plus these distances.

GG2 False. Although efficiency is a problem, and consistency is not, it must be noted that there are problems with inference.

GG4 It is possible because the computer output contains estimates of the variances, not the actual variances.

GG6 False. If variance is overestimated, then the t statistic will be too small, implying that the null will be accepted too often, implying that type I errors occur less frequently.

HH2 False. All data should be divided by the square root of x.

HH4 False. Divide through data by x and then regress y/x on a constant, producing the GLS estimator as $\Sigma(y/x)$, which is not $\Sigma y/\Sigma x$.

HH6 In (b) the error is heteroskedastic since the error variance is larger when income is larger, so OLS is inefficient and its estimated variance is biased. In (a) there is no heteroskedasticity, so the properties of OLS are unaffected.

HH8 **(a)** The relationship can be rewritten as $y = \alpha + \beta x + u$ where u is an error with mean zero and variance $\sigma^2(\alpha + \beta x)^2$. Estimate using an iterative procedure, beginning by using the OLS estimates of α and β to estimate the transformation for heteroskedasticity. Find the EGLS estimates, then use these EGLS estimates to re-estimate the transformation for heteroskedasticity, etc.
(b) Use MLE. The log-likelihood is $-(T/2)\ln 2\pi - (T/2)\ln\sigma^2 - \Sigma\ln(\alpha + \beta x) - (1/2\sigma^2)\Sigma[(y - \alpha - \beta x)^2/(\alpha + \beta x)^2]$.

HH10 The heteroskedasticity-consistent variance–covariance matrix estimate is given by the formula $(X'X)^{-1}X'WX(X'X)^{-1}$ where W is a diagonal matrix consisting of the squared residuals and in this application X is a column of ones. This produces

SSE/T^2. The usual estimator is $s^2/T = SSE/[T(T-1)]$.

HH12 (a) $\ln L = -(N/2)\ln 2\pi - (N/2)\ln\delta - (\theta/2)\Sigma\ln x - (1/2\delta)\Sigma[(y - \alpha - \beta x)^2/x^\theta]$
$+ (\lambda - 1)\Sigma\ln y$

(b) Do an LR test of the joint hypothesis that $\lambda = 1$ and $\theta = 0$.

(c) Do an LR test of the hypothesis that $\lambda = 1$ allowing θ to take on any value.

II2 False. A lagged value of the regressand appearing as a regressor introduces bias (which disappears asymptotically).

II4 A straight line fitted to a nonlinear functional form will tend to produce strings of positive errors and strings of negative errors, exactly what an autocorrelated error structure would tend to produce.

JJ2 Use a Goldfeld–Quandt test. Regress using only the fourth quarter data and estimate the variance of the error term. Regress using all the other data and estimate the variance of the error term. The ratio of these two estimates is distributed as an F with dfs the two divisors of the $SSEs$.

JJ4 (a) $\beta^{OLS} = 2$, producing OLS residuals 2, -1, 0 and -1, $s^2 = 2$, so estimated $V(\beta^{OLS})$ is $1/7$.

(b) The heteroskedasticity-consistent variance–covariance matrix estimate is given by the formula $(X'X)^{-1}X'WX(X'X)^{-1}$ where W is a diagonal matrix consisting of the squared OLS residuals. This produces $8/14^2 = 2/49$.

(c) White's test statistic is calculated as 4 times the R^2 from regressing the squared OLS residuals on an intercept and x^2.

(d) The studentized Breusch–Pagan test statistic is calculated as 4 times the R^2 from regressing the squared OLS residuals on an intercept and x^2.

KK2 Estimate by GLS of observations (2, 6, 12) on observations (1, 2, 3). Transforming to eliminate heteroskedasticity implies regressing observations (2, 3, 4) on observations (1, 1, 1), yielding GLS estimate 3.

KK4 (a) For the first 22 observations $SSR = 1,000$, so that $s^2 = 2$. For the next 32 observations $SSR = 2,916$, so that $s^2 = 8$. Their ratio is distributed as an F with dfs 30 and 20. Since the ratio 4 exceeds the critical value of 2.04 the null of equal variances is rejected.

(b) An appropriate transformation for the heteroskedasticity is to multiply the first period's data by 2, changing its Σxy to 400 and Σx^2 to 40. The EGLS estimator is $616/56 = 11$.

(c) Estimate OLS variance by $(X'X)^{-1}X'WX(X'X)^{-1}$ where W is a diagonal matrix with 22 twos followed by 32 eights. This yields $(1/26)^2(2 \times 10 + 8 \times 16) = 0.22$.

LL2 The variance–covariance matrix of ε is $\sigma^2 V$ where V has twos down the diagonal, ones beside the diagonal, and zero elsewhere. V^{-1} is one-quarter times a matrix Q with 3, 4, 3 down the diagonal, -2 beside the diagonal and 1 elsewhere. The GLS estimate of K is $(X'QX)^{-1}X'Qy$ where in this case X is a column of ones. This yields $7/2$.

LL4 (a) Unbiased because $E\varepsilon = 0$.

(b) $V(\beta^{OLS}) = (X'X)^{-1}X'WX(X'X)^{-1}$ where W is the variance–covariance matrix of the error vector, in this case ones on the diagonal and -0.6 on the off-diagonal. This yields 0.1.

(c) $V(\beta^{GLS}) = (X'W^{-1}X)^{-1} = 0.09$.

MM2 (a) Writing these two equations as a single equation we get a y vector consisting of y_1 followed by y_2 and an X matrix consisting of a column of 20 ones followed by 20 zeros and a column of 20 zeros followed by 20 ones. The error vector has a variance–covariance matrix consisting of four blocks. The upper left block is two times a 20×20 identity matrix, the lower right block is three times a 20×20 identity matrix, and the remaining blocks are identities. Estimating with GLS yields 3 and 5.

(b) The X matrix becomes a column of 20 ones followed by 20 twos and the parameter vector now contains only μ_1. Estimation yields 18/7 for μ_1 and thus 36/7 for μ_2.

NN2 **(a)** $V_1 = \sigma^2(X_1'M_2X_1)^{-1}$ and $V_2 = \sigma^2(X_2'M_1X_2)^{-1}$.

(b) $E(\beta_1^* = E(X_1'X_1)^{-1}X_1'(X_1\beta_1 + X_2\beta_2 + \varepsilon - X_2\beta_2^*) = \beta_1$.

(c) $W = V[(X_1'X_1)^{-1}X_1'\varepsilon] + V(X_1'X_1)^{-1}X_1'X_2\beta_2^*]$ assuming $E\varepsilon\beta_2^* = 0$. This yields $W = \sigma^2(X_1'X_1)^{-1} + (X_1'X_1)^{-1}X_1'X_2V_2^*X_2'X_1(X_1'X_1)^{-1}$.

(d) Using the hint we get
$V_1 - W = (X_1'X_1)^{-1}X_1'X_2[\sigma^2(X_2'M_1X_2)^{-1} - V_2^*]X_2'X_1(X_1'X_1)^{-1}$ which is nnd if $V_2 - V_2^*$ is nnd.

(e) If the unbiased estimate of β_2 from the previous study is better than the estimate of β_2 from the data at hand, in the sense that it has a smaller variance, one is better off using the previous study's estimate and ignoring the estimate obtainable from the data, rather than doing the opposite.

NN4 **(a)** We need to add an artificial observation y = 3, x = 1 plus an error with mean zero and variance 4. Using the hint the variance of ε is estimated to be $(360 - 40)/20 = 16$. To make the errors homoskedastic we must multiply through the artificial observation by 2 creating the extra observation y = 6 and x = 2. This causes Σxy to increase to 32 and Σx^2 to increase to 14, creating $\beta^* = 32/14 = 2.3$.

(b) In both cases the variance of the error is the same, so the relative variances are captured by the Σx^2 terms. The ratio of the new variance to the old is 10/14, a reduction of 29%.

NN6 **(a)** Instruct her to perform mixed estimation by appending to the 75×1 vector of observations on the dependent variable the 3×1 vector of coefficient estimates from the original regression and appending below the 75×3 X matrix a 3×3 identity matrix. GLS would have to be performed because the variance–covariance matrix of the errors would become a 78×78 matrix with the 3×3 variance–covariance matrix from the original regression in the bottom right hand corner.

(b) Yes. Tell her to pool the data and run a new regression, checking for whether the variance of the error term is the same in the two samples.

OO2 **(a)** $[X'(I + XVX')^{-1}X]^{-1}X'(I + XVX')^{-1}y$

$= \{X'[I - X(X'X + V^{-1})^{-1}X']X\}^{-1}X'[I - X(X'X + V^{-1})^{-1}X']y$

$= \{X'X - X'XQ^{-1}X'X\}^{-1}\{I - X'XQ^{-1}\}X'y$

where $Q = (X'X + V^{-1})$

$= \{(X'X)^{-1} - (X'X)^{-1}X'X[(X'X)(X'X)^{-1}(X'X)$
$\quad - Q]^{-1}(X'X)(X'X)^{-1}\}\{I - X'XQ^{-1}\}X'y$

$= \{(X'X)^{-1} - [(X'X) - Q]^{-1}\}\{I - X'XQ^{-1}\}X'y$

$= \{(X'X)^{-1} - (X'X)^{-1} + (X'X)^{-1}[(X'X)^{-1}$
$\quad - Q^{-1}]^{-1}(X'X)^{-1}\}\{I - X'XQ^{-1}\}X'y$

$= (X'X)^{-1}X'y$

(b) The extent to which GLS deviates from OLS depends on the design matrix X, so conclusions from Monte Carlo studies cannot be generalized.

PP2 The log-likelihood is $-(T/2)\ln 2\pi - (\alpha/2)\Sigma w_t - (1/2)\Sigma[(y_t - \beta x_t)^2 \exp(-\alpha w_t)]$. The second cross partial is $-\Sigma x w(y - \beta x)\exp(-\alpha w)$, the expected value of which is zero, so we need not worry about the second partial with respect to β. The second partial with respect to α is $-(1/2)\Sigma(y - \beta x)^2 w^2 \exp(-\alpha w)$, the expected value of which is $-(T/2)\Sigma w^2$, so the required Cramer–Rao lower bound is $2/T\Sigma w^2$.

PP4 The max log-likelihood restricted is $-(T/2)\ln(2\pi) - (T/2)\ln(\sigma_t^2)^* - (T/2)$ and the max log-likelihood unrestricted is $-(T/2)\ln(2\pi) - (1/2)\Sigma\ln(\sigma_t^2)^{**} - (T/2)$, so $LR = T\ln(\sigma_t^2)^* - \Sigma\ln(\sigma_t^2)^{**}$.

PP6 $V(Q^*) = (\partial Q^*/\partial P^*)^2 V(P^*) = [P(1 - P)]^{-2} P(1 - P)/N = [NP(1 - P)]^{-1}$.

QQ2 $E(\varepsilon_t - \varepsilon_{t-1})(\varepsilon_{t-1} - \varepsilon_{t-2}) = 2E\varepsilon_t\varepsilon_{t-1} - V\varepsilon - E\varepsilon_t\varepsilon_{t-2} = (2\rho - 1 - \rho^2)V\varepsilon$ and $V(\varepsilon_t - \varepsilon_{t-1}) = 2V\varepsilon - 2\rho V\varepsilon = 2(1 - \rho)V\varepsilon$ so that the condition is $|2\rho - 1 - \rho^2|/2(1 - \rho) < \rho$, satisfied when $|\rho| > 1/3$.

QQ4 **(a)** Transform x_t to $x_t - \rho x_{t-2}$, and transform the first two observations by multiplying them by the square root of $1 - \rho^2$.

RR2 False. Adding an error to the second equation gives rise to an estimating equation in which y is regressed on lagged y and x, with a spherical error.

RR4 **(a)** The first model gives rise to an estimating equation in which y is regressed on lagged y, x and w. The second model gives rise to an estimating equation in which y is regressed on lagged y, x, w, and lagged w. This suggests discriminating between the models by running this second regression and testing if the coefficient on lagged w is significantly different from zero.

(b) Both estimating equations involve regressing y on lagged y and x. The second equation has a moving average error, whereas the error in the first equation is spherical, so a test for this difference could serve as a way of discriminating between the models.

RR6 **(a)** Estimating equation involves regressing p on lagged p, x, lagged x, w, and lagged w. Assuming a spherical error attached to the original equation this estimating equation has a moving average error. Furthermore, it is over-identified: the estimated coefficient on x can be used in conjunction with the estimated coefficient on lagged x to estimate λ, but also the estimated coefficient on w can be used in conjunction with the estimated coefficient on lagged w to produce another estimate of λ.

(b) These estimates will be different. The search over λ builds in the over-identifying restriction and thus is preferred.

(c) If the coefficient on w is zero the equation is not over-identified; the two estimating methods should produce the same estimates.

RR8 **(a)** Multiplying through this equation by $(1 - \lambda L)(1 - \delta L)$ and rearranging we get $y_t = (1 - \delta - \lambda + \delta\lambda)\alpha + (\delta + 1)y_{t-1} - \delta\lambda y_{t-2} + \beta x_t - \beta\delta x_{t-1} + \theta z_t - \theta\lambda z_{t-1}$ which can be written generically as $y_t = \theta_0 + \theta_1 y_{t-1} + \theta_2 y_{t-2} + \theta_3 x_t + \theta_4 x_{t-1} + \theta_5 z_t + \theta_6 z_{t-1}$. It is overidentified because there are seven coefficient estimates but only five parameters to be estimated; there are consequently two over-identifying restrictions which can be written as $\theta_1 = -\theta_4/\theta_3 - \theta_6/\theta_5$ and $\theta_2 = -\theta_4\theta_6/\theta_3\theta_5$ or as $\theta_1\theta_3\theta_5 + \theta_4\theta_5 + \theta_6\theta_3 = 0$ and $\theta_2\theta_3\theta_5 + \theta_4\theta_6 = 0$.

(b) The numerators of the asymptotic t statistics would each be estimated by plugging in unrestricted estimates of the θs into the last forms of the restrictions given in (a). The denominator of the t statistic is the square root of the estimated variance of the numerator, calculated by using the formula for the variance of a nonlinear function. Because of the nonlinearities, all results are asymptotic and so do not rely on normally-distributed errors.

(c) Joint testing of these restrictions requires a Wald test, using the formula for the variance–covariance matrix of a vector of nonlinear functions of a vector.

SS2 (i) Select parameter values (including an error variance for the regression error, σ^2, and an error variance for the measurement error, σ_x^2), sample size, say 30, 30 x values, and 30 IV values (correlated with x). (ii) Get the computer to produce 30 errors with mean zero and variance σ^2. Use these errors and the true x values to calculate 30 y values. (iii) Get the computer to draw 30 errors with mean zero and variance σ_x^2 and use them to calculate the measured x values. (iv) Use the y values and the measured x values to calculate the OLS estimate and an IV estimate. Save them. (v) Repeat from (ii) to produce, say, 800 sets of estimates. (vi) Use the 800 OLS estimates to estimate bias, variance and MSE. Use the 800 IV estimates to estimate the same. Compare.

TT2 False. The consequences stated refer to measurement errors in the independent variable, not the dependent variable.

TT4 The two-group estimator is $(y2 - y1)/(x2 - x1)$ where $x2$ is the average of the high half of the x observations, etc. The IV estimator is $(W'X)^{-1}W'y$ where X is a column of ordered (from smallest to largest) observations on x, y is the corresponding column of observations on y, and W is a column the first half of which consists of minus ones and the second half of which consists of ones. This produces the same formula as that of the two-group estimator, if the $T/2$ divisors for the averaging are canceled.

TT6 The plim of OLS is $\beta - \beta\sigma_x^2/\text{plim}(x^2/T)$, so if β is positive it is biased downwards. The plim of inverse OLS is $\beta + \sigma_y^2/\beta\text{plim}(x^2/T)$, which is biased upwards.

UU2 Use the predicted values of lagged y from a regression of y on an intercept, x, and z. This is the "best" linear combination of the possible instruments x and z.

UU4 The relationship $Py = PX\beta + P\varepsilon$ has a spherical error. Use PW as an instrument for PX, producing $\beta^{IV} = (W'P'PX)^{-1}W'P'Py = (W'V^{-1}x)^{-1}W'V^{-1}y$ whose variance–covariance matrix is $(W'V^{-1}X)^{-1}W'V^{-1}W(X'V^{-1}W)^{-1}$.

UU6 (a) $\Sigma xe = \Sigma x(y - \beta x) = \Sigma xy - \beta\Sigma x^2$ which set to zero yields $\beta^* = \Sigma xy/\Sigma x^2 = \beta^{OLS}$.

(b) $\Sigma ze = \Sigma z(y - \beta x) = \Sigma zy - \beta\Sigma xz$ which set equal to zero yields $\beta^{**} = \Sigma zy/\Sigma xz = \beta^{iv}$.

(c) GMM requires minimization of a weighted sum of Σxe and Σze, namely $d'V^{-1}d$ where $d' = (\Sigma xe, \Sigma ze)$ and V is the variance–covariance matrix of d, with $\sigma^2\Sigma x^2$ and $\sigma^2\Sigma z^2$ in the two diagonal positions and $\sigma^2\Sigma xz$ in the off-diagonal position, where σ^2 is the variance of the error term and is irrelevant for maximization purposes.

VV2 False. It can be calculated, but one does not know of what the result is an estimate.

VV4 (a) $\beta_1^* = 8/4 = 2$; $\beta_0^* = 1 - 2\beta_1^* = -3$.

(b) β estimates unchanged; $\alpha_0^* = 2$ and $\alpha_2^* = 4$.

(c) β estimates unchanged; $\alpha_1^* = 2$; $\alpha_2^* = -12$.

VV6 The only identified parameter is α_1, the 2SLS estimate of which is obtained either by an IV regression of y_1 on y_2 using the reduced form prediction of y_2, call it y_2^*, as an instrument for y_2, or by regressing y_1 on y_2^*. Thus $\alpha_1^* = \Sigma y_1 y_2^*/\Sigma y_2 y_2^*$ or $\Sigma y_1 y_2^*/\Sigma(y_2^*)^2$, where $y_2^* = 3x_1 + 4x_2$. Both formulas yield 18/25.

VV8 Each reduced form equation has the same set of exogenous variables, so there is no gain from using a SURE technique.

VV10 (a) Reduced forms are $p = (v - u)/(\alpha - \beta)$ and $q = (\alpha v - \beta u)/(\alpha - \beta)$. plim $\Sigma qp/\Sigma p^2 = \text{plim}[\Sigma(v - u)(\alpha v - \beta u)/T]/\text{plim}[\Sigma(v - u)^2/T] = [\alpha V(v) + \beta V(u)]/[V(v) + V(u)]$.

(b) Follows from it being a weighted average of a positive and a negative number.

(c) Regress p on q. The plim of the estimate is $[\alpha V(v) + \beta V(u)]/[\alpha^2 V(v) + \beta^2 V(u)]$. Substituting $V(V) = kV(u)$ into both plims we get the plim of the first estimate equals $(\alpha k + \beta)/(k + 1)$ and the plim of the second estimate equals $(\alpha k + \beta)/(\alpha^2 k + \beta^2)$. This gives two equations which can be solved to produce estimates of α and β in terms of k and the two regression estimates.

(d) Knowledge about the relative magnitudes of the error variances can aid in identification.

WW2 Uncertain. Because of the measurement error, all coefficient estimates are biased, which suggests that the degrees of freedom should be equal to the number of parameters being estimated, as the original Hausman article stated. But there is some controversy on this – recent thinking is that the variance–covariance matrix of the difference between the OLS and IV estimates is singular and that only a relevant subset of this matrix (and of the parameter vector) can be used in constructing the test, reducing the degrees of freedom to one in this case.

WW4 (a) $\beta^{IV} = (Z'X)^{-1}Z'(X\beta^{OLS} + \varepsilon^{OLS})$ so $\beta^{IV} - \beta^{OLS} = (Z'X)^{-1}Z'\varepsilon^{OLS}$.

(b) $V(\beta^{IV} - \beta^{OLS}) = E[(Z'X)^{-1}Z'\varepsilon^{OLS}\varepsilon^{OLS'}Z(X'Z)^{-1}]$
$= E[(Z'X)^{-1}Z'M\varepsilon\varepsilon'MZ(X'Z)^{-1}]$
$= \sigma^2(Z'X)^{-1}Z'MZ(X'Z)^{-1}$
$= \sigma^2(Z'X)^{-1}Z'[I - X(X'X)^{-1}X']Z(X'Z)^{-1}$
$= \sigma^2(Z'X)^{-1}Z'Z(X'Z)^{-1} - \sigma^2(X'X)^{-1}$
$= V(\beta^{IV}) - V(\beta^{OLS})$.

WW6 $(IV - OLS) = (2, -1)'$ with estimated variance–covariance matrix V with 1 and 2 on the diagonal and -1 in the off-diagonal. The Hausman test statistic is $(2, -1)V^{-1}(2, -1)' = 5$, which is less than 5.99, the 5% critical value for 2 d.f., so the null of x being exogenous is accepted.

XX2 (i) Specify $y = \alpha + \beta x + \varepsilon$, select values for α, β and σ^2, choose the sample size (say 35), obtain 35 x values, and determine a limit value k above which, say, y is unobserved (and is set equal to k). Choose k so that about 10 observations, say, are expected to fall into this category in a typical sample. (ii) Have the computer generate 35 errors, calculate the 35 y values, and set any y greater than k equal to k. (iii) Use the y and x data to obtain OLS and Tobit estimates. Save them. (iv) Repeat from (ii) to obtain, say, 600 sets of estimates. (v) Use the 600 OLS estimates to estimate the bias of OLS, and use the 600 Tobit estimates to estimate the bias of the Tobit estimator.

XX4 (i) Select a sample size, say 90, choose α, β, δ and θ values, variances of the two error terms and a nonzero covariance between these two errors. In practice you can create one error as a random error and then the other as a constant times this error plus another random error. The δ and θ values must be chosen so as to ensure that a reasonable number of the $\delta + \theta w$ observations are negative, and the variance of the u error must be such as to allow the u term to cause a reasonable number of the $\delta + \theta w$ observations to change sign when u is added. (ii) Draw 90 ε and u values and use them to create 90 y values with the y value being set to zero if $\delta + \theta w + u$ is negative. (iii) Calculate β^{OLS} and β^* the Heckman two-stage estimator. (iv) Repeat from (ii) to calculate 3,000 β^{OLS} and β^* estimates. (v) Calculate the bias and variance of these estimators.

YY2   (a)   The likelihood is $[e^{\alpha}/(1 + e^{\alpha})]^{25}(1 + e^{\alpha})]^{-75}$. Maximizing the log-likelihood with respect to α yields the MLE of $e^{\alpha}/(1 + e^{\alpha})$, the probability of being a smoker, as $25/100 = 1/4$. Note the MLE of $e^{\alpha} = 1/3$.
   (b)   The likelihood is $[e^{\alpha}/(1 + e^{\alpha})]^{15}(1 + e^{\alpha})^{-40}[e^{\alpha+\beta}/(1 + e^{\alpha+\beta})]^{10}(1 + e^{\alpha+\beta})^{-35}$. The log-likelihood is $25\alpha + 10\beta - 55\ln(1 + e^{\alpha}) - 45\ln(1 + e^{\alpha+\beta})$. Maximizing with respect to α and β yields $\alpha^{MLE} = \ln(3/8)$ and $\beta^{MLE} = \ln(16/21)$.
   (c)   2/9 and 3/11, equal to the fraction of male smokers in the male data and the fraction of female smokers in the female data, respectively.
   (d)   Evaluate the likelihood of part (b) for $e^{\beta} = 3/8$ and $e^{\beta} = 16/21$ to get the maximized unrestricted likelihood. Evaluate the likelihood of part (a) above for $e^{\alpha} = 1/3$ to get the maximized restricted likelihood. Minus twice the logarithm of the ratio of the latter to the former produces the LR test statistic.

YY4   An ordered logit or ordered probit estimation procedure would be appropriate. Among the explanatory variables will be a dummy for gender and an interactive dummy of gender times experience. An LR test can be used to test if the coefficients on these two explanatory variables are zero.

YY6 $\text{prob(unsuccessful)} = \text{prob}(\alpha + \beta x + \varepsilon < \delta_1)$
     $= \text{prob}(\varepsilon < \delta_1 - \alpha - \beta x) = \exp(\delta_1 - \alpha - \beta x)/[1 + \exp(\delta_1 - \alpha - \beta x)]$
   $\text{prob(moderate)} = \text{prob}(\delta_1 < \alpha + \beta x + \varepsilon < \delta_2)$
     $= \text{prob}(\delta_1 - \alpha - \beta x < \varepsilon < \delta_2 - \alpha - \beta x)$
     $= \exp(\delta_2 - \alpha - \beta x)/[1 + \exp(\delta_2 - \alpha - \beta x)]$
     $- \exp(\delta_1 - \alpha - \beta x)/[1 + \exp(\delta_1 - \alpha - \beta x)]$
   $\text{prob(successful)} = \text{prob}(\alpha + \beta x + \varepsilon > \delta_2)$
     $= \text{prob}(\varepsilon > \delta_2 - \alpha - \beta x) = [1 + \exp(\delta_2 - \alpha - \beta x)]^{-1}$
By tradition δ_1 is set to zero for normalization. For sample size N the likelihood is the product of N of these probability expressions, each unsuccessful outcome contributing an expression given by prob (unsuccessful) above, each moderate outcome contributing an expression given by prob (moderate) above, and each successful observation contributing an expression given by prob (successful) above.

ZZ2   A sold-out rink reflects a game for which the demand exceeded the capacity of the rink. Treat these observations as limit observations in a Tobit model.

ZZ4   Estimate by using a double-limit Tobit estimation procedure, in which the likelihood term for a stock that does not trade is the integral from $P_b - \alpha - \beta x$ to $P_a - \alpha - \beta x$.

ZZ6   (a)   The graph follows the 45 degree line up from the SW quadrant until Δy^* becomes a_1, at which point it jumps up to the horizontal axis and along it until Δy^* becomes a_2, at which point it jumps up and becomes the 45 degree line again.
   (b)   The likelihood is the product of two types of terms. For an observation with Δy nonzero, its likelihood term is the formula for $N(0, \sigma^2)$ evaluated at

$\Delta y - \beta \Delta x$. For an observation with zero Δy, its likelihood term is the integral of this normal formula from $a_1 - \Delta y - \beta \Delta x$ to $a_2 - \Delta y - \beta \Delta x$.

AB2   **(a)**   The integral of $\beta e^{-\beta x}$ from x equals zero to p is $1 - e^{-\beta p}$ so the probability that a cost-of-repair exceeds a given p value is $e^{-\beta p}$. Using this, the likelihood can be written as $\alpha^N \exp(-\alpha \Sigma p)\beta^{N1} \exp(-\beta \Sigma_1 x)\exp(-\beta \Sigma_2 p)$ where N is the total number of observations. $N1$ is the number of observations for which a cost-of-repair figure is available, the one subscript denotes summation over these $N1$ observations, and the two subscript denotes summation over the write-offs. Maximizing the log-likelihood produces $\alpha^{MLE} = N/\Sigma p$ and $\beta^{MLE} = N1/(\Sigma_1 x + \Sigma_2 p)$.

(b)   Prob(scrapped) = prob(accident)prob($x > p$),   so   prob(accident) = 0.02/ prob($x > p$). For a given p value, the prob($x > p$) = $e^{-\beta p}$, so the unconditional prob($x > p$) = integral over all p values of $e^{-\beta p} \alpha e^{-\alpha p} = \alpha/(\alpha + \beta)$ which can be evaluated using the MLEs.

GLOSSARY

This glossary contains common econometric terms that are not explained in the body of this book. Terms not included here appear in the index.

a.c.f. – autocorrelation function, used in the identification stage of time series (Box–Jenkins) analysis.

a priori information – extraneous information.

admissible – see *inadmissible*.

aggregation (grouping) – the use of group sums or group means for regression purposes instead of individual observations. Although theoretically this leads to a loss in efficiency because of the loss in information arising from the data aggregation, in applications this is not necessarily so, since aggregation can to a certain extent cancel out errors in measurement or misspecifications of micro-relationships. See Grunfeld and Griliches (1960). R^2s are higher with grouped data because errors tend to cancel one another when summed. Care must be taken in determining the basis on which grouping is undertaken since different results are usually obtained with different grouping rules. See Maddala (1977, pp. 66–9). Note that heteroskedasticity results if each group does not contain the same number of observations. Johnston (1972, pp. 228–38) has a general discussion of grouping.

ANOVA – analysis of variance.

BAN – best asymptotically normal; a BAN estimator is consistent, distributed asymptotically normally and is asymptotically efficient.

beta coefficient – the coefficient estimate from a regression in which the variables have been standardized. It can be calculated by multiplying the usual coefficient estimate by the standard error of its regressor and dividing by the standard error of the regressand, and can be interpreted as the number of standard error changes in the dependent variable resulting from a standard error change in the independent variable. It is sometimes used as a measure of the relative strength of regressors in affecting the dependent variable.

bounds test – a test for which the critical value is known only to fall within known bounds, as is the case, for example, for the DW test.

bunch map analysis – a method developed by Frisch for analyzing multicollinearity. See Malinvaud (1966, pp. 32–6).

C(α) test – test akin to the LM test except that it is evaluated at an arbitrary root-n consistent estimate that satisfies the null hypothesis, rather than at the restricted maximum likelihood estimate. When evaluated at the restricted maximum likelihood estimate one of its two terms disappears, and the other becomes the LM test statistic.

canonical correlation – an analysis whereby linear combinations of two sets of variables are found such that the correlation between the two linear combinations is maximized. These linear combinations can be interpreted as indices representing their respective sets of variables. For example, an economist may be seeking an index to represent meat consumption, where there is a variety of differently priced meats, along with a corresponding price index.

Cholesky decomposition – a positive definite matrix such as a variance–covariance matrix Σ can be decomposed by the Cholesky decomposition into $\Sigma = PP'$ where P is a lower triangular matrix. It is in effect an easily computable "square root" of Σ, allowing a drawing ε from $N(0, I)$ to be transformed into a drawing from $N(0, \Sigma)$ by calculating $P\varepsilon$.

classical – an adjective used to describe statisticians who are not Bayesians.

cointegrating vector – if a linear combination of nonstationary variables is stationary, the coefficients of this linear combination are called the cointegrating vector.

collinearity – multicollinearity.

concentrated log-likelihood – a log-likelihood in which irrelevant terms have been omitted and some parameters have been replaced by their solution values in terms of the remaining parameters.

confluence analysis – see *bunch map analysis*.

consistent test – a test whose power increases to one as the sample size increases, holding size constant.

contemporaneous – an adjective used to indicate "in the same time period."

correlation coefficient – a measure of the linear association between two variables, calculated as the square root of the R^2 obtained by regressing one variable on the other (and signed to indicate whether the relationship is positive or negative). See also *partial correlation coefficient, multiple correlation coefficient,* and *Fisher's z.*

correlation matrix – a matrix displaying the correlation coefficients between different elements of a vector (the *ij*th element contains the correlation coefficient between the *i*th and the *j*th elements of the vector; all the diagonal elements are ones, since a variable is perfectly correlated with itself). Most computer regression packages produce this matrix for the vector of regressors since it is useful in analyzing multicollinearity.

covariance matrix – variance–covariance matrix.

degenerate distribution – a distribution concentrated entirely at one point.

degrees of freedom – the number of free or linearly independent sample observations used in the calculation of a statistic.

dominant variables – independent variables that account for so much of the variation in a dependent variable that the influence of other variables cannot be estimated. For an example in the context of material inputs dominating capital and labor in determining output, see Rao and Miller (1971, pp. 40–3).

double k-class estimator – a generalized version of the *k*-class estimator.

dummy variable trap – forgetting to omit the dummy variable for one category when an intercept is included, since if a dummy is included for all categories an exact linear relationship will exist between the dummies and the intercept.

ecological inference – use of aggregate data to study the behavior of individuals, usually in the context of examining transitions such as people changing their vote from one election to another. Because statistical results using aggregated data in this context do not necessarily reflect the underlying individual behavioral relationships, one must be very careful when specifying the "ecologial" regression run using aggregate data. See Aachen and Shively (1995) and King (1997).

ergodic – a time series is ergodic if it is stationary and in addition observations far apart in time can be considered uncorrelated.

exponential smoothing – a forecasting method in which the forecast is a weighted average of past values with weights declining geometrically.

Fisher's z – hypotheses concerning the population correlation coefficient ρ can be tested by using the fact that $z = \frac{1}{2}\ln[(r + 1)/(r - 1)]$, where r is the sample correlation coefficient, is approximately normally distributed (around the value of z calculated with $r = \rho$) with standard error $1/\sqrt{(T - 3)}$.

FIVE – full information instrumental variables efficient estimator, used when 3SLS is infeasible due to a large number of exogenous variables.

Gibbs sampler – a method of drawing random observations (x, y) from the joint distribution of x and y. It can be used when it is difficult to draw observations from the joint distribution of x and y, say, but easy to draw observations from the distribution of y conditional on x and from the distribution of x conditional on y. It works by drawing y_0 from the distribution of y conditional on an arbitrarily-determined x_0, then drawing an observation x_1 from the distribution of x conditional on y_0, then drawing an observation y_1 from the distribution of y conditional on x_1, and so on. After only a few iterations a pair of x, y observations can be viewed as a random drawing from the joint distribution of x and y. See Casella and George (1992).

Granger representation theorem – if two I(1) variables are cointegrated, then their dynamic specification can be written as an error correction model (ECM), and vice versa, if the dynamic relationship between two I(1) variables can be written as an ECM, they are cointegrated.

grouping – see *aggregation*.

hat matrix – the matrix $H = X(X'X)^{-1}X'$ whose diagonal elements are prominent in finding influential observations through measures such as DFFITS. Note that estimated $y = Hy$. Also called a *projection matrix* when used for other purposes.

Holt–Winters – a generalization of exponential smoothing to incorporate trend and seasonal variation.

inadmissible – an estimator of a parameter is inadmissible with respect to a particular definition of risk if there exists another estimator whose risk is less than or equal to that estimator's risk, for all values of the parameter.

jack-knife – a means of estimating an estimator's variance by computing the variance of the estimates produced by that estimator omitting each of the observations in turn.

Janus coefficient – a measure of forecast accuracy, calculated as the ratio of the average of the squared forecast errors for extra-sample data to the comparable average for in-sample data.

Jensen's inequality – the expected value of a concave function of x is less than the function evaluated at the expected value of x. (This can be deduced from the material in the technical notes to section 2.8.)

LIVE – limited information instrumental variables efficient estimator, used when there is a large number of exogenous variables, making 2SLS infeasible.

martingale – a data-generating mechanism that can for most purposes be considered a generalization of a random walk, permitting heteroskedasticity.

minimax – an estimator of a parameter is minimax with respect to a particular definition of risk if over all values of that parameter its maximum risk is less than or equal to the maximum risk of all other estimators.

minimum variance bound – Cramer–Rao bound.

multiple correlation coefficient – the square root of the coefficient of determination, R^2, from a multiple regression.

p value – the probability, under the null hypothesis, of obtaining a test statistic value bigger than its observed value. Alternatively, the smallest level of significance (type I error) for which the observed test statistic value results in a rejection of the null hypothesis.

p.a.c.f. – partial autocorrelation function, used in the identification stage of time series (Box–Jenkins) analysis.

partial correlation coefficient – a measure of the linear association between two variables when specified other variables are held constant. It is calculated as the correlation coefficient between the residuals obtained when the two variables in question are regressed on the variables to be held constant. See Goldberger (1968b, chapter 4).

partial regression coefficient – a regression coefficient whose calculation accounts for the influence of other regressors. ''Gross'' or ''simple'' regression coefficients, calculated ignoring the influence of other regressors, are seldom encountered. See Goldberger (1968b, chapter 3).

pivotal statistic – a statistic which is independent of the model parameters.

point optimal test – a test whose power is higher than that of all other tests with the same size, for a specific degree of falseness of the null hypothesis. It is particularly useful for situations in which theoretical considerations suggest a part of the parameter space in which we want our test to have good relative power. Contrast with *UMP test*.

precision – the accuracy of an estimator as measured by the inverse of its variance.

predetermined variable – exogenous or lagged endogenous variable.

prior information – extraneous information.

projection matrix – the matrix $P = X(X'X)^{-1}X'$ which ''projects'' the vector y into the column space of X, in the sense that estimated $y = Py$. Also called the *hat matrix* when used to examine influential observations.

risk function – the expected value of a loss function in Bayesian estimation; in classical analyses, usually interpreted as the sum of the MSEs of the parameter estimates.

sampling error – the error in estimating a parameter caused by the fact that in the sample at hand all the disturbances are not zero.

score statistic – the vector of first derivatives of the log-likelihood with respect to the parameter vector.

score test – another name for the LM test, since the LM test is in effect testing for the score statistic equal to the zero vector.

scoring, method of – an iterative method of maximizing a log-likelihood function which involves the use of the score vector.

serial correlation – autocorrelation.

size of a test – the probability of a type one error.

stationarity, strong vs weak – strong stationarity means that the moments of the variable in question are all independent of time, whereas for weak stationarity this is so only for the first two moments; the two concepts coincide in the case of normality.

stock-adjustment model – partial-adjustment model.

sufficient statistic – an estimator that uses all the information contained in the sample in the sense that we would make the same parameter estimate whether we were told the whole set of observations or only the value of the sufficient statistic.

threshold loss function – a loss function taking the value 0 if the error is less than some critical or threshold level, and a constant value if the error is greater than or equal to this critical level. It captures losses of a dichotomous nature, such as death resulting from an overdose.

truncated squared error loss – a loss function equal to the squared error, but with a maximum loss for any observation. It is used as a means of handling outliers.

unbiased test – test with power greater than or equal to size for all parameter values.

UMP – see *uniformly most powerful test.*

uniformly most powerful test – a test whose power is higher than that of all other tests with the same size, for all degrees of falseness of the null hypothesis. Contrast with *point optimal test.*

BIBLIOGRAPHY

ABRAHAM, W. (1976) Letter from Ethiopia. *New York Statistician* 27(3), 3.

ACHEN, C. and P. W. SHIVELY (1995) *Cross-Level Inference*. Chicago: University of Chicago Press.

ADAMS, G. (1965) Prediction with Consumer Attitudes: The Time Series – Cross Section Paradox. *Review of Economics and Statistics* 47, 367–78.

AIGNER, D. J. (1971) *Basic Econometrics*. Englewood Cliffs, NJ: Prentice-Hall.

AIGNER, D. J. (1974) MSE Dominance of Least Squares with Errors of Observation. *Journal of Econometrics* 2, 365–72.

AIGNER, D. J. (1988) On Econometric Methodology and the Search for Causal Laws. *Economic Record* 64, 323–5.

AIGNER, D. J. and G. G. JUDGE (1977) Application of Pre-test and Stein Estimators to Economics Data. *Econometrica* 45, 1279–88.

ALLISON, P. (1984) *Event History Analysis: Regression for Longitudinal Event Data*. Beverley Hills, CA: Sage Publications.

ALLISON, P. (1987) Introducing a Disturbance into Logit and Probit Regression Models. *Sociological Methods & Research* 15, 355–74.

ALOGOSKOUFIS, G. and R. SMITH (1991) On Error Correction Models: Specification, Interpretation, Estimation. *Journal of Economic Surveys* 5, 97–128. Reprinted in L. Oxley et al. (eds) *Surveys in Econometrics*. Oxford: Basil Blackwell, 139–70.

AMBLER, S. (1989) Does Money Matter in Canada? Evidence from a Vector Error Correction Model. *Review of Economics and Statistics* 71, 651–8.

AMEMIYA, T. (1974) The Nonlinear Two-Stage Least Squares Estimator. *Journal of Econometrics* 2, 105–10.

AMEMIYA, T. (1980) Selection of Regressors. *International Economic Review* 21, 331–54.

AMEMIYA, T. (1981) Qualitative Response Models: A Survey. *Journal of Economic Literature* 19, 1483–536.

AMEMIYA, T. (1983) Non-Linear Regression Models. In Z. Griliches and M. Intriligator (eds) *Handbook of Econometrics Vol. I*. Amsterdam: North Holland, 333–89.

AMEMIYA, T. (1984) Tobit Models: A Survey. *Journal of Econometrics* 24, 3–61.

AMES, E. and S. REITER (1961) Distributions of Correlation Coefficients in Economic Time Series. *Journal of the American Statistical Association* 56, 637–56.

ANDERSON, O. D. (1977) A Commentary on a Survey of Time Series. *International Statistical Review* 45, 273–97.

ANDERSON, R. G., J. M. JOHANNES and R. H. RASCHE (1983) A New Look at the Relationship between Time-series and Structural Equation Models. *Journal of Econometrics* 23, 235–51.

ANDERSON-SPRECHER, R. (1994) Model Comparisons and R^2. *American Statistician* 48, 113–17.

ANSCOMBE, F. J. (1973) Graphs in Statistical Analysis. *American Statistician* 27(1), 17–21.

ARMSTRONG, J. S. (1978) *Long-Range Forecasting: From Crystal Ball to Computer.* New York: John Wiley.

ARMSTRONG, J. S. et al. (1978) Symposium on Forecasting with Econometric Methods. *Journal of Business* 51, 547–600.

ASHLEY, R. (1983) On the Usefulness of Macroeconomic Forecasts as Inputs to Forecasting Models. *Journal of Forecasting* 2, 211–23.

ASHLEY, R. (1984) A Simple Test for Regression Parameter Stability. *Economic Inquiry* 22, 253–68.

ATTFIELD, C. (1982) An Adjustment to the Likelihood Ratio Statistic when Testing Hypotheses in the Multivariate Linear Model Using Large Samples. *Economics Letters* 9, 345–8.

BACKUS, D. (1986) The Canadian–U.S. Exchange Rate: Evidence from a Vector Autoregression. *Review of Economics and Statistics* 68, 628–37.

BACON, R. W. (1977) Some Evidence on the Largest Squared Correlation Coefficient from Several Samples. *Econometrica* 45, 1997–2001.

BAKAN, D. (1966) The Test of Significance in Psychological Research. *Psychological Bulletin* 66, 423–37.

BALTAGI, B. H. (1986) Pooling Under Misspecification: Some Monte Carlo Evidence on the Kmenta and the Error Components Techniques. *Econometric Theory* 2, 429–41.

BALTAGI, B. H. (1995) *Econometric Analysis of Panel Data.* New York: Wiley.

BALTAGI, B. H. and J. M. GRIFFIN (1984) Short and Long-run Effects in Pooled Models. *International Economic Review* 25, 631–45.

BANERJEE, A. et al. (1986) Exploring Equilibrium Relationships in Econometrics Through Static Models: Some Monte Carlo Evidence. *Oxford Bulletin of Economics and Statistics* 48, 253–77.

BANERJEE, A., J. J. DOLADO, J. W. GALBRAITH and D. F. HENDRY (1993) *Co-integration, Error Correction, and the Econometric Analysis of Non-Stationary Data.* Oxford: Oxford University Press.

BANERJEE, A., J. GALBRAITH and J. DOLADO (1990) Dynamic Specification and Linear Transformations of the Autoregressive Distributed Lag Model. *Oxford Bulletin of Economics and Statistics* 52, 95–104.

BANERJEE, A., R. L. LUMSDAINE and J. H. STOCK (1992) Recursive and Sequential Tests of the Unit-Root and Trend-Break Hypotheses: Theory and International Evidence. *Journal of Business and Economic Statistics* 10, 271–87.

BARDSEN, G. (1989) Estimation of Long-Run Coefficients in Error Correction Models. *Oxford Bulletin of Economics and Statistics* 51, 345–50.

BARTELS, L. M. (1991) Quasi-Instrumental Variables. *American Journal of Political Science* 35, 777–800.

BARTELS, R. (1977) On the Use of Limit Theorem Arguments in Economic Statistics. *American Statistician* 31, 85–7.

BAUER, P. W. (1990) Recent Developments in the Econometric Estimation of Frontiers. *Journal of Econometrics* 46, 39–56.

BEACH, C. M. and J. G. MACKINNON (1978a) A Maximum Likelihood Procedure for Regressions with Autocorrelated Errors. *Econometrica* 46, 51–8.

BEACH, C. M. and J. G. MACKINNON (1978b) Full Maximum Likelihood Estimation of Second-order Autoregressive Error Models. *Journal of Econometrics* 7, 187–98.

BEATON, A. E., D. B. RUBIN and J. L. BARONE (1976) The Acceptability of Regression Solutions: Another Look at Computational Accuracy. *Journal of the American Statistical Association* 71, 158–68.

BECK, N. and J. N. KATZ (1995) What to Do (And not to do) with Time-Series Cross-Section Data. *American Political Science Review* 89, 634–47.

BECKER, W. E. and P. E. KENNEDY (1992) A Graphical Exposition of Ordered Probit. *Econometric Theory* 8, 127–31.

BEGGS, J. J. (1988) Diagnostic Testing in Applied Econometrics. *Economic Record* 64, 81–101.

BELL, W. R. and S. C. HILLMER (1984) Issues Involved with the Seasonal Adjustment of Times Series. *Journal of Business and Economic Statistics* 2, 291–349 including commentary.

BELSLEY, D. A. (1984a) Collinearity and Forecasting. *Journal of Forecasting* 3, 183–96.

BELSLEY, D. A. (1984b) Demeaning Conditioning Diagnostics Through Centering. *American Statistician* 38, 73–93.

BELSLEY, D. A. (1986a) Model Selection in Regression Analysis, Regression Diagnostics and Prior Knowledge. *International Journal of Forecasting* 2, 41–6, and commentary 46–52.

BELSLEY D. A. (1986b) Centering, the Constant, First Differencing and Assessing Conditioning. In D. Belsley and E. Kuh (eds) *Model Reliability*. Cambridge, MA: MIT Press, 117–53.

BELSLEY, D. A. (1988a) Modelling and Forecast Reliability. *International Journal of Forecasting* 4, 427–47.

BELSLEY, D. A. (1988b) Two- or Three-Stage Least Squares? *Computer Science in Economics and Management* 1, 21–30.

BELSLEY, D. A. (1989) Conditioning in Models with Logs. *Journal of Econometrics* 38, 127–43.

BELSLEY, D. A., E. KUH and R. E. WELSCH (1980) *Regression Diagnostics: Identifying Influential Data and Sources of Collinearity*. New York: John Wiley.

BELSLEY, D. A. and R. E. WELSCH (1988) Modelling Energy Consumption – Using and Abusing Regression Diagnostics. *Journal of Business and Economic Statistics* 6, 442–7.

BENTLER, P. M. (1992) *EQS Structural Equation Program Manual*. Los Angeles: BMDP Statistical Software.

BERA, A. K. and M. L. HIGGINS (1993) ARCH Models: Properties, Estimation and Testing. *Journal of Economic Surveys* 7, 305–66. Reprinted in L. Oxley et al. (eds) *Surveys in Econometrics*. Oxford: Basil Blackwell, 215–72.

BERA, A. K. and C. M. JARQUE (1982) Model Specification Tests: A Simultaneous Approach. *Journal of Econometrics* 20, 59–82.

BERA, A. K., M. McALEER, M. H. PESARAN and M. J. YOON (1992) Joint Tests of

Non-Nested Models and General Error Specifications. *Econometric Reviews* 11, 97–117.

BERA, A. K. and C. R. McKENZIE (1986) Alternative Forms and Properties of the Score Test. *Journal of Applied Statistics* 13, 13–25.

BERGER, J. O. (1985) *Statistical Decision Theory and Bayesian Analysis*. New York: Springer-Verlag.

BERGMANN, B. (1987) "Measurement" or Finding Things Out in Economics. *Journal of Economic Education* 18, 191–201.

BERNDT, E. R. (1991) *The Practice of Econometrics: Classic and Contemporary*. Reading, MA: Addison-Wesley.

BERNDT, E. R. and N. E. SAVIN (1977) Conflict Among Criteria for Testing Hypotheses in the Multivariate Regression Model. *Econometrica* 45, 1263–78.

BHARGAVA, A. (1986) On the Theory of Testing for Unit Roots in Observed Time Series. *Review of Economic Studies* 53, 369–84.

BHAT, C. R. (1994) Imputing a Continuous Income Variable from Grouped and Missing Income Observations. *Economics Letters* 46, 311–19.

BIBBY, J. and H. TOUTENBURG (1977) *Prediction and Improved Estimation in Linear Models*. New York: John Wiley.

BINKLEY, J. K. and P. C. ABBOTT (1987) The Fixed X Assumption in Econometrics: Can the Textbooks be Trusted? *American Statistician* 41, 206–14.

BINKLEY, J. K. (1992) Finite Sample Behavior of Tests for Grouped Heteroskedasticity. *Review of Economics and Statistics* 74, 563–8.

BISHOP, R. V. (1979) The Construction and Use of Causality Tests. *Agricultural Economics Research* 31, 1–6.

BLANCHARD, O. J. (1987) Comment. *Journal of Business and Economic Statistics* 5, 449–51.

BLAUG, M. (1980) *The Methodology of Economics*. Cambridge: Cambridge University Press.

BLEANEY, M. (1990) Some Comparisons of the Relative Power of Simple Tests for Structural Change in Regression Models. *Journal of Economic Forecasting* 9, 437–44.

BLIEMEL, F. (1973) Theils Forecast Accuracy Coefficient: A Clarification. *Journal of Marketing Research* 10, 444–6.

BLOUGH, S. R. (1992) The Relationship between Power and Level for Generic Unit Root Tests in Finite Samples. *Journal of Applied Econometrics* 7, 295–308.

BLYTH, C. R. (1972) Subjective vs. Objective Methods in Statistics. *American Statistician* 26, 20–2.

BODKIN, R. G., L. R. KLEIN and K. MARWAH (1991) *A History of Macroeconometric Model-Building*. Brookfield, VT: Edward Elgar.

BOGGS, P. T. et al. (1988) A Computational Examination of Orthogonal Distance Regression. *Journal of Econometrics* 38, 169–201.

BOLLEN, K. A. (1989) *Structural Equations with Latent Variables*. New York: Wiley.

BOLLERSLEV, T. (1986) Generalized Autoregressive Conditional Heteroskedasticity. *Journal of Econometrics* 31, 307–27.

BOOTHE, P. and J. G. MACKINNON (1986) A Specification Test for Models Estimated by Generalized Least Squares. *Review of Economics and Statistics* 68, 711–14.

BOUND, J., JAEGER, D. A. and BAKER, R. M. (1995) Problems with Instrumental Variables Estimation when the Correlation between the Instruments and the

Endogenous Explanatory Variable is Weak. *Journal of the American Statistical Association* 90, 443–50.

BOX, G. E. P. and G. M. JENKINS (1970) *Time Series Analysis: Forecasting and Control*. San Francisco: Holden Day (revised edition 1976).

BREUER, J. B. and M. E. WOHAR (1996) The Road Less Travelled: Institutional Aspects of Data and their Influence on Empirical Estimates with an Application to Tests of Forward Rate Unbiasedness. *Economic Journal* 106, 26–38.

BREUSCH, T. S. (1978) Testing for Autocorrelation in Dynamic Linear Models. *Australian Economic Papers* 17, 334–55.

BREUSCH, T. S. and L. G. GODFREY (1981) A Review of Recent Work on Testing for Autocorrelation in Dynamic Simultaneous Models . In D. Currie, R. Nobay and D. Peel (eds) *Macroeconomic Analysis: Essays in Macroeconomics and Econometrics*. London: Croon Helm, 63–105.

BREUSCH, T. S. and L. G. GODFREY (1986) Data Transformation Tests. *Economic Journal* 96 Supplement, 47–58.

BREUSCH, T. S. and A. R. PAGAN (1979) A Simple Test for Heteroskedasticity and Random Coefficient Variation. *Econometrica* 47, 1287–94.

BREUSCH, T. S. and A. R. PAGAN (1980) The Lagrange Multiplier Test and its Application to Model Specification in Econometrics. *Review of Economic Studies* 47, 239–53.

BROWN, R., J. DURBIN and J. EVANS (1975) Techniques for Testing the Constancy of Regression Relationships Over Time. *Journal of the Royal Statistical Society* B37, 149–63.

BRUNNER, K. (1973) Review of B. Hickman (ed.) *Econometric Models of Cyclical Behavior* in *Journal of Economic Literature* 11, 926–33.

BURBIDGE, J. B., L. MAGEE and A. L. ROBB (1988) Alternative Transformations to Handle Extreme Values of the Dependent Variable. *Journal of the American Statistical Association* 83, 123–7.

BURKE, S. P., L. G. GODFREY and A. R. TREMAYNE (1990) Testing AR(1) Against MA(1) Disturbances in the Linear Regression Model: An Alternative Procedure. *Review of Economic Studies* 57, 135–46.

BURTLESS, G. (1995) The Case for Randomized Field Trials in Economic and Policy Research. *Journal of Economic Perspectives* 9, 63–84.

BUSCHE, K. and P. E. KENNEDY (1984) On Economists' Belief in the Law of Small Numbers. *Economic Inquiry* 22, 602–3.

BUSE, A. (1973) Goodness of Fit in Generalized Least Squares Estimation. *American Statistician* 27, 106–8.

BUSE, A. (1982) The Likelihood Ratio, Wald and Lagrange Multiplier Tests: An Expository Note. *American Statistician* 36, 153–7.

BUSE, A. (1988) Book Review. *Journal of Business and Economic Statistics* 6, 141–2.

BUTLER, R. J., J. B. McDONALD, R. D. NELSON and S. B. WHITE (1990) Robust and Partially Adaptive Estimation of Regression Models. *Review of Economics and Statistics* 72, 321–7.

BUTLER, R. J. and J. D. WORRALL (1991) Gamma Duration Models with Heterogeneity. *Review of Economics and Statistics* 73, 161–6.

CADSBY, C. B. and T. STENGOS (1986) Testing for Parameter Stability in a Regression Model with AR(1) Errors. *Economics Letters* 20, 29–32.

CAMERON, A. and P. TRIVEDI (1986) Econometric Models Based on Count Data: Comparisons and Applications of Some Estimators and Tests. *Journal of Applied Econometrics* 1, 29–54.

CAMERON, T. A. (1988) A New Paradigm for Valuing Non-market Goods Using Referendum Data: Maximum Likelihood Estimation by Censored Logistic Regression. *Journal of Environmental Economics and Management* 15, 355–79.

CAMPBELL, J. Y. and P. PERRON (1991) Pitfalls and Opportunities: What Macroeconomists Should Know about Unit Roots. *NBER Macroeconomics Annual* 141–201.

CAMPBELL, J. Y. AND R. J. SHILLER (1988) Interpreting Cointegrated Models. *Journal of Economic Dynamics and Control* 12, 505–22.

CASELLA, G. (1985) An Introduction to Empirical Bayes Data Analysis. *American Statistician* 39, 83–7.

CASELLA, G. and E. GEORGE (1992) Explaining the Gibbs Sampler. *American Statistician* 46, 167–74.

CAUDILL, S. B. (1988) The Necessity of Mining Data. *Atlantic Economic Journal* 16(3), 11–18.

CAUDILL, S. B., J. M. FORD and D. M. GROPPER (1995) Frontier Estimation and Firm-Specific Inefficiency Measures in the Presence of Heteroscedasticity. *Journal of Business and Economic Statistics* 13, 105–11.

CAUDILL, S. B. and J. D. JACKSON (1989) Measuring Marginal Effects in Limited Dependent Variable Models. *The Statistician* 38, 203–6.

CAUDILL, S. B. and J. D. JACKSON (1993) Heteroscedasticity and Grouped Data. *Southern Economic Journal* 60, 128–35.

CAUDILL, S. B. and F. G. MIXON (1995) Modeling Household Fertility Decisions: Estimation and Testing of Censored Regression Models for Count Data. *Empirical Economics* 20, 183–96.

CHALLEN, D. W. and A. J. HAGGER (1983) *Macroeconomic Systems: Construction, Validation and Applications.* New York: St. Martin's Press.

CHAREMZA, W. W. and D. F. DEADMAN (1992) *New Directions in Econometric Practice.* Aldershot: Edward Elgar.

CHARNES, A., COOPER, W. W., LEWIN, A. Y. and L. M. SEIFORD (1995) *Data Envelopment Analysis: Theory, Methodology and Applications.* Boston: Kluwer.

CHATFIELD, C. (1984) *The Analysis of Time Series: An Introduction.* London: Chapman and Hall.

CHATFIELD, C. (1988) The Future of Time-Series Forecasting. *International Journal of Forecasting* 4, 411–19.

CHATFIELD, C. (1991) Avoiding Statistical Pitfalls. *Statistical Science* 6, 240–68.

CHEUNG, Y-W. and K. S. LAI (1995) Lag Order and Critical Values of the Augmented Dickey–Fuller Test. *Journal of Business and Economic Statistics* 13, 277–80.

CHEUNG, Y-W. and K. S. LAI (1993) Finite-Sample Sizes of Johansen's Likelihood Ratio Tests for Cointegration. *Oxford Bulletin of Economics and Statistics* 55, 313–28.

CHINTAGUNTA, P. K. (1992) Estimating a Multinomial Probit Model of Brand Choice Using the Method of Simulated Moments. *Marketing Science* 11, 386–407.

CHOUDHURY, A., M. CHAUDHURY and S. POWER (1987) A New Approximate GLS Estimator for the Regression Model with MA(1) Disturbances. *Bulletin of Economic Research* 39, 171–7.

CHOW, G. C. (1983) *Econometrics.* New York: McGraw-Hill.

CHRIST, C. (1966) *Econometric Models and Methods*. New York: Wiley.

CHRISTIANO L. J. and M. EICHENBAUM (1990) Unit Roots in Real GNP: Do We Know, and Do We Care? *Carnegie–Rochester Conference Series on Public Policy* 327–62, and comment by J. Stock, 63–82.

CHRISTIE, A. A. (1990) Aggregation of Test Statistics. *Journal of Accounting and Economics* 12, 15–36.

CLEMENS, R. T. (1989) Combining Forecasts: A Review and Annotated Bibliography. *International Journal of Forecasting* 8, 559–83.

CLEVELAND, W. S., S. J. Devlin and E. GROSSE (1988) Regression by Local Fitting. *Journal of Econometrics* 37, 87–114.

COCHRANE, J. (1991) A Critique of the Application of Unit Root Tests. *Journal of Economic Dynamics and Control* 15, 275–84.

COHEN, J. and P. COHEN (1975) *Applied Multiple Regression/Correlation Analysis for the Behavioral Sciences*. Hillside, NJ: Laurence Erlbaum Associates.

CONLISK, J. (1971) When Collinearity is Desirable. *Western Economic Journal* 9, 393–407.

COOLEY, T. F. and S. F. LEROY (1985) Atheoretical Macroeconometrics: A Critique. *Journal of Monetary Economics* 16, 283–308.

COOLEY, T. F. and S. F. LEROY (1981) Identification and Estimation of Money Demand. *American Economic Review* 71, 825–44.

COPAS, J. (1966) Monte Carlo Results for Estimation in a Stable Markov Time Series. *Journal of the Royal Statistical Society* A129, 110–16.

CRAMER, J. S. (1987) Mean and Variance of R^2 in Small and Moderate Samples. *Journal of Econometrics* 35, 253–66.

CRATO, N. and P. ROTHMAN (1994) Fractional Integration Analysis of Long-Run Behavior for US Macroeconomic Time Series. *Economics Letters* 45, 287–91.

DAGENAIS, M. G. and J. M. DUFOUR (1991) Invariance, Nonlinear Models, and Asymptotic Tests. *Econometrica* 59, 1601–15.

DAGENAIS, M. G. and J. M. DUFOUR (1992) On the Lack of Invariance of some Asymptotic Tests to Rescaling. *Economics Letters* 38, 251–7.

DARNELL, A. C. (1994) *A Dictionary of Econometrics*. Aldershot: Edward Elgar.

DARNELL, A. C. and J. L. EVANS (1990) *The Limits of Econometrics*. Aldershot: Edward Elgar.

DASTOOR, N. K. (1981) A Note on the Interpretation of the Cox Procedure for Non-nested Hypotheses. *Economics Letters* 8, 113–19.

DAVIDSON, J., D. HENDRY, F. SRBA and S. YEO (1978) Econometric Modelling of the Aggregate Time-series Relationship between Consumers Expenditure and Income in the United Kingdom. *Economic Journal* 88, 661–92.

DAVIDSON, R., L. G. GODFREY and J. G. MACKINNON (1985) A Simplified Version of the Differencing Test. *International Economic Review* 26, 639–47.

DAVIDSON, R. and J. G. MACKINNON (1980) Estimating the Covariance Matrix for Regression Models with AR(1) Errors and Lagged Dependent Variables. *Economics Letters* 6, 119–23.

DAVIDSON, R. and J. G. MACKINNON (1983) Small Sample Properties of Alternative Forms of the Lagrange Multiplier Test. *Economics Letters* 12, 269–75.

DAVIDSON, R. and J. G. MACKINNON (1984) Convenient Specification Tests for Logit and Probit Models. *Journal of Econometrics* 25, 241–62.

DAVIDSON, R. and J. G. MACKINNON (1988) Double Length Artificial Regressions. *Oxford Bulletin of Economics and Statistics* 50, 203–17.

DAVIDSON, R. and J. G. MACKINNON (1993) *Estimation and Inference in Econometrics.* Oxford: Oxford University Press.

DEB, P. and M. SEFTON (1996) The Distribution of a Lagrange Multiplier Test of Normality. *Economics Letters* 51, 123–30.

DENBY, L. and D. PREGIBON (1987) An Example of the Use of Graphics in Regression. *American Statistician* 41, 33–8.

DENTON, F. (1985) Data Mining as an Industry. *Review of Economics and Statistics* 67 124–7.

DEWALD, W., J. THURSBY and R. ANDERSON (1986) Replication in Empirical Economics. *American Economic Review* 76, 587–603.

DEZHBAKHSH, H. (1990) The Inappropriate Use of Serial Correlation Tests in Dynamic Linear Models. *Review of Economics and Statistics* 72, 126–32.

DEZHBAKHSH, H. and J. G. THURSBY (1994) Testing for Autocorrelation in the Presence of Lagged Dependent Variables: A Specification Error Approach. *Journal of Econometrics* 60, 251–72.

DHARMAPALA, D. and M. McALEER (1996) Econometric Methodology and the Philosophy of Science. *Journal of Statistical Planning and Inference* 49, 9–37.

DHRYMES, P. et al. (1972) Criteria for Evaluation of Econometric Models. *Annals of Economic and Social Measurement* 1, 291–324.

DICKENS, W. T. (1990) Error Components in Grouped Data: Is It Ever Worth Weighting? *Review of Economics and Statistics* 72, 328–33.

DICKEY, D. A. and W. FULLER (1981) Likelihood Ratio Statistics for Autoregressive Time Series with a Unit Root. *Econometrica* 49, 1057–72.

DICKEY, D. A., D. W. JANSEN and D. L. THORNTON (1991) A Primer on Cointegration with an Application to Money and Income. *Federal Reserve Bank of St. Louis Review* 73(2), 58–78.

DIDERRICH, G. T. (1985) The Kalman Filter from the Perspective of Goldberger–Theil Estimators. *The American Statistician* 39(3), 193–8.

DIELMAN, T. E. (1983) Pooled Cross-sectional and Time Series Data: A Survey of Current Statistical Methodology. *American Statistician* 37, 111–22.

DIELMAN, T. E. and R. PFAFFENBERGER (1982) LAV (Least Absolute Value) Estimation in Linear Regression: A Review. *TIMS Studies in the Management Sciences* 19, 31–52.

DOAN, T., R. LITTERMAN and C. SIMS (1984) Forecasting and Conditional Projection Using Realistic Prior Distributions. *Econometric Reviews* 3, 1–100.

DODS, J. L. and D. E. A. GILES (1995) Alternative Strategies for "Augmenting" the Dickey–Fuller Test: Size-Robustness in the Face of Pre-testing. *Journal of Statistical and Computational Simulation* 53, 243–58.

DOLADO, J. J., T. JENKINSON and S. SOSVILLA-RIVERO (1990) Cointegration and Unit Roots. *Journal of Economic Surveys* 4, 249–73.

DOLTON, P. J. and G. H. MAKEPEACE (1987) Interpreting Sample Selection Effects. *Economics Letters* 24, 373–9.

DORAN, H. (1993) Testing Nonnested Models. *American Journal of Agricultural Economics* 75, 95–103.

DORFMAN, J. H. and K. A. FOSTER (1991) Estimating Productivity Changes with Flexible Coefficients. *Western Journal of Agricultural Economics* 16, 280–90.

DORFMAN, J. H. and C. S. McINTOSH (1990) Results of a Price Forecasting Competition. *American Journal of Agricultural Economics* 72, 804–8.

DOWLING, J. and F. GLAHE (1970) *Readings in Econometric Theory*. Boulder, CO: Colorado Associated University Press.

DRAPER, N. R. and R. C. VAN NOSTRAND (1979) Ridge Regression and James Stein Estimation: Review and Comments. *Technometrics* 21, 451–65.

DREZE, J. (1983) Nonspecialist Teaching of Econometrics: A Personal Comment and Personalistic Lament. *Econometric Reviews* 2, 291–9.

DUAN, N. (1983) Smearing Estimate: A Nonparametric Retransformation Method. *Journal of the American Statistical Association* 78, 605–10.

DUFOUR, J. M. (1980) Dummy Variables and Predictive Tests for Structural Change. *Economic Letters* 6, 241–7.

DUFOUR, J. M. (1982) Recursive Stability of Linear Regression Relationships. *Journal of Econometrics* 19, 31–76.

DUNN, L. F. (1993) Category versus Continuous Survey Responses in Economic Modelling: Monte Carlo and Empirical Evidence. *Review of Economics and Statistics* 75, 188–93.

DURBIN, J. (1953) A Note on Regression when there is Extraneous Information about one of the Coefficients. *Journal of the American Statistical Association* 48, 799–808.

DURBIN, J. (1970) Testing for Serial Correlation in Least Squares Regression When Some of the Regressors are Lagged Dependent Variables. *Econometrica* 38, 410–21.

DUTTA, M. (1975) *Econometric Methods*. Cincinnati: South-Western.

EDWARDS, J. B. (1969) The Relation between the F-Test and R^2. *American Statistician* 23, 28.

EDGERTON, D. and C. WELLS (1994) Critical Values for the CUSUMSQ Statistic in Medium and Large-Sized Samples. *Oxford Bulletin of Economics and Statistics* 56, 355–65.

EFRON, B. (1986) Why Isn't Everyone a Bayesian? *American Statistician* 40, 1–11.

EFRON, B. and C. MORRIS (1977) Stein's Paradox in Statistics. *Scientific American* 236 (May), 119–27.

EFRON, B. and R. J. TIBSHIRANI (1993) *An Introduction to the Bootstrap*. New York: Chapman and Hall.

ENDERS, W. (1995) *Applied Econometric Time Series*. New York: Wiley.

ENGLE, R. (1974) Specification of the Disturbances for Efficient Estimation. *Econometrica* 42, 135–46.

ENGLE, R. F. (1982) Autoregressive Conditional Heteroskedasticity with Estimates of the Variance of United Kingdom Inflation. *Econometrica* 50, 987–1001.

ENGLE, R. F. (1984) Wald, Likelihood Ratio and Lagrange Multiplier Tests in Econometrics. In Z. Griliches and M. Intriligator (eds), *Handbook of Econometrics Vol. II*. Amsterdam: North Holland, ch. 13.

ENGLE, R. and C. GRANGER (1987) Co-Integration and Error Correction: Representation, Estimation and Testing. *Econometrica* 55, 251–76.

ENGLE, R. F., D. F. HENDRY and D. TRUMBLE (1985) Small-Sample Properties of ARCH Estimators and Tests. *Canadian Journal of Economics* 18, 66–93.

ENGLE, R. F. and M. W. WATSON (1987) The Kalman Filter: Applications to Forecasting and Rational Expectations Models. In T. F. Bewley (ed.) *Advances in*

Econometrics: Fifth World Congress, Vol. 1. Cambridge: Cambridge University Press, 245–84.

ENGLE, R. and B. S. YOO (1987) Forecasting and Testing in Cointegrated Systems. *Journal of Econometrics* 35, 143–59.

EPPS, T. W. and M. L. EPPS (1977) The Robustness of Some Standard Tests for Autocorrelation and Heteroskedasticity when Both Problems are Present. *Econometrica* 45, 745–53.

EPSTEIN, R. J. (1987) *A History of Econometrics*. Amsterdam: North Holland.

ERLAT, H. Computing Heteroskedasticity-robust Tests of Linear Restrictions. *Oxford Bulletin of Economics and Statistics* 49, 439–46.

EVANS, M., Y. HAITOVSKY, and G. TREYZ (1972) An Analysis of the Forecasting Properties of US Econometric Models. In B. Hickman (ed.) *Econometric Models of Cyclic Behavior*. New York: Columbia University Press, 949–1158.

FADER, P. S., J. M. LATTIN and J. D. C. LITTLE (1992) Estimating Nonlinear Parameters in the Multinomial Logit Model. *Marketing Science* 11, 372–85.

FAIR, R. C. (1970) The Estimation of Simultaneous Equation Models with Lagged Endogenous Variables and First-order Serially Correlated Errors. *Econometrica* 38, 507–16.

FAIR, R. C. (1973) A Comparison of Alternative Estimators of Microeconomic Models. *International Economic Review* 14, 261–77.

FAIR, R. C. (1984) *Specification, Estimation and Analysis of Macroeconometric Models* Cambridge, MA: Harvard University Press.

FAIR, R. C. and D. M. JAFFEE (1972) Methods of Estimation for Markets in Disequilibrium. *Econometrica* 40, 497–514.

FAIR, R. C. and R. J. SHILLER (1989) The Informational Content of Ex Ante Forecasts. *Review of Economics and Statistics* 71, 325–31.

FAN, Y. and Q. LI (1995) Bootstrapping J-Type Tests for Non-Nested Regression Models. *Economics Letters* 48, 107–12.

FAREBROTHER, R. W. (1979) A Grouping Test for Misspecification. *Econometrica* 47, 209–10.

FARLEY, J. U., M. J. HINRICH and T. MCGUIRE (1975) Some Comparisons of Tests for a Shift in the Slopes of a Multivariate Linear Time Series Model. *Journal of Econometrics* 3, 297–318.

FARRAR, D. and R. GLAUBER (1967) Multicollinearity in Regression Analysis: The Problem Revisited. *Review of Economics and Statistics* 49, 92–107 (reprinted in J. Dowling and F. Glahe (eds) (1970) *Readings in Econometric Theory*. Boulder, CO: Colorado Associated University Press).

FAULHABER, G. R. and W. J. BAUMOL (1988) Economists as Innovators. *Journal of Economic Literature* 26, 577–600.

FAVERO, C. and D. F. Hendry (1992) Testing the Lucas Critique: A Review. *Econometric Reviews* 11, 265–306.

FEIGE, E. L. (1975) The Consequences of Journal Editorial Policies and a Suggestion for Revision. *Journal of Political Economy* 83, 1291–6.

FELDSTEIN, M. (1971) The Error of Forecast in Econometric Models when the Forecast-period Exogenous Variables are Stochastic. *Econometrica* 39, 55–60.

FELDSTEIN, M. (1973) Multicollinearity and the Mean Square Error of Alternative Estimators. *Econometrica* 41, 337–46.

FELDSTEIN, M. (1974) Errors in Variables: A Consistent Estimator with Smaller MSE in Finite Samples. *Journal of the American Statistical Association* 69, 990–6.

FELDSTEIN, M. S. (1982) Inflation, Tax Rules and Investment: Some Econometric Evidence. *Econometrica* 50, 825–62.

FIEBIG, D. G. (1985) Evaluating Estimators Without Moments. *Review of Economics and Statistics* 67, 529–34.

FILDES, R. and S. MAKRIDAKIS (1988) Forecasting and Loss Functions. *International Journal of Forecasting* 4, 545–50.

FILDES, R. and S. MAKRIDAKIS (1995) The Impact of Empirical Accuracy Studies on Time Series Analysis and Forecasting. *International Statistical Review* 63, 289–308.

FISHCHOFF, B. and R. BEYTH-MAROM (1983) Hypothesis Evaluation from a Bayesian Perspective. *Psychological Review* 90, 239–60.

FISHER, F. M. (1966) *The Identification Problem*. New York: McGraw-Hill.

FISHER, F. M. (1986) Statisticians, Econometricians and Adversary Proceedings. *Journal of the American Statistical Society* 81, 277–86.

FISHER, W. (1976) Normalization in Point Estimation. *Journal of Econometrics* 4, 243–52.

FOMBY, T. B. and R. C. HILL (1986) The Relative Efficiency of a Robust Generalized Bayes Estimator in a Linear Regression Model with Multicollinearity. *Economics Letters* 22, 33–8.

FOMBY, T. B., R. C. HILL and S. R. JOHNSON (1984) *Advanced Econometric Methods*. New York: Springer-Verlag.

FORSUND, F. R., C. A. K. LOVELL and P. SCHMIDT (1980) A Survey of Frontier Production Functions and of their Relationship to Efficiency Measurement. *Journal of Econometrics* 13, 5–25.

FRANSES, P. H. and G. BIESSEN (1992) Model Adequacy and Influential Observations. *Economics Letters* 38, 133–7.

FRANSES, P. H. and M. McALEER (1997) Testing for Unit Roots and Non-Linear Transformations. *Journal of Time Series Analysis* forthcoming.

FREED, N. and F. GLOVER (1982) Linear Programming and Statistical Discriminant – the LP Side. *Decision Sciences* 13, 172–3.

FRIEDMAN, D. and S. SUNDER (1994) *Experimental Methods: A Primer for Economists*. Cambridge: Cambridge University Press.

FRIEDMAN, M. and A. J. SCHWARTZ (1991) Alternative Approaches to Analysing Economic Data. *American Economic Review* 81, 39–49.

FROMM, G. and G. SCHINK (1973) Aggregation and Econometric Models. *International Economic Review* 14, 1–32.

FRY, T. R. L., R. D. BROOKS, B. R. COMLEY and J. ZHANG (1993) Economic Motivations for Limited Dependent and Qualitative Variable Models. *Economic Record* 69, 193–205.

FULLER, W. (1976) *Introduction to Statistical Time Series*. New York: Wiley.

GALLANT, A. R. (1975) Nonlinear Regression. *American Statistician* 29, 73–81.

GALPIN, J. S. and D. M. HAWKINS (1984) The Use of Recursive Residuals in Checking Model Fit in Linear Regression. *American Statistician* 38, 94–105.

GARCIA, J. and J. M. LABEAGA (1996) Alternative Approaches to Modelling Zero Expenditure: An Application to Spanish Demand for Tobacco. *Oxford Bulletin of Economics and Statistics* 58, 489–506.

GAUGER, J. (1989) The Generated Regressor Correction: Impacts Upon Inferences in Hypothesis Testing. *Journal of Macroeconomics* 11, 383–95.

GEARY, R. and C. LESER (1968) Significance Tests in Multiple Regression. *American Statistician* 22, 20–1.

GENCAY, R. and X. YANG (1996) A Forecast Comparison of Residential Housing Prices by Parametric versus Semiparametric Conditional Mean Estimators. *Economics Letters* 52, 129–35.

GERSOVITZ, M. and J. G. MACKINNON (1978) Seasonality in Regression: An Application of Smoothness Priors. *Journal of the American Statistical Association* 73, 264–73.

GEWEKE, J. (1986) Exact Inference in the Inequality Constrained Normal Linear Regression Model. *Journal of Applied Econometrics* 1, 127–42.

GILBERT, C. L. (1986) Professor Hendry's Econometric Methodology. *Oxford Bulletin of Economics and Statistics* 48, 283–307.

GILBERT, C. L. (1989) LSE and the British Approach to Time Series Econometrics. *Oxford Economic Papers* 41, 108–28.

GILES, D. (1973) *Essays on Econometric Topics: From Theory to Practice.* Research Paper no. 10, Reserve Bank of New Zealand. Wellington, New Zealand.

GILES, D. E. A. and G. N. SAXTON (1993) The Goldfeld–Quandt Test: A Re-Consideration of the "One Third" Rule of Thumb. *Journal of Quantitative Economics* 9, 111–22.

GILES, J. A. and D. E. A. GILES (1993) Pre-Test Estimation and Testing in Econometrics: Recent Developments. *Journal of Economic Surveys* 7, 145–97. Reprinted in L. Oxley et al. (eds) *Surveys in Econometrics.* Oxford: Basil Blackwell, 42–90.

GIORDANO, R. and M. R. VEALL (1989) A Note on Log-Log Regressions with Dummy Variables: Why Units Matter. *Oxford Bulletin of Economics and Statistics* 51, 95–6.

GLEJSER, H. (1969) A New Test for Heteroskedasticity. *Journal of the American Statistical Association* 64, 316–23.

GODFREY, L. G. (1976) Testing for Serial Correlation in Dynamic Simultaneous Equation Models. *Econometrica* 44, 1077–84.

GODFREY, L. G. (1978) Testing Against General Autoregressive and Moving Average Error Models When the Regressors Include Lagged Dependent Variables. *Econometrica* 46, 1293–302.

GODFREY, L. G. (1979) Testing the Adequacy of a Time Series Model. *Biometrika* 66, 67–72.

GODFREY, L. G. (1987) Discriminating Between Autocorrelation and Misspecification in Regression Analysis: An Alternative Test Strategy. *Review of Economics and Statistics* 69, 128–34.

GODFREY, L. G. (1988) *Misspecification Tests in Econometrics.* Cambridge: Cambridge University Press.

GODFREY, L. G. (1994) Testing for Serial Correlation by Variable Addition in Dynamic Models Estimated by Instrumental Variables. *Review of Economics and Statistics* 76, 550–9.

GODFREY, L. G. and J. P. HUTTON (1994) Discriminating between Errors-in-Variables/Simultaneity and Misspecification in Linear Regression Models. *Economics Letters* 44, 359–64.

GODFREY, L. G., M. McALEER and C. R. McKENZIE (1988) Variable Addition and Lagrange Multiplier Tests for Linear and Logarithmic Regression Models. *Review of Economics and Statistics* 70, 492–503.

GODFREY, L. G. and C. D. ORME (1991) Testing for Skewness of Regression Disturbances. *Economics Letters* 37, 31–4.

GODFREY, L. G. and A. R. TREMAYNE (1988) Checks of Model Adequacy for Univariate Time Series Models and their Application to Econometric Relationships. *Econometric Reviews* 7, 1–42.

GOLDBERGER, A. S. (1962) Best Linear Unbiased Prediction in the Generalized Linear Regression Model. *Journal of the American Statistical Association* 57, 369–75.

GOLDBERGER, A. S. (1964) *Econometric Theory.* New York: John Wiley.

GOLDBERGER, A. S. (1968a) The Interpretation and Estimation of Cobb–Douglas Functions. *Econometrica* 35, 464–72.

GOLDBERGER, A. S. (1968b) *Topics in Regression Analysis.* New York: Macmillan.

GOLDBERGER, A. S. (1972) Structural Equation Methods in the Social Sciences. *Econometrica* 40, 979–1002.

GOLDBERGER, A. S. (1989) The ET Interview. *Econometric Theory* 5, 133–60.

GOLDFELD, S. and R. QUANDT (1972) *Nonlinear Methods in Econometrics.* Amsterdam: North Holland.

GOLDFELD, S. and R. QUANDT (1976) *Studies in Nonlinear Estimation.* Cambridge, MA: Ballinger.

GOLDSTEIN, R. et al. (1989) Survival Analysis Software. *Journal of Applied Econometrics* 4, 393–414.

GONZALO, J. (1994) Five Alternative Methods of Estimating Long-Run Equilibrium Relationships. *Journal of Econometrics* 60, 203–33.

GOODHART, C. A. E. (1978) Problems of Monetary Management: the UK Experience. In A. S. Courakis (ed.) *Inflation, Depression and Economic Policy in the West: Lessons from the 1970s.* Oxford: Basil Blackwell.

GOODMAN, A. C. and R. A. DUBIN (1990) Sample Stratification with Non-nested Alternatives: Theory and a Hedonic Example. *Review of Economics and Statistics* 72, 168–73.

GRANGER, C. W. J. (1982) Acronyms in Time Series Analysis (ATSA). *Journal of Time Series Analysis* 3, 103–7.

GRANGER, C. W. J. (ed.) (1990) *Modelling Economic Series: Readings in Econometric Methodology.* Oxford: Oxford University Press.

GRANGER, C. W. J. (1993) Strategies for Modelling Nonlinear Time-Series Relationships. *Economic Record* 69, 233–8.

GRANGER, C. W. J. (1996) Can We Improve the Perceived Quality of Economic Forecasts? *Journal of Applied Econometrics* 11, 455–73.

GRANGER, C. W. J. (1997) On Modelling the Long Run in Applied Economics. *Economic Journal* 107, 169–77.

GRANGER, C. W. J. and R. F. ENGLE (1984) Applications of Spectral Analysis in Econometrics. In D. R. Brillinger and P. R. Kishnaiah (eds) *Handbook of Statistics Vol. 5.* Amsterdam: Elsevier.

GRANGER, C. W. J. and P. NEWBOLD (1973) Some Comments on the Evaluation of Economic Forecasts. *Applied Economics* 5, 35–47.

GRANGER, C. W. J. and P. NEWBOLD (1974) Spurious Regressions in Econometrics. *Journal of Econometrics* 2, 111–20.

GRANGER, C. W. J. and P. NEWBOLD (1976) R^2 and the Transformation of Regression Variables. *Journal of Econometrics* 4, 205–10.

GRANGER, C. W. J. and P. NEWBOLD (1986) *Forecasting Economic Time Series*, 2nd edn. London: Academic Press.

GRANGER, C. W. J. and R. RAMANATHAN (1984) Improved Methods of Combining Forecasts. *Journal of Forecasting* 3, 197–204.

GRANGER, C. and H. UHLIG (1990) Reasonable Extreme-Bounds Analysis. *Journal of Econometrics* 44, 159–70.

GREENBERG, E. and C. E. WEBSTER (1983) *Advanced Econometrics: A Bridge to the Literature*. New York: John Wiley.

GREENE, W. H. (1981) On the Asymptotic Bias of the Ordinary Least Squares Estimator of the Tobit Model. *Econometrica* 49, 505–13.

GREENE, W. H. (1997) *Econometric Analysis*, 3rd edn. New York: Macmillan.

GREENE, W. H., L. G. KNAPP and T. G. SEAKS (1995) Estimating the Functional Form of the Independent Variables in Probit Models. *Applied Economics* 27, 193–6.

GREENE, W. H. and T. G. SEAKS (1991) The Restricted Least Squares Estimator: A Pedagogical Note. *Review of Economics and Statistics* 73, 563–7.

GREGORY, A. W. and B. E. HANSEN (1996a) Residual-Based Tests for Cointegration in Models with Regime Shifts. *Journal of Econometrics* 70, 99–126.

GREGORY, A. W. and B. E. HANSEN (1996b) Tests for Cointegration in Models with Regime and Trend Shifts. *Oxford Bulletin of Economics and Statistics* 58, 555–60.

GREGORY, A. W. and M. R. VEALL (1985) Formulating Wald Tests of Nonlinear Restrictions. *Econometrica* 53, 1465–8.

GRIFFITHS, W. E. (1988) Bayesian Econometrics and How to Get Rid of Those Wrong Signs. *Review of Marketing and Agricultural Economics* 56, 36–56.

GRIFFITHS, W. E. and P. A. A. BEESLEY (1984) The Small-sample Properties of Some Preliminary Test Estimators in a Linear Model with Autocorrelated Errors. *Journal of Econometrics* 25, 49–61.

GRILICHES, Z. (1985) Data and Econometricians – The Uneasy Alliance. *American Economic Review* 74, 196–200.

GRILICHES, Z. (1986) Economic Data Issues. In Z. Griliches and M. Intriligator (eds), *Handbook of Econometrics Vol. III*. Amsterdam: North Holland, ch. 25.

GRILICHES, Z. (1994) Productivity, R&D, and the Data Constraint. *American Economic Review* 84, 1–23.

GRILICHES, Z. and P. RAO (1969) Small-sample Properties of Several Two-stage Regression Methods in the Context of Autocorrelated Errors. *Journal of the American Statistical Association* 64, 253–72.

GROGGER, J. (1990) A Simple Test for Exogeneity in Probit, Logit, and Poisson Regression Models. *Economics Letters* 33, 329–32.

GRUBB, D. and L. MAGEE (1988) A Variance Comparison of OLS and Feasible GLS Estimators. *Econometric Theory* 4, 329–35.

GRUNFELD, Y. and Z. GRILICHES (1960) Is Aggregation Necessarily Bad? *Review of Economics and Statistics* 42, 1–13 (reprinted in J. Dowling and F. Glahe (eds) (1970) Readings in Econometric Theory. Boulder, CO: Colorado Associated University Press).

GUILKEY, D. K. and P. SCHMIDT (1989) Extended Tabulations for Dickey–Fuller Tests. *Economics Letters* 31, 355–7.

GUJARATI, D. (1978) *Basic Econometrics*. New York: McGraw-Hill.

GUMPERTZ, M. and S. PANTULA (1989) A Simple Approach to Inference in Random Coefficient Models. *American Statistician* 43, 203–10.

GURNEY, A. (1989) Obtaining Estimates for the Standard Errors of Long-run Parameters. *National Institute Economic Review* 128, 89–90.

HACKL, P. and A. H. WESTLUND (1989) Statistical Analysis of Structural Change: An Annotated Bibliography. *Empirical Economics* 14, 167–92.

HAESSEL, W. (1978) Measuring Goodness of Fit in Linear and Nonlinear Models. *Southern Economic Journal* 44, 648–52.

HAFER, R. W. and R. G. SHEEHAN (1989) The Sensitivity of VAR Forecasts to Alternative Lag Structures. *International Journal of Forecasting* 8, 339–408.

HALL, A. (1989) On the Calculation of the Information Matrix Test in the Normal Linear Regression Model. *Economics Letters* 29, 31–5.

HALL, A. (1993) Some Aspects of Generalized Method of Moments Estimation. In G. S. Maddala, C. R. Rao and H. D. Vinod (eds) *Handbook of Statistics*, Vol. II. Amsterdam: Elsevier, 393–417.

HALL, A. D. and M. McALEER (1989) A Monte Carlo Study of Some Tests of Model Adequacy in Time Series Analysis. *Journal of Business and Economic Statitstics* 7, 95–106.

HALL, S. G. and S. J. BROOKS (1986) The Use of Prior Regressions in the Estimation of Error Correction Models. *Economics Letters* 20, 33–7.

HALL, S. G. , K. CUTHBERTSON and M. P. TAYLOR (1992) *Applied Econometric Techniques*. Hemel Hempstead, UK: Philip Allan.

HALVORSEN, R. and R. PALMQUIST (1980) The Interpretation of Dummy Variables in Semilogarithmic Equations. *American Economic Review* 70, 474–5.

HAMILTON, J. D. (1994) *Time Series Analysis*. Princeton: Princeton University Press.

HANSEN, B. E. (1992) Testing for Parameter Instability in Linear Models. *Journal of Policy Modeling* 14, 517–33.

HANSEN, B. E. (1995) Rethinking the Univariate Approach to Unit Root Testing: Using Covariates to Increase Power. *Econometric Theory* 11, 1148–71.

HANSEN, B. E. (1996) Methodology: Alchemy or Science? *Economic Journal* 106, 1398–413.

HANSEN, L. P. and J. J. HECKMAN (1996) The Empirical Foundations of Calibration. *Journal of Economic Perspectives* 10, 87–104.

HARDLE, W. (1990) *Applied Nonparametric Regression*. Cambridge: Cambridge University Press.

HARGREAVES, C. P. (1994) A Review of Methods of Estimating Cointegrating Relationships. In Hargreaves, C. P. (ed.) *Nonstationary Time Series Analysis and Cointegration*. Oxford: Oxford University Press, 87–132.

HARRIS, R. I. D. (1992) Testing for Unit Roots Using the Augmented Dickey–Fuller Test: Some Issues Relating to the Size, Power and Lag Structure of the Test. *Economics Letters* 38, 381–6.

HARRIS, R. I. D. (1994) Cointegration Analysis Using the Johansen Technique: A Practitioner's Guide to the Software. *Economic Journal* 104, 127–8.

HARRIS, R. I. D. (1995) *Using Cointegration Analysis in Econometric Modelling*. Hemel Hempstead: Prentice-Hall/Harvester Wheatsheaf.

HARTMAN, R. S. (1991) A Monte Carlo Analysis of Alternative Estimators in Models Involving Selectivity. *Journal of Business and Economic Statistics* 9, 41–9.

HARTWIG, F. and B. E. DEARING (1979) *Exploratory Data Analysis*. Beverly Hills, CA: Sage.

HARVEY, A. C. (1981) *The Econometric Analysis of Time Series*. Oxford: Philip Allan .

HARVEY, A. C. (1987) Applications of the Kalman Filter in Econometrics. In T. F. Bewley (ed.) *Advances in Econometrics: Fifth World Congress*, 1, Cambridge: Cambridge University Press, 285–313.

HARVEY, A. C. (1997) Trends, Cycles and Autoregressions. *Economic Journal* 107, 192–201.

HARVEY, A. C. and P. COLLIER (1977) Testing for Functional Misspecification in Regression Analysis. *Journal of Econometrics* 6, 103–19.

HATANAKA, M. (1974) An Efficient Two-step Estimator for the Dynamic Adjustment Model with Autoregressive Errors. *Journal of Econometrics* 2, 199–220.

HAUG, A. A. (1993) Residual Based Tests for Cointegration: A Monte Carlo Study of Size Distortions. *Economics Letters* 41, 345–51.

HAUG, A. A. (1996) Tests for Cointegration: A Monte Carlo Comparison. *Journal of Econometrics* 71, 89–115.

HAUSMAN, J. A. (1978) Specification Tests in Econometrics. *Econometrica* 46, 1251–71.

HAUSMAN, J. A. (1983) Specification and Estimation of Simultaneous Equation Models. In Z. Griliches and M. Intriligator (eds), *Handbook of Econometrics Vol. I*. Amsterdam: North Holland, ch. 7.

HAUSMAN, J., B. H. HALL and Z. GRILICHES (1984) Econometric Models for Count Data with an Application to the Patents–R&D Relationship. *Econometrica* 52, 909–38.

HAUSMAN, J. A. and D. McFADDEN (1984) Specification Tests for the Multinomial Logit Model. *Econometrica* 52, 1219–40.

HAYDUK, L. A. (1987) *Structural Equation Modeling with LISREL*. Baltimore: Johns Hopkins University Press.

HAYNES, S. E. and J. A. STONE (1985) A Neglected Method of Separating Demand and Supply in Time Series Regression. *Journal of Business and Economic Statistics* 3, 238–43.

HECKMAN, J. J. (1976) The Common Structure of Statistical Models of Truncation, Sample Selection and Limited Dependent Variables and a Simple Estimator for Such Models. *Annals of Economic and Social Measurement* 5, 475–92.

HECKMAN, J. J. and B. SINGER (1984) A Method for Minimizing the Impact of Distribution Assumptions in Econometric Models for Duration Data. *Econometrica* 52, 271–320.

HECKMAN, J. J. and J. A. SMITH (1995) Assessing the Case for Social Experiments. *Journal of Economic Perspectives* 9, 85–110.

HENDRY, D. F. (1973) On Asymptotic Theory and Finite Sample Experiments. *Economica* 40, 210–17.

HENDRY, D. F. (1980) Econometrics – Alchemy or Science? *Economica* 47, 387–406.

HENDRY, D. F. (1984) Monte Carlo Experimentation in Econometrics. In Z. Griliches and M. Intriligator (eds), *Handbook of Econometrics Vol. II*. Amsterdam: North Holland, ch. 16.

HENDRY, D. F. (1986) Econometric Modelling with Cointegrated Variables: An Overview. *Oxford Bulletin of Economics and Statistics* 48, 201–12.

HENDRY, D. F. (1993) *Econometrics: Alchemy or Science?* Oxford: Basil Blackwell.

HENDRY, D. F. (1995) *Dynamic Econometrics*. Oxford: Oxford University Press.

HENDRY, D. F. and N. R. ERICSSON (1991) An Econometric Analysis of UK Money Demand in "Monetary Trends in the United States and the United Kingdom" by Milton Friedman and Anna J. Schwartz. *American Economic Review* 81, 8–38.

HENDRY, D. F., E. E. LEAMER and D. J. POIRIER (1990) The ET Dialogue: A Conversation on Econometric Methodology. *Econometric Theory* 6, 171–261.

HENDRY, D. F. and G. E. MIZON (1978) Serial Correlation as a Convenient Simplification, Not a Nuisance: A Comment on a Study of the Demand for Money by the Bank of England. *Economic Journal* 88, 549–63.

HENDRY, D. F. and M. S. MORGAN (1995) *The Foundations of Econometric Analysis*. Cambridge: Cambridge University Press.

HENDRY, D. F., A. R. PAGAN and D. SARGAN (1984) Dynamic Specification. In Z. Griliches and M. Intriligator (eds) *Handbook of Econometrics Vol. II*. Amsterdam: North Holland, ch. 18.

HENDRY, D. F. and J. F. RICHARD (1983) The Econometric Analysis of Economic Time Series. *International Statistical Review* 51, 111–48.

HEY, J. (1983) *Data in Doubt*. Oxford: Martin Robertson.

HILL, G. and R. FILDES (1984) The Accuracy of Extrapolation Methods: An Automatic Box–Jenkins Package Sift. *Journal of Forecasting* 3, 319–23.

HILL, R. C. (1987) Modeling Multicollinearity and Extrapolation in Monte Carlo Experiments on Regression. In T. Fomby and G. Rhodes (eds) *Advances in Econometrics*. Greenwich, CT: JAI Press, 127–55.

HILL, R. C. and R. F. ZIEMER (1982) Small Sample Performance of the Stein Rule in Nonorthogonal Designs. *Economics Letters* 10, 285–92.

HILL, R. C. and R. F. ZIEMER (1984) The Risk of General Stein-like Estimators in the Presence of Multicollinearity. *Journal of Econometrics* 25, 205–16.

HILL, R. C., R. F. ZIEMER and F. C. WHITE (1981) Mitigating the Effects of Multicollinearity Using Exact and Stochastic Restrictions: The Case of an Agricultural Production Function in Thailand: Comment. *American Journal of Agricultural Economics* 63, 298–9.

HO, M. S. and B. E. SORENSEN (1996) Finding Cointegration Rank in High Dimensional Systems Using the Johansen Test: An Illustration Using Data Based on Monte Carlo Simulations. *Review of Economics and Statistics* 78, 726–32.

HOFF, J. C. (1983) *A Practical Guide to Box–Jenkins Forecasting*. Belmont, CA: Lifetime Learning.

HOFFMAN, D. and A. R. PAGAN (1989) Post Sample Prediction Tests for Generalized Method of Moments Estimators. *Oxford Bulletin of Economics and Statistics* 51, 333–43.

HOFFMAN, D. and P. SCHMIDT (1981) Testing the Restrictions Implied by the Rational Expectations Hypothesis. *Journal of Econometrics* 15, 265–88.

HOGARTH, R. M. (1975) Cognitive Processes and the Assessment of Subjective Probability Distributions. *Journal of the American Statistical Association* 70, 271–94.

HOGG, R. V. (1988) Comment. *Journal of Business and Economic Statistics* 6, 428.

HOLDEN, D. and PERMAN, R. (1994) Unit Roots and Cointegration for the Economist.

In Rao, B. B. (ed.) *Cointegration for the Applied Economist*. New York: St. Martin's Press, 47–112.

HOLDEN, K. and J. THOMPSON (1992) Co-Integration: An Introductory Survey. *British Review of Economic Issues* 14, 1–52.

HOROWITZ, J. L. and G. R. NEUMANN (1989) Specification Testing in Censored Regression Models: Parametric and Semi-Parametric Methods. *Journal of Applied Econometrics* 4 supplement, S61–S86.

HOWREY, E. et al. (1974) Notes on Testing the Predictive Performance of Econometric Models. *International Economic Review* 15, 366–83.

HSU, D. A. (1982) Robust Inferences for Structural Shift in Regression Models. *Journal of Econometrics* 19, 89–107.

HSU, Y-S. (1991) General Linear Hypotheses in a Two-stage Least Squares Estimation Model. *Economics Letters* 36, 275–9.

HSU, Y. S. et al. (1986) Monte Carlo Studies on the Effectiveness of the Bootstrap Method on 2SLS Estimates. *Economics Letters* 20, 233–9.

HURN, A. S. (1993) Seasonality, Cointegration and Error Correction: An Illustration Using South African Monetary Data. *Scottish Journal of Political Economy* 40, 311–22.

HYLLEBERG, S. (1986) *Seasonality in Regression*. Orlando, FA: Academic Press.

ILMAKUNNAS, P. (1990) Testing the Order of Differencing in Quarterly Data: An Illustration of the Testing Sequence. *Oxford Bulletin of Economics and Statistics* 52, 79–88.

INDER, B. A. (1984) Finite Sample Power of Tests for Autocorrelation in Models Containing Lagged Dependent Variables. *Economics Letters* 14, 179–85.

INDER, B. (1993) Estimating Long-run Relationships in Economics: A Comparison of Different Approaches. *Journal of Econometrics* 57, 53–68.

INTRILIGATOR, M. D., R. G. BODKIN and C. HSIAO (1996) *Econometric Models, Techniques and Applications*, 2nd edn. Upper Saddle River, NJ: Prentice-Hall.

IZADI, H. (1992) Estimating a Generalized Censored Regression Model: A New Method. *Economics Letters* 39, 19–22.

JANSON, M. (1988) Combining Robust and Traditional Least Squares Methods: A Critical Evaluation. *Journal of Business and Economic Statistics* 6, 415–28 (commentary, 428–52).

JARQUE, C. M. and A. K. BERA (1980) Efficient Tests for Normality, Heteroskedasticity, and Serial Independence of Regression Residuals. *Economics Letters* 6, 255–9.

JENKINS, G. M. (1979) *Practical Experiences with Modelling and Forecasting Time Series*. St Helier: Gwilym Jenkins and Partners (Overseas) Ltd.

JENKINS, S. P. (1995) Easy Estimation Methods for Discrete-time Duration Models. *Oxford Bulletin of Economics and Statistics* 57, 129–38.

JEONG, J. and G. S. MADDALA (1993) A Perspective on Application of Bootstrap Methods in Econometrics. In G. S. Maddala, C. R. Rao and H. D. Vinod (eds), *Handbook of Statistics, Vol. 11*. Amsterdam: North Holland, 573–610.

JOHANSEN, S. (1988) Statistical Analysis of Cointegrating Vectors. *Journal of Economic Dynamics and Control* 12, 231–54.

JOHNSON, H. G. (1971) The Keynesian Revolution and the Monetarist Counterrevolution. *American Economic Review* 61, 1–14.

JOHNSTON, J. (1972) *Econometric Methods*, 2nd edn. New York: McGraw-Hill.
JOHNSTON, J. (1984) *Econometric Methods*, 3rd edn. New York: McGraw-Hill.
JONES, J. (1977) *Introduction to Decision Theory*. Homewood, IL: Irwin.
JORESKOG, K. G. and D. SORBOM (1993) *LISREL 8: Structural Equation Modeling with the SIMPLIS Command Language*. Chicago: Scientific Software International.
JUDGE, G. G. and M. E. BOCK (1978) *The Statistical Implications of Pre-test and Stein-rule Estimators in Econometrics*. Amsterdam: North Holland.
JUDGE, G. G., W. E. GRIFFITHS, R. C. HILL and T. C. LEE (1980) *The Theory and Practice of Econometrics*. New York: John Wiley.
JUDGE, G. G., W. E. GRIFFITHS, R. C. HILL, H. LUTKEPOHL and T. C. LEE (1985) *The Theory and Practice of Econometrics*, 2nd edn. New York: John Wiley.
JUDGE, G. G., W. E. GRIFFITHS, R. C. HILL, H. LUTKEPOHL and T. C. LEE (1988) *Introduction to the Theory and Practice of Econometrics*, 2nd edn. New York: John Wiley.

KADANE, J. et al. (1980) Interactive Elicitation of Opinion for a Normal Linear Model. *Journal of the American Statistical Association* 75, 845–54.
KADIYALA, K. (1968) A Transformation Used to Circumvent the Problem of Autocorrelation. *Econometrica* 36, 93–6.
KADIYALA, K. (1972) Regression with Non-gaussian Stable Disturbances: Some Sampling Results. *Econometrica* 40, 719–22.
KAKIMOTO, S. and K. OHTANI (1985) On the Use of a Proxy Variable in the Test of Homoscedasticity. *Economics Letters* 18, 153–6.
KALAHA, R. and L. TESFATISON (1989) Time-Varying Linear Regression via Flexible Least Squares. *Computers and Mathematics with Applications* 17, 1215–45.
KAMSTRA, M. and P. E. KENNEDY (1997) Combining Qualitative Forecasts with Logit. *International Journal of Forecasting*, forthcoming.
KANE, E. (1968) *Economic Statistics and Econometrics*. New York: Harper and Row.
KANG, H. (1986) Univariate ARIMA Forecasts of Defined Variables. *Journal of Business and Economic Statistics* 4, 81–6.
KARNI, E. and SHAPIRO, B. (1980) Tales of Horror from Ivory Towers. *Journal of Political Economy* 88, 210–12.
KASS, R. E. and L. WASSERMAN (1996) The Selection of Prior Distributions by Formal Rules. *Journal of the American Statistical Association* 91, 1343–70.
KEANE, M. P. (1992) A Note on Identification in the Multinominal Probit Model. *Journal of Business and Economic Statistics* 10, 193–200.
KEMPTHORNE, O. and T. E. DOERFLER (1969) The Behaviour of Some Significance Tests under Experimental Randomization. *Biometrika* 56, 231–48.
KENNEDY, P. E. (1981a) Estimation with Correctly Interpreted Dummy Variables in Semilogarithmic Equations. *American Economic Review* 71, 802.
KENNEDY, P. E. (1981b) The "Ballentine": A Graphical Aid for Econometrics. *Australian Economic Papers* 20, 414–16.
KENNEDY, P. E. (1983) Logarithmic Dependent Variables and Prediction Bias. *Oxford Bulletin of Economics and Statistics* 45, 389–92.
KENNEDY, P. E. (1985) A Rule of Thumb for Mixed Heteroskedasticity. *Economics Letters* 18, 157–9.
KENNEDY, P. E. (1986) Interpreting Dummy Variables. *Review of Economics and Statistics* 68, 174–5.

KENNEDY, P. E. (1989) Non-nested Hypothesis Tests: A Diagrammatic Exposition. *Australian Economic Papers* 28, 160–5.

KENNEDY, P. E. (1990) An Exercise in Computing the Variance of the Forecast Error. *International Journal of Forecasting* 6, 275–6.

KENNEDY, P. E. (1991a) An Extension of Mixed Estimation, with an Application to Forecasting New Product Growth. *Empirical Economics* 16, 401–15.

KENNEDY, P. E. (1991b) Comparing Classification Techniques. *International Journal of Forecasting* 7, 403–6.

KENNEDY, P. E. (1995) Randomization Tests in Econometrics. *Journal of Business and Economic Statistics* 13, 85–94.

KENNEDY, P. E. (1998) Using Monte Carlo Studies for Teaching Econometrics. In W. Becker and M. Watts (eds) *Teaching Undergraduate Economics: Alternatives to Chalk and Talk*. Cincinnati: Southwestern Publishing Co., forthcoming.

KENNEDY, P. E. and S. ADJIBOLOSOO (1990) More Evidence on the Use of Bayesian Estimators for Nonspherical Errors. *Journal of Quantitative Economics* 6, 61–70.

KENNEDY, P. E. and B. CADE (1996) Randomization Tests for Multiple Regression. *Communications in Statistics – Computation and Simulation* 25, 923–36.

KENNEDY, P. E. and D. SIMONS (1991) Fighting the Teflon Factor: Comparing Classical and Bayesian Estimators for Autocorrelated Errors. *Journal of Econometrics* 48, 12–27.

KEYNES, J. M. (1940) On Methods of Statistical Research: Comment. *Economic Journal* 50, 154–6.

KIEFER, N. (1988) Economic Duration Data and Hazard Functions. *Journal of Economic Literature* 26, 646–79.

KING, G. (1997) *A Solution to the Ecological Inference Problem: Reconstructing Individual Behavior from Aggregate Data*. Princeton: Princeton University Press.

KING, G., KEOHANE, R. O. and S. VERBA (1994) *Designing Social Inquiry: Scientific Inference in Qualitative Research*. Princeton: Princeton University Press.

KING, M. L. (1987) Testing for Autocorrelation in Linear Regression Models: A Survey. In M. King and D. Giles (eds) *Specification Analysis in the Linear Model*. London: Routledge and Kegan Paul, ch.3.

KING, M. L. and D. E. A. GILES (1984) Autocorrelation Pre-testing in the Linear Model: Estimation, Testing and Prediction. *Journal of Econometrics* 25, 35–48.

KING, R. G. (1995) Quantitative Theory and Econometrics. *Federal Reserve Bank of Richmond Economic Quarterly* 81(3), 53–105.

KIVIET, J. F. (1985) Model Selection Test Procedures in a Single Linear Equation of a Dynamic Simultaneous System and their Defects in Small Samples. *Journal of Econometrics* 28, 327–62.

KIVIET, J. F. (1986) On the Rigour of some Misspecification Tests for Modelling Dynamic Relationships. *Review of Economic Studies* 53, 241–61.

KLEIN, L. R. (1984) The Importance of the Forecast. *Journal of Forecasting* 3, 1–9.

KLEIN, P. and G. MOORE (1983) The Leading Indicator Approach to Economic Forecasting – Retrospect and Prospect. *Journal of Forecasting* 2, 119–35.

KMENTA, J. (1972) Summary of the Discussion. In K. Brunner (ed.) *Problems and Issues in Current Econometric Practice*. Columbus: Ohio State University Press, 262–84.

KMENTA, J. (1986) *Elements of Econometrics,* 2nd edn. New York: Macmillan.

KMENTA, J. and R. GILBERT (1968) Small Sample Properties of Alternative

Estimators of Seemingly Unrelated Regressions. *Journal of the American Statistical Association* 63, 1180–1200.

KOENKER, R. (1981) A Note on Studentizing a Test for Heteroskedasticity. *Journal of Econometrics* 17, 107–12.

KOENKER, R. (1982) Robust Methods in Econometrics. *Econometric Reviews* 1, 213–55.

KOENKER, R. (1988) Asymptotic Theory and Econometric Practice. *Journal of Applied Econometrics* 3, 139–43.

KOENKER, R. and G. BASSETT (1978) Regression Quantiles. *Econometrica* 46, 33–50.

KOHLI, U. (1989) Consistent Estimation when the Left-hand Variable is Exogenous Over Part of the Sample Period. *Journal of Applied Econometrics* 4, 283–93.

KOOP, G. (1994) Recent Progress in Applied Bayesian Econometrics. *Journal of Economic Surveys* 8, 1–34.

KRAMER, W. et al. (1985) Diagnostic Checking in Practice. *Review of Economics and Statistics* 67, 118–23.

KRAMER, W., W. PLOBERGER and R. ALT (1988) Testing for Structural Change in Dynamic Models. *Econometrica* 56,1355–69.

KRAMER, W. and H. SONNBERGER (1986) *The Linear Regression Model Under Test.* Heidelberg: Physica-Verlag.

KRASKER, W. S., E. KUH and R. E. WELSCH (1983) Estimation for Dirty Data and Flawed Models. In Z. Griliches and M. Intriligator (eds), *Handbook of Econometrics Vol. I.* Amsterdam: North Holland, ch. 11.

KRASKER, W. S. and J. W. PRATT (1986) Bounding the Effects of Proxy Variables on Regression Coefficients. *Econometrica* 54, 641–55.

KUH, E. and J. MEYER (1957) How Extraneous are Extraneous Estimates? *Review of Economics and Statistics* 39, 380–93 (reprinted in J. Dowling and F. Glahe (eds) (1970) *Readings in Econometric Theory.* Boulder, CO: Colorado Associated University Press.

KWIATKOWSKI, D., P. C. B. PHILLIPS, P. SCHMIDT and Y. SHIN (1992) Testing the Null Hypothesis of Stationarity Against the Alternative of a Unit Root. *Journal of Econometrics* 54, 159–78.

KYDLAND, F. E. and E. C. PRESCOTT (1996) The Computational Experiment: An Econometric Tool. *Journal of Economic Perspectives* 10, 69–85.

LAHIRI, K. and D. EGY (1981) Joint Estimation and Testing for Functional Form and Heteroskedasticity. *Journal of Econometrics* 15, 299–307.

LANCASTER, T. (1990) *The Econometric Analysis of Transition Data.* Cambridge: Cambridge University Press.

LANDWEHR, J. M., D. PREGIBON and A. C. SHOEMAKER (1984) Graphical Methods for Assessing Logistic Regression Models. *Journal of the American Statistical Association* 79, 61–83.

LANKFORD, R. H. and J. H. WYCKOFF (1991) Modeling Charitable Giving Using a Box–Cox Standard Tobit Model. *Review of Economics and Statistics* 73, 460–70.

LAU, L. J. (1986) Functional Forms in Econometric Model Building. In Z. Griliches and M. D. Intriligator (eds), *Handbook of Econometrics Vol. III.* Amsterdam: North Holland, ch. 25.

LAYSON, S. K. and T. G. SEAKS (1984) Estimation and Testing for Functional Form in First Difference Models. *Review of Economics and Statistics* 66, 338–43.

LEAMER, E. E. (1978) *Specification Searches: Ad Hoc Inference with Nonexperimental Data*. New York: John Wiley.

LEAMER, E. E. (1981) Is It a Demand Curve or Is It a Supply Curve? Partial Identification Through Inequality Constraints. *Review of Economics and Statistics* 63, 319–27.

LEAMER, E. E. (1983a) Let's Take the Con out of Econometrics. *American Economic Review* 73, 31–43.

LEAMER, E. E. (1983b) Model Choice and Specification Analysis. In Z. Griliches and M. Intriligator (eds), *Handbook of Econometrics Vol. I*. Amsterdam: North Holland, ch. 5.

LEAMER, E. E. (1986) A Bayesian Analysis of the Determinants of Inflation. In D. Belsley and E. Kuh (eds) *Model Reliability*. Cambridge, MA: MIT Press.

LEAMER, E. E. (1988) Things That Bother Me. *Economic Record* 64, 331–5.

LEAMER, E. E. (1994) *Sturdy Econometrics*. Aldershot: Edward Elgar.

LEAMER, E. E. and H. LEONARD (1983) Reporting the Fragility of Regression Estimates. *Review of Economics and Statistics* 65, 306–17.

LECHNER, M. (1991) Testing Logit Models in Practice. *Empirical Economics* 16, 177–98.

LEECH, D. (1975) Testing the Error Specification in Nonlinear Regression. *Econometrica* 43, 719–25.

LEITCH, G. and J. E. TANNER (1995) Professional Economic Forecasts: Are They Worth their Costs? *Journal of Forecasting* 14, 143–57.

LEONTIEF, W. (1971) Theoretical Assumptions and Nonobserved Facts. *American Economic Review* 61, 1–7.

LEVI, M. (1973) Errors in the Variables Bias in the Presence of Correctly Measured Variables. *Econometrica* 41, 985–6.

LEVI, M. (1977) Measurement Errors and Bounded OLS Estimates. *Journal of Econometrics* 6, 165–71.

LEYBOURNE, S. J. (1994) Testing for Unit Roots: A Simple Alternative to Dickey–Fuller. *Applied Economics* 26, 721–9.

LEYBOURNE, S. J. (1995) Testing for Unit Roots Using Forward and Reverse Dickey–Fuller Regressions. *Oxford Bulletin of Economics and Statistics* 57, 559–71.

LEYBOURNE, S. J. and B. P. M. McCABE (1992) A Simple Test for Parameter Constancy in a Nonlinear Time Series Regression Model. *Economics Letters* 38, 157–62.

LEYBOURNE, S. J. and B. P. M. McCABE (1994) A Simple Test for Cointegration. *Oxford Bulletin of Economics and Statistics* 56, 97–103.

LI, H. and G. S. MADDALA (1996) Bootstrapping Time Series Models. *Econometric Reviews* 15, 115–95 including commentary.

LI, Y., G. S. MADDALA and M. RUSH (1995) New Small Sample Estimators for Cointegration Regression. *Economics Letters* 47, 123–9.

LIBERT, G. (1984) The M-Competition with a Fully Automatic Box–Jenkins Procedure. *Journal of Forecasting* 3, 325–8.

LIN. C-F. J. and T. TERASVIRTA (1994) Testing the Constancy of Regression Parameters against Continuous Structural Change. *Journal of Econometrics* 62, 211–28.

LIN, K. and J. KMENTA (1982) Ridge Regression under Alternative Loss Criteria. *Review of Economics and Statistics* 64, 488–94.

LINDLEY, D. V., A. TVERSKY and R. BROWN (1979) On the Reconciliation of Probability Assessments. *Journal of the Royal Statistical Society* A142, 146–80.

LITTERMAN, R. (1986) A Statistical Approach to Economic Forecasting. *Journal of Business and Economic Statistics* 4, 1–4.

LITTLE, R. J. A. (1992) Regression with Missing X's: A Review. *Journal of the American Statistical Association* 87, 1227–37.

LOTT, W. F. and S. RAY (1992) *Econometrics Problems and Data Sets*. San Diego: Harcourt, Brace Jovanovich.

LOVELL, M. C. (1983) Data Mining. *Review of Economics and Statistics* 65, 1–12.

LUCAS, R. E. (1973) Some International Evidence on Output–Inflation Tradeoffs. *American Economic Review* 63, 326–34.

LUCAS, R. E. (1976) Econometric Policy Evaluation: A Critique. *Carnegie Rochester Conferences on Public Policy* 1, 19–46.

MACDONALD, G. M. and J. G. MACKINNON (1985) Convenient Methods for Estimation of Linear Regression Models with MA(1) Errors. *Canadian Journal of Economics* 18, 106–16.

MACDONALD, J. B. and S. B. WHITE (1993) A Comparison of Some Robust, Adaptive and Partially Adaptive Estimators of Regression Models. *Econometric Reviews* 12, 103–24.

MACDONALD, M. (1995) Feminist Economics: From Theory to Research. *Canadian Journal of Economics* 28, 159–76.

MACHAK, J. A., W. A. SPIVEY and W. J. WROBLESKI (1985) A Framework for Time Varying Parameter Regression Modeling. *Journal of Business and Economic Statistics* 3, 104–11.

MACHLUP, F. (1974) Proxies and Dummies. *Journal of Political Economy* 82, 892.

MacKINNON, J. G. (1983) Model Specification Tests Against Nonnested Alternatives. *Econometric Reviews* 2, 85–110.

MacKINNON, J. G. (1991) Critical Values for Cointegration Tests. In R. F. Engle and C. W. J. Granger (eds) *Long-run Economic Relationships*. Oxford: Oxford University Press, 267–76.

MacKINNON, J. G. (1992) Model Specification Tests and Artificial Regressions. *Journal of Economic Literature* 30, 102–46.

MacKINNON, J. G. and L. MAGEE (1990) Transforming the Dependent Variable in Regression Models. *International Economic Review* 31, 315–39.

MacKINNON, J. G. and H. WHITE (1985) Some Heteroskedasticity-Consistent Covariance Matrix Estimators with Improved Finite Sample Properties. *Journal of Econometrics* 29, 305–25.

MADDALA, G. S. (1971) Generalized Least Squares with an Estimated Variance–Covariance Matrix. *Econometrica* 39, 23–33.

MADDALA, G. (1974) Some Small Sample Evidence on Tests of Significance in Simultaneous Equations Models. *Econometrica* 42, 841–51.

MADDALA, G. S. (1977) *Econometrics*. New York: McGraw-Hill.

MADDALA, G. S. (1983) *Limited-dependent and Qualitative Variables in Econometrics*. Cambridge: Cambridge University Press.

MADDALA, G. S. (1986) Disequilibrium, Self-Selection and Switching Models. In Z. Griliches and M. D. Intriligator (eds), *Handbook of Econometrics Vol. III*. Amsterdam: North Holland, ch.28.

MADDALA, G. S. (1988) *Introduction to Econometrics*. New York: Macmillan.

MADDALA, G. S. (1991) To Pool or Not to Pool: That is the Question. *Journal of Quantitative Economics* 7, 255–64.

MADDALA, G. S. (1995) Specification Tests in Limited Dependent Variable Models. In Maddala et al. (eds) *Advances in Econometrics and Quantitative Economics*. Oxford: Basil Blackwell, 1–49.

MAHMOUD, E. (1984) Accuracy in Forecasting: A Survey. *Journal of Forecasting* 3, 139–59.

MAKRIDAKIS, S. (1976) A Survey of Time Series. *International Statistical Review* 44, 29–70.

MAKRIDAKIS, S. (1978) Time-series Analysis and Forecasting: An Update and Evaluation. *International Statistical Review* 46, 255–78.

MAKRIDAKIS, S. et al. (1982) The Accuracy of Extrapolation (Time Series) Methods: Results of a Forecasting Competition. *Journal of Forecasting* 1, 111–53 (commentary, 2, 259–311).

MALINVAUD, E. (1966) *Statistical Methods of Econometrics*. Amsterdam: North Holland.

MALLEY, J. R. (1990) Dynamic Specification in Econometric Estimation. *Journal of Agricultural Economics Research* 42(2), 52–5.

MANSKI, C. (1988) *Analog Estimation Methods in Econometrics*. New York: Chapman and Hall.

MANSKI, C. (1991) Regression. *Journal of Economic Literature* 29, 34–50.

MAYER, L. S. (1980) The Use of Exploratory Methods in Economic Analysis: Analyzing Residential Energy Demand. In J. Kmenta and J. B. Ramsey (eds), *Evaluation and Econometric Models*. New York: Academic Press, 15–45 (commentary by V. K. Smith, 123–8).

MAYER, T. (1975) Selecting Economic Hypotheses by Goodness of Fit. *Economic Journal* 85, 877–83.

MAYER, T. (1980) Economics as a Hard Science: Realistic Goal or Wishful Thinking? *Economic Inquiry* 18, 165–78.

MAYER, T. (1993) *Truth versus Precision in Economics*. Aldershot: Edward Elgar.

McALEER, M. (1987) Specification Tests for Separate Models: A Survey. In M. King and D. Giles (eds) *Specification Analysis in the Linear Model*. London: Routledge and Kegan Paul, ch. 9.

McALEER, M. (1994) Sherlock Holmes and the Search for Truth: A Diagnostic Tale. *Journal of Economic Surveys* 8, 317–70. Reprinted in L. Oxley et al. (eds) *Surveys in Econometrics*. Oxford: Basil Blackwell, 91–138.

McALEER, M., C. R. McKENZIE and A. D. HALL (1988) Testing Separate Time Series Models. *Journal of Time Series Analysis* 9, 169–89.

McALEER, M., A. R. PAGAN and P. A. VOLKER (1985) What Will Take the Con Out of Econometrics? *American Economic Review* 75, 293–307 (comment by E. Leamer, 308–13).

McCABE, B. P. M. (1989) Misspecification Tests in Econometrics Based on Ranks. *Journal of Econometrics* 40, 261–78.

McCALLUM, B. T. (1972) Relative Asymptotic Bias from Errors of Omission and Measurement. *Econometrica* 40, 757–8.

McCARTHY, M. (1971) Notes on the Selection of Instruments for Two-stage Least

Squares and K-class Type Estimators of Large Models. *Southern Economic Journal* 37, 251–9.

McCLOSKEY, D. N. (1994) Why Don't Economists Believe Empirical Findings? *Eastern Economic Journal* 20, 357–60.

McCLOSKEY, D. N. and S. T. ZILIAK (1996) The Standard Error of Regression. *Journal of Economic Literature* 34, 97–114.

McCULLOCH, J. H. (1985) On Heteros*edasticity. *Econometrica* 53, 483.

McDERMOTT, C. J. (1990) Cointegration: Origins and Significance for Economists. *New Zealand Economic Papers* 24, 1–23.

McDONALD, J. F. and R. A. MOFFITT (1980) The Uses of Tobit Analysis. *Review of Economics and Statistics* 62, 318–21.

McGUIRK, A. M., P. DRISCOLL and J. ALWAY (1993) Misspecification Testing: A Comprehensive Approach. *American Journal of Agricultural Economics* 75, 1044–55.

McINTOSH, C. S. and J. H. DORFMAN (1992) Qualitative Forecast Evaluation: A Comparison of Two Performance Measures. *American Journal of Agricultural Economics* 74, 209–14.

McKELVEY, R. M. and W. ZAVOINA (1975) A Statistical Model for the Analysis of Ordered Level Dependent Variables. *Journal of Mathematical Sociology* 4, 103–22.

McNEES, S. (1982) The Role of Macroeconomic Models in Forecasting and Policy Analysis in the United States. *Journal of Forecasting* 1, 37–48.

McNEES, S. (1986) Forecasting Accuracy of Alternative Techniques: A Comparison of US Macroeconomic Forecasts. *Journal of Business and Economic Statistics* 4, 5–15.

McNOWN, R. F. and K. R. HUNTER (1980) A Test for Autocorrelation in Models with Lagged Dependent Variables. *Review of Economics and Statistics* 62, 313–17.

MESSER, K. and H. WHITE (1984) A Note on Computing the Heteroskedasticity-consistent Covariance Matrix Using Instrumental Variable Techniques. *Oxford Bulletin of Economics and Statistics* 46, 181–4.

MEYER, B. D. (1990) Unemployment Insurance and Unemployment Spells. *Econometrica* 58, 757–82.

MEYER, B. D. (1995) Natural and Quasi-experiments in Economics. *Journal of Business and Economic Statistics* 13, 151–61.

MILLER, D. M. (1984) Reducing Transformation Bias in Curve Fitting. *American Statistician* 38, 124–6.

MILLER, P. J. and W. T. ROBERDS (1991) The Quantitative Significance of the Lucas Critique. *Journal of Business and Economic Statistics* 9, 361–89.

MILLS, J. A. and K. PRASAD (1992) A Comparison of Model Selection Criteria. *Econometric Reviews* 11, 201–33.

MILLS, T. C. (1990) *Time Series Techniques for Economists.* Cambridge: Cambridge University Press.

MILLS, T. C. (1991) Nonlinear Time Series Models in Economics. *Journal of Economic Surveys* 5, 215–42. Reprinted in L. Oxley et al. (eds), *Surveys in Econometrics.* Oxford: Basil Blackwell, 273–98.

MITCHELL, D. and P. SPEAKER (1986) A Simple, Flexible Distributed Lag Technique: The Polynomial Inverse Lag. *Journal of Econometrics* 31, 329–40.

MITTELHAMMER, R. C. and D. L. YOUNG (1981) Mitigating the Effects of Multicollinearity Using Exact and Stochastic Restrictions: The Case of an Aggregate

Agricultural Production Function in Thailand: Reply. *American Journal of Agricultural Economics* 63, 301–4.

MIYAZAKI, S. and W. E. GRIFFITHS (1984) The Properties of Some Covariance Matrix Estimators in Linear Models with AR(1) Errors. *Economics Letters* 14, 351–6.

MIZON, G. E. (1984) The Encompassing Approach in Econometrics. In D. F. Hendry and K. F. Wallis (eds), *Econometrics and Quantitative Economics*. Oxford: Basil Blackwell, ch. 6.

MIZON, G. E. and J. F. RICHARD (1986) The Encompassing Principle and its Application to Testing Non-nested Hypotheses. *Econometrica* 54, 657–78.

MOCAN, H. N. (1994) Is There a Unit Root in US Real GNP? *Economics Letters* 45, 23–31.

MONTGOMERY, D. and D. MORRISON (1973) A Note on Adjusting R^2. *Journal of Finance* 28, 1009–13.

MOON, C. G. (1989) A Monte Carlo Comparison of Semiparametric Tobit Estimators. *Journal of Applied Econometrics* 4, 1361–82.

MOREY, M. J. (1984) The Statistical Implications of Preliminary Specification Error Testing. *Journal of Econometrics* 25, 63–72.

MORGAN, M. (1990) *The History of Econometric Ideas*. Cambridge: Cambridge University Press.

MORGAN, M. (1990a) Perspectives in the History of Econometrics: A Review Essay of R. J. Epstein: *A History of Econometrics*. *Econometric Theory* 6, 151–64.

MORGENSTERN, O. (1963) *On the Accuracy of Economic Observations*. Princeton: Princeton University Press.

MOSTELLER, F., A. F. SIEGAL, E. TRAPIDO and C. YOUTZ (1981) Eye Fitting Straight Lines. *American Statistician* 35, 150–2.

MOULTON, B. R. (1990) An Illustration of a Pitfall in Estimating the Effect of Aggregate Variables on Microeconomic Units. *Review of Economics and Statistics* 72, 334–8.

MOULTON, B. R. (1991) A Bayesian Approach to Regression Selection and Estimation, with Application to a Price Index for Radio Services. *Journal of Econometrics* 49, 169–93.

MUELLER, R. O. (1996) *Basic Principles of Structural Equation Modeling: An Introduction to LISREL and EQS*. New York: Springer-Verlag.

MURPHY, A. (1994) Artificial Regression Based Mis-specification Tests for Discrete Choice Models. *Economic and Social Review* 26, 69–74.

MURPHY, A. (1996) Simple LM Tests of Mis-specification for Ordered Logit Models. *Economics Letters* 52, 137–41.

MURPHY, J. (1973) *Introductory Econometrics*. Homewood, IL: Irwin.

MURRAY, M. P. (1994) A Drunk and Her Dog: An Illustration of Cointegration and Error Correction. *American Statistician* 48, 37–9.

MUSCATELLI, V. A. and S. HURN (1992) Cointegration and Dynamic Time Series Models. *Journal of Economic Surveys* 6, 1–43. Reprinted in L. Oxley et al. (eds), *Surveys in Econometrics*. Oxford: Basil Blackwell, 171–214.

NAKAMURA, A., M. NAKAMURA and H. DULEEP (1990) Alternative Approaches to Model Choice. *Journal of Economic Behavior and Organization* 14, 97–125.

NARULA, S. C. and J. F. WELLINGTON (1982) The Minimum Sum of Absolute Errors Regression: A State of the Art Survey. *International Statistical Review* 50, 317–26.

NAWATA, K. (1993) A Note on the Estimation of Models with Sample-Selection Biases. *Economics Letters* 42, 15–24.

NAWATA, K. (1994) Estimation of Sample Selection Bias Models by the Maximum Likelihood Estimator and Heckman's Two Step Estimator. *Economics Letters* 45, 33–40.

NAWATA, K. and N. NAGASE (1996) Estimation of Sample Selection Models. *Econometric Reviews* 15, 387–400.

NELSON, C. R. (1972) The Prediction Performance of the FRB-PENN Model of the US Economy. *American Economic Review* 62, 902–17.

NELSON, C. R. and H. KANG (1984) Pitfalls in the Use of Time as an Explanatory Variable in Regression. *Journal of Business and Economic Statistics* 2, 73–82.

NELSON, C. R. and C. PLOSSER (1982) Trends and Random Walks in Macroeconomic Time Series. *Journal of Monetary Economics* 10, 139–62.

NELSON, C. R. and R. STARTZ (1990a) Some Further Results on the Exact Small Sample Properties of the Instrumental Variable Estimator. *Econometrica* 58, 967–76.

NELSON, C. R. and R. STARTZ (1990b) The Distribution of the Instrumental Variables Estimator and its t-Ratio when the Instrument is a Poor One. *Journal of Business* 63, S125–S140.

NELSON, J. A. (1995) Feminism and Economics. *Journal of Economic Perspectives* 9, 131–48.

NEWBOLD, P. (1983) ARIMA Model Building and the Time Series Analysis Approach to Forecasting. *Journal of Forecasting* 2, 23–35.

NEWBOLD, P. and C. AGIAKLOGLOU (1994) Adventures with ARIMA Software. *International Journal of Forecasting* 10, 573–81.

NEWEY, W. K. (1985) Maximum Likelihood Specification Testing and Conditional Moment Tests. *Econometrica* 53, 1047–70.

NEWEY, W. K. and K. D. WEST (1987) A Simple, Positive Semi-Definite, Heteroskedasticity and Autocorrelation Consistent Covariance Matrix. *Econometrica* 55, 703–8.

NICHOLLS, D. F., A. R. PAGAN, and R. D. TERRELL (1975) The Estimation and Use of Models with Moving Average Disturbance Terms: A Survey. *International Economic Review* 16, 113–34.

NOVICK, M. R. and P. H. JACKSON (1974) *Statistical Methods for Educational and Psychological Research*. New York: McGraw-Hill.

NOVICK, M. et al. (1983) *The Computer-Assisted Data Analysis (CADA) Monitor*. CADA Research Group, University of Iowa.

OHTANI, K. (1982) Small Sample Properties of the Two-Step and Three-Step Estimators in a Heteroskedastic Linear Regression Model and the Bayesian Alternative. *Economics Letters* 10, 293–8.

OHTANI, K. (1985) A Note on the Use of a Proxy Variable in Testing Hypotheses. *Economics Letters* 17, 107–10.

OHTANI, K. and M. KOBIYASHI (1986) A Bounds Test for Equality Between Sets of Coefficients in Two Linear Regression Models Under Heteroskedasticity. *Econometric Theory* 2, 220–31.

ORCUTT, G. and H. WINOKUR (1969) First Order Autoregression: Inference Estimation and Prediction. *Econometrica* 37, 1–14.

OSBORN, D. R. (1990) A Survey of Seasonality in UK Macroeconomic Variables. *International Journal of Forecasting* 6, 327–36.

OXLEY, L. (1996) International Congress on Modelling and Simulation, Newcastle, New South Wales, 1995. *Journal of Economic Surveys* 10, 225–31.

OXLEY, L. and M. McALEER (1993) Econometric Issues in Macroeconomic Models with Generated Regressors. *Journal of Economic Surveys* 7, 1–40.

PAGAN, A. R. (1984a) Model Evaluation by Variable Addition. In D. F. Hendry and K. F. Wallis (eds), *Econometrics and Quantitative Economics*. Oxford: Basil Blackwell, ch. 5.

PAGAN, A. R. (1984b) Econometric Issues in the Analysis of Regressions with Generated Regressors. *International Economic Review* 25, 221–47.

PAGAN, A. R. (1987) Three Econometric Methodologies: A Critical Appraisal. *Journal of Economic Surveys* 1, 3–24. Reprinted in L. Oxley et al. (eds), *Surveys in Econometrics*. Oxford: Basil Blackwell, 9–29.

PAGAN, A. (1995) Three Econometric Methodologies: An Update. In L.Oxley et al. (eds), *Surveys in Econometrics*. Oxford: Basil Blackwell, 30–41.

PAGAN, A. R. and D. F. NICHOLLS (1984) Estimating Predictions, Prediction Errors and their Standard Errors Using Constructed Variables. *Journal of Econometrics* 24, 293–310.

PAGAN, A. R. and A. ULLAH (1997) *Non-parametric Econometrics*. Cambridge: Cambridge University Press.

PAGAN, A. R. and F. VELLA (1989) Diagnostic Checks for Models Based on Individual Data: A Survey. *Journal of Applied Econometrics* 4 supplement, S29–S59.

PANKRATZ, A. (1983) *Forecasting with Univariate Box–Jenkins Models: Concepts and Cases*. New York: John Wiley.

PARK, R. (1966) Estimation with Heteroskedastic Error Terms. *Econometrica* 34, 888.

PEACH, J. T. and J. L. WEBB (1983) Randomly Specified Macroeconomic Models: Some Implications for Model Selection. *Journal of Economic Issues* 17, 697–720.

PEITGEN, H. O. and P. H. RICHTER (1986) *The Beauty of Fractiles*. Heidelberg: Springer-Verlag.

PESARAN, M. H. (1987) Econometrics. In J. Eatwell, M. Milgate and P. Newman (eds), *The New Palgrave: A Dictionary of Economics*, 2, London: Macmillan, 8–22.

PESARAN, M. H. (1988) The Role of Theory in Applied Econometrics. *Economic Record* 64, 336–9.

PESARAN, M. H., R. P. SMITH and J. S. YEO (1985) Testing for Structural Stability and Prediction Failure: A Review. *Manchester School* 53, 280–95.

PHILLIPS, P. C. B. (1991) To Criticize the Critics: An Objective Bayesian Analysis of Stochastic Trends. *Journal of Applied Econometrics* 6, 333–61.

PHILLIPS, P. C. B. (1995) Nonstationary Time Series and Cointegration. *Journal of Applied Econometrics* 10, 87–94.

PHILLIPS, P. C. B. and P. PERRON (1988) Testing for a Unit Root in Time Series Regression. *Biometrika* 75, 335–46.

PIERCE, D. A. (1980) A Survey of Recent Developments in Seasonal Adjustment. *American Statisitician* 34, 125–34.

PINDYCK R. S. and D. L. RUBINFELD (1991) *Econometric Methods and Economic Forecasts*, 3rd edn. New York: McGraw-Hill.

POIRIER, D. (1976) *The Econometrics of Structural Change* Amsterdam: North Holland.

POIRIER, D. J. (1988) Frequentist and Subjectivist Perspectives on the Problems of Model Building in Economics. *Journal of Economic Perspectives* 2, 121–44 (commentary, 145–70).

POIRIER, D. J. (1989) A Report from the Battlefront. *Journal of Business and Economic Statistics* 7, 137–9.

POIRIER, D. J. (1991) Editor's Introduction. *Journal of Econometrics* 49, 1–4.

POIRIER, D. J. (1992) A Return to the Battlefront. *Journal of Business and Economic Statistics* 10, 473–4.

POIRIER, D. J., M. D. TELLO and S. E. ZIN (1986) A Diagnostic Test for Normality Within the Power Exponential Family. *Journal of Business and Economic Statistics* 4, 359–73.

PRESCOTT, D. and T. STENGOS (1987) Hypothesis Testing in Regression Models with AR(1) Errors and a Lagged Dependent Variable. *Economics Letters* 24, 237–42.

PRESS, S. J. (1980) Bayesian Computer Programs. In A. Zellner (ed.), *Bayesian Analysis in Econometrics and Statistics: Essays in Honor of Harold Jeffreys*. Amsterdam: North Holland, ch. 27.

PRESS, S. J. (1989) *Bayesian Statistics*. New York: Wiley.

PRESS, S. J. et al. (1986) *Numerical Recipes*. Cambridge: Cambridge University Press.

PRESS, S. J. and S. WILSON (1978) Choosing Between Logistic Regression and Discriminant Analysis. *Journal of the American Statistical Association* 73, 699–705.

QIN, D. (1993) *The Formation of Econometrics*. Oxford: Clarendon Press.

QIN, D. (1996) Bayesian Econometrics: The First Twenty Years. *Econometric Theory* 12, 500–16.

QUANDT, R. E. (1982) Econometric Disequilibrium Models. *Econometric Reviews* 1, 1–96 (with commentary).

QUANDT, R. E. (1983) Computational Problems and Methods. In Z. Griliches and M. D. Intriligator (eds), *Handbook of Econometrics Vol. I*. Amsterdam: North Holland, ch.12.

RAJ, B. and A. ULLAH (1981) *Econometrics: A Varying Coefficients Approach*. London: Croom Helm.

RAMSEY, J. B. (1969) Tests for Specification Error in Classical Linear Least Squares Regression Analysis. *Journal of the Royal Statistical Society* B31, 250–71.

RAO, P. and R. MILLER (1971) *Applied Econometrics*. Belmont, CA: Wadsworth.

RAPPOPORT, P. and L. REICHLIN (1989) Segmented Trends and Non-Stationary Time Series. *Economic Journal* 99, Supplement, 168–77.

RAVEH, A. (1984) Comments on Some Properties of X-ll. *Review of Economics and Statistics* 66, 343–8.

RAYNER, R. K. (1993) Testing for Serial Correlation in Regression Models with Lagged Dependent Variables. *Review of Economics and Statistics* 75, 716–21.

REUTER, P. (1982) The Irregular Economy and the Quality of Macroeconomic Statistics. In V. Tanzi (ed.), *The Underground Economy in the United States and Abroad*. Lexington: Lexington Books, 125–43.

RHODES, G. (1975) Non-theoretical Errors and Testing Economic Hypotheses. *Economic Inquiry* 13, 437–44.

RIISE, T. and D. TJOSTHEIN (1984) Theory and Practice of Multivariate ARMA Forecasting. *Journal of Forecasting*. 3, 309–17.

ROBB, A. L. (1980) Accounting for Seasonality with Spline Functions. *Review of Economics and Statistics* 62, 321–3.

ROBERTSON, D. and J. SYMONS (1992) Some Strange Properties of Panel Data Estimators. *Journal of Applied Econometrics* 7, 175–89.

ROBINSON, P. M. (1986) Non-Parametric Methods in Specification. *Economic Journal* 96 supplement, 134–41.

ROBINSON, P. M. (1988) Semi-Parametric Econometrics: A Survey. *Journal of Applied Econometrics* 3, 35–51.

ROSSANA, R. J. and J. J. SEATER (1995) Temporal Aggregation and Economic Time Series. *Journal of Business and Economic Statistics* 13, 441–51.

ROTHENBERG, T. (1973) *Efficient Estimation with A Priori Information*. New Haven. CT: Yale University Press.

RUBNER. A. (1970) *Three Sacred Cows of Economics*. London: MacGibbon and Kee.

RUNKLE, D. E. (1987) Vector Autoregression and Reality. *Journal of Business and Economic Statistics* 5, 437–54.

RUTEMILLER, H. and D. BOWERS (1968) Estimation in a Heteroskedastic Regression Model. *Journal of the American Statistical Association* 63, 552–7.

SALKEVER, D. (1976) The Use of Dummy Variables to Compute Predictions, Prediction Errors, and Confidence Intervals. *Journal of Econometrics* 4, 393–7.

SAMUELSON, P. (1965) Research in Macroeconomics (mimeo). Cambridge, MA.

SANINT, L. R. (1982) Applying Principal Components Regression Analysis to Time Series Demand Estimation. *Agricultural Economics Research* 34, 21–7.

SAVAGE, L. (1954) *The Foundations of Statistics*. New York: John Wiley.

SAVIN, N. E. and K. J. WHITE (1978) Estimation and Testing for Functional Form and Autocorrelation. *Journal of Econometrics* 8, 1–12.

SCHMIDT, P. (1990) Dickey–Fuller Tests with Drift. In T. B. Fomby and G. F. Rhodes, *Advances in Econometrics Vol. 8*. Greenwich, CT: JAI Press, 161–200.

SCHWERT, G. W. (1989) Tests for Unit Roots: A Monte Carlo Investigation. *Journal of Business and Economic Statistics* 7, 147–59.

SEAKS, T. G. (1990) The Computation of Test Statistics for Multivariate Regression Models in Event Studies. *Economics Letters* 33, 141–5.

SEAKS, T. G. and S. K. LAYSON (1983) Box–Cox Estimation with Standard Econometric Problems. *Review of Economics and Statistics* 65, 160–4.

SEAKS, T. G. and D. P. VINES (1990) A Monte Carlo Evaluation of the Box–Cox Difference Transformation. *Review of Economics and Statistics* 72, 506–10.

SEPHTON, P. S. (1995) Response Surface Estimates of the KPSS Stationarity Test. *Economics Letters* 47, 255–61.

SHABAN, S. A. (1980) Change-point Problem and Two-phase Regression: An Annotated Bibliography. *International Statistical Review* 48, 83–93.

SHOESMITH, G. L. (1995) Multiple Cointegrating Vectors, Error Correction, and Forecasting with Litterman's Model. *International Journal of Forecasting* 11, 557–67.

SHOURIE, A. (1972) The Use of Macroeconomic Regression Models of Developing Countries for Forecasts and Policy Prescription: Some Reflections on Current Practice. *Oxford Economic Papers* 24, 1–35.

SILVAPULLE, P. and M. L. KING (1991) Testing Moving Average Against Autoregressive Disturbances in the Linear-Regression Model. *Journal of Business and Economic Statistics* 9, 329–35.

SILVEY, S. (1969) Multicollinearity and Imprecise Estimation. *Journal of the Royal Statistical Society* B31, 539–52.

SIMON, J. L. (1994) The Art of Forecasting: A Wager. *Cato Journal* 14, 159–61.

SIMS, C. A. (1980) Macroeconomics and Reality. *Econometrica* 48, 1–47.

SIMS, C. A. (1988) Bayesian Skepticism on Unit Root Econometrics. *Journal of Economic Dynamics and Control* 12, 463–74.

SIMS, C. A. and H. UHLIG (1991) Understanding Unit Rooters: A Helicopter Tour. *Econometrica* 59, 1591–9.

SMALL, K. A. and C. HSIAO (1985) Multinomial Logit Specification Tests. *International Economic Review* 26, 619–27.

SMITH, M. (1993) *Neural Networks for Statistical Modeling*. New York: Van Nostrand Reinhold.

SMITH, G. and W. BRAINARD (1976) The Value of A Priori Information in Estimating a Financial Model. *Journal of Finance* 31, 1299–322.

SMITH, G. and F. CAMPBELL (1980) A Critique of Some Ridge Regression Methods. *Journal of the American Statistical Association* 75, 74–103 (commentary following).

SMITH, M. A. and D. J. SMYTH (1990) Choosing Among Multiple Nonlinear Non-nested Regression Models with Different Dependent Variables. *Economics Letters* 34, 147–50.

SMITH, V. K. (1973) *Monte Carlo Methods: Role for Econometrics*. Lexington, MA: Lexington Books.

SNEE, R. D. (1977) Validation of Regression Models: Methods and Examples. *Technometrics* 19, 415–28.

SOWELL, F. (1992) Modelling Long-Run Behavior with the Fractional ARIMA Model. *Journal of Monetary Economics* 29, 277–302.

SPANOS, A. (1986) *Statistical Foundations of Econometric Modelling*. Cambridge: University of Cambridge Press.

SPENCER, D. and K. BERK (1981) A Limited Information Specification Test. *Econometrica* 49, 1079–85.

SPIRO, P. (1989) Improving a Group Forecast by Removing the Conservative Bias in its Components International. *Journal of Forecasting* 8, 127–31.

SPITZER, J. J. (1982) A Primer on Box–Cox Estimation. *Review of Economics and Statistics* 64, 307–13.

SPITZER, J. J. (1984) Variances Estimates in Models with the Box–Cox Transformation: Implications for Estimation and Hypotheses-testing. *Review of Economics and Statistics* 66, 645–52.

SRIVASTAVA, V. K. (1980) Estimation of Linear Single Equation and Simultaneous Equation Models under Stochastic Linear Constraints: An Annotated Bibliography. *International Statistical Review* 48, 79–82.

STAMP, J. (1929) *Some Economic Factors in Modern Life*. London: King and Son.

STANLEY, T. D. and S. B. JARRELL (1989) Meta-Regression Analysis: A Quantitative Method of Literature Surveys. *Journal of Economic Surveys* 3, 161–70.

STERN, S. (1991) Imputing a Continuous Income Variable from a Bracketed Income Variable with Special Attention to Missing Observations. *Economics Letters* 37, 287–91.

STEWART, M. B. (1983) On Least Squares Estimation when the Dependent Variable is Grouped. *Review of Economic Studies* 55, 737–53.

STIGLER, G. (1961) The Economics of Information. *Journal of Political Economy* 69, 213–25.

STIGLER, S. (1973) Simon Newcomb, Percy Daniell, and the History of Robust Estimation 1885–1920. *Journal of the American Statistical Association* 68, 872–9.

STOCK, J. H. and M. W. WATSON (1988a) Variable Trends in Economic Time Series. *Journal of Economic Perspectives* 2, 147–74.

STOCK, J. H. and M. W. WATSON (1988b) Testing for Common Trends. *Journal of the American Statistical Association* 83, 1097–1107.

STOLZENBERG, R. M. and D. A. RELLES (1990) Theory Testing in a World of Constrained Research Design. *Sociological Methods & Research* 18, 395–415.

STONE, R. (1945) The Analysis of Market Demand. *Journal of the Royal Statistica/ Society* B7, 297.

STREISSLER, E. (1970) *Pitfalls in Econometric Forecasting*. London: Institute of Economic Affairs.

SUITS, D. (1984) Dummy Variables: Mechanics vs Interpretation. *Review of Economics and Statistics* 66, 177–80.

SUITS, D. B., A. MASON and L. CHAN (1978) Spline Functions Fitted by Standard Regression Methods. *Review of Economics and Statistics* 60, 132–9.

SUMMERS, L. (1991) The Scientific Illusion in Empirical Macroeconomics. *Scandinavian Journal of Economics* 93, 129–48.

SUREKHA, K. and W. E. GRIFFITHS (1984) A Monte Carlo Comparison of Some Bayesian and Sampling Theory Estimators in Two Heteroscedastic Error Models. *Communications in Statistics – Simulation and Computation* 13, 85–105.

SWAMY, P. A. V. B., R. K. CONWAY and M. R. LEBLANC (1988) The Stochastic Coefficients Approach to Econometric Modelling, Part I: A Critique of Fixed Coefficients Models. *Journal of Agricultural Economics Research* 40(2), 2–10.

SWAMY, P. A. V. B. and G. S. TAVLAS (1995) Random Coefficient Models: Theory and Applications. *Journal of Economic Surveys* 9, 165–96.

TAUCHEN, G. (1985) Diagnostic Testing and Evaluation of Maximum Likelihood Models. *Journal of Econometrics* 30, 415–43.

TAYLOR, L. D. (1974) Estimation by Minimizing the Sum of Absolute Errors in P. Zarembka (ed.) *Frontiers in Econometrics*. New York: Academic Press.

TAYLOR, W. (1976) Prior Information on the Coefficients When the Disturbance Covariance Matrix is Unknown. *Econometrica* 44, 725–39.

TERZA, J. V. (1987) Estimating Linear Models with Ordinal Qualitative Regressors. *Journal of Econometrics* 34, 275–92.

TERZA, J. and P. W. WILSON (1990) Analyzing Frequencies of Several Types of Events: A Mixed Multinomial Poisson Approach. *Review of Economics and Statistics* 72, 108–15.

THEIL, H. (1957) Specification Errors and the Estimation of Economic Relationships. *Review of the International Statistical Institute* 25, 41–51 (reprinted in J. Dowling and F. Glahe (eds) (1970) *Readings in Econometric Theory*. Boulder, CO: Colorado Associated University Press).

THEIL, H. (1963) On the Use of Incomplete Prior Information in Regression Analysis. *Journal of the American Statistical Association* 58, 401–14.

THEIL, H. (1966) *Applied Economic Forecasting*. Amsterdam: North Holland.

THEIL, H. (1971) *Principles of Econometrics*. New York: John Wiley.

THEIL, H. and A. S. GOLDBERGER (1961) On Pure and Mixed Statistical Estimation in Economics. *International Economic Review* 2, 65–78.

THOMAS, R. L. (1993) *Introductory Econometrics*, 3rd edn. Harlow, Essex: Longmans.

THURSBY, J. G. (1981) A Test Strategy for Discriminating Between Autocorrelation and Misspecification in Regression Analysis. *Review of Economics and Statistics* 63, 117–23.

THURSBY, J. G. (1982) Misspecification, Heteroskedasticity, and the Chow and Goldfeld–Quandt Tests. *Review of Economics and Statistics* 64, 314–21 .

THURSBY, J. G. (1989) A Comparison of Several Specification Error Tests for a General Alternative. *International Economic Review* 30, 217–30.

THURSBY, J. G. (1992) A Comparison of Several Exact and Approximate Tests for Structural Shift under Heteroscedasticity. *Journal of Econometrics* 53, 363–86.

THURSBY, J. and P. SCHMIDT (1977) Some Properties of Tests for Specification Error in a Linear Regression Model. *Journal of the American Statistical Association* 72, 635–41.

TIAO, G. C. and G. E. P. Box (1973) Some Comments on Bayes' Estimators. *American Statistician* 27, 12–14.

TINTNER G. (1953). The Definition of Econometrics. *Econometrica* 21, 31–40.

TOBIN, J. (1958) Estimation of Relationships for Limited Dependent Variables. *Econometrica* 26, 24–36.

TORO-VIZCARRONDO, C., and T. D. WALLACE (1968) A Test of the Mean Square Error Criterion for Restrictions in Linear Regression. *Journal of the American Statistical Association* 63, 558–72.

TSAY, R. S. (1989) Parsimonious Parameterization of Vector Autoregression Moving Average Models. *Journal of Business and Economic Statistics* 7, 327–41.

TSE, Y. K. (1984) Testing Linear and Log-Linear Regressions with Autocorrelated Errors. *Economics Letters* 14, 333–7.

TURKINGTON, D. A. (1989) Classical Tests for Contemporaneously Uncorrelated Disturbances in the Linear Simultaneous Equations Model. *Journal of Econometrics* 42, 299–317.

UHL, N. and T. EISENBERG (1970) Predicting Shrinkage in the Multiple Correlation Coefficient. *Educational and Psychological Measurement* 30, 487–9.

ULLAH, A. (1988) Non-Parametric Estimation of Econometric Functionals. *Canadian Journal of Economics* 21, 625–58.

UNWIN, A. (1992) How Interactive Graphics Will Revolutionize Statistical Practice. *The Statistician* 41, 365–9.

URZUA, C. M. (1996) On the Correct Use of Omnibus Tests for Normality. *Economics Letters* 53, 247–51.

UTTS, J. (1982) The Rainbow Test for Lack of Fit in Regression. *Communications in Statistics – Theory and Methods* 11, 1801–15.

VALAVANIS, S. (1959) *Econometrics*. New York: McGraw-Hill.

VAN OPHEM, H. and A. SCHRAM (1997) Sequential and Multinomial Logit: A Nested Model. *Empirical Economics* 22, 131–52.

VANDAELE. W. (1981) Wald, Likelihood Ratio, and Lagrange Multiplier Tests as an F Test. *Economics Letters* 8, 361–5.

VARIAN, H. R. (1974) A Bayesian Approach to Real Estate Assessment. In S. E. Fienberg and A. Zellner (eds), *Studies in Bayesian Econometrics and Statistics in Honor of Leonard J. Savage*. Amsterdam: North Holland, 195–208.

VEALL, M. R. (1987) Bootstrapping the Probability Distribution of Peak Electricity Demand. *International Economic Review* 28, 203–12.

VEALL, M. R. (1989) Applications of Computationally-Intensive Methods to Econometrics. *Bulletin of the International Statistical Institute, Proceedings of the 47th Session*, Book 3, 75–88.

VEALL, M. R. (1992) Bootstrapping the Process of Model Selection: An Econometric Example. *Journal of Applied Econometrics* 7, 93–9.

VEALL, M. (1998) Applications of the Bootstrap in Econometrics and Economic Statistics. In D. E. A. Giles and A. Ullah (eds), *Handbook of Applied Economic Statistics*. New York: Marcel Dekker, forthcoming.

VEALL, M. R. and K. F. ZIMMERMANN (1996) Pseudo-R^2 Measures for some Common Limited Dependent Variable Models. *Journal of Economic Surveys* 10, 241–59.

VINOD, H. D. and A. ULLAH (1981) *Recent Advances in Regression Methods*. New York: Marcel Dekker.

WALDMAN. D. M. (1983) A Note on Algebraic Equivalence of Whites Test and a Variation of the Godfrey/Breusch-Pagan Test for Heteroskedasticity. *Economics Letters* 13, 197–200.

WALLACE, T. D. (1972) Weaker Criteria and Tests for Linear Restrictions in Regression. *Econometrica* 40, 689–98.

WALLACE, T. D. (1977) Pretest Estimation in Regression: A Survey. *American Journal of Agricultural Economics* 59, 431–43.

WALLACE, T. D. and V. ASHAR (1972) Sequential Methods in Model Construction. *Review of Economics and Statistics* 54, 172–8.

WALLACE, T. D. and C. TORO-VIZCARRONDO (1969) Tables for the Mean Square Error Test for Exact Linear Restrictions in Regression. *Journal of the American Statistical Association* 64, 1649–63.

WALLIS, K. (1972) Testing for Fourth Order Autocorrelation in Quarterly Regression Equations. *Econometrica* 40, 617–36.

WALLSTEN, T. S. and D. V. BUDESCU (1983) Encoding Subjective Probabilities: A Psychological and Psychometric Review. *Management Science* 29, 151–73.

WARNER, B. and M. MISRA (1996) Understanding Neural Networks as Statistical Tools. *American Statistician* 50, 284–93.

WATSON, M. W. and R. F. ENGLE (1985) Testing for Regression Coefficient Stability with a Stationary AR(1) Alternative. *Review of Economics and Statistics* 67, 341–6.

WATTS, D. (1973) Transformations Made Transparently Easy, or, So That's What a Jacobian Is! *American Statistician* 27, 22–5.

WAUD, R. (1968) Misspecification in the "Partial Adjustment" and "Adaptive Expectations" Models. *International Economic Review* 9, 204–17.

WEBER, J. D. (1973) *Historical Aspects of the Bayesian Controversy*. Tucson: Division of Economic and Business Research, University of Arizona.

WELCH, M. E. (1987) A Kalman Filtering Perspective. *The American Statistician* 41(1), 90–1.

WELSCH, R. E. (1980) Regression Sensitivity Analysis and Bounded-Influence Estimation. In J. Kmenta and J. Ramsey (eds), *Evaluation of Econometric Models*. New York: Academic Press, 153–67.

WELSCH, R. E. (1986) Comment. *Statistical Science* 1, 403–5.

WHITE, H. (1980) A Heteroskedasticity-consistent Covariance Matrix Estimator and a Direct Test for Heteroskedasticity. *Econometrica* 48, 817–38.

WHITE, H. (1984) *Asymptotic Theory for Econometrics*. Orlando: Academic Press.

WHITE, H. and G. M. MACDONALD (1980) Some Large Sample Tests for Non-Normality in the Linear Regression Model. *Journal of the American Statistical Association* 75, 16–28.

WHITE, K. J. (1992) The Durbin–Watson Test for Autocorrelation in Nonlinear Models. *Review of Economics and Statistics* 74, 370–3.

WICKENS, M. R. (1972) A Note on the Use of Proxy Variables. *Econometrica* 40, 759–61.

WICKENS, M. and T. BREUSCH (1988) Dynamic Specification, the Long-Run and the Estimation of Transformed Regression Models. *Economic Journal* (Supplement) 98, 189–205.

WILTON, D. (1975) Structural Shift with an Interstructural Transition Function. *Canadian Journal of Economics* 8, 423–32.

WINKELMANN, R. (1995) Duration Dependence and Dispersion in Count-Data Models. *Journal of Business and Economic Statistics* 13, 467–74.

WINKELMANN, R. (1997) *Econometric Analysis of Count Data*, 2nd edn. Berlin: Springer-Verlag.

WINKELMANN, R. and K. F. ZIMMERMAN (1995) Recent Developments in Count Data Modelling: Theory and Application. *Journal of Economic Surveys* 9, 1–24.

WONG, K. (1996) Bootstrapping Hausman's Exogeneity Test. *Economics Letters* 53, 139–43.

WONNACOTT, R. and T. WONNACOTT (1970) *Econometrics*. New York: John Wiley.

WOOLDRIDGE, J. M. (1989) A Computationally Simple Heteroskedasticity and Serial Correlation Robust Standard Error for the Linear Regression Model. *Economics Letters* 31, 239–43.

WOOLDRIDGE, J. M. (1990) A Note on the Lagrange Multiplier and F-Statistics for Two Stage Least Squares Regressions. *Economics Letters* 34, 151–5.

WOOLDRIDGE, J. M. (1992) Some Alternatives to the Box–Cox Regression Model. *International Economic Review* 33, 935–55.

WORKING, (1927) What Do Statistical Demand Curves Show? *Quarterly Journal of Economics* 41, 212–35.

WORSWICK, G. D. N. (1972) Is Progress in Science Possible? *Economic Journal* 82, 73–86.

YI, G. (1991) Estimating the Variability of the Stein Estimator by Bootstrap. *Economics Letters* 37, 293–98.

YOUNG, R. (1982) Forecasting with an Econometric Model: The Issue of Judgemental Adjustment. *Journal of Forecasting* 1, 189–204.

ZAMAN, A. (1984) Avoiding Model Selection by the Use of Shrinkage Techniques. *Journal of Econometrics* 25, 73–85.

ZAMAN, A. (1996) *Statistical Foundations for Econometric Techniques*. San Diego, CA: Academic Press.

ZELLNER, A. (1962) An Efficient Method of Estimating Seemingly Unrelated

Regressions and Tests for Aggregation Bias. *Journal of the American Statistical Association* 57, 348–68; reprinted in Dowling and Glahe (1970).

ZELLNER, A. (1971) *An Introduction to Bayesian Inference in Econometrics.* New York: John Wiley.

ZELLNER, A. (1974) The Bayesian Approach and Alternatives in Econometrics. In S. E. Fienberg and A. Zellner (eds) *Studies in Bayesian Econometrics and Statistics in Honor of Leonard J. Savage.* Amsterdam: North Holland, 39–54 (reprinted in A. Zellner (1984) *Basic Issues in Econometrics.* Chicago: University of Chicago Press, 187–200).

ZELLNER, A. (1978) Estimation of Functions of Population Means and Regression Coefficients Including Structural Coefficients: A Minimum Expected Loss (MELO) Approach. *Journal of Econometrics* 8, 127–58.

ZELLNER, A. (1979) Statistical Analysis of Econometric Models. *Journal of the American Statistical Association* 74, 628–51 (reprinted in A. Zellner (1984) *Basic Issues in Econometrics.* Chicago: University of Chicago Press, 83–119).

ZELLNER, A. (1981) Philosophy and Objectives of Econometrics. In D. Currie, R. Nobay and D. Peel (eds), *Macroeconomic Analysis: Essays in Macroeconomics and Econometrics.* London: Croom Helm, 24–34.

ZELLNER, A. (1983) The Current State of Bayesian Econometrics in T. Dwivedi (ed.), *Topics in Applied Statistics.* New York: Marcel Dekker (reprinted in A. Zellner (1984) *Basic Issues in Econometrics.* Chicago: University of Chicago Press, 306–21).

ZELLNER, A. (1986) Biased Predictors, Rationality and the Evaluation of Forecasts. *Economics Letters* 21, 45–8.

ZELLNER, A. (1986a) Biased Predictors, Rationality and the Evaluation of Forecasts. *Economics Letters* 21, 45–8.

ZELLNER, A. (1986b) A Tale of Forecasting 1001 Series: The Bayesian Knight Strikes Again. *International Journal of Forecasting* 5, 491–4.

ZELLNER, A. (1986c) Bayesian Estimation and Prediction Using Asymmetric Loss Functions. *Journal of the American Statistical Association* 81, 446–51.

ZELLNER, A. (1988) Bayesian Analysis in Econometrics. *Journal of Econometrics* 37, 27–50.

ZELLNER, A. (1989) The ET Interview. *Econometric Theory* 5, 287–317.

ZELLNER, A. and J. F. RICHARD (1973) Use of Prior Information in the Analysis and Estimation of Cobb–Douglas Production Function Models. *International Economic Review* 14, 107–19.

ZHANG, J. and D. HOFFMAN (1993) Discrete Choice Logit Models: Testing the IIA Property. *Sociological Methods & Research* 22, 193–213.

ZIEMER, R. F. (1984) Reporting Econometric Results: Believe It or Not? *Land Economics* 60, 122–7.

ZUEHLKE, T. W. and A. R. ZEMAN (1991) A Comparison of Two-Stage Estimators of Censored Regression Models. *Review of Economics and Statistics* 73, 185–8.

NAME INDEX

SUBJECT INDEX